MW00650048

Modern Python Cookbook

Second Edition

133 recipes to develop flawless and expressive programs in Python 3.8

Steven F. Lott

Packt>

BIRMINGHAM - MUMBAI

Modern Python Cookbook

Second Edition

Producer: Tushar Gupta
Acquisition Editor – Peer Reviews: Divya Mudaliar
Project Editor: Tom Jacob
Content Development Editor: Alex Patterson
Technical Editor: Karan Sonawane
Copy Editor: Safis Editing
Proofreader: Safis Editing
Indexer: Priyanka Dhadke
Presentation Designer: Pranit Padwal

First published: November 2016
Second edition: July 2020

Production reference: 1280720

Published by Packt Publishing Ltd.
Livery Place
35 Livery Street
Birmingham B3 2PB, UK.

ISBN 978-1-80020-745-5

www.packt.com

Contributors

About the author

Steven F. Lott has been programming since the 70s, when computers were large, expensive, and rare. As a contract software developer and architect, he has worked on hundreds of projects, from very small to very large. He's been using Python to solve business problems for almost 20 years.

He's currently leveraging Python to implement cloud management tools. His other titles with Packt include *Python Essentials*, *Mastering Object-Oriented Python*, *Functional Python Programming*, and *Python for Secret Agents*.

Steven is currently a technomad who lives in various places on the east coast of the U.S.

About the reviewers

Alex Martelli is an Italian-born computer engineer, and Fellow and Core Committer of the Python Software Foundation. For over 15 years now, he has lived and worked in Silicon Valley, currently as Tech Lead for "long tail" community support for Google Cloud Platform.

Alex holds a Laurea (Master's degree) in Electrical Engineering from Bologna University; he is the author of *Python in a Nutshell* (co-author, in the current 3rd edition), co-editor of the Python Cookbook's first two editions, and has written many other (mostly Python-related) materials, including book chapters, interviews, and many tech talks. Check out `https://www.google.com/search?q=alex+martelli`, especially the **Videos** tab thereof.

Alex won the 2002 Activators' Choice Award, and the 2006 Frank Willison award for outstanding contributions to the Python community.

Alex has taught courses on programming, development methods, object-oriented design, cloud computing, and numerical computing, at Ferrara University and other universities and schools. Alex was also the keynote speaker for the *2008 SciPy Conference*, and for many editions of *Pycon APAC* and *Pycon Italia* conferences.

Anna Martelli Ravenscroft is an experienced speaker and trainer, with a diverse background from bus driving to bridge, disaster preparedness to cognitive science. A frequent track chair, program committee member, and speaker at Python and Open Source conferences, Anna also frequently provides technical reviewing for Python books. She co-edited the 2nd edition of the *Python Cookbook* and co-authored the 3rd edition of *Python in a Nutshell*. Anna is a Fellow of the Python Software Foundation and won a Frank Willison Memorial Award for her contributions to Python.

Table of Contents

Preface

Python is the preferred choice of developers, engineers, data scientists, and hobbyists everywhere. It is a great scripting language that can power your applications and provide great speed, safety, and scalability. By exposing Python as a series of simple recipes, you can gain insights into specific language features in a particular context. Having a tangible context helps make the language or standard library feature easier to understand.

This book takes a recipe-based approach, where each recipe addresses specific problems and issues.

What you need for this book

All you need to follow through the examples in this book is a computer running any Python 3.8.5 or newer. Some of the examples can be adapted to work with Python 3 versions prior to 3.8. A number of examples are specific to Python 3.8 features.

It's often easiest to install a fresh copy of Python. This can be downloaded from `https://www.python.org/downloads/`. An alternative is to start with `Miniconda` (`https://docs.conda.io/en/latest/miniconda.html`) and use the `conda` tool to create a Python 3.8 (or newer) environment.

Python 2 cannot easily be used any more. Some Linux distributions and older macOS releases included a version of Python 2. It should be thought of as part of the operating system, and not a general software development tool.

Who this book is for

The book is for web developers, programmers, enterprise programmers, engineers, and big data scientists. If you are a beginner also, this book will get you started. If you are experienced, it will expand your knowledge base. A basic knowledge of programming would help.

What this book covers

Chapter 1, Numbers, Strings, and Tuples, will look at the different kinds of numbers, work with strings, use tuples, and use the essential built-in types in Python. We will also exploit the full power of the unicode character set.

Chapter 2, Statements and Syntax, will cover some basics of creating script files first. Then we'll move on to looking at some of the complex statements, including `if`, `while`, `for`, `try`, `with`, and `raise`.

Chapter 3, Function Definitions, will look at a number of function definition techniques. We'll also look at the Python 3.5 `typing` module and see how we can create more formal annotations for our functions.

Chapter 4, Built-In Data Structures Part 1 – Lists and Sets, will look at an overview of the various structures that are available and what problems they solve. From there, we can look at lists and sets in detail.

Chapter 5, Built-In Data Structures Part 2 – Dictionaries, will continue examining the built-in data structures, looking at dictionaries in detail. This chapter will also look at some more advanced topics related to how Python handles references to objects.

Chapter 6, User Inputs and Outputs, will explain how to use the different features of the `print()` function. We'll also look at the different functions used to provide user input.

Chapter 7, Basics of Classes and Objects, will create classes that implement a number of statistical formulae.

Chapter 8, More Advanced Class Design, will dive a little more deeply into Python classes. We will combine some features we have previously learned about to create more sophisticated objects.

Chapter 9, Functional Programming Features, will examine ways Python can be used for functional programming. This will emphasize function definitions and stateless, immutable objects.

Chapter 10, Input/Output, Physical Format, and Logical Layout, will work with different file formats such as JSON, XML, and HTML.

Chapter 11, Testing, will give us a detailed description of the different testing frameworks used in Python.

Chapter 12, Web Services, will look at a number of recipes for creating RESTful web services and also serving static or dynamic content.

Chapter 13, Application Integration: Configuration, will start looking at ways that we can design applications that can be composed to create larger, more sophisticated composite applications.

Chapter 14, Application Integration: Combination, will look at ways that complications that can arise from composite applications and the need to centralize some features, such as command-line parsing.

Chapter 15, Statistical Programming and Linear Regression, will look at some basic statistical calculations that we can do with Python's built-in libraries and data structures. We'll look at the questions of correlation, randomness, and the `null` hypothesis.

To get the most out of this book

To get the most out of this book you can download the example code files and the color images as per the instructions below.

Download the example code files

You can download the example code files for this book from your account at `packtpub.com`. If you purchased this book elsewhere, you can visit `packtpub.com/support` and register to have the files emailed directly to you.

You can download the code files by following these steps:

1. Log in or register at `packtpub.com`.
2. Select the **SUPPORT** tab.
3. Click on **Code Downloads & Errata**.
4. Enter the name of the book in the **Search** box and follow the on-screen instructions.

Once the file is downloaded, please make sure that you unzip or extract the folder using the latest version of:

- WinRAR / 7-Zip for Windows
- Zipeg / iZip / UnRarX for Mac
- 7-Zip / PeaZip for Linux

The code bundle for the book is also hosted on GitHub at `https://github.com/PacktPublishing/Modern-Python-Cookbook-Second-Edition`. This repository is also the best places to start a conversation about specific topics discussed in the book. Feel free to open an issue if you want to engage with the authors or other readers. We also have other code bundles from our rich catalog of books and videos available at `https://github.com/PacktPublishing/`. Check them out!

Conventions used

In this book, you will find a number of text styles that distinguish between different kinds of information. Here are some examples of these styles and an explanation of their meaning.

Code words in text, database table names, folder names, filenames, file extensions, pathnames, dummy URLs, user input, and Twitter handles are shown as follows: "We can include other contexts through the use of the `include` directive."

A block of code is set as follows:

```
if distance is None:
    distance = rate * time
elif rate is None:
    rate = distance / time
elif time is None:
    time = distance / rate
```

Any command-line input or output is written as follows:

```
>>> import math
>>> math.factorial(52)
80658175170943878571660636856403766975289505440883277824000000000000
```

New terms and important words are shown in bold.

Warnings or important notes appear like this.

Tips and tricks appear like this.

Get in touch

Feedback from our readers is always welcome.

General feedback: Email `feedback@packtpub.com`, and mention the book's title in the subject of your message. If you have questions about any aspect of this book, please email us at `questions@packtpub.com`.

Errata: Although we have taken every care to ensure the accuracy of our content, mistakes do happen. If you have found a mistake in this book we would be grateful if you would report this to us. Please visit, `packtpub.com/support/errata`, selecting your book, clicking on the Errata Submission Form link, and entering the details.

Piracy: If you come across any illegal copies of our works in any form on the Internet, we would be grateful if you would provide us with the location address or website name. Please contact us at `copyright@packtpub.com` with a link to the material.

If you are interested in becoming an author: If there is a topic that you have expertise in and you are interested in either writing or contributing to a book, please visit `authors.packtpub.com`.

Reviews

Please leave a review. Once you have read and used this book, why not leave a review on the site that you purchased it from? Potential readers can then see and use your unbiased opinion to make purchase decisions, we at Packt can understand what you think about our products, and our authors can see your feedback on their book. Thank you!

For more information about Packt, please visit `packtpub.com`.

1

Numbers, Strings, and Tuples

This chapter will look at some of the central types of Python objects. We'll look at working with different kinds of numbers, working with strings, and using tuples. These are the simplest kinds of data Python works with. In later chapters, we'll look at data structures built on these foundations.

Most of these recipes assume a beginner's level of understanding of Python 3.8. We'll be looking at how we use the essential built-in types available in Python—numbers, strings, and tuples. Python has a rich variety of numbers, and two different division operators, so we'll need to look closely at the choices available to us.

When working with strings, there are several common operations that are important. We'll explore some of the differences between bytes—as used by our OS files, and strings—as used by Python. We'll look at how we can exploit the full power of the Unicode character set.

In this chapter, we'll show the recipes as if we're working from the `>>>` prompt in interactive Python. This is sometimes called the **read-eval-print loop** (**REPL**). In later chapters, we'll change the style so it looks more like a script file. The goal in this chapter is to encourage interactive exploration because it's a great way to learn the language.

We'll cover these recipes to introduce basic Python data types:

- Working with large and small integers
- Choosing between `float`, `decimal`, and `fraction`
- Choosing between `true division` and `floor division`
- Rewriting an immutable `string`

- `String` parsing with regular expressions
- Building complex strings with `f-strings`
- Building complex strings from lists of characters
- Using the Unicode characters that aren't on our keyboards
- Encoding strings – creating ASCII and UTF-8 bytes
- Decoding bytes – how to get proper characters from some bytes
- Using tuples of items
- Using `NamedTuples` to simplify item access in tuples

We'll start with integers, work our way through strings, and end up working with simple combinations of objects in the form of tuples and `NamedTuples`.

Working with large and small integers

Many programming languages make a distinction between integers, bytes, and long integers. Some languages include distinctions for *signed versus unsigned* integers. How do we map these concepts to Python?

The easy answer is that we don't. Python handles integers of all sizes in a uniform way. From bytes to immense numbers with hundreds of digits, they're all integers to Python.

Getting ready

Imagine you need to calculate something really big. For example, we want to calculate the number of ways to permute the cards in a 52-card deck. The *factorial* 52! = 52 × 51 × 50 × ... × 2 × 1, is a very, very large number. Can we do this in Python?

How to do it...

Don't worry. Really. Python has one universal type of integer, and this covers all of the bases, from individual bytes to numbers that fill all of the memory. Here are the steps to use integers properly:

1. Write the numbers you need. Here are some smallish numbers: 355, 113. There's no practical upper limit.
2. Creating a very small value—a single `byte`—looks like this:

   ```
   >>> 2
   2
   ```

   Or perhaps this, if you want to use base 16:

   ```
   >>> 0xff
   255
   ```

3. Creating a much, much bigger number with a calculation using the `**` operator ("raise to power") might look like this:

   ```
   >>> 2**2048
   323...656
   ```

This number has 617 digits. We didn't show all of them.

How it works...

Internally, Python has two representations for numbers. The conversion between these two is seamless and automatic.

For smallish numbers, Python will generally use 4-byte or 8-byte integer values. Details are buried in CPython's internals; they depend on the facilities of the C compiler used to build Python.

For numbers over `sys.maxsize`, Python switches to internally representing integer numbers as sequences of digits. Digit, in this case, often means a 30-bit value.

How many ways can we permute a standard deck of 52 cards? The answer is $52! \approx 8 \times 10^{67}$. Here's how we can compute that large number. We'll use the factorial function in the `math` module, shown as follows:

```
>>> import math
>>> math.factorial(52)
80658175170943878571660636856403766975289505440883277824000000000000
```

Yes, this giant number works perfectly.

The first parts of our calculation of 52! (from 52 × 51 × 50 × ... down to about 42) could be performed entirely using the smallish integers. After that, the rest of the calculation had to switch to largish integers. We don't see the switch; we only see the results.

For some of the details on the internals of integers, we can look at this:

```
>>> import sys
>>> import math
>>> math.log(sys.maxsize, 2)
63.0
>>> sys.int_info
sys.int_info(bits_per_digit=30, sizeof_digit=4)
```

The `sys.maxsize` value is the largest of the small integer values. We computed the log to base 2 to find out how many bits are required for this number.

This tells us that our Python uses 63-bit values for small integers. The range of smallish integers is from $-2^{63} \ldots 2^{63} - 1$. Outside this range, largish integers are used.

The values in `sys.int_info` tell us that large integers are a sequence of 30-bit digits, and each of these digits occupies 4 bytes.

A large value like 52! consists of 8 of these 30-bit-sized digits. It can be a little confusing to think of a digit as requiring 30 bits in order to be represented. Instead of the commonly used symbols, 0, 1, 2, 3, ..., 9, for base-10 numbers, we'd need 2^{30} distinct symbols for each digit of these large numbers.

A calculation involving big integer values can consume a fair bit of memory. What about small numbers? How can Python manage to keep track of lots of little numbers like one and zero?

For some commonly used numbers (-5 to 256), Python can create a secret pool of objects to optimize memory management. This leads to a small performance improvement.

There's more...

Python offers us a broad set of arithmetic operators: `+`, `-`, `*`, `/`, `//`, `%`, and `**`. The / and `//` operators are for division; we'll look at these in a separate recipe named *Choosing between true division and floor division*. The `**` operator raises a number to a power.

For dealing with individual bits, we have some additional operations. We can use `&`, `^`, `|`, `<<`, and `>>`. These operators work bit by bit on the internal binary representations of integers. These compute a binary **AND**, a binary **Exclusive OR**, **Inclusive OR**, **Left Shift**, and **Right Shift** respectively.

See also

- We'll look at the two division operators in the *Choosing between true division and floor division* recipe, later in this chapter.
- We'll look at other kinds of numbers in the *Choosing between float, decimal, and fraction* recipe, which is the next recipe in this chapter.
- For details on integer processing, see `https://www.python.org/dev/peps/pep-0237/`.

Choosing between float, decimal, and fraction

Python offers several ways to work with rational numbers and approximations of irrational numbers. We have three basic choices:

- Float
- Decimal
- Fraction

With so many choices, when do we use each?

Getting ready

It's important to be sure about our core mathematical expectations. If we're not sure what kind of data we have, or what kinds of results we want to get, we really shouldn't be coding yet. We need to take a step back and review things with a pencil and paper.

There are three general cases for math that involve numbers beyond integers, which are:

1. **Currency**: Dollars, cents, euros, and so on. Currency generally has a fixed number of decimal places. Rounding rules are used to determine what 7.25% of $2.95 is, rounded to the nearest penny.
2. **Rational Numbers or Fractions**: When we're working with American units like feet and inches, or cooking measurements in cups and fluid ounces, we often need to work in fractions. When we scale a recipe that serves eight, for example, down to five people, we're doing fractional math using a scaling factor of `5/8`. How do we apply this scaling to `2/3` cup of rice and still get a measurement that fits an American kitchen gadget?
3. **Irrational Numbers**: This includes all other kinds of calculations. It's important to note that digital computers can only approximate these numbers, and we'll occasionally see odd little artifacts of this approximation. Float approximations are very fast, but sometimes suffer from truncation issues.

When we have one of the first two cases, we should avoid floating-point numbers.

How to do it...

We'll look at each of the three cases separately. First, we'll look at computing with currency. Then, we'll look at rational numbers, and after that, irrational or floating-point numbers. Finally, we'll look at making explicit conversions among these various types.

Doing currency calculations

When working with currency, we should always use the `decimal` module. If we try to use the values of Python's built-in `float` type, we can run into problems with the rounding and truncation of numbers:

1. To work with currency, we'll do this. Import the `Decimal` class from the `decimal` module:

   ```
   >>> from decimal import Decimal
   ```

2. Create `Decimal` objects from strings or integers. In this case, we want 7.25%, which is 7.25/100. We can compute the value using `Decimal` objects. We could have used `Decimal('0.0725')` instead of doing the division explicitly. The result is a hair over $0.21. It's computed correctly to the full number of decimal places:

```
>>> tax_rate = Decimal('7.25')/Decimal(100)
>>> purchase_amount = Decimal('2.95')
>>> tax_rate * purchase_amount
Decimal('0.213875')
```

3. To round to the nearest penny, create a `penny` object:

```
>>> penny = Decimal('0.01')
```

4. Quantize your data using this `penny` object:

```
>>> total_amount = purchase_amount + tax_rate * purchase_amount
>>> total_amount.quantize(penny)
Decimal('3.16')
```

This shows how we can use the default rounding rule of `ROUND_HALF_EVEN`.

Every financial wizard (and many world currencies) have different rules for rounding. The `Decimal` module offers every variation. We might, for example, do something like this:

```
>>> import decimal
>>> total_amount.quantize(penny, decimal.ROUND_UP)
Decimal('3.17')
```

This shows the consequences of using a different rounding rule.

Fraction calculations

When we're doing calculations that have exact fraction values, we can use the `fractions` module. This provides us with handy rational numbers that we can use. In this example, we want to scale a recipe for eight down to five people, using `5/8` of each ingredient. When we need $2\frac{1}{2}$ cups of sugar, what does that turn out to be?

To work with fractions, we'll do this:

1. Import the `Fraction` class from the `fractions` module:

```
>>> from fractions import Fraction
```

2. Create `Fraction` objects from strings, integers, or pairs of integers. If you create fraction objects from floating-point values, you may see unpleasant artifacts of float approximations. When the denominator is a power of 2, - $\frac{1}{2}$, $\frac{1}{4}$, and so on, converting from float to fraction can work out exactly. We created one fraction from a string, `'2.5'`. We created the second fraction from a floating-point calculation, `5/8`. Because the denominator is a power of 2, this works out exactly:

```
>>> sugar_cups = Fraction('2.5')
>>> scale_factor = Fraction(5/8)
>>> sugar_cups * scale_factor
Fraction(25, 16)
```

3. The result, $\frac{25}{16}$, is a complex-looking fraction. What's a nearby fraction that might be simpler?

```
>>> Fraction(24,16)
Fraction(3, 2)
```

We can see that we'll use almost a cup and a half of sugar to scale the recipe for five people instead of eight.

Floating-point approximations

Python's built-in `float` type can represent a wide variety of values. The trade-off here is that `float` often involves an approximation. In a few cases—specifically when doing division that involves powers of 2—it can be as exact as `fraction`. In all other cases, there may be small discrepancies that reveal the differences between the implementation of `float` and the mathematical ideal of an irrational number:

1. To work with `float`, we often need to round values to make them look sensible. It's important to recognize that all `float` calculations are an approximation:

```
>>> (19/155)*(155/19)
0.9999999999999999
```

2. Mathematically, the value should be `1`. Because of the approximations used for `float`, the answer isn't exact. It's not wrong by much, but it's wrong. In this example, we'll use `round(answer, 3)` to round to three digits, creating a value that's more useful:

```
>>> answer = (19/155)*(155/19)
>>> round(answer, 3)
1.0
```

3. Know the error term. In this case, we know what the exact answer is supposed to be, so we can compare our calculation with the known correct answer. This gives us the general error value that can creep into floating-point numbers:

```
>>> 1-answer
1.1102230246251565e-16
```

For most floating-point errors, this is the typical value—about 10^{-16}. Python has clever rules that hide this error some of the time by doing some automatic rounding. For this calculation, however, the error wasn't hidden.

This is a very important consequence.

> Don't compare floating-point values for exact equality.

When we see code that uses an exact == test between floating-point numbers, there are going to be problems when the approximations differ by a single bit.

Converting numbers from one type into another

We can use the `float()` function to create a `float` value from another value. It looks like this:

```
>>> float(total_amount)
3.163875
>>> float(sugar_cups * scale_factor)
1.5625
```

In the first example, we converted a `Decimal` value into `float`. In the second example, we converted a `Fraction` value into `float`.

It rarely works out well to try to convert `float` into `Decimal` or `Fraction`:

```
>>> Fraction(19/155)
Fraction(8832866365939553, 72057594037927936)
>>> Decimal(19/155)
Decimal('0.12258064516129031640279123394066118635237216949462890625')
```

In the first example, we did a calculation among integers to create a `float` value that has a known truncation problem. When we created a `Fraction` from that truncated `float` value, we got some terrible - looking numbers that exposed the details of the truncation.

Similarly, the second example tries to create a `Decimal` value from a `float` value that has a truncation problem, resulting in a complicated value.

How it works...

For these numeric types, Python offers a variety of operators: `+`, `-`, `*`, `/`, `//`, `%`, and `**`. These are for addition, subtraction, multiplication, true division, truncated division, modulo, and raising to a power, respectively. We'll look at the two division operators in the *Choosing between true division and floor division* recipe.

Python is adept at converting numbers between the various types. We can mix `int` and `float` values; the integers will be promoted to floating-point to provide the most accurate answer possible. Similarly, we can mix `int` and `Fraction` and the results will be a `Fraction` object. We can also mix `int` and `Decimal`. We cannot casually mix `Decimal` with `float` or `Fraction`; we need to provide explicit conversions in that case.

> It's important to note that `float` values are really approximations. The Python syntax allows us to write numbers as decimal values; however, that's not how they're processed internally.

We can write a value like this in Python, using ordinary base-10 values:

```
>>> 8.066e+67
8.066e+67
```

The actual value used internally will involve a binary approximation of the decimal value we wrote. The internal value for this example, `8.066e+67`, is this:

```
>>> (6737037547376141/(2**53))*(2**226)
8.066e+67
```

The numerator is a big number, `6737037547376141`. The denominator is always 2^{53}. Since the denominator is fixed, the resulting fraction can only have 53 meaningful bits of data. This is why values can get truncated. This leads to tiny discrepancies between our idealized abstraction and actual numbers. The exponent (2^{226}) is required to scale the fraction up to the proper range.

Mathematically, $\frac{6737037547376141 \times 2^{226}}{2^{53}}$.

We can use `math.frexp()` to see these internal details of a number:

```
>>> import math
>>> math.frexp(8.066E+67)
(0.7479614202861186, 226)
```

The two parts are called the **mantissa** (or **significand**) and the **exponent**. If we multiply the mantissa by 2^{53}, we always get a whole number, which is the numerator of the binary fraction.

> The error we noticed earlier matches this quite nicely: $10^{-16} \approx 2^{-53}$.

Unlike the built-in `float`, a `Fraction` is an exact ratio of two integer values. As we saw in the *Working with large and small integers* recipe, integers in Python can be very large. We can create ratios that involve integers with a large number of digits. We're not limited by a fixed denominator.

A `Decimal` value, similarly, is based on a very large integer value, as well as a scaling factor to determine where the decimal place goes. These numbers can be huge and won't suffer from peculiar representation issues.

> **Why use floating-point? Two reasons**: Not all computable numbers can be represented as fractions. That's why mathematicians introduced (or perhaps discovered) irrational numbers. The built-in float type is as close as we can get to the mathematical abstraction of irrational numbers. A value like $\sqrt{2}$, for example, can't be represented as a fraction. Also, float values are very fast on modern processors.

There's more...

The Python `math` module contains several specialized functions for working with floating-point values. This module includes common elementary functions such as square root, logarithms, and various trigonometry functions. It also has some other functions such as gamma, factorial, and the Gaussian error function.

The `math` module includes several functions that can help us do more accurate floating-point calculations. For example, the `math.fsum()` function will compute a floating-point sum more carefully than the built-in `sum()` function. It's less susceptible to approximation issues.

We can also make use of the `math.isclose()` function to compare two floating-point values to see if they're nearly equal:

```
>>> (19/155)*(155/19) == 1.0
False
>>> math.isclose((19/155)*(155/19), 1)
True
```

This function provides us with a way to compare floating-point numbers meaningfully for near-equality.

Python also offers *complex* numbers. A complex number has a real and an imaginary part. In Python, we write `3.14+2.78j` to represent the complex number $3.14 + 2.78\sqrt{-1}$. Python will comfortably convert between float and complex. We have the usual group of operators available for complex numbers.

To support complex numbers, there's the `cmath` package. The `cmath.sqrt()` function, for example, will return a complex value rather than raise an exception when extracting the square root of a negative number. Here's an example:

```
>>> math.sqrt(-2)
Traceback (most recent call last):
  File "<stdin>", line 1, in <module>
ValueError: math domain error
>>> cmath.sqrt(-2)
1.4142135623730951j
```

This is essential when working with complex numbers.

See also

- We'll talk more about floating-point numbers and fractions in the *Choosing between true division and floor division* recipe.
- See `https://en.wikipedia.org/wiki/IEEE_floating_point`

Choosing between true division and floor division

Python offers us two kinds of division operators. What are they, and how do we know which one to use? We'll also look at the Python division rules and how they apply to integer values.

Getting ready

There are several general cases for division:

- A *div-mod* pair: We want both parts – the quotient and the remainder. The name refers to the division and modulo operations combined together. We can summarize the quotient and remainder as $q, r = (\lfloor \frac{a}{b} \rfloor, a \bmod b)$.

We often use this when converting values from one base into another. When we convert seconds into hours, minutes, and seconds, we'll be doing a *div-mod* kind of division. We don't want the exact number of hours; we want a truncated number of hours, and the remainder will be converted into minutes and seconds.

- The *true* value: This is a typical floating-point value; it will be a good approximation to the quotient. For example, if we're computing an average of several measurements, we usually expect the result to be floating-point, even if the input values are all integers.
- A *rational fraction* value: This is often necessary when working in American units of feet, inches, and cups. For this, we should be using the `Fraction` class. When we divide `Fraction` objects, we always get exact answers.

We need to decide which of these cases apply, so we know which division operator to use.

How to do it...

We'll look at these three cases separately. First, we'll look at truncated floor division. Then, we'll look at true floating-point division. Finally, we'll look at the division of fractions.

Doing floor division

When we are doing the *div-mod* kind of calculations, we might use the floor division operator, `//`, and the modulo operator, `%`. The expression `a % b` gives us the remainder from an integer division of `a // b`. Or, we might use the `divmod()` built-in function to compute both at once:

1. We'll divide the number of seconds by 3,600 to get the value of `hours`. The modulo, or remainder in division, computed with the `%` operator, can be converted separately into `minutes` and `seconds`:

```
>>> total_seconds = 7385
>>> hours = total_seconds//3600
>>> remaining_seconds = total_seconds % 3600
```

2. Next, we'll divide the number of seconds by 60 to get `minutes`; the remainder is the number of seconds less than 60:

```
>>> minutes = remaining_seconds//60
>>> seconds = remaining_seconds % 60
>>> hours, minutes, seconds
(2, 3, 5)
```

Here's the alternative, using the `divmod()` function to compute quotient and modulo together:

1. Compute quotient and remainder at the same time:

```
>>> total_seconds = 7385
>>> hours, remaining_seconds = divmod(total_seconds, 3600)
```

2. Compute quotient and remainder again:

```
>>> minutes, seconds = divmod(remaining_seconds, 60)
>>> hours, minutes, seconds
(2, 3, 5)
```

Doing true division

A true value calculation gives as a floating-point approximation. For example, about how many hours is 7,386 seconds? Divide using the true division operator:

```
>>> total_seconds = 7385
>>> hours = total_seconds / 3600
>>> round(hours, 4)
2.0514
```

> We provided two integer values, but got a floating-point exact result. Consistent with our previous recipe, when using floating-point values, we rounded the result to avoid having to look at tiny error values.

This true division is a feature of Python 3 that Python 2 didn't offer by default.

Rational fraction calculations

We can do division using `Fraction` objects and integers. This forces the result to be a mathematically exact rational number:

1. Create at least one `Fraction` value:

```
>>> from fractions import Fraction
>>> total_seconds = Fraction(7385)
```

2. Use the `Fraction` value in a calculation. Any integer will be promoted to a `Fraction`:

```
>>> hours = total_seconds / 3600
>>> hours
Fraction(1477, 720)
```

3. If necessary, convert the exact fraction into a floating-point approximation:

```
>>> round(float(hours),4)
2.0514
```

First, we created a `Fraction` object for the total number of seconds. When we do arithmetic on fractions, Python will promote any integers to be fractions; this promotion means that the math is done as precisely as possible.

How it works...

Python has two division operators:

- The / true division operator produces a true, floating-point result. It does this even when the two operands are integers. This is an unusual operator in this respect. All other operators preserve the type of the data. The true division operation - when applied to integers - produces a `float` result.
- The // truncated division operator always produces a truncated result. For two integer operands, this is the truncated quotient. When floating-point operands are used, this is a truncated floating-point result:

```
>>> 7358.0 // 3600.0
2.0
```

See also

- For more on the choice between floating-point and fractions, see the *Choosing between float, decimal, and fraction* recipe.
- See `https://www.python.org/dev/peps/pep-0238/`

Rewriting an immutable string

How can we rewrite an immutable string? We can't change individual characters inside a string:

```
>>> title = "Recipe 5: Rewriting, and the Immutable String"
>>> title[8] = ''
Traceback (most recent call last):
File "<stdin>", line 1, in <module>
TypeError: 'str' object does not support item assignment
```

Since this doesn't work, how do we make a change to a string?

Getting ready

Let's assume we have a string like this:

```
>>> title = "Recipe 5: Rewriting, and the Immutable String"
```

We'd like to do two transformations:

- Remove the part up to the `:`
- Replace the punctuation with _, and make all the characters lowercase

Since we can't replace characters in a string object, we have to work out some alternatives. There are several common things we can do, shown as follows:

- A combination of slicing and concatenating a string to create a new string.
- When shortening, we often use the `partition()` method.
- We can replace a character or a substring with the `replace()` method.
- We can expand the string into a list of characters, then join the string back into a single string again. This is the subject of a separate recipe, *Building complex strings with a list of characters*.

How to do it...

Since we can't update a string in place, we have to replace the string variable's object with each modified result. We'll use an assignment statement that looks something like this:

```
some_string = some_string.method()
```

Or we could even use an assignment like this:

```
some_string = some_string[:chop_here]
```

We'll look at a few specific variations of this general theme. We'll slice a piece of a string, we'll replace individual characters within a string, and we'll apply blanket transformations such as making the string lowercase. We'll also look at ways to remove extra _ that show up in our final string.

Slicing a piece of a string

Here's how we can shorten a string via slicing:

1. Find the boundary:

   ```
   >>> colon_position = title.index(':')
   ```

The `index` function locates a particular substring and returns the position where that substring can be found. If the substring doesn't exist, it raises an exception. The following expression will always be true: `title[colon_position] == ':'`.

2. Pick the substring:

```
>>> discard, post_colon = title[:colon_position], title[colon_
position+1:]
>>> discard
'Recipe 5'
>>> post_colon
' Rewriting, and the Immutable String'
```

We've used the slicing notation to show the `start:end` of the characters to pick. We also used multiple assignment to assign two variables, `discard` and `post_colon`, from the two expressions.

We can use `partition()`, as well as manual slicing. Find the boundary and partition:

```
>>> pre_colon_text, _, post_colon_text = title.partition(':')
>>> pre_colon_text
'Recipe 5'
>>> post_colon_text
' Rewriting, and the Immutable String'
```

The `partition` function returns three things: the part before the target, the target, and the part after the target. We used multiple assignment to assign each object to a different variable. We assigned the target to a variable named _ because we're going to ignore that part of the result. This is a common idiom for places where we must provide a variable, but we don't care about using the object.

Updating a string with a replacement

We can use a string's `replace()` method to create a new string with punctuation marks removed. When using `replace` to switch punctuation marks, save the results back into the original variable. In this case, `post_colon_text`:

```
>>> post_colon_text = post_colon_text.replace(' ', '_')
>>> post_colon_text = post_colon_text.replace(',', '_')
>>> post_colon_text
'_Rewriting__and_the_Immutable_String'
```

This has replaced the two kinds of punctuation with the desired _ characters. We can generalize this to work with all punctuation. This leverages the `for` statement, which we'll look at in *Chapter 2, Statements and Syntax*.

We can iterate through all punctuation characters:

```
>>> from string import whitespace, punctuation
>>> for character in whitespace + punctuation:
...     post_colon_text = post_colon_text.replace(character, '_')
>>> post_colon_text
'_Rewriting__and_the_Immutable_String'
```

As each kind of punctuation character is replaced, we assign the latest and greatest version of the string to the `post_colon_text` variable.

We can also use a string's `translate()` method for this. This relies on creating a dictionary object to map each source character's position to a resulting character:

```
>>> from string import whitespace, punctuation
>>> title = "Recipe 5: Rewriting an Immutable String"
>>> title.translate({ord(c): '_' for c in whitespace+punctuation})
Recipe_5__Rewriting_an_Immutable_String
```

We've created a mapping with `{ord(c): '_' for c in whitespace+punctuation}` to translate any character, `c`, in the `whitespace+punctuation` sequence of characters to the `'_'` character. This may have better performance than a sequence of individual character replacements.

Removing extra punctuation marks

In many cases, there are some additional steps we might follow. We often want to remove leading and trailing _ characters. We can use `strip()` for this:

```
>>> post_colon_text = post_colon_text.strip('_')
```

In some cases, we'll have multiple _ characters because we had multiple punctuation marks. The final step would be something like this to clean up multiple _ characters:

```
>>> while '__' in post_colon_text:
...     post_colon_text = post_colon_text.replace('__', '_')
```

This is yet another example of the same pattern we've been using to modify a string in place. This depends on the `while` statement, which we'll look at in *Chapter 2, Statements and Syntax*.

How it works...

We can't—technically—modify a string in place. The data structure for a string is immutable. However, we can assign a new string back to the original variable. This technique behaves the same as modifying a string in place.

When a variable's value is replaced, the previous value no longer has any references and is garbage collected. We can see this by using the `id()` function to track each individual string object:

```
>>> id(post_colon_text)
4346207968
>>> post_colon_text = post_colon_text.replace('_','-')
>>> id(post_colon_text)
4346205488
```

Your actual ID numbers may be different. What's important is that the original string object assigned to `post_colon_text` had one ID. The new string object assigned to `post_colon_text` has a different ID. It's a new string object.

When the old string has no more references, it is removed from memory automatically.

We made use of **slice notation** to decompose a string. A slice has two parts: `[start:end]`. A slice always includes the starting index. String indices always start with zero as the first item. A slice never includes the ending index.

> The items in a slice have an index from `start` to `end-1`. This is sometimes called a **half-open** interval.

Think of a slice like this: all characters where the index *i* is in the range *start* ≤ *i* < *end*.

We noted briefly that we can omit the start or end indices. We can actually omit both. Here are the various options available:

- `title[colon_position]`: A single item, that is, the `:` we found using `title.index(':')`.
- `title[:colon_position]`: A slice with the start omitted. It begins at the first position, index of zero.
- `title[colon_position+1:]`: A slice with the end omitted. It ends at the end of the string, as if we said `len(title)`.
- `title[:]`: Since both start and end are omitted, this is the entire string. Actually, it's a *copy* of the entire string. This is the quick and easy way to duplicate a string.

There's more...

There are more features for indexing in Python collections like a string. The normal indices start with 0 on the left. We have an alternate set of indices that use negative numbers that work from the right end of a string:

- `title[-1]` is the last character in the title, `'g'`
- `title[-2]` is the next-to-last character, `'n'`
- `title[-6:]` is the last six characters, `'String'`

We have a lot of ways to pick pieces and parts out of a string.

Python offers dozens of methods for modifying a string. The *Text Sequence Type — str* section of the *Python Standard Library* describes the different kinds of transformations that are available to us. There are three broad categories of string methods: we can ask about the string, we can parse the string, and we can transform the string to create a new one. Methods such as `isnumeric()` tell us if a string is all digits.

Here's an example:

```
>>> 'some word'.isnumeric()
False
>>> '1298'.isnumeric()
True
```

Before doing comparisons, it can help to change a string so that it has the same uniform case. It's frequently helpful to use the `lower()` method, thus assigning the result to the original variable:

```
>>> post_colon_text = post_colon_text.lower()
```

We've looked at parsing with the `partition()` method. We've also looked at transforming with the `lower()` method, as well as the `replace()` and `translate()` methods.

See also

- We'll look at the string as list technique for modifying a string in the *Building complex strings from lists of characters* recipe.
- Sometimes, we have data that's only a stream of bytes. In order to make sense of it, we need to convert it into characters. That's the subject of the *Decoding bytes - how to get proper characters from some bytes* recipe.

String parsing with regular expressions

How do we decompose a complex string? What if we have complex, tricky punctuation? Or—worse yet—what if we don't have punctuation, but have to rely on patterns of digits to locate meaningful information?

Getting ready

The easiest way to decompose a complex string is by generalizing the string into a pattern and then writing a regular expression that describes that pattern.

There are limits to the patterns that regular expressions can describe. When we're confronted with deeply nested documents in a language like HTML, XML, or JSON, we often run into problems, and can't use regular expressions.

The `re` module contains all of the various classes and functions we need to create and use regular expressions.

Let's say that we want to decompose text from a recipe website. Each line looks like this:

```
>>> ingredient = "Kumquat: 2 cups"
```

We want to separate the ingredient from the measurements.

How to do it...

To write and use regular expressions, we often do this:

1. Generalize the example. In our case, we have something that we can generalize as:

   ```
   (ingredient words): (amount digits) (unit words)
   ```

2. We've replaced literal text with a two-part summary: what it means and how it's represented. For example, `ingredient` is represented as `words`, while `amount` is represented as `digits`. Import the `re` module:

   ```
   >>> import re
   ```

3. Rewrite the pattern into **Regular expression** (**RE**) notation:

   ```
   >>> ingredient_pattern = re.compile(r'([\w\s]+):\s+(\d+)\s+(\w+)')
   ```

   We've replaced representation hints such as *ingredient words*, a mixture of letters and spaces, with `[\w\s]+`. We've replaced *amount digits* with `\d+`. And we've replaced *single spaces* with `\s+` to allow one or more spaces to be used as punctuation. We've left the colon in place because, in the regular expression notation, a colon matches itself.

For each of the fields of data, we've used `()` to capture the data matching the pattern. We didn't capture the colon or the spaces because we don't need the punctuation characters.

REs typically use a lot of \ characters. To make this work out nicely in Python, we almost always use *raw* strings. The `r'` prefix tells Python not to look at the \ characters and not to replace them with special characters that aren't on our keyboards.

4. Compile the pattern:

```
>>> pattern = re.compile(pattern_text)
```

5. Match the pattern against the input text. If the input matches the pattern, we'll get a `match` object that shows details of the matching:

```
>>> match = pattern.match(ingredient)
>>> match is None
False
>>> match.groups()
('Kumquat', '2', 'cups')
```

6. Extract the named groups of characters from the `match` object:

```
>>> match.group(1)
'Kumquat'
>>> match.group(2)
'2'
>>> match.group(3)
'cups'
```

Each group is identified by the order of the capture ()s in the regular expression. This gives us a tuple of the different fields captured from the string. We'll return to the use of tuples in the *Using tuples* recipe. This can be confusing in more complex regular expressions; there is a way to provide a name, instead of the numeric position, to identify a capture group.

How it works...

There are a lot of different kinds of string patterns that we can describe with RE.

We've shown a number of character classes:

- `\w` matches any alphanumeric character (a to z, A to Z, 0 to 9)
- `\d` matches any decimal digit
- `\s` matches any space or tab character

These classes also have inverses:

- \W matches any character that's not a letter or a digit
- \D matches any character that's not a digit
- \S matches any character that's not some kind of space or tab

Many characters match themselves. Some characters, however, have a special meaning, and we have to use \ to escape from that special meaning:

- We saw that + as a suffix means to match one or more of the preceding patterns. \d+ matches one or more digits. To match an ordinary +, we need to use \+.
- We also have * as a suffix, which matches zero or more of the preceding patterns. \w* matches zero or more characters. To match a *, we need to use *.
- We have ? as a suffix, which matches zero or one of the preceding expressions. This character is used in other places, and has a different meaning in the other context. We'll see it used in (?P<name>...), where it is inside () to define special properties for the grouping.
- . matches any single character. To match a . specifically, we need to use \..

We can create our own unique sets of characters using [] to enclose the elements of the set. We might have something like this:

```
(?P<name>\w+)\s*[=:]\s*(?P<value>.*)
```

This has a \w+ to match any number of alphanumeric characters. This will be collected into a group called name.

It uses \s* to match an optional sequence of spaces.

It matches any character in the set [=:]. Exactly one of the characters in this set must be present.

It uses \s* again to match an optional sequence of spaces.

Finally, it uses .* to match everything else in the string. This is collected into a group named value.

We can use this to parse strings, like this:

```
size = 12
weight: 14
```

By being flexible with the punctuation, we can make a program easier to use. We'll tolerate any number of spaces, and either an = or a : as a separator.

There's more...

A long regular expression can be awkward to read. We have a clever Pythonic trick for presenting an expression in a way that's much easier to read:

```
>>> ingredient_pattern = re.compile(
... r'(?P<ingredient>[\w\s]+):\s+' # name of the ingredient up to the ":"
... r'(?P<amount>\d+)\s+'          # amount, all digits up to a space
... r'(?P<unit>\w+)'               # units, alphanumeric characters
... )
```

This leverages three syntax rules:

- A statement isn't finished until the `()` characters match.
- Adjacent string literals are silently concatenated into a single long string.
- Anything between # and the end of the line is a comment, and is ignored.

We've put Python comments after the important clauses in our regular expression. This can help us understand what we did, and perhaps help us diagnose problems later.

We can also use the regular expression's "verbose" mode to add gratuitous whitespace and comments inside a regular expression string. To do this, we must use `re.X` as an option when compiling a regular expression to make whitespace and comments possible. This revised syntax looks like this:

```
>>> ingredient_pattern_x = re.compile(r'''
... (?P<ingredient>[\w\s]+):\s+ # name of the ingredient up to the ":"'
... (?P<amount>\d+)\s+          # amount, all digits up to a space'
... (?P<unit>\w+)               # units, alphanumeric characters
... ''', re.X)
```

We can either break the pattern up or make use of extended syntax to make the regular expression more readable.

See also

- The *Decoding Bytes – How to get proper characters from some bytes* recipe
- There are many books on Regular expressions and Python Regular expressions in particular, like *Mastering Python Regular Expressions* (`https://www.packtpub.com/application-development/mastering-python-regular-expressions`)

Building complex strings with f-strings

Creating complex strings is, in many ways, the polar opposite of parsing a complex string. We generally find that we use a template with substitution rules to put data into a more complex format.

Getting ready

Let's say we have pieces of data that we need to turn into a nicely formatted message. We might have data that includes the following:

```
>>> id = "IAD"
>>> location = "Dulles Intl Airport"
>>> max_temp = 32
>>> min_temp = 13
>>> precipitation = 0.4
```

And we'd like a line that looks like this:

```
IAD : Dulles Intl Airport : 32 / 13 / 0.40
```

How to do it...

1. Create an `f-string` from the result, replacing all of the data items with `{}` placeholders. Inside each placeholder, put a variable name (or an expression.) Note that the string uses the prefix of `f'`. The `f` prefix creates a sophisticated string object where values are interpolated into the template when the string is used:

   ```
   f'{id} : {location} : {max_temp} / {min_temp} / {precipitation}'
   ```

2. For each name or expression, an optional `:data type` can be appended to the names in the template string. The basic data type codes are:

   - `s` for string
   - `d` for decimal number
   - `f` for floating-point number

   It would look like this:

   ```
   f'{id:s}  : {location:s} : {max_temp:d} / {min_temp:d} /
   {precipitation:f}'
   ```

3. Add length information where required. Length is not always required, and in some cases, it's not even desirable. In this example, though, the length information ensures that each message has a consistent format. For strings and decimal numbers, prefix the format with the length like this: `19s` or `3d`. For floating-point numbers, use a two-part prefix like `5.2f` to specify the total length of five characters, with two to the right of the decimal point. Here's the whole format:

```
>>> f'{id:3d}  : {location:19s} : {max_temp:3d} / {min_temp:3d} /
{precipitation:5.2f}'
'IAD  : Dulles Intl Airport :   32 /  13 /  0.40'
```

How it works...

f-strings can do a lot of relatively sophisticated string assembly by interpolating data into a template. There are a number of conversions available.

We've seen three of the formatting conversions—`s`, `d`, `f`—but there are many others. Details can be found in the *Formatted string literals* section of the *Python Standard Library*: `https://docs.python.org/3/reference/lexical_analysis.html#formatted-string-literals`.

Here are some of the format conversions we might use:

- `b` is for binary, base 2.
- `c` is for Unicode character. The value must be a number, which is converted into a character. Often, we use hexadecimal numbers for these characters, so you might want to try values such as `0x2661` through `0x2666` to see interesting Unicode glyphs.
- `d` is for decimal numbers.
- `E` and `e` are for scientific notations. `6.626E-34` or `6.626e-34`, depending on which `E` or `e` character is used.
- `F` and `f` are for floating-point. For *not a number*, the `f` format shows lowercase `nan`; the `F` format shows uppercase `NAN`.
- `G` and `g` are for general use. This switches automatically between `E` and `F` (or `e` and `f`) to keep the output in the given sized field. For a format of `20.5G`, up to 20-digit numbers will be displayed using `F` formatting. Larger numbers will use `E` formatting.
- `n` is for locale-specific decimal numbers. This will insert `,` or `.` characters, depending on the current locale settings. The default locale may not have 1,000 separators defined. For more information, see the `locale` module.

- `o` is for octal, base 8.
- `s` is for string.
- `X` and `x` are for hexadecimal, base 16. The digits include uppercase `A-F` and lowercase `a-f`, depending on which `X` or `x` format character is used.
- `%` is for percentage. The number is multiplied by 100 and includes the `%`.

We have a number of prefixes we can use for these different types. The most common one is the length. We might use `{name:5d}` to put in a 5-digit number. There are several prefixes for the preceding types:

- **Fill and alignment**: We can specify a specific filler character (space is the default) and an alignment. Numbers are generally aligned to the right and strings to the left. We can change that using <, >, or ^. This forces left alignment, right alignment, or centering, respectively. There's a peculiar = alignment that's used to put padding after a leading sign.
- **Sign**: The default rule is a leading negative sign where needed. We can use `+` to put a sign on all numbers, `-` to put a sign only on negative numbers, and a space to use a space instead of a plus for positive numbers. In scientific output, we often use `{value: 5.3f}`. The space makes sure that room is left for the sign, ensuring that all the decimal points line up nicely.
- **Alternate form**: We can use the # to get an alternate form. We might have something like `{0:#x}`, `{0:#o}`, or `{0:#b}` to get a prefix on hexadecimal, octal, or binary values. With a prefix, the numbers will look like `0xnnn`, `0onnn`, or `0bnnn`. The default is to omit the two-character prefix.
- **Leading zero**: We can include `0` to get leading zeros to fill in the front of a number. Something like `{code:08x}` will produce a hexadecimal value with leading zeroes to pad it out to eight characters.
- **Width and precision**: For integer values and strings, we only provide the width. For floating-point values, we often provide `width.precision`.

There are some times when we won't use a `{name:format}` specification. Sometimes, we'll need to use a `{name!conversion}` specification. There are only three conversions available:

- `{name!r}` shows the representation that would be produced by `repr(name)`.
- `{name!s}` shows the string value that would be produced by `str(name)`; this is the default behavior if you don't specify any conversion. Using `!s` explicitly lets you add string-type format specifiers.
- `{name!a}` shows the ASCII value that would be produced by `ascii(name)`.
- Additionally, there's a handy debugging format specifier available in Python 3.8. We can include a trailing equals sign, `=`, to get a handy dump of a variable or expression. The following example uses both forms:

```
>>> value = 2**12-1
>>> f'{value=} {2**7+1=}'
'value=4095 2**7+1=129'
```

The `f-string` showed the value of the variable named `value` and the result of an expression, `2**7+1`.

In *Chapter 7, Basics of Classes and Objects*, we'll leverage the idea of the `{name!r}` format specification to simplify displaying information about related objects.

There's more...

The `f-string` processing relies on the string `format()` method. We can leverage this method and the related `format_map()` method for cases where we have more complex data structures.

Looking forward to *Chapter 4, Built-In Data Structures Part 1: Lists and Sets*, we might have a dictionary where the keys are simple strings that fit with the `format_map()` rules:

```
>>> data = dict(
... id=id, location=location, max_temp=max_temp,
... min_temp=min_temp, precipitation=precipitation
... )
>>> '{id:3s}  : {location:19s} :  {max_temp:3d} / {min_temp:3d} / {precipitation:5.2f}'.format_map(data)
'IAD  : Dulles Intl Airport :   32 /  13 /  0.40'
```

We've created a `dictionary` object, `data`, that contains a number of values with `keys` that are valid Python identifiers: `id`, `location`, `max_temp`, `min_temp`, and `precipitation`. We can then use this dictionary with `format_map()` to extract values from the dictionary using the `keys`.

Note that the formatting template here is not an `f-string`. It doesn't have the `f"` prefix. Instead of using the automatic formatting features of an `f-string`, we've done the interpolation "the hard way" using the `format_map()` method.

See also

- More details can be found in the *Formatted string literals* section of the *Python Standard Library*: `https://docs.python.org/3/reference/lexical_analysis.html#formatted-string-literals`

Building complicated strings from lists of characters

How can we make complicated changes to an immutable string? Can we assemble a string from individual characters?

In most cases, the recipes we've already seen give us a number of tools for creating and modifying strings. There are yet more ways in which we can tackle the string manipulation problem. In this recipe, we'll look at using a `list` object as a way to decompose and rebuild a string. This will dovetail with some of the recipes in *Chapter 4, Built-In Data Structures Part 1: Lists and Sets*.

Getting ready

Here's a string that we'd like to rearrange:

```
>>> title = "Recipe 5: Rewriting an Immutable String"
```

We'd like to do two transformations:

- Remove the part before `:`
- Replace the punctuation with `_` and make all the characters lowercase

We'll make use of the `string` module:

```
>>> from string import whitespace, punctuation
```

This has two important constants:

- `string.whitespace` lists all of the ASCII whitespace characters, including space and tab.
- `string.punctuation` lists the ASCII punctuation marks.

How to do it...

We can work with a string exploded into a list. We'll look at lists in more depth in *Chapter 4, Built-In Data Structures Part 1: Lists and Sets*:

1. Explode the string into a `list` object:

   ```
   >>> title_list = list(title)
   ```

2. Find the partition character. The `index()` method for a list has the same semantics as the `index()` method has for a string. It locates the position with the given value:

   ```
   >>> colon_position = title_list.index(':')
   ```

3. Delete the characters that are no longer needed. The `del` statement can remove items from a list. Unlike strings, lists are mutable data structures:

```
>>> del title_list[:colon_position+1]
```

4. Replace punctuation by stepping through each position. In this case, we'll use a `for` statement to visit every index in the string:

```
>>> for position in range(len(title_list)):
...     if title_list[position] in whitespace+punctuation:
...         title_list[position]= '_'
```

5. The expression `range(len(title_list))` generates all of the values between `0` and `len(title_list)-1`. This assures us that the value of `position` will be each value index in the list. Join the list of characters to create a new string. It seems a little odd to use a zero-length string, `''`, as a separator when concatenating strings together. However, it works perfectly:

```
>>> title = ''.join(title_list)
>>> title
'_Rewriting_an_Immutable_String'
```

We assigned the resulting string back to the original variable. The original string object, which had been referred to by that variable, is no longer needed: it's automatically removed from memory (this is known as "garbage collection"). The new string object replaces the value of the variable.

How it works...

This is a change in representation trick. Since a string is immutable, we can't update it. We can, however, convert it into a mutable form; in this case, a list. We can make whatever changes are required to the mutable list object. When we're done, we can change the representation from a list back to a string and replace the original value of the variable.

Lists provide some features that strings don't have. Conversely, strings provide a number of features lists don't have. As an example, we can't convert a list into lowercase the way we can convert a string.

There's an important trade-off here:

- Strings are immutable, which makes them very fast. Strings are focused on Unicode characters. When we look at mappings and sets, we can use strings as keys for mappings and items in sets because the value is immutable.
- Lists are mutable. Operations are slower. Lists can hold any kind of item. We can't use a list as a key for a mapping or an item in a set because the list value could change.

Strings and lists are both specialized kinds of sequences. Consequently, they have a number of common features. The basic item indexing and slicing features are shared. Similarly, a list uses the same kind of negative index values that a string does: `list[-1]` is the last item in a `list` object.

We'll return to mutable data structures in *Chapter 4, Built-In Data Structures Part 1: Lists and Sets*.

See also

- We can also work with strings using the internal methods of a string. See the *Rewriting an immutable string* recipe for more techniques.
- Sometimes, we need to build a string, and then convert it into bytes. See the *Encoding strings – creating ASCII and UTF-8 bytes* recipe for how we can do this.
- Other times, we'll need to convert bytes into a string. See the *Decoding Bytes – How to get proper characters from some bytes* recipe for more information.

Using the Unicode characters that aren't on our keyboards

A big keyboard might have almost 100 individual keys. Fewer than 50 of these are letters, numbers, and punctuation. At least a dozen are *function* keys that do things other than simply *insert* letters into a document. Some of the keys are different kinds of *modifiers* that are meant to be used in conjunction with another key—for example, we might have *Shift*, *Ctrl*, *Option*, and *Command*.

Most operating systems will accept simple key combinations that create about 100 or so characters. More elaborate key combinations may create another 100 or so less popular characters. This isn't even close to covering the vast domain of characters from the world's alphabets. And there are icons, emoticons, and dingbats galore in our computer fonts. How do we get to all of those glyphs?

Getting ready

Python works in Unicode. There are thousands of individual Unicode characters available.

We can see all the available characters at `https://en.wikipedia.org/wiki/List_of_Unicode_characters`, as well as at `http://www.unicode.org/charts/`.

We'll need the Unicode character number. We may also want the Unicode character name.

A given font on our computer may not be designed to provide glyphs for all of those characters. In particular, Windows computer fonts may have trouble displaying some of these characters. Using the following Windows command to change to code page 65001 is sometimes necessary:

```
chcp 65001
```

Linux and macOS rarely have problems with Unicode characters.

How to do it...

Python uses **escape sequences** to extend the ordinary characters we can type to cover the vast space of Unicode characters. Each escape sequence starts with a \ character. The next character tells us exactly how the Unicode character will be represented. Locate the character that's needed. Get the name or the number. The numbers are always given as hexadecimal, base 16. Websites describing Unicode often write the character as `U+2680`. The name might be `DIE FACE-1`. Use `\unnnn` with up to a four-digit number. Or, use `\N{name}` with the spelled-out name. If the number is more than four digits, use `\Unnnnnnnn` with the number padded out to exactly eight digits:

```
>>> 'You Rolled \u2680'
'You Rolled ⚀'
>>> 'You drew \u0001F000'
'You drew 🀄'
>>> 'Discard \N{MAHJONG TILE RED DRAGON}'
'Discard 🀄'
```

Yes, we can include a wide variety of characters in Python output. To place a \ character in the string, we need to use `\\`. For example, we might need this for Windows file paths.

How it works...

Python uses Unicode internally. The 128 or so characters we can type directly using the keyboard all have handy internal Unicode numbers.

When we write:

```
'HELLO'
```

Python treats it as shorthand for this:

```
'\u0048\u0045\u004c\u004c\u004f'
```

Once we get beyond the characters on our keyboards, the remaining thousands of characters are identified only by their number.

When the string is being compiled by Python, `\uxxxx`, `\Uxxxxxxxx`, and `\N{name}` are all replaced by the proper Unicode character. If we have something syntactically wrong—for example, `\N{name` with no closing `}`—we'll get an immediate error from Python's internal syntax checking.

Back in the *String parsing with regular expressions* recipe, we noted that regular expressions use a lot of \ characters and that we specifically do not want Python's normal compiler to touch them; we used the `r'` prefix on a regular expression string to prevent \ from being treated as an escape and possibly converted into something else. To use the full domain of Unicode characters, we cannot avoid using \ as an escape.

What if we need to use Unicode in a Regular expression? We'll need to use \\ all over the place in the Regular expression. We might see this: `'\\w+[\u2680\u2681\u2682\u2683\u2684\u2685]\\d+'`. We couldn't use the `r'` prefix on the string because we needed to have the Unicode escapes processed. This forced us to double the \ used for Regular expressions. We used `\uxxxx` for the Unicode characters that are part of the pattern. Python's internal compiler will replace `\uxxxx` with Unicode characters and `\\w` with a required `\w` internally.

> When we look at a string at the `>>>` prompt, Python will display the string in its canonical form. Python prefers to use `'` as a delimiter, even though we can use either `'` or `"` for a string delimiter. Python doesn't generally display raw strings; instead, it puts all of the necessary escape sequences back into the string:
>
> ```
> >>> r"\w+"
> '\\w+'
> ```
>
> We provided a string in raw form. Python displayed it in canonical form.

See also

- In the *Encoding strings - creating ASCII and UTF-8 bytes* and the *Decoding Bytes - How to get proper characters from some bytes* recipes, we'll look at how Unicode characters are converted into sequences of bytes so we can write them to a file. We'll look at how bytes from a file (or downloaded from a website) are turned into Unicode characters so they can be processed.
- If you're interested in history, you can read up on ASCII and EBCDIC and other old-fashioned character codes here: `http://www.unicode.org/charts/`.

Encoding strings – creating ASCII and UTF-8 bytes

Our computer files are bytes. When we upload or download from the internet, the communication works in bytes. A byte only has 256 distinct values. Our Python characters are Unicode. There are a lot more than 256 Unicode characters.

How do we map Unicode characters to bytes to write to a file or for transmission?

Getting ready

Historically, a character occupied 1 byte. Python leverages the old ASCII encoding scheme for bytes; this sometimes leads to confusion between bytes and proper strings of Unicode characters.

Unicode characters are encoded into sequences of bytes. There are a number of standardized encodings and a number of non-standard encodings.

Plus, there also are some encodings that only work for a small subset of Unicode characters. We try to avoid these, but there are some situations where we'll need to use a subset encoding scheme.

Unless we have a really good reason not to, we almost always use UTF-8 encoding for Unicode characters. Its main advantage is that it's a compact representation of the Latin alphabet, which is used for English and a number of European languages.

Sometimes, an internet protocol requires ASCII characters. This is a special case that requires some care because the ASCII encoding can only handle a small subset of Unicode characters.

How to do it...

Python will generally use our OS's default encoding for files and internet traffic. The details are unique to each OS:

1. We can make a general setting using the `PYTHONIOENCODING` environment variable. We set this outside of Python to ensure that a particular encoding is used everywhere. When using Linux or macOS, use `export` to `set` the environment variable. For Windows, use the `set` command, or the PowerShell `Set-Item` cmdlet. For Linux, it looks like this:

   ```
   export PYTHONIOENCODING=UTF-8
   ```

2. Run Python:

   ```
   python3.8
   ```

3. We sometimes need to make specific settings when we open a file inside our script. We'll return to this topic in *Chapter 10, Input/Output, Physical Format and, Logical Layout*. Open the file with a given encoding. Read or write Unicode characters to the file:

   ```
   >>> with open('some_file.txt', 'w', encoding='utf-8') as output:
   ...     print( 'You drew \U0001F000', file=output )
   >>> with open('some_file.txt', 'r', encoding='utf-8') as input:
   ...     text = input.read()
   >>> text
   'You drew 🀀'
   ```

We can also manually encode characters, in the rare case that we need to open a file in bytes mode; if we use a mode of `wb`, we'll need to use manual encoding:

```
>>> string_bytes = 'You drew \U0001F000'.encode('utf-8')
>>> string_bytes
b'You drew \xf0\x9f\x80\x80'
```

We can see that a sequence of bytes (`\xf0\x9f\x80\x80`) was used to encode a single Unicode character, `U+1F000`, 🀀.

How it works...

Unicode defines a number of encoding schemes. While UTF-8 is the most popular, there is also UTF-16 and UTF-32. The number is the typical number of bits per character. A file with 1,000 characters encoded in UTF-32 would be 4,000 8-bit bytes. A file with 1,000 characters encoded in UTF-8 could be as few as 1,000 bytes, depending on the exact mix of characters. In UTF-8 encoding, characters with Unicode numbers above `U+007F` require multiple bytes.

Various OSes have their own coding schemes. macOS files can be encoded in `Mac Roman` or `Latin-1`. Windows files might use `CP1252` encoding.

The point with all of these schemes is to have a sequence of bytes that can be mapped to a Unicode character and—going the other way—a way to map each Unicode character to one or more bytes. Ideally, all of the Unicode characters are accounted for. Pragmatically, some of these coding schemes are incomplete.

The historical form of ASCII encoding can only represent about 100 of the Unicode characters as bytes. It's easy to create a string that cannot be encoded using the ASCII scheme.

Here's what the error looks like:

```
>>> 'You drew \U0001F000'.encode('ascii')
Traceback (most recent call last):
  File "<stdin>", line 1, in <module>
UnicodeEncodeError: 'ascii' codec can't encode character '\U0001f000' in
position 9: ordinal not in range(128)
```

We may see this kind of error when we accidentally open a file with a poorly chosen encoding. When we see this, we'll need to change our processing to select a more useful encoding; ideally, UTF-8.

> **Bytes versus strings**: Bytes are often displayed using printable characters. We'll see `b'hello'` as shorthand for a five-byte value. The letters are chosen using the old ASCII encoding scheme, where byte values from `0x20` to `0x7F` will be shown as characters, and outside this range, more complex-looking escapes will be used.
>
> This use of characters to represent byte values can be confusing. The prefix of `b'` is our hint that we're looking at bytes, not proper Unicode characters.

See also

- There are a number of ways to build strings of data. See the *Building complex strings with f"strings"* and the *Building complex strings from lists of characters* recipes for examples of creating complex strings. The idea is that we might have an application that builds a complex string, and then we encode it into bytes.
- For more information on UTF-8 encoding, see `https://en.wikipedia.org/wiki/UTF-8`.
- For general information on Unicode encodings, see `http://unicode.org/faq/utf_bom.html`.

Decoding bytes – how to get proper characters from some bytes

How can we work with files that aren't properly encoded? What do we do with files written in ASCII encoding?

A download from the internet is almost always in bytes—not characters. How do we decode the characters from that stream of bytes?

Also, when we use the `subprocess` module, the results of an OS command are in bytes. How can we recover proper characters?

Much of this is also relevant to the material in *Chapter 10, Input/Output, Physical Format and Logical Layout*. We've included this recipe here because it's the inverse of the previous recipe, *Encoding strings - creating ASCII and UTF-8 bytes*.

Getting ready

Let's say we're interested in offshore marine weather forecasts. Perhaps this is because we own a large sailboat, or perhaps because good friends of ours have a large sailboat and are departing the **Chesapeake Bay** for the **Caribbean**.

Are there any special warnings coming from the **National Weather Services** office in Wakefield, Virginia?

Here's where we can get the warnings: `https://forecast.weather.gov/product.php?site=CRH&issuedby=AKQ&product=SMW&format=TXT`.

We can download this with Python's `urllib` module:

```
>>> import urllib.request
>>> warnings_uri= 'https://forecast.weather.gov/product.php?site=CRH&issuedby=AKQ&product=SMW&format=TXT'
>>> with urllib.request.urlopen(warnings_uri) as source:
...     warnings_text = source.read()
```

Or, we can use programs like `curl` or `wget` to get this. At the OS Terminal prompt, we might run the following (long) command:

```
$ curl 'https://forecast.weather.gov/product.php?site=CRH&issuedby=AKQ&product=SMW&format=TXT' -o AKQ.html
```

Typesetting this book tends to break the command onto many lines. It's really one very long line.

The code repository includes a sample file, `Chapter_01/National Weather Service Text Product Display.html`.

The `forecast_text` value is a stream of bytes. It's not a proper string. We can tell because it starts like this:

```
>>> warnings_text[:80]
b'<!DOCTYPE html PUBLIC "-//W3C//DTD XHTML 1.0 Transitional//EN" "http://www.w3.or'
```

The data goes on for a while, providing details from the web page. Because the displayed value starts with `b'`, it's bytes, not proper Unicode characters. It was probably encoded with UTF-8, which means some characters could have weird-looking `\xnn` escape sequences instead of proper characters. We want to have the proper characters.

While this data has many easy-to-read characters, the `b'` prefix shows that it's a collection of byte values, not proper text. Generally, a `bytes` object behaves somewhat like a `string` object. Sometimes, we can work with bytes directly. Most of the time, we'll want to decode the bytes and create proper Unicode characters from them.

How to do it...

1. Determine the coding scheme if possible. In order to decode bytes to create proper Unicode characters, we need to know what encoding scheme was used. When we read XML documents, there's a big hint provided within the document:

   ```
   <?xml version="1.0" encoding="UTF-8"?>
   ```

   When browsing web pages, there's often a header containing this information:

   ```
   Content-Type: text/html; charset=ISO-8859-4
   ```

   Sometimes, an HTML page may include this as part of the header:

   ```
   <meta http-equiv="Content-Type" content="text/html;
   charset=utf-8">
   ```

   In other cases, we're left to guess. In the case of US weather data, a good first guess is UTF-8. Other good guesses include ISO-8859-1. In some cases, the guess will depend on the language.

2. The *codecs – Codec registry and base classes* section of the *Python Standard Library* lists the standard encodings available. Decode the data:

   ```
   >>> document = forecast_text.decode("UTF-8")
   >>> document[:80]
   '<!DOCTYPE html PUBLIC "-//W3C//DTD XHTML 1.0 Transitional//EN"
   "http://www.w3.or'
   ```

   The `b'` prefix is no longer used to show that these are bytes. We've created a proper string of Unicode characters from the stream of bytes.

3. If this step fails with an exception, we guessed wrong about the encoding. We need to try another encoding. Parse the resulting document.

Since this is an HTML document, we should use **Beautiful Soup**. See `http://www.crummy.com/software/BeautifulSoup/`.

We can, however, extract one nugget of information from this document without completely parsing the HTML:

```
>>> import re
>>> title_pattern = re.compile(r"\<h3\>(.*?)\</h3\>")
>>> title_pattern.search( document )
<_sre.SRE_Match object; span=(3438, 3489), match='<h3>There are no
products active at this time.</h>
```

This tells us what we need to know: there are no warnings at this time. This doesn't mean smooth sailing, but it does mean that there aren't any major weather systems that could cause catastrophes.

How it works...

See the *Encoding strings – creating ASCII and UTF-8 bytes* recipe for more information on Unicode and the different ways that Unicode characters can be encoded into streams of bytes.

At the foundation of the operating system, files and network connections are built up from bytes. It's our software that decodes the bytes to discover the content. It might be characters, images, or sounds. In some cases, the default assumptions are wrong and we need to do our own decoding.

See also

- Once we've recovered the string data, we have a number of ways of parsing or rewriting it. See the *String parsing with regular expressions* recipe for examples of parsing a complex string.
- For more information on encodings, see `https://en.wikipedia.org/wiki/UTF-8` and `http://unicode.org/faq/utf_bom.html`.

Using tuples of items

What's the best way to represent simple (*x,y*) and (*r,g,b*) groups of values? How can we keep things that are pairs, such as latitude and longitude, together?

Getting ready

In the *String parsing with regular expressions* recipe, we skipped over an interesting data structure.

We had data that looked like this:

```
>>> ingredient = "Kumquat: 2 cups"
```

We parsed this into meaningful data using a regular expression, like this:

```
>>> import re
>>> ingredient_pattern = re.compile(r'(?P<ingredient>\w+):\s+(?P<amount>\
d+)\s+(?P<unit>\w+)')
>>> match = ingredient_pattern.match(ingredient)
>>> match.groups()
('Kumquat', '2', 'cups')
```

The result is a tuple object with three pieces of data. There are lots of places where this kind of grouped data can come in handy.

How to do it...

We'll look at two aspects to this: putting things into tuples and getting things out of tuples.

Creating tuples

There are lots of places where Python creates tuples of data for us. In the *Getting ready* section of the *String parsing with regular expressions* recipe, we showed you how a regular expression match object will create a tuple of text that was parsed from a string.

We can create our own tuples, too. Here are the steps:

1. Enclose the data in `()`.
2. Separate the items with `,`:

    ```
    >>> from fractions import Fraction
    >>> my_data = ('Rice', Fraction(1/4), 'cups')
    ```

There's an important special case for the `one-tuple`, or `singleton`. We have to include an extra `,`, even when there's only one item in the tuple:

```
>>> one_tuple = ('item', )
>>> len(one_tuple)
1
```

> The `()` characters aren't always required. There are a few times where we can omit them. It's not a good idea to omit them, but we can see funny things when we have an extra comma:
>
> ```
> >>> 355,
> (355,)
> ```
>
> The extra comma after `355` turns the value into a `singleton` tuple.

Extracting items from a tuple

The idea of a tuple is for it to be a container with a number of items that's fixed by the problem domain: for example, for (`red`, `green`, `blue`) color numbers, the number of items is always three.

In our example, we've got an `ingredient`, and `amount`, and `units`. This must be a three-item collection. We can look at the individual items in two ways:

- By index position; that is, positions are numbered starting with zero from the left:

  ```
  >>> my_data[1]
  Fraction(1, 4)
  ```

- Using multiple assignment:

  ```
  >>> ingredient, amount, unit = my_data
  >>> ingredient
  'Rice'
  >>> unit
  'cups'
  ```

Tuples—like strings—are immutable. We can't change the individual items inside a tuple. We use tuples when we want to keep the data together.

How it works...

Tuples are one example of the more general `Sequence` class. We can do a few things with sequences.

Here's an example tuple that we can work with:

```
>>> t = ('Kumquat', '2', 'cups')
```

Here are some operations we can perform on this tuple:

- How many items in `t`?

  ```
  >>> len(t)
  3
  ```

- How many times does a particular value appear in `t`?

```
>>> t.count('2')
1
```

- Which position has a particular value?

```
>>> t.index('cups')
2
>>> t[2]
'cups'
```

- When an item doesn't exist, we'll get an exception:

```
>>> t.index('Rice')
Traceback (most recent call last):
  File "<stdin>", line 1, in <module>
ValueError: tuple.index(x): x not in tuple
```

- Does a particular value exist?

```
>>> 'Rice' in t
False
```

There's more...

A tuple, like a string, is a sequence of items. In the case of a string, it's a sequence of characters. In the case of a tuple, it's a sequence of many things. Because they're both sequences, they have some common features. We've noted that we can pluck out individual items by their index position. We can use the `index()` method to locate the position of an item.

The similarities end there. A string has many methods it can use to create a new string that's a transformation of a string, plus methods to parse strings, plus methods to determine the content of the strings. A tuple doesn't have any of these bonus features. It's—perhaps—the simplest possible data structure.

See also

- We looked at one other sequence, the list, in the *Building complex strings from lists of characters* recipe.
- We'll also look at sequences in *Chapter 4, Built-In Data Structures Part 1: Lists and Sets.*

Using NamedTuples to simplify item access in tuples

When we worked with tuples, we had to remember the positions as numbers. When we use a (*r*,*g*,*b*) tuple to represent a color, can we use "red" instead of zero, "green" instead of 1, and "blue" instead of 2?

Getting ready

Let's continue looking at items in recipes. The regular expression for parsing the string had three attributes: ingredient, amount, and unit. We used the following pattern with names for the various substrings:

```
r'(?P<ingredient>\w+):\s+(?P<amount>\d+)\s+(?P<unit>\w+)')
```

The resulting data tuple looked like this:

```
>>> item = match.groups()
('Kumquat', '2', 'cups')
```

While the matching between `ingredient`, `amount`, and `unit` is pretty clear, using something like the following isn't ideal. What does "1" mean? Is it really the quantity?

```
>>> Fraction(item[1])
Fraction(2, 1)
```

We want to define tuples with names, as well as positions.

How to do it...

1. We'll use the `NamedTuple` class definition from the typing package:

   ```
   >>> from typing import NamedTuple
   ```

2. With this base class definition, we can define our own unique tuples, with names for the items:

   ```
   >>> class Ingredient(NamedTuple):
   ...     ingredient: str
   ...     amount: str
   ...     unit: str
   ```

3. Now, we can create an instance of this unique kind of tuple by using the classname:

   ```
   >>> item_2 = Ingredient('Kumquat', '2', 'cups')
   ```

4. When we want a value, we can use `name` instead of the position:

```
>>> Fraction(item_2.amount)
Fraction(2, 1)
>>> f"Use {item_2.amount} {item_2.unit} fresh {item_2.ingredient}"
'Use 2 cups fresh Kumquat'
```

How it works...

The `NamedTuple` class definition introduces a core concept from *Chapter 7, Basics of Classes and Objects*. We've extended the base class definition to add unique features for our application. In this case, we've named the three attributes each `Ingredient` tuple must contain.

Because a `NamedTuple` class is a tuple, the order of the attribute names is fixed. We can use a reference like the expression `item_2[0]` as well as the expression `item_2.ingredient`. Both names refer to the item in index 0 of the tuple, `item_2`.

The core tuple types can be called "anonymous tuples" or maybe "index-only tuples." This can help to distinguish them from the more sophisticated "named tuples" introduced through the `typing` module.

Tuples are very useful as tiny containers of closely related data. Using the `NamedTuple` class definition makes them even easier to work with.

There's more...

We can have a mixed collection of values in a tuple or a named tuple. We need to perform conversion before we can build the tuple. It's important to remember that a tuple cannot ever be changed. It's an immutable object, similar in many ways to the way strings and numbers are immutable.

For example, we might want to work with amounts that are exact fractions. Here's a more sophisticated definition:

```
>>> class IngredientF(NamedTuple):
...     ingredient: str
...     amount: Fraction
...     unit: str
```

These objects require some care to create. If we're using a bunch of strings, we can't simply build this object from three string values; we need to convert the amount into a `Fraction` instance. Here's an example of creating an item using a `Fraction` conversion:

```
>>> item_3 = IngredientF('Kumquat', Fraction('2'), 'cups')
```

This tuple has a more useful value for the amount of each ingredient. We can now do mathematical operations on the amounts:

```
>>> f'{item_3.ingredient} doubled: {item_3.amount*2}'
'Kumquat doubled: 4'
```

It's very handy to specifically state the data type within `NamedTuple`. It turns out Python doesn't use the type information directly. Other tools, for example, `mypy`, can check the type hints in `NamedTuple` against the operations in the rest of the code to be sure they agree.

See also

- We'll look at class definitions in *Chapter 7, Basics of Classes and Objects*.

2
Statements and Syntax

Python syntax is designed to be simple. There are a few rules; we'll look at some of the interesting statements in the language as a way to understand those rules. Concrete examples can help clarify the language's syntax.

We'll cover some basics of creating script files first. Then we'll move on to looking at some of the more commonly-used statements. Python only has about 20 or so different kinds of imperative statements in the language. We've already looked at two kinds of statements in *Chapter 1, Numbers, Strings, and Tuples*, the assignment statement and the expression statement.

When we write something like this:

```
>>> print("hello world")
hello world
```

We're actually executing a statement that contains only the evaluation of a function, `print()`. This kind of statement—where we evaluate a function or a method of an object—is common.

The other kind of statement we've already seen is the assignment statement. Python has many variations on this theme. Most of the time, we're assigning a single value to a single variable. Sometimes, however, we might be assigning two variables at the same time, like this:

```
quotient, remainder = divmod(355, 113)
```

These recipes will look at some of the more common of the complex statements, including `if`, `while`, `for`, `try`, and `with`. We'll touch on a few of the simpler statements as we go, like `break` and `raise`.

In this chapter, we'll look at the following recipes:

- Writing Python script and module files - syntax basics
- Writing long lines of code
- Including descriptions and documentation
- Better RST markup in `docstrings`
- Designing complex `if...elif` chains
- Saving intermediate results with the `:=` "walrus"
- Avoiding a potential problem with `break` statements
- Leveraging exception matching rules
- Avoiding a potential problem with an `except:` clause
- Concealing an exception root cause
- Managing a context using the `with` statement

We'll start by looking at the big picture – scripts and modules – and then we'll move down into details of individual statements. New with Python 3.8 is the assignment operator, sometimes called the "walrus" operator. We'll move into exception handling and context management as more advanced recipes in this section.

Writing Python script and module files – syntax basics

We'll need to write Python script files in order to do anything that's fully automated. We can experiment with the language at the interactive `>>>` prompt. We can also use JupyterLab interactively. For automated work, however, we'll need to create and run script files.

How can we make sure our code matches what's in common use? We need to look at some common aspects of *style*: how we organize our programming to make it readable.

We'll also look at a number of more technical considerations. For example, we need to be sure to save our files in UTF-8 encoding. While ASCII encoding is still supported by Python, it's a poor choice for modern programming. We'll also need to be sure to use spaces instead of tabs. If we use Unix newlines as much as possible, we'll also find it slightly simpler to create software that runs on a variety of operating systems.

Most text editing tools will work properly with Unix (newline) line endings as well as Windows or DOS (return-newline) line endings. Any tool that can't work with both kinds of line endings should be avoided.

Getting ready

To edit Python scripts, we'll need a good programming text editor. Python comes with a handy editor, IDLE. It works well for simple projects. It lets us jump back and forth between a file and an interactive `>>>` prompt, but it's not a good programming editor for larger projects.

There are dozens of programming editors. It's nearly impossible to suggest just one. So we'll suggest a few.

The JetBrains PyCharm editor has numerous features. The community edition version is free. See `https://www.jetbrains.com/pycharm/download/`.

ActiveState has Komodo IDE, which is also very sophisticated. The Komodo Edit version is free and does some of the same things as the full Komodo IDE. See `http://komodoide.com/komodo-edit/`.

Notepad++ is good for Windows developers. See `https://notepad-plus-plus.org`.

BBEdit is very nice for macOS X developers. See `http://www.barebones.com/products/bbedit/`.

For Linux developers, there are several built-in editors, including VIM, gedit, and Kate. These are all good. Since Linux tends to be biased toward developers, the editors available are all suitable for writing Python.

What's important is that we'll often have two windows open while we're working:

- The script or file that we're working on in our editor of choice.
- Python's `>>>` prompt (perhaps from a shell or perhaps from IDLE) where we can try things out to see what works and what doesn't. We may be creating our script in Notepad++ but using IDLE to experiment with data structures and algorithms.

We actually have two recipes here. First, we need to set some defaults for our editor. Then, once the editor is set up properly, we can create a generic template for our script files.

How to do it...

First, we'll look at the general setup that we need to do in our editor of choice. We'll use Komodo examples, but the basic principles apply to all editors. Once we've set the edit preferences, we can create our script files:

1. Open your editor of choice. Look at the preferences page for the editor.
2. Find the settings for preferred file encoding. With Komodo Edit Preferences, it's on the **Internationalization** tab. Set this to UTF-8.

3. Find the settings for indentation. If there's a way to use spaces instead of tabs, check this option. With Komodo Edit, we actually do this backward—we uncheck "prefer spaces over tabs." Also, set the spaces per indent to four. That's typical for Python code. It allows us to have several levels of indentation and still keep the code fairly narrow.

> The rule is this: we want spaces; we do not want tabs.

Once we're sure that our files will be saved in UTF-8 encoding, and we're also sure we're using spaces instead of tabs, we can create an example script file:

1. The first line of most Python script files should look like this:

   ```
   #!/usr/bin/env python3
   ```

   This sets an association between the file you're writing and Python.

   For Windows, the filename-to-program association is done through a setting in one of the Windows control panels. Within the **Default Programs** control panel, there's a panel to **Set Associations**. This control panel shows that `.py` files are bound to the Python program. This is normally set by the installer, and we rarely need to change it or set it manually.

> Windows developers can include the preamble line anyway. It will make macOS X and Linux folks happy when they download the project from GitHub.

2. After the preamble, there should be a triple-quoted block of text. This is the documentation string (called a **docstring**) for the file we're going to create. It's not technically mandatory, but it's essential for explaining what a file contains:

   ```
   """
   A summary of this script.
   """
   ```

   Because Python triple-quoted strings can be indefinitely long, feel free to write as much as necessary. This should be the primary vehicle for describing the script or library module. This can even include examples of how it works.

3. Now comes the interesting part of the script: the part that really does something. We can write all the statements we need to get the job done. For now, we'll use this as a placeholder:

```
print('hello world')
```

This isn't much, but at least the script does something. In other recipes, we'll look at more complex processing. It's common to create function and class definitions, as well as to write statements to use the functions and classes to do things.

For our first, simple script, all of the statements must begin at the left margin and must be complete on a single line. There are many Python statements that have blocks of statements nested inside them. These internal blocks of statements must be indented to clarify their scope. Generally—because we set indentation to four spaces—we can hit the *Tab* key to indent.

Our file should look like this:

```
#!/usr/bin/env python3
"""
My First Script: Calculate an important value.
"""

print(355/113)
```

How it works...

Unlike other languages, there's very little *boilerplate* in Python. There's only one line of *overhead* and even the `#!/usr/bin/env python3` line is generally optional.

Why do we set the encoding to UTF-8? While the entire language is designed to work using just the original 128 ASCII characters, we often find that ASCII is limiting. It's easier to set our editor to use UTF-8 encoding. With this setting, we can simply use any character that makes sense. We can use characters like μ as Python variables if we save our programs in UTF-8 encoding.

This is legal Python if we save our file in UTF-8:

```
π = 355/113
print(π)
```

> It's important to be consistent when choosing between spaces and tabs in Python. They are both more or less invisible, and mixing them can easily lead to confusion. Spaces are suggested.

When we set up our editor to use a four-space indent, we can then use the button labeled *Tab* on our keyboard to insert four spaces. Our code will align properly, and the indentation will show how our statements nest inside each other.

The initial `#!` line is a comment. Because the two characters are sometimes called sharp and bang, the combination is called "shebang." Everything between a # and the end of the line is ignored. The Linux loader (a program named `execve`) looks at the first few bytes of a file to see what the file contains. The first few bytes are sometimes called *magic* because the loader's behavior seems magical. When present, this two-character sequence of `#!` is followed by the path to the program responsible for processing the rest of the data in the file. We prefer to use `/usr/bin/env` to start the Python program for us. We can leverage this to make Python-specific environment settings via the `env` program.

There's more...

The *Python Standard Library* documents are derived, in part, from the documentation strings present in the module files. It's common practice to write sophisticated docstrings in modules. There are tools like pydoc and Sphinx that can reformat the module docstrings into elegant documentation. We'll look at this in other recipes.

Additionally, unit test cases can be included in the docstrings. Tools like `doctest` can extract examples from the document string and execute the code to see if the answers in the documentation match the answers found by running the code. Most of this book is validated with **doctest**.

Triple-quoted documentation strings are preferred over # comments. While all text between # and the end of the line is ignored, this is limited to a single line, and it is used sparingly. A docstring can be of indefinite size; they are used widely.

Prior to Python 3.6, we might sometimes see this kind of thing in a script file:

```
color = 355/113  # type: float
```

The `# type: float` comment can be used by a type inferencing system to establish that the various data types can occur when the program is actually executed. For more information on this, see **Python Enhancement Proposal** (**PEP**) 484: `https://www.python.org/dev/peps/pep-0484/`.

The preferred style is this:

```
color: float = 355/113
```

The type hint is provided immediately after the variable name. This is based on PEP 526, `https://www.python.org/dev/peps/pep-0526`. In this case, the type hint is obvious and possibly redundant. The result of exact integer division is a floating-point value, and type inferencing tools like `mypy` are capable of figuring out the specific type for obvious cases like this.

There's another bit of overhead that's sometimes included in a file. The VIM and gedit editors let us keep edit preferences in the file. This is called a **modeline**. We may see these; they can be ignored. Here's a typical modeline that's useful for Python:

```
# vim: tabstop=8 expandtab shiftwidth=4 softtabstop=4
```

This sets the Unicode `u+0009` TAB characters to be transformed to eight spaces; when we hit the *Tab* key, we'll shift four spaces. This setting is carried in the file; we don't have to do any VIM setup to apply these settings to our Python script files.

See also

- We'll look at how to write useful document strings in the *Including descriptions and documentation* and *Writing better RST markup in docstrings* recipes.
- For more information on suggested style, see `https://www.python.org/dev/peps/pep-0008/`

Writing long lines of code

There are many times when we need to write lines of code that are so long that they're very hard to read. Many people like to limit the length of a line of code to 80 characters or fewer. It's a well-known principle of graphic design that a narrower line is easier to read. See `http://webtypography.net/2.1.2` for a deeper discussion of line width and readability.

While shorter lines are easier on the eyes, our code can refuse to cooperate with this principle. Long statements are a common problem. How can we break long Python statements into more manageable pieces?

Getting ready

Often, we'll have a statement that's awkwardly long and hard to work with. Let's say we've got something like this:

```
>>> import math
>>> example_value = (63/25) * (17+15*math.sqrt(5)) / (7+15*math.sqrt(5))
>>> mantissa_fraction, exponent = math.frexp(example_value)
>>> mantissa_whole = int(mantissa_fraction*2**53)
>>> message_text = f'the internal representation is {mantissa_
whole:d}/2**53*2**{exponent:d}'
>>> print(message_text)
the internal representation is 7074237752514592/2**53*2**2
```

This code includes a long formula, and a long format string into which we're injecting values. This looks bad when typeset in a book; the f-string line may be broken incorrectly. It looks bad on our screen when trying to edit this script.

We can't haphazardly break Python statements into chunks. The syntax rules are clear that a statement must be complete on a single *logical* line.

The term "logical line" provides a hint as to how we can proceed. Python makes a distinction between logical lines and physical lines; we'll leverage these syntax rules to break up long statements.

How to do it...

Python gives us several ways to wrap long statements so they're more readable:

- We can use \ at the end of a line to continue onto the next line.
- We can leverage Python's rule that a statement can span multiple logical lines because the `()`, `[]`, and `{}` characters must balance. In addition to using `()` or \, we can also exploit the way Python automatically concatenates adjacent string literals to make a single, longer literal; `("a" "b")` is the same as `"ab"`.
- In some cases, we can decompose a statement by assigning intermediate results to separate variables.

We'll look at each one of these in separate parts of this recipe.

Using a backslash to break a long statement into logical lines

Here's the context for this technique:

```
>>> import math
>>> example_value = (63/25) * (17+15*math.sqrt(5)) / (7+15*math.sqrt(5))
>>> mantissa_fraction, exponent = math.frexp(example_value)
>>> mantissa_whole = int(mantissa_fraction*2**53)
```

Python allows us to use \ to break the logical line into two physical lines:

1. Write the whole statement on one long line, even if it's confusing:

   ```
   >>> message_text = f'the internal representation is {mantissa_
   whole:d}/2**53*2**{exponent:d}'
   ```

2. If there's a *meaningful* break, insert the \ to separate the statement:

   ```
   >>> message_text = f'the internal representation is \
   ...     {mantissa_whole:d}/2**53*2**{exponent:d}'
   ```

For this to work, the \ must be the last character on the line. We can't even have a single space after the \. An extra space is fairly hard to see; for this reason, we don't encourage using back-slash continuation like this. PEP 8 provides guidelines on formatting and discourages this.

In spite of this being a little hard to see, the \ can always be used. Think of it as the last resort in making a line of code more readable.

Using the () characters to break a long statement into sensible pieces

1. Write the whole statement on one line, even if it's confusing:

```
>>> import math
>>> example_value1 = (63/25) * (17+15*math.sqrt(5)) / (7+15*math.
sqrt(5))
```

2. Add the extra () characters, which don't change the value, but allow breaking the expression into multiple lines:

```
>>> example_value2 = (63/25) * ( (17+15*math.sqrt(5)) /
(7+15*math.sqrt(5)) )
>>> example_value2 == example_value1
True
```

3. Break the line inside the () characters:

```
>>> example_value3 = (63/25) * (
...       (17+15*math.sqrt(5))
...     / (7+15*math.sqrt(5))
... )
>>> example_value3 == example_value1
True
```

The matching () character's technique is quite powerful and will work in a wide variety of cases. This is widely used and highly recommended.

We can almost always find a way to add extra () characters to a statement. In rare cases when we can't add () characters, or adding () characters doesn't improve readability, we can fall back on using \ to break the statement into sections.

Using string literal concatenation

We can combine the () characters with another rule that joins adjacent string literals. This is particularly effective for long, complex format strings:

1. Wrap a long string value in the () characters.

2. Break the string into substrings:

```
>>> message_text = (
...     f'the internal representation '
...     f'is {mantissa_whole:d}/2**53*2**{exponent:d}'
... )
>>> message_text
'the internal representation is 7074237752514592/2**53*2**2'
```

We can always break a long string into adjacent pieces. Generally, this is most effective when the pieces are surrounded by `()` characters. We can then use as many physical line breaks as we need. This is limited to those situations where we have particularly long string literals.

Assigning intermediate results to separate variables

Here's the context for this technique:

```
>>> import math
>>> example_value = (63/25) * (17+15*math.sqrt(5)) / (7+15*math.sqrt(5))
```

We can break this into three intermediate values:

1. Identify sub-expressions in the overall expression. Assign these to variables:

   ```
   >>> a = (63/25)
   >>> b = (17+15*math.sqrt(5))
   >>> c = (7+15*math.sqrt(5))
   ```

   This is generally quite simple. It may require a little care to do the algebra to locate sensible sub-expressions.

2. Replace the sub-expressions with the variables that were created:

   ```
   >>> example_value = a * b / c
   ```

We can always take a sub-expression and assign it to a variable, and use the variable everywhere the sub-expression was used. The `15*sqrt(5)` product is repeated; this, too, is a good candidate for refactoring the expression.

We didn't give these variables descriptive names. In some cases, the sub-expressions have some semantics that we can capture with meaningful names. In this case, however, we chose short, arbitrary identifiers instead.

How it works...

The Python Language Manual makes a distinction between logical lines and physical lines. A logical line contains a complete statement. It can span multiple physical lines through techniques called **line joining**. The manual calls the techniques **explicit line joining** and **implicit line joining**.

The use of \ for explicit line joining is sometimes helpful. Because it's easy to overlook, it's not generally encouraged. PEP 8 suggests this should be the method of last resort.

The use of `()` for implicit line joining can be used in many cases. It often fits semantically with the structure of the expressions, so it is encouraged. We may have the `()` characters as a required syntax. For example, we already have `()` characters as part of the syntax for the `print()` function. We might do this to break up a long statement:

```
>>> print(
...     'several values including',
...     'mantissa =', mantissa,
...     'exponent =', exponent
... )
```

There's more...

Expressions are used widely in a number of Python statements. Any expression can have `()` characters added. This gives us a lot of flexibility.

There are, however, a few places where we may have a long statement that does not specifically involve an expression. The most notable example of this is the `import` statement—it can become long, but doesn't use any expressions that can be parenthesized. In spite of not having a proper expression, it does, however, still permit the use of `()`. The following example shows we can surround a very long list of imported names:

```
>>> from math import (
...     sin, cos, tan,
...     sqrt, log, frexp)
```

In this case, the `()` characters are emphatically not part of an expression. The `()` characters are available syntax, included to make the statement consistent with other statements.

See also

- Implicit line joining also applies to the matching `[]` and `{}` characters. These apply to collection data structures that we'll look at in *Chapter 4, Built-In Data Structures Part 1: Lists and Sets.*

Including descriptions and documentation

When we have a useful script, we often need to leave notes for ourselves—and others—on what it does, how it solves some particular problem, and when it should be used.

Because clarity is important, there are some formatting recipes that can help make the documentation very clear. This recipe also contains a suggested outline so that the documentation will be reasonably complete.

Getting ready

If we've used the *Writing Python script and module files - syntax basics* recipe to build a script file, we'll have to put a small documentation string in our script file. We'll expand on this documentation string in this recipe.

There are other places where documentation strings should be used. We'll look at these additional locations in *Chapter 3, Function Definitions*, and *Chapter 7, Basics of Classes and Objects*.

We have two general kinds of modules for which we'll be writing summary docstrings:

- **Library modules**: These files will contain mostly function definitions as well as class definitions. In this case, the docstring summary can focus on what the module is more than what it does. The docstring can provide examples of using the functions and classes that are defined in the module. In *Chapter 3, Function Definitions*, and *Chapter 7, Basics of Classes and Objects*, we'll look more closely at this idea of a package of functions or classes.
- **Scripts**: These are files that we generally expect will do some real work. In this case, we want to focus on doing rather than being. The docstring should describe what it does and how to use it. The options, environment variables, and configuration files are important parts of this docstring.

We will sometimes create files that contain a little of both. This requires some careful editing to strike a proper balance between doing and being. In most cases, we'll provide both kinds of documentation.

How to do it...

The first step in writing documentation is the same for both library modules and scripts:

1. Write a brief summary of what the script or module is or does. The summary doesn't dig too deeply into how it works. Like a lede in a newspaper article, it introduces the who, what, when, where, how, and why of the module. Details will follow in the body of the docstring.

The way the information is displayed by tools like `Sphinx` and `pydoc` suggests a specific style for the summaries we write. In the output from these tools, the context is pretty clear, therefore it's common to omit a subject in the summary sentence. The sentence often begins with the verb.

For example, a summary like this: *This script downloads and decodes the current Special Marine Warning (SMW) for the area AKQ has a needless This script. We can drop that and begin with the verb phrase Downloads and decodes....*

We might start our module docstring like this:

```
"""
Downloads and decodes the current Special Marine Warning (SMW)
for the area 'AKQ'.
"""
```

We'll separate the other steps based on the general focus of the module.

Writing docstrings for scripts

When we document a script, we need to focus on the needs of a person who will use the script.

1. Start as shown earlier, creating a summary sentence.
2. Sketch an outline for the rest of the docstring. We'll be using **ReStructuredText** (**RST**) markup. Write the topic on one line, then put a line of = under the topic to make it a proper section title. Remember to leave a blank line between each topic.

   Topics may include:

   - **SYNOPSIS**: A summary of how to run this script. If the script uses the `argparse` module to process command-line arguments, the help text produced by `argparse` is the ideal summary text.
   - **DESCRIPTION**: A more complete explanation of what this script does.
   - **OPTIONS**: If `argparse` is used, this is a place to put the details of each argument. Often, we'll repeat the `argparse` help parameter.
   - **ENVIRONMENT**: If `os.environ` is used, this is the place to describe the environment variables and what they mean.

- **FILES**: Names of files that are created or read by a script are very important pieces of information.
- **EXAMPLES**: Some examples of using the script are always helpful.
- **SEE ALSO**: Any related scripts or background information.

Other topics that might be interesting include **EXIT STATUS**, **AUTHOR**, **BUGS**, **REPORTING BUGS**, **HISTORY**, or **COPYRIGHT**. In some cases, advice on reporting bugs, for instance, doesn't really belong in a module's docstring, but belongs elsewhere in the project's GitHub or SourceForge pages.

3. Fill in the details under each topic. It's important to be accurate. Since we're embedding this documentation within the same file as the code, it needs to be correct, complete, and consistent.
4. For code samples, there's a cool bit of RST markup we can use. Recall that all elements are separated by blank lines. In one paragraph, use `::` by itself. In the next paragraph, provide the code example indented by four spaces.

Here's an example of a docstring for a script:

```
"""
Downloads and decodes the current Special Marine Warning (SMW)
for the area 'AKQ'

SYNOPSIS
========

::

    python3 akq_weather.py

DESCRIPTION
===========

Downloads the Special Marine Warnings

Files
=====

Writes a file, ''AKW.html''.

EXAMPLES
========
```

```
Here's an example::

    slott$ python3 akq_weather.py
    <h3>There are no products active at this time.</h3>
"""
```

In the `SYNOPSIS` section, we used `::` as a separate paragraph. In the `EXAMPLES` section, we used `::` at the end of a paragraph. Both versions are hints to the RST processing tools that the indented section that follows should be typeset as code.

Writing docstrings for library modules

When we document a library module, we need to focus on the needs of a programmer who will import the module to use it in their code:

1. Sketch an outline for the rest of the docstring. We'll be using RST markup. Write the topic on one line. Include a line of = under each topic to make the topic into a proper heading. Remember to leave a blank line between each paragraph.
2. Start as shown previously, creating a summary sentence:
   - **DESCRIPTION**: A summary of what the module contains and why the module is useful
   - **MODULE CONTENTS**: The classes and functions defined in this module
   - **EXAMPLES**: Examples of using the module
3. Fill in the details for each topic. The module contents may be a long list of class or function definitions. This should be a summary. Within each class or function, we'll have a separate docstring with the details for that item.
4. For code examples, see the previous examples. Use `::` as a paragraph or the ending of a paragraph. Indent the code example by four spaces.

How it works...

Over the decades, the *man page* outline has evolved to contain a complete description of Linux commands. This general approach to writing documentation has proven useful and resilient. We can capitalize on this large body of experience, and structure our documentation to follow the man page model.

These two recipes for describing software are based on summaries of many individual pages of documentation. The goal is to leverage the well-known set of topics. This makes our module documentation mirror the common practice.

We want to prepare module docstrings that can be used by the Sphinx Python Documentation Generator (see `http://www.sphinx-doc.org/en/stable/`). This is the tool used to produce Python's documentation files. The `autodoc` extension in Sphinx will read the docstring headers on our modules, classes, and functions to produce the final documentation that looks like other modules in the Python ecosystem.

There's more...

RST markup has a simple, central syntax rule: paragraphs are separated by blank lines.

This rule makes it easy to write documents that can be examined by the various RST processing tools and reformatted to look extremely nice.

When we want to include a block of code, we'll have some special paragraphs:

- Separate the code from the text with blank lines.
- Indent the code by four spaces.
- Provide a prefix of `::`. We can either do this as its own separate paragraph or as a special double-colon at the end of the lead-in paragraph:

  ```
  Here's an example::

      more_code()
  ```

- The `::` is used in the lead-in paragraph.

There are places for novelty and art in software development. Documentation is not really the place to push the envelope.

> A unique voice or quirky presentation isn't fun for users who simply want to use the software. An amusing style isn't helpful when debugging. Documentation should be commonplace and conventional.

It can be challenging to write good software documentation. There's a broad chasm between too little information and documentation that simply recapitulates the code. Somewhere, there's a good balance. What's important is to focus on the needs of a person who doesn't know too much about the software or how it works. Provide this *semi-knowledgeable* user with the information they need to describe what the software does and how to use it.

In many cases, we need to separate two parts of the use cases:

- The intended use of the software
- How to customize or extend the software

These may be two distinct audiences. There may be users who are distinct from developers. Each has a unique perspective, and different parts of the documentation need to respect these two perspectives.

See also

- We look at additional techniques in *Writing better RST markup in docstrings*.
- If we've used the *Writing Python script and module files – syntax basics* recipe, we'll have put a documentation string in our script file. When we build functions in *Chapter 3, Function Definitions*, and classes in *Chapter 7, Basics of Classes and Objects*, we'll look at other places where documentation strings can be placed.
- See `http://www.sphinx-doc.org/en/stable/` for more information on Sphinx.
- For more background on the man page outline, see `https://en.wikipedia.org/wiki/Man_page`

Writing better RST markup in docstrings

When we have a useful script, we often need to leave notes on what it does, how it works, and when it should be used. Many tools for producing documentation, including docutils, work with RST markup. What RST features can we use to make documentation more readable?

Getting ready

In the *Including descriptions and documentation* recipe, we looked at putting a basic set of documentation into a module. This is the starting point for writing our documentation. There are a large number of RST formatting rules. We'll look at a few that are important for creating readable documentation.

How to do it...

1. Be sure to write an outline of the key points. This may lead to creating RST section titles to organize the material. A section title is a two-line paragraph with the title followed by an underline using =, -, ^, ~, or one of the other docutils characters for underlining.

   A heading will look like this:

   ```
   Topic
   =====
   ```

The heading text is on one line and the underlining characters are on the next line. This must be surrounded by blank lines. There can be more underline characters than title characters, but not fewer.

The RST tools will infer our pattern of using underlining characters. As long as the underline characters are used consistently, the algorithm for matching underline characters to the desired heading will detect the pattern. The keys to this are consistency and a clear understanding of sections and subsections.

When starting out, it can help to make an explicit reminder sticky note like this:

Character	**Level**
=	1
-	2
^	3
~	4

Example of heading characters

2. Fill in the various paragraphs. Separate paragraphs (including the section titles) with blank lines. Extra blank lines don't hurt. Omitting blank lines will lead the RST parsers to see a single, long paragraph, which may not be what we intended.

   We can use inline markup for emphasis, strong emphasis, code, hyperlinks, and inline math, among other things. If we're planning on using Sphinx, then we have an even larger collection of text roles that we can use. We'll look at these techniques soon.

3. If the programming editor has a spell checker, use that. This can be frustrating because we'll often have code samples that may include abbreviations that fail spell checking.

How it works...

The docutils conversion programs will examine the document, looking for sections and body elements. A section is identified by a title. The underlines are used to organize the sections into a properly nested hierarchy. The algorithm for deducing this is relatively simple and has these rules:

- If the underline character has been seen before, the level is known
- If the underline character has not been seen before, then it must be indented one level below the previous outline level
- If there is no previous level, this is level one

A properly nested document might have the following sequence of underline characters:

```
TITLE
=====

SOMETHING
---------

MORE
^^^^

EXTRA
^^^^^

LEVEL 2
-------

LEVEL 3
^^^^^^^
```

We can see that the first title underline character, =, will be level one. The next, -, is unknown but appears after a level one, so it must be level two. The third headline has ^, which is previously unknown, is inside level two, and therefore must be level three. The next ^ is still level three. The next two, - and ^, are known to be level two and three respectively.

> From this overview, we can see that inconsistency will lead to confusion.

If we change our mind partway through a document, this algorithm can't detect that. If—for inexplicable reasons—we decide to skip over a level and try to have a level four heading inside a level two section, that simply can't be done.

There are several different kinds of body elements that the RST parser can recognize. We've shown a few. The more complete list includes:

- **Paragraphs of text**: These might use inline markup for different kinds of emphasis or highlighting.
- **Literal blocks**: These are introduced with `::` and indented four spaces. They may also be introduced with the `.. parsed-literal::` directive. A **doctest** block is indented four spaces and includes the Python `>>>` prompt.

- **Lists, tables, and block quotes**: We'll look at these later. These can contain other body elements.
- **Footnotes**: These are special paragraphs. When rendered, they may be put on the bottom of a page or at the end of a section. These can also contain other body elements.
- **Hyperlink targets, substitution definitions, and RST comments**: These are specialized text items.

There's more...

For completeness, we'll note here that RST paragraphs are separated by blank lines. There's quite a bit more to RST than this core rule.

In the *Including descriptions and documentation* recipe, we looked at several different kinds of body elements we might use:

- **Paragraphs of Text**: This is a block of text surrounded by blank lines. Within these, we can make use of inline markup to emphasize words, or to use a font to show that we're referring to elements of our code. We'll look at inline markup in the *Using inline markup* recipe.
- **Lists**: These are paragraphs that begin with something that looks like a number or a bullet. For bullets, use a simple `-` or `*`. Other characters can be used, but these are common. We might have paragraphs like this.

  It helps to have bullets because:

  - They can help clarify
  - They can help organize
- **Numbered Lists**: There are a variety of patterns that are recognized. We might use a pattern like one of the four most common kinds of numbered paragraphs:
  1. Numbers followed by punctuation like `.` or `)`.
  2. A letter followed by punctuation like `.` or `)`.
  3. A Roman numeral followed by punctuation.
  4. A special case of # with the same punctuation used on the previous items. This continues the numbering from the previous paragraphs.
- **Literal Blocks**: A code sample must be presented literally. The text for this must be indented. We also need to prefix the code with `::`. The `::` character must either be a separate paragraph or the end of a lead-in to the code example.

- **Directives**: A directive is a paragraph that generally looks like `.. directive::`. It may have some content that's indented so that it's contained within the directive. It might look like this:

```
.. important::

     Do not flip the bozo bit.
```

The `.. important::` paragraph is the directive. This is followed by a short paragraph of text indented within the directive. In this case, it creates a separate paragraph that includes the admonition of *important*.

Using directives

Docutils has many built-in directives. Sphinx adds a large number of directives with a variety of features.

Some of the most commonly used directives are the admonition directives: `attention`, `caution`, `danger`, `error`, `hint`, `important`, `note`, `tip`, `warning`, and the generic `admonition`. These are compound body elements because they can have multiple paragraphs and nested directives within them.

We might have things like this to provide appropriate emphasis:

```
.. note:: Note Title

    We need to indent the content of an admonition.
    This will set the text off from other material.
```

One of the other common directives is the `parsed-literal` directive:

```
.. parsed-literal::

    any text
        *almost* any format
    the text is preserved
        but **inline** markup can be used.
```

This can be handy for providing examples of code where some portion of the code is highlighted. A literal like this is a simple body element, which can only have text inside. It can't have lists or other nested structures.

Using inline markup

Within a paragraph, we have several inline markup techniques we can use:

- We can surround a word or phrase with * for *emphasis*. This is commonly typeset as *italic*.
- We can surround a word or phrase with ** for **strong**. This is commonly typeset as **bold**.
- We surround references with single back-ticks (`, it's on the same key as the ~ on most keyboards). Links are followed by an underscore, "_". We might use `section title`_ to refer to a specific section within a document. We don't generally need to put anything around URLs. The docutils tools recognize these. Sometimes we want a word or phrase to be shown and the URL concealed. We can use this: `the Sphinx documentation <http://www.sphinx-doc.org/en/stable/>`_.
- We can surround code-related words with a double back-tick (``) to make them look like ``code``.

There's also a more general technique called a text role. A role is a little more complex-looking than simply wrapping a word or phrase in * characters. We use :word: as the role name followed by the applicable word or phrase in single ` back-ticks. A text role looks like this :strong:`this`.

There are a number of standard role names, including :emphasis:, :literal:, :code:, :math:, :pep-reference:, :rfc-reference:, :strong:, :subscript:, :superscript:, and :title-reference:. Some of these are also available with simpler markup like *emphasis* or **strong**. The rest are only available as explicit roles.

Also, we can define new roles with a simple directive. If we want to do very sophisticated processing, we can provide docutils with class definitions for handling roles, allowing us to tweak the way our document is processed. Sphinx adds a large number of roles to support detailed cross-references among functions, methods, exceptions, classes, and modules.

See also

- For more information on RST syntax, see http://docutils.sourceforge.net. This includes a description of the docutils tools.
- For information on **Sphinx Python Documentation Generator**, see http://www.sphinx-doc.org/en/stable/
- The Sphinx tool adds many additional directives and text roles to basic definitions.

Designing complex if...elif chains

In most cases, our scripts will involve a number of choices. Sometimes the choices are simple, and we can judge the quality of the design with a glance at the code. In other cases, the choices are more complex, and it's not easy to determine whether or not our `if` statements are designed properly to handle all of the conditions.

In the simplest case, we have one condition, *C*, and its inverse, $\neg C$` . These are the two conditions for an `if...else` statement. One condition, *C*, is stated in the `if` clause, the other condition, *C*'s inverse, is implied in `else`.

This is the **Law of the Excluded Middle**: we're claiming there's no missing alternative between the two conditions, *C* and $\neg C$. For a complex condition, though, this isn't always true.

If we have something like:

```
if weather == RAIN and plan == GO_OUT:
    bring("umbrella")
else:

    bring("sunglasses")
```

It may not be immediately obvious, but we've omitted a number of possible alternatives. The `weather` and `plan` variables have four different combinations of values. One of the conditions is stated explicitly, the other three are assumed:

- `weather == RAIN` and `plan == GO_OUT`. Bringing an umbrella seems right.
- `weather != RAIN` and `plan == GO_OUT`. Bringing sunglasses seems appropriate.
- `weather == RAIN` and `plan != GO_OUT`. If we're staying in, then neither accessory seems right.
- `weather != RAIN` and `plan != GO_OUT`. Again, the accessory question seems moot if we're not going out.

How can we be sure we haven't missed anything?

Getting ready

Let's look at a concrete example of an `if...elif` chain. In the casino game of *Craps*, there are a number of rules that apply to a roll of two dice. These rules apply on the first roll of the game, called the *come-out* roll:

- 2, 3, or 12 is *Craps*, which is a loss for all bets placed on the **pass line**
- 7 or 11 is a winner for all bets placed on the **pass line**
- The remaining numbers establish a **point**

Many players place their bets on the **pass line**. We'll use this set of three conditions as an example for looking at this recipe because it has a potentially vague clause in it.

How to do it...

When we write an `if` statement, even when it appears trivial, we need to be sure that all conditions are covered.

1. Enumerate the conditions we know. In our example, we have three rules: (2, 3, 12), (7, 11), and a vague statement of "the remaining numbers." This forms a first draft of the `if` statement.
2. Determine the universe of all possible alternatives. For this example, there are 11 alternative outcomes: the numbers from 2 to 12, inclusive.
3. Compare the conditions, *C*, with the universe of alternatives, *U*. There are three possible outcomes of this comparison:

   - More conditions than are possible in the universe of alternatives, $C \supset U$. The most common cause is failing to completely enumerate all possible alternatives in the universe. We might, for example, have modeled dice using 0 to 5 instead of 1 to 6. The universe of alternatives appears to be the values from 0 to 10, yet there are conditions for 11 and 12.
   - Gaps in the conditions, $U \setminus C \neq \emptyset$. There are one or more alternatives without a condition. The most common cause is failing to fully understand the various conditions. We might, for example, have enumerated the vales as two tuples instead of sums. (1, 1), (1, 2), (2, 1), and (6, 6) have special rules. It's possible to miss a condition like this and have a condition untested by any clause of the `if` statement.
   - Match between conditions and the universe of alternatives, $U = C$. This is ideal. The universe of all possible alternatives matches of all the conditions in the `if` statement.

The first outcome is a rare problem where the conditions in our code seem to describe too many alternative outcomes. It helps to uncover these kinds of problems as early as possible to permit rethinking the design from the foundations. Often, this suggests the universe of alternatives is not fully understood; either we wrote too many conditions or failed to identify all the alternative outcomes.

A more common problem is to find a gap between the designed conditions in the draft `if` statement and the universe of possible alternatives. In this example, it's clear that we haven't covered all of the possible alternatives. In other cases, it takes some careful reasoning to understand the gap. Often, the outcome of our design effort is to replace any vague or poorly defined terms with something much more precise.

In this example, we have a vague term, which we can replace with something more specific. The term **remaining numbers** appears to be the list of values (4, 5, 6, 8, 9, 10). Supplying this list removes any possible gaps and doubts.

The goal is to have the universe of known alternatives match the collection of conditions in our `if` statement. When there are exactly two alternatives, we can write a condition expression for one of the alternatives. The other condition can be implied; a simple `if` and `else` will work.

When we have more than two alternatives, we'll have more than two conditions. We need to use this recipe to write a chain of `if` and `elif` statements, one statement per alternative:

1. Write an `if...elif...elif` chain that covers all of the known alternatives. For our example, it will look like this:

```
dice = die_1 + die_2
if dice in (2, 3, 12):
    game.craps()
elif dice in (7, 11):
    game.winner()
elif dice in (4, 5, 6, 8, 9, 10):
    game.point(die)
```

2. Add an `else` clause that raises an exception, like this:

```
else:
    raise Exception('Design Problem')
```

This extra `else` gives us a way to positively identify when a logic problem is found. We can be sure that any design error we made will lead to a conspicuous problem when the program runs. Ideally, we'll find any problems while we're unit testing.

In this case, it is clear that all 11 alternatives are covered by the `if` statement conditions. The extra `else` can't ever be used. Not all real-world problems have this kind of easy proof that all the alternatives are covered by conditions, and it can help to provide a noisy failure mode.

How it works...

Our goal is to be sure that our program always works. While testing helps, we can still have the same wrong assumptions when doing design and creating test cases.

While rigorous logic is essential, we can still make errors. Further, someone doing ordinary software maintenance might introduce an error. Adding a new feature to a complex `if` statement is a potential source of problems.

This `else-raise` design pattern forces us to be explicit for each and every condition. Nothing is assumed. As we noted previously, any error in our logic will be uncovered if the exception gets raised.

The `else-raise` design pattern doesn't have a significant performance impact. A simple `else` clause is slightly faster than an `elif` clause with a condition. However, if we think that our application performance depends in any way on the cost of a single expression, we've got more serious design problems to solve. The cost of evaluating a single expression is rarely the costliest part of an algorithm.

Crashing with an exception is sensible behavior in the presence of a design problem. An alternative is to write a message to an error log. However, if we have this kind of logic gap, the program should be viewed as fatally broken. It's important to find and fix this as soon as the problem is known.

There's more...

In many cases, we can derive an `if...elif...elif` chain from an examination of the desired post condition at some point in the program's processing. For example, we may need a statement that establishes something simple, like: *m* is equal to the larger of *a* or *b*.

(For the sake of working through the logic, we'll avoid Python's handy `m = max(a, b)`, and focus on the way we can compute a result from exclusive choices.)

We can formalize the final condition like this:

$$(m = a \vee m = b) \wedge m \geq a \wedge m \geq b$$

We can work backward from this final condition, by writing the goal as an `assert` statement:

```
# do something
assert (m == a or m == b) and m >= a and m >= b
```

Once we have the goal stated, we can identify statements that lead to that goal. Clearly assignment statements like `m = a` or `m = b` would be appropriate, but each of these works only under certain conditions.

Each of these statements is part of the solution, and we can derive a precondition that shows when the statement should be used. The preconditions for each assignment statement are the `if` and `elif` expressions. We need to use `m = a` when `a >= b`; we need to use `m = b` when `b >= a`. Rearranging logic into code gives us this:

```
if a >= b:
    m = a
elif b >= a:
    m = b
```

```
    else:
        raise Exception('Design Problem')

    assert (m == a or m == b) and m >= a and m >= b
```

Note that our universe of conditions, $U = \{a \geq b, b \geq a\}$, is complete; there's no other possible relationship. Also notice that in the edge case of $a = b$, we don't actually care which assignment statement is used. Python will process the decisions in order, and will execute `m = a`. The fact that this choice is consistent shouldn't have any impact on our design of `if...elif...elif` chains. We should always write the conditions without regard to the order of evaluation of the clauses.

See also

- This is similar to the syntactic problem of a dangling else. See `http://www.mathcs.emory.edu/~cheung/Courses/561/Syllabus/2-C/dangling-else.html`
- Python's indentation removes the dangling else syntax problem. It doesn't remove the semantic issue of trying to be sure that all conditions are properly accounted for in a complex `if...elif...elif` chain.

Saving intermediate results with the := "walrus"

Sometimes we'll have a complex condition where we want to preserve an expensive intermediate result for later use. Imagine a condition that involves a complex calculation; the cost of computing is high measured in time, or input-output, or memory, or network resource use. Resource use defines the cost of computation.

An example includes doing repetitive searches where the result of the search may be either a useful value or a sentinel value indicating that the target was not found. This is common in the Regular Expression (`re`) package where the `match()` method either returns a match object or a `None` object as a sentinel showing the pattern wasn't found. Once this computation is completed, we may have several uses for the result, and we emphatically do not want to perform the computation again.

This is an example where it can be helpful to assign a name to the value of an expression. We'll look at how to use the "assignment expression" or "walrus" operator. It's called the walrus because the assignment expression operator, `:=`, looks like the face of a walrus to some people.

Getting ready

Here's a summation where – eventually – each term becomes so small that there's no point in continuing to add it to the overall total:

$$\sum_{0 \le n < \infty} \left(\frac{1}{2n+1}\right)^2$$

In effect, this is something like the following summation function:

```
>>> s = sum((1/(2*n+1))**2 for n in range(0, 20_000))
```

What's not clear is the question of how many terms are required. In the example, we've summed 20,000. But what if 16,000 are enough to provide an accurate answer?

We don't want to write a summation like this:

```
>>> b = 0
>>> for n in range(0, 20_000):
...     if (1/(2*n+1))**2 >= 0.000_000_001:
...         b = b + (1/(2*n+1))**2
```

This example repeats an expensive computation, `(1/(2*n+1))**2`. That's likely to be a waste of time.

How to do it...

1. Isolate an expensive operation that's part of a conditional test. In this example, the variable `term` is used to hold the expensive result:

   ```
   >>> p = 0
   >>> for n in range(0, 20_000):
   ...     term = (1/(2*n+1))**2
   ...     if term >= 0.000_000_001:
   ...         p = p + term
   ```

2. Rewrite the assignment statement to use the `:=` assignment operator. This replaces the simple condition of the `if` statement.
3. Add an `else` condition to break out of the `for` statement if no more terms are needed. Here's the results of these two steps:

```
>>> q = 0
>>> for n in range(0, 20_000):
...     if (term := (1/(2*n+1))**2) >= 0.000_000_001:
...         q = q + term
...     else:
...         break
```

The assignment expression, `:=`, lets us do two things in the `if` statement. We can both compute a value and also check to see that the computed value meets some useful criteria. We can provide the computation and the test criteria adjacent to each other.

How it works...

The assignment expression operator, `:=`, saves an intermediate result. The operator's result value is the same as the right-hand side operand. This means that the expression `a + (b:= c+d)` has the same as the expression `a+(c+d)`. The difference between the expression `a + (b:= c+d)` and the expression `a+(c+d)` is the side-effect of setting the value of the `b` variable partway through the evaluation.

An assignment expression can be used in almost any kind of context where expressions are permitted in Python. The most common cases are `if` statements. Another good idea is inside a `while` condition.

They're also forbidden in a few places. They cannot be used as the operator in an expression statement. We're specifically prohibited from writing `a := 2` as a statement: there's a perfectly good assignment statement for this purpose and an assignment expression, while similar in intent, is potentially confusing.

There's more...

We can do some more optimization of our infinite summation example, shown earlier in this recipe. The use of a `for` statement and a `range()` object seems simple. The problem is that we want to end the `for` statement early when the terms being added are so small that they have no significant change in the final sum.

We can combine the early exit with the term computation:

```
>>> r = 0
>>> n = 0
>>> while (term := (1/(2*n+1))**2) >= 0.000_000_001:
...     r += term
...     n += 1
```

We've used a `while` statement with the assignment expression operator. This will compute a value using `(1/(2*n+1))**2`, and assign this to term. If the value is significant, we'll add it to the sum, `r`, and increment the value for the `n` variable. If the value is too small to be significant, the `while` statement will end.

Here's another example, showing how to compute running sums of a collection of values. This looks forward to concepts in *Chapter 4, Built-In Data Structures Part 1: Lists and Sets*. Specifically, this shows a list comprehension built using the assignment expression operator:

```
>>> data = [11, 13, 17, 19, 23, 29]
>>> total = 0
>>> running_sum = [(total := total + d) for d in data]
>>> total
112
>>> running_sum
[11, 24, 41, 60, 83, 112]
```

We've started with some data, in the `data` variable. This might be minutes of exercise each day for most of a week. The value of `running_sum` is a list object, built by evaluating the expression `(total := total + d)` for each value, `d`, in the `data` variable. Because the assignment expression changes the value of the `total` variable, the resulting list is the result of each new value being accumulated.

See also

- For details on assignment expression, see PEP 572 where the feature was first described: `https://www.python.org/dev/peps/pep-0572/`

Avoiding a potential problem with break statements

The common way to understand a `for` statement is that it creates a *for all* condition. At the end of the statement, we can assert that, for all items in a collection, some processing has been done.

This isn't the only meaning for a `for` statement. When we introduce the `break` statement inside the body of a `for`, we change the semantics to *there exists*. When the `break` statement leaves the `for` (or `while`) statement, we can assert only that there exists at least one item that caused the statement to end.

There's a side issue here. What if the `for` statement ends without executing `break`? Either way, we're at the statement after the `for` statement.

The condition that's true upon leaving a `for` or `while` statement with a `break` can be ambiguous. Did it end normally? Did it execute `break`? We can't *easily* tell, so we'll provide a recipe that gives us some design guidance.

This can become an even bigger problem when we have multiple `break` statements, each with its own condition. How can we minimize the problems created by having complex conditions?

Getting ready

When parsing configuration files, we often need to find the first occurrence of a `:` or `=` character in a string. This is common when looking for lines that have a similar syntax to assignment statements, for example, `option = value` or `option : value`. The properties file format uses lines where `:` (or `=`) separate the property name from the property value.

This is a good example of a *there exists* modification to a `for` statement. We don't want to process *all* characters; we want to know where there is the leftmost `:` or `=`.

Here's the sample data we're going use as an example:

```
>>> sample_1 = "some_name = the_value"
```

Here's a small `for` statement to locate the leftmost `"="` or `":"` character in the sample string value:

```
>>> for position in range(len(sample_1)):
...     if sample_1[position] in '=:':
...         break
>>> print(f"name={sample_1[:position]!r}",
...       f"value={sample_1[position+1:]!r}")
name='some_name ' value=' the_value'
```

When the `"="` character is found, the `break` statement stops the `for` statement. The value of the `position` variable shows where the desired character was found.

What about this edge case?

```
>>> sample_2 = "name_only"
>>> for position in range(len(sample_2)):
...     if sample_2[position] in '=:':
...         break
>>> print(f"name={sample_2[:position]!r}",
...       f"value={sample_2[position+1:]!r}")
name='name_onl' value=''
```

The result is awkwardly wrong: the `y` character got dropped from the value of name. Why did this happen? And, more importantly, how can we make the condition at the end of the `for` statement more clear?

How to do it...

Every statement establishes a post condition. When designing a `for` or `while` statement, we need to articulate the condition that's true at the end of the statement. In this case, the post condition of the `for` statement is quite complicated.

Ideally, the post condition is something simple like `text[position] in '=:'`. In other words, the value of `position` is the location of the `"="` or `":"` character. However, if there's no `=` or `:` in the given text, the overly simple post condition can't be true. At the end of the `for` statement, one of two things are true: either (a) the character with the index of `position` is `"="` or `":"`, or (b) all characters have been examined and no character is `"="` or `":"`.

Our application code needs to handle both cases. It helps to carefully articulate all of the relevant conditions.

1. Write the obvious post condition. We sometimes call this the *happy-path* condition because it's the one that's true when nothing unusual has happened:

   ```
   text[position] in '=:'
   ```

2. Create the overall post condition by adding the conditions for the edge cases. In this example, we have two additional conditions:

   - There's no `=` or `:`.
   - There are no characters at all. `len()` is zero, and the `for` statement never actually does anything. In this case, the `position` variable will never be created. In this example, we have three conditions:

   ```
   (len(text) == 0
    or not('=' in text or ':' in text)
    or text[position] in '=:')
   ```

3. If a `while` statement is being used, consider redesigning it to have the overall post condition in the `while` clause. This can eliminate the need for a `break` statement.
4. If a `for` statement is being used, be sure a proper initialization is done, and add the various terminating conditions to the statements after the loop. It can look redundant to have `x = 0` followed by `for x = ...`. It's necessary in the case of a `for` statement that doesn't execute the `break` statement. Here's the resulting `for` statement and a complicated `if` statement to examine all of the possible post conditions:

```
>>> position = -1
>>> for position in range(len(sample_2)):
...     if sample_2[position] in '=:':
...         break
...
>>> if position == -1:
...     print(f"name=None value=None")
... elif not(sample_2[position] == ':' or sample_2[position] ==
'='):
...     print(f"name={sample_2!r} value=None")
... else:
...     print(f"name={sample_2[:position]!r}",
...         f"value={sample_2[position+1:]!r}")
name= name_only value= None
```

In the statements after the `for`, we've enumerated all of the terminating conditions explicitly. If the position found is `-1`, then the `for` loop did not process any characters. If the position is not the expected character, then all the characters were examined. The third case is one of the expected characters were found. The final output, `name='name_only' value=None`, confirms that we've correctly processed the sample text.

How it works...

This approach forces us to work out the post condition carefully so that we can be absolutely sure that we know all the reasons for the loop terminating.

In more complex, nested `for` and `while` statements—with multiple `break` statements—the post condition can be difficult to work out fully. A `for` statement's post condition must include *all* of the reasons for leaving the loop: the *normal* reasons plus all of the `break` conditions.

In many cases, we can refactor the `for` statement. Rather than simply asserting that `position` is the index of the `=` or `:` character, we include the next processing steps of assigning substrings to the `name` and `value` variables. We might have something like this:

```
>>> if len(sample_2) > 0:
...     name, value = sample_2, None
... else:
...     name, value = None, None
>>> for position in range(len(sample_2)):
...     if sample_2[position] in '=:':
...         name, value = sample_2[:position], sample2[position:]
```

```
...         break
>>> print(f"{name=} {value=}")
name='name_only' value=None
```

This version pushes some of the processing forward, based on the complete set of post conditions evaluated previously. The initial values for the `name` and `value` variables reflect the two edge cases: there's no `=` or `:` in the data or there's no data at all. Inside the `for` statement, the `name` and `value` variables are set prior to the `break` statement, assuring a consistent post condition.

The idea here is to forego any assumptions or intuition. With a little bit of discipline, we can be sure of the post conditions. The more we think about post conditions, the more precise our software can be. It's imperative to be explicit about the condition that's true when our software works. This is the goal for our software, and you can work backward from the goal by choosing the simplest statements that will make the goal conditions true.

There's more...

We can also use an `else` clause on a `for` statement to determine if the statement finished normally or a `break` statement was executed. We can use something like this:

```
>>> for position in range(len(sample_2)):
...     if sample_2[position] in '=:':
...         name, value = sample_2[:position], sample_2[position+1:]
...         break
... else:
...     if len(sample_2) > 0:
...         name, value = sample_2, None
...     else:
...         name, value = None, None
>>> print(f"{name=} {value=}")
name='name_only' value=None
```

Using an `else` clause in a `for` statement is sometimes confusing, and we don't recommend it. It's not clear if its version is substantially better than any of the alternatives. It's too easy to forget the reason why `else` is executed because it's used so rarely.

See also

- A classic article on this topic is by David Gries, *A note on a standard strategy for developing loop invariants and loops*. See `http://www.sciencedirect.com/science/article/pii/0167642383900151`

Leveraging exception matching rules

The `try` statement lets us capture an exception. When an exception is raised, we have a number of choices for handling it:

- **Ignore it**: If we do nothing, the program stops. We can do this in two ways—don't use a `try` statement in the first place, or don't have a matching `except` clause in the `try` statement.
- **Log it**: We can write a message and use a `raise` statement to let the exception propagate after writing to a log; generally, this will stop the program.
- **Recover from it**: We can write an `except` clause to do some recovery action to undo any effects of the partially completed `try` clause.
- **Silence it**: If we do nothing (that is, use the `pass` statement), then processing is resumed after the `try` statement. This silences the exception.
- **Rewrite it**: We can raise a different exception. The original exception becomes a context for the newly raised exception.

What about nested contexts? In this case, an exception could be ignored by an inner `try` but handled by an outer context. The basic set of options for each `try` context is the same. The overall behavior of the software depends on the nested definitions.

Our design of a `try` statement depends on the way that Python exceptions form a class hierarchy. For details, see *Section 5.4*, *Python Standard Library*. For example, `ZeroDivisionError` is also an `ArithmeticError` and an `Exception`. For another example, `FileNotFoundError` is also an `OSError` as well as an `Exception`.

This hierarchy can lead to confusion if we're trying to handle detailed exceptions as well as generic exceptions.

Getting ready

Let's say we're going to make use of the `shutil` module to copy a file from one place to another. Most of the exceptions that might be raised indicate a problem too serious to work around. However, in the specific event of `FileNotFoundError`, we'd like to attempt a recovery action.

Here's a rough outline of what we'd like to do:

```
>>> from pathlib import Path
>>> import shutil
>>> import os

>>> source_dir = Path.cwd()/"data"
>>> target_dir = Path.cwd()/"backup"
>>> for source_path in source_dir.glob('**/*.csv'):
...     source_name = source_path.relative_to(source_dir)
...     target_path = target_dir/source_name
...     shutil.copy(source_path, target_path)
```

We have two directory paths, `source_dir` and `target_dir`. We've used the `glob()` method to locate all of the directories under `source_dir` that have `*.csv` files.

The expression `source_path.relative_to(source_dir)` gives us the tail end of the filename, the portion after the directory. We use this to build a new, similar path under the `target_dir` directory. This assures that a file named `wc1.csv` in the `source_dir` directory will have a similar name in the `target_dir` directory.

The problems arise with handling exceptions raised by the `shutil.copy()` function. We need a `try` statement so that we can recover from certain kinds of errors. We'll see this kind of error if we try to run this:

```
FileNotFoundError: [Errno 2] No such file or directory: '/Users/slott/
Documents/Writing/Python/Python Cookbook 2e/Modern-Python-Cookbook-
Second-Edition/backup/wc1.csv'
```

This happens when the backup directory hasn't been created. It will also happen when there are subdirectories inside the `source_dir` directory tree that don't also exist in the `target_dir` tree. How do we create a `try` statement that handles these exceptions and creates the missing directories?

How to do it...

1. Write the code we want to use indented in the `try` block:

   ```
   >>>     try:
   ...         shutil.copy(source_path, target_path)
   ```

2. Include the most specific exception classes first. In this case, we have a meaningful response to the specific `FileNotFoundError`.

3. Include any more general exceptions later. In this case, we'll report any generic `OSError` that's encountered. This leads to the following:

```
>>>     try:
...         target = shutil.copy(source_path, target_path)
...     except FileNotFoundError:
...         target_path.parent.mkdir(exist_ok=True,
parents=True)
...         target = shutil.copy(source_path, target_path)
...     except OSError as ex:
...         print(f"Copy {source_path} to {target_path} error
{ex}")
```

We've matched exceptions with the most specific first and the more generic after that.

We handled `FileNotFoundError` by creating the missing directories. Then we did `copy()` again, knowing it would now work properly.

We logged any other exceptions of the class `OSError`. For example, if there's a permission problem, that error will be written to a log and the next file will be tried. Our objective is to try and copy all of the files. Any files that cause problems will be logged, but the copying process will continue.

How it works...

Python's matching rules for exceptions are intended to be simple:

- Process `except` clauses in order.
- Match the actual exception against the exception class (or tuple of exception classes). A match means that the actual exception object (or any of the base classes of the exception object) is of the given class in the `except` clause.

These rules show why we put the most specific exception classes first and the more general exception classes last. A generic exception class like `Exception` will match almost every kind of exception. We don't want this first, because no other clauses will be checked. We must always put generic exceptions last.

There's an even more generic class, the `BaseException` class. There's no good reason to ever handle exceptions of this class. If we do, we will be catching `SystemExit` and `KeyboardInterrupt` exceptions; this interferes with the ability to kill a misbehaving application. We only use the `BaseException` class as a superclass when defining new exception classes that exist outside the normal exception hierarchy.

There's more...

Our example includes a nested context in which a second exception can be raised. Consider this `except` clause:

```
...     except FileNotFoundError:
...         target_path.parent.mkdir(exist_ok=True, parents=True)
...         target = shutil.copy(source_path, target_path)
```

If the `mkdir()` method or `shutil.copy()` functions raise an exception while handling the `FileNotFoundError` exception, it won't be handled. Any exceptions raised within an `except` clause can crash the program as a whole. Handling this can involve nested `try` statements.

We can rewrite the exception clause to include a nested `try` during recovery:

```
...     try:
...         target = shutil.copy(source_path, target_path)
...     except FileNotFoundError:
...         try:
...             target_path.parent.mkdir(exist_ok=True,
parents=True)
...             target = shutil.copy(source_path, target_path)
...         except OSError as ex2:
...             print(f"{target_path.parent} problem: {ex2}")
...     except OSError as ex:
...         print(f"Copy {source_path} to {target_path} error {ex}")
```

In this example, a nested context writes one message for `OSError`. In the outer context, a slightly different error message is used to log the error. In both cases, processing can continue. The distinct error messages make it slightly easier to debug the problems.

See also

- In the *Avoiding a potential problem with an except: clause* recipe, we look at some additional considerations when designing exception handling statements.

Avoiding a potential problem with an except: clause

There are some common mistakes in exception handling. These can cause programs to become unresponsive.

One of the mistakes we can make is to use the `except:` clause with no named exceptions to match. There are a few other mistakes that we can make if we're not cautious about the exceptions we try to handle.

This recipe will show some common exception handling errors that we can avoid.

Getting ready

When code can raise a variety of exceptions, it's sometimes tempting to try and match as many as possible. Matching too many exceptions can interfere with stopping a misbehaving Python program. We'll extend the idea of *what not to do* in this recipe.

How to do it...

We need to avoid using the bare `except:` clause. Instead, use `except Exception:` to match the most general kind of exception that an application can reasonably handle.

Handling too many exceptions can interfere with our ability to stop a misbehaving Python program. When we hit *Ctrl* + *C*, or send a `SIGINT` signal via the OS's `kill -2` command, we generally want the program to stop. We rarely want the program to write a message and keep running. If we use a bare `except:` clause, we can accidentally silence important exceptions.

There are a few other classes of exceptions that we should be wary of attempting to handle:

- `SystemError`
- `RuntimeError`
- `MemoryError`

Generally, these exceptions mean things are going badly somewhere in Python's internals. Rather than silence these exceptions, or attempt some recovery, we should allow the program to fail, find the root cause, and fix it.

How it works...

There are two techniques we should avoid:

- Don't capture the `BaseException` class.
- Don't use `except:` with no exception class. This matches all exceptions, including exceptions we should avoid trying to handle.

Using either of the above techniques can cause a program to become unresponsive at exactly the time we need to stop it. Further, if we capture any of these exceptions, we can interfere with the way these internal exceptions are handled:

- `SystemExit`
- `KeyboardInterrupt`
- `GeneratorExit`

If we silence, wrap, or rewrite any of these, we may have created a problem where none existed. We may have exacerbated a simple problem into a larger and more mysterious problem.

> It's a noble aspiration to write a program that never crashes. Interfering with some of Python's internal exceptions, however, doesn't create a more reliable program. Instead, it creates a program where a clear failure is masked and made into an obscure mystery.

See also

- In the *Leveraging the exception matching rules* recipe, we look at some considerations when designing exception-handling statements.

Concealing an exception root cause

In Python 3, exceptions contain a root cause. The default behavior of internally raised exceptions is to use an implicit `__context__` to include the root cause of an exception. In some cases, we may want to deemphasize the root cause because it's misleading or unhelpful for debugging.

This technique is almost always paired with an application or library that defines a unique exception. The idea is to show the unique exception without the clutter of an irrelevant exception from outside the application or library.

Getting ready

Assume we're writing some complex string processing. We'd like to treat a number of different kinds of detailed exceptions as a single generic error so that users of our software are insulated from the implementation details. We can attach details to the generic error.

How to do it...

1. To create a new exception, we can do this:

```
>>> class MyAppError(Exception):
...     pass
```

   This creates a new, unique class of exception that our library or application can use.

2. When handling exceptions, we can conceal the root cause exception like this:

```
>>> try:
...     None.some_method(42)
... except AttributeError as exception:
...     raise MyAppError("Some Known Problem") from None
```

In this example, we raise a new exception instance of the module's unique `MyAppError` exception class. The new exception will not have any connection with the root cause `AttributeError` exception.

How it works...

The Python exception classes all have a place to record the cause of the exception. We can set this `__cause__` attribute using the `raise Visible from RootCause` statement. This is done implicitly using the exception context as a default if the `from` clause is omitted.

Here's how it looks when this exception is raised:

```
>>> try:
...     None.some_method(42)
... except AttributeError as exception:
...     raise MyAppError("Some Known Problem") from None
Traceback (most recent call last):
  File "/Applications/PyCharm CE.app/Contents/helpers/pycharm/docrunner.
py", line 139, in __run
    exec(compile(example.source, filename, "single",
  File "<doctest examples.txt[67]>", line 4, in <module>
    raise MyAppError("Some Known Problem") from None
MyAppError: Some Known Problem
```

The underlying cause has been concealed. If we omit `from None`, then the exception will include two parts and will be quite a bit more complex. When the root cause is shown, the output looks like this:

```
Traceback (most recent call last):
  File "<doctest examples.txt[66]>", line 2, in <module>
    None.some_method(42)
AttributeError: 'NoneType' object has no attribute 'some_method'


During handling of the above exception, another exception occurred:


Traceback (most recent call last):
  File "/Applications/PyCharm CE.app/Contents/helpers/pycharm/docrunner.
py", line 139, in __run
    exec(compile(example.source, filename, "single",
  File "<doctest examples.txt[66]>", line 4, in <module>
    raise MyAppError("Some Known Problem")
MyAppError: Some Known Problem
```

This shows the underlying `AttributeError`. This may be an implementation detail that's unhelpful and better left off the printed display of the exception.

There's more...

There are a number of internal attributes of an exception. These include `__cause__`, `__context__`, `__traceback__`, and `__suppress_context__`. The overall exception context is in the `__context__` attribute. The cause, if provided via a `raise from` statement, is in `__cause__`. The context for the exception is available but can be suppressed from being printed.

See also

- In the *Leveraging the exception matching rules* recipe, we look at some considerations when designing exception-handling statements.
- In the *Avoiding a potential problem with an except: clause* recipe, we look at some additional considerations when designing exception-handling statements.

Managing a context using the with statement

There are many instances where our scripts will be entangled with external resources. The most common examples are disk files and network connections to external hosts. A common bug is retaining these entanglements forever, tying up these resources uselessly. These are sometimes called memory **leaks** because the available memory is reduced each time a new file is opened without closing a previously used file.

We'd like to isolate each entanglement so that we can be sure that the resource is acquired and released properly. The idea is to create a context in which our script uses an external resource. At the end of the context, our program is no longer bound to the resource and we want to be guaranteed that the resource is released.

Getting ready

Let's say we want to write lines of data to a file in CSV format. When we're done, we want to be sure that the file is closed and the various OS resources—including buffers and file handles—are released. We can do this in a context manager, which guarantees that the file will be properly closed.

Since we'll be working with CSV files, we can use the `csv` module to handle the details of the formatting:

```
>>> import csv
```

We'll also use the `pathlib` module to locate the files we'll be working with:

```
>>> from pathlib import Path
```

For the purposes of having something to write, we'll use this silly data source:

```
>>> some_source = [[2,3,5], [7,11,13], [17,19,23]]
```

This will give us a context in which to learn about the `with` statement.

How to do it...

1. Create the context by opening the path, or creating the network connection with `urllib.request.urlopen()`. Other common contexts include archives like `zip` files and `tar` files:

```
>>> target_path = Path.cwd()/"data"/"test.csv"
>>> with target_path.open('w', newline='') as target_file:
```

2. Include all the processing, indented within the with statement:

```
>>> target_path = Path.cwd()/"data"/"test.csv"
>>> with target_path.open('w', newline='') as target_file:
...     writer = csv.writer(target_file)
...     writer.writerow(['column', 'data', 'heading'])
...     writer.writerows(some_source)
```

3. When we use a file as a context manager, the file is automatically closed at the end of the indented context block. Even if an exception is raised, the file is still closed properly. Outdent the processing that is done after the context is finished and the resources are released:

```
>>> target_path = Path.cwd()/"data"/"test.csv"
>>> with target_path.open('w', newline='') as target_file:
...     writer = csv.writer(target_file)
...     writer.writerow(['column', 'data', 'heading'])
...     writer.writerows(some_source)
>>> print(f'finished writing {target_path.name}')
```

The statements outside the `with` context will be executed after the context is closed. The named resource—the file opened by `target_path.open()`—will be properly closed.

Even if an exception is raised inside the `with` statement, the file is still properly closed. The context manager is notified of the exception. It can close the file and allow the exception to propagate.

How it works...

A context manager is notified of three significant events surrounding the indented block of code:

- Entry
- Normal exit with no exception
- Exit with an exception pending

The context manager will—under all conditions—disentangle our program from external resources. Files can be closed. Network connections can be dropped. Database transactions can be committed or rolled back. Locks can be released.

We can experiment with this by including a manual exception inside the `with` statement. This can show that the file was properly closed:

```
>>> try:
...     with target_path.open('w', newline='') as target_file:
...         writer = csv.writer(target_file)
...         writer.writerow(['column', 'data', 'heading'])
...         writer.writerow(some_source[0])
...         raise Exception("Testing")
... except Exception as exc:
...     print(f"{target_file.closed=}")
...     print(f"{exc=}")
>>> print(f"Finished Writing {target_path.name}")
```

In this example, we've wrapped the real work in a `try` statement. This allows us to raise an exception after writing the first line of data to the CSV file. Because the exception handling is outside the `with` context, the file is closed properly. All resources are released and the part that was written is properly accessible and usable by other programs.

The output confirms the expected file state:

```
target_file.closed=True
exc=Exception('Testing')
```

This shows us that the file was properly closed. It also shows us the message associated with the exception to confirm that it was the exception we raised manually. This kind of technique allows us to work with expensive resources like database connections and network connections and be sure these don't "leak." A resource leak is a common description used when resources are not released properly back to the OS; it's as if they slowly drain away, and the application stops working because there are no more available OS network sockets or file handles. The `with` statement can be used to properly disentangle our Python application from OS resources.

There's more...

Python offers us a number of context managers. We noted that an open file is a context, as is an open network connection created by `urllib.request.urlopen()`.

For all file operations, and all network connections, we should always use a `with` statement as a context manager. It's very difficult to find an exception to this rule.

It turns out that the `decimal` module makes use of a context manager to allow localized changes to the way decimal arithmetic is performed. We can use the `decimal.localcontext()` function as a context manager to change rounding rules or precision for calculations isolated by a `with` statement.

We can define our own context managers, also. The `contextlib` module contains functions and decorators that can help us create context managers around resources that don't explicitly offer them.

When working with locks, the `with` statement context manager is the ideal way to acquire and release a lock. See `https://docs.python.org/3/library/threading.html#with-locks` for the relationship between a lock object created by the `threading` module and a context manager.

See also

- See `https://www.python.org/dev/peps/pep-0343/` for the origins of the with statement.
- Numerous recipes in *Chapter 9, Functional Programming Features*, will make use of this technique. The recipes *Reading delimited files with the cvs module*, *Reading complex formats using regular expressions*, and *Reading HTML documents*, among others, will make use of the `with` statement.

3 Function Definitions

Function definitions are a way to decompose a large problem into smaller problems. Mathematicians have been doing this for centuries. It's a way to package our Python programming into intellectually manageable chunks.

We'll look at a number of function definition techniques in these recipes. This will include ways to handle flexible parameters and ways to organize the parameters based on some higher-level design principles.

We'll also look at the `typing` module and how we can create more formal annotations for our functions. We will start down the road toward using the `mypy` project to make more formal assertions about the data types in use.

In this chapter, we'll look at the following recipes:

- Function parameters and type hints
- Designing functions with optional parameters
- Type hints for optional parameters
- Using super flexible keyword parameters
- Forcing keyword-only arguments with the * separator
- Defining position-only parameters with the / separator
- Writing hints for more complicated types
- Picking an order for parameters based on partial functions
- Writing clear documentation strings with RST markup
- Designing recursive functions around Python's stack limits
- Writing testable scripts with the script library switch

Function parameters and type hints

Python 3 added syntax for type hints. The `mypy` tool is one way to validate these type hints to be sure the hints and the code agree. All the examples shown in this book have been checked with the `mypy` tool.

This extra syntax for the hints is optional. It's not used at runtime and has no performance costs. If hints are present, tools like `mypy` can use them. The tool checks that the operations on the `n` parameter inside the function agree with the type hint about the parameter. The tool also tries to confirm that the return expressions both agree with the type hint. When an application has numerous function definitions, this extra scrutiny can be very helpful.

Getting ready

For an example of type hints, we'll look at some color computations. The first of these is extracting the Red, Green, and Blue values from the color codes commonly used in the style sheets for HTML pages. There are a variety of ways of encoding the values, including strings, integers, and tuples. Here are some of the varieties of types:

- A string of six hexadecimal characters with a leading #; for example, `"#C62D42"`.
- A string of six hexadecimal characters without the extra #; for example, `"C62D42"`.
- A numeric value; for example, `0xC62D42`. In this case, we've allowed Python to translate the literal value into an internal integer.
- A three-tuple of R, G, and B numeric values; for example, `(198, 45, 66)`.

Each of these has a specific type hint. For strings and numbers, we use the type name directly, `str` or `int`. For tuples, we'll need to import the `Tuple` type definition from the `typing` module.

The conversion from string or integer into three values involves two separate steps:

1. If the value is a string, convert it into an integer using the `int()` function.
2. For integer values, split the integer into three separate values using the `>>` and `&` operators. This is the core computation for converting an integer, `hx_int`, into `r`, `g`, and `b`:

   ```
   r, g, b = (hx_int >> 16) & 0xFF, (hx_int >> 8) & 0xFF, hx_int &
   0xFF.
   ```

A single RGB integer has three separate values that are combined via bit shifting. The red value is shifted left 16 bits, the green value is shifted left eight bits, and the blue value occupies the least-significant eight bits. A shift left by 16 bits is mathematically equivalent to multiplying by 2^{16}. Recovering the value via a right shift is similar to dividing by 2^{16}. The `>>` operator does the bit shifting, while the `&` operator applies a "mask" to save a subset of the available bits.

How to do it...

For functions that work with Python's atomic types (strings, integers, floats, and tuples), it's generally easiest to write the function without type hints and then add the hints. For more complex functions, it's sometimes easier to organize the type hints first. Since this function works with atomic types, we'll start with the function's implementation:

1. Write the function without any hints:

```
def hex2rgb(hx_int):
    if isinstance(hx_int, str):
        if hx_int [0] == "#":
            hx_int = int(hx_int [1:], 16)
        else:
            hx_int = int(hx_int, 16)
    r, g, b = (hx_int >> 16) & 0xff, (hx_int >> 8) & 0xff, hx_
int & 0xff
    return r, g, b
```

2. Add the result hint; this is usually the easiest way to do this. It's based on the return statement. In this example, the return is a tuple of three integers. We can use `Tuple[int, int, int]` for this. We'll need the `Tuple` definition from the `typing` module. Note the capitalization of the `Tuple` type hint, which is distinct from the underlying type object:

```
from typing import Tuple
```

3. Add the parameter hints. In this case, we've got two alternative types for the parameter: it can be a string or an integer. In the formal language of the type hints, this is a union of two types. The parameter is described as `Union[str, int]`. We'll need the `Union` definition from the `typing` module as well.

Combining the hints into a function leads to the following definition:

```
def hex2rgb(hx_int: Union[int, str]) -> Tuple[int, int, int]:
    if isinstance(hx_int, str):
        if hx_int[0] == "#":
            hx_int = int(hx_int[1:], 16)
        else:
            hx_int = int(hx_int, 16)
    r, g, b = (hx_int >> 16)&0xff, (hx_int >> 8)&0xff, hx_int&0xff
    return r, g, b
```

How it works...

The type hints have no impact when the Python code is executed. The hints are designed for people to read and for external tools, like mypy, to process.

When mypy is examining this block of code, it will confirm that the hx_int variable is always used as either an integer or a string. If inappropriate methods or functions are used with this variable, mypy will report the potential problem. The mypy tool relies on the presence of the isinstance() function to discern that the body of the first if statement is only used on a string value, and never used on an integer value.

In the r, g, b = assignment statement, the value for hx_int is expected to be an integer. If the isinstance(hx_int, str) value was true, the int() function would be used to create an integer. Otherwise, the parameter would be an integer to start with. The mypy tool will confirm the >> and & operations are appropriate for the expected integer value.

We can observe mypy's analysis of a type by inserting the reveal_type(hx_int) function into our code. This statement has function-like syntax; it's only used when running the mypy tool. We will only see output from this when we run mypy, and we have to remove this extra line of code before we try to do anything else with the module.

A temporary use of reveal_type() looks like this example:

```
def hex2rgb(hx_int: Union[int, str]) -> Tuple[int, int, int]:
    if isinstance(hx_int, str):
        if hx_int[0] == "#":
            hx_int = int(hx_int[1:], 16)
        else:
            hx_int = int(hx_int, 16)
    reveal_type(hx_int)  # Only used by mypy. Must be removed.
    r, g, b = (hx_int >> 16)&0xff, (hx_int >> 8)&0xff, hx_int&0xff
    return r, g, b
```

The output looks like this when we run mypy on the specific module:

```
(cookbook) % mypy Chapter_03/ch03_r01.py
Chapter_03/ch03_r01.py:55: note: Revealed type is 'builtins.int'
```

The output from the reveal_type(hx_int) line tells us mypy is certain the variable will have an integer value after the first if statement is complete.

Once we've seen the revealed type information, we need to delete the reveal_type(hx_int) line from the file. In the example code available online, reveal_type() is turned into a comment on line 55 to show where it can be used. Pragmatically, these lines are generally deleted when they're no longer used.

There's more...

Let's look at a related computation. This converts RGB numbers into Hue-Saturation-Lightness values. These HSL values can be used to compute complementary colors. An additional algorithm required to convert from HSL back into RGB values can help encode colors for a web page:

- RGB to HSL: We'll look at this closely because it has complex type hints.
- HSL to complement: There are a number of theories on what the "best" complement might be. We won't look at this function. The *hue* value is in the range of 0 to 1 and represents degrees around a color circle. Adding (or subtracting) 0.5 is equivalent to a 180° shift, and is the complementary color. Offsets by 1/6 and 1/3 can provide a pair of related colors.
- HSL to RGB: This will be the final step, so we'll ignore the details of this computation.

We won't look closely at all of the implementations. Information is available at `https://www.easyrgb.com/en/math.php` if you wish to create working implementations of most of these functions.

We can rough out a definition of the function by writing a stub definition, like this:

```
def rgb_to_hsl(rgb: Tuple[int, int, int]) -> Tuple[float, float,
float]:
```

This can help us visualize a number of related functions to be sure they all have consistent types. The other two functions have stubs like these:

```
def hsl_complement(hsl: Tuple[float, float, float]) -> Tuple[float,
float, float]:

def hasl_to_rgb(hsl: Tuple[float, float, float]) -> Tuple[int, int,
int]:
```

After writing down this initial list of stubs, we can identify that type hints are repeated in slightly different contexts. This suggests we need to create a separate type to avoid repetition of the details. We'll provide a name for the repeated type detail:

```
RGB = Tuple[int, int, int]
HSL = Tuple[float, float, float]
def rgb_to_hsl(color: RGB) -> HSL:
def hsl_complement(color: HSL) -> HSL:

def hsl_to_rgb(color: HSL) -> RGB:
```

This overview of the various functions can be very helpful for assuring that each function does something appropriate for the problem being solved, and has the proper parameters and return values.

As noted in *Chapter 1, Numbers, Strings, and Tuples, Using NamedTuples to Simplify Item Access in Tuples* recipe, we can provide a more descriptive set of names for these tuple types:

```
from typing import NamedTuple
class RGB(NamedTuple):
    red: int
    green: int
    blue: int

def hex_to_rgb2(hx_int: Union[int, str]) -> RGB:
    if isinstance(hx_int, str):
        if hx_int[0] == "#":
            hx_int = int(hx_int[1:], 16)
        else:
            hx_int = int(hx_int, 16)
    # reveal_type(hx_int)
    return RGB(
        (hx_int >> 16)&0xff,
        (hx_int >> 8)&0xff,
        (hx_int&0xff)
    )
```

We've defined a unique, new `Tuple` subclass, the `RGB` named tuple. This has three elements, available by name or position. The expectation stated in the type hints is that each of the values will be an integer.

In this example, we've included a `reveal_type()` to show where it might be useful. In the long run, once the author understands the types in use, this kind of code can be deleted.

The `hex_to_rgb2()` function creates an `RGB` object from either a string or an integer. We can consider creating a related type, `HSL`, as a named tuple with three float values. This can help clarify the intent behind the code. It also lets the `mypy` tool confirm that the various objects are used appropriately.

See also

- The `mypy` project contains a wealth of information. See `https://mypy.readthedocs.io/en/latest/index.html` for more information on the way type hints work.

Designing functions with optional parameters

When we define a function, we often have a need for optional parameters. This allows us to write functions that are more flexible and easier to read.

We can also think of this as a way to create a family of closely-related functions. We can think of each function as having a slightly different collection of parameters - called the **signature** - but all sharing the same simple name. This is sometimes called an "overloaded" function. Within the typing module, an `@overload` decorator can help create type hints in very complex cases.

An example of an optional parameter is the built-in `int()` function. This function has two signatures:

- `int(str)`: For example, the value of `int('355')` has a value of `355`. In this case, we did not provide a value for the optional base parameter; the default value of `10` was used.
- `int(str, base)`: For example, the value of `int('163', 16)` is `355`. In this case, we provided a value for the base parameter.

Getting ready

A great many games rely on collections of dice. The casino game of *Craps* uses two dice. A game like *Zonk* (or *Greed* or *Ten Thousand*) uses six dice. Variations of the game may use more.

It's handy to have a dice-rolling function that can handle all of these variations. How can we write a dice simulator that works for any number of dice, but will use two as a handy default value?

How to do it...

We have two approaches to designing a function with optional parameters:

- **General to Particular**: We start by designing the most general solution and provide handy defaults for the most common case.
- **Particular to General**: We start by designing several related functions. We then merge them into one general function that covers all of the cases, singling out one of the original functions to be the default behavior. We'll look at this first, because it's often easier to start with a number of concrete examples.

Particular to General design

When following the particular to general strategy, we'll design several individual functions and look for common features. Throughout this example, we'll use slightly different names as the function evolves. This simplifies unit testing the different versions and comparing them:

1. Write one game function. We'll start with the *Craps* game because it seems to be the simplest:

    ```
    import random
    def die() -> int:
        return random.randint(1, 6)

    def craps() -> Tuple[int, int]:
        return (die(), die())
    ```

    We defined a function, `die()`, to encapsulate a basic fact about standard dice. There are five platonic solids that can be pressed into service, yielding four-sided, six-sided, eight-sided, twelve-sided, and twenty-sided dice. The six-sided die has a long history, starting as *Astragali* bones, which were easily trimmed into a six-sided cube.

2. Write the next game function. We'll move on to the *Zonk* game because it's a little more complex:

    ```
    def zonk() -> Tuple[int, ...]:
        return tuple(die() for x in range(6))
    ```

    We've used a generator expression to create a `tuple` object with six dice. We'll look at generator expressions in depth online in *Chapter 9, Functional Programming Features* (link provided in the *Preface*).

    The generator expression in the body of the `zonk()` function has a variable, `x`, which is required syntax, but the value is ignored. It's also common to see this written as `tuple(die() for _ in range(6))`. The variable _ is a valid Python variable name; this name can be used as a hint that we don't ever want to use the value of this variable.

    Here's an example of using the `zonk()` function:

    ```
    >>> zonk()
    (5, 3, 2, 4, 1, 1)
    ```

    This shows us a roll of six individual dice. There's a short straight (1-5), as well as a pair of ones. In some versions of the game, this is a good scoring hand.

    Locate the common features in the `craps()` and `zonk()` functions. This may require some refactoring of the various functions to locate a common design. In many cases, we'll wind up introducing additional variables to replace constants or other assumptions.

In this case, we can refactor the design of `craps()` to follow the pattern set by `zonk()`. Rather than building exactly two evaluations of the `die()` function, we can introduce a generator expression based on `range(2)` that will evaluate the `die()` function twice:

```
def craps_v2() -> Tuple[int, ...]:
    return tuple(die() for x in range(2))
```

Merge the two functions. This will often involve exposing a variable that had previously been a literal or other hardwired assumption:

```
def dice_v2(n: int) -> Tuple[int, ...]:
    return tuple(die() for x in range(n))
```

This provides a general function that covers the needs of both *Craps* and *Zonk*.

3. Identify the most common use case and make this the default value for any parameters that were introduced. If our most common simulation was *Craps*, we might do this:

```
def dice_v3(n: int = 2) -> Tuple[int, ...]:
    return tuple(die() for x in range(n))
```

Now, we can simply use `dice_v3()` for *Craps*. We'll need to use `dice_v3(6)` for *Zonk*.

4. Check the type hints to be sure they describe the parameters and the return values. In this case, we have one parameter with an integer value, and the return is a tuple of integers, described by `Tuple[int, ...]`.

Throughout this example, the name evolved from `dice` to `dice_v2` and then to `dice_v3`. This makes it easier to see the differences here in the recipe. Once a final version is written, it makes sense to delete the others and rename the final versions of these functions to `dice()`, `craps()`, and `zonk()`. The story of their evolution may make an interesting blog post, but it doesn't need to be preserved in the code.

General to Particular design

When following the general to particular strategy, we'll identify all of the needs first. It can be difficult to foresee all the alternatives, so this may be difficult in practice. We'll often do this by introducing variables to the requirements:

1. Summarize the requirements for dice-rolling. We might start with a list like this:
   - *Craps*: Two dice
   - First roll in *Zonk*: Six dice
   - Subsequent rolls in *Zonk*: One to six dice

   This list of requirements shows a common theme of rolling *n* dice.

2. Rewrite the requirements with an explicit parameter in place of any literal value. We'll replace all of our numbers with a parameter, *n*, and show the values for this new parameter that we've introduced:

    - *Craps*: *n* dice, where *n* = 2
    - First roll in *Zonk*: *n* dice, where *n* = 6
    - Subsequent rolls in Zonk: n dice, where $1 \le n \le 6$

    The goal here is to be absolutely sure that all of the variations really have a common abstraction. We also want to be sure we've properly parameterized each of the various functions.

3. Write the function that fits the General pattern:

    ```
    def dice(n):
        return tuple(die() for x in range(n))
    ```

    In the third case – subsequent rolls in *Zonk* – we identified a constraint of $1 \le n \le 6$. We need to determine if this is a constraint that's part of our `dice()` function, or if this constraint is imposed on the dice by the simulation application that uses the `dice` function. In this example, the upper bound of six is part of the application program to play Zonk; this not part of the general `dice()` function.

4. Provide a default value for the most common use case. If our most common simulation was *Craps*, we might do this:

    ```
    def dice(n=2):
        return tuple(die() for x in range(n))
    ```

5. Add type hints. These will describe the parameters and the return values. In this case, we have one parameter with an integer value, and the return is a tuple of integers, described by `Tuple[int, ...]`:

    ```
    def dice(n: int=2) -> Tuple[int, ...]:
        return tuple(die() for x in range(n))
    ```

Now, we can simply use `dice()` for *Craps*. We'll need to use `dice(6)` for *Zonk*.

In this recipe, the name didn't need to evolve through multiple versions. This version looks precisely like `dice_v2()` from the previous recipe. This isn't an accident – the two design strategies often converge on a common solution.

How it works...

Python's rules for providing parameter values are very flexible. There are several ways to ensure that each parameter is given an argument value when the function is evaluated. We can think of the process like this:

1. Set each parameter to its default value. Not all parameters have defaults, so some parameters will be left undefined.
2. For arguments without names – for example, `dice(2)` – the argument values are assigned to the parameters by position.
3. For arguments with names – for example, `dice(n: int = 2)` – the argument values are assigned to parameters by name. It's an error to assign a parameter both by position and by name.
4. If any parameter still doesn't have a value, this raises a `TypeError` exception.

These rules allow us to create functions that use default values to make some parameters optional. The rules also allow us to mix positional values with named values.

The use of optional parameters stems from two considerations:

- Can we parameterize the processing?
- What's the most common argument value for that parameter?

Introducing parameters into a process definition can be challenging. In some cases, it helps to have concrete example code so that we can replace literal values (such as 2 or 6) with a parameter.

In some cases, however, the literal value doesn't need to be replaced with a parameter. It can be left as a literal value. Our `die()` function, for example, has a literal value of 6 because we're only interested in standard, cubic dice. This isn't a parameter because we don't see a need to make a more general kind of die. For some popular role-playing games, it may be necessary to parameterize the number of faces on the die to support monsters and wizards.

There's more...

If we want to be very thorough, we can write functions that are specialized versions of our more generalized function. These functions can simplify an application:

```
def craps():
    return dice(2)

def zonk():
    return dice(6)
```

Our application features – `craps()` and `zonk()` – depend on a general function, `dice()`. This, in turn, depends on another function, `die()`. We'll revisit this idea in the *Picking an order for parameters based on partial functions* recipe.

Each layer in this stack of dependencies introduces a handy abstraction that saves us from having to understand too many details in the lower layers. This idea of layered abstractions is sometimes called **chunking**. It's a way of managing complexity by isolating the details.

In this example, our stack of functions only has two layers. In a more complex application, we may have to introduce parameters at many layers in a hierarchy.

See also

- We'll extend on some of these ideas in the *Picking an order for parameters based on partial functions* recipe, later in this chapter.
- We've made use of optional parameters that involve immutable objects. In this recipe, we focused on numbers. In *Chapter 4, Built-In Data Structures Part 1: Lists and Sets,* we'll look at mutable objects, which have an internal state that can be changed. In the *Avoiding mutable default values for function parameters* recipe, we'll look at some additional considerations that are important for designing functions that have optional values, which are mutable objects.

Designing type hints for optional parameters

This recipe combines the two previous recipes. It's common to define functions with fairly complex options and then add type hints around those definitions. For atomic types like strings and integers, it can make sense to write a function first, and then add type hints to the function.

In later chapters, when we look at more complex data types, it often makes more sense to create the data type definitions first, and then define the functions (or methods) related to those types. This philosophy of type first is one of the foundations for object-oriented programming.

Getting ready

We'll look at the two dice-based games, *Craps* and *Zonk*. In the *Craps* game, the players will be rolling two dice. In the *Zonk* game, they'll roll a number of dice, varying from one to six. The games have a common, underlying requirement to be able to create collections of dice. As noted in the *Designing functions with optional parameters* recipe, there are two broad strategies for designing the common function for both games; we'll rely on the General to Particular strategy and create a very general dice function.

How to do it...

1. Define a function with the required and optional parameters. This can be derived from combining a number of examples. Or, it can be designed through careful consideration of the alternatives. For this example, we have a function where one parameter is required and one is optional:

    ```
    def dice(n, sides=6):
        return tuple(random.randint(1, sides) for _ in range(n))
    ```

2. Add the type hint for the return value. This is often easiest because it is based on the `return` statement. In this case, it's a tuple of indefinite size, but all the elements are integers. This is represented as `Tuple[int, ...]`. (`...` is valid Python syntax for a tuple with an indefinite number of items.)
3. Add required parameter type hints. The parameter `n` must be an integer, so we'll replace the simple `n` parameter with `n: int` to include a type hint.
4. Add optional parameter type hints. The syntax is more complex for these because we're inserting the hint between the name and the default value. In this case, the sides parameter must also be an integer, so we'll replace `sides = 6` with `sides: int = 6`.

Here's the final definition with all of the type hints included. We've changed the name to make it distinct from the `dice()` example shown previously:

```
def dice_t(n: int, sides: int = 6) -> Tuple[int, ...]:
    return tuple(random.randint(1, sides) for _ in range(n))
```

The syntax for the optional parameter contains a wealth of information, including the expected type and a default value.

`Tuple[int, ...]`, as a description of a tuple that's entirely filled with int values, can be a little confusing at first. Most tuples have a fixed, known number of items. In this case, we're extending the concept to include a fixed, but not fully defined number of items in a tuple.

How it works...

The type hint syntax can seem unusual at first. The hints can be included wherever variables are created:

- Function (and class method) parameter definitions. The hints are right after the parameter name, separated by a colon. As we've seen in this recipe, any default value comes after the type hint.
- Assignment statements. We can include a type hint after the variable name on the left-hand side of a simple assignment statement. It might look like this:

    ```
    Pi: float = 355/113
    ```

Additionally, we can include type hints on function (and class method) return types. The hints are after the function definition, separated by a ->. The extra syntax makes them easy to read and helpful for a person to understand the code.

The type hint syntax is optional. This keeps the language simple, and puts the burden of type checking on external tools like mypy.

There's more...

In some cases, the default value can't be computed in advance. In other cases, the default value would be a mutable object, like a list, which we don't want to provide in the parameter definitions.

Here, we'll look at a function with very complex default values. We're going to be simulating a very wide domain of games, and our assumptions about the number of dice and the shape of the dice are going to have to change dramatically.

There are two fundamental use cases:

- When we're rolling six-sided dice, the default number of dice is two. This fits with two-dice games like *Craps*. If we call the function with no argument values, this is what we'd like to happen. We can also explicitly provide the number of dice in order to support multi-dice games.
- When we're rolling other dice, the default number of dice changes to one. This fits with games that use polyhedral dice of four, eight, twelve, or twenty sides. It even fits with irregular dice with ten sides.

These rules will dramatically change the way default values need to be handled in our dice() and dice_t() functions. We can't trivially provide a default value for the number of dice. A common practice is to provide a special value like None, and compute an appropriate default when the None value is provided.

The None value also expands the type hint requirement. When we can provide a value for an int or None, this is effectively Union[None, int]. The typing module lets us use Optional[int] for values for which None is a possibility:

```
from typing import Optional, Tuple
def polydice(n: Optional[int] = None, sides: int = 6) -> Tuple[int,
...]:
    if n is None:
        n = 2 if sides == 6 else 1
    return tuple(random.randint(1, sides) for _ in range(n))
```

In this example, we've defined the n parameter as having a value that will either be an integer or None. Since the actual default value depends on other arguments, we can't provide a simple, fixed default in the function definition. We've used a default value of None to show the parameter is optional.

Here are four examples of using this function with a variety of argument values:

```
>>> random.seed(113)
>>> polydice()
(1, 6)
>>> polydice(6)
(6, 3, 1, 4, 5, 3)
>>> polydice(sides=8)
(4,)
>>> polydice(n=8, sides=4)
(4, 1, 1, 3, 2, 3, 4, 3)
```

In the first example, neither the `n` nor `sides` parameters were provided. In this case, the value used for `n` was two because the value of `sides` was six.

The second example provides a value for the `n` parameter. The expected number of six-sided dice were simulated.

The third example provides a value for the `sides` parameter. Since there's no value for the `n` parameter, a default value for the `n` parameter was computed based on the value of the `sides` parameter.

The fourth example provides values for both the `n` and the `sides` parameters. No defaults are used here.

See also

- See the *Using super flexible keyword parameters* recipe for more examples of how parameters and defaults work in Python.

Using super flexible keyword parameters

Some design problems involve solving a simple equation for one unknown when given enough known values. For example, rate, time, and distance have a simple linear relationship. We can solve any one when given the other two.

Here are the three rules that we can use as an example:

- $d = r \times t$
- $r = d / t$
- $t = d / r$

When designing electrical circuits, for example, a similar set of equations is used based on Ohm's Law. In that case, the equations tie together resistance, current, and voltage.

In some cases, we want to provide a simple, high-performance software implementation that can perform any of the three different calculations based on what's known and what's unknown. We don't want to use a general algebraic framework; we want to bundle the three solutions into a simple, efficient function.

Getting ready

We'll build a single function that can solve a **Rate-Time-Distance** (**RTD**) calculation by embodying all three solutions, given any two known values. With minor variable name changes, this applies to a surprising number of real-world problems.

There's a trick here. We don't necessarily want a single value answer. We can slightly generalize this by creating a small Python dictionary with the three values in it. We'll look at dictionaries in more detail in *Chapter 4, Built-In Data Structures Part 1: Lists and Sets.*

We'll use the `warnings` module instead of raising an exception when there's a problem:

```
>>> import warnings
```

Sometimes, it is more helpful to produce a result that is doubtful than to stop processing.

How to do it...

1. Solve the equation for each of the unknowns. We can base all of this on the $d = r \times t$ RTD calculation. This leads to three separate expressions:
   - Distance = rate * time
   - Rate = distance / time
   - Time = distance / rate
2. Wrap each expression in an `if` statement based on one of the values being `None` when it's unknown:

```
if distance is None:
    distance = rate * time
elif rate is None:
    rate = distance / time
elif time is None:
    time = distance / rate
```

3. Refer to the *Designing complex if...elif chains* recipe from *Chapter 2, Statements and Syntax*, for guidance on designing these complex `if...elif` chains. Include a variation of the `else` crash option:

```
else:
    warnings.warning( "Nothing to solve for" )
```

4. Build the resulting dictionary object. In some very simple cases, we can use the `vars()` function to simply emit all of the local variables as a resulting dictionary. In other cases, we'll need to build the dictionary object explicitly:

```
return dict(distance=distance, rate=rate, time=time)
```

5. Wrap all of this as a function using keyword parameters with default values of `None`. This leads to parameter types of `Optional[float]`. The return type is a dictionary with string keys and `Optiona[float]` values, summarized as `Dict[str, Optional[float]]`:

```
def rtd(
    distance: Optional[float] = None,
    rate: Optional[float] = None,
    time: Optional[float] = None,
) -> Dict[str, Optional[float]]:
    if distance is None and rate is not None and time is not 
None:
        distance = rate * time
    elif rate is None and distance is not None and time is not 
None:
        rate = distance / time
    elif time is None and distance is not None and rate is not 
None:
        time = distance / rate
    else:
        warnings.warn("Nothing to solve for")
    return dict(distance=distance, rate=rate, time=time)
```

The type hints tend to make the function definition so long it has to be spread across five physical lines of code. The presence of so many optional values is difficult to summarize!

We can use the resulting function like this:

```
>>> rtd(distance=31.2, rate=6)
{'distance': 31.2, 'rate': 6, 'time': 5.2}
```

This shows us that going `31.2` nautical miles at a rate of `6` knots will take `5.2` hours.

For a nicely formatted output, we might do this:

```
>>> result = rtd(distance=31.2, rate=6)
>>> ('At {rate}kt, it takes '
... '{time}hrs to cover {distance}nm').format_map(result)
'At 6kt, it takes 5.2hrs to cover 31.2nm'
```

To break up the long string, we used our knowledge from the *Designing complex if...elif chains* recipe from *Chapter 2, Statements and Syntax*.

How it works...

Because we've provided default values for all of the parameters, we can provide argument values for any two of the three parameters, and the function can then solve for the third parameter. This saves us from having to write three separate functions.

Returning a dictionary as the final result isn't essential to this. It's a handy way to show inputs and outputs. It allows the function to return a uniform result, no matter which parameter values were provided.

There's more...

We have an alternative formulation for this, one that involves more flexibility. Python functions have an *all other keywords* parameter, prefixed with `**`. It is often shown like this:

```
def rtd2(distance, rate, time, **keywords):
    print(keywords)
```

We can leverage the flexible `keywords` parameter and insist that all arguments be provided as keywords:

```
def rtd2(**keywords: float) -> Dict[str, Optional[float]]:
    rate = keywords.get('rate')
    time = keywords.get('time')
    distance = keywords.get('distance')
etc.
```

The `keywords` type hint states that all of the values for these parameters will be `float` objects. In some rare case, not all of the keyword parameters are the same type; in this case, some redesign may be helpful to make the types clearer.

This version uses the dictionary `get()` method to find a given key in the dictionary. If the key is not present, a default value of `None` is provided.

The dictionary's `get()` method permits a second parameter, the default, which is provided if the key is not present. If you don't enter a default, the default value is set to `None`, which works out well for this function.

This kind of open-ended design has the potential advantage of being much more flexible. It has some disadvantages. One potential disadvantage is that the actual parameter names are hard to discern, since they're not part of the function definition, but instead part of the function's body.

We can follow the *Writing clear documentation strings with RST markup* recipe and provide a good docstring. It seems somehow better, though, to provide the parameter names explicitly as part of the Python code rather than implicitly through documentation.

This has another, and more profound, disadvantage. The problem is revealed in the following bad example:

```
>>> rtd2(distnace=31.2, rate=6)
{'distance': None, 'rate': 6, 'time': None}
```

This isn't the behavior we want. The misspelling of "distance" is not reported as a `TypeError` exception. The misspelled parameter name is not reported anywhere. To uncover these errors, we'd need to add some programming to pop items from the `keywords` dictionary and report errors on names that remain after the expected names were removed:

```
def rtd3(**keywords: float) -> Dict[str, Optional[float]]:
    rate = keywords.pop("rate", None)
    time = keywords.pop("time", None)
    distance = keywords.pop("distance", None)
    if keywords:
        raise TypeError(
            f"Invalid keyword parameter: {', '.join(keywords.
keys())}")
```

This design will spot spelling errors, but has a more complex procedure for getting the values of the parameters. While this can work, it is often an indication that explicit parameter names might be better than the flexibility of an unbounded collection of names.

See also

- We'll look at the documentation of functions in the *Writing clear documentation strings with RST markup* recipe.

Forcing keyword-only arguments with the * separator

There are some situations where we have a large number of positional parameters for a function. Perhaps we've followed the *Designing functions with optional parameters* recipe and that led us to designing a function with so many parameters that it gets confusing.

Pragmatically, a function with more than about three parameters can be confusing. A great deal of conventional mathematics seems to focus on one and two-parameter functions. There don't seem to be too many common mathematical operators that involve three or more operands.

When it gets difficult to remember the required order for the parameters, there are too many parameters.

Getting ready

We'll look at a function that has a large number of parameters. We'll use a function that prepares a wind-chill table and writes the data to a CSV format output file.

We need to provide a range of temperatures, a range of wind speeds, and information on the file we'd like to create. This is a lot of parameters.

A formula for the apparent temperature, the wind chill, is this:

$$T_{wc}(T_a, V) = 13.12 + 0.6215T_a - 11.37V^{0.16} + 0.3965T_aV^{0.16}$$

The wind chill temperature, T_{wc}, is based on the air temperature, T_a, in degrees, *C*, and the wind speed, *V*, in KPH.

For Americans, this requires some conversions:

- Convert from *F* into *C*: $C = 5(F-32) / 9$
- Convert windspeed from MPH, V_m , into KPH, V_k: $V_k = V_m \times 1.609344$
- The result needs to be converted from *C* back into *F*: $F = 32 + C(9/5)$

We won't fold these conversions into this solution. We'll leave that as an exercise for you.

The function to compute the wind-chill temperature, `Twc()`, is based on the definition provided previously. It looks like this:

```
def Twc(T: float, V: float) -> float:
    return 13.12 + 0.6215*T - 11.37*V**0.16 + 0.3965*T*V**0.16
```

One approach to creating a wind-chill table is to create something like this:

```
import csv

def wind_chill(
    start_T: int, stop_T: int, step_T: int,
    start_V: int, stop_V: int, step_V: int,
    target: TextIO
) -> None:
    """Wind Chill Table."""
    writer= csv.writer(target)
    heading = ['']+[str(t) for t in range(start_T, stop_T, step_T)]
    writer.writerow(heading)
    for V in range(start_V, stop_V, step_V):
```

```
        row = [float(V)] + [
            Twc(T, V) for T in range(start_T, stop_T, step_T)
        ]
        writer.writerow(row)
```

Before we get to the design problem, let's look at the essential processing. We've opened an output file using the with context. This follows the *Managing a context using the with statement* recipe in *Chapter 2, Statements and Syntax*. Within this context, we've created a write for the CSV output file. We'll look at this in more depth in *Chapter 10, Input/Output, Physical Format, and Logical Layout*.

We've used an expression, `['']+[str(t) for t in range(start_T, stop_T, step_T)]`, to create a heading row. This expression includes a list literal and a generator expression that builds a list. We'll look at lists in *Chapter 4, Built-In Data Structures Part 1: Lists and Sets*. We'll look at the generator expression online in *Chapter 9, Functional Programming Features* (link provided in the *Preface*).

Similarly, each cell of the table is built by a generator expression, `[Twc(T, V)for T in range(start_T, stop_T, step_T)]`. This is a comprehension that builds a `list` object. The list consists of values computed by the wind-chill function, `Twc()`. We provide the wind velocity based on the row in the table. We provide a temperature based on the column in the table.

The `def wind_chill` line presents a problem: the function has seven distinct positional parameters. When we try to use this function, we wind up with code like the following:

```
>>> p = Path('data/wc1.csv')
>>> with p.open('w', newline='') as target:
...     wind_chill(0, -45, -5, 0, 20, 2, target)
```

What are all those numbers? Is there something we can do to help explain the purposes behind all those numbers?

How to do it...

When we have a large number of parameters, it helps to use keyword arguments instead of positional arguments.

In Python 3, we have a technique that mandates the use of keyword arguments. We can use the `*` as a separator between two groups of parameters:

- Before `*`, we list the argument values that can be *either* positional or named by keyword. In this example, we don't have any of these parameters.
- After `*`, we list the argument values that must be given with a keyword. For our example, this is all of the parameters.

For our example, the resulting function definition has the following stub definition:

```
def wind_chill(
    *,
    start_T: int, stop_T: int, step_T: int,
    start_V: int, stop_V: int, step_V: int,
    path: Path
) -> None:
```

Let's see how it works in practice with different kinds of parameters.

1. When we try to use the confusing positional parameters, we'll see this:

```
>>> wind_chill(0, -45, -5, 0, 20, 2, target)
Traceback (most recent call last):
  File "<stdin>", line 1, in <module>
TypeError: wind_chill() takes 0 positional arguments but 7 were
given
```

2. We must use the function with explicit parameter names, as follows:

```
>>> p = Path('data/wc1.csv')
>>> with p.open('w', newline='') as output_file:
...     wind_chill(start_T=0, stop_T=-45, step_T=-5,
...     start_V=0, stop_V=20, step_V=2,
...     target=output_file)
```

This use of mandatory keyword parameters forces us to write a clear statement each time we use this complex function.

How it works...

The * character has a number of distinct meanings in the definition of a function:

- * is used as a prefix for a special parameter that receives all the unmatched positional arguments. We often use `*args` to collect all of the positional arguments into a single parameter named `args`.
- ** is used a prefix for a special parameter that receives all the unmatched named arguments. We often use `**kwargs` to collect the named values into a parameter named `kwargs`.
- *, when used by itself as a separator between parameters, separates those parameters. It can be applied positionally or by keyword. The remaining parameters can only be provided by keyword.

The `print()` function exemplifies this. It has three keyword-only parameters for the output file, the field separator string, and the line end string.

There's more...

We can, of course, combine this technique with default values for the various parameters. We might, for example, make a change to this, thus introducing a single default value:

```
import sys
def wind_chill(
    *,
    start_T: int, stop_T: int, step_T: int,
    start_V: int, stop_V: int, step_V: int,
    target: TextIO=sys.stdout
) -> None:
```

We can now use this function in two ways:

- Here's a way to print the table on the console, using the default target:

```
wind_chill(
    start_T=0, stop_T=-45, step_T=-5,
    start_V=0, stop_V=20, step_V=2)
```

- Here's a way to write to a file using an explicit target:

```
path = pathlib.Path("code/wc.csv")
with path.open('w', newline='') as output_file:
    wind_chill(target=output_file,
        start_T=0, stop_T=-45, step_T=-5,
        start_V=0, stop_V=20, step_V=2)
```

We can be more confident in these changes because the parameters must be provided by name. We don't have to check carefully to be sure about the order of the parameters.

As a general pattern, we suggest doing this when there are more than three parameters for a function. It's easy to remember one or two. Most mathematical operators are unary or binary. While a third parameter may still be easy to remember, the fourth (and subsequent) parameter will become very difficult to recall, and forcing the named parameter evaluation of the function seems to be a helpful policy.

See also

- See the *Picking an order for parameters based on partial functions* recipe for another application of this technique.

Defining position-only parameters with the / separator

In Python 3.8, an additional annotation was added to function definitions. We can use the / character in the parameter list to separate the parameters into two groups. Before /, all parameters work positionally, or names may not be used with argument values. After /, parameters may be given in order, or names may be used.

This should be used for functions where the following conditions are all true:

- A few positional parameters are used (no more than three)
- They are all required
- The order is so obvious that any change might be confusing

This has always been a feature of the standard library. As an example, the `math.sin()` function can only use positional parameters. The formal definition is as follows:

```
>>> help(math.sin)


Help on built-in function sin in module math:


sin(x, /)
    Return the sine of x (measured in radians).
```

Even though there's an `x` parameter name, we can't use this name. If we try to, we'll see the following exception:

```
>>> import math
>>> math.sin(x=0.5)
Traceback (most recent call last):
  File "<stdin>", line 1, in <module>
TypeError: sin() takes no keyword arguments
```

The `x` parameter can only be provided positionally. The output from the `help()` function provides a suggestion of how the / separator can be used to make this happen.

Getting ready

Position-only parameters are used by some of the internal built-ins; the design pattern can also be helpful, though, in our functions. To be useful, there must be very few position-only parameters. Since most mathematical operators have one or two operands, this suggests one or two position-only parameters can be useful.

We'll consider two functions for conversion of units from the Fahrenheit system used in the US and the Centigrade system used almost everywhere else in the world:

- Convert from *F* into *C*: *C* = 5(*F*-32) / 9
- Convert from *C* into *F*: *F* = 32 + *C*(9/5)

Each of these functions has a single argument, making it a reasonable example for a position-only parameter.

How to do it...

1. Define the function:

```
def F(c: float) -> float:
    return 32 + c*(9/5)
```

2. Add the / parameter separator after the position-only parameters:

```
def F(c: float, /) -> float:
    return 32 + c*(9/5)
```

How it works...

The / separator divides the parameter names into two groups. In front of / are parameters where the argument values must be provided positionally: named argument values cannot be used. After / are parameters where names are permitted.

Let's look at a slightly more complex version of our temperature conversions:

```
def C(f: float, /, truncate: bool=False) -> float:
    c = 5*(f-32) / 9
    if truncate:
        return round(c, 0)

    return c
```

This function has a position-only parameter named `f`. It also has the `truncate` parameter, which can be provided by name. This leads to three separate ways to use this function, as shown in the following examples:

```
>>> C(72)
22.2222222222222
>>> C(72, truncate=True)
22.0
>>> C(72, True)
22.0
```

The first example shows the position-only parameter and the output without any rounding. This is an awkwardly complex-looking value.

The second example uses the named parameter style to set the non-positional parameter, `truncate`, to `True`. The third example provides both argument values positionally.

There's more...

This can be combined with the * separator to create very sophisticated function signatures. The parameters can be decomposed into three groups:

- Parameters before the / separator must be given by position. These must be first.
- Parameters after the / separator can be given by position or name.
- Parameters after the * separator must be given by name only. These names are provided last, since they can never be matched by position.

See also

- See the *Forcing keyword-only arguments with the * separator* recipe for details on the * separator.

Writing hints for more complex types

The Python language allows us to write functions (and classes) that are entirely generic with respect to data type. Consider this function as an example:

```
def temperature(*, f_temp=None, c_temp=None):
    if c_temp is None:
        return {'f_temp': f_temp, 'c_temp': 5*(f_temp-32)/9}
    elif f_temp is None:
        return {'f_temp': 32+9*c_temp/5, 'c_temp': c_temp}
    else:

        raise TypeError("One of f_temp or c_temp must be
provided")
```

This follows three recipes shown earlier: *Using super flexible keyword parameters*, *Forcing keyword-only arguments with the * separator*, and *Designing complex if...elif chains*, from *Chapter 2, Statements and Syntax*.

This function produces a fairly complex data structure as a result. It's not very clear what the data structure is. Worse, it's difficult to be sure functions are using the output from this function correctly. The parameters don't provide type hints, either.

This is valid, working Python. It lacks a formal description that would help a person understand the intent.

We can also include docstrings. Here's the recommended style:

```
def temperature(*, f_temp=None, c_temp=None):
    """Convert between Fahrenheit temperature and
    Celsius temperature.

    :key f_temp: Temperature in °F.
    :key c_temp: Temperature in °C.
    :returns: dictionary with two keys:
        :f_temp: Temperature in °F.
        :c_temp: Temperature in °C.
    """
```

The docstring doesn't support sophisticated, automated testing to confirm that the documentation actually matches the code. The two could disagree with each other.

The `mypy` tool performs the needed automated type-checking. For this to work, we need to add type hints about the type of data involved. How can we provide meaningful type hints for more complex data structures?

Getting ready

We'll implement a version of the `temperature()` function. We'll need two modules that will help us provide hints regarding the data types for parameters and return values:

```
from typing import Optional, Union, Dict
```

We've opted to import a few of the type names from the `typing` module. If we're going to supply type hints, we want them to be terse. It's awkward having to write `typing.List[str]`. We prefer to omit the module name by using this kind of explicit import.

How to do it...

Python 3.5 introduced type hints to the language. We can use them in three places: function parameters, function returns, and type hint comments:

1. Annotate parameters to functions, like this:

```
def temperature(*,
    f_temp: Optional[float]=None,
    c_temp: Optional[float]=None):
```

We've added `:` and a type hint as part of the parameter. The type `float` tells `mypy` any number is allowed here. We've wrapped this with the `Optional[]` type operation to state that the argument value can be either a number or `None`.

2. Annotate return values from functions, like this:

```
def temperature(*,
    f_temp: Optional[float]=None,
    c_temp: Optional[float]=None) -> Dict[str, float]:
```

   We've added `->` and a type hint for the return value of this function. In this case, we've stated that the result will be a dictionary object with keys that are strings, `str`, and values that are numbers, `float`.

   The `typing` module introduces the type hint names, such as `Dict`, that describes a data structure. This is different from the `dict` class, which actually builds objects. `typing.Dict` is merely a description of possible objects.

3. If necessary, we can add type hints as comments to assignment statements. These are sometimes required to clarify a long, complex series of statements. If we wanted to add them, the annotations could look like this:

```
result: Dict[str, float] = {"c_temp": c_temp, "f_temp": f_temp}
```

   We've added a `Dict[str, float]` type hint to the statement that builds the final dictionary object.

How it works...

The type information we've added are called **hints**. They're not requirements that are somehow checked by the Python compiler. They're not checked at runtime either.

These type hints are used by a separate program, `mypy`. See `http://mypy-lang.org` for more information.

The `mypy` program examines the Python code, including the type hints. It applies some formal reasoning and inference techniques to determine if the various type hints will always be true. For larger and more complex programs, the output from `mypy` will include warnings and errors that describe potential problems with either the code itself, or the type hints decorating the code.

For example, here's a mistake that's easy to make. We've assumed that our function returns a single number. Our `return` statement, however, doesn't match our expectation:

```
def temperature_bad(
        *, f_temp: Optional[float] = None, c_temp: Optional[float] =
None
    ) -> float:
```

```
if f_temp is not None:
    c_temp = 5 * (f_temp - 32) / 9
elif f_temp is not None:8888889
    f_temp = 32 + 9 * c_temp / 5
else:
    raise TypeError("One of f_temp or c_temp must be provided")
result = {"c_temp": c_temp, "f_temp": f_temp}

return result
```

When we run `mypy`, we'll see this:

```
Chapter_03/ch03_r07.py:45: error: Incompatible return value type (got
"Dict[str, float]", expected "float")
```

We can see that line 45, the `return` statement, doesn't match the function definition. The result was a `Dict[str, float]` object but the definition hint was a `float` object. Ideally, a unit test would also uncover a problem here.

Given this error, we need to either fix the return or the definition to be sure that the expected type and the actual type match. It's not clear which of the two type hints is *right*. Either of these could be the intent:

- Return a single value, consistent with the definition that has the `-> float` hint. This means the return statement needs to be fixed.
- Return the dictionary object, consistent with the `return` statement where a `Dict[str, float]` object was created. This means we need to correct the `def` statement to have the proper return type. Changing this may spread ripples of change to other functions that expect the `temperature()` function to return a `float` object.

The extra syntax for parameter types and return types has no real impact on performance, and only a very small cost when the source code is first compiled into byte code. They are—after all—merely hints.

The docstring is an important part of the code. The code describes data and processing, but can't clarify intent. The docstring comments can provide insight into what the values in the dictionary are and why they have specific key names.

There's more...

A dictionary with specific string keys is a common Python data structure. It's so common there's a type hint in the `mypy_extensions` library that's perfect for this situation. If you've installed `mypy`, then `mypy_extensions` should also be present.

The `TypedDict` class definition is a way to define a dictionary with specific string keys, and has an associated type hint for each of those keys:

```
from mypy_extensions import TypedDict

TempDict = TypedDict(
    "TempDict",
    {
        "c_temp": float,
        "f_temp": float,
    }
)
```

This defines a new type, `TempDict`, which is a kind of `Dict[str, Any]`, a dictionary mapping a string key to another value. This further narrows the definition by listing the expected string keys should be from the defined set of available keys. It also provides unique types for each individual string key. These constraints aren't checked at runtime as they're used by `mypy`.

We can make another small change to make use of this type:

```
def temperature_d(
        *,
        f_temp: Optional[float] = None,
        c_temp: Optional[float] = None
    ) -> TempDict:
    if f_temp is not None:
        c_temp = 5 * (f_temp - 32) / 9
    elif c_temp is not None:
        f_temp = 32 + 9 * c_temp / 5
    else:
        raise TypeError("One of f_temp or c_temp must be provided")
    result: TempDict = {"c_temp": c_temp, "f_temp": f_temp}

    return result
```

We've made two small changes to the `temperature()` function to create this `temperature_d()` variant. First, we've used the `TempDict` type to define the resulting type of data. Second, the assignment for the `result` variable has had the type hint added to assert that we're building an object conforming to the `TempDict` type.

See also

- See `https://www.python.org/dev/peps/pep-0484/` for more information on type hints.

- See `https://mypy.readthedocs.io/en/latest/index.html` for the current `mypy` project.

Picking an order for parameters based on partial functions

When we look at complex functions, we'll sometimes see a pattern in the ways we use the function. We might, for example, evaluate a function many times with some argument values that are fixed by context, and other argument values that are changing with the details of the processing.

It can simplify our programming if our design reflects this concern. We'd like to provide a way to make the common parameters slightly easier to work with than the uncommon parameters. We'd also like to avoid having to repeat the parameters that are part of a larger context.

Getting ready

We'll look at a version of the Haversine formula. This computes distances between two points, p_1 and p_2, on the surface of the Earth, $p_1 = (lon_1, lat_1)$ and $p_2 = (lon_2, lat_2)$:

$$a = \sqrt{\sin^2 \frac{lat_2 - lat_1}{2} + \cos(lat_1)\cos(lat_2)\sin^2 \frac{lat_2 - lat_1}{2}}$$

$$c = 2 \sin^{-1} a$$

The essential calculation yields the central angle, c, between two points. The angle is measured in radians. We convert it into distance by multiplying by the Earth's mean radius in some units. If we multiply the angle c by a radius of 3,959 miles, the distance, we'll convert the angle into miles.

Here's an implementation of this function. We've included type hints:

```
from math import radians, sin, cos, sqrt, asin

MI= 3959
NM= 3440
KM= 6372

def haversine(lat_1: float, lon_1: float,
    lat_2: float, lon_2: float, R: float) -> float:
    """Distance between points.
```

```
    R is Earth's radius.
    R=MI computes in miles. Default is nautical miles.

    >>> round(haversine(36.12, -86.67, 33.94, -118.40, R=6372.8), 5)
    2887.25995
    """
    Δ_lat = radians(lat_2) - radians(lat_1)
    Δ_lon = radians(lon_2) - radians(lon_1)
    lat_1 = radians(lat_1)
    lat_2 = radians(lat_2)

    a = sqrt(
        sin(Δ_lat / 2) ** 2 + cos(lat_1) * cos(lat_2) * sin(Δ_lon /
2) ** 2
    )

    return R * 2 * asin(a)
```

> Note on the doctest example: The example uses an Earth radius with an extra decimal point that's not used elsewhere. This example will match other examples online. The Earth isn't spherical. Around the equator, a more accurate radius is 6378.1370 km. Across the poles, the radius is 6356.7523 km. We're using common approximations in the constants, separate from the more precise value used in the unit test case.

The problem we often have is that the value for `R` rarely changes. In a practical application, we may be consistently working in kilometers or nautical miles. We'd like to have a consistent, default value like `R = NM` to get nautical miles throughout our application.

There are several common approaches to providing a consistent value for an argument. We'll look at al.l of them.

How to do it...

In some cases, an overall context will establish a single value for a parameter. The value will rarely change. There are several common approaches to providing a consistent value for an argument. These involve wrapping the function in another function. There are several approaches:

- Wrap the function in a new function.

- Create a partial function. This has two further refinements:
    - We can provide keyword parameters
    - We can provide positional parameters

We'll look at each of these in separate variations in this recipe.

Wrapping a function

We can provide contextual values by wrapping a general function in a context-specific wrapper function:

1. Make some parameters positional and some parameters keywords. We want the contextual features—the ones that rarely change—to be keywords. The parameters that change more frequently should be left as positional. We can follow the *Forcing keyword-only arguments with the * separator* recipe to do this. We might change the basic `haversine` function so that it looks like this:

    ```
    def haversine(lat_1: float, lon_1: float,
        lat_2: float, lon_2: float, *, R: float) -> float:
    ```

2. We can then write a wrapper function that will apply all of the positional arguments, unmodified. It will supply the additional keyword argument as part of the long-running context:

    ```
    def nm_haversine_1(*args):
        return haversine(*args, R=NM)
    ```

    We have the `*args` construct in the function declaration to accept all positional argument values in a single tuple, `args`. We also have `*args`, when evaluating the `haversine()` function, to expand the tuple into all of the positional argument values to this function.

The lack of type hints in the `nm_haversine_1()` function is not an oversight. Using the `*args` construct, to pass a sequence of argument values to a number of parameters, makes it difficult to be sure each of the parameter type hints are properly reflected in the `*args` tuple. This isn't ideal, even though it's simple and passes the unit tests.

Creating a partial function with keyword parameters

A partial function is a function that has some of the argument values supplied. When we evaluate a partial function, we're mixing the previously supplied parameters with additional parameters. One approach is to use keyword parameters, similar to wrapping a function:

1. We can follow the *Forcing keyword-only arguments with the * separator* recipe to do this. We might change the basic `haversine` function so that it looks like this:

    ```
    def haversine(lat_1: float, lon_1: float,
        lat_2: float, lon_2: float, *, R: float) -> float:
    ```

2. Create a partial function using the keyword parameter:

```
from functools import partial
nm_haversine_3 = partial(haversine, R=NM)
```

The `partial()` function builds a new function from an existing function and a concrete set of argument values. The `nm_haversine_3()` function has a specific value for `R` provided when the partial was built.

We can use this like we'd use any other function:

```
>>> round(nm_haversine_3(36.12, -86.67, 33.94, -118.40), 2)
1558.53
```

We get an answer in nautical miles, allowing us to do boating-related calculations without having to patiently check that each time we used the `haversine()` function, it had `R=NM` as an argument.

Creating a partial function with positional parameters

A partial function is a function that has some of the argument values supplied. When we evaluate a partial function, we're supplying additional parameters. An alternative approach is to use positional parameters.

If we try to use `partial()` with positional arguments, we're constrained to providing the leftmost parameter values in the partial definition. This leads us to think of the first few arguments to a function as candidates for being hidden by a partial function or a wrapper:

1. We might change the basic `haversine` function to put the radius parameter first. This makes it slightly easier to define a partial function. Here's how we'd change things:

```
def p_haversine(
    R: float,
    lat_1: float, lon_1: float, lat_2: float, lon_2: float
) -> float:
```

2. Create a partial function using the positional parameter:

```
from functools import partial
nm_haversine_4 = partial(p_haversine, NM)
```

   The `partial()` function builds a new function from an existing function and a concrete set of argument values. The `nm_haversine_4()` function has a specific value for the first parameter, `R`, that's provided when the partial was built.

We can use this like we'd use any other function:

```
>>> round(nm_haversine_4(36.12, -86.67, 33.94, -118.40), 2)
1558.53
```

We get an answer in nautical miles, allowing us to do boating-related calculations without having to patiently check that each time we used the `haversine()` function, it had `R=NM` as an argument.

How it works...

The partial function is—essentially—identical to the wrapper function. While it saves us a line of code, it has a more important purpose. We can build partials freely in the middle of other, more complex, pieces of a program. We don't need to use a `def` statement for this.

Note that creating partial functions leads to a few additional considerations when looking at the order for positional parameters:

- If we try to use `*args`, it must be defined last. This is a language requirement. It means that the parameters in front of this can be identified specifically; all the others become anonymous and can be passed - *en masse* - to the wrapped function. This anonymity means `mypy` can't confirm the parameters are being used correctly.
- The leftmost positional parameters are easiest to provide a value for when creating a partial function.
- The keyword-only parameters, after the `*` separator, are also a good choice.

These considerations can lead us to look at the leftmost argument as being more of a context: these are expected to change rarely and can be provided by partial function definitions.

There's more...

There's a third way to wrap a function—we can also build a `lambda` object. This will also work:

```
nm_haversine_L = lambda *args: haversine(*args, R=NM)
```

Notice that a `lambda` object is a function that's been stripped of its name and body. It's reduced to just two essentials:

- The parameter list, `*args`, in this example
- A single expression, which is the result, `haversine(*args, R=NM)`

A `lambda` cannot have any statements. If statements are needed in the body, we have to create a definition that includes a name and a body with multiple statements.

The lambda approach makes it difficult to create type hints. While it passes unit tests, it's difficult to work with. Creating type hints for lambdas is rather complex and looks like this:

```
NM_Hav = Callable[[float, float, float, float], float]

nm_haversine_5: NM_Hav = lambda lat_1, lon_1, lat_2, lon_2:
```

```
haversine(
    lat_1, lon_1, lat_2, lon_2, R=NM
)
```

First, we define a callable type named `NM_Hav`. This callable accepts four float values and returns a float value. We can then create a lambda object, `nm_haversine_5`, of the `NM_Hav` type. This lambda uses the underlying `haversine()` function, and provides argument values by position so that the types can be checked by `mypy`. This is rather complex, and a function definition might be simpler than assigning a lambda object to a variable.

See also

- We'll also look at extending this design further in the *Writing testable scripts with the script library switch* recipe.

Writing clear documentation strings with RST markup

How can we clearly document what a function does? Can we provide examples? Of course we can, and we really should. In the *Including descriptions and documentation* recipe in *Chapter 2, Statements and Syntax*, and in the *Better RST markup in docstrings* recipes, we looked at some essential documentation techniques. Those recipes introduced **ReStructuredText** (**RST**) for module docstrings.

We'll extend those techniques to write RST for function docstrings. When we use a tool such as Sphinx, the docstrings from our function will become elegant-looking documentation that describes what our function does.

Getting ready

In the *Forcing keyword-only arguments with the * separator* recipe, we looked at a function that had a large number of parameters and another function that had only two parameters.

Here's a slightly different version of one of those functions, `Twc()`:

```
>>> def Twc(T, V):
...     """Wind Chill Temperature."""
...     if V < 4.8 or T > 10.0:
...         raise ValueError("V must be over 4.8 kph, T must be below 10°C")
...     return 13.12 + 0.6215*T - 11.37*V**0.16 + 0.3965*T*V**0.16
```

We need to annotate this function with some more complete documentation.

Ideally, we've got Sphinx installed to see the fruits of our labor. See `http://www.sphinx-doc.org`.

How to do it...

We'll generally write the following things (in this order) for a function description:

- Synopsis
- Description
- Parameters
- Returns
- Exceptions
- Test cases
- Anything else that seems meaningful

Here's how we'll create nice documentation for a function. We can apply a similar method to a function, or even a module:

1. Write the synopsis. A proper subject isn't required—we don't write *This function computes...*; we start with *Computes....* There's no reason to overstate the context:

   ```
   def Twc(T, V):
       """Computes the wind chill temperature."""
   ```

2. Write the description and provide details:

   ```
   def Twc(T, V):
       """Computes the wind chill temperature

       The wind-chill, :math:'T_{wc}', is based on
       air temperature, T, and wind speed, V.
       """
   ```

   In this case, we used a little block of typeset math in our description. The `:math:` interpreted text role uses LaTeX math typesetting. Sphinx can use MathJax or JSMath to do JavaScript math typesetting.

3. Describe the parameters: For positional parameters, it's common to use `:param name: description`. Sphinx will tolerate a number of variations, but this is common. For parameters that must be keywords, it's common to use `:key name: description`.

The word `key` instead of `param` shows that it's a keyword-only parameter:

```
def Twc(T: float, V: float):
    """Computes the wind chill temperature

    The wind-chill, :math:'T_{wc}', is based on
    air temperature, T, and wind speed, V.

    :param T: Temperature in °C
    :param V: Wind Speed in kph
    """
```

There are two ways to include type information:

- Using Python 3 type hints
- Using RST `:type name:` markup

We generally don't use both techniques. Type hints seem to be a better idea than the RST `:type:` markup.

4. Describe the return value using `:returns:`:

```
def Twc(T: float, V: float) -> float:
    """Computes the wind chill temperature

    The wind-chill, :math:'T_{wc}', is based on
    air temperature, T, and wind speed, V.

    :param T: Temperature in °C
    :param V: Wind Speed in kph
    :returns: Wind-Chill temperature in °C
    """
```

There are two ways to include return type information:

- Using Python 3 type hints
- Using RST `:rtype:` markup

We generally don't use both techniques. The RST `:rtype:` markup has been superseded by type hints.

5. Identify the important exceptions that might be raised. Use the `:raises exception:` reason markup. There are several possible variations, but `:raises exception:` seems to be the most popular:

```
def Twc(T: float, V: float) -> float:
```

```
    """Computes the wind chill temperature

    The wind-chill, :math:'T_{wc}', is based on
    air temperature, T, and wind speed, V.

    :param T: Temperature in °C
    :param V: Wind Speed in kph
    :returns: Wind-Chill temperature in °C
    :raises ValueError: for wind speeds under 4.8 kph or T
above 10°C
    """
```

6. Include a doctest test case, if possible:

```
def Twc(T: float, V: float) -> float:
    """Computes the wind chill temperature

    The wind-chill, :math:'T_{wc}', is based on
    air temperature, T, and wind speed, V.

    :param T: Temperature in °C
    :param V: Wind Speed in kph
    :returns: Wind-Chill temperature in °C
    :raises ValueError: for wind speeds under 4.8 kph or T
above 10°C

    >>> round(Twc(-10, 25), 1)
    -18.8

    """
```

7. Write any additional notes and helpful information. We could add the following to the docstring:

```
See https://en.wikipedia.org/wiki/Wind_chill

..  math::

    T_{wc}(T_a, V) = 13.12 + 0.6215 T_a - 11.37 V^{0.16} +
0.3965
    T_a V^{0.16}
```

We've included a reference to a Wikipedia page that summarizes wind-chill calculations and has links to more detailed information. For more information, see `https://web.archive.org/web/20130627223738/http://climate.weatheroffice.gc.ca/prods_servs/normals_documentation_e.html`.

We've also included a `math::` directive with the LaTeX formula that's used in the function. This will often typeset nicely, providing a very readable version of the code. Note that the LaTeX formula is indented four spaces inside the `.. math::` directive.

How it works...

For more information on docstrings, see the *Including descriptions and documentation* recipe in *Chapter 2, Statements and Syntax*. While Sphinx is popular, it isn't the only tool that can create documentation from the docstring comments. The pydoc utility that's part of the Python Standard Library can also produce good-looking documentation from the docstring comments.

The `Sphinx` tool relies on the core features of RST processing in the `docutils` package. See `https://pypi.python.org/pypi/docutils` for more information.

The RST rules are relatively simple. Most of the additional features in this recipe leverage the *interpreted text roles* of RST. Each of our `:param T:`, `:returns:`, and `:raises ValueError:` constructs is a text role. The RST processor can use this information to decide on style and structure for the content. The style usually includes a distinctive font. The context might be an HTML **definition list** format.

There's more...

In many cases, we'll also need to include cross-references among functions and classes. For example, we might have a function that prepares a wind-chill table. This function might have documentation that includes a reference to the `Twc()` function.

Sphinx will generate these cross-references using a special `:func:` text role:

```
def wind_chill_table():
    """Uses :func:'Twc' to produce a wind-chill
    table for temperatures from -30°C to 10°C and
    wind speeds from 5kph to 50kph.
    """
```

We've used `:func:'Twc'` to cross-reference one function in the RST documentation for a different function. Sphinx will turn these into proper hyperlinks.

See also

- See the *Including descriptions and documentation and Writing better RST markup in docstrings* recipes in *Chapter 2, Statements and Syntax*, for other recipes that show how RST works.

Designing recursive functions around Python's stack limits

Some functions can be defined clearly and succinctly using a recursive formula. There are two common examples of this.

The factorial function has the following recursive definition:

$$n! = \begin{cases} 1 & \text{if } n = 0 \\ n \times (n-1)! & \text{if } n > 0 \end{cases}$$

The recursive rule for computing a Fibonacci number, F_n, has the following definition:

$$F_n = \begin{cases} 1 & \text{if } n = 0 \vee n = 1 \\ F_{n-1} + F_{n-2} & \text{if } n > 0 \end{cases}$$

Each of these involves a case that has a simple defined value and a case that involves computing the function's value, based on other values of the same function.

The problem we have is that Python imposes a limitation on the upper limit for these kinds of recursive function definitions. While Python's integers can easily represent *1000!*, the stack limit prevents us from doing this casually.

Computing F_n Fibonacci numbers involves an additional problem. If we're not careful, we'll compute a lot of values more than once:

$$F_5 = F_4 + F_3$$

$$F_5 = (F_3 + F_2) + (F_2 + F_1)$$

And so on.

To compute F_5, we'll compute F_3 twice, and F_2 three times. This can become extremely costly as computing one Fibonacci number involves also computing a cascading torrent of other numbers.

Pragmatically, the filesystem is an example of a recursive data structure. Each directory contains subdirectories. The essential design for a simple numeric recursion also applies to the analysis of the directory tree. Similarly, a document serialized in JSON notation is a recursive collection of objects; often, a dictionary of dictionaries. Understanding such simple cases for recursion make it easier to work with more complex recursive data structures.

In all of these cases, we're seeking to eliminate the recursion and replace it with iteration. In addition to recursion elimination, we'd like to preserve as much of the original mathematical clarity as we can.

Getting ready

Many recursive function definitions follow the pattern set by the factorial function. This is sometimes called **tail recursion** because the recursive case can be written at the tail of the function body:

```
def fact(n: int) -> int:
    if n == 0:
        return 1
    return n*fact(n-1)
```

The last expression in the function refers to the function with a different argument value.

We can restate this, avoiding the recursion limits in Python.

How to do it...

A tail recursion can also be described as a **reduction**. We're going to start with a collection of values, and then reduce them to a single value:

1. Expand the rule to show all of the details: $n! = nx(n-1) \times (n-2) \times (n-3) \ldots \times 1$. This helps ensure we understand the recursive rule.
2. Write a loop or generator to create all the values: $N = \{n, n-1, n-2, \ldots, 1\}$. In Python, this can be as simple as `range(1, n+1)`. In some cases, though, we might have to apply some transformation function to the base values: $N = \{f(i): 1 \leq i < n+1\}$. Applying a transformation often looks like this in Python:

   ```
   N = (f(i) for i in range(1, n+1))
   ```

3. Incorporate the reduction function. In this case, we're computing a large product, using multiplication. We can summarize this using $\prod x$ notation. For this example, we're computing a product of values in a range:

$$\prod_{1 \le x < n+1} x$$

Here's the implementation in Python:

```
def prod(int_iter: Iterable[int]) -> int:
    p = 1
    for x in int_iter:
        p *= x
    return p
```

We can refactor the `fact()` function to use the `prod()` function like this:

```
def fact(n: int):
    return prod(range(1, n+1))
```

This works nicely. We've optimized a recursive solution to combine the `prod()` and `fact()` functions into an iterative function. This revision avoids the potential stack overflow problems the recursive version suffers from.

Note that the Python 3 `range` object is lazy: it doesn't create a big `list` object. The `range` object returns values as they are requested by the `prod()` function. This makes the overall computation relatively efficient.

How it works...

A tail recursion definition is handy because it's short and easy to remember. Mathematicians like this because it can help clarify what a function means.

Many static, compiled languages are optimized in a manner similar to the technique we've shown here. There are two parts to this optimization:

- Use relatively simple algebraic rules to reorder the statements so that the recursive clause is actually last. The `if` clauses can be reorganized into a different physical order so that `return fact(n-1) * n` is last. This rearrangement is necessary for code organized like this:

  ```
  def ugly_fact(n: int) -> int:
      if n > 0:
          return fact(n-1) * n
      elif n == 0:
          return 1
  ```

```
    else:
        raise ValueError(f"Unexpected {n=}")
```

- Inject a special instruction into the virtual machine's byte code—or the actual machine code—that re-evaluates the function without creating a new stack frame. Python doesn't have this feature. In effect, this special instruction transforms the recursion into a kind of `while` statement:

```
p = n
while n != 1:
    n = n-1
    p *= n
```

This purely mechanical transformation leads to rather ugly code. In Python, it may also be remarkably slow. In other languages, the presence of the special byte code instruction will lead to code that runs quickly.

We prefer not to do this kind of mechanical optimization. First, it leads to ugly code. More importantly - in Python - it tends to create code that's actually slower than the alternative we developed here.

There's more...

The Fibonacci problem involves two recursions. If we write it naively as a recursion, it might look like this:

```
def fibo(n: int) -> int:
    if n <= 1:
        return 1
    else:
        return fibo(n-1)+fibo(n-2)
```

It's difficult to do a simple mechanical transformation to turn something into a tail recursion. A problem with multiple recursions like this requires some more careful design.

We have two ways to reduce the computation complexity of this:

- Use memoization
- Restate the problem

The **memoization** technique is easy to apply in Python. We can use `functools.lru_cache()` as a decorator. This function will cache previously computed values. This means that we'll only compute a value once; every other time, `lru_cache` will return the previously computed value.

It looks like this:

```
from functools import lru_cache


@lru_cache(128)
def fibo_r(n: int) -> int:
if n < 2:
    return 1
else:
    return fibo_r(n - 1) + fibo_r(n - 2)
```

Adding a decorator is a simple way to optimize a more complex multi-way recursion.

Restating the problem means looking at it from a new perspective. In this case, we can think of computing all Fibonacci numbers up to, and including, F_n. We only want the last value in this sequence. We compute all the intermediates because it's more efficient to do it that way. Here's a generator function that does this:

```
def fibo_iter() -> Iterator[int]:
    a = 1
    b = 1
    yield a
    while True:
        yield b
        a, b = b, a + b
```

This function is an infinite iteration of Fibonacci numbers. It uses Python's `yield` so that it emits values in a lazy fashion. When a client function uses this iterator, the next number in the sequence is computed as each number is consumed.

Here's a function that consumes the values and also imposes an upper limit on the otherwise infinite iterator:

```
def fibo_i(n: int) -> int:
    for i, f_i in enumerate(fibo_iter()):
        if i == n:
            break
    return f_i
```

This function consumes each value from the `fibo_iter()` iterator. When the desired number has been reached, the `break` statement ends the `for` statement.

When we looked at the *Avoiding a potential problem with break statements* recipe in *Chapter 2, Statements and Syntax*, we noted that a `while` statement with a `break` may have multiple reasons for terminating. In this example, there is only one way to end the `for` statement.

We can always assert that `i == n` at the end of the loop. This simplifies the design of the function. We've also optimized the recursive solution and turned it into an iteration that avoids the potential for stack overflow.

See also

- See the *Avoiding a potential problem with break statements* recipe in *Chapter 2, Statements and Syntax*.

Writing testable scripts with the script-library switch

It's often very easy to create a Python script file. A script file is very easy to use because when we provide the file to Python, it runs immediately. In some cases, there are no function or class definitions; the script file is the sequence of Python statements.

These simple script files are very difficult to test. More importantly, they're also difficult to reuse. When we want to build larger and more sophisticated applications from a collection of script files, we're often forced to re-engineer a simple script into a function.

Getting ready

Let's say that we have a handy implementation of the haversine distance function called `haversine()`, and it's in a file named `ch03_r11.py`.

Initially, the file might look like this:

```
import csv
from pathlib import Path
from math import radians, sin, cos, sqrt, asin
from functools import partial

MI = 3959
NM = 3440
KM = 6373
```

```
def haversine(lat_1: float, lon_1: float,
    lat_2: float, lon_2: float, *, R: float) -> float:
... and more ...

nm_haversine = partial(haversine, R=NM)

source_path = Path("waypoints.csv")
with source_path.open() as source_file:
    reader = csv.DictReader(source_file)
        start = next(reader)
        for point in reader:
            d = nm_haversine(
                float(start['lat']), float(start['lon']),
                float(point['lat']), float(point['lon'])
            )
            print(start, point, d)
            start = point
```

We've omitted the body of the `haversine()` function, showing only `... and more...`, since it's exactly the same code we've already shown in the *Picking an order for parameters based on partial functions* recipe. We've focused on the context in which the function is in a Python script, which also opens a file, `wapypoints.csv`, and does some processing on that file.

How can we import this module without it printing a display of distances between waypoints in our `waypoints.csv` file?

How to do it...

Python scripts can be simple to write. Indeed, it's often too simple to create a working script. Here's how we transform a simple script into a reusable library:

1. Identify the statements that do the work of the script: we'll distinguish between *definition* and *action*. Statements such as `import`, `def`, and `class` are clearly definitional—they define objects but don't take a direct action to compute or produce the output. Almost all other statements take some action. The distinction is entirely one of intent.
2. In our example, we have some assignment statements that are more definition than action. These actions are like `def` statements; they only set variables that are used later. Here are the generally definitional statements:

```
MI = 3959
NM = 3440
```

```
KM = 6373

def haversine(lat_1: float, lon_1: float,
    lat_2: float, lon_2: float, *, R: float) -> float:
    ... and more ...

nm_haversine = partial(haversine, R=NM)
```

The rest of the statements clearly take an action toward producing the printed results.

So, the testability approach is as follows:

3. Wrap the actions into a function:

```
def distances():
    source_path = Path("waypoints.csv")
    with source_path.open() as source_file:
        reader = csv.DictReader(source_file)
        start = next(reader)
        for point in reader:
            d = nm_haversine(
                float(start['lat']), float(start['lon']),
                float(point['lat']), float(point['lon'])
            )
            print(start, point, d)
            start = point
```

4. Where possible, extract literals and turn them into parameters. This is often a simple movement of the literal to a parameter with a default value. From this:

```
def distances():
    source_path = Path("waypoints.csv")
```

To this:

```
def distances(source_path: Path = Path("waypoints.csv")) ->
None:
```

This makes the script reusable because the path is now a parameter instead of an assumption.

5. Include the following as the only high-level action statements in the script file:

```
if __name__ == "__main__":
    distances()
```

We've packaged the action of the script as a function. The top-level action script is now wrapped in an `if` statement so that it isn't executed during import.

How it works...

The most important rule for Python is that an `import` of a module is essentially the same as running the module as a script. The statements in the file are executed, in order, from top to bottom.

When we import a file, we're generally interested in executing the `def` and `class` statements. We might be interested in some assignment statements.

When Python runs a script, it sets a number of built-in special variables. One of these is `__name__`. This variable has two different values, depending on the context in which the file is being executed:

- The top-level script, executed from the command line: In this case, the value of the built-in special name of `__name__` is set to `__main__`.
- A file being executed because of an `import` statement: In this case, the value of `__name__` is the name of the module being created.

The standard name of `__main__` may seem a little odd at first. Why not use the filename in all cases? This special name is assigned because a Python script can be read from one of many sources. It can be a file. Python can also be read from the `stdin` pipeline, or it can be provided on the Python command line using the `-c` option.

When a file is being imported, however, the value of `__name__` is set to the name of the module. It will not be `__main__`. In our example, the value `__name__` during `import` processing will be `ch03_r08`.

There's more...

We can now build useful work around a reusable library. We might make several files that look like this:

File `trip_1.py`:

```
from ch03_r11 import distances
distances('trip_1.csv')
```

Or perhaps something even more complex:

File `all_trips.py`:

```
from ch03_r11 import distances
for trip in 'trip_1.csv', 'trip_2.csv':
    distances(trip)
```

The goal is to decompose a practical solution into two collections of features:

- The definition of classes and functions
- A very small action-oriented script that uses the definitions to do useful work

To get to this goal, we'll often start with a script that conflates both sets of features. This kind of script can be viewed as a **spike solution**. Our spike solution should evolve towards a more refined solution as soon as we're sure that it works. A *spike* or *piton* is a piece of removable mountain-climbing gear that doesn't get us any higher on the route, but it enables us to climb safely.

See also

- In *Chapter 7, Basics of Classes and Objects*, we'll look at class definitions. These are another kind of widely used definitional statement, in addition to function definitions.

4

Built-In Data Structures Part 1: Lists and Sets

Python has a rich collection of built-in data structures. These data structures are sometimes called "containers" or "collections" because they contain a collection of individual items. These structures cover a wide variety of common programming situations.

We'll look at an overview of the various collections that are built-in and what problems they solve. After the overview, we will look at the list and set collections in detail in this chapter, and then dictionaries in *Chapter 5, Built-In Data Structures Part 2: Dictionaries*.

The built-in tuple and string types have been treated separately. These are sequences, making them similar in many ways to the list collection. In *Chapter 1, Numbers, Strings, and Tuples*, we emphasized the way strings and tuples behave more like immutable numbers than like the mutable list collection.

The next chapter will look at dictionaries, as well as some more advanced topics also related to lists and sets. In particular, it will look at how Python handles references to mutable collection objects. This has consequences in the way functions need to be defined that accept lists or sets as parameters.

In this chapter, we'll look at the following recipes, all related to Python's built-in data structures:

- Choosing a data structure
- Building lists – literals, appending, and comprehensions
- Slicing and dicing a `list`
- Deleting from a `list` – deleting, removing, popping, and filtering

- Writing list-related type hints
- Reversing a copy of a `list`
- Building sets – literals, adding, comprehensions, and operators
- Removing items from a `set` – `remove()`, `pop()`, and difference
- Writing set-related type hints

Choosing a data structure

Python offers a number of built-in data structures to help us work with collections of data. It can be confusing to match the data structure features with the problem we're trying to solve.

How do we choose which structure to use? What are the features of lists, sets, and dictionaries? Why do we have tuples and frozen sets?

Getting ready

Before we put data into a collection, we'll need to consider how we'll gather the data, and what we'll do with the collection once we have it. The big question is always how we'll identify a particular item within the collection.

We'll look at a few key questions that we need to answer to decide which of the built-in structures is appropriate.

How to do it...

1. Is the programming focused on simple existence? Are items present or absent from a collection? An example of this is validating input values. When the user enters something that's in the collection, their input is valid; otherwise, their input is invalid. Simple membership tests suggest using a `set`:

```
def confirm() -> bool:
    yes = {"yes", "y"}
    no = {"no", "n"}
    while (answer := input("Confirm: ")).lower() not in
(yes|no):
        print("Please respond with yes or no")
    return answer in yes
```

A `set` holds items in no particular order. Once an item is a member, we can't add it again:

```
>>> yes = {"yes", "y"}
>>> no = {"no", "n"}
>>> valid_inputs = yes | no
>>> valid_inputs.add("y")
>>> valid_inputs
{'yes', 'no', 'n', 'y'}
```

We have created a `set`, `valid_inputs`, by performing a `set` union using the `|` operator among sets. We can't add another `y` to a `set` that already contains `y`. There is no exception raised if we try such an addition, but the contents of the set don't change.

Also, note that the order of the items in the `set` isn't exactly the order in which we initially provided them. A `set` can't maintain any particular order to the items; it can only determine if an item exists in the `set`. If order matters, then a `list` is more appropriate.

2. Are we going to identify items by their position in the collection? An example includes the lines in an input file—the line number is its position in the collection. When we must identify an item using an index or position, we must use a `list`:

```
>>> month_name_list = ["Jan", "Feb", "Mar", "Apr",
...     "May", "Jun", "Jul", "Aug",
...     "Sep", "Oct", "Nov", "Dec"]
>>> month_name_list[8]
'Sep'
>>> month_name_list.index("Feb")
```

We have created a list, `month_name_list`, with 12 string items in a specific order. We can pick an item by providing its position. We can also use the `index()` method to locate the index of an item in the list. List index values in Python always start with a position of zero. While a list has a simple membership test, the test can be slow for a very large list, and a set might be a better idea if many such tests will be needed.

If the number of items in the collection is fixed—for example, RGB colors have three values—this suggests a `tuple` instead of a `list`. If the number of items will grow and change, then the `list` collection is a better choice than the `tuple` collection.

3. Are we going to identify the items in a collection by a key value that's distinct from the item's position? An example might include a mapping between strings of characters—words—and integers that represent the frequencies of those words, or a mapping between a color name and the RGB tuple for that color. We'll look at mappings and dictionaries in the next chapter; the important distinction is mappings don't locate items by position the way lists do.

In contrast to a list, here's an example of a dictionary:

```
>>> scheme = {"Crimson": (220, 14, 60),
... "DarkCyan": (0, 139, 139),
... "Yellow": (255, 255, 00)}
>>> scheme['Crimson']
(220, 14, 60)
```

In this dictionary, `scheme`, we've created a mapping from color names to the RGB color tuples. When we use a key, for example `"Crimson"`, to get an item from the dictionary, we can retrieve the value bound to that key.

4. Consider the mutability of items in a `set` collection and the keys in a `dict` collection. Each item in a `set` must be an immutable object. Numbers, strings, and tuples are all immutable, and can be collected into sets. Since `list`, `dict`, are `set` objects and are mutable, they can't be used as items in a `set`. It's impossible to build a `set` of `list` objects, for example.

   Rather than create a `set` of `list` items, we must transform each `list` item into an immutable `tuple`. Similarly, dictionary keys must be immutable. We can use a number, a string, or a `tuple` as a dictionary key. We can't use a `list`, or a `set`, or any another mutable mapping as a dictionary key.

How it works...

Each of Python's built-in collections offers a specific set of unique features. The collections also offer a large number of overlapping features. The challenge for programmers new to Python is to identify the unique features of each collection.

The `collections.abc` module provides a kind of roadmap through the built-in container classes. This module defines the **Abstract Base Classes** (**ABC**s) underlying the concrete classes we use. We'll use the names from this set of definitions to guide us through the features.

From the ABCs, we can see that there are actually places for a total of six kinds of collections:

- **Set**: Its unique feature is that items are either members or not. This means duplicates are ignored:
  - **Mutable set**: The `set` collection
  - **Immutable set**: The `frozenset` collection
- **Sequence**: Its unique feature is that items are provided with an index position:
  - **Mutable sequence**: The `list` collection
  - **Immutable sequence**: The `tuple` collection

- **Mapping**: Its unique feature is that each item has a key that refers to a value:
  - **Mutable mapping**: The `dict` collection.
  - **Immutable mapping**: Interestingly, there's no built-in frozen mapping.

Python's libraries offer a large number of additional implementations of these core collection types. We can see many of these in the *Python Standard Library*.

The `collections` module contains a number of variations of the built-in collections. These include:

- `namedtuple`: A `tuple` that offers names for each item in a `tuple`. It's slightly clearer to use `rgb_color.red` than `rgb_color[0]`.
- `deque`: A double-ended queue. It's a mutable sequence with optimizations for pushing and popping from each end. We can do similar things with a `list`, but `deque` is more efficient when changes at both ends are needed.
- `defaultdict`: A `dict` that can provide a default value for a missing key.
- `Counter`: A `dict` that is designed to count occurrences of a key. This is sometimes called a multiset or a bag.
- `OrderedDict`: A `dict` that retains the order in which keys were created.
- `ChainMap`: A `dict` that combines several dictionaries into a single mapping.

There's still more in the *Python Standard Library*. We can also use the `heapq` module, which defines a priority queue implementation. The `bisect` module includes methods for searching a sorted list very quickly. This allows a list to have performance that is a little closer to the fast lookups of a dictionary.

There's more...

We can find lists of data structures in summary web pages, like this one: `https://en.wikipedia.org/wiki/List_of_data_structures`.

Different parts of the article provide slightly different summaries of data structures. We'll take a quick look at four additional classifications of data structures:

- **Arrays**: The Python `array` module supports densely packed arrays of values. The `numpy` module also offers very sophisticated array processing. See `https://numpy.org`. (Python has no built-in or standard library data structure related to linked lists).
- **Trees**: Generally, tree structures can be used to create sets, sequential lists, or key-value mappings. We can look at a tree as an implementation technique for building sets or dicts, rather than a data structure with unique features. (Python has no built-in or standard library data structure implemented via trees).

- **Hashes**: Python uses hashes to implement dictionaries and sets. This leads to good speed but potentially large memory consumption.
- **Graphs**: Python doesn't have a built-in graph data structure. However, we can easily represent a graph structure with a dictionary where each node has a list of adjacent nodes.

We can—with a little cleverness—implement almost any kind of data structure in Python. Either the built-in structures have the essential features, or we can locate a built-in structure that can be pressed into service. We'll look at mappings and dictionaries in the next chapter: they provide a number of important features for organizing collections of data.

See also

- For advanced graph manipulation, see `https://networkx.github.io`.

Building lists – literals, appending, and comprehensions

If we've decided to create a collection based on each item's position in the container—a `list`—we have several ways of building this structure. We'll look at a number of ways we can assemble a list object from the individual items.

In some cases, we'll need a list because it allows duplicate values. This is common in statistical work, where we will have duplicates but we don't require the index positions. A different structure, called a multiset, would be useful for a statistically oriented collection that permits duplicates. This kind of collection isn't built-in (although `collections.Counter` is an excellent multiset, as long as items are immutable), leading us to use a `list` object.

Getting ready

Let's say we need to do some statistical analyses of some file sizes. Here's a short script that will provide us with the sizes of some files:

```
>>> from pathlib import Path
>>> home = Path.cwd()
>>> for path in home.glob('data/*.csv'):
...     print(path.stat().st_size, path.name)
1810 wc1.csv
28 ex2_r12.csv
```

```
1790 wc.csv
215 sample.csv
45 craps.csv
28 output.csv
225 fuel.csv
166 waypoints.csv
412 summary_log.csv
156 fuel2.csv
```

We've used a `pathlib.Path` object to represent a directory in our filesystem. The `glob()` method expands all names that match a given pattern. In this case, we used a pattern of `'data/*.csv'` to locate all CSV-formatted data files. We can use the `for` statement to assign each item to the `path` variable. The `print()` function displays the size from the file's OS `stat` data and the name from the `Path` instance, `path`.

We'd like to accumulate a `list` object that has the various file sizes. From that, we can compute the total size and average size. We can look for files that seem too large or too small.

How to do it...

We have many ways to create `list` objects:

- **Literal**: We can create a literal display of a `list` using a sequence of values surrounded by `[]` characters. It looks like this: `[value, ... ]`. Python needs to match the `[` and `]` to see a complete logical line, so the literal can span physical lines. For more information, refer to the *Writing long lines of code* recipe in *Chapter 2, Statements and Syntax*.
- **Conversion Function**: We can convert some other data collection into a list using the `list()` function. We can convert a `set`, or the keys of a `dict`, or the values of a `dict`. We'll look at a more sophisticated example of this in the *Slicing and dicing a list* recipe.
- **Append Method**: We have `list` methods that allow us to build a `list` one item a time. These methods include `append()`, `extend()`, and `insert()`. We'll look at `append()` in the *Building a list with the append() method* section of this recipe. We'll look at the other methods in the *How to do it...* and *There's more...* sections of this recipe.
- **Comprehension**: A comprehension is a specialized generator expression that describes the items in a list using a sophisticated expression to define membership. We'll look at this in detail in the *Writing a list comprehension* section of this recipe.
- **Generator Expression**: We can use generator expressions to build `list` objects. This is a generalization of the idea of a list comprehension. We'll look at this in detail in the *Using the list function on a generator expression* section of this recipe.

The first two ways to create lists are single Python expressions. We won't provide recipes for these. The last three are more complex, and we'll show recipes for each of them.

Building a list with the append() method

1. Create an empty list using literal syntax, `[]`, or the `list()` function:

```
>>> file_sizes = []
```

2. Iterate through some source of data. Append the items to the list using the `append()` method:

```
>>> home = Path.cwd()
>>> for path in home.glob('data/*.csv'):
...     file_sizes.append(path.stat().st_size)
>>> print(file_sizes)
[1810, 28, 1790, 160, 215, 45, 28, 225, 166, 39, 412, 156]
>>> print(sum(file_sizes))
5074
```

We used the path's `glob()` method to find all files that match the given pattern. The `stat()` method of a path provides the OS **stat** data structure, which includes the size, `st_size`, in bytes.

When we print the `list`, Python displays it in literal notation. This is handy if we ever need to copy and paste the list into another script.

It's very important to note that the `append()` method does not return a value. The `append()` method mutates the `list` object, and does not return anything.

> Generally, almost all methods that mutate an object have no return value. Methods like `append()`, `extend()`, `sort()`, and `reverse()` have no return value. They adjust the structure of the list object itself. The notable exception is the `pop()` method, which mutates a collection and returns a value.
>
> It's surprisingly common to see wrong code like this:
>
> ```
> a = ['some', 'data']
> a = a.append('more data')
> ```
>
> This is emphatically wrong. This will set `a` to `None`. The correct approach is a statement like this, without any additional assignment:
>
> ```
> a.append('more data')
> ```

Writing a list comprehension

The goal of a `list` comprehension is to create an object that occupies a syntax role, similar to a list literal:

1. Write the wrapping `[]` brackets that surround the `list` object to be built.
2. Write the source of the data. This will include the target variable. Note that there's no `:` at the end because we're not writing a complete statement:

   ```
   for path in home.glob('data/*.csv')
   ```

3. Prefix this with the expression to evaluate for each value of the target variable. Again, since this is only a single expression, we cannot use complex statements here:

   ```
   [path.stat().st_size
      for path in home.glob('data/*.csv')]
   ```

In some cases, we'll need to add a filter. This is done with an `if` clause, included after the `for` clause. We can make the generator expression quite sophisticated.

Here's the entire `list` object construction:

```
>>> [path.stat().st_size
...     for path in home.glob('data/*.csv')]
[1810, 28, 1790, 160, 215, 45, 28, 225, 166, 39, 412, 156]
```

Now that we've created a `list` object, we can assign it to a variable and do other calculations and summaries on the data.

The list comprehension is built around a central generator expression, called a **comprehension** in the language manual. The generator expression at the heart of the comprehension has a data expression clause and a `for` clause. Since this generator is an expression, not a complete statement, there are some limitations on what it can do. The data expression clause is evaluated repeatedly, driven by the variables assigned in the `for` clause.

Using the list function on a generator expression

We'll create a `list` function that uses the generator expression:

1. Write the wrapping `list()` function that surrounds the generator expression.
2. We'll reuse *steps 2* and *3* from the list comprehension version to create a generator expression. Here's the generator expression:

   ```
   list(path.stat().st_size
      for path in home.glob('data/*.csv'))
   ```

Here's the entire `list` object:

```
>>> list(path.stat().st_size
...     for path in home.glob('data/*.csv'))
[1810, 28, 1790, 160, 215, 45, 28, 225, 166, 39, 412, 156]
```

Using the explicit `list()` function had an advantage when we consider the possibility of changing the data structure. We can easily replace `list()` with `set()`. In the case where we have a more advanced collection class, which is the subject of *Chapter 6, User Inputs and Outputs*, we may use one of our own customized collections here. List comprehension syntax, using `[]`, can be a tiny bit harder to change because `[]` are used for many things in Python.

How it works...

A Python `list` object has a dynamic size. The bounds of the array are adjusted when items are appended or inserted, or `list` is extended with another `list`. Similarly, the bounds shrink when items are popped or deleted. We can access any item very quickly, and the speed of access doesn't depend on the size of the `list`.

In rare cases, we might want to create a `list` with a given initial size, and then set the values of the items separately. We can do this with a list comprehension, like this:

```
sieve = [True for i in range(100)]
```

This will create a `list` with an initial size of 100 items, each of which is `True`. It's rare to need this, though, because lists can grow in size as needed. We might need this kind of initialization to implement the Sieve of Eratosthenes:

```
>>> sieve[0] = sieve[1] = False
>>> for p in range(100):
...     if sieve[p]:
...         for n in range(p*2, 100, p):
...             sieve[n] = False
>>> prime = [p for p in range(100) if sieve[p]]
```

The list comprehension syntax, using `[]`, and the `list()` function both consume items from a generator and append them to create a new `list` object.

There's more...

A common goal for creating a `list` object is to be able to summarize it. We can use a variety of Python functions for this. Here are some examples:

```
>>> sizes = list(path.stat().st_size
...     for path in home.glob('data/*.csv'))
```

```
>>> sum(sizes)
5074
>>> max(sizes)
1810
>>> min(sizes)
28
>>> from statistics import mean
>>> round(mean(sizes), 3)
422.833
```

We've used the built-in `sum()`, `min()`, and `max()` methods to produce some descriptive statistics of these document sizes. Which of these index files is the smallest? We want to know the position of the minimum in the list of values. We can use the `index()` method for this:

```
>>> sizes.index(min(sizes))
1
```

We found the minimum, and then used the `index()` method to locate the position of that minimal value.

Other ways to extend a list

We can extend a `list` object, as well as insert one into the middle or beginning of a `list`. We have two ways to extend a `list`: we can use the `+` operator or we can use the `extend()` method. Here's an example of creating two lists and putting them together with `+`:

```
>>> home = Path.cwd()
>>> ch3 = list(path.stat().st_size
...     for path in home.glob('Chapter_03/*.py'))
>>> ch4 = list(path.stat().st_size
...     for path in home.glob('Chapter_04/*.py'))
>>> len(ch3)
12
>>> len(ch4)
16
>>> final = ch3 + ch4
>>> len(final)
28
>>> sum(final)
61089
```

We have created a list of sizes of documents with names like `chapter_03/*.py`. We then created a second list of sizes of documents with a slightly different name pattern, `chapter_04/*.py`. We then combined the two lists into a final list.

We can do this using the `extend()` method as well. We'll reuse the two lists and build a new list from them:

```
>>> final_ex = []
>>> final_ex.extend(ch3)
>>> final_ex.extend(ch4)
>>> len(final_ex)
28
>>> sum(final_ex)
61089
```

Previously, we noted that the `append()` method does not return a value. Similarly, the `extend()` method does not return a value either. Like `append()`, the `extend()` method mutates the list object "in-place."

We can insert a value prior to any particular position in a list as well. The `insert()` method accepts the position of an item; the new value will be before the given position:

```
>>> p = [3, 5, 11, 13]
>>> p.insert(0, 2)
>>> p
[2, 3, 5, 11, 13]
>>> p.insert(3, 7)
>>> p
[2, 3, 5, 7, 11, 13]
```

We've inserted two new values into a `list` object. As with the `append()` and `extend()` methods, the `insert()` method does not return a value. It mutates the `list` object.

See also

- Refer to the *Slicing and dicing a list* recipe for ways to copy lists and pick sublists from a list.
- Refer to the *Deleting from a list – deleting, removing, popping, and filtering* recipe for other ways to remove items from a list.

- In the *Reversing a copy of a list* recipe, we'll look at reversing a list.
- This article provides some insights into how Python collections work internally: `https://wiki.python.org/moin/TimeComplexity`. When looking at the tables, it's important to note the expression **O**(`1`) means that the cost is essentially constant. The expression **O**(`n`) means the cost varies with the index of the item we're trying to process; the cost grows as the size of the collection grows.

Slicing and dicing a list

There are many times when we'll want to pick items from a `list`. One of the most common kinds of processing is to treat the first item of a `list` as a special case. This leads to a kind of *head-tail* processing where we treat the head of a list differently from the items in the tail of a list.

We can use these techniques to make a copy of a `list` too.

Getting ready

We have a spreadsheet that was used to record fuel consumption on a large sailboat. It has rows that look like this:

Date	**Engine on**	**Fuel height**
	Engine off	
	Other notes	
10/25/2013	08:24	29
	13:15	27
	Calm seas—Anchor in Solomon's Island	
10/26/2013	09:12	27
	18:25	22
	choppy—Anchor in Jackson's Creek	

Example of sailboat fuel use

In this dataset, fuel is measured by height. This is because a **sight-gauge** is used, calibrated in inches of depth. For all practical purposes, the tank is rectangular, so the depth shown can be converted into volume since we know 31 inches of depth is about 75 gallons.

This example of spreadsheet data is not properly normalized. Ideally, all rows follow the **first normal form** for data: a row should have identical content, and each cell should have only atomic values. In this data, there are three subtypes of row: one with starting measurements, one with ending measurements, and one with additional data.

The denormalized data has these two problems:

- It has four rows of headings. This is something the `csv` module can't deal with directly. We need to do some slicing to remove the rows from other notes.
- Each day's travel is spread across two rows. These rows must be combined to make it easier to compute an elapsed time and the number of inches of fuel used.

We can read the data with a function defined like this:

```
import csv
from pathlib import Path
from typing import List, Any

def get_fuel_use(path: Path) -> List[List[Any]]:
    with path.open() as source_file:
        reader = csv.reader(source_file)
        log_rows = list(reader)
    return log_rows
```

We've used the `csv` module to read the log details. `csv.reader()` is an iterable object. In order to collect the items into a single list, we applied the `list()` function. We looked at the first and last item in the list to confirm that we really have a list-of-lists structure.

Each row of the original CSV file is a list. Here's what the first and last rows look like:

```
>>> log_rows[0]
['date', 'engine on', 'fuel height']
>>> log_rows[-1]
['', "choppy -- anchor in jackson's creek", '']
```

For this recipe, we'll use an extension of a list index expression to slice items from the list of rows. The slice, like the index, follows the list object in `[]` characters. Python offers several variations of the slice expression so that we can extract useful subsets of the list of rows.

Let's go over how we can slice and dice the raw list of rows to pick out the rows we need.

How to do it...

1. The first thing we need to do is remove the four lines of heading from the list of rows. We'll use two partial slice expressions to divide the list by the fourth row:

```
>>> head, tail = log_rows[:4], log_rows[4:]
>>> head[0]
['date', 'engine on', 'fuel height']
>>> head[-1]
['', '', '']
>>> tail[0]
['10/25/13', '08:24:00 AM', '29']
>>> tail[-1]
['', "choppy -- anchor in jackson's creek", '']
```

   We've sliced the list into two sections using `log_rows[:4]` and `log_rows[4:]`. The first slice expression selects the four lines of headings; this is assigned to the `head` variable. We don't really want to do any processing with the head, so we ignore that variable. (Sometimes, the variable name _ is used for data that will be ignored.) The second slice expression selects rows from 4 to the end of the list. This is assigned to the `tail` variable. These are the rows of the sheet we care about.

2. We'll use slices with steps to pick the interesting rows. The `[start:stop:step]` version of a slice will pick rows in groups based on the step value. In our case, we'll take two slices. One slice starts on row zero and the other slice starts on row one.

   Here's a slice of every third row, starting with row zero:

```
>>> pprint(tail[0::3])
[['10/25/13', '08:24:00 AM', '29'], ['10/26/13', '09:12:00 AM',
'27']]
```

   We'll also want every third row, starting with row one:

```
>>> pprint(tail[1::3])
[['', '01:15:00 PM', '27'], ['', '06:25:00 PM', '22']]
```

3. These two slices can then be zipped together to create pairs:

```
>>> list(zip(tail[0::3], tail[1::3]))
[(['10/25/13', '08:24:00 AM', '29'], ['', '01:15:00 PM', '27']),
 (['10/26/13', '09:12:00 AM', '27'], ['', '06:25:00 PM', '22'])]
```

We've sliced the list into two parallel groups:

- The `[0::3]` slice starts with the first row and includes every third row. This will be rows zero, three, six, nine, and so on.
- The `[1::3]` slice starts with the second row and includes every third row. This will be rows one, four, seven, ten, and so on.

We've used the `zip()` function to interleave these two sequences from the `list`. This gives us a sequence of three tuples that's very close to something we can work with.

4. Flatten the results:

```
>>> paired_rows = list( zip(tail[0::3], tail[1::3]) )
>>> [a+b for a, b in paired_rows]
[['10/25/13', '08:24:00 AM', '29', '', '01:15:00 PM', '27'],
 ['10/26/13', '09:12:00 AM', '27', '', '06:25:00 PM', '22']]
```

We've used a list comprehension from the *Building lists – literals, appending, and comprehensions* recipe to combine the two elements in each pair of rows to create a single row. Now, we're in a position to convert the date and time into a single `datetime` value. We can then compute the difference in times to get the running time for the boat, and the difference in heights to estimate the fuel burned.

How it works...

The slice operator has several different forms:

- `[:]`: The start and stop are implied. The expression `S[:]` will create a copy of sequence `S`.
- `[:stop]`: This makes a new list from the beginning to just before the stop value.
- `[start:]`: This makes a new list from the given start to the end of the sequence.
- `[start:stop]`: This picks a sublist, starting from the start index and stopping just before the stop index. Python works with half-open intervals. The start is included, while the end is not included.

- `[::step]`: The start and stop are implied and include the entire sequence. The step—generally not equal to one—means we'll skip through the list from the start using the step. For a given step, s, and a list of size $|L|$, the index values are $i \in \left\{s \times n : 0 \leq n < \frac{|L|}{s}\right\}$.
- `[start::step]`: The start is given, but the stop is implied. The idea is that the start is an offset, and the step applies to that offset. For a given start, a, step, s, and a list of size $|L|$, the index values are $i \in \left\{a + s \times n : 0 \leq n < \frac{|L| - a}{s}\right\}$.
- `[:stop:step]`: This is used to prevent processing the last few items in a list. Since the step is given, processing begins with element zero.
- `[start:stop:step]`: This will pick elements from a subset of the sequence. Items prior to start and at or after stop will not be used.

The slicing technique works for lists, tuples, strings, and any other kind of sequence. Slicing does not cause the collection to be mutated; rather, slicing will make a copy of some part of the sequence. The items within the source collection are now shared between collections.

There's more...

In the *Reversing a copy of a list* recipe, we'll look at an even more sophisticated use of slice expressions.

The copy is called a **shallow copy** because we'll have two collections that contain references to the same underlying objects. We'll look at this in detail in the *Making shallow and deep copies of objects* recipe.

For this specific example, we have another way of restructuring multiple rows of data into single rows of data: we can use a generator function. We'll look at functional programming techniques online in *Chapter 9, Functional Programming Features* (link provided in the *Preface*).

See also

- Refer to the *Building lists – literals, appending, and comprehensions* recipe for ways to create lists.
- Refer to the *Deleting from a list – deleting, removing, popping, and filtering* recipe for other ways to remove items from a list.
- In the *Reversing a copy of a list* recipe, we'll look at reversing a list.

Deleting from a list – deleting, removing, popping, and filtering

There will be many times when we'll want to remove items from a `list` collection. We might delete items from a list, and then process the items that are left over.

Removing unneeded items has a similar effect to using `filter()` to create a copy that has only the needed items. The distinction is that a filtered copy will use more memory than deleting items from a list. We'll show both techniques for removing unwanted items from a list.

Getting ready

We have a spreadsheet that is used to record fuel consumption on a large sailboat. It has rows that look like this:

Date	**Engine on**	**Fuel height**
	Engine off	
	Other notes	
10/25/2013	08:24	29
	13:15	27
	Calm seas—Anchor in Solomon's Island	
10/26/2013	09:12	27
	18:25	22
	Choppy—Anchor in Jackson's Creek	

Example of sailboat fuel use

For more background on this data, refer to the *Slicing and dicing a list* recipe earlier in this chapter.

We can read the data with a function, like this:

```
import csv
from pathlib import Path
from typing import List, Any

def get_fuel_use(path: Path) -> List[List[Any]]:
    with path.open() as source_file:
```

```
        reader = csv.reader(source_file)
        log_rows = list(reader)
    return log_rows
```

We've used the `csv` module to read the log details. `csv.reader()` is an `iterable` object. In order to collect the items into a single list, we applied the `list()` function. We looked at the first and last item in the list to confirm that we really have a list-of-lists structure.

Each row of the original CSV file is a list. Each of those lists contains three items.

How to do it...

We'll look at several ways to remove things from a list:

- The `del` statement.
- The `remove()` method.
- The `pop()` method.
- Using the `filter()` function to create a copy that rejects selected rows.
- We can also replace items in a list using slice assignment.

The del statement

We can remove items from a list using the `del` statement. We can provide an object and a slice to remove a group of rows from the list object. Here's how the `del` statement looks:

```
>>> del log_rows[:4]
>>> log_rows[0]
['10/25/13', '08:24:00 AM', '29']
>>> log_rows[-1]
['', "choppy -- anchor in jackson's creek", '']
```

The `del` statement removed the first four rows, leaving behind the rows that we really need to process. We can then combine these and summarize them using the *Slicing and dicing a list* recipe.

The remove() method

We can remove items from a list using the `remove()` method. This removes matching items from a list.

We might have a list that looks like this:

```
>>> row = ['10/25/13', '08:24:00 AM', '29', '', '01:15:00 PM', '27']
```

We can remove the useless `''` item from the list:

```
>>> row.remove('')
>>> row
['10/25/13', '08:24:00 AM', '29', '01:15:00 PM', '27']
```

Note that the `remove()` method does not return a value. It mutates the list in place. This is an important distinction that applies to mutable objects.

> The `remove()` method does not return a value. It mutates the list object. It's surprisingly common to see wrong code like this:
>
> ```
> a = ['some', 'data']
> a = a.remove('data')
> ```
>
> This is emphatically wrong. This will set `a` to `None`.

The pop() method

We can remove items from a list using the `pop()` method. This removes items from a list based on their index.

We might have a list that looks like this:

```
>>> row = ['10/25/13', '08:24:00 AM', '29', '', '01:15:00 PM', '27']
```

This has a useless `''` string in it. We can find the index of the item to pop and then remove it. The code for this has been broken down into separate steps in the following example:

```
>>> target_position = row.index('')
>>> target_position
3
>>> row.pop(target_position)
''
>>> row
['10/25/13', '08:24:00 AM', '29', '01:15:00 PM', '27']
```

Note that the `pop()` method does two things:

- It mutates the `list` object.
- It also returns the value that was removed.

This combination of mutation and returning a value is rare, making this method distinctive.

Rejecting items with the filter() function

We can also remove items by building a copy that passes the desirable items and rejects the undesirable items. Here's how we can do this with the `filter()` function:

1. Identify the features of the items we wish to pass or reject. The `filter()` function expects a rule for passing data. The logical inverse of that function will reject data. In our case, the rows we want have a numeric value in column two. We can best detect this with a little helper function.
2. Write the filter `test` function. If it's trivial, use a `lambda` object. Otherwise, write a separate function:

   ```
   def number_column(row, column=2):
       try:
           float(row[column])
           return True
       except ValueError:
           return False
   ```

   We've used the built-in `float()` function to see if a given string is a proper number. If the `float()` function does not raise an exception, the data is a valid number, and we want to pass this row. If an exception is raised, the data was not numeric, and we'll reject the row.

3. Use the filter `test` function (or `lambda`) with the data in the `filter()` function:

   ```
   >>> tail_rows = list(filter(number_column, log_rows))
   >>> len(tail_rows)
   4
   >>> tail_rows[0]
   ['10/25/13', '08:24:00 AM', '29']
   >>> tail_rows[-1]
   ['', '06:25:00 PM', '22']
   ```

   We provided our test, `number_column()` and the original data, `log_rows`. The output from the `filter()` function is an iterable. To create a list from the iterable result, we'll use the `list()` function. The result contains just the four rows we want; the remaining rows were rejected.

This design doesn't mutate the original `log_rows` list object. Instead of deleting the rows, this creates a copy that omits those rows.

Slice assignment

We can replace items in a list by using a slice expression on the left-hand side of the assignment statement. This lets us replace items in a list. When the replacement is a different size, it lets us expand or contract a list. This leads to a technique for removing items from a list using slice assignment.

We'll start with a row that has an empty value in position `3`. This looks like this:

```
>>> row = ['10/25/13', '08:24:00 AM', '29', '', '01:15:00 PM', '27']
>>> target_position = row.index('')
>>> target_position
3
```

We can assign an empty list to the slice that starts at index position `3` and ends just before index position `4`. This will replace a one-item slice with a zero-item slice, removing the item from the list:

```
>>> row[3:4] = []
>>> row
['10/25/13', '08:24:00 AM', '29', '01:15:00 PM', '27']
```

The `del` statement and methods like `remove()` and `pop()` seem to clearly state the intent to eliminate an item from the collection. The slice assignment can be less clear because it doesn't have an obvious method name. It does work well, however, for removing a number of items that can be described by a slice expression.

How it works...

Because a list is a `mutable` object, we can remove items from the `list`. This technique doesn't work for `tuples` or `strings`. All three collections are sequences, but only the list is mutable.

We can only remove items with an index that's present in the list. If we attempt to remove an item with an index outside the allowed range, we'll get an `IndexError` exception.

For example, here, we're trying to delete an item with an index of three from a list where the index values are zero, one, and two:

```
>>> row = ['', '06:25:00 PM', '22']
>>> del row[3]
Traceback (most recent call last):
  File "/Users/slott/miniconda3/envs/cookbook/lib/python3.8/doctest.py", line 1328, in __run
    compileflags, 1), test.globs)
```

```
  File "<doctest examples.txt[80]>", line 1, in <module>
    del row[3]
IndexError: list assignment index out of range
```

There's more...

There are a few places in Python where deleting from a `list` object may become complicated. If we use a `list` object in a `for` statement, we can't delete items from the list. Doing so will lead to unexpected conflicts between the iteration control and the underlying object.

Let's say we want to remove all even items from a list. Here's an example that does not work properly:

```
>>> data_items = [1, 1, 2, 3, 5, 8, 10,
...     13, 21, 34, 36, 55]
>>> for f in data_items:
...     if f%2 == 0:
...         data_items.remove(f)
>>> data_items
[1, 1, 3, 5, 10, 13, 21, 36, 55]
```

The source list had several even values. The result is clearly not right; the values of `10` and `36` remain in the list. Why are some even-valued items left in the list?

Let's look at what happens when processing `data_items[5]`; it has a value of eight. When the `remove(8)` method is evaluated, the value will be removed, and all the subsequent values slide forward one position. `10` will be moved into position `5`, the position formerly occupied by `8`. The list's internal index will move forward to the next position, which will have `13` in it. `10` will never be processed.

Similarly, confusing things will also happen if we insert the driving iterable in a `for` loop into the middle of a list. In that case, items will be processed twice.

We have several ways to avoid the *skip-when-delete* problem:

- Make a copy of the `list`:

  ```
  >>> for f in data_items[:]:
  ```

- Use a `while` statement and maintain the index value explicitly:

  ```
  >>> position = 0
  >>> while position != len(data_items):
  ...     f = data_items[position]
  ```

```
...     if f%2 == 0:
...         data_items.remove(f)
...     else:
...         position += 1
```

We've designed a loop that only increments the `position` value if the value of `data_items[position]` is odd. If the value is even, then it's removed, which means the other items are moved forward one position in the `list`, and the value of the `position` variable is left unchanged.

- We can also traverse the `list` in reverse order. Because of the way negative index values work in Python, the `range()` object works well. We can use the expression `range(len(row)-1, -1, -1)` to traverse the `data_items` list in reverse order, deleting items from the end, where a change in position has no consequence on subsequent positions.

See also

- Refer to the *Building lists – literals, appending, and comprehensions* recipe for ways to create lists.
- Refer to the *Slicing and dicing a list* recipe for ways to copy lists and pick sublists from a list.
- In the *Reversing a copy of a list* recipe, we'll look at reversing a list.

Writing list-related type hints

The `typing` module provides a few essential type definitions for describing the contents of a `list` object. The primary type definition is `List`, which we can parameterize with the types of items in the list.

There are two common patterns to the types of items in lists in Python:

- **Homogenous**: Each item in the `list` has a common type or protocol. A common superclass is also a kind of homogeneity. A list of mixed integer and floating-point values can be described as a list of float values, because both `int` and `float` support the same numeric protocols.
- **Heterogenous**: The items in the `list` come from a union of a number of types with no commonality. This is less common, and requires more careful programming to support it. This will often involve the `Union` type definition from the `typing` module.

Getting ready

We'll look at a list that has two kinds of tuples. Some tuples are simple RGB colors. Other tuples are RGB colors that are the result of some computations. These are built from float values instead of integers. We might have a heterogenous list structure that looks like this:

```
scheme = [
    ('Brick_Red', (198, 45, 66)),
    ('color1', (198.00, 100.50, 45.00)),
    ('color2', (198.00, 45.00, 142.50)),
]
```

Each item in the list is a two-tuple with a color name, and a tuple of RGB values. The RGB values are represented as a three-tuple with either integer or float values. This is potentially difficult to describe with type hints.

We have two related functions that work with this data. The first creates a color code from RGB values. The hints for this aren't very complicated:

```
def hexify(r: float, g: float, b: float) -> str:
    return f'#{int(r)<<16 | int(g)<<8 | int(b):06X}'
```

An alternative is to treat each color as a separate pair of hex digits with an expression like `f"#{int(r):02X}{int(g):02X}{int(b):02X}"` in the `return` statement.

When we use this function to create a color string from an RGB number, it looks like this:

```
>>> hexify(198, 45, 66)
'#C62D42'
```

The other function, however, is potentially confusing. This function transforms a complex list of colors into another list with the color codes:

```
def source_to_hex(src):
    return [
        (n, hexify(*color)) for n, color in src
    ]
```

We need type hints to be sure this function properly transforms a list of colors from numeric form into string code form.

How to do it...

We'll start by adding type hints to describe the individual items of the input list, exemplified by the `scheme` variable, shown previously:

1. Define the resulting type first. It often helps to focus on the outcomes and work backward toward the source data required to produce the expected results. In this case, the result is a list of two-tuples with the color name and the hexadecimal code for the color. We could describe this as `List[Tuple[str, str]]`, but that hides some important details:

   ```
   ColorCode = Tuple[str, str]
   ColorCodeList = List[ColorCode]
   ```

   This list can be seen as being homogenous; each item will match the `ColorCode` type definition.

2. Define the source type. In this case, we have two slightly different kinds of color definitions. While they tend to overlap, they have different origins, and the processing history is sometimes helpful as part of a type hint:

   ```
   RGB_I = Tuple[int, int, int]
   RGB_F = Tuple[float, float, float]
   ColorRGB = Tuple[str, Union[RGB_I, RGB_F]]
   ColorRGBList = List[ColorRGB]
   ```

   We've defined the two integer-based RGB three-tuple as `RGB_I`, and the float-based RGB three-tuple as `RGB_F`. These two alternative types are combined into the `ColorRGB` tuple definition. This is a two-tuple; the second element may be an instance of either the `RGB_I` type or the `RGB_F` type. The presence of a `Union` type means that this list is effectively heterogenous.

3. Update the function to include the type hints. The input will be a list like the `schema` object, shown previously. The result will be a list that matches the `ColorCodeList` type description:

   ```
   def source_to_hex(src: ColorRGBList) -> ColorCodeList:
       return [
           (n, hexify(*color)) for n, color in src
       ]
   ```

How it works...

The `List[]` type hint requires a single value to describe all of the object types that can be part of this list. For homogenous lists, the type is stated directly. For heterogenous lists, a `Union` must be used to define the various kinds of types.

The approach we've taken breaks type hinting down into two layers:

- A "foundation" layer that describes the individual items in a collection. We've defined three types of primitive items: the `RGB_I` and `RGB_F` types, as well as the resulting `ColorCode` type.
- A number of "composition" layers that combine foundational types into descriptions of composite objects. In this case, `ColorRGB`, `ColorRGBList`, and `ColorCodeList` are all composite type definitions.

Once the types have been named, then the names are used with definition functions, classes, and methods.

It's important to define types in stages to avoid long, complex type hints that don't provide any useful insight into the objects being processed. It's good to avoid type descriptions like this:

```
List[Tuple[str, Union[Tuple[int, int, int], Tuple[float, float,
float]]]]
```

While this is technically correct, it's difficult to understand because of its complexity. It helps to decompose complex types into useful component descriptions.

There's more...

There are a number of ways of describing tuples, but only one way to describe lists:

- The various color types could be described with a `NamedTuple` class. Refer to the recipe in *Chapter 1, Numbers, Strings, and Tuples, Using named tuples to simplify item access in tuples* recipe, for examples of this.
- When all the items in a tuple are the same type, we can slightly simplify the type hint to look like this: `RGB_I = Tuple[int, ...]` and `RGB_F = Tuple[float, ...]`. This has the additional implication of an unknown number of values, which isn't true in this example. We have precisely three values in each RGB tuple, and it makes sense to retain this narrow, focused definition.
- As we've seen in this recipe, the `RGB_I = Tuple[int, int, int]` and `RGB_F = Tuple[float, float, float]` type definitions provide very narrow definitions of what the data structure should be at runtime.

See also

- In *Chapter 1, Numbers, Strings, and Tuples*, the *Using named tuples to simplify item access in tuples* recipe provides some alternative ways to clarify types hints for tuples.

- The *Writing set-related type hints* recipe covers this from the view of Set types.
- The *Writing dictionary-related type hints* recipe discusses types with respect to dictionaries and mappings.

Reversing a copy of a list

Once in a while, we need to reverse the order of the items in a `list` collection. Some algorithms, for example, produce results in a reverse order. We'll look at the way numbers converted into a specific base are often generated from least-significant to most-significant digit. We generally want to display the values with the most-significant digit first. This leads to a need to reverse the sequence of digits in a list.

We have three ways to reverse a list. First, there's the `reverse()` method. We can also use the `reversed()` function, as well as a slice that visits items in reverse order.

Getting ready

Let's say we're doing a conversion among number bases. We'll look at how a number is represented in a base, and how we can compute that representation from a number.

Any value, *v*, can be defined as a polynomial function of the various digits, d_n, in a given base, *b*:

$$v = d_n \times b^n + d_{n-1} \times b^{n-1} + d_{n-2} \times b^{n-2} + \ldots + d_1 \times b + d_0$$

A rational number has a finite number of digits. An irrational number would have an infinite series of digits.

For example, the number `0xBEEF` is a base 16 value. The digits are {`B = 11, E = 14, F = 15`}, while the base *b* = 16:

$$48879 = 11 \times 16^3 + 14 \times 16^2 + 14 \times 16 + 15$$

We can restate this in a form that's slightly more efficient to compute:

$$v = (((d_n \times b + d_{n-1}) \times b + d_{n-2}) \times b + \ldots + d_1) \times b + d_0$$

There are many cases where the base isn't a consistent power of some number. The ISO date format, for example, has a mixed base that involves 7 days per week, 24 hours per day, 60 minutes per hour, and 60 seconds per minute.

Given a week number, a day of the week, an hour, a minute, and a second, we can compute a timestamp of seconds, t_s, within the given year:

$$t_s = (((w \times 7 + d) \times 24 + h) \times 60 + m) \times 60 + s$$

For example:

```
>>> week = 13
>>> day = 2
>>> hour = 7
>>> minute = 53
>>> second = 19
>>> t_s = (((week*7+day)*24+hour)*60+minute)*60+second
>>> t_s
8063599
```

This shows how we convert from the given moment into a timestamp. How do we invert this calculation? How do we get the various fields from the overall timestamp?

We'll need to use `divmod` style division. For some background, refer to the *Choosing between true division and floor division* recipe.

The algorithm for converting a timestamp in seconds, t_s, into individual week, day, and time fields looks like this:

$$t_m, s \leftarrow t_s/60, t_s \bmod 60$$

$$t_h, m \leftarrow t_m/60, t_m \bmod 60$$

$$t_d, h \leftarrow t_h/60, t_h \bmod 24$$

$$w, d \leftarrow t_d/60, t_d \bmod 7$$

This has a handy pattern that leads to a very simple implementation. It has a consequence of producing the values in reverse order:

```
>>> t_s = 8063599
>>> fields = []
>>> for b in 60, 60, 24, 7:
...     t_s, f = divmod(t_s, b)
...     fields.append(f)
```

```
>>> fields.append(t_s)
>>> fields
[19, 53, 7, 2, 13]
```

We've applied the `divmod()` function four times to extract seconds, minutes, hours, days, and weeks from a timestamp, given in seconds. These are in the wrong order. How can we reverse them?

How to do it...

We have three approaches: we can use the `reverse()` method, we can use a `[::-1]` slice expression, or we can use the `reversed()` built-in function. Here's the `reverse()` method:

```
>>> fields_copy1 = fields.copy()
>>> fields_copy1.reverse()
>>> fields_copy1
[13, 2, 7, 53, 19]
```

We made a copy of the original list so that we could keep an unmutated copy to compare with the mutated copy. This makes it easier to follow the examples. We applied the `reverse()` method to reverse a copy of the list.

This will mutate the list. As with other mutating methods, it does not return a useful value. It's an error to use a statement like `a = b.reverse()`; the value of `a` will always be `None`.

Here's a slice expression with a negative step:

```
>>> fields_copy2 = fields[::-1]
>>> fields_copy2
[13, 2, 7, 53, 19]
```

In this example, we made a slice `[::-1]` that uses an implied start and stop, and the step was `-1`. This picks all the items in the list in reverse order to create a new list.

The original list is emphatically *not* mutated by this `slice` operation. This creates a copy. Check the value of the `fields` variable to see that it's unchanged.

Here's how we can use the `reversed()` function to create a reversed copy of a list of values:

```
>>> fields_copy3 = list(reversed(fields))
>>> fields_copy3
[13, 2, 7, 53, 19]
```

It's important to use the `list()` function in this example. The `reversed()` function is a generator, and we need to consume the items from the generator to create a new list.

How it works...

As we noted in the *Slicing and dicing a list* recipe, the slice notation is quite sophisticated. Using a slice with a negative step size will create a copy (or a subset) with items processed in right to left order, instead of the default left to right order.

It's important to distinguish between these three methods:

- The `reverse()` method modifies the `list` object itself. As with methods like `append()` and `remove()`, there is no return value from this method. Because it changes the list, it doesn't return a value.
- The `[::-1]` slice expression creates a new list. This is a shallow copy of the original list, with the order reversed.
- The `reversed()` function is a generator that yields the values in reverse order. When the values are consumed by the `list()` function, it creates a copy of the list.

See also

- Refer to the *Making shallow and deep copies of objects* recipe for more information on what a shallow copy is and why we might want to make a deep copy.
- Refer to the *Building lists - literals, appending, and comprehensions* recipe for ways to create lists.
- Refer to the *Slicing and dicing a list* recipe for ways to copy lists and pick sublists from a list.
- Refer to the *Deleting from a list - deleting, removing, popping, and filtering* recipe for other ways to remove items from a list.

Building sets - literals, adding, comprehensions, and operators

If we've decided to create a collection based on only an item being present—a `set` —we have several ways of building this structure. Because of the narrow focus of sets, there's no ordering to the items - no relative positions - and no concept of duplication. We'll look at a number of ways we can assemble a set collection from individual items.

In some cases, we'll need a set because it prevents duplicate values. It's common to summarize data by reducing a large collection to a set of distinct items. An interesting use of sets is for locating repeated items when examining a connected graph. We often think of the directories in the filesystem forming a tree from the root directory through a path of directories to a particular file. Because there are links in the filesystem, the path is not a simple directed tree, but can have cycles. It can be necessary to keep a set of directories that have been visited to avoid endlessly following a circle of file links.

The set operators parallel the operators defined by the mathematics of set theory. These can be helpful for doing bulk comparisons between sets. We'll look at these in addition to the methods of the `set` class.

Sets have an important constraint: they only contain immutable objects. Informally, immutable objects have no internal state that can be changed. Numbers are immutable, as are strings, and tuples of immutable objects. As we noted in the *Rewriting an immutable string* recipe in *Chapter 1, Numbers, Strings, and Tuples*, strings are complex objects, but we cannot update them; we can only create new ones. Formally, immutable objects have an internal hash value, and the `hash()` function will show this value.

Here's how this looks in practice:

```
>>> a = "string"
>>> hash(a)
4964286962312962439
>>> b = ["list", "of", "strings"]
>>> hash(b)
Traceback (most recent call last):
  File "<input>", line 1, in <module>
TypeError: unhashable type: 'list'
```

The value of the `a` variable is a string, which is immutable, and has a hash value. The `b` variable, on the other hand, is a mutable list, and doesn't have a hash value. We can create sets of immutable objects like strings, but the `TypeError: unhashable type` exception will be raised if we try to put mutable objects into a set.

Getting ready

Let's say we need to do some analysis of the dependencies among modules in a complex application. Here's one part of the available data:

```
import_details = [
 ('Chapter_12.ch12_r01', ['typing', 'pathlib']),
 ('Chapter_12.ch12_r02', ['typing', 'pathlib']),
```

```
    ('Chapter_12.ch12_r03', ['typing', 'pathlib']),
    ('Chapter_12.ch12_r04', ['typing', 'pathlib']),
    ('Chapter_12.ch12_r05', ['typing', 'pathlib']),
    ('Chapter_12.ch12_r06', ['typing', 'textwrap', 'pathlib']),
    ('Chapter_12.ch12_r07',
     ['typing', 'Chapter_12.ch12_r06', 'Chapter_12.ch12_r05',
   'concurrent']),
    ('Chapter_12.ch12_r08', ['typing', 'argparse', 'pathlib']),
    ('Chapter_12.ch12_r09', ['typing', 'pathlib']),
    ('Chapter_12.ch12_r10', ['typing', 'pathlib']),
    ('Chapter_12.ch12_r11', ['typing', 'pathlib']),
    ('Chapter_12.ch12_r12', ['typing', 'argparse'])
  ]
```

Each item in this list describes a module and the list of modules that it imports. There are a number of questions we can ask about this collection of relationships among modules. We'd like to compute the short list of dependencies, thereby removing duplication from this list.

We'd like to accumulate a `set` object that has the various imported modules. We'd also like to separate the overall collection into subsets with modules that have names matching a common pattern.

How to do it...

We have many ways to create `set` objects. There are important restrictions on what kinds of items can be collected into a set. Items in a `set` must be immutable.

Here are ways to build sets:

- **Literal**: We can create literal display of a `set` using a sequence of values surrounded by {} characters. It looks like this: `{value, ... }`. Python needs to match the { and } to see a complete logical line, so the literal can span physical lines. For more information, refer to the *Writing long lines of code* recipe in *Chapter 2, Statements and Syntax*. Note that we can't create an empty set with {}; this is an empty dictionary. We must use `set()` to create an empty set.
- **Conversion Function**: We can convert some other data collection into a `set` using the `set()` function. We can convert a `list`, or the keys of a `dict`, or a `tuple`. This will remove duplicates from the collection. It's also subject to the constraint that the items are all immutable objects like strings, numbers, or tuples of immutable objects.
- **Add Method**: The `set` method `add()` will add an item to a set. Additionally, sets can be created by a number of set operators for performing union, intersection, difference, and symmetrical difference.

- **Comprehension**: A comprehension is a specialized generator expression that describes the items in a set using a sophisticated expression to define membership. We'll look at this in detail in the *Writing a set comprehension* section of this recipe.
- **Generator Expression**: We can use generator expressions to build `set` objects. This is a generalization of the idea of a set comprehension. We'll look at this in detail in the *Using the set function on a generator expression* section of this recipe.

The first two ways to create sets are single Python expressions. We won't provide recipes for these. The last three are more complex, and we'll show recipes for each of them.

Building a set with the add method

Our collection of data is a list with sublists. We want to summarize the items inside each of the sublists:

1. Create an empty set into which items can be added. Unlike lists, there's no abbreviated syntax for an empty set, so we must use the `set()` function:

   ```
   >>> all_imports = set()
   ```

2. Write a for statement to iterate through each two-tuple in the `import_details` collection. This needs a nested for statement to iterate through each name in the list of imports in each pair. Use the `add()` method of the `all_imports` set to create a complete set with duplicates removed:

   ```
   >>> for item, import_list in import_details:
   ...     for name in import_list:
   ...         all_imports.add(name)
   >>> print(all_imports)
   {'Chapter_12.ch12_r06', 'Chapter_12.ch12_r05', 'textwrap',
   'concurrent', 'pathlib', 'argparse', 'typing'}
   ```

This result summarizes many lines of details, showing the set of distinct items imported. Note that the order here is arbitrary and can vary each time the example is executed.

Writing a set comprehension

The goal of a set comprehension is to create an object that occupies a syntax role, similar to a set literal:

1. Write the wrapping `{}` braces that surround the `set` object to be built.
2. Write the source of the data. This will include the target variable. We have two nested lists, so we'll two for clauses. Note that there's no `:` at the end because we're not writing a complete statement:

```
for item, import_list in import_details for name in import_
list
```

3. Prefix the `for` clauses with the expression to evaluate for each value of the target variable. In this case, we only want the name from the import list within each pair of items in the overall import details list-of-lists:

```
{name for item, import_list in import_details for name in
import_list}
```

A set comprehension cannot have duplicates, so this will always be a set of distinct values.

As with the list comprehension, a set comprehension is built around a central generator expression. The generator expression at the heart of the comprehension has a data expression clause and a `for` clause. As with list comprehensions, we can include `if` clauses to act as a filter.

Using the set function on a generator expression

We'll create a `set` function that uses the generator expression:

1. Write the wrapping `set()` function that surrounds the generator expression.
2. We'll reuse *steps 2* and *3* from the list comprehension version to create a generator expression. Here's the generator expression:

```
set(name
...     for item, import_list in import_details
...         for name in import_list
... )
```

Here's the entire `set` object:

```
>>> all_imports = set(name
...     for item, import_list in import_details
...         for name in import_list
... )
>>> all_imports
{'Chapter_12.ch12_r05', 'Chapter_12.ch12_r06', 'argparse',
'concurrent', 'pathlib', 'textwrap', 'typing'}
```

Using the explicit `list()` function had an advantage when we consider the possibility of changing the data structure. We can easily replace `set()` with `list()`.

How it works...

A `set` can be thought of as a collection of immutable objects. Each immutable Python object has a hash value, and this numeric code is used to optimize locating items in the set. We can imagine the implementation relies on an array of buckets, and the hash value directs us to a bucket to see if the item is present in that bucket or not.

Hash values are not necessarily unique. The array of hash buckets is finite, meaning collisions are possible. This leads to some overhead to handle these collisions and grow the array of buckets when collisions become too frequent.

The hash values of integers, interestingly, are the integer values. Because of this, we can create integers that will have a hash collision:

```
>>> v1 = 7
>>> v2 = 7+sys.hash_info.modulus
>>> v1
7
>>> v2
2305843009213693958
>>> hash(v1)
7
>>> hash(v2)
7
```

In spite of these two objects having the same hash value, hash collision processing keeps these two objects separate from each other in a set.

There's more...

We have several ways to add items to a `set`:

- The example used the `add()` method. This works with a single item.
- We can use the `union()` method. This is like an operator—it creates a new result `set`. It does not mutate either of the operand sets.
- We can use the | union operator to compute the union of two sets.
- We can use the `update()` method to update one set with items from another set. This mutates a set and does not return a value.

For most of these, we'll need to create a singleton `set` from the item we're going to add. Here's an example of adding a single item, `3`, to a set by turning it into a singleton `set`:

```
>>> collection = {1}
>>> collection
{1}
>>> item = 3
>>> collection.union({item})
{1, 3}
>>> collection
{1}
```

In the preceding example, we've created a singleton set, `{item}`, from the value of the `item` variable. We then used the `union()` method to compute a new set, which is the union of `collection` and `{item}`.

Note that `union()` returns a resulting object and leaves the original `collection` set untouched. We would need to use this as `collection = collection.union({item})` to update the `collection` object. This is yet another alternative that uses the union operator, `|`:

```
>>> collection = collection | {item}
>>> collection
{1, 3}
```

We can also use the `update()` method:

```
>>> collection.update({4})
>>> collection
{1, 3, 4}
```

Methods like `update()` and `add()` mutate the `set` object. Because they mutate the set, they do not return a value. This is similar to the way methods of the `list` collection work. Generally, a method that mutates the collection does not return a value. The only exception to this pattern is the `pop()` method, which both mutates the `set` object and returns the popped value.

Python has a number of `set` operators. These are ordinary operator symbols that we can use in complex expressions:

- `|` for set union, often typeset as $A \cup B$.
- `&` for set intersection, often typeset as $A \cap B$.
- `^` for set symmetric difference, often typeset as $A \Delta B$.
- `-` for set subtraction, often typeset as $A - B$.

See also

- In the *Removing items from a set – remove, pop, and difference* recipe, we'll look at how we can update a set by removing or replacing items.

Removing items from a set – remove(), pop(), and difference

Python gives us several ways to remove items from a `set` collection. We can use the `remove()` method to remove a specific item. We can use the `pop()` method to remove (and return) an arbitrary item.

Additionally, we can compute a new set using the set intersection, difference, and symmetric difference operators: `&`, `-`, and `^`. These will produce a new set that is a subset of a given input set.

Getting ready

Sometimes, we'll have log files that contain lines with complex and varied formats. Here's a small snippet from a long, complex log:

```
[2016-03-05T09:29:31-05:00] INFO: Processing ruby_block[print IP] action run (@recipe_files::/home/slott/ch4/deploy.rb line 9)
[2016-03-05T09:29:31-05:00] INFO: Installed IP: 111.222.111.222
[2016-03-05T09:29:31-05:00] INFO: ruby_block[print IP] called

 - execute the ruby block print IP
[2016-03-05T09:29:31-05:00] INFO: Chef Run complete in 23.233811181 seconds

Running handlers:
[2016-03-05T09:29:31-05:00] INFO: Running report handlers
Running handlers complete
[2016-03-05T09:29:31-05:00] INFO: Report handlers complete
Chef Client finished, 2/2 resources updated in 29.233811181 seconds
```

We need to find all of the IP: `111.222.111.222` lines in this log.

Here's how we can create a `set` of `matches`:

```
>>> import re
>>> pattern = re.compile(r"IP: \d+\.\d+\.\d+\.\d+")
>>> matches = set(pattern.findall(log))
>>> matches
{'IP: 111.222.111.222'}
```

The problem we have is extraneous matches. The log file has lines that look similar but are examples we need to ignore. In the full log, we'll also find lines containing text like `IP: 1.2.3.4`, which need to be ignored. It turns out that there is a set irrelevant of values that need to be ignored.

This is a place where set intersection and set subtraction can be very helpful.

How to do it...

1. Create a `set` of items we'd like to ignore:

   ```
   >>> to_be_ignored = {'IP: 0.0.0.0', 'IP: 1.2.3.4'}
   ```

2. Collect all entries from the log. We'll use the `re` module for this, as shown earlier. Assume we have data that includes good addresses, plus dummy and placeholder addresses from other parts of the log:

   ```
   >>> matches = {'IP: 111.222.111.222', 'IP: 1.2.3.4'}
   ```

3. Remove items from the `set` of matches using a form of set subtraction. Here are two examples:

   ```
   >>> matches - to_be_ignored
   {'IP: 111.222.111.222'}
   >>> matches.difference(to_be_ignored)
   {'IP: 111.222.111.222'}
   ```

Both of these are operators that return new sets as their results. Neither of these will mutate the underlying set objects.

It turns out the `difference()` method can work with any iterable collection, including lists and tuples. While permitted, mixing sets and lists can be confusing, and it can be challenging to write type hints for them.

We'll often use these in statements, like this:

```
>>> valid_matches = matches - to_be_ignored
>>> valid_matches
{'IP: 111.222.111.222'}
```

This will assign the resulting set to a new variable, `valid_matches`, so that we can do the required processing on this new set.

We can also use the `remove()` and `pop()` methods to remove specific items. The `remove()` method raises an exception when an item cannot be removed. We can use this behavior to both confirm that an item is in the set and remove it. In this example, we have an item in the `to_be_ignored` set that doesn't need to exist in the original `matches` object, so these methods aren't helpful.

How it works...

A `set` object tracks membership of items. An item is either in the `set` or not. We specify the item we want to remove. Removing an item doesn't depend on an index position or a key value.

Because we have `set` operators, we can remove any of the items in one `set` from a target `set`. We don't need to process the items individually.

There's more...

We have several other ways to remove items from a set:

- In this example, we used the `difference()` method and the `-` operator. The `difference()` method behaves like an operator and creates a new set.
- We can also use the `difference_update()` method. This will mutate a set in place. It does not return a value.
- We can remove an individual item with the `remove()` method.
- We can also remove an arbitrary item with the `pop()` method. This doesn't apply to this example very well because we can't control which item is popped.

Here's how the `difference_update()` method looks:

```
>>> valid_matches = matches.copy()
>>> valid_matches.difference_update(to_be_ignored)
>>> valid_matches
{'IP: 111.222.111.222'}
```

We applied the `difference_update()` method to remove the undesirable items from the `valid_matches` set. Since the `valid_matches` set was mutated, no value is returned. Also, since the set is a copy, this operation doesn't modify the original `matches` set.

We could do something like this to use the `remove()` method. Note that `remove()` will raise an exception if an item is not present in the set:

```
>>> valid_matches = matches.copy()
>>> for item in to_be_ignored:
...     if item in valid_matches:
...         valid_matches.remove(item)
>>> valid_matches
{'IP: 111.222.111.222'}
```

We tested to see if the item was in the `valid_matches` set before attempting to remove it. Using an `if` statement is one way to avoid raising a `KeyError` exception. An alternative is to use a `try:` statement to silence the exception that's raised when an item is not present:

```
>>> valid_matches = matches.copy()
>>> for item in to_be_ignored:
...     try:
...         valid_matches.remove(item)
...     except KeyError:
...         pass
>>> valid_matches
{'IP: 111.222.111.222'}
```

We can also use the `pop()` method to remove an arbitrary item. This method is unusual in that it both mutates the set and returns the item that was removed. For this application, it's nearly identical to `remove()`.

Writing set-related type hints

The `typing` module provides a few essential type definitions for describing the contents of a `set` object. The primary type definition is `set`, which we can parameterize with the types of items in the set. This parallels the *Writing list-related type hints* recipe.

There are two common patterns for the types of items in sets in Python:

- **Homogenous**: Each item in the set has a common type or protocol.
- **Heterogenous**: The items in the set come from a union of a number of types with no commonality.

Getting ready

A dice game like *Zonk* (also called *10,000* or *Greed*) requires a random collection of dice to be grouped into "hands." While rules vary, there a several patterns for hands, including:

- Three of a kind.
- A "small straight" of five ascending dice (1-2-3-4-5 or 2-3-4-5-6 are the two combinations).
- A "large straight" of six ascending dice.
- An "ace" hand. This has at least one 1 die that's not part of a three of a kind or straight.

More complex games, like Yatzy poker dice (or Yahtzee™) introduce a number of other patterns. These might include two pairs, four or five of a kind, and a full house. We'll limit ourselves to the simpler rules for Zonk.

We'll use the following definitions to create the hands of dice:

```
from enum import Enum
class Die(str, Enum):
    d_1 = "\u2680"
    d_2 = "\u2681"
    d_3 = "\u2682"
    d_4 = "\u2683"
    d_5 = "\u2684"
    d_6 = "\u2685"

def zonk(n: int = 6) -> Tuple[Die, ...]:
    faces = list(Die)
    return tuple(random.choice(faces) for _ in range(n))
```

The `Die` class definition enumerates the six faces of a standard die by providing the Unicode character with the appropriate value.

When we evaluate the `zonk()` function, it looks like this.

```
>>> zonk()
(<Die.d_6: '⚅'>, <Die.d_1: '⚀'>, <Die.d_1: '⚀'>, <Die.d_6: '⚅'>,
<Die.d_3: '⚂'>, <Die.d_2: '⚁'>)
```

This shows us a hand with two sixes, two ones, a two, and a three. When examining the hand for patterns, we will often create complex sets of objects.

How to do it...

In our analysis of the patterns of dice in a six-dice hand, creating a `Set[Die]` object from the six dice reveals a great deal of information:

- When there is one dice in the set of unique values, then all six dice have the same value.
- When there are five distinct dice in the set of unique values, then this could be a small straight. This requires an additional check to see if the set of unique values is 1-5 or 2-6, which are the two valid small straights.
- When there are six distinct items in the set of unique values, then this must be a large straight.
- For two unique dice in the set, there must be three of a kind. While there may also be four of a kind or five of a kind, these other combinations aren't scoring combinations.
- The three and four matching dice cases are ambiguous. For three distinct values, the patterns are *xxxyyz* and *xxyyzz*. For four distinct values, the patterns are *wwwxyz*, and *wwxxyz*.

We can distinguish many of the patterns by looking at the cardinality of the set of distinct dice. The remaining distinctions can be made by looking at the pattern of counts. We'll also create a set for the values created by a `collections.Counter` object. The underlying value is int, so this will be `Set[int]`:

1. Define the type for each item in the set. In this example, the class `Die` is the item class.
2. Create the `Set` object from the hand of `Die` instances. Here's how the evaluation function can begin:

    ```
    def eval_zonk_6(hand: Tuple[Die, ...]) -> str:
        assert len(hand) == 6, "Only works for 6-dice zonk."
        unique: Set[Die] = set(hand)
    ```

3. We'll need the two small straight definitions. We'll include this in the body of the function to show how they're used. Pragmatically, the value of `small_straights` should be global and computed only once:

    ```
    faces = list(Die)
    small_straights = [
        set(faces[:-1]), set(faces[1:])
    ]
    ```

4. Examine the simple cases. The number of distinct elements in the set identifies several kinds of hands directly:

```
if len(unique) == 6:
    return "large straight"
elif len(unique) == 5 and unique in small_straights:
    return "small straight"
elif len(unique) == 2:
    return "three of a kind"
elif len(unique) == 1:
    return "six of a kind!"
```

5. Examine the more complex cases. When there are three or four distinct values, the patterns can be summarized using the counts in a simple histogram. This will use a distinct type for the elements of the set. This is `Set[int]`, which will collect the counts instead of `Set[Die]` to create the unique `Die` values:

```
elif len(unique) in {3, 4}:
    frequencies: Set[int] = set(collections.Counter(hand).
values())
```

6. Compare the items in the frequency set to determine what kind of hand this is. For the cases of four distinct `Die` values, these can form one of two patterns: *wwwxyz* and *wwxxyz*. The first of these has a `frequencies` object with `Die` w occurring three times and the other `Die` values occurring once each. The second has no `Die` that occurred three times, showing it's non-scoring. Similarly, when there are three distinct values, they have three patterns, two of which have the required three of a kind. The third pattern is three pairs. Interesting, but non-scoring. If one of the `Die` has a frequency of three or four, that's a scoring combination. If nothing else matches and there's a one, that's a minimal score:

```
    if 3 in frequencies or 4 in frequencies:
        return "three of a kind"
    elif Die.d_1 in unique:
        return "ace"
```

7. Are there any conditions left over? Does this cover all possible cardinalities of dice and frequencies of dice? The remaining case is some collection of pairs and singletons without any "one" showing. This is a non-scoring *Zonk*:

```
return "Zonk!"
```

This shows two ways of using sets to evaluate the pattern of a collection of data items. The first set, `Set[Die]`, looked at the overall pattern of unique `Die` values. The second set, `Set[int]`, looked at the pattern of frequencies of die values.

Here's the whole function:

```
def eval_zonk_6(hand: Tuple[Die, ...]) -> str:
    assert len(hand) == 6, "Only works for 6-dice zonk."
    faces = list(Die)
    small_straights = [
        set(faces[:-1]), set(faces[1:])
    ]
    unique: Set[Die] = set(hand)

    if len(unique) == 6:
        return "large straight"
    elif len(unique) == 5 and unique in small_straights:
        return "small straight"
    elif len(unique) == 2:
        return "three of a kind"
    elif len(unique) == 1:
        return "six of a kind!"
    elif len(unique) in {3, 4}:
        # len(unique) == 4: wwwxyz (good) or wwxxyz (non-scoring)
        # len(unique) == 3: xxxxyz, xxxyyz (good) or xxyyzz (non-
scoring)
        frequencies: Set[int] = set(collections.Counter(hand).
values())
        if 3 in frequencies or 4 in frequencies:
            return "three of a kind"
        elif Die.d_1 in unique:
            return "ace"

    return "Zonk!"
```

This shows the two kinds of `set` objects. A simple set of dice is assigned to the variable `unique`. When the number of unique values is `3` or `4`, then a second `set` object is created, `frequencies`. If `3` is in the set of frequencies, then there was a three of a kind. If `4` was in the set of frequencies, then there was a four of a kind.

How it works...

The essential property of a set is membership. When we compute a set from a collection of `Die` instances, the `Set[Die]` object will only show the distinct values. We use `Set[Die]` to provide guidance to the `mypy` program that only instances of the `Die` class will be collected in the set.

Similarly, when we look at the distribution of frequencies, there are only a few distinct patterns, and they can be identified by transforming the frequencies into a set of distinct values. The presence of a `3` or a `4` value in the set of frequencies provides all of the information required to discern the kind of hand. The `3` (or `4`) value in the frequencies will always be the largest value, making it possible to use `max(collections.Counter(hand).values())` instead of `set(collections.Counter(hand).values())`. Changing from a collection to an individual item will require some additional changes. We leave those for you to figure out.

There's more...

Computing the score of the hand depends on which dice were part of the winning pattern. This means that the evaluation function needs to return a more complex result when the outcome is three of a kind. To determine the points, there are two cases we need to consider:

- The value of the dice that occurred three or more times.
- It's possible to roll two triples; this pattern must be distinguished too.

We have two separate conditions to identify the patterns of unique values indicating a three of a kind pattern. The function needs some refactoring to properly identify the values of the dice occurring three or more times. We'll leave this refactoring as an exercise for you.

See also

- Refer to the *Writing list-related type hints* recipe in this chapter for more about type hints for lists.
- The *Writing dictionary-related type hints* recipe covers type hints for dictionaries.

5

Built-In Data Structures Part 2: Dictionaries

Python has a rich collection of built-in data structures. These data structures are sometimes called "containers" or "collections" because they contain a collection of individual items. These structures cover a wide variety of common programming situations.

In this chapter, we'll build on some of the basics introduced in *Chapter 4, Built-In Data Structures Part 1: Lists and Sets*. This chapter covers the dictionary structure. This is a mapping from keys to values, sometimes called an associative array.

This chapter will also look at some more advanced topics related to how Python handles references to mutable collection objects. This has consequences in the way functions need to be defined.

In this chapter, we'll look at the following recipes, all related to Python's built-in data structures:

- Creating dictionaries – inserting and updating
- Removing items from dictionaries – the `pop()` method and the `del` statement
- Controlling the order of dictionary keys
- Writing dictionary-related type hints
- Understanding variables, references, and assignment
- Making shallow and deep copies of objects
- Avoiding mutable default values for function parameters

We'll start with how to create a dictionary.

Creating dictionaries – inserting and updating

A dictionary is one kind of Python mapping. The built-in type `dict` class provides a number of common features. There are some common variations on these features defined in the `collections` module.

As we noted in the *Choosing a data structure* recipe at the beginning of the previous chapter, we'll use a dictionary when we have a key that we need to map to a given value. For example, we might want to map a single word to a long, complex definition of the word, or perhaps some value to a count of the number of times that value has occurred in a dataset.

A dictionary with keys and integer counts is very common. We'll look at a detailed recipe that shows how to initialize the dictionary and update the counter.

Getting ready

We'll look at an algorithm for locating the various stages in transaction processing. This relies on assigning a unique ID to each request and including that ID with each log record written during the transaction starting with that request. Because a multi-threaded server may be handling a number of requests concurrently, the stages for each request's transaction will be interleaved unpredictably. Reorganizing the log by request ID helps segregate the various threads.

Here's a simulated sequence of log entries for three concurrent requests:

```
[2019/11/12:08:09:10,123] INFO #PJQXB^eRwnEGG?2%32U path="/openapi.yaml"
method=GET

[2019/11/12:08:09:10,234] INFO 9DiC!B^nXxnEGG?2%32U path="/items?limit=x"
method=GET

[2019/11/12:08:09:10,235] INFO 9DiC!B^nXxnEGG?2%32U error="invalid query"

[2019/11/12:08:09:10,345] INFO #PJQXB^eRwnEGG?2%32U status="200"
bytes="11234"

[2019/11/12:08:09:10,456] INFO 9DiC!B^nXxnEGG?2%32U status="404"
bytes="987"

[2019/11/12:08:09:10,567] INFO >UL>PB_R>&nEGG?2%32U path="/category/42"
method=GET
```

Each line has a timestamp. The severity level is `INFO` for each record shown in the example. The next string of 20 characters is a transaction ID. This is followed by log information for a particular step in the transaction.

The following regular expression defines the log records:

```
log_parser = re.compile(r"\[(.*?)\] (\w+) (\S+) (.*)")
```

This defines four fields. The timestamp is enclosed by `[]`. This is followed a word (`\w+`) and a sequence without any spaces (`\S+`). The balance of the line is the fourth group of characters.

Parsing these lines will produce a sequence of four-tuples. The data looks like this:

```
[('2019/11/12:08:09:10,123', 'INFO', '#PJQXB^eRwnEGG?2%32U', 'path="/
openapi.yaml" method=GET'),
 ('2019/11/12:08:09:10,234', 'INFO', '9DiC!B^nXxnEGG?2%32U', 'path="/
items?limit=x" method=GET'),
 ('2019/11/12:08:09:10,235', 'INFO', '9DiC!B^nXxnEGG?2%32U',
'error="invalid query"'),
 ('2019/11/12:08:09:10,345', 'INFO', '#PJQXB^eRwnEGG?2%32U',
'status="200" bytes="11234"'),
 ('2019/11/12:08:09:10,456', 'INFO', '9DiC!B^nXxnEGG?2%32U',
'status="404" bytes="987"'),
 ('2019/11/12:08:09:10,567', 'INFO', '>UL>PB_R>&nEGG?2%32U', 'path="/
category/42" method=GET')]
```

We need to know how often each unique path is requested. This means ignoring some log records and collecting data from the other records. A mapping from the path string to a count is an elegant way to gather this data. It's so elegant that the collections module provides some alternatives for handling this use case.

How to do it...

We have a number of ways to build dictionary objects:

- **Literal**: We can create a display of a dictionary by using a sequence of key/value pairs surrounded by `{}` characters. The `{}` characters overlap with the way set literals are created. The difference is the use of `:` between keys and values. Literals look like this: `{"num": 355, "den": 113}`.
- **Conversion function**: A sequence of two-tuples can be turned into a dictionary like this: `dict([('num', 355), ('den', 113)])`. Each two-tuple becomes a key/value pair. The keys must be immutable objects like strings, numbers, or tuples of immutable objects. We can also build dictionaries like this: `dict(num=355, den=113)`. Each of the parameter names becomes a key. This limits the dictionary keys to strings that are also valid Python variable names.
- **Insertion**: We can use the dictionary `[key] = value` syntax to set or replace a value in a dictionary. We'll look at this later in this recipe.
- **Comprehensions**: Similar to lists and sets, we can write a dictionary comprehension to build a dictionary from some source of data.

Building a dictionary by setting items

We build a dictionary by creating an empty dictionary and then setting items to it:

1. Create an empty dictionary to map paths to counts with `{}`. We can also use `dict()` to create an empty dictionary. Since we're going to create a histogram that counts the number of times a path is used, we'll call it `histogram`. The type hint is something we'll look at in the *Writing dictionary-related type hints* recipe later in this chapter:

   ```
   >>> histogram = {}
   ```

2. For each of the log lines, filter out the ones that do not have a value that starts with `path` in the item with an index of 3:

   ```
   >>> for line in log_lines:
   ...     path_method = line[3]  # group(4) of the original match
   ...     if path_method.startswith("path"):
   ```

3. If the path is not in the dictionary, we need to add it. Once the value of the `path_method` string is in the dictionary, we can increment the value in the dictionary, based on the key from the data:

   ```
   ...         if path_method not in histogram:
   ...             histogram[path_method] = 0
   ...         histogram[path_method] += 1
   ```

This technique adds each new `path_method` value to the dictionary. Once it has been established that the `path_method` key is in the dictionary, we can increment the value associated with the key.

Building a dictionary as a comprehension

The last field of each log line had one or two fields inside. There may have been a value like `path="/openapi.yaml" method=GET` with two attributes, `path` and `method`; or a value like `error="invalid query"` with only one attribute, `error`.

Use the following regular expression to decompose this final field:

```
param_parser = re.compile(r'(\w+)=(".*?"|\w+)')
```

This regular expression matches the word in from of the =, saving that as group one. The text after the = sign has one of two forms: it's either a quote and an arbitrary string of characters to the next quote, or it's a simple word of one or more characters without quotes. This will become group two.

The `findall()` method of this regular expression object can decompose the fields. Each matching group becomes a two-tuple with the name and the value separated by the =. We can then build a dictionary from the list of matched groups:

1. For each of the log lines, apply the regular expression to create a list of groups:

```
>>> for line in log_lines:
...     name_value_pairs = param_parser.findall(line[3])
```

2. Use a dictionary comprehension to use the name as the key and the value as the value of a dictionary:

```
...     params = {match[0]: match[1] for match in name_value_
pairs}
```

We can print the `params` values and we'll see the following dictionaries:

```
{'path': '"/openapi.yaml"', 'method': 'GET'}
{'path': '"/items?limit=x"', 'method': 'GET'}
{'error': '"invalid query"'}
{'status': '"200"', 'bytes': '"11234"'}
{'status': '"404"', 'bytes': '"987"'}
{'path': '"/category/42"', 'method': 'GET'}
```

Using a dictionary for the final fields of each log record makes it easy to separate the important pieces of information.

How it works...

The core feature of a dictionary is a mapping from an immutable key to a value object of any kind. In the first example, we've used an immutable string as the key, and an integer as the value. We describe it as `Dict[str, int]` in the type hint.

As we count, we replace each value associated with a given key. It's important to understand how the following statement works:

```
histogram[customer] += 1
```

The implementation is essentially this:

```
histogram[customer] = histogram[customer] + 1
```

The expression `histogram[customer] + 1` computes a new integer object from two other integer objects. This new object replaces the old value in the dictionary. This construct works elegantly because the dictionary as a whole is mutable.

It's essential that dictionary key objects be immutable. We cannot use a `list`, `set`, or `dict` as the key in a dictionary mapping. We can, however, transform a list into an immutable tuple, or make a `set` into a `frozenset` so that we can use one of these more complex objects as a key. In both examples, we had immutable strings as the keys to each dictionary.

There's more...

We don't have to use an `if` statement to add missing keys. We can use the `setdefault()` method of a dictionary instead. Our code to compute the path and method histogram would look like this:

```
>>> histogram = {}
>>> for line in log_lines:
...     path_method = line[3]  # group(4) of the match
...     if path_method.startswith("path"):
...         histogram.setdefault(path_method, 0)
...         histogram[path_method] += 1
```

If the key, `path_method`, doesn't exist, a default value of zero is provided. If the key does exist, the `setdefault()` method does nothing.

The `collections` module provides a number of alternative mappings that we can use instead of the default `dict` mapping:

- `defaultdict`: This collection saves us from having to write step two explicitly. We provide an initialization function as part of creating a `defaultdict` instance. We'll look at an example soon.
- `Counter`: This collection does the entire **key-and-count** algorithm as it is being created. We'll look at this soon too.

Here's the version using the `defaultdict` class:

```
>>> from collections import defaultdict
>>> histogram = defaultdict(int)
>>> for line in log_lines:
...     path_method = line[3]  # group(4) of the match
...     if path_method.startswith("path"):
...         histogram[path_method] += 1
```

We've created a `defaultdict` instance that will initialize any unknown key values using the `int()` function. We provide `int`—the function—to the `defaultdict` constructor. `Defaultdict` will evaluate the `int()` function to create default values.

This allows us to simply use `histogram[path_method] += 1`. If the value associated with the `path_method` key was previously in the dictionary, it will be incremented. If the `path_method` value was not in the dictionary, the `int` function is called with no argument; the return value, `0`, is used to create a new entry in the dictionary. Once the new default value is present, it can be incremented.

The other way we can accumulate frequency counts is by creating a `Counter` object. We need to import the `Counter` class so that we can build the `Counter` object from the raw data:

```
>>> from collections import Counter
>>> histogram = Counter(line[3]
...     for line in log_lines
...     if line[3].startswith("path")
... )
```

When we create a `Counter` from a source of data, the `Counter` class will scan the data and count the distinct occurrences.

See also

- In the *Removing from dictionaries – the pop() method and the del statement* recipe, we'll look at how dictionaries can be modified by removing items.
- In the *Controlling the order of dictionary keys* recipe, we'll look at how we can control the order of keys in a dictionary.

Removing from dictionaries – the pop() method and the del statement

A common use case for a dictionary is as an **associative store**: we can keep an association between key and value objects. This means that we may be doing any of the **CRUD** operations on an item in the dictionary:

- Create a new key and value pair
- Retrieve the value associated with a key
- Update the value associated with a key
- Delete the key (and the corresponding value) from the dictionary

We have two common variations on this theme:

- We have the in-memory dictionary, `dict`, and the variations on this theme in the `collections` module. The collection only exists while our program is running.
- We also have persistent storage in the `shelve` and `dbm` modules. The data collection is a persistent file in the filesystem, with a dict-like mapping interface.

These are similar, while the distinctions between a `shelf.Shelf` and `dict` object are minor. This allows us to experiment with a `dict` object and switch to a `Shelf` object without making dramatic changes to a program.

A server process will often have multiple concurrent sessions. When sessions are created, they can be placed into `dict` or `shelf`. When the session exits, the item can be deleted or perhaps archived.

We'll simulate this concept of a service that handles multiple requests. We'll define a service that works in a simulated environment with a single processing thread. We'll avoid concurrency and multi-processing considerations.

Getting ready

A great deal of processing supports the need to group items around one (or more) different common values. We might have web log records grouped by time, or by the resource requested. With more sophisticated websites, we might use cookies to group transactions around sessions defined by the value of a cookie.

We'll look at an algorithm for locating the various stages in transaction processing. This relies on assigning a unique ID to each request and including that ID with each log record written while handling a request. Because a multi-threaded server may be handling a number of sessions concurrently, the steps for each of a number of requests will be interleaved unpredictably. Reorganizing the log by request ID helps segregate the various threads.

Here's a simulated sequence of log entries for three concurrent requests:

```
[2019/11/12:08:09:10,123] INFO #PJQXB^eRwnEGG?2%32U path="/openapi.yaml"
method=GET

[2019/11/12:08:09:10,234] INFO 9DiC!B^nXxnEGG?2%32U path="/items?limit=x"
method=GET

[2019/11/12:08:09:10,235] INFO 9DiC!B^nXxnEGG?2%32U error="invalid query"

[2019/11/12:08:09:10,345] INFO #PJQXB^eRwnEGG?2%32U status="200"
bytes="11234"

[2019/11/12:08:09:10,456] INFO 9DiC!B^nXxnEGG?2%32U status="404"
bytes="987"

[2019/11/12:08:09:10,567] INFO >UL>PB_R>&nEGG?2%32U path="/category/42"
method=GET
```

Each line has a timestamp. The severity level is `INFO` for each record shown in the example. The next string of 20 characters is a transaction ID. This is followed by log information for a particular step in the transaction.

The following regular expression defines the log records:

```
log_parser = re.compile(r"\[(.*?)\] (\w+) (\S+) (.*)")
```

This defines four fields. The timestamp is enclosed by `[]`. This is followed a word (`\w+`) and a sequence without any spaces (`\S+`). The balance of the line is the fourth group of characters.

A transaction's end is marked with a `status=` in the fourth group of characters. This shows the final disposition of the web request.

We'll use an algorithm that uses the transaction ID as a key in a dictionary. The value is the sequence of steps for the transaction. With a very long log, we don't-generally-want to save every transaction in a gigantic dictionary. When we reach the termination, we can yield the list of log entries for a complete transaction.

How to do it...

The context will include `match := log_parser.match(line)` to apply the regular expression. Given that context, the processing to use each match to update or delete from a dictionary is as follows:

1. Define a `defaultdict` object to hold transaction steps. The keys are 20-character strings. The values are lists of log records. In this case, each log record will have been parsed from the source text into a tuple of individual strings:

   ```
   LogRec = Tuple[str, ...]
   requests: DefaultDict[str, List[LogRec]] = collections.
   defaultdict(list)
   ```

2. Define the key for each cluster of log entries:

   ```
   id = match.group(2)
   ```

3. Update a dictionary item with a log record:

   ```
   requests[id].append(match.groups())
   ```

4. If this log record completes a transaction, yield the group as part of a generator function. Then remove the transaction from the dictionary, since it's complete:

   ```
   if match.group(3).startswith('status'):
       yield requests[id]
       del requests[id]
   ```

Here's the essential algorithm wrapped up as a generator function:

```
def request_iter_t(source: Iterable[str]) -> Iterator[List[LogRec]]:
    requests: DefaultDict[str, List[LogRec]] = collections.
defaultdict(list)
    for line in source:
        if match := log_parser.match(line):
            id = match.group(2)
            requests[id].append(tuple(match.groups()))
            if match.group(3).startswith('status'):
                yield requests[id]
```

```
                del requests[id]
        if requests:
            print("Dangling", requests)
```

This shows how the individual lines are parsed by the regular expression, then organized into clusters around the `id` value in group number two.

How it works...

Because a dictionary is a mutable object, we can remove keys from a dictionary. This will delete both the key and the value object associated with the key. We do this when a transaction is complete. A moderately busy web server handling an average of ten transactions per second will see 864,000 transactions in a 24-hour period. If there are an average of 2.5 log entries per transaction, there will be at least 2,160,000 lines in the file.

If we only want to know the elapsed time per resource, we don't want to keep the entire dictionary of 864,000 transactions in memory. We'd rather transform the log into a clustered intermediate file for further analysis.

This idea of transient data leads us to accumulate the parsed log lines into a list instance. Each new line is appended to the appropriate list for the transaction in which the line belongs. When the final line has been found, the group of lines can be purged from the dictionary. In the example, we used the `del` statement, but the `remove()` or `pop()` method can also be used.

There's more...

The example relies on the way a regular expression `Match` object's `groups()` method produces a `Tuple[str, ...]` object. This isn't ideal because it leads to the opaque `group(3)` and `group(4)` references. It's not at all clear what these groups mean in the overall log record.

If we change the regular expression pattern, we can get a dictionary for each row. The match object's `groupdict()` method produces a dictionary. Here's the revised regular expression, with named groups:

```
log_parser_d = re.compile(
    r"\[(?P<time>.*?)\] "
    r"(?P<sev>\w+) "
    r"(?P<id>\S+) "
    r"(?P<msg>.*)"
)
```

This leads to a small but helpful variation on the preceding example, as shown in the following example:

```
LogRecD = Dict[str, str]

def request_iter_d(source: Iterable[str]) -> Iterator[List[LogRecD]]:
    requests: DefaultDict[str, List[LogRecD]] = collections.
defaultdict(list)
    for line in source:
        if match := log_parser_d.match(line):
            record = match.groupdict()
            id = record.pop('id')
            requests[id].append(record)
            if record['msg'].startswith('status'):
                yield requests[id]
                del requests[id]
    if requests:
        print("Dangling", requests)
```

This example has a slightly different type for the log records. In the example, each log record is a dictionary created by a `Match` object's `groupdict()` method.

The `id` field is popped from each record. There's no benefit in keeping this as a field in the dictionary as well as the key used to find the list of record dictionaries.

The result of running this is a sequence of `List[Dict[str, str]]` instances. It looks like the following example:

```
>>> for r in request_iter_d(log.splitlines()):
...     print(r)
[{'time': '2019/11/12:08:09:10,123', 'sev': 'INFO', 'msg': 'path="/
openapi.yaml" method=GET'}, {'time': '2019/11/12:08:09:10,345', 'sev':
'INFO', 'msg': 'status="200" bytes="11234"'}]
[{'time': '2019/11/12:08:09:10,234', 'sev': 'INFO', 'msg': 'path="/
items?limit=x" method=GET'}, {'time': '2019/11/12:08:09:10,235',
'sev': 'INFO', 'msg': 'error="invalid query"'}, {'time':
'2019/11/12:08:09:10,456', 'sev': 'INFO', 'msg': 'status="404"
bytes="987"'}]
Dangling defaultdict(<class 'list'>, {'>UL>PB_R>&nEGG?2%32U': [{'time':
'2019/11/12:08:09:10,567', 'sev': 'INFO', 'msg': 'path="/category/42"
method=GET'}]})
```

This shows the two complete transactions, assembled from multiple log records. It also shows the `Dangling` log record, where the completion of the transaction was not found in the log. This may represent a problem, but it's more likely to represent either a transaction in process when one log file was closed and the next log file opened, or it may represent a user that walked away from the browser and never finished the transaction.

See also

- In the *Creating dictionaries – inserting and updating* recipe, we look at how we create dictionaries and fill them with keys and values.
- In the *Controlling the order of dictionary keys* recipe, we look at how we can control the order of keys in a dictionary.

Controlling the order of dictionary keys

In the *Creating dictionaries – inserting and updating* recipe, we looked at the basics of creating a dictionary object. In many cases, we'll put items into a dictionary and fetch items from a dictionary individually. The idea of an order to the keys isn't central to using a dictionary.

Here are two common cases where key order may be important:

- **Entry order**: When working with documents in JSON or YAML notation, it can help to preserve the order of keys from the source documents.
- **Sorted order**: When summarizing data, it often helps to provide the keys in some easier-to-visualize order.

A Python dictionary's keys – since version 3.6 – are saved in the order in which they were initially inserted. This can be made explicit using the `collections.OrderedDict` class instead of the built-in `dict` class.

In the case when a dictionary contains a summary, we may want to sort the keys before displaying the contents of the dictionary. This is done with the `sorted()` function.

Getting ready

We'll look at the process of working with spreadsheet data. When we use a `csv.DictReader()` each row becomes a dictionary. It can be very helpful for people using the data to preserve the order of the original columns. Here's a simple table of data from a spreadsheet:

```
date,engine on,fuel height on,engine off,fuel height off
10/25/13,08:24:00,29,13:15:00,27
10/26/13,09:12:00,27,18:25:00,22
10/28/13,13:21:00,22,06:25:00,14
```

When displaying this data, it's helpful to keep the columns in the original order.

How to do it...

We have two common cases where we want to control the ordering of the keys of a dictionary:

- Keys in the order the items were inserted:
  - Use the built-in `dict` class to preserve the order in which keys are inserted.
  - Use `collections.OrderedDict` to explicitly state the keys are kept in the order they were inserted.
- Keys in some other order. The ordering can be imposed by using `sorted()` to iterate over the keys in the desired order. This can be done when making a copy of a dictionary, but it's more commonly done when emitting a final report or summary from dictionary data.

Here's how using the built-in `dict` class will preserve the order of the columns in the original `.csv` file:

```
import csv
from pathlib import Path
from typing import List, Dict

def get_fuel_use(source_path: Path) -> List[Dict[str, str]]:
    with source_path.open() as source_file:
        rdr= csv.DictReader(source_file)
        data: List[Dict[str, str]] = list(rdr)
    return data
```

Each row in the list collection that's created is a dictionary. The order of the keys in each dictionary will match the order of the columns in the source file. The items in the list will match the original rows.

The output looks like this:

```
>>> source_path = Path("data/fuel2.csv")
>>> fuel_use = get_fuel_use(source_path)
>>> for row in fuel_use:
...     print(row)
{'date': '10/25/13', 'engine on': '08:24:00', 'fuel height on': '29',
'engine off': '13:15:00', 'fuel height off': '27'}
{'date': '10/26/13', 'engine on': '09:12:00', 'fuel height on': '27',
'engine off': '18:25:00', 'fuel height off': '22'}
```

```
{'date': '10/28/13', 'engine on': '13:21:00', 'fuel height on': '22',
'engine off': '06:25:00', 'fuel height off': '14'}
```

How it works...

Since Python 3.6, the `dict` class keeps the keys in the order they are inserted. This property of the built-in `dict` collection class is very handy for ensuring keys remain in an order that's easy to understand.

This is a change from other, older implementations of the `dict` class. It's also different from the way a `set` object works. Old implementations of `dict` (and the current implementation of `set`) rely on the hash values of the keys. This tends to put keys into a difficult-to-predict order.

We can impose a specific order by creating a dictionary object from a list of two-tuples. This gives us complete control over the ordering of the keys. In these cases, it can be more clear to use the `colllections.OrderedDict` class, but this is no longer necessary.

For example, we might have a row like this:

```
>>> row = {'columns': 42, 'data': 3.14, 'of': 2.718, 'some': 1.618}
```

From this dictionary, we can build a new dictionary with keys in a specific order:

```
>>> import collections


>>> key_order = ['some', 'columns', 'of', 'data']
>>> collections.OrderedDict(
...     [(name, row[name]) for name in key_order]
... )
OrderedDict([('some', 1.618), ('columns', 42), ('of', 2.718), ('data',
3.14)])
```

This provides ways to create dictionaries that can be serialized with the attributes in a predictable order. When we do JSON serialization, for example, this can be helpful.

There's more...

There's another time when we can enforce an ordering of dictionary keys. That happens when we iterate through the keys. Implicitly, the `keys()` method is used as an iterator over a dictionary. Consider this code snippet:

```
for field in row:
    print(field, row[field])
```

By definition, the statement `for field in row.keys():` has the same behavior as the statement `for field in row:`. We can use this to explicitly sort the keys into a more useful order for presentation.

Consider this summary of simplified web server log entries:

```
>>> log_rows = [
...     {'date': '2019-11-12T13:14:15', 'path': '/path/to/resource'},
...     {'date': '2019-11-14T15:16:17', 'path': '/path/to/resource'},
...     {'date': '2019-11-19T20:21:11', 'path': '/path/to/resource'},
...     {'date': '2019-11-20T21:22:23', 'path': '/path/to/resource'},
...     {'date': '2019-11-26T07:08:09', 'path': '/path/to/resource'},
... ]
>>> summary = collections.Counter()
>>> for row in log_rows:
...     date = datetime.datetime.strptime(row['date'], "%Y-%m-
%dT%H:%M:%S")
...     summary[date.weekday()] += 1
>>> summary
Counter({1: 3, 3: 1, 2: 1})
```

The `summary` object has day of week, as a number, and the number of times a particular path was referenced. We'd like to change this to show the names of the days of the week. And, also very important for understanding the data, we'd like the days to be in proper calendar order, not in alphabetical order by day name.

We can sort the `Counter` dictionary keys and use the `calendar` module to provide day names from the day numbers. The following snippet shows the essence of this operation:

```
>>> import calendar
>>> for k in sorted(summary):
...     print(calendar.day_name[k], summary[k])
Tuesday 3
Wednesday 1
Thursday 1
```

This shows how the `sorted()` function can be applied to the keys of a `collections.Counter` dictionary to produce the keys in a meaningful order.

See also

- In the *Creating dictionaries – inserting and updating* recipe, we'll look at how we can create dictionaries.
- In the *Removing from dictionaries – the pop() method and the del statement* recipe, we'll look at how dictionaries can be modified by removing items.

Writing dictionary-related type hints

When we look at sets and lists, we generally expect each item within a `list` (or a `set`) to be the same type. When we look at object-oriented class designs, in *Chapter 7, Basics of Classes and Objects,* we'll see how a common superclass can be the common type for a closely related family of object types. While it's possible to have heterogeneous types in a list or set collection, it often becomes quite complex to process.

Dictionaries are used in a number of different ways.

- **Homogeneous types for values**: This is common for dictionaries based on `collections.Counter` or `collections.defaultdict`. The input from a `csv.DictReader` will also be homogeneous, since every value from a CSV file is a string.
- **Heterogeneous types for values**: This is common for dictionaries used to represent complex objects that have been serialized into JSON notation. It's also common for internal data structures created as part of more complex processing.

This flexibility leads to two kinds of type hints for dictionary objects.

Getting ready

We'll look at two kinds of dictionary type hints for homogeneous value types as well as heterogeneous value types. We'll look at data that starts out as one of these kinds of dictionaries but is transformed to have more complex type definitions.

We'll be starting with the following CSV file:

```
date,engine on,fuel height on,engine off,fuel height off
10/25/13,08:24:00,29,13:15:00,27
10/26/13,09:12:00,27,18:25:00,22
10/28/13,13:21:00,22,06:25:00,14
```

This describes three separate legs of a multi-day trip in a sailboat. The fuel is measured by the height in the tank, rather than some indirect method using a float or other gauges. Because the tank is approximately rectangular, there's a relatively simple transformation from height to gallons. For this tank, 31 inches of depth is about 75 gallons of fuel.

How to do it...

The initial use of `csv.DictReader` will lead to dictionaries with homogeneous type definitions:

1. Locate the type of the keys in the dictionary. When reading CSV files, the keys are strings, with the type `str`.
2. Locate the type of the values in the dictionary. When reading CSV files, the values are strings, with the type `str`.
3. Combine the types using the `typing.Dict` type hint. This yields `Dict[str, str]`.

Here's an example function for reading data from a CSV file:

```
def get_fuel_use(source_path: Path) -> List[Dict[str, str]]:
    with source_path.open() as source_file:
        rdr = csv.DictReader(source_file)
        data: List[Dict[str, str]] = list(rdr)
    return data
```

The `get_fuel_use()` function yields values that match the source data. In this case, it's a dictionary that maps string column names to string cell values.

This data, by itself, is difficult to work with. A common second step is to apply transformations to the source rows to create more useful data types. We can describe the results with a type hint:

1. Identify the various value types that will be needed. In this example, there are five fields with three different types, shown here:
   - The `date` field is a `datetime.date` object.
   - The `engine on` field is a `datetime.time` object.
   - The `fuel height on` field is an integer, but we know that it will be used in a float context, so we'll create a float directly.
   - The `engine off` field is a `datetime.time` object.
   - The `fuel height off` field is also a float value.
2. Import the `TypedDict` type definition from the `mypy_extensions` module.
3. Define `TypedDict` with the new heterogeneous dictionary types:

```
from mypy_extensions import TypedDict
History = TypedDict(
    'History',
    {
        'date': datetime.date,
```

```
                'start_time': datetime.time,
                'start_fuel': float,
                'end_time': datetime.time,
                'end_fuel': float
            }
        )
```

In this example, we've also renamed the fields to make them shorter and slightly easier to understand.

The function to perform the transformation can look like the following example:

```
def make_history(source: Iterable[Dict[str, str]]) ->
Iterator[History]:
    for row in source:
        yield dict(
            date=datetime.datetime.strptime(
                row['date'], "%m/%d/%y").date(),
            start_time=datetime.datetime.strptime(
                row['engine on'], '%H:%M:%S').time(),
            start_fuel=float(row['fuel height on']),
            end_time=datetime.datetime.strptime(
                row['engine off'], '%H:%M:%S').time(),
            end_fuel=float(row['fuel height off']),
        )
```

This function consumes instances of the initial `Dict[str, str]` dictionary and creates instances of the dictionary described by the `History` type hint. Here's how these two functions work together:

```
>>> source_path = Path("data/fuel2.csv")
>>> fuel_use = make_history(get_fuel_use(source_path))
>>> for row in fuel_use:
...     print(row)
{'date': datetime.date(2013, 10, 25), 'start_time': datetime.time(8, 24),
'start_fuel': 29.0, 'end_time': datetime.time(13, 15), 'end_fuel': 27.0}
{'date': datetime.date(2013, 10, 26), 'start_time': datetime.time(9, 12),
'start_fuel': 27.0, 'end_time': datetime.time(18, 25), 'end_fuel': 22.0}
{'date': datetime.date(2013, 10, 28), 'start_time': datetime.time(13,
21), 'start_fuel': 22.0, 'end_time': datetime.time(6, 25), 'end_fuel':
14.0}
```

This shows how the output from the `get_fuel_use()` function can be processed by the `make_history()` function to create an iterable sequence of dictionaries. Each of the resulting dictionaries has the source data converted to a more useful type.

How it works...

The core type hint for a dictionary names the key type and the value type, in the form `Dict[key, value]`. The `mypy` extension type, `TypedDict`, lets us be more specific about bindings between dictionary keys and a very broad domain of values.

It's important to note that type hints are only checked by the `mypy` program. These hints have no runtime impact. We could, for example, write a statement like the following:

```
result: History = {'date': 42}
```

This statement claims that the `result` dictionary will match the type hints in the `History` type definition. The dictionary literal, however, has the wrong type for the `date` field and a number of other fields are missing. While this will execute, it will raise errors from `mypy`.

There's more...

One of the common cases for heterogeneity is optional items. The type hint `Optional[str]` is the same as `Union[str, None]`. This optional or union specification is a very specialized kind of heterogeneity. This is rarely needed with a dictionary, since it can be simpler to omit the `key: value` pair entirely.

There are some parallels between `TypedDict` and the `NamedTuple` type definitions. We can, for example, make a few small syntax changes to create a named tuple instead of a typed dictionary. The alternative looks like this:

```
from typing import NamedTuple
HistoryT = NamedTuple(
    'HistoryT',
    [
        ('date', datetime.date),
        ('start_time', datetime.time),
        ('start_fuel', float),
        ('end_time', datetime.time),
        ('end_fuel', float)
    ]
)
```

Because a `HistoryT` object has an `_asdict()` method, it's possible to produce a dictionary that matches the `History` typed dict shown above.

The similarities allow us the flexibility to define types with similar syntax. A dictionary that matches the `TypedDict` hint is a dictionary and is mutable. The `HistoryT` subclass of `NamedTuple`, however, is immutable. This is one central difference between these two type hints. More importantly, a dictionary uses `row['date']` syntax to refer to one item using the key. `NamedTuple` uses `row.date` syntax to refer to one item using a name.

See also

- The *Using NamedTuples to simplify item access in tuples* recipe provides more details on the `NamedTuple` type hint.
- See the *Writing list-related type hints* recipe in this chapter for more about type hints for lists.
- The *Writing set-related type hints* recipe covers this from the view of set types.

Understanding variables, references, and assignment

How do variables really work? What happens when we assign a mutable object to two variables? We can easily have two variables that share references to a common object; this can lead to potentially confusing results when the shared object is mutable.

We'll focus on this principle: **Python shares references; it doesn't copy data**.

To see what this rule on reference sharing means, we'll create two data structures: one is mutable and one is immutable.

Getting ready

We'll create two data structures; one is mutable and one is immutable. We'll use two kinds of sequences, although we could do something similar with two kinds of sets:

```
>>> mutable = [1, 1, 2, 3, 5, 8]
>>> immutable = (5, 8, 13, 21)
```

We'll look at what happens when references to these objects are shared.

We can do a similar comparison with a `set` and a `frozenset`. We can't easily do this with a mapping because Python doesn't offer a handy immutable mapping.

How to do it...

This recipe will show how to observe the spooky action at a distance when there are two references to an underlying mutable object. We'll look at ways to prevent this in the *Making shallow and deep copies of objects* recipe. Here are the steps for seeing the difference between mutable and immutable collections:

1. Assign each collection to an additional variable. This will create two references to the structure:

   ```
   >>> mutable_b = mutable
   >>> immutable_b = immutable
   ```

   We now have two references to the list `[1, 1, 2, 3, 5, 8]` and two references to the tuple `(5, 8, 13, 21)`.

2. We can confirm this using the `is` operator. This determines if two variables refer to the same underlying object:

   ```
   >>> mutable_b is mutable
   True
   >>> immutable_b is immutable
   True
   ```

3. Make a change to one of the two references to the collection. For the list type, we have methods like `extend()`, `append()`, or `add()`:

   ```
   >>> mutable += [mutable[-2] + mutable[-1]]
   ```

4. We can do a similar thing with the immutable structure:

   ```
   >>> immutable += (immutable[-2] + immutable[-1],)
   ```

5. Look at the other two variables that reference the mutable structure. Because the two variables are references to the same underlying `list` object, each variable shows the current state:

   ```
   >>> mutable_b
   [1, 1, 2, 3, 5, 8, 13]
   >>> mutable is mutable_b
   True
   ```

- Look at the two variables referring to immutable structures. Initially, the two variables shared a common object. When the assignment statement was executed, a new tuple was created and only one variable changed to refer to the new tuple:

```
>>> immutable_b
(5, 8, 13, 21)
>>> immutable
(5, 8, 13, 21, 34)
```

How it works...

The two variables `mutable` and `mutable_b` still refer to the same underlying object. Because of that, we can use either variable to change the object and see the change reflected in the other variable's value.

The two variables, `immutable_b` and `immutable`, started out referring to the same object. Because the object cannot be mutated in place, a change to one variable means that a new object is assigned to that variable. The other variable remains firmly attached to the original object.

In Python, a variable is a label that's attached to an object. We can think of them like adhesive notes in bright colors that we stick on an object temporarily. Multiple labels can be attached to an object. An assignment statement places a reference on an object.

Consider the following statement:

```
immutable += (immutable[-2] + immutable[-1],)
```

The expression on the right side of += creates a new tuple from the previous value of the `immutable` tuple. The assignment statement then assigns the label `immutable` to the resulting object.

When we use a variable on an assignment statement there are two possible actions:

- For mutable objects that provide definitions for appropriate assignment operators like +=, the assignment is transformed into a special method; in this case, `__iadd__()`. The special method will mutate the object's internal state.
- For immutable objects that do not provide definitions for assignment like +=, the assignment is transformed into = and +. A new object is built by the + operator and the variable name is attached to that new object. Other variables that previously referred to the object being replaced are not affected; they will continue to refer to old objects.

Python counts the number of places from which an object is referenced. When the count of references becomes zero, the object is no longer used anywhere, and can be removed from memory.

There's more...

Languages like C++ or Java have primitive types in addition to objects. In these languages, a += statement leverages a feature of the hardware instructions or the Java Virtual Machine instructions to tweak the value of a primitive type.

Python doesn't have this kind of optimization. Numbers are immutable objects. When we do something like this:

```
>>> a = 355
>>> a += 113
```

we're not tweaking the internal state of the object `355`. This does not rely on the internal `__iadd__()` special method. This behaves as if we had written:

```
>>> a = a + 113
```

The expression `a + 113` is evaluated, and a new immutable integer object is created. This new object is given the label `a`. The old value previously assigned to `a` is no longer needed, and the storage can be reclaimed.

See also

- In the *Making shallow and deep copies of objects* recipe, we'll look at ways we can copy mutable structures to prevent shared references.
- Also, see *Avoiding mutable default values for function parameters* for another consequence of the way references are shared in Python.

Making shallow and deep copies of objects

Throughout this chapter, we've talked about how assignment statements share references to objects. Objects are not normally copied. When we write:

```
a = b
```

we now have two references to the same underlying object. If the object of `b` has a mutable type, like the `list`, `set`, or `dict` types, then both `a` and `b` are references to the same mutable object.

As we saw in the *Understanding variables, references, and assignment* recipe, a change to the `a` variable changes the list object that both `a` and `b` refer to.

Most of the time, this is the behavior we want. There are rare situations in which we want to actually have two independent objects created from one original object.

There are two ways to break the connection that exists when two variables are references to the same underlying object:

- Making a shallow copy of the structure
- Making a deep copy of the structure

Getting ready

Python does not automatically make a copy of an object. We've seen several kinds of syntax for making a copy:

- Sequences - `list`, as well as `str`, `bytes`, and `tuple`: We can use `sequence[:]` to copy a sequence by using an empty slice expression. This is a special case for sequences.
- Almost all collections have a `copy()` method. We can also use `object.copy()` to make a copy of a variable named `object`.
- Calling a type, with an instance of the type as the only argument, returns a copy. For example, if `d` is a dictionary, `dict(d)` creates a shallow copy of `d`.

What's important is that these are all *shallow* copies. When two collections are shallow copies, they each contain references to the same underlying objects. If the underlying objects are immutable, such as tuples, numbers, or strings, this distinction doesn't matter.

For example, if we have `a = [1, 1, 2, 3]`, we can't perform any mutation on `a[0]`. The number `1` in `a[0]` has no internal state. We can only replace the object.

Questions arise, however, when we have a collection that involves mutable objects. First, we'll create an object, then we'll create a copy:

```
>>> some_dict = {'a': [1, 1, 2, 3]}
>>> another_dict = some_dict.copy()
```

This example created a shallow copy of the dictionary. The two copies will look alike because they both contain references to the same objects. There's a shared reference to the immutable string `a` and a shared reference to the mutable list `[1, 1, 2, 3]`. We can display the value of `another_dict` to see that it looks like the `some_dict` object we started with:

```
>>> another_dict
{'a': [1, 1, 2, 3]}
```

Here's what happens when we update the shared list that's inside the copy of the dictionary:

```
>>> some_dict['a'].append(5)
>>> another_dict
{'a': [1, 1, 2, 3, 5]}
```

We made a change to a mutable `list` object that's shared between the two `dict` instances, `some_dict` and `another_dict`. We can see that the item is shared by using the `id()` function:

```
>>> id(some_dict['a']) == id(another_dict['a'])
True
```

Because the two `id()` values are the same, these are the same underlying object. The value associated with the key `a` is the same mutable list in both `some_dict` and `another_dict`. We can also use the `is` operator to see that they're the same object.

This mutation of a shallow copy works for `list` collections that contain other `list` objects as items as well:

```
>>> some_list = [[2, 3, 5], [7, 11, 13]]
>>> another_list = some_list.copy()
>>> some_list is another_list
False
>>> some_list[0] is another_list[0]
True
```

We've made a copy of an object, `some_list`, and assigned it to the variable `another_list`. The top-level `list` object is distinct, but the items within the `list` are shared references. We used the `is` operator to show that item zero in each list are both references to the same underlying objects.

Because we can't make a `set` of mutable objects, we don't really have to consider making shallow copies of sets that share items.

What if we want to completely disconnect two copies? How do we make a deep copy instead of a shallow copy?

How to do it...

Python generally works by sharing references. It only makes copies of objects reluctantly. The default behavior is to make a shallow copy, sharing references to the items within a collection. Here's how we make deep copies:

1. Import the `copy` module:

   ```
   >>> import copy
   ```

2. Use the `copy.deepcopy()` function to duplicate an object and all of the mutable items contained within that object:

   ```
   >>> some_dict = {'a': [1, 1, 2, 3]}
   >>> another_dict = copy.deepcopy(some_dict)
   ```

This will create copies that have no shared references. A change to one copy's mutable internal items won't have any effect anywhere else:

```
>>> some_dict['a'].append(5)
>>> some_dict
{'a': [1, 1, 2, 3, 5]}
>>> another_dict
{'a': [1, 1, 2, 3]}
```

We updated an item in `some_dict` and it had no effect on the copy in `another_dict`. We can see that the objects are distinct with the `id()` function:

```
>>> id(some_dict['a']) == id(another_dict['a'])
False
```

Since the `id()` values are different, these are distinct objects. We can also use the `is` operator to see that they're distinct objects.

How it works...

Making a shallow copy is relatively easy. We can write our own version of the algorithm using comprehensions (containing generator expressions):

```
>>> copy_of_list = [item for item in some_list]
>>> copy_of_dict = {key:value for key, value in some_dict.items()}
```

In the `list` case, the items for the new `list` are references to the items in the source list. Similarly, in the `dict` case, the keys and values are references to the keys and values of the source dictionary.

The `deepcopy()` function uses a recursive algorithm to look inside each mutable collection.

For an object with a `list` type, the conceptual algorithm is something like this:

```
immutable = (numbers.Number, tuple, str, bytes)
def deepcopy_list(some_list:
    copy = []
    for item in some_list:
        if isinstance(item, immutable):
            copy.append(item)
        else:

            copy.append(deepcopy(item))
```

The actual code doesn't look like this, of course. It's a bit more clever in the way it handles each distinct Python type. This does, however, provide some insight as to how the `deepcopy()` function works.

See also

- In the *Understanding variables, references, and assignment* recipe, we'll look at how Python prefers to create references to objects.

Avoiding mutable default values for function parameters

In *Chapter 3, Function Definitions*, we looked at many aspects of Python function definitions. In the *Designing functions with optional parameters* recipe, we showed a recipe for handling optional parameters. At the time, we didn't dwell on the issue of providing a reference to a mutable structure as a default. We'll take a close look at the consequences of a mutable default value for a function parameter.

Getting ready

Let's imagine a function that either creates or updates a mutable `Counter` object. We'll call it `gather_stats()`.

Ideally, a small data gathering function could look like this:

```
import collections
from random import randint, seed
from typing import Counter, Optional, Callable

def gather_stats_bad(
    n: int,
    samples: int = 1000,
    summary: Counter[int] = collections.Counter()
) -> Counter[int]:
    summary.update(
        sum(randint(1, 6)
            for d in range(n)) for _ in range(samples)
    )
    return summary
```

This shows a *bad* design for a function with two stories. The first story offers no argument value for the `summary` parameter. When this is omitted, the function creates and returns a collection of statistics. Here's the example of this story:

```
>>> seed(1)
>>> s1 = gather_stats_bad(2)
>>> s1
Counter({7: 168, 6: 147, 8: 136, 9: 114, 5: 110, 10: 77, 11: 71, 4: 70,
3: 52, 12: 29, 2: 26})
```

The second story allows us to provide an explicit argument value for the `summary` parameter. When this argument is provided this function updates the given object. Here's an example of this story:

```
>>> seed(1)
>>> mc = Counter()
>>> gather_stats_bad(2, summary=mc)
Counter...
>>> mc
Counter({7: 168, 6: 147, 8: 136, 9: 114, 5: 110, 10: 77, 11: 71, 4: 70,
3: 52, 12: 29, 2: 26})
```

We've set the random number seed to be sure that the two sequences of random values are identical. This makes it easy to confirm that the results are the same in both stories. If we provide a `Counter` object or use the default `Counter` object, we get identical results.

The `gather_stats_bad()` function returns a value. When writing a script, we'd simply ignore the returned value. When working with Python's interactive REPL the output is printed. We've shown `Counter...` instead of the lengthy output.

The problem arises when we do the following operation:

```
>>> seed(1)
>>> s3b = gather_stats_bad(2)
>>> s3b
Counter({7: 336, 6: 294, 8: 272, 9: 228, 5: 220, 10: 154, 11: 142, 4:
140, 3: 104, 12: 58, 2: 52})
```

The count values in this example are doubled. Something has gone wrong. This only happens when we use the default story more than once. This code can pass a unit test suite and appear correct.

As we saw in the *Making shallow and deep copies of objects* recipe, Python prefers to share references. A consequence of that sharing is the object referenced by the `s1` variable and the object referenced by the `s3b` variable are the same object:

```
>>> s1 is s3b
True
```

This means the value of the s1 variable changed when the value for the s3b variable was created. From this, it should be apparent the function is updating some shared collection and returning the reference to the shared collection.

The default value used for the summary parameter of this gather_stats_bad() function seems to be sharing a single object. How can we avoid this?

How to do it...

There are two approaches to solving this problem of a mutable default parameter:

- Provide an immutable default
- Change the design

We'll look at the immutable default first. Changing the design is generally a better idea. In order to see why it's better to change the design, we'll show the purely technical solution.

When we provide default values for functions, the default object is created exactly once and shared forever after. Here's the alternative:

1. Replace any mutable default parameter value with None:

   ```
   def gather_stats_good(
       n: int, samples: int = 1000, summary:
   Optional[Counter[int]] = None
   ) -> Counter[int]:
   ```

2. Add an if statement to check for an argument value of None and replace it with a fresh, new mutable object:

   ```
   if summary is None:
       summary = Counter()
   ```

3. This will assure us that every time the function is evaluated with no argument value for a parameter, we create a fresh, new mutable object. We will avoid sharing a single mutable object over and over again.

How it works...

As we noted earlier, Python prefers to share references. It rarely creates copies of objects without explicit use of the copy module or the copy() method of an object. Therefore, default values for function parameter values will be shared objects. Python does not create fresh, new objects for default parameter values.

The rule is very important and often confuses programmers new to Python.

> Don't use mutable defaults for functions. A mutable object (`set`, `list`, `dict`) should not be a default value for a function parameter.

Providing a mutable object as a default parameter value is often a very bad idea. In most cases, we should consider changing the design, and not offering a default value at all. The best approach is to use two separate functions, distinguished by the user stories. One function creates a value, the second function updates the value.

We'd refactor one function to create two functions, `create_stats()` and `update_stats()`, with unambiguous parameters:

```
def create_stats(n: int, samples: int = 1000) -> Counter[int]:
    return update_stats(n, samples, Counter())

def update_stats(
    n: int, samples: int = 1000, summary: Counter[int]
) -> Counter[int]:
    summary.update(
        sum(randint(1, 6)
            for d in range(n)) for _ in range(samples))
    return summary
```

We've created two separate functions. This will separate the two stories so that there's no confusion. The idea of optional mutable arguments was not a good idea. The mutable object provided as a default value is reused. This reuse of a mutable object means the default value will be updated, a potential source of confusion. It's very unlikely to want a default value that is updated as an application executes.

There's more...

In the standard library, there are some examples of a cool technique that shows how we can create fresh default objects. A number of functions use a key function to create comparable values from a complex object. We can look at `sorted()`, `min()`, and `max()` for examples of this. A default key function does nothing; it's `lambda item: item`. A non-default key function requires an item and produces some object that is a better choice for comparison.

In order to leverage this technique, we need to modify the design of our example function. We will no longer update an existing counter object in the function. We'll always create a fresh, new object. We can modify what class of object is created.

Here's a function that allows us to plug in a different class in the case where we don't want the default `Counter` class to be used:

```
T = TypeVar('T')
Summarizer = Callable[[Iterable[T]], Counter[T]]

def gather_stats_flex(
    n: int,
    samples: int = 1000,
    summary_func: Summarizer = collections.Counter
) -> Counter[int]:
    summary = summary_func(
        sum(randint(1, 6)
            for d in range(n)) for _ in range(samples))
    return summary
```

For this version, we've defined an initialization value to be a function of one argument. The default will apply this one-argument function to a generator function for the random samples. We can override this function with another one-argument function that will collect data. This will build a fresh object using any kind of object that can gather data.

Here's an example using `list` instead of `collections.Counter`:

```
test_flex = """
>>> seed(1)
>>> gather_stats_flex(2, 12, summary_func=list)
[7, 4, 5, 8, 10, 3, 5, 8, 6, 10, 9, 7]
>>> seed(1)
>>> gather_stats_flex(2, 12, summary_func=list)
[7, 4, 5, 8, 10, 3, 5, 8, 6, 10, 9, 7]
"""
```

In this case, we provided the `list()` function to create a list with the individual random samples in it.

Here's an example without an argument value. It will create a `collections.Counter` object:

```
>>> seed(1)
>>> gather_stats_flex(2, 12)
Counter({7: 2, 5: 2, 8: 2, 10: 2, 4: 1, 3: 1, 6: 1, 9: 1})
```

In this case, we've used the default value. The function created a `Counter()` object from the random samples.

See also

- See the *Creating dictionaries – inserting and updating* recipe, which shows how `defaultdict` works.

6

User Inputs and Outputs

The key purpose of software is to produce useful output. One simple type of output is text displaying some useful result. Python supports this with the `print()` function.

The `input()` function has a parallel with the `print()` function. The `input()` function reads text from a console, allowing us to provide data to our programs.

There are a number of other common ways to provide input to a program. Parsing the command line is helpful for many applications. We sometimes need to use configuration files to provide useful input. Data files and network connections are yet more ways to provide input. Each of these methods is distinct and needs to be looked at separately. In this chapter, we'll focus on the fundamentals of `input()` and `print()`.

In this chapter, we'll look at the following recipes:

- Using the features of the `print()` function
- Using `input()` and `getpass()` for user input
- Debugging with `f"{value=}"` strings
- Using `argparse` to get command-line input
- Using `cmd` to create command-line applications
- Using the OS environment settings

It seems best to start with the `print()` function and show a number of the things it can do. After all, it's often the output from an application that creates the most value.

Using the features of the print() function

In many cases, the `print()` function is the first function we learn about. The first script is often a variation on the following:

```
>>> print("Hello, world.")
Hello, world.
```

The `print()` function can display multiple values, with helpful spaces between items.

When we write this:

```
>>> count = 9973
>>> print("Final count", count)
Final count 9973
```

We see that a space separator is included for us. Additionally, a line break, usually represented by the `\n` character, is printed after the values provided in the function.

Can we control this formatting? Can we change the extra characters that are supplied?

It turns out that there are some more things we can do with `print()`.

Getting ready

Consider this spreadsheet, used to record fuel consumption on a large sailboat. It has rows that look like this:

date	engine on	fuel height on	engine off	fuel height off
10/25/13	08:24:00	29	13:15:00	27
10/26/13	09:12:00	27	18:25:00	22
10/28/13	13:21:00	22	06:25:00	14

Example of fuel use by a sailboat

For more information on this data, refer to the *Removing items from a set – remove(), pop(), and difference* and *Slicing and dicing a list* recipes in *Chapter 4, Built-In Data Structures Part 1: Lists and Sets*. Instead of a sensor inside the tank, the depth of fuel is observed through a glass panel on the side of the tank. Knowing the tank is approximately rectangular, with a full depth of about 31 inches and a volume of about 72 gallons, it's possible to convert depth to volume.

Here's an example of using this CSV data. This function reads the file and returns a list of fields built from each row:

```
from pathlib import Path
import csv
from typing import Dict, List


def get_fuel_use(source_path: Path) -> List[Dict[str, str]]:
    with source_path.open() as source_file:
        rdr = csv.DictReader(source_file)
        return list(rdr)
```

This example uses a given `Path` object to identify a file. The opened file is used to create a dictionary-based reader for the `CSV` file. The list of rows represents the spreadsheet as Python objects.

Here's an example of reading and printing rows from the `CSV` file:

```
>>> source_path = Path("data/fuel2.csv")
>>> fuel_use = get_fuel_use(source_path)
>>> for row in fuel_use:
...     print(row)
{'date': '10/25/13', 'engine on': '08:24:00', 'fuel height on': '29',
'engine off': '13:15:00', 'fuel height off': '27'}
{'date': '10/26/13', 'engine on': '09:12:00', 'fuel height on': '27',
'engine off': '18:25:00', 'fuel height off': '22'}
{'date': '10/28/13', 'engine on': '13:21:00', 'fuel height on': '22',
'engine off': '06:25:00', 'fuel height off': '14'}
```

We used a `pathlib.Path` object to define the location of the raw data. We evaluated the `get_fuel_use()` function to open and read the file with the given path. This function creates a list of rows from the source spreadsheet. Each line of data is represented as a `Dict[str, str]` object.

The output from `print()`, shown here in long lines, could be seen as challenging for some folks to read. Let's look at how we can improve this output using additional features of the `print()` function.

How to do it...

We have two ways to control the `print()` formatting:

- Set the inter-field separator string, `sep`, which has the single space character as its default value
- Set the end-of-line string, `end`, which has the single `\n` character as its default value

We'll show several examples of changing `sep` and `end`. The examples are similar.

The default case looks like this. This example has no change to `sep` or `end`:

1. Read the data:

   ```
   >>> fuel_use = get_fuel_use(Path("data/fuel2.csv"))
   ```

2. For each item in the data, do any useful data conversions:

   ```
   >>> for leg in fuel_use:
   ...     start = float(leg["fuel height on"])
   ...     finish = float(leg["fuel height off"])
   ```

3. Print labels and fields using the default values of `sep` and `end`:

   ```
   ...     print("On", leg["date"],
   ...     "from", leg["engine on"],
   ...     "to", leg["engine off"],
   ...     "change", start-finish, "in.")
   On 10/25/13 from 08:24:00 to 13:15:00 change 2.0 in.
   On 10/26/13 from 09:12:00 to 18:25:00 change 5.0 in.
   On 10/28/13 from 13:21:00 to 06:25:00 change 8.0 in.
   ```

When we look at the output, we can see where a space was inserted between each item. The `\n` character at the end of each collection of data items means that each `print()` function produces a separate line.

When preparing data, we might want to use a format that's similar to CSV, perhaps using a column separator that's not a simple comma. Here's an example using |:

```
>>> print("date", "start", "end", "depth", sep=" | ")
date | start | end | depth
```

This is a modification to *step 3* of the recipe shown before:

1. Print labels and fields using a string value of `" | "` for the `sep` parameter:

   ```
   ...     print(leg["date"], leg["engine on"],
   ...     leg["engine off"], start-finish, sep=" | ")
   10/25/13 | 08:24:00 | 13:15:00 | 2.0
   10/26/13 | 09:12:00 | 18:25:00 | 5.0
   10/28/13 | 13:21:00 | 06:25:00 | 8.0
   ```

In this case, we can see that each column has the given separator string. Since there were no changes to the `end` setting, each `print()` function produces a distinct line of output.

Here's how we might change the default punctuation to emphasize the field name and value.

This is a modification to *step 3* of the recipe shown before:

1. Print labels and fields using a string value of `"="` for the `sep` parameter and `',  '` for the `end` parameter:

```
...     print("date", leg["date"], sep="=", end=",  ")
...     print("on", leg["engine on"], sep="=", end=",  ")
...     print("off", leg["engine off"], sep="=", end=",  ")
...     print("change", start-finish, sep="=")
date=10/25/13, on=08:24:00, off=13:15:00, change=2.0
date=10/26/13, on=09:12:00, off=18:25:00, change=5.0
date=10/28/13, on=13:21:00, off=06:25:00, change=8.0
```

Since the string used at the end of the line was changed to `',  '`, each use of the `print()` function no longer produces separate lines. In order to see a proper end of line, the final `print()` function has a default value for `end`. We could also have used an argument value of `end='\n'` to make the presence of the newline character explicit.

How it works...

We can imagine that `print()` has a definition something like this:

```
def print_like(*args, sep=None, end=None, file=sys.stdout):
    if sep is None: sep = " "
    if end is None: end = "\n"

    arg_iter = iter(args)
    value = next(arg_iter)
    file.write(str(value))
    for value in arg_iter:
        file.write(sep)
        file.write(str(value))
        file.write(end)

    file.flush()
```

This only has a few of the features of the actual `print()` function. The purpose is to illustrate how the separator and ending strings work. If no value is provided, the default value for the separator is a single space character, and the default value at end-of-line is a single newline character, `"\n"`.

This print-like function creates an explicit iterator object, `arg_iter`. Using `next(arg_iter)` allows us to treat the first item as special, since it won't have a separator in front of it. The `for` statement then iterates through the remaining argument values, inserting the separator string, `sep`, in front of each item after the first.

The end-of-line string, `end`, is printed after all of the values. It is always written. We can effectively turn it off by setting it to a zero-length string, `""`.

Using the `print()` function's `sep` and `end` parameters can get quite complex for anything more sophisticated than these simple examples. Rather than working with a complex sequence of `print()` function requests, we can use the `format()` method of a string, or use an f-string.

There's more...

The `sys` module defines the two standard output files that are always available: `sys.stdout` and `sys.stderr`. In the general case, the `print()` function is a handy wrapper around `stdout.write()`.

We can use the `file=` keyword argument to write to the standard error file instead of writing to the standard output file:

```
>>> import sys
>>> print("Red Alert!", file=sys.stderr)
```

We've imported the `sys` module so that we have access to the standard error file. We used this to write a message that would not be part of the standard output stream.

Because these two files are always available, using OS file redirection techniques often works out nicely. When our program's primary output is written to `sys.stdout`, it can be redirected at the OS level. A user might enter a command line like this:

```
python3 myapp.py <input.dat >output.dat
```

This will provide the `input.dat` file as the input to `sys.stdin`. When a Python program writes to `sys.stdout`, the output will be redirected by the OS to the `output.dat` file.

In some cases, we need to open additional files. In that case, we might see programming like this:

```
>>> from pathlib import Path
>>> target_path = Path("data")/"extra_detail.log"
>>> with target_path.open('w', encoding='utf-8') as target_file:
...     print("Some detailed output", file=target_file)
...     print("Ordinary log")
Ordinary log
```

In this example, we've opened a specific path for the output and assigned the open file to `target_file` using the `with` statement. We can then use this as the `file=` value in a `print()` function to write to this file. Because a file is a context manager, leaving the `with` statement means that the file will be closed properly; all of the OS resources will be released from the application. All file operations should be wrapped in a `with` statement context to ensure that the resources are properly released.

In large, long-running applications like web servers, the failure to close files and release resources is termed a "leak." A memory leak, for example, can arise when files are not closed properly and buffers remain allocated. Using a `with` statement assures that resources are released, eliminating a potential source of resource management problems.

See also

- Refer to the *Debugging with "format".format_map(vars())* recipe.
- For more information on the input data in this example, refer to the *Removing items from a set – remove(), pop(), and difference* and *Slicing and dicing a list* recipes in *Chapter 4, Built-In Data Structures Part 1: Lists and Sets.*
- For more information on file operations in general, refer to *Chapter 8, More Advanced Class Design.*

Using input() and getpass() for user input

Some Python scripts depend on gathering input from a user. There are several ways to do this. One popular technique is to use the console to prompt a user for input.

There are two relatively common situations:

- **Ordinary input**: We can use the `input()` function for this. This will provide a helpful echo of the characters being entered.
- **Secure, no echo input**: This is often used for passwords. The characters entered aren't displayed, providing a degree of privacy. We use the `getpass()` function in the `getpass` module for this.

The `input()` and `getpass()` functions are just two implementation choices for reading from the console. It turns out that getting the string of characters is only the first step in gathering valid, useful data. The input also needs to be validated.

When gathering input from a user there are several tiers of considerations for us to make, including the following:

1. The user interaction: This is the process of writing a prompt and reading input characters from the user.
2. Validation: The user's input needs to be checked to see whether it belongs in the expected domain of values. We might be looking for digits, yes/no values, or days of the week. In most cases, there are two parts to the validation tier:
    - We check whether the input fits some general domain – for example, numbers.
    - We check whether the input fits some more specific subdomain. For example, this might include a check to see whether the number is greater than or equal to zero, or between zero and six.

3. Validating the input in some larger context to ensure that it's consistent with other inputs. For example, we can check whether a collection of inputs represents a date, and that the date is prior to today.

Gathering user input isn't a trivial operation. However, Python provides several libraries to help us implement the required tiers of input validation.

Above and beyond these techniques, we'll look at some other approaches in the *Using argparse to get command-line input* recipe later in this chapter.

Getting ready

We'll look at a technique for reading a complex structure from a person. In this case, we'll use `year`, `month`, and `day` as separate items. These items are then combined to create a complete `date`.

Here's a quick example of user input that omits all of the validation considerations. This is poor design:

```
from datetime import date

def get_date1() -> date:
    year = int(input("year: "))
    month = int(input("month [1-12]: "))
    day = int(input("day [1-31]: "))
    result = date(year, month, day)
    return result
```

This illustrates how easy it is to use the `input()` function. This will behave badly when the user enters an invalid date. Raising an exception for bad data isn't an ideal user experience. The recipe will take a different approach than this example.

We often need to wrap this in additional processing to make it more useful. The calendar is complex, and we'd hate to accept February 31 without warning a user that it is not a proper date.

How to do it...

1. If the input is a password or something equally subject to redaction, the `input()` function isn't the best choice. If passwords or other secrets are involved, then use the `getpass.getpass()` function. This means we need the following import when secrets are involved:

```
from getpass import getpass
```

Otherwise, when secret input is not required, we'll use the built-in `input()` function, and no additional import is required.

2. Determine which prompt will be used. In our example, we provided a field name and a hint about the type of data expected as the prompt string argument to the `input()` or `getpass()` function. It can help to separate the input from the text-to-integer conversion. This recipe doesn't follow the snippet shown previously; it breaks the operation into two separate steps. First, get the text value:

```
year_text = input("year: ")
```

3. Determine how to validate each item in isolation. The simplest case is a single value with a single rule that covers everything. In more complex cases – like this one – each individual element is a number with a range constraint. In a later step, we'll look at validating the composite item:

```
year = int(year_text)
```

4. Wrap the input and validation into a `while-try` block that looks like this:

```
year = None
while year is None:
    year_text = input("year: ")
    try:
        year = int(year_text)
    except ValueError as ex:
        print(ex)
```

This applies a single validation rule, the `int(year_txt)` expression, to ensure that the input is an integer. If the `int()` function works without raising an exception, the resulting `year` object is the desired integer. If the `int()` function raises an exception, this is reported with an error message. The `while` statement leads to a repeat of the input and conversion sequence of steps until the value of the `year` variable is not `None`.

Raising an exception for faulty input allows us the most flexibility. We can extend this with additional exception classes for other conditions the input must meet. In some cases, we may need to define our own unique customized exceptions for data validation.

In some cases, the error message can be printed to `sys.stderr` instead of `sys.stdout`. To do this, we could use `print(ex, file=sys.stderr)`. Mixing standard output and standard error may not work out well because the OS-level buffering for these two files is sometimes different, leading to confusing output. It's often a good idea to stick to a single channel.

This processing only covers the `year` field. We still need to get values for the `month` and `day` fields. This means we'll need three nearly identical loops for each of these three fields of a complex date object. Rather than copying and pasting nearly identical code, we need to restructure this input and validate the sequence into a separate function. We'll call the new function `get_integer()`.

Here's the definition:

```
def get_integer(prompt: str) -> int:
    while True:
        value_text = input(prompt)
        try:
            value = int(value_text)
            return value
        except ValueError as ex:
            print(ex)
```

This function will use the built-in `input()` function to prompt the user for input. It uses the `int()` function to try and create an integer value. If the conversion works, the value is returned. If the conversion raises a `ValueError` exception, this is displayed to the user and the input is attempted again.

We can combine this into an overall process for getting the three integers of a date. This will involve the same `while-try`, but applied to the composite object. It will look like this:

```
def get_date2() -> date:
    while True:
        year = get_integer("year: ")
        month = get_integer("month [1-12]: ")
        day = get_integer("day [1-31]: ")
        try:
            result = date(year, month, day)
            return result
        except ValueError as ex:
            problem = f"invalid, {ex}"
```

This uses individual `while-try` processing sequences in the `get_integer()` function to get the individual values that make up a date. Then it uses the `date()` constructor to create a `date` object from the individual fields. If the `date` object – as a whole – can't be built because the pieces are invalid, then the `year`, `month`, and `day` must be re-entered to create a valid `date`.

Given a year and a month, we can actually determine a slightly narrower range for the number of days. This is complex because months have different numbers of days, varying from 28 to 31, and February has a number of days that varies with the type of year.

We can compute the starting date of the next month and use a `timedelta` object to provide the number of days between the two dates:

```
day_1_date = date(year, month, 1)
if month == 12:
```

```
        next_year, next_month = year+1, 1
    else:
        next_year, next_month = year, month+1
    day_end_date = date(next_year, next_month, 1)
    stop = (day_end_date - day_1_date).days

    day = get_integer(f"day [1-{stop}]: ")
```

This will compute the length of any given month for a given year. The algorithm works by computing the first day of a given year and month. It then computes the first day of the next month (which may be the first month of the next year).

The number of days between these dates is the number of days in the given month. The `(day_end_date - day_1_date).days` expression extracts the number of days from the `timedelta` object. This can be used to display a more helpful prompt for the number of days that are valid in a given month.

How it works...

We need to decompose the input problem into several separate but closely related problems. We can imagine a tower of conversion steps. At the bottom layer is the initial interaction with the user. We identified two of the common ways to handle this:

- `input()`: This prompts and reads from a user
- `getpass.getpass()`: This prompts and reads passwords without an echo

These two functions provide the essential console interaction. There are other libraries that can provide more sophisticated interactions, if that's required. For example, the `click` project has sophisticated prompting capabilities. See `https://click.palletsprojects.com/en/7.x/`.

On top of the foundation, we've built several tiers of validation processing. The tiers are as follows:

- A **general domain** validation: This uses built-in conversion functions such as `int()` or `float()`. These raise `ValueError` exceptions for invalid text.
- A **subdomain** validation: This uses an `if` statement to determine whether values fit any additional constraints, such as ranges. For consistency, this should also raise a `ValueError` exception if the data is invalid.
- **Composite object** validation: This is application-specific checking. For our example, the composite object was an instance of `datetime.date`. This also tends to raise `ValueError` exceptions for dates that are invalid.

There are a lot of potential kinds of constraints that might be imposed on values. For example, we might want only valid OS process IDs, called PIDs. This requires checking the `/proc/<pid>` path on most Linux systems.

For BSD-based systems such as macOS X, the `/proc` filesystem doesn't exist. Instead, something like the following needs to be done to determine if a PID is valid:

```
>>> import subprocess
>>> status = subprocess.run(["ps", str(PID)], check=True, text=True)
```

For Windows, the command would look like this:

```
>>> status = subprocess. run(
...     ["tasklist", "/fi", f'"PID eq {PID}"'], check=True, text=True)
```

Either of these two functions would need to be part of the input validation to ensure that the user is entering a proper PID value. This check can only be made safely when the value of the `PID` variable is a number.

There's more...

We have several alternatives for user input that involve slightly different approaches. We'll look at these two topics in detail:

- **Complex text**: This will involve the simple use of `input()` with clever parsing of the source text.
- **Interaction via the `cmd` module**: This involves a more complex class and somewhat simpler parsing.

We'll start by looking at ways to process more complex text using more sophisticated parsing.

Complex text parsing

A simple date value requires three separate fields. A more complex date-time that includes a time zone offset from UTC involves seven separate fields: year, month, day, hour, minute, second, and time zone. Prompting for each individual field can be tedious for the person entering all those details. The user experience might be improved by reading and parsing a complex string rather than a large number of individual fields:

```
def get_date3() -> date:
    while True:
        raw_date_str = input("date [yyyy-mm-dd]: ")
        try:
            input_date = datetime.strptime(
                raw_date_str, "%Y-%m-%d").date()
            return input_date
        except ValueError as ex:
            print(f"invalid date, {ex}")
```

We've used the `strptime()` function to parse a time string in a given format. We've emphasized the expected date format in the prompt that's provided in the `input()` function. The `datetime` module provides a `ValueError` exception for data that's not in the right format as well as for non-dates that are in the right format; `2019-2-31`, for example, also raises a `ValueError` exception.

This style of input requires the user to enter a more complex string. Since it's a single string that includes all of the details for a date, many people find it easier to use than a number of individual prompts.

Note that both techniques - gathering individual fields and processing a complex string - depend on the underlying `input()` function.

Interaction via the cmd module

The `cmd` module includes the `Cmd` class, which can be used to build an interactive interface. This takes a dramatically different approach to the notion of user interaction. It does not rely on using `input()` explicitly.

We'll look at this closely in the *Using cmd for creating command-line applications* recipe.

See also

In the reference material for the SunOS operating system, which is now owned by Oracle, there is a collection of commands that prompt for different kinds of user inputs:

`https://docs.oracle.com/cd/E19683-01/816-0210/6m6nb7m5d/index.html`

Specifically, all of these commands beginning with `ck` are for gathering and validating user input. This could be used to define a module of input validation rules:

- `ckdate`: This prompts for and validates a date
- `ckgid`: This prompts for and validates a group ID
- `ckint`: This displays a prompt, verifies, and returns an integer value
- `ckitem`: This builds a menu, prompts for, and returns a menu item
- `ckkeywd`: This prompts for and validates a keyword
- `ckpath`: This displays a prompt, verifies, and returns a pathname
- `ckrange`: This prompts for and validates an integer
- `ckstr`: This displays a prompt, verifies, and returns a string answer
- `cktime`: This displays a prompt, verifies, and returns a time of day
- `ckuid`: This prompts for and validates a user ID
- `ckyorn`: This prompts for and validates yes/no

This is a handy summary of the various kinds of user inputs used to support a command-line application. Another list of validation rules can be extracted from JSON schema definitions; this includes `None`, `Boolean`, `integer`, `float`, and `string`. A number of common string formats include date-time, time, date, email, hostname, IP addresses in version 4 and version 6 format, and URIs. Another source of user input types can be found in the definition of the HTML5 `<input>` tag; this includes `color`, `date`, `datetime-local`, `email`, `file`, `month`, `number`, `password`, `telephone numbers`, `time`, `URL`, and `week-year`.

Debugging with f"{value=}" strings

One of the most important debugging and design tools available in Python is the `print()` function. There are some kinds of formatting options available; we looked at these in the *Using features of the print() function* recipe.

What if we want more flexible output? We have more flexibility with `f"string"` formatting.

Getting ready

Let's look at a multistep process that involves some moderately complex calculations. We'll compute the mean and standard deviation of some sample data. Given these values, we'll locate all items that are more than one standard deviation above the mean:

```
>>> import statistics
>>> size = [2353, 2889, 2195, 3094,
... 725, 1099, 690, 1207, 926,
... 758, 615, 521, 1320]

>>> mean_size = statistics.mean(size)
>>> std_size = statistics.stdev(size)
>>> sig1 = round(mean_size + std_size, 1)
>>> [x for x in size if x > sig1]
[2353, 2889, 3094]
```

This calculation has several working variables. The final list comprehension involves three other variables, `mean_size`, `std_size`, and `sig1`. With so many values used to filter the `size` list, it's difficult to visualize what's going on. It's often helpful to know the steps in the calculation; showing the values of the intermediate variables can be very helpful.

How to do it...

The `f"{name=}"` string will have both the literal `name=` and the value for the `name` variable. Using this with a `print()` function looks as follows:

```
>>> print(
...     f"{mean_size=:.2f}, {std_size=:.2f}"
... )
mean_size=1414.77, std_size=901.10
```

We can use `{name=}` to put any variable into the f-string and see the value. These examples in the code above include `:.2f` as the format specification to show the values rounded to two decimal places. Another common suffix is `!r`; to show the internal representation of the object, we might use `f"{name=!r}"`.

How it works...

For more background on the formatting options, refer to the *Building complex strings with f"strings"* recipe in *Chapter 1, Numbers, Strings, and Tuples*. Python 3.8 extends the basic f-string formatting to introduce the `"="` formatting option to display a variable and the value of the variable.

There is a very handy extension to this capability. We can actually use any expression on the left of the `"="` option in the f-string. This will show the expression and the value computed by the expression, providing us with even more debugging information.

There's more...

For example, we can use this more flexible format to include additional calculations that aren't simply local variables:

```
>>> print(
...     f"{mean_size=:.2f}, {std_size=:.2f},"
...     f" {mean_size+2*std_size=:.2f}"
... )
mean_size=1414.77, std_size=901.10, mean_size+2*std_size=3216.97
```

We've computed a new value, `mean_size+2*std_size`, that appears only inside the formatted output. This lets us display intermediate computed results without having to create an extra variable.

See also

- Refer to the *Building complex strings with f"strings"* recipe in *Chapter 1, Numbers, Strings, and Tuples*, for more of the things that can be done with the `format()` method.
- Refer to the *Using features of the print() function* recipe earlier in this chapter for other formatting options.

Using argparse to get command-line input

For some applications, it can be better to get the user input from the OS command line without a lot of human interaction. We'd prefer to parse the command-line argument values and either perform the processing or report an error.

For example, at the OS level, we might want to run a program like this:

```
% python3 ch05_r04.py -r KM 36.12,-86.67 33.94,-118.40
From (36.12, -86.67) to (33.94, -118.4) in KM = 2887.35
```

The OS prompt is `%`. We entered a command of `python3 ch05_r04.py`. This command had an optional argument, `-r KM`, and two positional arguments of `36.12,-86.67` and `33.94,-118.40`.

The program parses the command-line arguments and writes the result back to the console. This allows a very simple kind of user interaction. It keeps the program very simple. It allows the user to write a shell script to invoke the program or merge the program with other Python programs to create a higher-level program.

If the user enters something incorrect, the interaction might look like this:

```
% python3 ch05_r04.py -r KM 36.12,-86.67 33.94,-118asd
usage: ch05_r04.py [-h] [-r {NM,MI,KM}] p1 p2
ch05_r04.py: error: argument p2: could not convert string to float:
'-118asd'
```

An invalid argument value of `-118asd` leads to an error message. The program stopped with an error status code. For the most part, the user can hit the up-arrow key to get the previous command line back, make a change, and run the program again. The interaction is delegated to the OS command line.

The name of the program – `ch05_r04` – isn't too informative. We could perhaps have chosen a more informative name. The positional arguments are two (latitude, longitude) pairs. The output shows the distance between the two in the given units.

How do we parse argument values from the command line?

Getting ready

The first thing we need to do is to refactor our code to create three separate functions:

- A function to get the arguments from the command line. To fit well with the `argparse` module, this function will almost always return an `argparse.Namespace` object.

- A function that does the real work. It helps if this function is designed so that it makes no reference to the command-line options in any direct way. The intent is to define a function to be reused in a variety of contexts, one of which is with parameters from the command line.
- A `main` function that gathers options and invokes the *real work* function with the appropriate argument values.

Here's our *real work* function, `display()`:

```
from ch03_r05 import haversine, MI, NM, KM
def display(lat1: float, lon1: float, lat2: float, lon2: float, r:
str) -> None:
    r_float = {"NM": NM, "KM": KM, "MI": MI}[r]
    d = haversine(lat1, lon1, lat2, lon2, r_float)
    print(f"From {lat1},{lon1} to {lat2},{lon2} in {r} = {d:.2f}")
```

We've imported the core calculation, `haversine()`, from another module. We've provided argument values to this function and used an f-string to display the final result message.

We've based this on the calculations shown in the examples in the *Picking an order for parameters based on partial functions* recipe in *Chapter 3, Function Definitions*:

$$a = \sqrt{\sin^2 \frac{lat_2 - lat_1}{2} + \cos(lat_1)\cos(lat_2)\sin^2 \frac{lat_2 - lat_1}{2}}$$

$$c = 2\sin^{-1} a$$

The essential calculation yields the central angle, c, between two points. The angle is measured in radians. We convert it into distance by multiplying by the Earth's mean radius in whatever unit we like. If we multiply angle c by a radius of 3,959 miles, the distance, we'll convert the angle to miles.

Note that we expect the distance conversion factor, *r*, to be provided as a string. This function will then map the string to an actual floating-point value, `r_float`. The `"MI"` string, for example, maps to the conversion value from radians to miles, `MI`, equal to 3,959.

Here's how the function looks when it's used inside Python:

```
>>> from ch05_r04 import display
>>> display(36.12, -86.67, 33.94, -118.4, 'NM')
From 36.12,-86.67 to 33.94,-118.4 in NM = 1558.53
```

This function has two important design features. The first feature is it avoids references to features of the `argparse.Namespace` object that's created by argument parsing. Our goal is to have a function that we can reuse in a number of alternative contexts. We need to keep the input and output elements of the user interface separate.

The second design feature is this function displays a value computed by another function. This is a helpful decomposition of the problem. We've separated the user experience of printed output from the essential calculation. This fits the general design pattern of separating processing into tiers and isolating the presentation tier from the application tier.

How to do it...

1. Define the overall argument parsing function:

   ```
   def get_options(argv: List[str]) -> argparse.Namespace:
   ```

2. Create the `parser` object:

   ```
       parser = argparse.ArgumentParser()
   ```

3. Add the various types of arguments to the `parser` object. Sometimes this is difficult because we're still refining the user experience. It's difficult to imagine all the ways in which people will use a program and all of the questions they might have. For our example, we have two mandatory, positional arguments, and an optional argument:

   - Point 1 latitude and longitude
   - Point 2 latitude and longitude
   - Optional units of distance; we'll provide nautical miles as the default:

   ```
   parser.add_argument(
       "-u", "--units",
       action="store", choices=("NM", "MI", "KM"), default="NM")
   parser.add_argument(
       "p1", action="store", type=point_type)
   parser.add_argument(
       "p2", action="store", type=point_type)
   options = parser.parse_args(argv)
   ```

   We've added optional and mandatory arguments. The first is the `-u` argument, which starts with a single dash, `-`, to mark it as optional. Additionally, a longer double dash version was added, `--units`, in this case. These are equivalent, and either can be used on the command line.

   The action of `'store'` will store any value that follows the `-r` option in the command line. We've listed the three possible choices and provided a default. The parser will validate the input and write appropriate errors if the input isn't one of these three values.

The mandatory arguments are named without a - prefix. These also use an action of `'store'`; since this is the default action it doesn't really need to be stated. The function provided as the `type` argument is used to convert the source string to an appropriate Python object. We'll look at the `point_type()` validation function in this section.

4. Evaluate the `parse_args()` method of the parser object created in *step 2*:

```
options = parser.parse_args(argv)
```

By default, the parser uses the values from `sys.argv`, which are the command-line argument values entered by the user. Testing is much easier when we can provide an explicit argument value.

Here's the final function:

```
def get_options(argv: List[str]) -> argparse.Namespace:
    parser = argparse.ArgumentParser()
    parser.add_argument("-r", action="store",
                        choices=("NM", "MI", "KM"), default="NM")
    parser.add_argument("p1", action="store", type=point_type)
    parser.add_argument("p2", action="store", type=point_type)
    options = parser.parse_args(argv)
    return options
```

This relies on the `point_type()` function to both validate the string and convert it to an object of a more useful type. We might use `type = int` or `type = float` to convert to a number.

In our example, we used `point_type()` to convert a string to a (latitude, longitude) two-tuple. Here's the definition of this function:

```
def point_type(text: str) -> Tuple[float, float]:
    try:
        lat_str, lon_str = text.split(",")
        lat = float(lat_str)
        lon = float(lon_str)
        return lat, lon
    except ValueError as ex:
        raise argparse.ArgumentTypeError(ex)
```

The `point_type()` function parses the input values. First, it separates the two values at the `,` character. It attempts a floating-point conversion on each part. If the `float()` functions both work, we have a valid latitude and longitude that we can return as a pair of floating-point values.

If anything goes wrong, an exception will be raised. From this exception, we'll raise an `ArgumentTypeError` exception. This is caught by the `argparse` module and causes it to report the error to the user.

Here's the main script that combines the option parser and the output display functions:

```
def main(argv: List[str] = sys.argv[1:]) -> None:
    options = get_options(argv)
    lat_1, lon_1 = options.p1
    lat_2, lon_2 = options.p2
    display(lat_1, lon_1, lat_2, lon_2, options.r)


if __name__ == "__main__":
    main()
```

This main script connects the user inputs to the displayed output. It does this by parsing the command-line options. Given the values provided by the user, these are decomposed into values required by the `display()` function, isolating the processing from the input parsing. Let's take a closer look at how argument parsing works.

How it works...

The argument parser works in three stages:

1. Define the overall context by creating a parser object as an instance of `ArgumentParser`. We can provide information such as the overall program description. We can also provide a formatter and other options here.
2. Add individual arguments with the `add_argument()` method. These can include optional arguments as well as required arguments. Each argument can have a number of features to provide different kinds of syntax. We'll look at a number of the alternatives in the *There's more...* section.
3. Parse the actual command-line inputs. The parser's `parse()` method will use `sys.argv` automatically. We can provide an explicit value instead of the `sys.argv` values. The most common reason for providing an override value is to allow more complete unit testing.

Some simple programs will have a few optional arguments. A more complex program may have many optional arguments.

It's common to have a filename as a positional argument. When a program reads one or more files, the filenames are provided in the command line, as follows:

```
python3 some_program.py *.rst
```

We've used the Linux shell's **globbing** feature: the `*.rst` string is expanded into a list of all files that match the naming rule. This is a feature of the Linux shell, and it happens before the Python interpreter starts. This list of files can be processed using an argument defined as follows:

```
parser.add_argument('file', nargs='*')
```

All of the names on the command line that do not start with the - character will be collected into the `file` value in the object built by the parser.

We can then use the following:

```
for filename in options.file:
    process(filename)
```

This will process each file given in the command line.

For Windows programs, the shell doesn't glob filenames from wildcard patterns, and the application must deal with filenames that contain wildcard characters like "*" and "?" in them. The Python `glob` module can help with this. Also, the `pathlib` module can create `Path` objects, which include globbing features.

To support Windows, we might have something like this inside the `get_options()` function. This will expand file strings into all matching names:

```
if platform.system() == "Windows":
    options.file = list(
        name
            for wildcard in options.file
                for name in Path().glob(wildcard)
    )
```

This will expand all of the names in the `file` parameter to create a new list similar to the list created by the Linux and macOS platforms.

It can be difficult to refer to a file with an asterisk or question mark in the name. For example, a file named `something*.py` appears to be a pattern for **globbing**, not a single filename. We can enclose the pattern wildcard character in `[]` to create a name that matches literally: `something[*].py` will only match the file named `something*.py`.

Some applications have very complex argument parsing options. Very complex applications may have dozens of individual commands. As an example, look at the `git` version control program; this application uses dozens of separate commands, such as `git clone`, `git commit`, and `git push`. Each of these commands has unique argument parsing requirements. We can use `argparse` to create a complex hierarchy of these commands and their distinct sets of arguments.

There's more...

What kinds of arguments can we process? There are a lot of argument styles in common use. All of these variations are defined using the `add_argument()` method of a parser:

- **Simple options**: The `-o` or `-option` arguments are often used to enable or disable features of a program. These are often implemented with `add_argument()` parameters of `action='store_true', default=False`. Sometimes the implementation is simpler if the application uses `action='store_false', default=True`. The choice of default value and stored value may simplify the programming, but it won't change the user's experience.
- **Simple options with non-trivial objects**: The user sees this is as simple `-o` or `--option` arguments. We may want to implement this using a more complex object that's not a simple Boolean constant. We can use `action='store_const', const=some_object`, and `default=another_object`. As modules, classes, and functions are also objects, a great deal of sophistication is available here.
- **Options with values**: We showed `-r unit` as an argument that accepted the string name for the units to use. We implemented this with an `action='store'` assignment to store the supplied string value. We can also use the `type=function` option to provide a function that validates or converts the input into a useful form.
- **Options that increment a counter**: One common technique is to have a debugging log that has multiple levels of detail. We can use `action='count', default=0` to count the number of times a given argument is present. The user can provide `-v` for verbose output and `-vv` for very verbose output. The argument parser treats `-vv` as two instances of the `-v` argument, which means that the value will increase from the initial value of `0` to `2`.
- **Options that accumulate a list**: We might have an option for which the user might want to provide more than one value. We could, for example, use a list of distance values. We could have an argument definition with `action='append', default=[]`. This would allow the user to use `-r NM -r KM` to get a display in both nautical miles and kilometers. This would require a significant change to the `display()` function, of course, to handle multiple units in a collection.
- **Show the help text**: If we do nothing, then `-h` and `--help` will display a help message and exit. This will provide the user with useful information. We can disable this or change the argument string, if we need to. This is a widely used convention, so it seems best to do nothing so that it's a feature of our program.
- **Show the version number**: It's common to have `-Version` as an argument to display the version number and exit. We implement this with `add_argument("--Version", action="version", version="v 3.14")`. We provide an action of `version` and an additional keyword argument that sets the version to display.

This covers most of the common cases for command-line argument processing. Generally, we'll try to leverage these common styles of arguments when we write our own applications. If we strive to use simple, widely used argument styles, our users are somewhat more likely to understand how our application works.

There are a few Linux commands that have even more complex command-line syntax. Some Linux programs, such as `find` or `expr`, have arguments that can't easily be processed by `argparse`. For these edge cases, we would need to write our own parser using the values of `sys.argv` directly.

See also

- We looked at how to get interactive user input in the *Using input() and getpass() for user input* recipe.
- We'll look at a way to add even more flexibility to this in the *Using the OS environment settings* recipe.

Using cmd to create command-line applications

There are several ways of creating interactive applications. The *Using input() and getpass() for user input* recipe looked at functions such as `input()` and `getpass.getpass()`. The *Using argparse to get command-line input* recipe showed us how to use `argparse` to create applications with which a user can interact from the OS command line.

We have a third way to create interactive applications: using the `cmd` module. This module will prompt the user for input, and then invoke a specific method of the class we provide.

Here's how the interaction will look – we've marked user input like this: "`help`":

```
A dice rolling tool. ? for help.
] help

Documented commands (type help <topic>):
========================================
dice  help  reroll  roll

Undocumented commands:
======================
EOF  quit

] help roll
```

```
Roll the dice. Use the dice command to set the number of dice.
] help dice
Sets the number of dice to roll.
] dice 5
Rolling 5 dice
] roll
[6, 6, 4, 3, 3]
]
```

There's an introductory message from the application with a very short explanation. The application displays a prompt, `]`. The user can then enter any of the available commands.

When we enter `help` as a command, we see a display of the commands. Four of the commands have further details. The other two, `EOF` and `quit`, have no further details available.

When we enter `help roll`, we see a brief summary for the `roll` command. Similarly, entering `help dice` displays information about the `dice` command. We entered the `dice 5` command to set the number of dice, and then the `roll` command showed the results of rolling five dice. This shows the essence of how an interactive command-line application prompts for input, reads commands, evaluates, and prints a result.

Getting ready

The core feature of the `cmd.Cmd` application is a **read-evaluate-print loop** (**REPL**). This kind of application works well when there are a large number of individual state changes and a large number of commands to make those state changes.

We'll make use of a simple, stateful dice game. The idea is to have a handful of dice, some of which can be rolled and some of which are frozen. This means our `Cmd` class definition will have some attributes that describe the current state of the handful of dice.

We'll define a small domain of commands, to roll and re-roll a handful of dice. The interaction will look like the following:

```
] roll
[4, 4, 1, 6, 4, 6]
] reroll 2 3 5
[4, 4, 6, 5, 4, 5] (reroll 1)
] reroll 2 3 5
[4, 4, 1, 3, 4, 3] (reroll 2)
```

In this example, the `roll` command rolled six dice. The two `reroll` commands created a hand for a particular game by preserving the dice from positions 0, 1, and 4, and rerolling the dice in positions 2, 3, and 5.

How can we create stateful, interactive applications with an REPL?

How to do it...

1. Import the `cmd` module to make the `cmd.Cmd` class definition available:

```
import cmd
```

2. Define an extension to `cmd.Cmd`:

```
class DiceCLI(cmd.Cmd):
```

3. Define any initialization required in the `preloop()` method:

```
def preloop(self):
    self.n_dice = 6
    self.dice = None  # no initial roll.
    self.reroll_count = 0
```

   This `preloop()` method is evaluated just once when the processing starts. The `self` argument is a requirement for methods within a class. For now, it's a simply required syntax. In *Chapter 7, Basics of Classes and Objects*, we'll look at this more closely.

   Initialization can also be done in an `__init__()` method. Doing this is a bit more complex, though, because it must collaborate with the `Cmd` class initialization. It's easier to do initialization separately in the `preloop()` method.

4. For each command, create a `do_command()` method. The name of the method will be the command, prefixed by `do_`. The user's input text after the command will be provided as an argument value to the method. The docstring comment in the method definition is the help text for the command. Here are two examples for the `roll` command and the `reroll` command:

```
def do_roll(self, arg: str) -> bool:
    """Roll the dice. Use the dice command to set the number
of dice."""
    self.dice = [random.randint(1, 6) for _ in range(self.n_
dice)]
    print(f"{self.dice}")
    return False

def do_reroll(self, arg: str) -> bool:      """Reroll selected
dice. Provide the 0-based positions."""
    try:
        positions = map(int, arg.split())
    except ValueError as ex:
        print(ex)
```

```
            return False
        for p in positions:
            self.dice[p] = random.randint(1, 6)
        self.reroll_count += 1
        print(f"{self.dice} (reroll {self.reroll_count})")
        return False
```

5. Parse and validate the arguments to the commands that use them. The user's input after the command will be provided as the value of the first positional argument to the method. If the arguments are invalid, the method prints a message and returns, making no state change. If the arguments are valid, the method can continue past the validation step. In this example, the only validation is to be sure the number is valid. Additional checks could be added to ensure that the number is in a sensible range:

```
    def do_dice(self, arg: str) -> bool:
        """Sets the number of dice to roll."""
        try:
            self.n_dice = int(arg)
        except ValueError:
            print(f"{arg!r} is invalid")
            return False
        self.dice = None
        print(f"Rolling {self.n_dice} dice")
        return False
```

6. Write the main script. This will create an instance of this class and execute the `cmdloop()` method:

```
if __name__ == "__main__":
    game = DiceCLI()
    game.cmdloop()
```

We've created an instance of our `DiceCLI` subclass of `Cmd`. When we execute the `cmdloop()` method, the class will write any introductory messages that have been provided, write the prompt, and read a command.

How it works...

The `Cmd` module contains a large number of built-in features for displaying a prompt, reading input from a user, and then locating the proper method based on the user's input.

For example, when we enter `dice 5`, the built-in methods of the `Cmd` superclass will strip the first word from the input, `dice`, prefix this with `do_`, and then evaluate the method that implements the command. The argument value will be the string `"5"`.

If we enter a command for which there's no matching `do_` method, the command processor writes an error message. This is done automatically; we don't need to write any code to handle invalid commands.

Some methods, such as `do_help()`, are already part of the application. These methods will summarize the other `do_*` methods. When one of our methods has a docstring, this can be displayed by the built-in help feature.

The `Cmd` class relies on Python's facilities for introspection. An instance of the class can examine the method names to locate all of the methods that start with `do_`. They're available in a class-level `__dict__` attribute. Introspection is an advanced topic, one that will be touched on in *Chapter 8, More Advanced Class Design*.

There's more...

The `Cmd` class has a number of additional places where we can add interactive features:

- We can define specific `help_*()` methods that become part of the help topics.
- When any of the `do_*` methods return a non-`False` value, the loop will end. We might want to add a `do_quit()` method that has `return True` as its body. This will end the command-processing loop.
- We might provide a method named `emptyline()` to respond to blank lines. One choice is to do nothing quietly. Another common choice is to have a default action that's taken when the user doesn't enter a command.
- The `default()` method is evaluated when the user's input does not match any of the `do_*` methods. This might be used for more advanced parsing of the input.
- The `postloop()` method can be used to do some processing just after the loop finishes. This would be a good place to write a summary. This also requires a `do_*` method that returns a value - any non-`False` value - to end the command loop.

Also, there are a number of attributes we can set. These are class-level variables that would be peers of the method definitions:

- The `prompt` attribute is the prompt string to write. For our example, we can do the following:

```
class DiceCLI(cmd.Cmd):
    prompt="] "
```

- The `intro` attribute is the introductory message.

- We can tailor the help output by setting `doc_header`, `undoc_header`, `misc_header`, and `ruler` attributes. These will all alter how the help output looks.

The goal is to be able to create a tidy class that handles user interaction in a way that's simple and flexible. This class creates an application that has a lot of features in common with Python's REPL. It also has features in common with many command-line programs that prompt for user input.

One example of these interactive applications is the command-line FTP client in Linux. It has a prompt of `<ftp>`, and it parses dozens of individual FTP commands. Entering `help` will show all of the various internal commands that are part of FTP interaction.

See also

- We'll look at class definitions in *Chapter 7, Basics of Classes and Objects*, and *Chapter 8, More Advanced Class Design.*

Using the OS environment settings

There are several ways to look at inputs provided by the users of our software:

- **Interactive input**: This is provided by the user on demand, as they interact with the application or service.
- **Command-line arguments**: These are provided once, when the program is started.
- **Environment variables**: These are OS-level settings. There are several ways these can be set, as shown in the following list:
  - Environment variables can be set at the command line, when the application starts.
  - They can be configured for a user in a configuration file for the user's selected shell. For example, if using **zsh**, these files are the `~/.zshrc` file and the `~/.profile` file. There can also be system-wide files, like `/etc/zshrc`. This makes the values persistent and less interactive than the command line. Other shells offer other filenames for settings and configurations unique to the shell.
  - In Windows, there's the Advanced Settings option, which allows someone to set a long-term configuration.
- **Configuration files**: These vary widely by application. The idea is to edit the text configuration file and make these options or arguments available for long periods of time. These might apply to multiple users or even to all users of a given system. Configuration files often have the longest time span.

In the *Using input() and getpass() for user input* and *Using cmd for creating command-line applications* recipes, we looked at interaction with the user. In the *Using argparse to get command-line input* recipe, we looked at how to handle command-line arguments. We'll look at configuration files in *Chapter 13, Application Integration: Configuration*.

The environment variables are available through the `os` module. How can we get an application's configuration based on these OS-level settings?

Getting ready

We may want to provide information of various types to a program via OS environment variable settings. There's a profound limitation here: the OS settings can only be string values. This means that many kinds of settings will require some code to parse the value and create proper Python objects from the string.

When we work with `argparse` to parse command-line arguments, this module can do some data conversions for us. When we use `os` to process environment variables; we'll have to implement the conversion ourselves.

In the *Using argparse to get command-line input* recipe, we wrapped the `haversine()` function in a simple application that parsed command-line arguments.

At the OS level, we created a program that worked like this:

```
% python3 ch05_r04.py -r KM 36.12,-86.67 33.94,-118.40
From (36.12, -86.67) to (33.94, -118.4) in KM = 2887.35
```

After using this version of the application for a while, we found that we're often using nautical miles to compute distances from where our boat is anchored. We'd really like to have default values for one of the input points as well as the `-r` argument.

Since a boat can be anchored in a variety of places, we need to change the default without having to tweak the actual code.

We'll set an OS environment variable, `UNITS`, with the distance units. We can set another variable, `HOME_PORT`, with the home point. We want to be able to do the following:

```
% UNITS=NM
% HOME_PORT=36.842952,-76.300171
% python3 ch05_r06.py 36.12,-86.67
From 36.12,-86.67 to 36.842952,-76.300171 in NM = 502.23
```

The units and the home point values are provided to the application via the OS environment. This can be set in a configuration file so that we can make easy changes. It can also be set manually, as shown in the example.

How to do it...

1. Import the `os` module. The OS environment is available through this module:

```
import os
```

2. Import any other classes or objects needed for the application:

```
from Chapter_03.ch03_r08 import haversine, MI, NM, KM
from Chapter_05.ch05_r04 import point_type, display
```

3. Define a function that will use the environment values as defaults for optional command-line arguments. The default set of arguments to parse comes from `sys.argv`, so it's important to also import the `sys` module:

```
def get_options(argv: List[str] = sys.argv[1:]) -> argparse.
Namespace:
```

4. Gather default values from the OS environment settings. This includes any validation required:

```
default_units = os.environ.get("UNITS", "KM")
if default_units not in ("KM", "NM", "MI"):
    sys.exit(f"Invalid UNITS, {default_units!r} not KM, NM, or
MI")
default_home_port = os.environ.get("HOME_PORT")
```

The `sys.exit()` function handles the error processing nicely. It will print the message and exit with a non-zero status code.

5. Create the `parser` attribute. Provide any default values for the relevant arguments. This depends on the `argparse` module, which must also be imported:

```
parser = argparse.ArgumentParser()

parser.add_argument(
    "-u", "--units",
    action="store", choices=("NM", "MI", "KM"),
default=default_units
)
parser.add_argument("p1", action="store", type=point_type)
parser.add_argument(
    "p2", nargs="?", action="store", type=point_type,
default=default_home_port
)
options = parser.parse_args(argv)
```

6. Do any additional validation to ensure that arguments are set properly. In this example, it's possible to have no value for `HOME_PORT` and no value provided for the second command-line argument. This requires an `if` statement and a call to `sys.exit()`:

```
if options.p2 is None:
    sys.exit("Neither HOME_PORT nor p2 argument provided.")
```

7. Return the `options` object with the set of valid arguments:

```
return options
```

This will allow the `-r` argument and the second point to be completely optional. The argument parser will use the configuration information to supply default values if these are omitted from the command line.

Use the *Using argparse to get command-line input* recipe for ways to process the options created by the `get_options()` function.

How it works...

We've used the OS environment variables to create default values that can be overridden by command-line arguments. If the environment variable is set, that string is provided as the default to the argument definition. If the environment variable is not set, then an application-level default value is used.

In the case of the `UNITS` variable, in this example, the application uses kilometers as the default if the OS environment variable is not set.

This gives us three tiers of interaction:

- We can define settings in a configuration file appropriate to the shell in use. For **bash** it is the `.bashrc` file; for **zsh**, it is the `.zshrc` file. For Windows, we can use the **Windows Advanced Settings** option to make a change that is persistent. This value will be used each time we log in or create a new command window.
- We can set the OS environment interactively at the command line. This will last as long as our session lasts. When we log out or close the command window, this value will be lost.
- We can provide a unique value through the command-line arguments each time the program is run.

Note that there's no built-in or automatic validation of the values retrieved from environment variables. We'll need to validate these strings to ensure that they're meaningful.

Also note that we've repeated the list of valid units in several places. This violates the **Don't Repeat Yourself** (**DRY**) principle. A global variable with a valid collection of values is a good improvement to make. (Python lacks formal constants, which are variables that cannot be changed. It's common to treat globals as if they are constants that should not be changed.)

There's more...

The *Using argparse to get command-line input* recipe shows a slightly different way to handle the default command-line arguments available from `sys.argv`. The first of the arguments is the name of the Python application being executed and is not often relevant to argument parsing.

he value of `sys.argv` will be a list of strings:

```
['ch05_r06.py', '-r', 'NM', '36.12,-86.67']
```

We have to skip the initial value in `sys.argv[0]` at some point in the processing. We have two choices:

- In this recipe, we discard the extra item as late as possible in the parsing process. The first item is skipped when providing `sys.argv[1:]` to the parser.
- In the previous example, we discarded the value earlier in the processing. The `main()` function used `options = get_options(sys.argv[1:])` to provide the shorter list to the parser.

Generally, the only relevant distinction between the two approaches is the number and complexity of the unit tests. This recipe will require a unit test that includes an initial argument string, which will be discarded during parsing.

See also

- We'll look at numerous ways to handle configuration files in *Chapter 13, Application Integration: Configuration.*

7
Basics of Classes and Objects

The point of computing is to process data. We often encapsulate the processing and the data into a single definition. We can organize objects into classes with a common collection of attributes to define their internal state and common behavior. Each instance of a class is a distinct object with unique internal state.

This concept of state and behavior applies particularly well to the way games work. When building something like an interactive game, the user's actions update the game state. Each of the player's possible actions is a method to change the state of the game. In many games this leads to a lot of animation to show the transition from state to state. In a single-player arcade-style game, the enemies or opponents will often be separate objects, each with an internal state that changes based on other enemy actions and the player's actions.

On the other hand, when we think of a casino game, such as *Craps*, there are only two game states, called "point off" and "point on." The transitions are shown to players by moving markers and chips around on a casino table. The game state changes based on rolls of the dice, irrespective of the player's betting actions.

The point of object-oriented design is to define current state with attributes of an object. The object is a member of a broader class of similar objects. The methods of each member of the class will lead to state changes on that object.

In this chapter, we will look at the following recipes:

- Using a class to encapsulate data and processing
- Essential type hints for class definitions
- Designing classes with lots of processing

- Using `typing.NamedTuple` for immutable objects
- Using dataclasses for mutable objects
- Using frozen dataclasses for immutable objects
- Optimizing small objects with `__slots__`
- Using more sophisticated collections
- Extending a built-in collection – a `list` that does statistics
- Using properties for lazy attributes
- Creating contexts and context managers
- Managing multiple contexts with multiple resources

The subject of object-oriented design is quite large. In this chapter, we'll cover some of the essentials. We'll start with some foundational concepts, such as how a class definition encapsulates state and processing details for all instances of a class.

Using a class to encapsulate data and processing

Class design is influenced by the SOLID design principles. The Single Responsibility and Interface Segregation principles offer helpful advice. Taken together, these principles advise us that a class should have methods narrowly focused on a single, well-defined responsibility.

Another way of considering a class is as a group of closely-related functions working with common data. We call these methods for working with the data. A class definition should contain the smallest collection of methods for working with the object's data.

We'd like to create class definitions based on a narrow allocation of responsibilities. How can we define responsibilities effectively? What's a good way to design a class?

Getting ready

Let's look at a simple, stateful object—a pair of dice. The context for this is an application that simulates a simple game like *Craps*. This simulation can help measure the house edge, showing exactly how much money we can lose playing *Craps*.

There's an important distinction between a class definition and the various instances of the class, called **objects** or **instances** of the class. Our focus is on writing class definitions that describe the objects' state and behavior. Our overall application works by creating instances of the classes. The behavior that emerges from the collaboration of the objects is the overall goal of the design process.

This idea is called **emergent behavior**. It is an essential ingredient in object-oriented programming. We don't enumerate every behavior of a program. Instead, we decompose the program into objects, with state and behavior captured in class definitions. The interactions among the objects lead to the observable behavior. Because the definition is not in a single block of code, the behavior emerges from the ways separate objects collaborate.

A software object can be viewed as analogous to a thing—a noun. The behaviors of the class can then be viewed as verbs. This identification of nouns and verbs gives us a hint as to how we can proceed to design classes to work effectively.

This leads us to several steps of preparation. We'll provide concrete examples of these steps using a pair of dice for game simulation. We proceed as follows:

1. Write down simple sentences that describe what an instance of the class does. We can call these the problem statements. It's essential to focus on single-verb sentences, with a focus on only the nouns and verbs. Here are some examples:
   - The game of *Craps* has two standard dice.
   - Each die has six faces, with point values from one to six.
   - Dice are rolled by a player. (Or, using active-voice verbs, "A player rolls the dice.")
   - The total of the dice changes the state of the *Craps* game. Those rules are separate from the dice.
   - If the two dice match, the number was rolled the hard way. If the two dice do not match, the roll was made the easy way. Some bets depend on this hard-easy distinction.
2. Identify all of the nouns in the sentences. In this example, the nouns include dice, faces, point values, and player. Nouns may identify different classes of objects. These are **collaborators**. Examples of collaborators include player and game. Nouns may also identify attributes of objects in questions. Examples include face and point value.
3. Identify all the verbs in the sentences. Verbs are generally methods of the class in question. In this example, verbs include roll and match. Sometimes, they are methods of other classes. One example is to change the state of a game, which applies to a `Craps` object more than the dice object.
4. Identify any adjectives. Adjectives are words or phrases that clarify a noun. In many cases, some adjectives will clearly be properties of an object. In other cases, the adjectives will describe relationships among objects. In our example, a phrase such as *the total of the dice* is an example of a prepositional phrase taking the role of an adjective. The *the total of* phrase modifies the noun *the dice*. The total is a property of the pair of dice.

This information is essential for defining the state and behavior of the objects. Having his background information will help us write the class definition.

How to do it...

Since the simulation we're writing involves random throws of dice, we'll depend on `from random import randint` to provide the useful `randint()` function. Given a low and a high value, this returns a random number between the two values; both end values are included in the domain of possible results:

1. Start writing the class with the `class` statement:

```
class Dice:
```

2. Initialize the object's attributes with an `__init__()` method. We'll model the internal state of the dice with a `faces` attribute. The `self` variable is required to be sure that we're referencing an attribute of a given instance of a class. Prior to the first roll of the dice, the faces don't really have a well-defined value, so we'll use the tuple `(0, 0)`. We'll provide a type hint on each attribute to be sure it's used properly throughout the class definition:

```
    def __init__(self) -> None:
        self.faces: Tuple[int, int] = (0, 0)
```

3. Define the object's methods based on the various verbs. When the player rolls the dice, a `roll()` method can set the values shown on the faces of the two dice. We implement this with a method to set the `faces` attribute of the `self` object:

```
    def roll(self) -> None:
        self.faces = (randint(1,6), randint(1,6))
```

   This method mutates the internal state of the object. We've elected to not return a value. This makes our approach somewhat like the approach of Python's built-in collection classes where a method that mutates the object does not return a value.

4. After a player rolls the dice, a `total()` method helps compute the total of the dice. This can be used by a separate object to change the state of the game based on the current state of the dice:

```
    def total(self) -> int:
        return sum(self.faces)
```

5. To resolve bets, two more methods can provide Boolean answers to the hard-way and easy-way questions:

```
    def hardway(self) -> bool:
        return self.faces[0] == self.faces[1]
    def easyway(self) -> bool:
        return self.faces[0] != self.faces[1]
```

It's rare for a casino game to have a rule that has a simple logical inverse. It's more common to have a rare third alternative that has a remarkably bad payoff rule. These two methods are a rare exception to the common pattern.

Here's an example of using this `Dice` class:

1. First, we'll seed the random number generator with a fixed value so that we can get a fixed sequence of results. This is a way of creating a unit test for this class:

```
>>> import random
>>> random.seed(1)
```

2. We'll create a `Dice` object, `d1`. We can then set its state with the `roll()` method. We'll then look at the `total()` method to see what was rolled. We'll examine the state by looking at the `faces` attribute:

```
>>> from ch06_r01 import Dice
>>> d1 = Dice()
>>> d1.roll()
>>> d1.total()
7
>>> d1.faces
(6, 1)
```

3. We'll create a second `Dice` object, `d2`. We can then set its state with the `roll()` method. We'll look at the result of the `total()` method, as well as the `hardway()` method. We'll examine the state by looking at the `faces` attribute:

```
>>> d2 = Dice()
>>> d2.roll()
>>> d2.total()
7
>>> d2.hardway()
False
>>> d2.faces
(1, 6)
```

4. Since the two objects are independent instances of the `Dice` class, a change to `d2` has no effect on `d1`.

How it works...

The core idea here is to use ordinary rules of grammar—nouns, verbs, and adjectives—as a way to identify basic features of a class. In our example, dice are real things. We try to avoid using abstract terms such as randomizers or event generators. It's easier to describe the tangible features of real things, and then define an implementation to match the tangible features.

The idea of rolling the dice is an example physical action that we can model with a method definition. This action of rolling the dice changes the state of the object. In rare cases—1 time in 36—the next state will happen to match the previous state.

Adjectives often hold the potential for confusion. The following are descriptions of the most common ways in which adjectives operate:

- Some adjectives, such as first, last, least, most, next, and previous, will have a simple interpretation. These can have a lazy implementation as a method, or an eager implementation as an attribute value.
- Some adjectives are a more complex phrase, such as *the total of the dice*. This is an adjective phrase built from a noun (*total*) and a preposition (*of*). This, too, can be seen as a method or an attribute.
- Some adjectives involve nouns that appear elsewhere in our software. We might have a phrase such as *the state of the Craps game*, where *state of* modifies another object, *the Craps game*. This is clearly only tangentially related to the dice themselves. This may reflect a relationship between dice and game.
- We might add a sentence to the problem statement such as *the dice are part of the game*. This can help clarify the presence of a relationship between game and dice. Prepositional phrases, such as *are part of*, can always be reversed to create the statement from the other object's point of view: for example, *The game contains dice*. This can help clarify the relationships among objects.

In Python, the attributes of an object are by default dynamic. We don't specify a fixed list of attributes. We can initialize some (or all) of the attributes in the `__init__()` method of a class definition. Since attributes aren't static, we have considerable flexibility in our design.

There's more...

Capturing the essential internal state and methods that cause state change is the first step in good class design. We can summarize some helpful design principles using the acronym **SOLID** :

- **Single Responsibility Principle**: A class should have one clearly defined responsibility.
- **Open/Closed Principle**: A class should be open to extension - generally via inheritance - but closed to modification. We should design our classes so that we don't need to tweak the code to add or change features.
- **Liskov Substitution Principle**: We need to design inheritance so that a subclass can be used in place of the superclass.
- **Interface Segregation Principle**: When writing a problem statement, we want to be sure that collaborating classes have as few dependencies as possible. In many cases, this principle will lead us to decompose large problems into many small class definitions.

- **Dependency Inversion Principle**: It's less than ideal for a class to depend directly on other classes. It's better if a class depends on an abstraction, and a concrete implementation class is substituted for the abstract class.

The goal is to create classes that have the necessary behavior and also adhere to the design principles so they can be extended and reused.

See also

- See the *Using properties for lazy attributes* recipe, where we'll look at the choice between an eager attribute and a lazy property.
- In *Chapter 8, More Advanced Class Design*, we'll look in more depth at class design techniques.
- See *Chapter 11, Testing*, for recipes on how to write appropriate unit tests for the class.

Essential type hints for class definitions

A class name is also a type hint, allowing a direct reference between a variable and the class that should define the objects associated with the variable. This relationship lets tools such as `mypy` reason about our programs to be sure that object references and method references appear to match the type hints in our code.

We'll use type hints in three common places in a class definition:

- In method definitions, we'll use type hints to annotate the parameters and the return type.
- In the `__init__()` method, we may need to provide hints for the instance variables that define the state of the object.
- Any attributes of the class overall. These are not common and type hints are rare here.

Getting ready

We're going to examine a class with a variety of type hints. In this example, our class will model a handful of dice. We'll allow rerolling selected dice, making the instance of the class stateful.

The collection of dice can be set by a first roll, where all the dice are rolled. The class allows subsequent rolls of a subset of dice. The number of rolls is counted, as well.

The type hints will reflect the nature of the collection of dice, the integer counts, a floating-point average value, and a string representation of the hand as a whole. This will show a number of type hints and how to write them.

How to do it...

1. This definition will involve random numbers as well as type hints for sets and lists. We import the `random` module. From the `typing` module, we'll import only the types we need, `Set` and `List`:

```
import random
from typing import Set, List
```

2. Define the class. This is a new type as well:

```
class Dice:
```

3. It's rare for class-level variables to require a type hint. They're almost always created with assignment statements that make the type information clear to a person or a tool like `mypy`. In this case, we want all instances of our class of dice to share a common random number generator:

```
    RNG = random.Random()
```

4. The `__init__()` method creates the instance variables that define the state of the object. In this case, we'll save some configuration details, plus some internal state. The `__init__()` method also has the initialization parameters. Generally, we'll put the type hints on these parameters. Other internal state variables may require type hints to show what kinds of values will be assigned by other methods of the class. In this example, the `faces` attribute has no initial value; we state that when it is set, it will be a `List[int]` object:

```
    def __init__(self, n: int, sides: int = 6) -> None:
        self.n_dice = n
        self.sides = sides
        self.faces: List[int]
        self.roll_number = 0
```

5. Methods that compute new derived values can be annotated with their return type information. Here are three examples to return a string representation, compute the total, and also compute an average of the dice. These functions have return types of `str`, `int`, and `float`, as shown:

```
    def __str__(self) -> str:
        return ", ".join(
            f"{i}: {f}"
            for i, f in enumerate(self.faces)
        )


    def total(self) -> int:
        return sum(self.faces)
```

```
    def average(self) -> float:
        return sum(self.faces) / self.n_dice
```

6. For methods with parameters, we include type hints on the parameters as well as a return type. In this case, the methods that change the internal state also return values. The return value from both methods is a list of dice faces, described as `List[int]`. The parameter for the `reroll()` method is a set of dice to be rolled again, this is shown as a `Set[int]` requiring a set of integers. Python is a little more flexible than this, and we'll look at some alternatives:

```
    def first_roll(self) -> List[int]:
        self.roll_number = 0
        self.faces = [
            self.RNG.randint(1, self.sides)
            for _ in range(self.n_dice)
        ]
        return self.faces

    def reroll(self, positions: Set[int]) -> List[int]:
        self.roll_number += 1
        for p in positions:
            self.faces[p] = self.RNG.randint(1, self.sides)
        return self.faces
```

How it works...

The type hint information is used by programs such as `mypy` to be sure the instances of the class are used properly through the application.

If we try to write a function like the following:

```
def example_mypy_failure() -> None:
    d = Dice(2.5)
    d.first_roll()
    print(d)
```

This attempt to create an instance of the `Dice()` class using a float value for the `n` parameter represents a conflict with the type hints. The hint for the `Dice` class `__init__()` method claimed the argument value should be an integer. The `mypy` program reports the following:

```
Chapter_07/ch07_r02.py:49: error: Argument 1 to "Dice" has incompatible
type "float"; expected "int"
```

If we try to execute this, it will raise a `TypeError` exception on using the `d.first_roll()` method. The exception is raised here because the body of the `__init__()` method works well with values of any type. The hints claim specific types are expected, but at runtime, any object can be provided. The hints are not checked during execution.

Similarly, when we use other methods, the `mypy` program checks to be sure our use of the method matches the expectations defined by the type hints. Here's another example:

```
r1: List[str] = d.first_roll()
```

This assignment statement has a type hint for the `r1` variable that doesn't match the type hint for the return type from the `first_roll()` method. This conflict is found by `mypy` and reported as `Incompatible types in assignment`.

There's more...

One of the type hints in this example is too specific. The function for re-rolling the dice, `reroll()`, has a `positions` parameter. The `positions` parameter is used in a `for` statement, which means the object must be some kind of iterable object.

The mistake was providing a type hint, `Set[int]`, which is only one of many kinds of iterable objects. We can generalize this definition by switching the type hint from the very specific `Set[int]` to the more general `Iterable[int]`.

Relaxing the hint means that a `set`, `list`, or `tuple` object is a valid argument value for this parameter. The only other code change required is to add `Iterable` to the `from` typing `import` statement.

The `for` statement has a specific protocol for getting the `iterator` object from an iterable collection, assigning values to a variable, and executing the indented body. This protocol is defined by the `Iterable` type hint. There are many such protocol-based types, and they allow us to provide type hints that match Python's inherent flexibility with respect to type.

See also

- In *Chapter 4, Built-In Data Structures Part 1: Lists and Sets*, the recipes *Writing list-related type hints*, *Writing set-related type hints*, and *Writing dictionary-related type hints* address additional detailed type hinting.
- In *Chapter 3, Function Definitions*, in the recipe *Function Parameters and Type Hints*, a number of similar concepts are shown.

Designing classes with lots of processing

Some of the time, an object will contain all of the data that defines its internal state. There are cases, however, where a class doesn't hold the data, but instead is designed to consolidate processing for data held in separate containers.

Some prime examples of this design are statistical algorithms, which are often outside the data being analyzed. The data might be in a built-in `list` or `Counter` object; the processing defined in a class separate from the data container.

In Python, we have to make a design choice between a module and a class. A number of related operations can be implemented using a module with many functions. See *Chapter 3, Function Definitions*, for more information on this.

A class definition can be an alternative to a module with a number of functions. How can we design a class that makes use of Python's sophisticated built-in collections as separate objects?

Getting ready

In *Chapter 4, Built-In Data Structures Part 1: Lists and Sets*, specifically the *Using set methods and operators* recipe, we looked at a statistical test called the **Coupon Collector's Test**. The concept is that each time we perform some process, we save a coupon that describes some aspect or parameter for the process. The question is, how many times do I have to perform the process before I collect a complete set of coupons?

If we have customers assigned to different demographic groups based on their purchasing habits, we might ask how many online sales we have to make before we've seen someone from each of the groups. If the groups are all about the same size, we can predict the average number of customers we encounter before we get a complete set of coupons. If the groups are different sizes, it's a little more complex to compute the expected time before collecting a full set of coupons.

Let's say we've collected data using a `Counter` object. In this example, the customers fall into eight categories with approximately equal numbers.

The data looks like this:

```
Counter({15: 7, 17: 5, 20: 4, 16: 3, ... etc., 45: 1})
```

The keys (15, 17, 20, 16, and so on) are the number of customer visits needed to get a full set of coupons from all the demographic groups. We've run the experiment many times, and the value associated with this key is the number of experiment trials with the given number of visits. In the preceding data, `15` visits were required on seven different trials. `17` visits were required for five different trials. This has a long tail. For one of the experimental trials, there were `45` individual visits before a full set of eight coupons was collected.

We want to compute some statistics on this `Counter`. We have two general strategies for storing the data:

- **Extend**: We can extend the `Counter` class definition to add statistical processing. The complexity of this varies with the kind of processing that we want to introduce. We'll cover this in detail in the *Extending a built-in collection – a list that does statistics* recipe, as well as *Chapter 8, More Advanced Class Design*.
- **Wrap**: We can wrap the `Counter` object in another class that provides just the features we need. When we do this, though, we'll often have to expose some additional methods that are an important part of Python, but that don't matter much for our application. We'll look at this in *Chapter 8, More Advanced Class Design*.

There's a variation on the **wrap** strategy where we define a statistical computation class that contains a `Counter` object. This often leads to an elegant solution.

We have two ways to design this separate processing. These two design alternatives apply to all of the architectural choices for storing the data:

- **Eager**: This means that we'll compute the statistics as soon as possible. The values can then be attributes of the class. While this can improve performance, it also means that any change to the data collection will invalidate the eagerly computed values, leading to a need to recompute them to keep them consistent with the data. We have to examine the overall context to see if this can happen.
- **Lazy**: This means we won't compute anything until it's required via a method function or property. We'll look at this in the *Using properties for lazy attributes* recipe.

The essential math for both designs is the same. The only question is when the computation is done.

We compute the mean using a sum of the expected values. The expected value is the frequency of a value multiplied by the value. The mean, μ, is this:

$$\mu = \frac{\sum_{k \in C}(f_k \times k)}{\sum_{k \in C} f_k}$$

Here, k is the key from the `Counter`, C, and f_k is the frequency value for the given key from the `Counter`. We weight each key with the number of times it was found in the `Counter` collection out of the total size of the collection, the sum of all the counts.

The standard deviation, σ, depends on the mean, μ. This also involves computing a sum of values, each of which is weighted by frequency. The following is the formula:

$$\sigma = \sqrt{\frac{\sum_{k \in C} f_k \times (k - \mu)^2}{C + 1}}$$

Here, k is the key from the `Counter`, C, and f_k is the frequency value for the given key from the `Counter`. The total number of items in the `Counter` is $C = \sum_{k \in C} f_k$. This is the sum of the frequencies.

How to do it...

1. Import the `collections` module as well as the type hint for the collection that will be used:

```
import collections
from typing import Counter
```

2. Define the class with a descriptive name:

```
class CounterStatistics:
```

3. Write the `__init__()` method to include the object where the data is located. In this case, the type hint is `Counter[int]` because the keys used in the `collections.Counter` object will be integers. The `typing.Collection` and `counter.Collection` names are similar. To avoid confusion, it's slightly easier if the names from the `typing` module are imported directly, and the related `collection.Counter` class uses the full name, qualified by module:

```
    def __init__(self, raw_counter: Counter[int]) -> None:
        self.raw_counter = raw_counter
```

4. Initialize any other local variables in the `__init__()` method that might be useful. Since we're going to calculate values eagerly, the most eager possible time is when the object is created. We'll write references to some yet to be defined functions:

```
        self.mean = self.compute_mean()
        self.stddev = self.compute_stddev()
```

5. Define the required methods for the various values. Here's the calculation of the mean:

```
    def compute_mean(self) -> float:
        total, count = 0.0, 0
        for value, frequency in self.raw_counter.items():
            total += value * frequency
            count += frequency
        return total / count
```

6. Here's how we can calculate the standard deviation:

```
def compute_stddev(self) -> float:
    total, count = 0.0, 0
    for value, frequency in self.raw_counter.items():
        total += frequency * (value - self.mean) ** 2
        count += frequency
    return math.sqrt(total / (count - 1))
```

Note that this calculation requires that the mean is computed first and the `self.mean` instance variable has been created. Also, this uses `math.sqrt()`. Be sure to add the needed `import math` statement in the Python file.

Here's how we can create some sample data:

```
from Chapter_15.collector import (
    samples, arrival1, coupon_collector
)
import collections
ArrivalF = Callable[[int], Iterator[int]]


def raw_data(
    n: int = 8, limit: int = 1000,
    arrival_function: ArrivalF = arrival1
) -> Counter[int]:
    data = samples(limit, arrival_function(n))
    wait_times = collections.Counter(coupon_collector(n, data))
    return wait_times
```

We've imported functions such as `expected()`, `arrival1()`, and `coupon_collector()` from the `Chapter_15.collector` module. We've also imported the standard library `collections` module.

The type definition for `ArrivalF` describes a function used to compute individual arrivals. For our simulation purposes, we've defined a number of these functions, each of which emits a sequence of customer coupons. When working with actual sales receipts, this can be replaced with a function that reads source datasets. All the functions have a common structure of accepting a domain size and emitting a sequence of values from the domain.

The `raw_data()` function will generate a number of customer visits. By default, it will be 1,000 visits. The domain will be eight different classes of customers; each class will have an equal number of members. We'll use the `coupon_collector()` function to step through the data, emitting the number of visits required to collect a full set of eight coupons.

This data is then used to assemble a `collections.Counter` object. This will have the number of customers required to get a full set of coupons. Each number of customers will also have a frequency showing how often that number of visits occurred. Because the key is the integer count of the number of visits, the type hint is `Counter[int]`.

Here's how we can analyze the `Counter` object:

```
>>> import random
>>> from ch07_r03 import CounterStatistics
>>> random.seed(1)
>>> data = raw_data()
>>> stats = CounterStatistics(data)
>>> print("Mean: {0:.2f}".format(stats.mean))
Mean: 20.81
>>> print("Standard Deviation: {0:.3f}".format(stats.stddev))
Standard Deviation: 7.025
```

First, we imported the `random` module so that we could pick a known seed value. This makes it easier to test and demonstrate an application because the random numbers are consistent. We also imported the `CounterStatistics` class from the `ch07_r03` module.

Once we have all of the items defined, we can force the `seed` to a known value, and generate the coupon collector test results. The `raw_data()` function will emit a `Counter` object, which we called `data`.

We'll use the `Counter` object to create an instance of the `CounterStatistics` class. We'll assign this to the `stats` variable. Creating this instance will also compute some summary statistics. These values are available as the `stats.mean` attribute and the `stats.stddev` attribute.

For a set of eight coupons, the theoretical average is `21.7` visits to collect all coupons. It looks like the results from `raw_data()` show behavior that matches the expectation of random visits. This is sometimes called the **null hypothesis**—the data is random.

How it works...

This class encapsulates two complex algorithms, but doesn't include any of the data for those algorithms. The data is kept separately, in a `Counter` object. We wrote a high-level specification for the processing and placed it in the `__init__()` method. Then we wrote methods to implement the processing steps that were specified. We can set as many attributes as are needed, making this a very flexible approach.

The advantage of this design is that the attribute values can be used repeatedly. The cost of computation for the mean and standard deviation is paid once; each time an attribute value is used, no further calculating is required.

The disadvantage of this design is changes to the state of the underlying `Counter` object will render the `CounterStatistics` object's state obsolete and incorrect. If, for example, we added a few hundred more trial runs, the mean and standard deviation would need to be recomputed. A design that eagerly computes values is appropriate when the underlying `Counter` isn't going to change. An eager design works well for batches of data with few changes.

There's more...

If we need to have stateful, mutable objects, we can add update methods that can change the `Counter` object's internal state. For example, we can introduce a method to add another value by delegating the work to the associated `Counter`. This switches the design pattern from a simple connection between computation and collection to a proper wrapper around the collection.

The method might look like this:

```
def add(self, value: int) -> None:
    self.raw_counter[value] += 1
    self.mean = self.compute_mean()
    self.stddev = self.compute_stddev()
```

First, we updated the state of the `Counter`. Then, we recomputed all of the derived values. This kind of processing might create tremendous computation overheads. There needs to be a compelling reason to recompute the mean and standard deviation after every value is changed.

There are considerably more efficient solutions. For example, if we save two intermediate sums and an intermediate count, we can update the sums and counts and compute the mean and standard deviation more efficiently.

For this, we might have an `__init__()` method that looks like this:

```
def __init__(self, counter: Counter = None) -> None:
    if counter is not None:
        self.raw_counter = counter
        self.count = sum(
            self.raw_counter[k] for k in self.raw_counter)
        self.sum = sum(
            self.raw_counter[k] * k for k in self.raw_counter)
        self.sum2 = sum(
            self.raw_counter[k] * k ** 2
                for k in self.raw_counter)
        self.mean: Optional[float] = self.sum / self.count
```

```
            self.stddev: Optional[float] = math.sqrt(
                (self.sum2 - self.sum ** 2 / self.count)
                / (self.count - 1)
            )
        else:
            self.raw_counter = collections.Counter()
            self.count = 0
            self.sum = 0
            self.sum2 = 0
            self.mean = None
            self.stddev = None
```

We've written this method to work either with a `Counter` object or without an initialized `Counter` instance. If no data is provided, it will start with an empty collection, and zero values for the count and the various sums. When the count is zero, the mean and standard deviation have no meaningful value, so `None` is provided.

If a `Counter` is provided, then `count`, `sum`, and the sum of squares are computed. These can be incrementally adjusted easily, quickly recomputing the `mean` and standard deviation.

When a single new value needs to be added to the collection, the following method will incrementally recompute the derived values:

```
    def add(self, value: int) -> None:
        self.raw_counter[value] += 1
        self.count += 1
        self.sum += value
        self.sum2 += value ** 2
        self.mean = self.sum / self.count
        if self.count > 1:
            self.stddev = math.sqrt(
                (self.sum2 - self.sum ** 2 / self.count)
                / (self.count - 1)
            )
```

Updating the `Counter` object, the `count`, the `sum`, and the sum of squares is clearly necessary to be sure that the `count`, `sum`, and sum of squares values match the `self.raw_counter` collection at all times. Since we know the `count` must be at least `1`, the mean is easy to compute. The standard deviation requires at least two values, and is computed from the `sum` and the sum of squares.

Here's the formula for this variation on standard deviation:

$$\sigma = \sqrt{\frac{\sum_{k \in C} f_k \times k^2 - \frac{(\sum_{k \in C} f_k \times k)^2}{C}}{C - 1}}$$

This involves computing two sums. One sum involves the frequency times the value squared. The other sum involves the frequency and the value, with the overall sum being squared. We've used *C* to represent the total number of values; this is the sum of the frequencies.

See also

- In the *Extending a built-in collection – a list that does statistics* recipe, we'll look at a different design approach where these functions are used to extend a class definition.
- We'll look at a different approach in the *Using properties for lazy attributes* recipe. This alternative recipe will use properties and compute the attributes as needed.
- In the *Designing classes with little unique processing* recipe, we'll look at a class with no real processing. It acts as a polar opposite of this class.

Using typing.NamedTuple for immutable objects

In some cases, an object is a container of rather complex data, but doesn't really do very much processing on that data. Indeed, in many cases, we'll define a class that doesn't require any unique method functions. These classes are relatively passive containers of data items, without a lot of processing.

In many cases, Python's built-in container classes – `list`, `set`, or `dict` – can cover the use cases. The small problem is that the syntax for a dictionary or a list isn't quite as elegant as the syntax for attributes of an object.

How can we create a class that allows us to use `object.attribute` syntax instead of `object['attribute']`?

Getting ready

There are two cases for any kind of class design:

- Is it stateless (immutable)? Does it embody attributes with values that never change? This is a good example of a `NamedTuple`.

- Is it stateful (mutable)? Will there be state changes for one or more attributes? This is the default for Python class definitions. An ordinary class is stateful. We can simplify creating stateful objects using the recipe *Using dataclasses for mutable objects*.

We'll define a class to describe simple playing cards that have a rank and a suit. Since a card's rank and suit don't change, we'll create a small stateless class for this. `typing.NamedTuple` serves as a handy base class for this class definition.

How to do it...

1. We'll define stateless objects as a subclass of `typing.NamedTuple`:

   ```
   from typing import NamedTuple
   ```

2. Define the class name as an extension to `NamedTuple`. Include the attributes with their individual type hints:

   ```
   class Card(NamedTuple):
       rank: int
       suit: str
   ```

Here's how we can use this class definition to create `Card` objects:

```
>>> eight_hearts = Card(rank=8, suit='\N{White Heart Suit}')
>>> eight_hearts
Card(rank=8, suit='♡')
>>> eight_hearts.rank
8
>> eight_hearts.suit
'♡'
>>> eight_hearts[0]
8
```

We've created a new class, named `Card`, which has two attribute names: `rank` and `suit`. After defining the class, we can create an instance of the class. We built a single card object, `eight_hearts`, with a rank of eight and a suit of ♡.

We can refer to attributes of this object with their name or their position within the tuple. When we use `eight_hearts.rank` or `eight_hearts[0]`, we'll see the `rank` attribute because it's defined first in the sequence of attribute names.

This kind of object is immutable. Here's an example of attempting to change the instance attributes:

```
>>> eight_hearts.suit = '\N{Black Spade Suit}'
Traceback (most recent call last):
  File "/Users/slott/miniconda3/envs/cookbook/lib/python3.8/doctest.py", line 1328, in __run
    compileflags, 1), test.globs)
  File "<doctest examples.txt[30]>", line 1, in <module>
    eight_hearts.suit = '\N{Black Spade Suit}'
AttributeError: can't set attribute
```

We attempted to change the `suit` attribute of the `eight_hearts` object. This raised an `AttributeError` exception showing that instances of `NamedTuple` are immutable.

How it works...

The `typing.NamedTuple` class lets us define a new subclass that has a well-defined list of attributes. A number of methods are created automatically to provide a minimal level of Python behavior. We can see an instance will display a readable text representation showing the values of the various attributes.

In the case of a `NamedTuple` subclass, the behavior is based on the way a built-in `tuple` instance works. The order of the attributes defines the comparison between tuples. Our definition of `Card`, for example, lists the `rank` attribute first. This means that we can easily sort cards by rank. For two cards of equal rank, the suits will be sorted into order. Because a `NamedTuple` is also a tuple, it works well as a member of a set or a key for a dictionary.

The two attributes, `rank` and `suit` in this example, are named as part of the class definition, but are implemented as instance variables. A variation on the tuple's `__new__()` method is created for us. This method has two parameters matching the instance variable names. This automatically created method will assign the instance variables automatically when the object is created.

There's more...

We can add methods to this class definition. For example, if each card has a number of points, we might want to extend the class to look like this example:

```
class CardPoints(NamedTuple):
    rank: int
    suit: str

    def points(self) -> int:
```

```
        if 1 <= self.rank < 10:
            return self.rank
        else:
            return 10
```

We've written a `CardsPoint` class with a `points()` method that returns the points assigned to each rank. This point rule applies to games like *Cribbage*, not to games like *Blackjack*.

Because this is a tuple, the methods cannot add new attributes or change the attributes. In some cases, we build complex tuples built from other tuples.

See also

- In the *Designing classes with lots of processing* recipe, we looked at a class that is entirely processing and almost no data. It acts as the polar opposite of this class.

Using dataclasses for mutable objects

There are two cases for any kind of class design:

- Is it stateless (immutable)? Does it embody attributes with values that never change? If so, see the *Using typing.NamedTuple for immutable objects* recipe for a way to build class definitions for stateless objects.
- Is it stateful (mutable)? Will there be state changes for one or more attributes? In this case, we can either build a class from the ground up, or we can leverage the `@dataclass` decorator to create a class definition from a few attributes and type hints.

Getting ready

We'll look closely at a stateful object that holds a hand of cards. Cards can be inserted into a hand and removed from a hand. In a game like Cribbage, the hand has a number of state changes. Initially, six cards are dealt to both players. The players will each place a pair of cards in a special pile, called the crib. The remaining four cards are played alternately to create scoring opportunities. After each hand's scoring combinations are totalled, the dealer will count the additional scoring combinations in the crib.

We'll look at a simple collection to hold the cards and discard two that form the crib.

How to do it...

1. To define data classes, we'll import the `dataclass` decorator:

```
from dataclasses import dataclass
from typing import List
```

2. Define the new class as a `dataclass`:

```
@dataclass
class CribbageHand:
```

3. Define the various attributes with appropriate type hints. For this example, we'll expect a player to have a collection of cards represented by `List[CardPoints]`. Because each card is unique, we could also use a `Set[CardPoints]` type hint:

```
    cards: List[CardPoints]
```

4. Define any methods that change the state of the object:

```
    def to_crib(self, card1, card2):
        self.cards.remove(card1)
        self.cards.remove(card2)
```

Here's the complete class definition, properly indented:

```
@dataclass
class CribbageHand:
    cards: List[CardPoints]

    def to_crib(self, card1, card2):
        self.cards.remove(card1)
        self.cards.remove(card2)
```

This definition provides a single instance variable, `self.cards`, that can be used by any method that is written. Because we provided a type hint, the `mypy` program can check the class to be sure that it is being used properly.

Here's how it looks when we create an instance of this `CribbageHand` class:

```
>>> cards = [
... CardPoints(rank=3, suit='◊'),
... CardPoints(rank=6, suit='♠'),
.. CardPoints(rank=7, suit='◊'),
... CardPoints(rank=1, suit='♠'),
... CardPoints(rank=6, suit='◊'),
... CardPoints(rank=10, suit='♡')]
```

```
>>> ch1 = CribbageHand(cards)
>>> ch1
CribbageHand(cards=[CardPoints(rank=3, suit='◊'), CardPoints(rank=6,
suit='♠'), CardPoints(rank=7, suit='◊'), CardPoints(rank=1, suit='♠'),
CardPoints(rank=6, suit='◊'), CardPoints(rank=10, suit='♡')])
>>> [c.points() for c in ch1.cards]
[3, 6, 7, 1, 6, 10]
```

We've created six individual `CardPoints` objects. This collection is used to initialize the `CribbageHand` object with six cards. In a more elaborate game, we might define a deck of cards and select from the deck.

The `@dataclass` decorator built a `__repr__()` method that returns a useful display string for the `CribbageHand` object. It shows the value of the card's instance variable. Because it's a display of six `CardPoints` objects, the text is long and sprawls over many lines. While the display may not be the prettiest, we wrote none of the code, making it very easy to use as a starting point for further development.

We built a small list comprehension showing the point values of each `CardPoints` object in the `CribbageHand` instance, `ch1`. A person uses this information (along with other details) to decide which cards to contribute to the dealer's crib.

In this case, the player decided to lay away the 3 ◊ and A ♠ cards for the crib:

```
>>> ch1.to_crib(CardPoints(rank=3, suit='◊'), CardPoints(rank=1, suit='♠
'))
>>> ch1
CribbageHand(cards=[CardPoints(rank=6, suit='♠'), CardPoints(rank=7,
suit='◊'), CardPoints(rank=6, suit='◊'), CardPoints(rank=10, suit='♡')])
>>> [c.points() for c in ch1.cards]
[6, 7, 6, 10]
```

After the `to_crib()` method removed two cards from the hand, the remaining four cards were displayed. Another list comprehension was created with the point values of the remaining four cards.

How it works...

The `@dataclass` decorator helps us define a class with several useful methods as well as a list of attributes drawn from the named variables and their type hints. We can see that an instance displays a readable text representation showing the values of the various attributes.

The attributes are named as part of the class definition, but are actually implemented as instance variables. In this example, there's only one attribute, `cards`. A very sophisticated `__init__()` method is created for us. In this example, it will have a parameter that matches the name of each instance variable and will assign a matching instance variable for us.

The `@dataclass` decorator has a number of options to help us choose what features we want in the class. Here are the options we can select from and the default settings:

- `init=True`: By default, an `__init__()` method will be created with parameters to match the instance variables. If we use `@dataclass(init=False)`, we'll have to write our own `__init__()` method.
- `repr=True`: By default, a `__repr__()` method will be created to return a string showing the state of the object.
- `eq=True`: By default the `__eq__()` and `__ne__()` methods are provided. These will compare all of the instance variables. In the event this isn't appropriate, we can use `@dataclass(eq=False)` to turn this feature off. In some cases, equality doesn't apply, and the methods aren't needed. In other cases, the generated methods aren't appropriate for the class, and more specialized methods need to be written.
- `order=False`: The `__lt__()`, `__le__()`, `__gt__()`, and `__ge__()` methods are not created automatically. If these are built automatically, they will use all of the `dataclass` instance variables, which isn't always desirable.
- `unsafe_hash=False`: Normally, mutable objects do not have hash values, and cannot be used as keys for dictionaries or elements of a set. It's possible to have a `__hash__()` function added automatically, but this is rarely a sensible choice for mutable objects.
- `frozen=False`: This creates an immutable object. Using `@dataclass(frozen=True)` overlaps with `typing.NamedTuple` in many ways.

Because this code is written for us, it lets us focus on the attributes of the class definition. We can write the methods that are truly distinctive and avoid writing "boilerplate" methods that have obvious definitions.

There's more...

Building a deck of cards is an example of a `dataclass` without an initialization. A single deck of cards uses an `__init__()` method without any parameters, it creates a collection of 52 `Card` objects.

Many `@dataclass` definitions provide class-level names that are used to define the instance variables and the initialization method, `__init__()`. In this case, we want a class-level variable with a list of suit strings. This is done with the `ClassVar` type hint. The `ClassVar` type's parameters define the class-level variable's type. In this case, it's a tuple of strings:

```
from typing import List, ClassVar, Tuple

@dataclass(init=False)
class Deck:
    suits: ClassVar[Tuple[str, ...]] = (
```

```
        '\N{Black Club Suit}', '\N{White Diamond Suit}',
        '\N{White Heart Suit}', '\N{Black Spade Suit}'
    )
    cards: List[CardPoints]

    def __init__(self) -> None:
        self.cards = [
            CardPoints(rank=r, suit=s)
                for r in range(1, 14)
                    for s in self.suits
        ]
        random.shuffle(self.cards)
```

This example class definition provides a class-level variable, `suits`, which is shared by all instances of the `Deck` class. This variable is a tuple of the characters used to define the suits.

The `cards` variable has a hint claiming it will have the `List[CardPoints]` type. This information is used by the `mypy` program to confirm that the body of the `__init__()` method performs the proper initialization of this attribute. It also confirms this attribute is used appropriately by other classes.

The `__init__()` method creates the value of the `self.cards` variable. A list comprehension is used to create all combinations of 13 ranks and 4 suits. Once the list has been built, the `random.shuffle()` method puts the cards into a random order.

See also

- See the *Using typing.NamedTuple for immutable objects* recipe for a way to build class definitions for stateless objects.
- The *Using a class to encapsulate data and processing* recipe covers techniques for building a class without the additional methods created by the `@dataclass` decorator.

Using frozen dataclasses for immutable objects

In the *Using typing.NamedTuple for immutable objects* recipe, we saw how to define a class that has a fixed set of attributes. The attributes can be checked by the `mypy` program to ensure that they're being used properly. In some cases, we might want to make use of the slightly more flexible `dataclass` to create an immutable object.

One potential reason for using a `dataclass` is because it can have more complex field definitions than a `NamedTuple` subclass. Another potential reason is the ability to customize initialization and the hashing function that is created. Because a `typing.NamedTuple` is essentially a tuple, there's limited ability to fine-tune the behavior of the instances in this class.

Getting ready

We'll revisit the idea of defining simple playing cards with `rank` and `suit`. The `rank` can be modeled by an integer between 1 (ace) and 13 (king.) The `suit` can be modeled by a single Unicode character from the set {'♣', '♠', '♡', '♢'}. Since a card's rank and suit don't change, we'll create a small, frozen `dataclass` for this.

How to do it...

1. From the `dataclasses` module, import the `dataclass` decorator:

   ```
   from dataclasses import dataclass
   ```

2. Start the class definition with the `@dataclass` decorator, using the `frozen=True` option to ensure that the objects are immutable. We've also included `order=True` so that the comparison operators are defined, allowing instances of this class to be sorted into order:

   ```
   @dataclass(frozen=True, order=True)
   class Card:
   ```

3. Provide the attribute names and type hints for the attributes of each instance of this class:

   ```
       rank: int
       suit: str
   ```

We can use these objects in code like the following:

```
>>> eight_hearts = Card(rank=8, suit='\N{White Heart Suit}')
>>> eight_hearts
Card(rank=8, suit='♡')
>>> eight_hearts.rank
8
>>> eight_hearts.suit
'♡'
```

We've created an instance of the `Card` class with a specific value for the `rank` and `suit` attributes. Because the object is immutable, any attempt to change the state will result in an exception that looks like the following example:

```
>>> eight_hearts.suit = '\N{Black Spade Suit}'
Traceback (most recent call last):
  File "/Users/slott/miniconda3/envs/cookbook/lib/python3.8/doctest.py",
line 1328, in __run
    compileflags, 1), test.globs)
  File "<doctest examples.txt[30]>", line 1, in <module>
    eight_hearts.suit = '\N{Black Spade Suit}'
dataclasses.FrozenInstanceError: cannot assign to field 'suit'
```

This shows an attempt to change an attribute of a frozen `dataclass` instance. The `dataclasses.FrozenInstanceError` exception is raised to signal that this kind of operation is not permitted.

How it works...

This `@dataclass` decorator adds a number of built-in methods to a class definition. As we noted in the *Using dataclasses for mutable objects* recipe, there are a number of features that can be enabled or disabled. Each feature may have one or several individual methods.

The type hints are incorporated into all of the generated methods. This assures consistency that can be checked by the `mypy` program.

There's more...

The `dataclass` initialization is quite sophisticated. We'll look at one feature that's sometimes handy for defining optional attributes.

Consider a class that can hold a hand of cards. While the common use case provides a set of cards to initialize the hand, we can also have hands that might be built incrementally, starting with an empty collection and adding cards during the game.

We can define this kind of optional attribute using the `field()` function from the `dataclasses` module. The `field()` function lets us provide a function to build default values, called `default_factory`. We'd use it as shown in the following example:

```
from dataclasses import field
from typing import List

@dataclass(frozen=True, order=True)
class Hand:
    cards: List[CardPoints] = field(default_factory=list)
```

The `Hand` `dataclass` has a single attribute, `cards`, which is a list of `CardPoints` objects. The `field()` function provides a default factory: in the event no initial value is provided, the `list()` function will be executed to create a new, empty list.

We can create two kinds of hands with this `dataclass`. Here's the conventional example, where we deal six cards:

```
>>> cards = [
... CardPoints(rank=3, suit='◊'),
... CardPoints(rank=6, suit='♠'),
... CardPoints(rank=7, suit='◊'),
... CardPoints(rank=1, suit='♠'),
... CardPoints(rank=6, suit='◊'),
... CardPoints(rank=10, suit='♡')]
>>>
>>> h = Hand(cards)
```

The `Hands()` type expects a single attribute, matching the definition of the attributes in the class. This is optional, and we can build an empty hand as shown in this example:

```
>>> crib = Hand()
>>> d3 = CardPoints(rank=3, suit='◊')
>>> h.cards.remove(d3)
>>> crib.cards.append(d3)
```

In this example, we've created a `Hand()` instance with no argument values. Because the `cards` attribute was defined with a field that provided a `default_factory`, the `list()` function will be used to create an empty list for the `cards` attribute.

See also

- The *Using dataclasses for mutable objects* recipe covers some additional topics on using dataclasses to avoid some of the complexities of writing class definitions.

Optimizing small objects with __slots__

The general case for an object allows a dynamic collection of attributes. There's a special case for an immutable object with a fixed collection of attributes based on the `tuple` class. We looked at both of these in the *Designing classes with little unique processing* recipe.

There's a middle ground. We can also define an object with a fixed number of attributes, but the values of the attributes can be changed. By changing the class from an unlimited collection of attributes to a fixed set of attributes, it turns out that we can also save memory and processing time.

How can we create optimized classes with a fixed set of attributes?

Getting ready

Let's look at the idea of a hand of playing cards in the casino game of *Blackjack*. There are two parts to a hand:

- The bet
- The cards

Both have dynamic values. Generally, each hand starts with a bet and an empty collection of cards. The dealer then deals two initial cards to the hand. It's common to get more cards. It's also possible to raise the bet via a double-down play.

Generally, Python allows adding attributes to an object. This can be undesirable, particularly when working with a large number of objects. The flexibility of using a dictionary has a high cost in memory use. Using specific `__slots__` names limits the class to precisely the `bet` and the `cards` attributes, saving memory.

How to do it...

We'll leverage the `__slots__` special name when creating the class:

1. Define the class with a descriptive name:

    ```
    class Hand:
    ```

2. Define the list of attribute names. This identifies the only two attributes that are allowed for instances of this class. Any attempt to add another attribute will raise an `AttributeError` exception:

    ```
    __slots__ = ('cards', 'bet')
    ```

3. Add an initialization method. In this example, we've allowed three different kinds of initial values for the cards. The type hint, `Union["Hand", List[Card], None]`, permits a `Hand` instance, a `List[Card]` instance, or nothing at all. For more information on this, see the *Designing functions with optional parameters* recipe in *Chapter 3, Function Definitions*. Because the `__slot__` names don't have type hints, we need to provide them in the `__init__()` method:

    ```
    def __init__(
            self,
            bet: int,
            hand: Union["Hand", List[Card], None] = None
    ) -> None:
        self.cards: List[Card] = (
    ```

```
        [] if hand is None
            else hand.cards if isinstance(hand, Hand)
                else hand
    )
    self.bet: int = bet
```

4. Add a method to update the collection. We've called it `deal` because it's used to deal a new card to the `hand`:

```
    def deal(self, card: Card) -> None:
        self.cards.append(card)
```

5. Add a `__repr__()` method so that it can be printed easily:

```
def __repr__(self) -> str:
    return (
        f"{self.__class__.__name__}("
        f"bet={self.bet}, hand={self.cards})"
    )
```

Here's how we can use this class to build a hand of cards. We'll need the definition of the `Card` class based on the example in the *Designing classes with little unique processing* recipe:

```
>>> from Chapter_07.ch07_r07 import Card, Hand
>>> h1 = Hand(2)
>>> h1.deal(Card(rank=4, suit='♣'))
>>> h1.deal(Card(rank=8, suit='♡'))
>>> h1
Hand(bet=2, hand=[Card(rank=4, suit='♣'), Card(rank=8, suit='♡')])
```

We've imported the `Card` and `Hand` class definitions. We built an instance of a `Hand`, `h1`, with a `bet` of `2`. We then added two cards to the hand via the `deal()` method of the `Hand` class. This shows how the `h1.hand` value can be mutated.

This example also displays the instance of `h1` to show the bet and the sequence of cards. The `__repr__()` method produces output that's in Python syntax.

We can replace the `h1.bet` value when the player doubles down (yes, this is a crazy thing to do when showing 12):

```
>>> h1.bet *= 2
>>> h1
Hand(bet=4, hand=[Card(rank=4, suit='♣'), Card(rank=8, suit='♡')])
```

When we displayed the Hand object, h1, it showed that the bet attribute was changed.

A better design than changing the bet attribute value is to introduce a double_down() method that makes appropriate changes to the Hand object.

Here's what happens if we try to create a new attribute:

```
>>> h1.some_other_attribute = True
Traceback (most recent call last):
  File "/Users/slott/miniconda3/envs/cookbook/lib/python3.8/doctest.py",
line 1336, in __run
    exec(compile(example.source, filename, "single",
  File "<doctest examples.txt[34]>", line 1, in <module>
    h1.some_other_attribute = True
AttributeError: 'Hand' object has no attribute 'some_other_attribute'
```

We attempted to create an attribute named some_other_attribute on the Hand object, h1. This raised an AttributeError exception. Using __slots__ means that new attributes cannot be added to the object.

How it works...

When we create an object instance, the steps in the process are defined in part by the object's class and the built-in type() function. Implicitly, a class is assigned a special __new__() method that handles the internal house-keeping required to create a new, empty object. After this, the __init__() method creates and initializes the attributes.

Python has three essential paths for creating instances of a class:

- The default behavior, defined by a built-in object and type(): This is used when we define a class with or without the @dataclass decorator. Each instance contains a __dict__ attribute that is used to hold all other attributes. Because the object's attributes are kept in a dictionary, we can add, change, and delete attributes freely. This flexibility requires the use of a relatively large amount of memory for the dictionary object inside each instance.
- The __slots__ behavior: This avoids creating the __dict__ attribute. Because the object has only the attributes named in the __slots__ sequence, we can't add or delete attributes. We can change the values of the defined attributes. This lack of flexibility means that less memory is used for each object.
- The subclass of tuple behavior: These are immutable objects. An easy way to create these classes is with typing.NamedTuple as a parent class. Once built, the instances are immutable and cannot be changed.

A large application might be constrained by the amount of memory used, and switching just the class with the largest number of instances to `__slots__` can lead to a dramatic improvement in performance.

There's more...

It's possible to tailor the way the `__new__()` method works to replace the default `__dict__` attribute with a different kind of dictionary. This is an advanced technique because it exposes the inner workings of classes and objects.

Python relies on a metaclass to create instances of a class. The default metaclass is the `type` class. The idea is that the metaclass provides a few pieces of functionality that are used to create the object. Once the empty object has been created, then the class's `__init__()` method will initialize the empty object.

Generally, a metaclass will provide a definition of `__new__()`, and perhaps `__prepare__()`, if there's a need to customize the namespace object. There's a widely used example in the Python Language Reference document that tweaks the namespace used to create a class.

For more details, see `https://docs.python.org/3/reference/datamodel.html#metaclass-example`.

See also

- The more common cases of an immutable object or a completely flexible object are covered in the *Designing classes with little unique processing* recipe.

Using more sophisticated collections

Python has a wide variety of built-in collections. In *Chapter 4, Built-In Data Structures Part 1: Lists and Sets*, we looked at them closely. In the *Choosing a data structure* recipe, we provided a kind of decision tree to help locate the appropriate data structure from the available choices.

When we consider built-ins and other data structures in the standard library, we have more choices, and more decisions to make. How can we choose the right data structure for our problem?

Getting ready

Before we put data into a collection, we'll need to consider how we'll gather the data, and what we'll do with the collection once we have it. The big question is always how we'll identify a particular item within the collection. We'll look at a few key questions that we need to answer to help select a proper collection for our needs.

Here's an overview of some of the alternative collections. The `collections` module contains a number of variations on the built-in collections. These include the following:

- `deque`: A double-ended queue. It's a mutable sequence with optimizations for pushing and popping from each end. Note that the class name starts with a lowercase letter; this is atypical for Python.
- `defaultdict`: A mapping that can provide a default value for a missing key. Note that the class name starts with a lowercase letter; this is atypical for Python.
- `Counter`: A mapping that is designed to count the number of occurrences of distinct keys. This is sometimes called a multiset or a bag.
- `OrderedDict`: A mapping that retains the order in which keys where created.
- `ChainMap`: A mapping that combines several dictionaries into a single mapping.

The `heapq` module includes a priority queue implementation. This is a specialized library that leverages the built-in `list` sequence to maintain items in a sorted order.

The `bisect` module includes methods for searching a sorted list. This creates some overlap between the dictionary features and the list features.

How to do it...

There are a number of questions we need to answer to decide if we need a library data collection instead of one of the built-in collections:

1. Is the structure a buffer between the producer and the consumer? Does some part of the algorithm produce data items and another part consume the data items?
    - A queue is used for **First-In-First-Out** (**FIFO**) processing. Items are inserted at one end and consumed from the other end. We can use `list.append()` and `list.pop(0)` to simulate this, though `collections.deque` will be more efficient; we can use `deque.append()` and `deque.popleft()`.
    - A stack is used for **Last-In-First-Out** (**LIFO**) processing. Items are inserted and consumed from the same end. We can use `list.append()` and `list.pop()` to simulate this, though `collections.deque` will be more efficient; we can use `deque.append()` and `deque.pop()`.
    - A priority queue (or heap queue) keeps the queue sorted in some order, distinct from the arrival order. We can try to simulate this by using the `list.append()`, `list.sort(key=lambda x:x.priority)`, and `list.pop(-1)` operations to keep items in order. Performing a sort after each insert can make it inefficient. Folding an item into a previously sorted list doesn't necessarily touch all items. Using the `heapq` module can be more efficient. The `heapq` module has functions for creating and updating heaps.

2. How do we want to deal with missing keys from a dictionary?
   - Raise an exception. This is the way the built-in `dict` class works.
   - Create a default item. This is how `collections.defaultdict` works. We must provide a function that returns the default value. Common examples include `defaultdict(int)` and `defaultdict(float)` to use a default value of zero. We can also use `defauldict(list)` and `defauldict(set)` to create dictionary-of-list or dictionary-of-set structures.
   - The `defaultdict(int)` used to count items is so common that the `collections.Counter` class does exactly this.
3. How do we want to handle the order of keys in a dictionary? Generally, Python newer than version 3.6 keeps the keys in insertion order. If we want a different order, we'll have to sort them manually. See the *Controlling the order of dict keys* recipe for more details.
4. How will we build the dictionary?
   - We have a simple algorithm to create items. In this case, a built-in `dict` object may be sufficient.
   - We have multiple dictionaries that will need to be merged. This can happen when reading configuration files. We might have an individual configuration, a system-wide configuration, and a default application configuration that all need to be merged into a single dictionary using a `ChainMap` collection.

How it works...

There are two principle resource constraints on data processing:

- Storage
- Time

All of our programming must respect these constraints. In most cases, the two are in opposition: anything we do to reduce storage use tends to increase processing time, and anything we do to reduce processing time increases storage use. Algorithm and data structure design seeks to find an optimal balance among the constraints.

The time aspect is formalized via a complexity metric. There are several ways to describe the complexity of an algorithm:

- Complexity $\mathbf{O}(1)$ happens in constant time; the complexity doesn't change with the volume of data. For some collections, the actual overall long-term average is nearly $\mathbf{O}(1)$ with minor exceptions. List `append` operations are an example: they're all about the same complexity. Once in a while, though, a behind-the-scenes memory management operation will add some time.

- Complexity described as $\mathbf{O}(n)$ happens in linear time. The cost grows as the volume of data, *n*, grows. Finding an item in a list has this complexity. Finding an item in a dictionary is closer to $\mathbf{O}(1)$ because it's (nearly) the same low complexity, no matter how large the dictionary is.
- A complexity described as $\mathbf{O}(n \log n)$ grows more quickly than the volume of data. Often the base two logarithm is used because each step in an algorithm considers only half the data. The `bisect` module includes search algorithms that have this complexity.
- There are even worse cases. Some algorithms have a complexity of $\mathbf{O}(n^2)$, $\mathbf{O}(2^n)$, or even $\mathbf{O}(n!)$. We'd like to avoid these kinds of very expensive algorithms through clever design and good choice of data structure. These can be deceptive in practice. We may be able to work out an $\mathbf{O}(2^n)$ algorithm where *n* is 3 or 4 because there are only 8 or 16 combinations, and the processing seems fast. If real data involves 70 items, the number of combinations has 22 digits.

The various data structures reflect unique time and storage trade-offs.

There's more...

As a concrete and extreme example, let's look at searching a web log file for a particular sequence of events. We have two overall design strategies:

- Read all of the events into a list structure with something like `file.read().splitlines()`. We can then use a `for` statement to iterate through the list looking for the combination of events. While the initial read may take some time, the search will be very fast because the log is all in memory.
- Read and process each individual event from a log file. If the event is part of the pattern, save just this event. We might use a `defaultdict` with the IP address as the key and a list of events as the value. This will take longer to read the logs, but the resulting structure in memory will be much smaller.

The first algorithm, reading everything into memory, is often wildly impractical. On a large web server, the logs might involve hundreds of gigabytes, or perhaps even terabytes, of data. Logs can easily be too large to fit into any computer's memory.

The second approach has a number of alternative implementations:

- **Single process**: The general approach to most of the Python recipes here assumes that we're creating an application that runs as a single process.
- **Multiple processes**: We might expand the row-by-row search into a multi-processing application using the `multiprocessing` or `concurrent.futures` package. These packages let us create a collection of worker processes, each of which can process a subset of the available data and return the results to a consumer that combines the results. On a modern multiprocessor, multi-core computer, this can be a very effective use of resources.

- **Multiple hosts**: The extreme case requires multiple servers, each of which handles a subset of the data. This requires more elaborate coordination among the hosts to share result sets. Generally, it can work out well to use a framework such as `Dask` or `Spark` for this kind of processing. While the `multiprocessing` module is quite sophisticated, tools like `Dask` are even more suitable for large-scale computation.

We'll often decompose a large search into map and reduce processing. The map phase applies some processing or filtering to every item in the collection. The reduce phase combines map results into summary or aggregate objects. In many cases, there is a complex hierarchy of `MapReduce` operations applied to the results of previous `MapReduce` operations.

See also

- See the *Choosing a data structure* recipe in *Chapter 4, Built-In Data Structures Part 1: Lists and Sets*, for a foundational set of decisions for selecting data structures.

Extending a built-in collection – a list that does statistics

In the *Designing classes with lots of processing* recipe, we looked at a way to distinguish between a complex algorithm and a collection. We showed how to encapsulate the algorithm and the data into separate classes. The alternative design strategy is to extend the collection to incorporate a useful algorithm.

How can we extend Python's built-in collections? How can we add features to the built-in list?

Getting ready

We'll create a sophisticated list class where each instance can compute the sums and averages of the items in the list. This will require an application to only put numbers in the list; otherwise, there will be `ValueError` exceptions.

We're going to show methods that explicitly use generator expressions as places where additional processing can be included. Rather than use `sum(self)`, we're going to emphasize `sum(v for v in self)` because there are two common future extensions: `sum(m(v) for v in self)` and `sum(v for v in self if f(v))`. These are the mapping and filtering alternatives where a mapping function, `m(v)`, is applied to each item; or a filter function, `f(v)`, is applied to each item. Computing a sum of squares, for example, applies a mapping to each value before summing.

How to do it...

1. Pick a name for the list that also does simple statistics. Define the class as an extension to the built-in `list` class:

    ```
    class StatsList(list):
    ```

2. Define the additional processing as new methods. The `self` variable will be an object that has inherited all of the attributes and methods from the superclass. When working with numeric data, `mypy` treats the `float` type as a superclass for both `float` and `int`, saving us from having to define an explicit `Union[float, int]`. We'll use a generator expression here as a place where future changes might be incorporated. Here's a `sum()` method:

    ```
        def sum(self) -> float:
            return sum(v for v in self)
    ```

3. Here's another method that we often apply to a list. This counts items and returns the size. We've used a generator expression to make it easy to add mappings or filter criteria if that ever becomes necessary:

    ```
        def size(self) -> float:
            return sum(1 for v in self)
    ```

4. Here's the `mean` function:

    ```
        def mean(self):
            return self.sum() / self.count()
    ```

5. Here are some additional methods. The `sum2()` method computes the sum of squares of values in the list. This is used to compute variance. The variance is then used to compute the standard deviation of the values in the list. Unlike with the previous `sum()` and `count()` methods, where there's no mapping, in this case, the generator expression includes a mapping transformation:

    ```
        def sum2(self) -> float:
            return sum(v ** 2 for v in self)

        def variance(self) -> float:
            return (
                (self.sum2() - self.sum() ** 2 / self.size())
                / (self.size() - 1)
            )

        def stddev(self) -> float:
            return math.sqrt(self.variance())
    ```

The StatsList class definition inherits all the features of a list object. It is extended by the methods that we added. Here's an example of creating an instance in this collection:

```
>>> from Chapter_07.ch07_r09 import StatsList
>>> subset1 = StatsList([10, 8, 13, 9, 11])
>>> data = StatsList([14, 6, 4, 12, 7, 5])
>>> data.extend(subset1)
```

We've created two StatsList objects, subset1 and data, from literal lists of objects. We used the extend() method, inherited from the list superclass, to combine the two objects. Here's the resulting object:

```
>>> data
[14, 6, 4, 12, 7, 5, 10, 8, 13, 9, 11]
```

Here's how we can use the additional methods that we defined on this object:

```
>>> data.mean()
9.0
>>> data.variance()
11.0
```

We've displayed the results of the mean() and variance() methods. All the features of the built-in list class are also present in our extension.

How it works...

One of the essential features of class definition is the concept of inheritance. When we create a superclass-subclass relationship, the subclass inherits all of the features of the superclass. This is sometimes called the generalization-specialization relationship. The superclass is a more generalized class; the subclass is more specialized because it adds or modifies features.

All of the built-in classes can be extended to add features. In this example, we added some statistical processing that created a subclass that's a specialized kind of list of numbers.

There's an important tension between the two design strategies:

- **Extending**: In this case, we extended a class to add features. The features are deeply entrenched with this single data structure, and we can't easily use them for a different kind of sequence.
- **Wrapping**: In designing classes with lots of processing, we kept the processing separate from the collection. This leads to some more complexity in juggling two objects.

It's difficult to suggest that one of these is inherently superior to the other. In many cases, we'll find that wrapping may have an advantage because it seems to be a better fit to the SOLID design principles. However, there will always be cases where it's appropriate to extend a built-in collection.

There's more...

The idea of generalization can lead to superclasses that are abstractions. Because an abstract class is incomplete, it requires a subclass to extend it and provide missing implementation details. We can't make an instance of an abstract class because it would be missing features that make it useful.

As we noted in the *Choosing a data structure* recipe in *Chapter 4, Built-In Data Structures Part 1: Lists and Sets*, there are abstract superclasses for all of the built-in collections. Rather than starting from a concrete class, we can also start our design from an abstract base class.

We could, for example, start a class definition like this:

```
from collections.abc import MutableMapping
class MyFancyMapping(MutableMapping):

etc.
```

In order to finish this class, we'll need to provide an implementation for a number of special methods:

- `__getitem__()`
- `__setitem__()`
- `__delitem__()`
- `__iter__()`
- `__len__()`

Each of these methods is missing from the abstract class; they have no concrete implementation in the `Mapping` class. Once we've provided workable implementations for each method, we can then make instances of the new subclass.

See also

- In the *Designing classes with lots of processing* recipe, we took a different approach. In that recipe, we left the complex algorithms in a separate class.

Using properties for lazy attributes

In the *Designing classes with lots of processing* recipe, we defined a class that eagerly computed a number of attributes of the data in a collection. The idea there was to compute the values as soon as possible, so that the attributes would have no further computational cost.

We described this as **eager** processing, since the work was done as soon as possible. The other approach is **lazy** processing, where the work is done as late as possible.

What if we have values that are used rarely, and are very expensive to compute? What can we do to minimize the up-front computation, and only compute values when they are truly needed?

Getting ready...

Let's say we've collected data using a `Counter` object. For more information on the various collections, see *Chapter 4, Built-In Data Structures Part 1: Lists and Sets*; specifically the *Using set methods and operators* and *Avoiding mutable default values for function parameters* recipes. In this case, the customers fall into eight categories with approximately equal numbers.

The data looks like this:

```
Counter({15: 7, 17: 5, 20: 4, 16: 3, ... etc., 45: 1})
```

In this collection, each key is the number of visits needed to get a full set of coupons. The values are the numbers of times that the visits occurred. In the preceding data that we saw, there were seven occasions where `15` visits were needed to get a full set of coupons. We can see from the sample data that there were five occasions where `17` visits were needed. This has a long tail. At only one point, there were `45` individual visits before a full set of eight coupons was collected.

We want to compute some statistics on this `Counter`. We have two overall strategies for doing this:

- **Extend**: We covered this in detail in the *Extending a built-in collection – a list that does statistics* recipe, and we will cover this in *Chapter 8, More Advanced Class Design*.
- **Wrap**: We can wrap the `Counter` object in another class that provides just the features we need. We'll look at this in *Chapter 8, More Advanced Class Design*.

A common variation on wrapping uses a statistical computation object with a separate data collection object. This variation on wrapping often leads to an elegant solution.

No matter which class architecture we choose, we have two ways to design the processing:

- **Eager**: This means that we'll compute the statistics as soon as possible. This was the approach followed in the *Designing classes with lots of processing* recipe.
- **Lazy**: This means we won't compute anything until it's required via a method function or property. In the *Extending a built-in collection - a list that does statistics* recipe, we added methods to a collection class. These additional methods are examples of lazy calculation. The statistical values are computed only when required.

The essential math for both designs is the same. The only question is when the computation is done.

The mean, μ, is this:

$$\mu = \frac{\sum_{k \in C}(f_k \times k)}{\sum_{k \in C} f_k}$$

Here, k is the key from the `Counter`, C, and f_k is the frequency value for the given key from the `Counter`. The sum of all the frequencies is the total count of all the original samples.

The standard deviation, σ, depends on the mean, μ. The formula is this:

$$\sigma = \sqrt{\frac{\sum_{k \in C} f_k \times (k - \mu)^2}{C + 1}}$$

Here, k is the key from the `Counter`, C, and f_k is the frequency value for the given key from the `Counter`. The total number of items in the counter is $C = \sum_{k \in C} f_k$.

How to do it...

1. Define the class with a descriptive name:

```
class LazyCounterStatistics:
```

2. Write the initialization method to include the object to which this object will be connected. We've defined a method function that takes a `Counter` object as an argument value. This `counter` object is saved as part of the `Counter_Statistics` instance:

```
    def __init__(self, raw_counter: Counter) -> None:
        self.raw_counter = raw_counter
```

3. Define some useful helper methods. Each of these is decorated with `@property` to make it behave like a simple attribute:

```
@property
def sum(self) -> float:
    return sum(
        f * v
        for v, f in self.raw_counter.items()
    )
@property
def count(self) -> float:
    return sum(
        f
        for v, f in self.raw_counter.items()
    )
```

4. Define the required methods for the various values. Here's the calculation of the mean. This too is decorated with `@property`. The other methods can be referenced as if they are attributes, even though they are proper method functions:

```
@property
def mean(self) -> float:
    return self.sum / self.count
```

5. Here's how we can calculate the standard deviation. Note that we've been using `math.sqrt()`. Be sure to add the required `import math` statement in the Python module:

```
@property
def sum2(self) -> float:
    return sum(
        f * v ** 2
        for v, f in self.raw_counter.items()
    )

@property
def variance(self) -> float:
    return (
        (self.sum2 - self.sum ** 2 / self.count) /
        (self.count - 1)
    )
```

```
    @property
    def stddev(self) -> float:
        return math.sqrt(self.variance)
```

To show how this works, we'll apply an instance of this class to the data created by the coupon collector function. The data from that function was organized as a `Counter` object that had the counts of visits required to get a full set of coupons. For each count of visits, the `Counter` instance kept the number of times it occurred. This provided a handy histogram showing a minimum and a maximum. The question we had was whether or not real data matched the statistical expectation.

Here's how we can create some sample data:

```
from Chapter_15.collector import *
import collections
from typing import Counter, Callable, Iterator
ArrivalF = Callable[[int], Iterator[int]]

def raw_data(
    n: int = 8,
    limit: int = 1000,
    arrival_function: ArrivalF = arrival1
  -> Counter[int]:

    data = samples(limit, arrival_function(n))
    wait_times = collections.Counter(coupon_collector(n,
data))
    return wait_times
```

We've imported functions such as `expected()`, `arrival1()`, and `coupon_collector()` from the `Chapter_15.collector` module. We've imported the standard library `collections` module. We've also imported the `Counter` type hint to provide a description the results of the `raw_data()` function.

We defined a function, `raw_data()`, that will generate a number of customer visits. The default for the resulting data will contain 1,000 visits. The domain will be eight different classes of customers; each class will have an equal number of members. We'll use the `coupon_collector()` function to step through the data, emitting the number of visits required to collect a full set of eight coupons.

This data is then used to assemble a `Counter` object. This will have the number of customers required to get a full set of coupons. Each number of customers will also have a frequency showing how often that number of visits occurred.

Here's how we can analyze the `Counter` object:

```
>>> import random
>>> random.seed(1)
>> data = raw_data(8)
>>> stats = LazyCounterStatistics(data)
>>> round(stats.mean, 2)

20.81
>>> round(stats.stddev, 2)
7.02
```

First, we imported the `random` module so that we could pick a known `seed` value. This makes it easier to test and demonstrate an application because the random numbers are consistent.

Setting the random number seed to a known value generates predictable, testable coupon collector test results. The results are randomized, but depend on the seed value. The `raw_data()` function will emit a `Counter` object, which we called `data`.

We'll use the `Counter` object to create an instance of the `LazyCounterStatistics` class. We'll assign this to the `stats` variable. When we print the value for the `stats.mean` property and the `stats.stddev` property, the methods are invoked to do the appropriate calculations of the various values.

For a set of eight coupons, the theoretical average is 21.7 visits to collect all coupons. It looks like the results from `raw_data()` show behavior that matches the expectation of random visits. This is sometimes called the null hypothesis—the data is random. Our customers are visiting us in nearly random orders, distributed fairly.

This might be a good thing because we've been trying to get a wider variety of customers to visit. It might be a bad thing because a promotional program has not moved the visits away from a random distribution. The subsequent decisions around this data depend on a great deal of context.

In this case, the generated data really was random. Using this is a way to validate the statistical testing approach. We can now use this software on real-world data with some confidence that it behaves correctly.

How it works...

The idea of lazy calculation works out well when the value is used rarely. In this example, the count is computed twice as part of computing the variance and standard deviation.

A naïve lazy design may not be optimal in some cases when values are recomputed frequently. This is an easy problem to fix, in general. We can always create additional local variables to cache intermediate results instead of recomputing them.

To make this class look like a class performing eager calculations, we used the `@property` decorator. This makes a method function appear to be an attribute. This can only work for method functions that have no argument values.

In all cases, an attribute that's computed eagerly can be replaced by a lazy property. The principle reason for creating eager attribute variables is to optimize computation costs. In the case where a value is used rarely, a lazy property can avoid an expensive calculation.

There's more...

There are some situations in which we can further optimize a property to limit the amount of additional computation that's done when a value changes. This requires a careful analysis of the use cases in order to understand the pattern of updates to the underlying data.

In the situation where a collection is loaded with data and an analysis is performed, we can cache results to save computing them a second time.

We might do something like this:

```
class CachingLazyCounterStatistics:
    def __init__(self, raw_counter: Counter) -> None:
        self.raw_counter = raw_counter
        self._sum: Optional[float] = None
        self._count: Optional[float] = None

    @property
    def sum(self) -> float:
        if self._sum is None:
            self._sum = sum(
                f * v
                for v, f in self.raw_counter.items()
            )
        return cast(float, self._sum)
```

This technique uses two attributes to save the results of the sum and count calculations, `self._sum` and `self._count`. This value can be computed once and returned as often as needed with no cost for recalculation.

The type hints show these attributes as being optional. Once the values for `self._sum` and `self._count` have been computed, the values are no longer optional, but will be present. We describe this to `mypy` with the `cast()` type hint. This hint tells `mypy` to consider `self._sum` as being a `float` object, not an `Optional[float]` object.

This caching optimization is only helpful if the state of the `raw_counter` object never changes. In an application that updates the underlying `Counter`, this cached value would become out of date. That kind of application would need to recreate the `LazyCounterStatistics` every time the `Counter` was updated.

See also...

- In the *Designing classes with lots of processing* recipe, we defined a class that eagerly computed a number of attributes. This represents a different strategy for managing the cost of the computation.

Creating contexts and context managers

A number of Python objects behave like context managers. Some of the most visible examples are file objects. We often use `with path.open() as file:` to process a file and guarantee the resources are released. In *Chapter 2, Statements and Syntax*, the recipe *Context management and the "with" statement* covers the basics of using a file-based context manager.

How can we create our own classes that act as context managers?

Getting ready

We'll look at a function from *Chapter 3, Function Definitions*, in the *Picking an order for parameters based on partial functions* recipe. This recipe introduced a function, `haversine()`, which has a context-like parameter used to adjust the answer from dimensionless radians to a useful unit of measure, such as kilometers, nautical miles, or US statute miles. In many ways, this distance factor is a kind of context, used to define the kinds of computations that are done.

What we want is to be able to use the `with` statement to describe an object that doesn't change very quickly; indeed the change acts as a kind of boundary, defining the scope of computations. We might want to use code like the following:

```
>>> with Distance(r=NM) as nm_dist:
...     print(f"{nm_dist(p1, p2)=:.2f}")
...     print(f"{nm_dist(p2, p3)=:.2f}")
```

The `Distance(r=NM)` constructor provides the definition of the context, providing a new object, `nm_dist`, that has been configured to perform the required calculation in nautical miles. This can be used only within the body of the `with` statement.

This `Distance` class definition can be seen as creating a partial function, `nm_dist()`. This function provides a fixed unit-of-measure parameter, `r`, for a number of following computations using the `haversine()` function.

There are a number of other ways to create partial functions, including a `lambda` object, the `functools.partial()` function, and callable objects. We looked at the partial function alternative in *Chapter 3, Function Definitions*, in the *Picking an order for parameters based on partial functions* recipe.

How to do it...

A context manager class has two special methods that we need to define:

1. Start with a meaningful class name:

   ```
   class Distance:
   ```

2. Define an initializer that creates any unique features of the context. In this case, we want to set the units of distance that are used:

   ```
       def __init__(self, r: float) -> None:
           self.r = r
   ```

3. Define the `__enter__()` method. This is called when the `with` statement block begins. The statement `with Distance(r=NM) as nm_dist` does two things. First it creates the instance of the `Distance` class, then it calls the `__enter__()` method of that object to start the context. The return value from `__enter__()` is what's assigned to a local variable via the `as` clause. This isn't always required. For simple cases, the context manager often returns itself. If this method needs to return an instance in the same class, the class hasn't been fully defined yet, and the class name has to be given as a string. For this recipe, we'll return a function, with the type hint based on `Callable`:

   ```
       def __enter__(self) -> Callable[[Point, Point], float]:
           return self.distance
   ```

4. Define the `__exit__()` method. When the context finishes, this method is invoked. This is where resources are released and cleanup can happen. In this example, nothing more needs to be done. The details of any exception are provided to this method; it can silence the exception or allow it to propagate. If the return value is `True`, the exception is silenced. `False` or `None` return values will allow the exception to be seen outside the `with` statement:

   ```
       def __exit__(
           self,
   ```

```
        exc_type: Optional[Type[Exception]],
        exc_val: Optional[Exception],
        exc_tb: Optional[TracebackType]
    ) -> Optional[bool]:
        return None
```

5. Create the class (or define the methods if an instance of this class is returned) that works within the context. In this case, we're using the `haversine()` function from *Chapter 3, Function Definitions*:

```
    def distance(self, p1: Point, p2: Point) -> float:
        return haversine(
            p1.lat, p1.lon, p2.lat, p2.lon, self.r
        )
```

This class requires a fairly large number of imports:

```
from types import TracebackType
from typing import Optional, Type, Callable, NamedTuple
```

This class has been defined to work with objects of the class `Point`. This can be a `NamedTuple`, `dataclass`, or some other class that provides the required two attributes. Here's the `NamedTuple` definition of `Point`:

```
class Point(NamedTuple):
    lat: float
    lon: float
```

Do remember, however, that this class works with any object of class `Point`.

How it works...

The context manager relies on the `with` statement doing a large number of things.

We'll put the following construct under a microscope:

```
>>> nm_distance = Distance(r=NM)
>>> with nm_distance as nm_calc:
...     print(f"{nm_calc(p1, p2)=:.2f}")
```

The first line creates an instance of the `Distance` class. This has a value for the `r` parameter equal to the constant `NM`, allowing us to do computations in nautical miles. The `Distance` instance is assigned to the `nm_distance` variable.

When the `with` statement starts execution, the context manager object is notified by having the `__enter__()` method executed. In this case, the value returned by the `__enter__()` method is a function, with the type `Callable[[Point, Point], float]`. The `as` clause assigns this object to the `nm_calc` variable.

The `print()` function does its work using the `nm_calc` object. This object is a function which will compute a distance from two `Point` instances.

When the `with` statement finishes, the `__exit__()` method will be executed. For more complex context managers, this may involve closing files or releasing network connections. There are a great many kinds of context cleanup that might be necessary. In this case, there's nothing that needs to be done to clean up the context.

This has the advantage of providing a fixed context boundary in which the partial function is being used. In some cases, the computation inside the context manager might involve a database or complex web services, leading to a more complex `__exit__()` method.

There's more...

The operation of the `__exit__()` method is central to making best use of a context manager. In the previous example, we use the following "do nothing" `__exit__()` method:

```
def __exit__(
    self,
    exc_type: Optional[Type[Exception]],
    exc_val: Optional[Exception],
    exc_tb: Optional[TracebackType]
) -> Optional[bool]:
    # Cleanup goes here.

    return None
```

The point here is to allow any exception to propagate normally. We often see any cleanup processing replacing the `# Cleanup goes here.` comment. This is where buffers are flushed, files are closed, and error log messages are written. In more complex applications, the backup copy of a file may be restored.

Sometimes, we'll need to handle specific exception details. Consider the following snippet of an interactive session:

```
>>> p1 = Point(38.9784, -76.4922)
>>> p2 = Point(36.8443, -76.2922)
>>> with Distance(None) as nm_dist:
...     print(f"{nm_dist(p1, p2)=:.2f}")
Traceback (most recent call last):
  ...
```

```
TypeError: unsupported operand type(s) for *: 'NoneType' and 'int'
```

The `Distance()` class was initialized with the `r` argument value set to `None`. While this code will lead to warnings from `mypy`, it's syntactically valid. The type error traceback, however, doesn't point to the `Distance` class, but points to a line of code within the `haversine()` function.

We might want to report a `ValueError` instead of this `TypeError`. Here's a variation on the `Distance` class, called `Distance_2`. This class conceals the `TypeError`, replacing it with a `ValueError`:

```
class Distance_2:
    def __init__(self, r: float) -> None:
        self.r = r

    def __enter__(self) -> Callable[[Point, Point], float]:
        return self.distance

    def __exit__(
        self,
        exc_type: Optional[Type[Exception]],
        exc_val: Optional[Exception],
        exc_tb: Optional[TracebackType]
    ) -> Optional[bool]:
        if exc_type is TypeError:
            raise ValueError(f"Invalid r={self.r}")
        return None

    def distance(self, p1: Point, p2: Point) -> float:
        return haversine(p1.lat, p1.lon, p2.lat, p2.lon, self.r)
```

This shows how we can examine the details of the exception in the `__exit__()` method. The information provided parallels the `sys.exc_info()` function, and includes the exception's type, the exception object, and a traceback object with the `types.TracebackType` type.

See also

- In the *Context management and the "with" statement* recipe in *Chapter 2, Statements and Syntax*, we cover the basics of using a file-based context manager.

Managing multiple contexts with multiple resources

We often use context managers with open files. Because the context manager can guarantee the OS resources are released, doing so prevents resource leaks and files that are damaged from being closed without having all of the bytes properly written to persistent storage.

When multiple resources are being processed, it often means multiple context managers will be needed. If we have two or three open files, does this mean we have deeply nested `with` statements? How can we optimize or simplify multiple `with` statements?

Getting ready

We'll look at creating a plan for a journey with multiple legs. Our starting data collection is a list of points that define our route. For example, traveling through Chesapeake Bay may involve starting in Annapolis, Maryland, sailing to Solomon's Island, Deltaville, Virginia, and then Norfolk, Virginia. For planning purposes, we'd like to think of this as three legs, instead of four points. A leg has a distance and takes time to traverse: the time and distance are the essence of the planning problem.

We'll start with some foundational definitions before we run the recipe. First is the definition of a single point, with attributes of latitude and longitude:

```
@dataclass(frozen=True)
class Point:
    lat: float

    lon: float
```

A point can be built with a statement like this: `p = Point(38.9784, -76.4922)`. This lets us refer to `p.lat` and `p.lon` in subsequent computations. The use of attribute names makes the code much easier to read.

A leg is a pair of points. We can define it as follows:

```
@dataclass
lass Leg:
    start: Point
    end: Point

    distance: float = field(init=False)
```

We've created this as a mutable object. The `distance` attribute has an initial value defined by the `dataclasses.field()` function. The use of `init=False` means the attribute is not provided when the object is initialized; it must be supplied after initialization.

Here's a context manager to create `Leg` objects from `Point` instances. This is similar to the context managers shown in the *Using contexts and context managers* recipe. There is a tiny but important difference here. The `__init__()` saves a value for `self.r` to set the distance unit context. The default value is nautical miles:

```
class LegMaker:
    def __init__(self, r: float=NM) -> None:
        self.last_point: Optional[Point] = None
        self.last_leg: Optional[Leg] = None
        self.r = r

    def __enter__(self) -> 'LegMaker':
        return self

    def __exit__(
        self,
        exc_type: Optional[Type[Exception]],
        exc_val: Optional[Exception],
        exc_tb: Optional[TracebackType]
    ) -> Optional[bool]:

        return None
```

The important method, `waypoint()`, accepts a waypoint and creates a `Leg` object. The very first waypoint, the starting point for the voyage, will return `None`. All subsequent points will return a `Leg` object:

```
def waypoint(self, next_point: Point) -> Optional[Leg]:
    leg: Optional[Leg]
    if self.last_point is None:
        # Special case for the first leg
        leg = None
    else:
        leg = Leg(self.last_point, next_point)
        d = haversine(
            leg.start.lat, leg.start.lon,
            leg.end.lat, leg.end.lon, self.r
        )
        leg.distance = round(d)
    self.last_point = next_point

    return leg
```

This method uses a cached point, `self.last_point`, and the next point, `next_point`, to create a `Leg` instance.

If we want to create an output file in CSV format, we'll need to use two context managers: one to create `Leg` objects, and another to manage the open file. We'll put this complex multi-context processing into a single function.

How to do it...

1. Define the headers to be used for the CSV output:

```
HEADERS = ["start_lat", "start_lon", "end_lat", "end_lon",
"distance"]
```

2. Define a function to transform complex objects into a dictionary suitable for writing each individual row. The input is a `Leg` object; the output is a dictionary with keys that match the `HEADERS` list of column names:

```
def flat_dict(leg: Leg) -> Dict[str, float]:
    struct = asdict(leg)
    return dict(
        start_lat=struct["start"]["lat"],
        start_lon=struct["start"]["lon"],
        end_lat=struct["end"]["lat"],
        end_lon=struct["end"]["lon"],
        distance=struct["distance"],
    )
```

3. Define the function with a meaningful name. We'll provide two parameters: a list of `Point` objects and a `Path` object showing where the CSV file should be created. We've used `Iterable[Point]` as a type hint so this function can accept any iterable collection of `Point` instances:

```
def make_route_file(
    points: Iterable[Point], target: Path
) -> None:
```

4. Start the two contexts with a single `with` statement. This will invoke both `__enter__()` methods to prepare both contexts for work. This line can get long, and parentheses can't easily be used to extend it, so a \ is often used for complex `with` statements:

```
with LegMaker(r=NM) as legger, \
    target.open('w', newline='') as csv_file:
```

5. Once the contexts are ready for work, we can create a CSV writer and begin writing rows:

```
writer = csv.DictWriter(csv_file, HEADERS)
writer.writeheader()
for point in points:
    leg = legger.waypoint(point)
    if leg is not None:
        writer.writerow(flat_dict(leg))
```

6. At the end of the context, do any final summary processing. This is not indented within the `with` statement's body; it is at the same indentation level as the `with` keyword itself:

```
print(f"Finished creating {target}")
```

How it works...

The compound `with` statement created a number of context managers for us. All of the managers will have their `__enter__()` methods used to both start processing and, optionally, return an object usable within the context. The `LegMaker` class defined an `__enter__()` method that returned the `LegMaker` instance. The `Path.open()` method returns a `TextIO` object; these are also context managers.

When the context exits at the end of the `with` statement, all of the context manager `__exit__()` methods are called. This allows each context manager to do any finalization. In the case of `TextIO` objects, this closes the external files, releasing any of the OS resources being used. In the cast of the `LegMaker` object, there is no finalization processing on context exit.

There's more...

A context manager's job is to isolate details of resource management. The most common examples are files and network connections. We've shown using a context manager around an algorithm to help manage a cache with a single `Point` object.

In this example, we specifically strove to avoid accumulating a large number of `Leg` instances. For some kinds of data science applications, the entire dataset doesn't fit in memory, and it's challenging to work with all the data in a single list or pandas `DataFrame`.

When working with very large datasets, it's often helpful to use compression. This can create a different kind of context around the processing. The built-in `open()` method is generally assigned to the `io.open()` function in the `io` module. This means we can often replace `io.open()` with a function such as `bz2.open()` to work with compressed files.

We can replace the context manager with something like this:

```
def make_route_bz2(
    points: Iterable[Point], target: Path
) -> None:
    with LegMaker(r=NM) as legger, \
            bz2.open(target, "wt") as archive:
        writer = csv.DictWriter(archive, HEADERS)
        writer.writeheader()
        for point in points:
            leg = legger.waypoint(point)
            if leg is not None:
                writer.writerow(flat_dict(leg))

    print(f"Finished creating {target}")
```

We've replaced the original `path.open()` method with `bz2.open(path)`. The rest of the context processing remains identical. This flexibility allows us to work with text files initially and convert to compressed files when the volume of data grows or when we move away from testing and experimenting into full-sized production use of the software.

See also

- In the *Context management and the "with" statement* recipe in *Chapter 2, Statements and Syntax*, we cover the basics of using a file-based context manager.
- The *Creating contexts and context managers* recipe covers the core of creating a class that is a context manager.

8
More Advanced Class Design

In *Chapter 7, Basics of Classes and Objects*, we looked at some recipes that covered the basics of class design. In this chapter, we'll dive more deeply into Python classes.

In the *Designing classes with lots of processing* and *Using properties for lazy attributes* recipes in *Chapter 7, Basics of Classes and Objects*, we identified a design choice that's central to object-oriented programming, the "wrap versus extend" decision. One way to add features is to create a new subclass via an extension. The other technique for adding features is to wrap an existing class, making it part of a new class.

In addition to direct inheritance, there are some other class extension techniques available in Python. A Python class can inherit features from more than one superclass. We call this design pattern a **mixin**.

In *Chapter 4, Built-In Data Structures Part 1: Lists and Sets*, and *Chapter 5, Built-In Data Structures Part 2: Dictionaries*, we looked at the core built-in data structures. We can combine and extend these collection definition features to create more complex data structures or data structures with additional features.

In this chapter, we'll look at the following recipes:

- Choosing between `inheritance` and `composition` - the "`is-a`" question
- Separating concerns via multiple `inheritance`
- Leveraging Python's duck typing
- Managing `global` and `singleton` objects

- Using more complex structures – maps of lists
- Creating a `class` that has orderable objects
- Improving performance with an ordered `collection`
- Deleting from a `list` of complicated objects

There are a great many techniques of object-oriented class design available in Python. We'll start with a foundational concept: making the design choice between using inheritance from a base class and wrapping a class to extend it.

Choosing between inheritance and composition – the "is-a" question

In the *Using cmd for creating command-line applications* recipe in *Chapter 6, User Inputs and Outputs*, and the *Extending a collection – a list that does statistics* recipe in *Chapter 7, Basics of Classes and Objects*, we looked at extending a class. In both cases, the class implemented in the recipe was a subclass of one of Python's built-in classes. In *Chapter 7, Basics of Classes and Objects*, we defined the `DiceCLI` class to extend the `cmd.Cmd` class via inheritance. In We also defined a `StatsList` class to extend the built-in `list` class.

The idea of extension via inheritance is sometimes called the generalization-specialization relationship. It's sometimes also called an **is-a relationship**.

There's an important semantic issue here: it's sometimes referred to as the **wrap versus extend problem**. There are two common choices:

- Do we mean that instances of the subclass are also examples of the superclass? This is an **is-a** relationship. An example in Python is the built-in `Counter`, which extends the base class `dict`. A `Counter` instance is a dictionary with a few extra features.
- Or do we mean something else? Perhaps there's an association, sometimes called a **has-a relationship**. An example of this is in the *Designing classes with lots of processing* recipe in *Chapter 7, Basics of Classes and Objects*, where `CounterStatistics` wraps a `Counter` object. In this case, the `CounterStatistics` object has a `Counter`, but is not a kind of `Counter`, nor is it a dictionary.

We'll look at both the inheritance and composition techniques for creating new features for existing classes. Seeing both solutions to the same problem can help clarify the differences.

Getting ready

For this recipe, we'll use models for a deck of playing cards as concrete examples. We have two ways to model a deck of playing cards:

- As a class of objects that extends the built-in `list` class. The deck **is a** list.
- As a wrapper that combines the built-in `list` class with some other features. The deck **has a** list as an attribute.

The core ingredient for both implementations is the underlying `Card` object. We can define this using `typing.NamedTuple`:

```
>>> from typing import NamedTuple
>>> class Card(NamedTuple):
...     rank: int
...     suit: str
>>> Spades, Hearts, Diamonds, Clubs = '\u2660\u2661\u2662\u2663'
```

We've created the class definition, `Card`, by extending the `NamedTuple` class. This creates a new subclass with two attributes of `rank` and `suit`. We've provided the type hints to suggest `rank` should be an integer value, and `suit` should be a string. The `mypy` tool can be used to confirm the type hints are followed by the code using this class.

We also defined the various suits as four different Unicode character strings, each of length one. The four-character literal was decomposed into four single-character substrings. The `"\u2660"` string, for example, is a single Unicode character that displays the black spade character.

Here's how we can build a `Card` object with a rank and suit:

```
>>> Card(2, Spades)
Card(rank=2, suit='♠')
```

We could provide an `Enum` class to define the collection of suit values. We'll leave this as an exercise for the reader.

We'll use this `Card` class in the rest of this recipe. In some card games, a single 52-card deck is used. In other games, a dealing shoe is used; this is a box that allows a dealer to shuffle and deal from multiple decks.

What's important is that the various kinds of collection—deck, shoe, and the built-in `list` type—all have considerable overlaps in the kinds of features they support. This means that both inheritance and wrapping will work. The two techniques make different claims and can lead to different ways of understanding the resulting code.

How to do it...

This recipe has three overall sections. In the first section, we'll take a close look at a previous recipe. We'll be working with the *Using a class to encapsulate data and processing* recipe in *Chapter 7, Basics of Classes and Objects*, with this recipe. After looking at the design changes, we'll show how to implement them using both inheritance and composition.

Here's the first part of the recipe to examine and plan the design changes:

1. Use the nouns and verbs from the original story or problem statement to identify all of the classes.
2. Look for overlaps in the feature sets of various classes. In many cases, the relationships will come directly from the problem statement itself. In the preceding example, a game can deal cards from a deck, or deal cards from a shoe. In this case, we might state one of these two views:
    - A shoe is a specialized deck that starts with multiple copies of the 52-card domain
    - A deck is a specialized shoe with only one copy of the 52-card domain
3. Clarify the relationships among the classes where necessary. We expected `Deck` to have one copy of each `Card`. `Shoe`, however, will have many copies of each `Card`. A large number of cards can share rank numbers and suit strings. There are a number of common patterns to these dependencies:
    - **Aggregation**: Some objects are bound into collections, but the objects have a properly independent existence. Our `Card` objects might be aggregated into a `Hand` collection. When the game ends, the `Hand` objects can be deleted, but the `Card` objects continue to exist.
    - **Composition**: Some objects are bound into collections, but do not have an independent existence. When looking at card games, a `Hand` of cards cannot exist without a `Player`. We might say that a `Player` object is composed—in part—of a `Hand`. If a `Player` is eliminated from a game, then the `Hand` objects must also be removed. While this is important for understanding the relationships among objects, there are some practical considerations that we'll look at in the next section.
    - **An is-a relationship among classes (also called inheritance)**: This is the idea that a `Shoe` is a `Deck` with an extra feature (or two). This may be central to our design. We'll look into this in detail in the *Extending - inheritance* section of this recipe.

We've identified several paths for implementing the associations. The **aggregation** and **composition** cases are generally implemented by some kind of "wrapping" design techniques. The **inheritance** or is-a case is the "extending" technique. We'll look at these techniques separately.

Wrapping – aggregation and composition

Wrapping is a way to understand a collection. It can be a class that is an aggregate of independent objects. This could be implemented as a class that wraps an existing `list` object, meaning that the underlying `Card` objects will be shared by a `list` collection and a `Deck` collection.

We can implement the desired design changes through composition using this portion of the overall recipe:

1. Define the independent collection. It might be a built-in collection, for example, a `set`, `list`, or `dict`. For this example, it will be a `list` that contains the individual `Card` instances:

   ```
   >>> domain = list(
   ...     Card(r+1,s)
   ...         for r in range(13)
   ...             for s in (Spades, Hearts, Diamonds, Clubs))
   ```

2. Define the aggregate class. To distinguish similar examples in this book, the name has a `_W` suffix. This not a generally recommended practice; it's only used here to emphasize the distinctions between class definitions in this recipe. (A short suffix like `"_W"` doesn't add much clarity in the long run; in this context, it's helpful to keep the example code short.) Later, we'll see a slightly different variation on this design. Here's the definition of the class:

   ```
   class Deck_W:
   ```

3. Use the `__init__()` method of this class as one way to provide the underlying collection object. This will also initialize any stateful variables. We might create an iterator for dealing:

   ```
       def __init__(self, cards: List[Card]) -> None:
           self.cards = cards
           self.deal_iter = iter(cards)
   ```

   This uses a type hint, `List[Card]`. The `typing` module provides the necessary definition of the `List` type hint. (This can be generalized to use a parameter annotation of `Iterable[Card]` and `self.cards = list(cards)`. It's not clear that this generalization is helpful for this application.)

4. If needed, provide other methods to either replace the collection or update the collection. This is rare in Python, since the underlying attribute, `cards`, can be accessed directly. However, it might be helpful to provide a method that replaces the `self.cards` value.

5. Provide the methods appropriate to the aggregate object. In this case, we've included two additional processing methods that encapsulate some of the behaviors of a deck of cards. The `shuffle()` method randomizes the internal list object, `self.cards`. It also creates an iterator used to step through the `self.cards` list by the `deal()` method. We've provided a type hint on `deal()` to clarify that it returns a `Card` instance:

```
def shuffle(self) -> None:
    random.shuffle(self.cards)
    self.deal_iter = iter(self.cards)

def deal(self) -> Card:
    return next(self.deal_iter)
```

Here's how we can use the `Deck_W` class. We'll be working with a list of `Card` objects. In this case, the `domain` variable was created from a list comprehension that generated all 52 combinations of 13 ranks and four suits:

```
>>> domain = list(
...     Card(r+1,s)
...         for r in range(13)
...             for s in (Spades, Hearts, Diamonds, Clubs))
>>> len(domain)
52
```

We can use the items in this collection, `domain`, to create a second aggregate object that shares the same underlying `Card` objects. We'll build the `Deck_W` object from the list of objects in the `domain` variable:

```
>>> import random
>>> from Chapter_08.ch08_r01 import Deck_W
>>> d = Deck_W(domain)
```

Once the `Deck_W` object is available, it's possible to use the unique features:

```
>>> random.seed(1)
>>> d.shuffle()
>>> [d.deal() for _ in range(5)]
[Card(rank=13, suit='♡'),
 Card(rank=3, suit='♡'),
 Card(rank=10, suit='♡'),
 Card(rank=6, suit='◊'),
 Card(rank=1, suit='◊')]
```

We've seeded the random number generator to force the shuffle operation to leave the cards in a known order. We can deal five cards from the deck. This shows how the `Deck_W` object, `d`, shares the same pool of objects as the `domain` list.

We can delete the `Deck_W` object, `d`, and create a new deck from the `domain` list. This is because the `Card` objects are not part of a composition. The cards have an existence independent of the `Deck_W` collection.

Extending – inheritance

Here's an approach to defining a class that extends one of the built-in collections of objects. We'll define a `Deck_X` class as an aggregate that wraps an existing list. The underlying `Card` objects will be part of the `Deck_X` list.

We can implement the desired design changes through inheritance using the steps from this portion of the overall recipe:

1. Start by defining the extension class as a subclass of a built-in collection. To distinguish similar examples in this book, the name has an `_X` suffix. A short suffix like this is not a generally recommended practice; it's used here to emphasize the distinctions between class definitions in this recipe. The subclass relationship is a formal statement—a `Deck_X` is also a kind of list. Here's the class definition:

    ```
    class Deck_X(list):
    ```

2. No additional code is needed to initialize the instance, as we'll use the `__init__()` method inherited from the `list` class.
3. No additional code is needed to update the list, as we'll use other methods of the `list` class for adding, changing, or removing items from the `Deck`.
4. Provide the appropriate methods to the extended object. The `shuffle()` method randomizes the object as a whole. The collection here is `self`, because this method is an extension of the `list` class. The `deal()` object relies on an iterator created by the `shuffle()` method to step through the `self.cards` list. Exactly like in `Deck_W`, we've provided a type hint on `deal()` to clarify that it returns a `Card` instance:

    ```
    def shuffle(self) -> None:
        random.shuffle(self)
        self.deal_iter = iter(self)

    def deal(self) -> Card:
        return next(self.deal_iter)
    ```

Here's how we can use the Deck_X class. First, we'll build a deck of cards:

```
>>> from Chapter_08.ch08_r01 import Deck_X
>>> d2 = Deck_X(
...     Card(r+1,s)
...         for r in range(13)
...             for s in (Spades, Hearts, Diamonds, Clubs))
>>> len(d2)
52
```

We used a generator expression to build individual Card objects. We can use the Deck_X() class in exactly the same way we'd use the list() class to create a new instance. In this case, we built a Deck_X object from the generator expression. We could build a list similarly.

We did not provide an implementation for the built-in __len__() method. This was inherited from the list class; it works nicely.

Using the deck-specific features for this implementation looks exactly like the other implementation, Deck_W:

```
>>> random.seed(1)
>>> d2.shuffle()
>>> [d2.deal() for _ in range(5)]
[Card(rank=13, suit='♡'),
 Card(rank=3, suit='♡'),
 Card(rank=10, suit='♡'),
 Card(rank=6, suit='◊'),
 Card(rank=1, suit='◊')]
```

We've seeded the random number generator, shuffled the deck, and dealt five cards. The extension methods work as well for Deck_X as they do for Deck_W. The shuffle() and deal() methods do their jobs.

There are some huge differences between these two definitions. When wrapping, we get precisely the methods we defined and no others. When using inheritance, we receive a wealth of method definitions from the superclass. This leads to some additional behaviors in the Deck_X class that may not be desirable:

- We can use a variety of collections to create Deck_X instances. The Deck_W class will only work for sequences offering the methods used by shuffling. We used a type hint to suggest that only List[Card] was sensible.

- A `Deck_X` instance can be sliced and indexed outside the core sequential iteration supported by the `deal()` method.
- Both classes create an internal `deal_iter` object to iterate through the cards and expose this iterator through the `deal()` method. `Deck_X`, being a list, also offers the special method `__iter__()`, and can be used as an iterable source of `Card` objects without the `deal()` method.

These differences are also important parts of deciding which technique to use. If the additional features are desirable, that suggests inheritance. If the additional features create problems, then composition might be a better choice.

How it works...

This is how Python implements the idea of inheritance. It uses a clever search algorithm for finding methods (and attributes.) The search works like this:

1. Examine the object's class for the method or attribute.
2. If the name is not defined in the immediate class, then search in all of the parent classes for the method or attribute.

Searching through the parent classes assures two things:

- Any method defined in any superclass is available to all subclasses
- Any subclass can override a method to replace a superclass method

Because of this, a subclass of the `list` class inherits all the features of the parent class. It is a specialized variation of the built-in `list` class.

This also means that all methods have the potential to be overridden by a subclass. Some languages have ways to lock a method against extension. Because Python doesn't have this, a subclass can override any method.

To explicitly refer to methods from a superclass, we can use the `super()` function to force a search through the superclasses. This allows a subclass to add features by wrapping the superclass version of a method. We use it like this:

```
def some_method(self):
    # do something extra
    super().some_method()
```

In this case, the `some_method()` method of a class will do something extra and then do the superclass version of the method. This allows us a handy way to extend selected methods of a class. We can preserve the superclass features while adding features unique to the subclass.

When designing a class, we must choose between several essential techniques:

- **Wrapping**: This technique creates a new class. All the methods you want the new class to have, you must explicitly define. This can be a lot of code to provide the required methods. Wrapping can be decomposed into two broad implementation choices:
    - **Aggregation**: The objects being wrapped have an independent existence from the wrapper. The `Deck_W` example showed how the `Card` objects and even the list of cards were independent of the class. When any `Deck_W` object is deleted, the underlying list will continue to exist; it's included as a reference only.
    - **Composition**: The objects being wrapped don't have any independent existence; they're an essential part of the composition. This involves a subtle difficulty because of Python's reference counting. We'll look at this shortly in some detail.
- **Extension via inheritance**: This is the is-a relationship. When extending a built-in class, then a great many methods are available from the superclass. The `Deck_X` example showed this technique by creating a deck as an extension to the built-in `list` class.

There's more...

When looking at the independent existence of objects, there's an additional consideration regarding memory use. Python uses a technique called reference counting to track how many times an object is used. A statement such as `del deck` doesn't directly remove the `deck` object. A `del` statement removes the `deck` *variable*, which decrements the reference count for the underlying *object*. When the reference count reaches zero, the underlying object is no longer used by any variable and can be removed (that removal is known as "garbage collection").

Consider the following example:

```
>>> c_2s = Card(2, Spades)
>>> c_2s
Card(rank=2, suit='♠')
>>> another = c_2s
>>> another
Card(rank=2, suit='♠')
```

After the above four statements, we have a single object, `Card(2, Spades)`, and two *variables* that refer to the object: both `c_2s` and `another`. We can confirm this by comparing their respective `id` values:

```
>>> id(c_2s) == id(another)
True
>>> c_2s is another
True
```

If we remove one of those variables with the `del` statement, the other variable still has a reference to the underlying object. The object won't be removed from memory until sometime after both variables are removed.

This consideration minimizes the distinction between aggregation and composition for Python programmers. In languages that don't use automatic garbage collection or reference counts, composition becomes an important part of memory management. In Python, we generally focus on aggregation over composition because the removal of unused objects is entirely automatic.

See also

- We've looked at built-in collections in *Chapter 4, Built-In Data Structures Part 1: Lists and Sets*. Also, in *Chapter 7, Basics of Classes and Objects*, we looked at how to define simple collections.
- In the *Designing classes with lots of processing* recipe, we looked at wrapping a class with a separate class that handles the processing details. We can contrast this with the *Using properties for lazy attributes* recipe of *Chapter 7, Basics of Classes and Objects*, where we put the complicated computations into the class as properties; this design relies on extension.

Separating concerns via multiple inheritance

In the *Choosing between inheritance and extension – the is-a question* recipe earlier in the chapter, we looked at the idea of defining a `Deck` class that was a composition of playing card objects. For the purposes of that example, we treated each `Card` object as simply having a rank and a suit. This created two small problems:

- The display for the card always showed a numeric rank. We didn't see J, Q, or K. Instead we saw 11, 12, and 13. Similarly, an ace was shown as 1 instead of A.

- Many games, such as *Blackjack* and *Cribbage*, assign a point value to each rank. Generally, the face cards have 10 points. For *Blackjack*, an ace has two different point values; depending on the total of other cards in the hand, it can be worth 1 point or 10 points.

Python's multiple inheritance lets us handle all of these variations in card game rules while keeping a single, essential `Card` class. Using multiple inheritance lets us separate rules for specific games from generic properties of playing cards. We can define a base class with mixin features.

Getting ready

A practical extension to the `Card` class needs to be a mixture of two feature sets:

1. The essential features, such as rank and suit. This includes a method to show the `Card` object's value nicely as a string (perhaps including "K," "Q," and so on, for court cards and aces, and numbers for spot cards).
2. Other, less essential, game-specific features, such as the number of points allotted to each particular card.

Python lets us define a class that includes features from multiple parents. A class can have both a `Card` superclass and a `GameRules` superclass.

In order to make sense of this kind of design, we'll often partition the various class hierarchies into two subsets of features:

- **Essential features**: These include the `rank` and `suit` attributes that apply to all `Card` instances.
- **Mixin features**: These features are *mixed in* to the class definition; they cover additional, more specialized use cases.

The idea is to define concrete classes from both essential and mixin features.

How to do it...

This recipe will create two hierarchies of classes, one for the essential `Card` and one for game-specific features including *Cribbage* point values. The essential class and mixin classes are then combined to create final, concrete classes appropriate to a specific game:

1. Define the essential class. This is a generic `Card` class, suitable for ranks 2 to 10:

```
@dataclass(frozen=True)
class Card:
    """Superclass for cards"""
    rank: int
```

```
    suit: str

    def __str__(self) -> str:
        return f"{self.rank:2d} {self.suit}"
```

2. Define the subclasses to implement specializations. We need two subclasses of the `Card` class—the `AceCard` class and the `FaceCard` class, as defined in the following code:

```
class AceCard(Card):
    def __str__(self) -> str:
        return f" A {self.suit}"


class FaceCard(Card):
    def __str__(self) -> str:
        names = {11: "J", 12: "Q", 13: "K"}
        return f" {names[self.rank]} {self.suit}"
```

3. Define the core features required by the mixin classes. In Python parlance, this is called a "protocol" that the mixin classes implement. (In other languages, it might be called an *interface*.) We've used the `typing.Protocol` type hint as the superclass. The type annotation requires each card to possess an integer rank attribute:

```
class PointedCard(Protocol):
    rank: int
```

4. Define a mixin subclass that identifies the additional features that will be added. For the game of *Cribbage*, the points for some cards are equal to the rank of the card. In this example, we'll use a concrete class that handles the rules for ace through 10:

```
class CribbagePoints(PointedCard):
    def points(self: PointedCard) -> int:
        return self.rank
```

5. Define concrete mixin subclasses for other kinds of features. For the three ranks of face cards, the points are always 10:

```
class CribbageFacePoints(PointedCard):
    def points(self: PointedCard) -> int:
        return 10
```

6. Create the final, concrete class definitions that combine one of the essential base classes and any required mixin classes. While it's technically possible to add unique method definitions here, this example has sets of features entirely defined in separate classes:

```
class CribbageCard(Card, CribbagePoints):
    pass


class CribbageAce(AceCard, CribbagePoints):
    pass


class CribbageFace(FaceCard, CribbageFacePoints):
    pass
```

7. Define a factory function (or factory class) to create the appropriate objects based on the input parameters. Even with the mixins, the objects being created will all be considered as subclasses of `Card` because it's first in the list of base classes:

```
def make_cribbage_card(rank: int, suit: str) -> Card:
    if rank == 1:
        return CribbageAce(rank, suit)
    if 2 <= rank < 11:
        return CribbageCard(rank, suit)
    if 11 <= rank:
        return CribbageFace(rank, suit)
    raise ValueError(f"Invalid rank {rank}")
```

We can use the `make_cribbage_card()` function to create a shuffled deck of cards as shown in this example interactive session:

```
>>> import random
>>> random.seed(1)
>>> deck = [make_cribbage_card(rank+1, suit) for rank in range(13) for suit in SUITS]
>>> random.shuffle(deck)
>>> len(deck)
52
>>> [str(c) for c in deck[:5]]
[' K ♡', ' 3 ♡', '10 ♡', ' 6 ◊', ' A ◊']
```

We've seeded the random number generator to assure that the results are the same each time we evaluate the `shuffle()` function. Having a fixed seed makes unit testing easier with predictable results.

We use a list comprehension to generate a list of cards that include all 13 ranks and 4 suits. This is a collection of 52 individual objects. The objects belong to two class hierarchies. Each object is a subclass of `Card` as well as being a subclass of `CribbagePoints`. This means that both collections of features are available for all of the objects.

For example, we can evaluate the `points()` method of each `Card` object:

```
>>> sum(c.points() for c in deck[:5])
30
```

The hand has two face cards, plus three, six, and ace, so the total points are `30`.

How it works...

Python's mechanism for finding a method (or attribute) of an object works like this:

1. Search the instance for the attribute.
2. Search in the class for the method or attribute.
3. If the name is not defined in the immediate class, then search all of the parent classes for the method or attribute. The parent classes are searched in a sequence called, appropriately, the **Method Resolution Order** (**MRO**).

We can see the method resolution order using the `mro()` method of a class. Here's an example:

```
>>> c = deck[5]
>>> str(c)
'10 ◊'
>>> c.__class__.__name__
'CribbageCard'
>>> c.__class__.mro()
[<class 'Chapter_08.ch08_r02.CribbageCard'>, <class 'Chapter_08.ch08_r02.
Card'>, <class 'Chapter_08.ch08_r02.CribbagePoints'>, <class 'Chapter_08.
ch08_r02.PointedCard'>, <class 'typing.Protocol'>, <class 'typing.
Generic'>, <class 'object'>]
```

We picked a card from the deck, `c`. The card's `__class__` attribute is a reference to the class. In this case, the class name is `CribbageCard`. The `mro()` method of this class shows us the order that's used to resolve names:

1. First, search the class itself, `CribbageCard`.
2. If it's not there, search `Card`.

3. Try to find it in `CribbagePoints` next.
4. Try to find it in the `PointedCard` protocol definition. This leads to a potential search of `Protocol`, and `Generic`, also.
5. Use `object` last.

Class definitions generally use internal `dict` objects to store method definitions. This means that the search is an extremely fast hash-based lookup of the name.

There's more...

There are several kinds of design concerns we can separate in the form of mixins:

- **Persistence and representation of state**: We might add methods to manage conversion to a consistent external representation. For example, methods to represent the state of an object in CSV or JSON notation.
- **Security**: This may involve a mixin class that performs a consistent authorization check that becomes part of each object.
- **Logging**: A mixin class could create a logger that's consistent across a variety of classes.
- **Event signaling and change notification**: In this case, we might have objects that produce state change notifications; objects can subscribe to those notifications. These are sometimes called the **Observable** and **Observer** design patterns. A GUI widget might observe the state of an object; when the object changes, the mixin feature notifies the GUI widget so that the display is refreshed.

In many cases, these concerns can be handled by separating the core state definition from these additional concerns. Mixin classes provide a way to isolate the various considerations.

As an example, we'll create a mixin to introduce logging to cards. We'll define this class in a way that must be provided first in the list of superclasses. Since it's early in the MRO list, it uses the `super()` function to use methods defined by subsequent classes in the MRO list.

This class will add the `logger` attribute to each class that has the `PointedCard` protocol defined:

```
class Logged(PointedCard):

    def __init__(self, *args, **kw):
        self.logger = logging.getLogger(self.__class__.__name__)
        super().__init__(*args, **kw)

    def points(self):
        p = super().points()
```

```
        self.logger.debug("points {0}", p)
        return p
```

Note that we've used `super().__init__()` to perform the `__init__()` method of any other classes defined. The order for these initializations comes from the class MRO. As we just noted, it's generally the simplest approach to have one class that defines the essential features of an object, and all other mixins add features to the essential object.

It's common to see the `super().__init__()` method called first. We've established the logger before performing other initializations so that mixin classes can depend on the presence of a logger prior to their initialization. This can help in debugging initialization problems.

We've provided a definition for `points()`. This will search other classes in the MRO list for an implementation of `points()`. Then it will log the results computed by the method from another class.

Here are some classes that include the `Logged` mixin features:

```
class LoggedCribbageAce(Logged, AceCard, CribbagePoints):
    pass


class LoggedCribbageCard(Logged, Card, CribbagePoints):
    pass


class LoggedCribbageFace(Logged, FaceCard, CribbageFacePoints):
    pass
```

Each of these classes are built from three separate class definitions. Since the `Logged` class is provided first, we're assured that all classes have consistent logging. We're also assured that any method in `Logged` can use `super()` to locate an implementation in the class list that follows it in the sequence of classes in the definition.

To make use of these classes, we'd need to make one more small change to an application:

```
def make_logged_card(rank: int, suit: str) -> Card:
    if rank == 1:
        return LoggedCribbageAce(rank, suit)
    if 2 <= rank < 11:
        return LoggedCribbageCard(rank, suit)
    if 11 <= rank:
        return LoggedCribbageFace(rank, suit)
    raise ValueError(f"Invalid rank {rank}")
```

We need to use this function instead of make_cribbage_card(). This function will use the set of class definitions that creates logged cards.

Here's how we use this function to build a deck of card instances:

```
deck = [make_logged_card(rank+1, suit)
        for rank in range(13)
            for suit in SUITS]
```

We've replaced make_card() with make_logged_card() when creating a deck. Once we do this, we now have detailed debugging information available from a number of classes in a consistent fashion.

See also

- The method resolution order is computed when the class is created. The algorithm used is called C3. More information is available at https://dl.acm.org/doi/10.1145/236337.236343. The process was originally developed for the Dylan language and is now also used by Python. The C3 algorithm assures that each parent class is searched exactly once. It also assures that the relative ordering of superclasses is preserved; subclasses will be searched before any of their parent classes are examined.
- When considering multiple inheritance, it's always essential to also consider whether or not a wrapper is a better design than a subclass. See the *Choosing between inheritance and extension – the is-a question* recipe.

Leveraging Python's duck typing

When a design involves inheritance, there is often a clear relationship from a superclass to one or more subclasses. In the *Choosing between inheritance and extension – the is-a question* recipe of this chapter, as well as the *Extending a collection – a list that does statistics* recipe in *Chapter 7*, *Basics of Classes and Objects*, we've looked at extensions that involve a proper subclass-superclass relationship.

In order to have classes that can be used in place of one another ("polymorphic" classes), some languages require a common superclass. In many cases, the common class doesn't have concrete implementations for all of the methods; it's called an abstract superclass.

Python doesn't *require* common superclasses. The standard library, however, does offer the abc module. This provides optional support creating abstract classes in cases where it can help to clarify the relationships among classes.

Instead of defining polymorphic classes with common superclasses, Python relies on **duck typing** to establish equivalence. This name comes from the quote:

> *"When I see a bird that walks like a duck and swims like a duck and quacks like a duck, I call that bird a duck."*

In the case of Python class relationships, if two objects have the same methods, and the same attributes, these similarities have the same effect as having a common superclass. No formal definition of a common class is required.

This recipe will show how to exploit the concept of duck typing to create polymorphic classes. Instances of these classes can be used in place of each other, giving us more flexible designs.

Getting ready

In some cases, it can be awkward to define a superclass for a number of loosely related implementation choices. For example, if an application is spread across several modules, it might be challenging to factor out a common superclass and put this by itself in a separate module where it can be imported into other modules.

Instead of factoring out a common abstraction, it's sometimes easier to create two equivalent classes that will pass the "duck test"—the two classes have the same methods and attributes, therefore, they are effectively interchangeable, polymorphic classes. The alternative implementations can be used interchangeably.

How to do it...

We'll define a pair of classes to show how this works. These classes will both simulate rolling a pair of dice. We'll create two distinct implementations that have enough common features that they are interchangeable:

1. Start with a class, `Dice1`, with the required methods and attributes. In this example, we'll have one attribute, `dice`, that retains the result of the last roll, and one method, `roll()`, that changes the state of the dice:

    ```
    class Dice1:
        def __init__(self, seed=None) -> None:
            self._rng = random.Random(seed)
            self.roll()

        def roll(self) -> Tuple[int, ...]:
            self.dice = (
                self._rng.randint(1, 6),
    ```

```
                self._rng.randint(1, 6))
            return self.dice
```

2. Define another class, `Dice2`, with the same methods and attributes. Here's a somewhat more complex definition that creates a class that has the same signature as the `Dice1` class:

```
class Die:
    def __init__(self, rng: random.Random) -> None:
        self._rng = rng

    def roll(self) -> int:
        return self._rng.randint(1, 6)


class Dice2:
    def __init__(self, seed: Optional[int] = None) -> None:
        self._rng = random.Random(seed)
        self._dice = [Die(self._rng) for _ in range(2)]
        self.roll()

    def roll(self) -> Tuple[int, ...]:
        self.dice = tuple(d.roll() for d in self._dice)
        return self.dice
```

At this point, the two classes, `Dice1` and `Dice2`, can be interchanged freely. Here's a function that accepts either class as an argument, creates an instance, and yields several rolls of the dice:

```
def roller(
    dice_class: Type[Dice2],
    seed: int = None,
    *,
    samples: int = 10
) -> Iterator[Tuple[int, ...]]:
    dice = dice_class(seed)
    for _ in range(samples):
        yield dice.roll()
```

We can use this function with either the `Dice1` class or `Dice2` class. This interactive session shows the `roller()` function being applied to both classes:

```
>>> from Chapter_08.ch08_r03 import roller, Dice1, Dice2
>>> list(roller(Dice1, 1, samples=5))
[(1, 3), (1, 4), (4, 4), (6, 4), (2, 1)]
>>> list(roller(Dice2, 1, samples=5))
[(1, 3), (1, 4), (4, 4), (6, 4), (2, 1)]
```

The objects built from `Dice1` and `Dice2` have enough similarities that they're indistinguishable.

How it works...

We've created two classes with identical collections of attributes and methods. This is the essence of duck typing. Because of the way Python searches through a sequence of dictionaries for matching names, classes do not need to have a common superclass to be interchangeable.

This leads to two techniques for creating related families of classes:

- When several subclasses have a common superclass, any search that fails to find a name in a subclass will search the common superclass. This assures common behavior.
- When several classes have common method names, then they can be used in place of each other. This is not as strong a guarantee as having a common superclass, but careful design and unit testing can make sure the various kinds of classes are all interchangeable.

There's more...

When we look at the `decimal` module, we see an example of a numeric type that is distinct from all of the other numeric types. In order to make this work out well, the `numbers` module includes the concept of registering a class as a part of the `Number` class hierarchy. This process of registration makes a class usable as a number without relying on inheritance.

Previously, we noted that the search for a method of a class involves the concept of a descriptor. Internally, Python uses descriptor objects to create gettable and settable properties of an object. In some cases, we may want to leverage explicit descriptors to create classes that appear equivalent because they have the same methods and attributes.

A descriptor object must implement some combination of the special methods `__get__`, `__set__`, and `__delete__`. When the attribute appears in an expression (or in a call to the `getattr()` built-in function), then `__get__` will be used to locate the value. When the attribute appears on the left side of an assignment (or in a call to the `setattr()` built-in function), then `__set__` is used. In a `del` statement, (or in a call to the `delattr()` built-in function), the `__delete__` method is used.

The descriptor object acts as an intermediary so that a simple attribute can be used in a variety of contexts. It's rare to use descriptors directly. We can use the `@property` decorator to build descriptors for us. This can be used to provide attribute names that are similar to other classes; they will pass the "duck test" and can be substituted for each other to create alternative implementations.

See also

- The duck type question is implicit in the *Choosing between inheritance and extension – the is-a question* recipe; if we leverage duck typing, we're also making a claim that two classes are not the same thing. When we bypass inheritance, we are implicitly claiming that the is-a relationship doesn't hold.
- When looking at the *Separating concerns via multiple inheritance* recipe, we're also able to leverage duck typing to create composite classes that may not have a simple inheritance hierarchy.

Managing global and singleton objects

The Python environment contains a number of implicit global objects. These objects provide a convenient way to work with a collection of other objects. Because the collection is implicit, we're saved from the annoyance of explicit initialization code.

One example of this is an implicit random number generating object that's part of the `random` module. When we evaluate `random.random()`, we're actually making use of an instance of the `random.Random` class that's an implicit part of the `random` module.

Other examples of this include the following:

- The collection of data encode/decode methods (`codecs`) available. The `codecs` module lists the available encoders and decoders. This also involves an implicit registry. We can add encodings and decodings to this registry.

- The `webbrowser` module has a registry of known browsers. For the most part, the operating system default browser is the one preferred by the user and the right one to use, but it's possible for an application to launch a browser other than the user's preferred browser, as long as it's installed on the system. It's also possible to register a new browser that's unique to an application.
- The logging module maintains a collection of named loggers. The `getLlogger()` function tries to find an existing logger; it creates a new logger if needed.

This recipe will show to work with an implicit global object like the registries used for codecs, browsers, and logger instances.

Getting ready

A collection of functions can all work with an implicit, global object, created by a module. The benefit is to allow other modules to share the common object without having to write any code that explicitly coordinates between the modules by passing variables explicitly.

For a simple example, let's define a module with a global singleton object. We'll look more at modules in *Chapter 13, Application Integration: Configuration*.

Our global object will be a counter that we can use to accumulate centralized data from several independent modules or objects. We'll provide an interface to this object using a number of separate functions.

The goal is to be able to write something like this:

```
for row in source:
    count('input')
    some_processing()
print(counts())
```

This implies two functions that refer to a shared, global counter:

- `count()`: It will increment the counter and return the current value
- `counts()`: It will provide all of the various counter values

How to do it...

There are two ways to handle global state information. One technique uses a module global variable because modules are singleton objects. The other uses a class-level variable (called `static` in some programming languages.) In Python, a class definition is a singleton object and can be shared without creating duplicates.

Global module variables

We can do the following to create a variable that is global to a module:

1. Create a module file. This will be a `.py` file with the definitions in it. We'll call it `counter.py`.
2. If necessary, define a class for the global singleton. In our case, we can use this definition to create a `collections.Counter` with a type hint of `Counter`:

```
import collections
from typing import List, Tuple, Any, Counter
```

3. Define the one and only instance of the global singleton object. We've used a leading _ in the name to make it slightly less visible. It's not—technically—private. It is, however, gracefully ignored by many Python tools and utilities:

```
_global_counter: Counter[str] = collections.Counter()
```

4. Define the two functions to use the global object, `_global_counter`. These functions encapsulate the detail of how the counter is implemented:

```
def count(key: str, increment: int = 1) -> None:
    _global_counter[key] += increment

def count_summary() -> List[Tuple[str, int]]:
    return _global_counter.most_common()
```

Now we can write applications that use the `count()` function in a variety of places. The counted events, however, are fully centralized in a single object, defined as part of the module.

We might have code that looks like this:

```
>>> from Chapter_08.ch08_r04 import *
>>> from Chapter_08.ch08_r03 import Dice1
>>> d = Dice1(1)
>>> for _ in range(1000):
...     if sum(d.roll()) == 7: count('seven')
...     else: count('other')
>>> print(count_summary())
[('other', 833), ('seven', 167)]
```

We've imported the `count()` and `count_summary()` functions from the `ch08_r04` module. We've also imported the `Dice1` object as a handy object that we can use to create a sequence of events. When we create an instance of `Dice1`, we provide an initialization to force a particular random seed. This gives repeatable results.

We can then use the object, d, to create random events. For this demonstration, we've categorized the events into two simple buckets, labeled seven and other. The count() function uses an implied global object.

When the simulation is done, we can dump the results using the count_summary() function. This will access the global object defined in the module.

The benefit of this technique is that several modules can all share the global object within the ch08_r04 module. All that's required is an import statement. No further coordination or overheads are necessary.

Class-level "static" variable

We can do the following to create a variable that is global to all instances of a class definition:

1. Define a class and provide a variable outside the __init__ method. This variable is part of the class, not part of each individual instance. It's shared by all instances of the class. In this example, we've decided to use a leading _ so the class-level variable is not seen as part of the public interface:

```
import collections
from typing import List, Tuple, Any, Counter
class EventCounter:
    _class_counter: Counter[str] = collections.Counter()
```

2. Add methods to update and extract data from the class-level _class_counter attribute:

```
def count(self, key: str, increment: int = 1) -> None:
    EventCounter._class_counter[key] += increment

def summary(self) -> List[Tuple[str, int]]:
    return EventCounter._class_counter.most_common()
```

It's very important to note that the _class_counter attribute is part of the class, and is referred to as EventCounterl._class_counter. We don't use the self instance variable because we aren't referring to an instance of the class, we're referring to a variable that's part of the overall class definition.

When we use self.name on the left side of the assignment, it may create an instance variable, local to the instance. Using EventCounter.name guarantees that a class-level variable is updated instead of creating an instance variable.

All of the augmented assignment statements, for example, `+=`, are implemented by an "in-place" special method name based on the operator. A statement like `x += 1` is implemented by `x.__iadd__(1)`. If the `__iadd__()` method is defined by the class of `x`, it must perform an in-place update. If the `__iadd__()` method returns the special `NotImplemented` value, the fall-back plan is to compute `x.__add__(1)` and then assign this to variable `x`. This means `self.counter[key] += increment` will tend to work for the large variety of Python collections that provide `__iadd__()` special methods.

Because explicit is better than implicit, it's generally a good practice to make sure class-level variables are explicitly part of the class namespace, not the instance namespace. While `self._class_counter` will work, it may not be clear to all readers that this is a class-level variable. Using `EventCounter._class_counter` is explicit.

The various application components can create objects, but the objects all share a common class-level value:

```
>>> from Chapter_08.ch08_r04 import *
>>> c1 = EventCounter()
>>> c1.count('input')
>>> c2 = EventCounter()
>>> c2.count('input')
>>> c3 = EventCounter()
>>> c3.counts()
[('input', 2)]
```

In this example, we've created three separate objects, `c1`, `c2`, and `c3`. Since all three share a common variable, defined in the `EventCounter` class, each can be used to increment that shared variable. These objects could be part of separate modules, separate classes, or separate functions, yet still share a common global state.

Clearly, shared global state must be used carefully. The examples cited at the beginning of this recipe mentioned codec registry, browser registry, and logger instances. These all work with shared global state. The documentation for how to use these registries needs to be explicitly clear on the presence of global state.

How it works...

The Python import mechanism uses `sys.modules` to track which modules are loaded. Once a module is in this mapping, it is not loaded again. This means that any variable defined within a module will be a singleton: there will only be one instance.

We have two ways to share these kinds of global singleton variables:

- Using the module name, explicitly. We could have created an instance of `Counter` in the module and shared this via `counter.counter`. This can work, but it exposes an implementation detail.
- Using wrapper functions, as shown in this recipe. This requires a little more code, but it permits a change in implementation without breaking other parts of the application.

The defined functions provide a way to identify relevant features of the global variable while encapsulating details of how it's implemented. This gives us the freedom to consider changing the implementation details. As long as the wrapper functions have the same semantics, the implementation can be changed freely.

Since we can only provide one definition of a class, the Python import mechanism tends to assure us that the class definition is a proper singleton object. If we make the mistake of copying a class definition and pasting the definition into two or more modules used by a single application, we would not share a single global object among these class definitions. This is an easy mistake to avoid.

How can we choose between these two mechanisms? The choice is based on the degree of confusion created by having multiple classes sharing a global state. As shown in the previous example, three variables share a common `Counter` object. The presence of an implicitly shared global state can be confusing. A module-level global is often more clear.

There's more...

A shared global state can be called the opposite of object-oriented programming. One ideal of object-oriented programming is to encapsulate all state changes in individual objects. Used too broadly, global variables break the idea of encapsulation of state within a single object.

A common global state often arises when trying to define configuration parameters for an application. It can help to have a single, uniform configuration that's shared widely throughout multiple modules. When these objects are used for pervasive features such as configuration, audits, logging, and security, they can be helpful for segregating a cross-cutting concern into a generic class separate from application-specific classes.

An alternative is to create a configuration object explicitly and make it part of the application in some obvious way. For example, an application's startup can provide a configuration object as a parameter to other objects throughout the application.

See also

- *Chapter 14, Application Integration: Combination*, covers additional topics in module and application design.

Using more complex structures – maps of lists

In *Chapter 4, Built-In Data Structures Part 1: Lists and Sets*, we looked at the basic data structures available in Python. The recipes generally looked at the various structures in isolation.

We'll look at a common combination structure—the mapping from a single key to a list of related values. This can be used to accumulate detailed information about an object identified by a given key. This recipe will transform a flat list of details into details structurally organized by shared key values.

Getting ready

In order to create a more complex data structure, like a map that contains lists, we're going to need more complex data. To get ready, we're going to start with some raw log data, decompose it into individual fields, and then create individual `Event` objects from the fields of data. We can then reorganize and regroup the `Event` objects into lists associated with common attribute values.

We'll start with an imaginary web log that's been transformed from the raw web format to the **comma-separated value** (**CSV**) format. This kind of transformation is often done with a regular expression that picks out the various syntactic groups. See the *String parsing with regular expressions* recipe in *Chapter 1, Numbers, Strings, and Tuples*, for information on how the parsing might work.

The raw data looks like the following:

```
[2016-04-24 11:05:01,462] INFO in module1: Sample Message One
[2016-04-24 11:06:02,624] DEBUG in module2: Debugging
[2016-04-24 11:07:03,246] WARNING in module1: Something might have gone wrong
```

Each line in the file has a timestamp, a severity level, a module name, and some text. We need to decompose the text into four separate fields. We can then define a class of `Event` objects and collections of `Event` instances.

Each row can be parsed into the component fields with a regular expression. We can create a single `NamedTuple` class that has a special static method, `from_line()`, to create instances of the class using these four fields. Because the attribute names match the regular expression group names, we can build instances of the class using the following definition:

```
class Event(NamedTuple):
    timestamp: str
    level: str
    module: str
    message: str

    @staticmethod
    def from_line(line: str) -> Optional['Event']:
        pattern = re.compile(
            r"\[(?P<timestamp>.*?)\]\s+"
            r"(?P<level>\w+)\s+"
            r"in\s+(?P<module>\w+)"
            r":\s+(?P<message>\w+)"
        )
        if log_line := pattern.match(line):
            return Event(
                **cast(re.Match, log_line).groupdict()
            )
        return None
```

The attributes of the `Event` subclass of the `NamedTuple` class are the fields from the log entry: a timestamp, a severity level, the module producing the message, and the body of the message. We've made sure the regular expression group names match the attribute names.

We've used the "walrus" operator in the `if` statement to assign the `log_line` variable and also check to see if the variable has a non-`None` value. This lets us work with the `match.groupdict()` dictionary. The `cast()` function is required to help the current release of `mypy` understand that the `log_line` variable will have a non-`None` value in the body of the `if` clause.

We can simulate applying the `from_line()` method to each line of a file with some test data. At the Python prompt, it looks like the following example:

```
>>> Event.from_line(
...     "[2016-04-24 11:05:01,462] INFO in module1: Sample Message One")
Event(timestamp='2016-04-24 11:05:01,462', level='INFO',
module='module1', message='Sample Message One')
```

Our objective is to see messages grouped by the module name attribute, like this:

```
'module1': [
    ('2016-04-24 11:05:01,462', 'INFO', 'module1', 'Sample Message One'),
    ('2016-04-24 11:07:03,246', 'WARNING', 'module1', 'Something might
have gone wrong')
]


'module2': [
    ('2016-04-24 11:06:02,624', 'DEBUG', 'module2', 'Debugging')
]
```

We'd like to examine the source log file, creating a list of all the messages organized by module, instead of sequentially through time. This kind of restructuring can make analysis simpler.

How to do it...

In order to create a mapping that includes list objects, we'll need to start with some core definition. Then we can write a `summize()` function to restructure the log data as follows:

1. Import the required `collections` module and some type hints for various kinds of collections:

   ```
   import re
   from typing import List, DefaultDict, cast, NamedTuple,
   Optional, Iterable
   ```

2. Define the source data type, an `Event NamedTuple`. This class definition was shown above, in the *Getting ready* section.
3. Define an overall type hint for the summary dictionary we'll be working with:

   ```
   Summary = DefaultDict[str, List[Event]]
   ```

4. Start the definition of a function to summarize an iterable source of the `Event` instances, and produce a `Summary` object:

   ```
   def summarize(data: Iterable[Event]) -> Summary:
   ```

5. Use the `list` function as the default value for a `defaultdict`. It's also helpful to create a type hint for this collection:

```
module_details: Summary = collections.defaultdict(list)
```

6. Iterate through the data, appending to the list associated with each key. The `defaultdict` object will use the `list()` function to build an empty list as the value corresponding to each new key the first time each key is encountered:

```
for event in data:
    module_details[event.module].append(event)
return module_details
```

The result of this will be a dictionary that maps from a module name string to a list of all log rows for that module name. The data will look like the following:

```
{'module1': [
    Event(timestamp='2016-04-24 11:05:01,462', level='INFO',
module='module1', message='Sample'),
    Event(timestamp='2016-04-24 11:07:03,246', level='WARNING',
module='module1', message='Something')],

 'module2': [
    Event(timestamp='2016-04-24 11:06:02,624', level='DEBUG',
module='module2', message='Debugging')]
}
```

The key for this mapping is the module name and the value in the mapping is the list of rows for that module name. We can now focus the analysis on a specific module.

How it works...

There are two choices for how a mapping behaves when a key that we're trying to access in that mapping is not found:

- The built-in `dict` class raises an exception when a key is missing. This makes it difficult to accumulate values associated with keys that aren't known in advance.
- The `defaultdict` class evaluates a function that creates a default value when a key is missing. In many cases, the function is `int` or `float` to create a default numeric value. In this case, the function is `list` to create an empty list.

We can imagine using the `set` function to create an empty `set` object for a missing key. This would be suitable for a mapping from a key to a set of objects that share that key.

There's more...

We can also build a version of this as an extension to the built-in `dict` class:

```
class ModuleEvents(dict):
    def add_event(self, event: Event) -> None:
        if event.module not in self:
            self[event.module] = list()
        self[event.module].append(event)
```

We've defined a method that's unique to this class, `add_event()`. This will add the empty list if the key, the module name in `event[2]`, is not currently present in the dictionary. After the `if` statement, a postcondition could be added to assert that the key is now in the dictionary.

We've used the `list()` function to create an empty list. This can be extended to create other empty collection types by using the class name. Using the empty `[]` has to be replaced with `set()` to replace a list with a set, a change that can be a little less clear than replacing `list()` with `set()`. Also, the class name here parallels the way the class name is used by the `collections.defaultdict()` function.

This allows us to use code such as the following:

```
>>> module_details = ModuleEvents()
>>> for event in event_iter:
...     module_details.add_event(event)
```

The resulting structure is very similar to `defaultdict`.

See also

- In the *Creating dictionaries – inserting and updating* recipe in *Chapter 4, Built-In Data Structures Part 1: Lists and Sets*, we looked at the basics of using a mapping.
- In the *Avoiding mutable default values for function parameters* recipe of *Chapter 4, Built-In Data Structures Part 1: Lists and Sets*, we looked at other places where default values are used.
- In the *Using more sophisticated collections* recipe of *Chapter 7, Basics of Classes and Objects*, we looked at other examples of using the `defaultdict` class.

Creating a class that has orderable objects

We often need objects that can be sorted into order. Log records are often ordered by date and time. When simulating card games, it's often essential to be able to sort the `Card` objects into a defined order. When cards form a sequence, sometimes called a straight, this can be an important way to score points. This is part of games such as *Poker*, *Cribbage*, and *Pinochle*.

Most of our class definitions have not included the features necessary for sorting objects into order. Many of the recipes have kept objects in mappings or sets based on the internal hash value computed by the `__hash__()` method, and an equality test defined by the `__eq__()` method.

In order to keep items in a sorted collection, we'll need the comparison methods that implement `<`, `>`, `<=`, and `>=`. These are in addition to `==` and `!=`. These comparisons are all based on the attribute values of each object and are distinct for every class we might define.

Getting ready

The game of *Pinochle* generally involves a deck with 48 cards. There are 6 ranks—9, 10, Jack, Queen, King, and ace—organized in the standard four suits. Each of these 24 kinds of cards appears twice in the deck. We have to be careful to avoid a structure such as a `dict` or `set` collection because cards are not unique in *Pinochle*; duplicates in a hand are very likely.

In the *Separating concerns via multiple inheritance* recipe, we defined playing cards using two class definitions. The `Card` class hierarchy defined essential features of each card. A second set of mixin classes provided game-specific features for each card.

We'll need to add features to those cards to create objects that can be ordered properly. Here are the first two elements of the design:

```
from Chapter_08.ch08_r02 import AceCard, Card, FaceCard, SUITS,
PointedCard

class PinochlePoints(PointedCard):
    def points(self: PointedCard) -> int:
        _points = {9: 0, 10: 10, 11: 2, 12: 3, 13: 4, 14: 11}
        return _points[self.rank]
```

We've imported the existing `Card` hierarchy. We've also defined a rule for computing the points for each card taken in a trick during play, the `PinochlePoints` class. This has a mapping from card ranks to the potentially confusing points for each card.

A 10 is worth 10 points, and an ace is worth 11 points, but the King, Jack, and Queen are worth four, three, and two points respectively. The nine is worthless. This can be confusing for new players.

Because an ace ranks above a King for purposes of identifying a straight, we've made the rank of the ace 14. This slightly simplifies the processing.

In order to use a sorted collection of cards, we need to add yet another feature to the card class definitions. We'll need to define the comparison operations. There are four special methods used for object ordering comparison. These require some additional type hints to make them applicable to other objects.

How to do it...

To create an orderable class definition, we'll create a comparison protocol, and then define a class that implements the protocol, as follows:

1. We're defining a new protocol for `mypy` to be used when comparing objects. This formal protocol definition describes what kinds of objects the mixin will apply to. We've called it `CardLike` because it applies to any kind of class with at least the two attributes of `rank` and `suit`:

    ```
    class CardLike(Protocol):
        rank: int
        suit: str
    ```

2. Using this protocol, we can create the `SortedCard` subclass for the comparison features. This subclass can be mixed into any class that fits the protocol definition:

    ```
    class SortedCard(CardLike):
    ```

3. Add the four order comparison methods to the `SortedCard` subclass. In this case, we've converted the relevant attributes of any class that fits the `CardLike` protocol into a tuple and relied on Python's built-in tuple comparison to handle the details of comparing the items in the tuple in order, starting with rank. Here are the methods:

    ```
        def __lt__(self: CardLike, other: Any) -> bool:
            return (self.rank, self.suit) < (other.rank, other.
    suit)

        def __le__(self: CardLike, other: Any) -> bool:
            return (self.rank, self.suit) <= (other.rank, other.
    suit)
    ```

```
    def __gt__(self: CardLike, other: Any) -> bool:
        return (self.rank, self.suit) > (other.rank, other.
suit)

    def __ge__(self: CardLike, other: Any) -> bool:
        return (self.rank, self.suit) >= (other.rank, other.
suit)
```

4. Write the composite class definitions, built from an essential `Card` class and two mixin classes to provide the *Pinochle* and comparison features:

```
class PinochleAce(AceCard, SortedCard, PinochlePoints):
    pass

class PinochleFace(FaceCard, SortedCard, PinochlePoints):
    pass

class PinochleNumber(Card, SortedCard, PinochlePoints):
    pass
```

5. There's no simple superclass for this hierarchy of classes. To an extent, we can consider these all as subclasses of the `Card` class. When we look at all the features that were added, the `Card` class could be misleading to any person reading our code. We'll add a type hint to create a common definition for these three classes:

```
PinochleCard = Union[PinochleAce, PinochleFace,
PinochleNumber]
```

6. Now we can create a function that will create individual card objects from the classes defined previously:

```
def make_card(rank: int, suit: str) -> PinochleCard:
    if rank in (9, 10):
        return PinochleNumber(rank, suit)
    elif rank in (11, 12, 13):
        return PinochleFace(rank, suit)
    else:
        return PinochleAce(rank, suit)
```

Even though the point rules are dauntingly complex, the complexity is hidden in the `PinochlePoints` class. Building composite classes as a base subclass of `Card` plus `PinochlePoints` leads to an accurate model of the cards without too much overt complexity.

We can now make cards that respond to comparison operators, using the following sequence of interactive commands:

```
>>> from Chapter_08.ch08_r06 import make_card
>>> c1 = make_card(9, '♡')
>>> c2 = make_card(10, '♡')
>>> c1 < c2
True
>>> c1 == c1
True
>>> c1 == c2
False
>>> c1 > c2
False
```

The equality comparisons to implement `==` and `!=` are defined in the base class, `Card`. This is a frozen `dataclass`. We didn't need to implement these methods. By default, dataclasses contain equality test methods.

Here's a function that builds the 48-card deck by creating two copies of each of the 24 different rank and suit combinations:

```
def make_deck() -> List[PinochleCard]:
    return [
        make_card(r, s)
            for _ in range(2)
                for r in range(9, 15)
                    for s in SUITS]
```

The value of the `SUITS` variable is one of the four Unicode characters for the suits. The generator expression inside the `make_deck()` function builds two copies of each card using the 6 ranks from 9 to the special rank of 14 for the ace, and four characters in the `SUITS` variable.

How it works...

Python uses special methods for a vast number of things. Almost every visible behavior in the language is due to some special method name. In this recipe, we've leveraged the four ordering operators.

When we write the following expression:

```
c1 <= c2
```

The preceding code is evaluated as if we'd written `c1.__le__(c2)`. This kind of transformation happens for all of the expression operators. By defining the comparison special methods, including the `__le__()` method, in our classes, we make these comparison operators work for us.

Careful study of *Section 3.3* of the *Python Language Reference* shows that the special methods can be organized into several distinct groups:

- Basic customization
- Customizing attribute access
- Customizing class creation
- Customizing instance and subclass checks
- Emulating callable objects
- Emulating container types
- Emulating numeric types
- `with` statement context managers

In this recipe, we've looked at only the first of these categories. The others follow some similar design patterns.

Here's how it looks when we work with instances of this class hierarchy. The first example will create a 48-card *Pinochle* deck:

```
>>> from Chapter_08.ch08_r06 import make_deck
>>> deck = make_deck()
>>> len(deck)
48
```

If we look at the first eight cards, we can see how they're built from all the combinations of rank and suit:

```
>>> [str(c) for c in deck[:8]]
[' 9 ♠', ' 9 ♡', ' 9 ◊', ' 9 ♣', '10 ♠', '10 ♡', '10 ◊', '10 ♣']
```

If we look at the second half of the unshuffled deck, we can see that it has the same cards as the first half of the deck:

```
>>> [str(c) for c in deck[24:32]]
[' 9 ♠', ' 9 ♡', ' 9 ◊', ' 9 ♣', '10 ♠', '10 ♡', '10 ◊', '10 ♣']
```

Since the `deck` variable is a simple list, we can shuffle the `list` object and pick a dozen cards:

```
>>> import random
>>> random.seed(4)
>>> random.shuffle(deck)
>>> [str(c) for c in sorted(deck[:12])]
[' 9 ♣', '10 ♣', ' J ♠', ' J ◊', ' J ◊', ' Q ♠', ' Q ♣', ' K ♠', ' K ♠',
' K ♣', ' A ♡', ' A ♣']
```

The important part is the use of the `sorted()` function. Because we've defined proper comparison operators, we can sort the `Card` instances, and they are presented in the expected order from low rank to high rank. Interestingly, this set of cards has `Q` ♠ and `J` ◊, the combination called a *Pinochle*.

There's more...

A little formal logic suggests that we really only need to implement two of the comparisons in detail. From an equality method and an ordering method, all the remaining methods can be built. For example, if we build the operations for less than (`__lt__()`) and equal to (`__eq__()`), we could compute the missing three following these equivalence rules:

- $a \leq b \equiv a < b \vee a = b$
- $a \geq b \equiv a > b \vee a = b$
- $a \neq b \equiv \neg(a = b)$

Python emphatically does not do any of this kind of advanced algebra for us. We need to do the algebra carefully and implement the necessary comparison methods.

The `functools` library includes a decorator, `@total_ordering`, that can generate these missing comparison methods. As of the writing of this chapter, issue 4610 in the `mypy` project is still open, and the type hint analysis is not quite correct. See `https://github.com/python/mypy/issues/4610` for details.

The comparison special methods all have a form similar to `__lt__(self, other: Any) -> bool`. The `other` parameter has a type hint of `Any`. Because this is part of the `CardLike` protocol, `mypy` narrows the meaning of `other` to other objects of the same protocol. This allows us to assume each `CardLike` object is compared against another `CardLike` object with the expected `rank` attribute.

The use of the `Any` type hint is very broad and permits some code that doesn't really work. Try this:

```
>>> c1 = make_card(9, '♡')
>>> c1 <= 10
```

This raises an `AttributeError` exception because the integer object `10` doesn't have a rank. This is the expected behavior; if we want to compare only the rank of a card, we should always be explicit and use `c1.rank <= 10`.

An implicit comparison between the rank of the `CardLike` object and an integer is possible. We can extend or modify the comparison special methods to handle two kinds of comparisons:

- `CardLike` against `CardLike`, using the existing comparison implementation
- `CardLike` against `int`, which will require some additional code

Comparing a `CardLike` object against an integer is done by using the `isinstance()` function to discriminate between the actual argument types.

Each of our comparison methods could be changed to look like this:

```
def __lt__(self: CardLike, other: Any) -> bool:
    if isinstance(other, int):
        return self.rank < other
    return (self.rank, self.suit) < (other.rank, other.suit)
```

This isn't the only change that's required for comparison against integers. The base class, `Card`, is a `dataclass` and introduced the `__eq__()` and `__ne__()` equality tests. These methods are not aware of the possibility of integer comparisons and would need to be modified, also. The complexity of these changes, and the implicit behavior, suggest we should avoid going down this path.

See also

- See the *Defining an ordered collection* recipe, which relies on sorting these cards into order.

Improving performance with an ordered collection

When simulating card games, the player's hand can be modeled as a set of cards or a list of cards. With most conventional single-deck games, a set collection works out nicely because there's only one instance of any given card, and the set class can do very fast operations to confirm whether a given card is or is not in the set.

When modeling *Pinochle*, however, we have a challenging problem. The *Pinochle* deck is 48 cards; it has two each of the 9, 10, Jack, Queen, King, and ace cards. A simple `set` object won't work well when duplicates are possible; we would need a **multiset** or **bag**. A multiset is a set-like collection that permits duplicate items.

In a multiset, a membership test becomes a bit more complex. For example, we can add the `Card(9,'◊')` object to a bag collection more than once, and then also remove it more than one time.

We have a number of ways to create a multiset:

- We can base a multiset collection on the built-in `list` collection. Appending an item to a `list` has a nearly fixed cost, characterized as $\mathbf{O}(1)$. The complexity of testing for membership tends to grow with the size of the collection, *n*; it is characterized as $\mathbf{O}(n)$. This search cost makes a `list` undesirable.
- We can base a multiset on the built-in `dict` collection. The value can be an integer count of the number of times a duplicated element shows up. Dictionary operations are on average characterized as $\mathbf{O}(1)$. (The amortized worst case is $\mathbf{O}(n)$, but worst cases are a rarity.) While this can seem ideal, it limits us to immutable items that are hashable. We have three ways of implementing this extension to the built-in `dict` class:
  - Define our own subclass of the `dict` class with methods to count duplicate entries. This requires overriding a number of special methods.
  - Use a `defaultdict`. See the *Using more complex structures – maps of lists* recipe, which uses `defaultdict(list)` to create a list of values for each key. The `len()` of each `list` is the number of times the key occurred. This can become rather complex when cards are added and removed from the multiset, leaving keys with zero-length lists.
  - Use `Counter`. We've looked at `Counter` in a number of recipes. See the *Avoiding mutable default values for function parameters* recipe in *Chapter 4, Built-In Data Structures Part 1: Lists and Sets*, the *Designing classes with lots of processing* and *Using properties for lazy attributes* recipes in *Chapter 7, Basics of Classes and Objects*, and the *Managing global and singleton objects* recipe of this chapter for other examples.
- We can base our multiset implementation on a sorted `list`. Maintaining the items in order means inserting an item will be slightly more expensive than inserting into a list. The complexity varies with the length of the list but grows more slowly. It is characterized as $\mathbf{O}(n \log_2 n)$. Searching, however, is less expensive than an unsorted list; it's $\mathbf{O}(\log_2 n)$. The `bisect` module provides functions that help us maintain a sorted list.

In this recipe, we will build a sorted collection of objects, and a multiset or bag using a sorted collection.

Getting ready

In the *Creating a class that has orderable objects* recipe, we defined cards that could be sorted. This is essential for using `bisect`. The algorithms in this module require a full set of comparisons among objects.

We'll define a multiset to keep 12-card *Pinochle* hands. Because of the duplication, there will be more than one card of a given rank and suit.

In order to view a hand as a kind of set, we'll also need to define some set operators on hand objects. The idea is to define set membership and subset operators.

We'd like to have Python code that's equivalent to the following:

$$c \in H$$

That means for a given card, *c*, and a hand of cards, $H = \{c_1, c_2, c_3, \ldots\}$, whether or not the given card is in the hand. We'd like this to be faster than a search through each individual card.

We'd also like code equivalent to this:

$$\{J, Q\} \subset H$$

This is for a specific pair of cards, called the *Pinochle*, and a hand of cards, *H*; we want to know if the pair of cards is a proper subset of the cards in the hand. We'd like this to be faster than two searches through all the cards of the hand.

We'll need to import two things:

```
from Chapter_08.ch08_r06 import make_deck, make_card
import bisect
```

The first import brings in our orderable card definitions from the *Creating a class that has orderable objects* recipe. The second import brings in the various bisect functions that we'll use to maintain an ordered set with duplicates.

How to do it...

We'll define a `Hand` collection that maintains `Card` items in order, as follows:

1. Define the `Hand` class with an initialization that can load the collection from any iterable source of data. We can use this to build a `Hand` from a list or possibly a generator expression. If the list is non-empty, we'll need to sort the items into order. The `sort()` method of the `self.cards` list will rely on the comparison operators implemented by the `Card` objects. (Technically, we only care about objects that are subclasses of `SortedCard`, since that is where the comparison methods are defined.):

```
class Hand:
    def __init__(self, card_iter: Iterable[Card]) -> None:
```

```
        self.cards = list(card_iter)
        self.cards.sort()
```

2. Define an `add()` method to add cards to a hand. We'll use the `bisect` module to assure that the card is properly inserted in the correct position in the `self.cards` list:

```
    def add(self, aCard: Card) -> None:
        bisect.insort(self.cards, aCard)
```

3. Define an `index()` method to find the position of a given card instance in a `Hand` collection. We'll use the `bisect` module for locating a given card. The additional `if` test is recommended in the documentation for `bisect.bisect_left()` to properly handle an edge case in the processing:

```
    def index(self, aCard: Card) -> int:
        i = bisect.bisect_left(self.cards, aCard)
        if i != len(self.cards) and self.cards[i] == aCard:
            return i
        raise ValueError
```

4. Define the `__contains__()` special method to implement the `in` operator. When we write the expression `card in some_hand` in Python, it's evaluated as if we had written `some_hand.__contains__(card)`. We've used the `index()` method to either find the card or raise an exception. The exception is transformed into a return value of `False`:

```
    def __contains__(self, aCard: Card) -> bool:
        try:
            self.index(aCard)
            return True
        except ValueError:
            return False
```

5. Define an iterator over the items in a `Hand` collection. This is a delegation to the `self.cards` collection. When we write the expression `iter(some_hand)` in Python, it's evaluated as if we had written `some_hand.__iter__()`. While we could also use the `yield from` statement, it seems a little misleading to use `yield from` outside the context of a recursive function; we'll delegate the `__iter__()` request to an `iter()` function in a direct and hopefully obvious way:

```
    def __iter__(self) -> Iterator[Card]:
        return iter(self.cards)
```

6. Define a subset operation between two `Hand` instances:

```
def __le__(self, other: Any) -> bool:
    for card in self:
        if card not in other:
            return False
    return True
```

Python doesn't have the a ⊂ b or a ⊆ b symbols, so the < and <= operators are conventionally pressed into service for comparing sets. When we write `pinochle <= some_hand` to see if the hand contains a specific combination of cards, it's evaluated as if we'd written `pinochle.__le__(some_hand)`.

The `in` operator is implemented by the `__contains__()` method. This shows how the Python operator syntax is implemented by the special methods.

We can use this `Hand` class like this:

```
>>> from Chapter_08.ch08_r06 import make_deck, make_card
>>> from Chapter_08.ch08_r07 import Hand
>>> import random
>>> random.seed(4)
>>> deck = make_deck()
>>> random.shuffle(deck)
>> h = Hand(deck[:12])
>>> [str(c) for c in h.cards]
[' 9 ♣', '10 ♣', ' J ♠', ' J ◊', ' J ◊', ' Q ♠', ' Q ♣', ' K ♠',
' K ♠', ' K ♣', ' A ♡', ' A ♣']
```

The cards are properly sorted in the `Hand` collection. This is a consequence of the way the `Hand` instance was created; cards were put into order by the collection.

Here's an example of using the subset operator, <=, to compare a specific pattern to the hand as a whole. In this case, the pattern is a pair of cards called the pinochle, a Jack of diamonds and a Queen of spades. First, we'll build a small tuple of two `Card` instances, then we can use the operator we've defined for comparing two collections of `Card` objects, as shown in this example:

```
>>> pinochle = Hand([make_card(11,'◊'), make_card(12,'♠')])
>>> pinochle <= h
True
```

Because a `Hand` is a collection, it supports iteration. We can use generator expressions that reference the `Card` objects within the overall `Hand` object, `h`:

```
>>> sum(c.points() for c in h)
56
```

How it works...

Our `Hand` collection works by wrapping an internal `list` object and applying an important constraint to that object. The items are kept in sorted order. This increases the cost of inserting a new item but reduces the cost of searching for an item.

The core algorithms for locating the position of an item are from the `bisect` module, saving us from having to write (and debug) them. The algorithms aren't really very complex. But it is more efficient to leverage existing code.

The module's name comes from the idea of bisecting the sorted list to look for an item. The essence is shown in this snippet of code:

```
while lo < hi:
    mid = (lo + hi)//2
    if x < a[mid]: hi = mid
    else: lo = mid+1
```

This code searches a list, `a`, for a given value, `x`. The value of `lo` is initially zero and the value of `hi` is initially the size of the list, `len(a)`.

First, the midpoint index, `mid`, is computed. If the target value, `x`, is less than the value at the midpoint of the list, `a[mid]`, then it must be in the first half of the list: the value of `hi` is shifted so that only the first half is considered.

If the target value, `x`, is greater than or equal to the midpoint value, `a[mid]`, then `x` must be in the second half of the list: the value of `lo` is shifted so that only the second half is considered.

Since the list is chopped in half at each operation, it requires $\mathbf{O}(\log_2 n)$ steps before the values of `lo` and `hi` converge on the position that should have the target value. If the item is not present, the `lo` and `hi` values will converge on a non-matching item. The documentation for the `bisect` module suggests using `bisect_left()` to consistently locate either the target item or an item less than the target, allowing an insert operation to put the new item into the correct position.

If we have a hand with 12 cards, then the first comparison discards 6. The next comparison discards 3 more. The next comparison discards 1 of the final 3. The fourth comparison will locate the position the card should occupy.

If we use an ordinary `list`, with cards stored in the random order of arrival, then finding a card will take an average of 6 comparisons. The worst possible case means it's the last of 12 cards, requiring all 12 to be examined.

With `bisect`, the number of comparisons is always $O(\log_2 n)$. This means that each time the list doubles in size, only one more operation is required to search the items.

There's more...

The `collections.abc` module defines abstract base classes for various collections. If we want our `Hand` to behave more like other kinds of sets, we can leverage these definitions.

We can add numerous set operators to this class definition to make it behave more like the built-in `MutableSet` abstract class definition.

A `MutableSet` is an extension to `Set`. The `Set` class is a composite built from three class definitions: `Sized`, `Iterable`, and `Container`. Because the `Set` class is built from three sets of features, it must define the following methods:

- `__contains__()`
- `__iter__()`
- `__len__()`
- `add()`
- `discard()`

We'll also need to provide some other methods that are part of being a mutable set:

- `clear()`, `pop()`: These will remove items from the set
- `remove()`: Unlike `discard()`, this will raise an exception when attempting to remove a missing item

In order to have unique set-like features, it also needs a number of additional methods. We provided an example of a subset, based on `__le__()`. We also need to provide the following subset comparisons:

- `__le__()`
- `__lt__()`
- `__eq__()`
- `__ne__()`
- `__gt__()`
- `__ge__()`
- `isdisjoint()`

These are generally not trivial one-line definitions. In order to implement the core set of comparisons, we'll often write two and then use logic to build the remainder based on those two.

In order to do set operations, we'll need to also provide the following special methods:

- `__and__()` and `__iand__()`. These methods implement the Python `&` operator and the `&=` assignment statement. Between two sets, this is a set intersection or $a \cap b$.
- `__or__()` and `__ior__()`. These methods implement the Python | operator and the |= assignment statement. Between two sets, this is a set union or $a \cup b$.
- `__sub__()` and `__isub__()`. These methods implement the Python `-` operator and the `-=` assignment statement. Between sets, this is the set difference, often written as $a - b$.
- `__xor__()` and `__ixor__()`. These methods implement the Python ^ operator and the ^= assignment statement. When applied between two sets, this is the symmetric difference, often written as $a \Delta b$.

The abstract class permits two versions of each operator. There are two cases:

- If we provide `__iand__()`, for example, then the statement `A &= B` will be evaluated as `A.__iand__(B)`. This might permit an efficient implementation.
- If we do not provide `__iand__()`, then the statement `A &= B` will be evaluated as `A = A.__and__(B)`. This might be somewhat less efficient because we'll create a new object. The new object is given the label `A`, and the old object will be removed from memory.

There are almost two dozen methods that would be required to provide a proper replacement for the built-in `Set` class. On one hand, it's a lot of code. On the other hand, Python lets us extend the built-in classes in a way that's transparent and uses the same operators with the same semantics as the existing classes.

See also

- See the *Creating a class that has orderable objects* recipe for the companion recipe that defines *Pinochle* cards.

Deleting from a list of complicated objects

Removing items from a list has an interesting consequence. Specifically, when item `list[x]` is removed, all the subsequent items move forward. The rule is this:

> Items `list[y+1]` take the place of items `list[y]` for all valid values of $y \geq x$.

This is a side-effect that happens in addition to removing the selected item. Because things can move around in a list, it makes deleting more than one item at a time potentially challenging.

When the list contains items that have a definition for the `__eq__()` special method, then the list `remove()` method can remove each item. When the list items don't have a simple `__eq__()` test, then it becomes more challenging to remove multiple items from the list.

We'll look at ways to delete multiple items from a list when they are complicated objects like instances of the built-in `dict` collection or of a `NamedTuple` or dataclass.

Getting ready

In order to create a more complex data structure, like a list that contains dictionaries, we're going to need more complex data. In order to get ready, we're going to start with a database-like structure, a list of dictionaries.

After creating the list of dictionaries, we'll look at the problem with a naïve approach to removing items. It's helpful to see what can go wrong with trying repeatedly to search a list for an item to delete.

In this case, we've got some data that includes a song name, the writers, and a duration. The dictionary objects are rather long. The data looks like this:

```
>>> song_list = [
...     {'title': 'Eruption', 'writer': ['Emerson'], 'time': '2:43'},
...     {'title': 'Stones of Years', 'writer': ['Emerson', 'Lake'],
'time': '3:43'},
...     {'title': 'Iconoclast', 'writer': ['Emerson'], 'time': '1:16'},
...     {'title': 'Mass', 'writer': ['Emerson', 'Lake'], 'time': '3:09'},
...     {'title': 'Manticore', 'writer': ['Emerson'], 'time': '1:49'},
...     {'title': 'Battlefield', 'writer': ['Lake'], 'time': '3:57'},
...     {'title': 'Aquatarkus', 'writer': ['Emerson'], 'time': '3:54'}
... ]
```

The type hint for each row of this complex structure can be defined with the `typing.TypedDict` hint. The definition looks like the following:

```
from typing import TypedDict, List
SongType = TypedDict(
    'SongType',
    {'title': str, 'writer': List[str], 'time': str}
)
```

The list of songs as a whole can be described as `List[SongType]`.

We can traverse the list of dictionary objects with the `for` statement. The following snippet shows the items we'd like to remove:

```
>>> for item in song_list:
...     if 'Lake' in item['writer']:
...         print("remove", item['title'])
remove Stones of Years
remove Mass
remove Battlefield
```

To properly delete items from a list, we must work with index positions in the list. Here's a naïve approach that emphatically does not work:

```
def naive_delete(data: List[SongType], writer: str) -> None:
    for index in range(len(data)):
        if 'Lake' in data[index]['writer']:
            del data[index]
```

The idea is to compute the index positions of the writers we'd like to remove. This fails with an index error as shown in the following output:

```
>>> naive_delete(song_list, 'Lake')
Traceback (most recent call last):
  File "/Applications/PyCharm CE.app/Contents/plugins/python-ce/helpers/pycharm/docrunner.py", line 138, in __run
    exec(compile(example.source, filename, "single",
  File "<doctest ch07_r08.__test__.test_naive_delete[2]>", line 1, in <module>
    naive_delete(song_list, 'Lake')
  File "Chapter_08/ch08_r08.py", line 72, in naive_delete
    if 'Lake' in data[index]['writer']:
IndexError: list index out of range
```

We can't use `range(len(data))` in a `for` statement because the `range` object's limits are fixed to the *original* size of the list. As items are removed, the list gets smaller, but the upper bound on the `range` object doesn't change. The value of the index will eventually be set to a value that's too large.

Here's another approach that doesn't work. When removing items with a direct equality test, we could try to use something like this:

```
while x in list:
    list.remove(x)
```

The problem here is the `List[SongType]` collection we're using doesn't have an implementation of `__contains__()` to identify an item with `Lake` in the `item['writer']` collection. We don't have a simple test usable by the `remove()` method.

If we want to use the list `remove()` method, we could consider creating a subclass of `dict` that implements `__eq__()` as a comparison against the string parameter value in `self['writer']`. This may violate the semantics of dictionary equality in general because it only checks for membership in a single field, something that might be a problem elsewhere in an application. We'll suggest that this is a potentially bad idea and abandon using `remove()`.

To parallel the basic `while in...remove` loop, we could define a function to find the index of an item we'd like to remove from the list:

```
def index_of_writer(data: List[SongType], writer: str) ->
Optional[int]:
    for i in range(len(data)):
        if writer in data[i]['writer']:
            return i
```

This `index_of_writer()` function will either return the index of an item to delete, or it will return `None` because there are no items to be deleted:

```
def multi_search_delete(data: List[SongType], writer: str) -> None:
    while (position := index_of_writer(data, 'Lake')) is not None:
        del data[position]  # or data.pop(position)
```

More importantly, this approach is wildly inefficient. Consider what happens when a target value occurs *x* times in a list of *n* items. There will be *x* trips through this loop. Each trip through the loop examines an average of $\mathbf{O}(x \times \frac{n}{2})$ trips through the list. The worst case is that all items need to be removed, leading to $\mathbf{O}(n^2)$ processing iterations. For a large data collection, this can be a terrible cost. We can do better.

How to do it...

To efficiently delete multiple items from a list, we'll need to implement our own list index processing as follows:

1. Define a function to update a `list` object by removing selected items:

    ```
    def incremental_delete(
        data: List[SongType], writer: str) -> None:
    ```

2. Initialize an index value, `i`, to zero to begin with the first item in the list:

    ```
        i = 0
    ```

3. While the value for the `i` variable is not equal to the length of the list, we want to make a state change to either increment the `i` variable or shrink the list:

```
while i != len(data):
```

4. The decision is written as an `if` statement. If the `data[i]` dictionary is a target, we can remove it, shrinking the list:

```
    if 'Lake' in data[i]['writer']:
        del data[i]
```

5. Otherwise, if the `data[i]` dictionary is not a target, we can increment the index value, `i`, one step closer to the length of the list. The post-condition for this `if` statement guarantees that we'll get closer to the termination condition of `i == len(data)`:

```
    else:
        i += 1
```

This leads to the expected behavior of removing the items from the list without suffering from index errors or making multiple passes through the list items. The rows with `'Lake'` are removed from the collection, the remaining rows are left intact, and no index errors are raised, nor are items skipped.

This makes exactly one pass through the data removing the requested items without raising index errors or skipping items that should have been deleted.

How it works...

The goal is to examine each item exactly once and either remove it or step over it. The loop design reflects the way that Python list item removal works. When an item is removed, all of the subsequent items are shuffled forward in the list.

A naïve process to update a list will often have one or both of the following problems:

- Items will be skipped when they have shifted forward after a deletion. This is common when using a naïve `for` loop with a `range()` object. It will always increment, skipping items after a deletion.
- The index can go beyond the end of the list structure after items are removed because `len()` was used once to get the original size and create a `range()` object.

Because of these two problems, the design of the invariant condition in the body of the loop is important. This reflects the two possible state changes:

- If an item is removed, the index must not change. The list itself will change.
- If an item is preserved, the index must change.

We can argue that the `incremental_delete()` function defined earlier makes one trip through the data, and has a complexity that can be summarized as $\mathbf{O}(n)$. What's not considered in this summary is the relative cost of each deletion. Deleting an item from a list means that each remaining item is shuffled forward one position. The cost of each deletion is effectively $\mathbf{O}(n)$. Therefore, the complexity is more like $\mathbf{O}(x \times n)$, where x items are removed from a list of *n* items.

While removing items from a mutable list is appealing and simple, it's rarely the ideal solution. Technically, $\mathbf{O}(x \times n)$ is equivalent to $\mathbf{O}(n^2)$, which reveals the potential cost of large operations. In many cases, we might want to use a mapping for complex updates.

There's more...

An alternative is to create a new list with some items rejected. Making a shallow copy of items is much faster than removing items from a list, but uses more storage. This is a common time versus memory trade-off.

We can use a list comprehension like the following one to create a new list of selected items:

```
[
    item
    for item in data
    if writer not in item['writer']
]
```

This will create a shallow copy of the `data` list, retaining the items in the list that we want to keep. The items we don't want to keep will be ignored. For more information on the idea of a shallow copy, see the *Making shallow and deep copies of objects* recipe in *Chapter 4, Built-In Data Structures Part 1: Lists and Sets*.

We can also use a higher-order function, `filter()`, as shown in this example:

```
list(
    filter(
        lambda item: writer not in item['writer'],
        data
    )
)
```

The `filter()` function has two arguments: a `lambda` object, and the original set of data. The `lambda` object is a kind of degenerate case for a function: it has arguments and a single expression, but no name. In this case, the single expression is used to decide which items to pass. Items for which the lambda is `False` are rejected.

The `filter()` function is a generator. This means that we need to collect all of the items to create a final list object. A `for` statement is one way to process all results from a generator. The `list()` and `tuple()` functions will also consume all items from a generator, stashing them in the collection object they create and return.

See also

- We've leveraged two other recipes: *Making shallow and deep copies of objects* and *Slicing and dicing a list* in *Chapter 4, Built-In Data Structures Part 1: Lists and Sets*.
- We'll look closely at filters and generator expressions in *Chapter 9, Functional Programming Features*.

9

Functional Programming Features

Introduction

The idea of **functional programming** is to focus on writing small, expressive functions that perform the required data transformations. Combinations of functions can often create code that is more succinct and expressive than long strings of procedural statements or the methods of complex, stateful objects. This chapter focuses on functional programming features of Python more than procedural or object-oriented programming.

This provides an avenue for software design distinct from the strictly object-oriented approach used elsewhere in this book. The combination of objects with functions permits flexibility in assembling an optimal collection of components.

Conventional mathematics defines many things as functions. Multiple functions can be combined to build up a complex result from previous transformations. When we think of mathematical operators as functions, an expression like $p = n \log_2 n$, can be expressed as two separate functions. We might think of this as $p = f(n, b)$ and $b = g(n)$. We can combine them as $p = f(n, g(n))$.

Ideally, we can also create a composite function from these two functions:

$$p = f\big(n, g(n)\big) = (g \circ f)(x)$$

Creating a new composite function, $g \circ f$, can help to clarify how a program works. It allows us to take a number of small details and combine them into a larger knowledge chunk.

Since programming often works with collections of data, we'll often be applying a function to all the items of a collection. This happens when doing data extraction and transformation. It also happens when summarizing data. This fits nicely with the mathematical idea of a **set builder** or **set comprehension**.

There are three common patterns for applying one function to a set of data:

- **Mapping**: This applies a function to all the elements of a collection, $\{m(x) \mid x \in S\}$. We apply some function, $m(x)$, to each item, x, of a larger collection, S.
- **Filtering**: This uses a function to select elements from a collection, $\{x \mid x \in S \textbf{ if } f(x)\}$. We use a function, $f(x)$, to determine whether to pass or reject each item, x, from the larger collection, S.
- **Reducing**: This summarizes the items of a collection. One of the most common reductions is creating a sum of all items in a collection, S, written as $\sum_{x \in S} x$. Other common reductions include finding the smallest item, the largest one, and the product of all items.

We'll often combine these patterns to create more complex composite applications. What's important here is that small functions, such as $m(x)$ and $f(x)$, can be combined via built-in higher-order functions such as `map()`, `filter()`, and `reduce()`. The `itertools` module contains many other higher-order functions we can use to build an application.

The items in a collection can be any of Python's built-in types. In some cases, we'll want to use our own class definitions to create stronger `mypy` type-checking. In this chapter, we'll look at three data structures that can be validated more strictly: immutable `NamedTuples`, immutable frozen dataclasses, and mutable dataclasses. There's no single "best" or "most optimal" approach. Immutable objects can be slightly easier to understand because the internal state doesn't change. Using one of these structures leads us to write functions to consume objects of one type and produce a result built from objects of a distinct type.

Some of these recipes will show computations that could also be defined as properties of a class definition created using the `@property` decorator. This is yet another design alternative that can limit the complexity of stateful objects. In this chapter, however, we'll try to stick to a functional approach, that is, transforming objects rather than using properties.

In this chapter, we'll look at the following recipes:

- Writing generator functions with the `yield` statement
- Applying transformations to a collection
- Using stacked generator expressions
- Picking a subset – three ways to filter
- Summarizing a collection – how to reduce
- Combining map and reduce transformations

- Implementing "there exists" processing
- Creating a partial function
- Simplifying complicated algorithms with immutable data structures
- Writing recursive generator functions with the `yield from` statement

Most of the recipes we'll look at in this chapter will work with all of the items in a single collection. The approach Python encourages is to use a `for` statement to assign each item within the collection to a variable. The variable's value can be mapped to a new value, used as part of a filter to create a subset of the collection, or used to compute a summary of the collection.

We'll start with a recipe where we will create functions that yield an iterable sequence of values. Rather than creating an entire list (or set, or some other collection), a generator function yields the individual items of a collection. Processing items individually saves memory and may save time.

Writing generator functions with the yield statement

A generator function is designed to apply some kind of transformation to each item of a collection. The generator is called "lazy" because of the way values must be consumed from the generator by a client. Client functions like the `list()` function or implicit `iter()` function used by a `for` statement are common examples of consumers. Each time a function like `list()` consumes a value, the generator function must consume values from its source and use the `yield` statement to yield one result back to the `list()` consumer.

In contrast, an ordinary function can be called "eager." Without the `yield` statement, a function will compute the entire result and return it via the `return` statement.

A consumer-driven approach is very helpful in cases where we can't fit an entire collection in memory. For example, analyzing gigantic web log files is best done in small doses rather than by creating a vast in-memory collection.

This lazy style of function design can be helpful for decomposing complex problems into a collection of simpler steps. Rather than building a single function with a complex set of transformations, we can create separate transformations that are easier to understand, debug, and modify. This combination of smaller transformations builds the final result.

In the language of Python's `typing` module, we'll often be creating a function that is an `Iterator`. We'll generally clarify this with a type, like `Iterator[str]`, to show that a function generates string objects. The `typing` module's `Generator` type is an extension of the `typing` module's `Iterator` protocol with a few additional features that won't figure in any of these recipes. We'll stick with the more general `Iterator`.

The items that are being consumed will often be from a collection described by the `Iterable` type. All of Python's built-in collections are `Iterable`, as are files. A list of string values, for example, can be viewed as an `Iterable[str]`.

The general template for these kinds of functions looks like this:

```
def some_iter(source: Iterable[P]) -> Iterator[Q]: …
```

The source data will be an `iterable` object – possibly a collection, or possibly another generator – over some type of data, shown with the type variable `P`. This results in an iterator over some type of data, shown as the type variable `Q`.

The generator function concept has a sophisticated extension permitting interaction between generators. Generators that interact are termed coroutines. To write type annotations for coroutines, the `Generator` type hint is required. This can provide the type value that's sent, as well as the type value of a final return. When these additional features aren't used, `Generator[Q, None, None]` is equivalent to `Iterator[Q]`.

Getting ready

We'll apply a generator to some web log data using the generator to transform raw text into more useful structured objects. The generator will isolate transformation processing so that a number of filter or summary operations can be performed.

The log data has date-time stamps represented as string values. We need to parse these to create proper `datetime` objects. To keep things focused in this recipe, we'll use a simplified log produced by a web server written with Flask.

The entries start out as lines of text that look like this:

```
[2016-06-15 17:57:54,715] INFO in ch10_r10: Sample Message One
[2016-06-15 17:57:54,715] DEBUG in ch10_r10: Debugging
[2016-06-15 17:57:54,715] WARNING in ch10_r10: Something might have
gone wrong
```

We've seen other examples of working with this kind of log in the *Using more complex structures – maps of lists* recipe in *Chapter 8, More Advanced Class Design*. Using REs from the *String parsing with regular expressions* recipe in *Chapter 1, Numbers, Strings, and Tuples*, we can decompose each line into a more useful structure.

The essential parsing can be done with the regular expression shown here:

```
pattern = re.compile(
    r"\[   (?P<date>.*?)  \]\s+"
    r"     (?P<level>\w+)    \s+"
    r"in\s+(?P<module>.+?)"
```

```
        r":\s+ (?P<message>.+)",
        re.X
    )
```

This regular expression describes a single line and decomposes the timestamp, severity level, module name, and message into four distinct capture groups. We can match this pattern with a line of text from the log and create a `match` object. The `match` object will have four individual groups of characters without the various bits of punctuation like `[`, `]`, and `:`.

It's often helpful to capture the details of each line of the log in an object of a distinct type. This helps make the code more focused, and it helps us use `mypy` to confirm that types are used properly. Here's a `NamedTuple` that can be used to save data from the regular expression shown previously:

```
class RawLog(NamedTuple):
    date: str
    level: str
    module: str
    message: str
```

The idea is to use the regular expression and the `RawLog` class to create objects like the ones shown in the following example:

```
RawLog(date='2016-04-24 11:05:01,462', level='INFO',
module='module1', message='Sample Message One')
```

This shows a `RawLog` instance with values assigned to each attribute. This will be much easier to use than a single string of characters or a tuple of character strings.

We have many choices for converting the log from a sequence of strings into a more useful `RawLog` data type. Here are a couple of ideas:

1. We can read the entire log into memory. Once the entire log is in memory, we can use the `splitlines()` method of the string to break the data into a list of log lines. If the log is large, this may be difficult.
2. What seems like a better idea is to convert each line, separately, from a string into a `RawLog` instance. This will consume much less memory. We can apply filters or do summarization on the lines without having to create large lists of objects.

The second approach can be built using a generator function to consume source lines and emit transformed `RawLog` results from each line. A generator function is a function that uses a `yield` statement. When a function has a `yield`, it builds the results incrementally, yielding each individual value in a way that can be consumed by a client. The consumer might be a `for` statement or it might be another function that needs a sequence of values, like the `list()` function.

This problem needs two separate examples of generator functions. We'll look at the transformation of a string into a tuple of fields in detail, and then apply the same recipe to transforming the date into a useful `datetime` object.

How to do it...

To use a generator function for transforming each individual line of text into a more useful `RawLog` tuple, we'll start by defining the function, as follows:

1. Import the `re` module to parse the line of the log file:

    ```
    import re
    ```

2. Define a function that creates `RawLog` objects. It seems helpful to include `_iter` in the function name to emphasize that the result is an iterator over `RawLog` tuples, not a single value. The parameter is an iterable source of log lines:

    ```
    def parse_line_iter(
            source: Iterable[str]) -> Iterator[RawLog]:
    ```

3. The `parse_line_iter()` transformation function relies on a regular expression to decompose each line. We can define this inside the function to keep it tightly bound with the rest of the processing:

    ```
    pattern = re.compile(
        r"\[   (?P<date>.*?)  \]\s+"
        r"     (?P<level>\w+)    \s+"
        r"in\s+(?P<module>.+?)"
        r":\s+ (?P<message>.+)",
        re.X
    )
    ```

4. A `for` statement will consume each line of the iterable source, allowing us to create and then yield each `RawLog` object in isolation:

    ```
        for line in source:
    ```

5. The body of the `for` statement can map each string instance that matches the pattern to a new `RawLog` object using the match groups:

    ```
            if match := pattern.match(line):
                yield RawLog(*cast(Match, match).groups())
    ```

Here's some sample data, shown as a list of string values:

```
>>> log_lines = [
...     '[2016-04-24 11:05:01,462] INFO in module1: Sample Message One',
...     '[2016-04-24 11:06:02,624] DEBUG in module2: Debugging',
```

```
...     '[2016-04-24 11:07:03,246] WARNING in module1: Something might
have gone wrong'
... ]
```

Here's how we use this function to emit a sequence of `RawLog` instances:

```
>>> for item in parse_line_iter(log_lines):
...     pprint(item)
RawLog(date='2016-04-24 11:05:01,462', level='INFO', module='module1',
message='Sample Message One')
RawLog(date='2016-04-24 11:06:02,624', level='DEBUG', module='module2',
message='Debugging')
RawLog(date='2016-04-24 11:07:03,246', level='WARNING', module='module1',
message='Something might have gone wrong')
```

We've used a `for` statement to iterate through the results of the `parse_line_iter()` function, one object at a time. We've used the `pprint()` function to display each `RawLog` instance.

We could also collect the items into a list collection using something like this:

```
>>> details = list(parse_date_iter(data))
```

In this example, the `list()` function consumes all of the items produced by the `parse_line_iter()` function. It's essential to use a function such as `list()` or a `for` statement to consume all of the items from the generator. A generator is a relatively passive construct: until data is demanded, it doesn't do any work.

If we don't use a function or `for` statement to consume the data, we'll see something like this:

```
>>> parse_line_iter(data)
<generator object parse_line_iter at 0x10167ddb0>
```

The value of the `parse_line_iter()` function is a generator. It's not a collection of items, but a function that will produce items, one at a time, on demand from a consumer.

How it works...

Python has a sophisticated construct called an **iterator** that lies at the heart of generators and collections. An iterator will provide each value from a collection while doing all of the internal bookkeeping required to maintain the state of the process. A generator function fits the protocol of an iterator: it provides a sequence of values and maintains its own internal state.

Consider the following common piece of Python code:

```
for i in some_collection:
    process(i)
```

Behind the scenes, something like the following is going on:

```
the_iterator = iter(some_collection)
try:
    while True:
        i = next(the_iterator)
        process(i)
except StopIteration:
    pass
```

Python evaluates the `iter()` function on a collection to create an `iterator` object for the collection, assigning it to the `the_iterator` variable. The iterator is bound to the collection and maintains some internal state information. The example code shown previously uses `next()` on `the_iterator` to get each value. When there are no more values in the collection, the `next()` function raises the `StopIteration` exception.

Each of Python's collection types implements the special method, `__iter__()`, required to produce an iterator object. The iterator produced by a `Sequence` or `Set` will visit each item in the collection. The iterator produced by a `Mapping` will visit each key for the mapping. We can use the `values()` method of a mapping to iterate over the values instead of the keys. We can use the `items()` method of a mapping to visit a sequence of `(key, value)` two-tuples. The iterator for a `file` will visit each line in the file.

The iterator concept can also be applied to functions. A function with a `yield` statement is called a `generator function`. It implements the protocol for an iterator. To do this, the generator returns itself in response to the `iter()` function. In response to the `next()` function, it yields the next value.

When we apply `list()` to a collection or a generator function, the same essential mechanism used by the `for` statement (the `iter()` and `next()` functions) will consume the individual values. The items are then combined into a sequence object.

Evaluating `next()` on a generator function is interesting. The statements of the generator function's body are evaluated until the `yield` statement. The value computed by the expression in `yield` becomes the result of `next()`. Each time `next()` is evaluated, the function resumes processing with the statement after `yield` and continues to the next `yield` statement, until the `return` statement, or until there are no more statements in the function's body.

To see how the `yield` statement works, look at this small function, which yields two objects:

```
>>> def gen_func():
```

```
...     print("pre-yield")
...     yield 1
...     print("post-yield")
...     yield 2
```

Here's what happens when we evaluate `next()`:

```
>>> y = gen_func()
>>> next(y)
pre-yield
1
>>> next(y)
post-yield
2
```

The first time we evaluated `next()`, the first `print()` function was evaluated, then the `yield` statement produced a value. The function's processing was suspended and the `>>>` prompt was given. The second time we evaluated the `next()` function, the statements between the two `yield` statements were evaluated. The function was again suspended and a `>>>` prompt was displayed.

What happens next? There are no more `yield` statements in the function's body, so we observe the following:

```
>>> next(y)
Traceback (most recent call last):
  File "<pyshell...>", line 1, in <module>
    next(y)
StopIteration
```

The `StopIteration` exception is raised at the end of a generator function. Generally, a function's processing is ended by a `return` statement. Python allows us to omit the `return` statement, using an implicit `return` at the end of the indented block of statements.

In this example, the creation of the `RawLog` object depends on the order of the fields in `NamedTuple` precisely matching the order of the collected data from the regular expression used to parse each line. In the event of a change to the format, we may need to change the regular expression and the order of the fields in the class.

There's more...

The core value of creating applications around generator functions comes from being able to break complex processing into two parts:

- The transformation or filter to map to each item in the source of the data
- The source set of data with which to work

We can apply this recipe a second time to clean up the date attributes in each `RawLog` object. The more refined kind of data from each log line will follow this class definition:

```
class DatedLog(NamedTuple):
    date: datetime.datetime
    level: str
    module: str
    message: str
```

This has a proper `datetime.datetime` object for the timestamp. The other fields remain as strings. Instances of `DatedLog` are easier to sort and filter by date or time than instances of `RawLog`.

Here's a generator function that's used to refine each `RawLog` object into a `DatedLog` object:

```
def parse_date_iter(
        source: Iterable[RawLog]) -> Iterator[DatedLog]:
    for item in source:
        date = datetime.datetime.strptime(
            item.date, "%Y-%m-%d %H:%M:%S,%f"
        )
        yield DatedLog(
            date, item.level, item.module, item.message
        )
```

Breaking overall processing into several small generator functions confers several significant advantages. First, the decomposition makes each function succinct and focused on a specific task. Second, it makes the overall composition somewhat more expressive of the work being done.

We can combine these two generators in the following kind of composition:

```
>>> for item in parse_date_iter(parse_line_iter(log_lines)):
...     pprint(item)
DatedLog(date=datetime.datetime(2016, 4, 24, 11, 5, 1, 462000),
level='INFO', module='module1', message='Sample Message One')
DatedLog(date=datetime.datetime(2016, 4, 24, 11, 6, 2, 624000),
```

```
level='DEBUG', module='module2', message='Debugging')
DatedLog(date=datetime.datetime(2016, 4, 24, 11, 7, 3, 246000),
level='WARNING', module='module1', message='Something might have gone
wrong')
```

The `parse_line_iter()` function will consume lines from the source data, creating `RawLog` objects when they are demanded by a consumer. The `parse_data_iter()` function is a consumer of `RawLog` objects; from this, it creates `DatedLog` objects when demanded by a consumer. The outer `for` statement is the ultimate consumer, demanding `DataLog` objects.

At no time will there be a large collection of intermediate objects in memory. Each of these functions works with a single object, limiting the amount of memory used.

See also

- In the *Using stacked generator expressions* recipe, we'll combine generator functions to build complex processing stacks from simple components.
- In the *Applying transformations to a collection* recipe, we'll see how the built-in `map()` function can be used to create complex processing from a simple function and an iterable source of data.
- In the *Picking a subset – three ways to filter* recipe, we'll see how the built-in `filter()` function can also be used to build complex processing from a simple function and an iterable source of data.

Applying transformations to a collection

Once we've defined a generator function, we'll need to apply the function to a collection of data items. There are a number of ways that generators can be used with collections.

In the *Writing generator functions with the yield statement* recipe earlier in this chapter, we created a generator function to transform data from a string into a more complex object. Generator functions have a common structure, and generally look like this:

```
def new_item_iter(source: Iterable) -> Iterator:
    for item in source:
        new_item = some transformation of item
        yield new_item
```

The function's type hints emphasize that it consumes items from the source collection. Because a generator function is a kind of `Iterator`, it will produce items for another consumer. This template for writing a generator function exposes a common design pattern.

Mathematically, we can summarize this as follows:

$$N = \{ m(x) \mid x \in S \}$$

The new collection, *N*, is a transformation, $m(x)$, applied to each item, x, of the source, S. This emphasizes the transformation function, $m(x)$, separating it from the details of consuming the source and producing the result.

This mathematical summary suggests the `for` statement can be understood as a kind of scaffold around the transformation function. There are two additional forms this scaffolding can take. We can write a generator expression and we can use the built-in `map()` function. This recipe will examine all three techniques.

Getting ready...

We'll look at the web log data from the *Writing generator functions with the yield statement* recipe. This had `date` as a string that we would like to transform into a proper `datetime` object to be used for further computations. We'll make use of the `DatedLog` class definition from that earlier recipe.

The text lines from the log were converted into `RawLog` objects. While these are a handy starting point because the attributes were cleanly separated from each other, this representation had a problem. Because the attribute values are strings, the datetime value is difficult to work with. Here's the example data, shown as a sequence of `RawLog` objects:

```
>>> data = [
...     RawLog("2016-04-24 11:05:01,462", "INFO", "module1", "Sample
Message One"),
...     RawLog("2016-04-24 11:06:02,624", "DEBUG", "module2",
"Debugging"),
...     RawLog(
...         "2016-04-24 11:07:03,246",
...         "WARNING",
...         "module1",
...         "Something might have gone wrong",
...     ),
... ]
```

We can write a generator function like this to transform each `RawLog` object into a more useful `DatedLog` instance:

```
import datetime
def parse_date_iter(
```

```
        source: Iterable[RawLog]) -> Iterator[DatedLog]:
    for item in source:
        date = datetime.datetime.strptime(
            item.date, "%Y-%m-%d %H:%M:%S,%f"
        )
        yield DatedLog(
            date, item.level, item.module, item.message
        )
```

This `parse_date_iter()` function will examine each item in the source using a `for` statement. A new `DatedLog` item is built from the `datetime` object and three selected attributes of the original `RawLog` object.

This `parse_date_iter()` function has a significant amount of scaffolding code around an interesting function. The `for` and `yield` statements are examples of scaffolding. The date parsing, on the other hand, is the distinctive, interesting part of the function. We need to extract this distinct function, then we'll look at the three ways we can use the function with simpler scaffolding around it.

How to do it...

To make use of different approaches to applying a generator function, we'll start with a definition of a `parse_date()` generator, then we'll look at three ways the generator can be applied to a collection of data:

1. Refactor the transformation into a function that can be applied to a single row of the data. It should produce an item of the result type from an item of the source type:

    ```
    def parse_date(item: RawLog) -> DatedLog:
        date = datetime.datetime.strptime(
            item.date, "%Y-%m-%d %H:%M:%S,%f")
        return DatedLog(
            date, item.level, item.module, item.message)
    ```

2. Create a unit test case for this isolated from the collection processing. Here's a doctest example:

    ```
    >>> item = RawLog("2016-04-24 11:05:01,462", "INFO", "module1",
    "Sample Message One")
    >>> parse_date(item)
    DatedLog(date=datetime.datetime(2016, 4, 24, 11, 5, 1, 462000),
    level='INFO', module='module1', message='Sample Message One')
    ```

This transformation can be applied to a collection of data in three ways: a generator function, a generator expression, and via the `map()` function.

Using a for statement

We can apply the `parse_date()` function to each item of a collection using a `for` statement. This was shown in the *Writing generator functions with the yield statement* recipe earlier in this chapter. Here's what it looks like:

```
def parse_date_iter(
        source: Iterable[RawLog]) -> Iterator[DatedLog]:
    for item in source:
        yield parse_date(item)
```

This version of the `parse_date_iter()` generator function uses the `for` statement to collect each item in the source collection. The results of the `parse_date()` function are yielded one at a time to create the `DatedLog` values for the iterator.

Using a generator expression

We can apply the `parse_date()` function to each item of a collection using a generator expression. A generator expression includes two parts – the mapping function, and a `for` clause enclosed by `()`:

1. Write the mapping function, applied to a variable. The variable will be assigned to each individual item from the overall collection:

   ```
   parse_date(item)
   ```

2. Write a `for` clause that assigns objects to the variable used previously. This value comes from some iterable collection, `source`, in this example:

   ```
   for item in source
   ```

3. The expression can be the return value from a function that provides suitable type hints for the source and the resulting expression. Here's the entire function, since it's so small:

   ```
   def parse_date_iter(
           source: Iterable[RawLog]) -> Iterator[DatedLog]:
       return (parse_date(item) for item in source)
   ```

This is a generator expression that applies the `parse_date()` function to each item in the `source` collection.

Using the map() function

We can apply the `parse_date()` function to each item of a collection using the `map()` built-in function. Writing the `map()` function includes two parts – the mapping function and the source of data – as arguments:

1. Use the `map()` function to apply the transformation to the source data:

```
map(parse_date, source)
```

2. The expression can be the return value from a function that provides suitable type hints for the source and the resulting expression. Here's the entire function, since it's so small:

```
def parse_date_iter(
        source: Iterable[RawLog]) -> Iterator[DatedLog]:
    return map(parse_date, source)
```

The `map()` function is an iterator that applies the `parse_date()` function to each item from the `source` iterable. It yields objects created by the `parse_date()` function.

It's important to note that the `parse_date` name, without `()` is a reference to the function object. It's a common error to think the function must be evaluated, and include extra, unnecessary uses of `()`.

Superficially, all three techniques are equivalent. There are some differences, and these will steer design in a particular direction. The differences include:

- Only the `for` statement allows additional statements like context managers or a `try` block to handle exceptions. In the case of very complex processing, this can be an advantage.
- The generator expression has a relatively fixed structure with `for` clauses and `if` clauses. It fits the more general mathematical pattern of a generator, allowing Python code to better match the underlying math. Because the expression is not limited to a named function or a lambda object, this can be very easy to read.
- The `map()` function can work with multiple, parallel iterables. Using `map(f, i1, i2, i3)` may be easier to read than `map(f, zip(i1, i2, i3))`. Because this requires a named function or a lambda object, this works well when the function is heavily reused by other parts of an application.

How it works...

The `map()` function replaces some common code that acts as a scaffold around the processing. We can imagine that the definition looks something like this:

```
def map(f: Callable, source: Iterable) -> Iterator:
    for item in source:
        yield f(item)
```

Or, we can imagine that it looks like this:

```
def map(f: Callable, source: Iterable) -> Iterator:
    return (f(item) for item in iterable)
```

Both of these conceptual definitions of the `map()` function summarize the core feature of applying a function to a collection of data items. Since they're equivalent, the final decision must emphasize code that seems both succinct and expressive to the target audience.

To be more exacting, we can introduce type variables to show how the `Callable`, `Iterable`, and `Iterator` types are related by the `map()` function:

```
P = TypeVar("P")
Q = TypeVar("Q")
F = Callable[[P], Q]
def map(transformation: F, source: Iterable[P]) -> Iterator[Q]: ...
```

This shows how the callable can transform objects of type `P` to type `Q`. The source is an iterable of objects of type `P`, and the result will be an iterator that yields objects of type `Q`. The transformation is of type `F`, a function we can describe with the `Callable[[P], Q]` annotation.

There's more...

In this example, we've used the `map()` function to apply a function that takes a single parameter to each individual item of a single iterable collection. It turns out that the `map()` function can do a bit more than this.

Consider this function:

```
>>> def mul(a, b):
...     return a*b
```

And these two sources of data:

```
>>> list_1 = [2, 3, 5, 7]
>>> list_2 = [11, 13, 17, 23]
```

We can apply the `mul()` function to pairs drawn from each source of data:

```
>>> list(map(mul, list_1, list_2))
[22, 39, 85, 161]
```

This allows us to merge two sequences of values using different kinds of operators. The `map()` algorithm takes values from each of the input collections and provides that group of values to the `mul()` function in this example. In effect, this is `[mul(2, 11), mul(3, 13), mul(5, 17), mul(7, 23)]`.

This builds a mapping using pairs. It's similar to the built-in `zip()` function. Here's the code, which is - in effect - `zip()` built using this feature of `map()`:

```
>>> def bundle(*args):
...     return args
>>> list(map(bundle, list_1, list_2))
[(2, 11), (3, 13), (5, 17), (7, 23)]
```

We needed to define a small helper function, `bundle()`, that takes any number of arguments and returns the internal tuple created by assigning positional arguments via the `*args` parameter definition.

When we start looking at generator expressions like this, we can see that a great deal of programming fits some common overall patterns:

- **Map**: $\{m(x) \mid x \in S\}$ becomes `(m(x) for x in S)`.
- **Filter**: $\{x \mid x \in S \textbf{ if } f(x)\}$ becomes `(x for x in S if f(x))`.
- **Reduce**: This is a bit more complex, but common reductions include sums and counts. For example, $\sum_{x \in S} x$ becomes `sum(x for x in S)`. Other common reductions include finding the maximum or the minimum of a set of a data collection.

See also

- In the *Using stacked generator expressions* recipe, later in this chapter, we will look at stacked generators. We will build a composite function from a number of individual mapping operations, written as various kinds of generator functions.

Using stacked generator expressions

In the *Writing generator functions with the yield statement* recipe, earlier in this chapter, we created a simple generator function that performed a single transformation on a piece of data. As a practical matter, we often have several functions that we'd like to apply to incoming data.

How can we stack or combine multiple generator functions to create a composite function?

Getting ready

This recipe will apply several different kinds of transformations to source data. There will be restructuring of the rows to combine three rows into a single row, data conversions to convert the source strings into useful numbers or date-time stamps, and filtering to reject rows that aren't useful.

We have a spreadsheet that is used to record fuel consumption on a large sailboat. It has rows that look like this:

Date	**Engine on**	**Fuel height**
	Engine off	**Fuel height**
	Other notes	
10/25/2013	08:24	29
	13:15	27
	calm seas - anchor solomon's island	
10/26/2013	09:12	27
	18:25	22
	choppy - anchor in jackson's creek	

Example of saiboat fuel use

For more background on this data, see the *Slicing and dicing a list* recipe in *Chapter 4, Built-In Data Structures Part 1: Lists and Sets*.

As a sidebar, we can gather this data from a source file. We'll look at this in detail in the *Reading delimited files with the csv module* recipe in *Chapter 10, Input/Output, Physical Format, and Logical Layout*:

```
>>> from pathlib import Path
>>> import csv
>>> with Path('data/fuel.csv').open() as source_file:
...     reader = csv.reader(source_file)
...     log_rows = list(reader)

>>> log_rows[0]
['date', 'engine on', 'fuel height']
>>> log_rows[-1]
['', "choppy -- anchor in jackson's creek", '']
```

We've used the `csv` module to read the log details. `csv.reader()` is an iterable object. In order to collect the items into a single list, we applied the `list()` function to the generator function. We printed at the first and last item in the list to confirm that we really have a list-of-lists structure.

We'd like to apply transformations to this list-of-lists object:

- Convert the date and time strings into two date-time values
- Merge three rows into one row
- Exclude header rows that are present in the data

If we create a useful group of generator functions, we can have software that looks like this:

```
>>> total_time = datetime.timedelta(0)
>>> total_fuel = 0
>>> for row in datetime_gen:
...     total_time += row.engine_off-row.engine_on
...     total_fuel += (
...         float(row.engine_on_fuel_height)-
...         float(row.engine_off_fuel_height)
...     )
>>> print(
...     f"{total_time.total_seconds()/60/60 =:.2f}, "
...     f"{total_fuel =:.2f}")
```

The combined generator function output has been assigned to the `datetime_gen` variable. This generator will yield a sequence of single rows with starting information, ending information, and notes. We can then compute time and fuel values and write summaries.

When we have more than two or three functions that are used to create the `datetime_gen` generator, the statement can become very long. In this recipe, we'll build a number of transformational steps into a single pipeline of processing.

How to do it...

We'll decompose this into three separate sub-recipes:

- Restructure the rows. The first part will create the `row_merge()` function to restructure the data.
- Exclude the header row. The second part will create a `skip_header_date()` filter function to exclude the header row.
- Create more useful row objects. The final part will create a function for additional data transformation, starting with `create_datetime()`.

Restructuring the rows

The first part of this three-part recipe will create the `row_merge()` function to restructure the data. We need to combine three rows into a useful structure. To describe this transformation, we'll define two handy types; one for the raw data, and one for the combined rows:

1. Define the input and output data structures. The `csv.Reader` class will create lists of strings. We've described it with the `RawRow` type. We'll restructure this into a `CombinedRow` instance. The combined row will have some extra attributes; we've called them `filler_1`, `filler_2`, and `filler_3`, with values of cells that will be empty in the input data. It's slightly easier to keep the structure similar to the original CSV columns. We'll remove the filler fields later:

```
RawRow = List[str]

class CombinedRow(NamedTuple):
    # Line 1
    date: str
    engine_on_time: str
    engine_on_fuel_height: str
    # Line 2
    filler_1: str
    engine_off_time: str
    engine_off_fuel_height: str
    # Line 3
    filler_2: str
    other_notes: str
    filler_3: str
```

2. The function's definition will accept an iterable of `RawRow` instances. It will behave as an iterator over `CombinedRow` objects:

```
def row_merge(
        source: Iterable[RawRow]) -> Iterator[CombinedRow]:
```

3. The body of the function will consume rows from the `source` iterator. The first column provides a handy way to detect the beginning of a new three-row cluster of data. When the first column is empty, this is additional data. When the first column is non-empty, the previous cluster is complete, and we're starting a new cluster. The very last cluster of three rows also needs to be emitted:

```
    cluster: RawRow = []
    for row in source:
        if len(row[0]) != 0:
            if len(cluster) == 9:
```

```
                    yield CombinedRow(*cluster)
                cluster = row.copy()
            else:
                cluster.extend(row)
        if len(cluster) == 9:
            yield CombinedRow(*cluster)
```

This initial transformation can be used to convert a sequence of lines of CSV cell values into `CombinedRow` objects where each of the field values from three separate rows have their own, unique attributes:

```
>>> pprint(list(row_merge(log_rows)))

[CombinedRow(date='date', engine_on_time='engine on', engine_on_fuel_
height='fuel height', filler_1='', engine_off_time='engine off', engine_
off_fuel_height='fuel height', filler_2='', other_notes='Other notes',
filler_3=''),

 CombinedRow(date='10/25/13', engine_on_time='08:24:00 AM', engine_on_
fuel_height='29', filler_1='', engine_off_time='01:15:00 PM', engine_off_
fuel_height='27', filler_2='', other_notes="calm seas -- anchor solomon's
island", filler_3=''),

 CombinedRow(date='10/26/13', engine_on_time='09:12:00 AM', engine_on_
fuel_height='27', filler_1='', engine_off_time='06:25:00 PM', engine_off_
fuel_height='22', filler_2='', other_notes="choppy -- anchor in jackson's
creek", filler_3='')]
```

We've extracted three `CombinedRow` objects from nine rows of source data. The first of these `CombinedRow` instances has the headings and needs to be discarded. The other two, however, are examples of raw data restructured.

We don't exclude the rows in the function we've written. It works nicely for doing row combinations. We'll stack another function on top of it to exclude rows that aren't useful. This separates the two design decisions and allows us to change the filter function without breaking the `row_merge()` function shown here.

There are several transformation steps required to make the data truly useful. We need to create proper `datetime.datetime` objects, and we need to convert the fuel height measurements into `float` objects. We'll tackle each of these as a separate, tightly focused transformation.

Excluding the header row

The first three rows from the source CSV file create a `CombinedRow` object that's not very useful. We'll exclude this with a function that processes each of the `CombinedRow` instances but discards the one with the labels in it:

1. Define a function to work with an `Iterable` collection of `CombinedRow` objects, creating an iterator of `CombinedRow` objects:

```
def skip_header_date(
        source: Iterable[CombinedRow]
        ) -> Iterator[CombinedRow]:
```

2. The function's body is a `for` statement to consume each row of the source:

```
    for row in source:
```

3. The body of the `for` statement yields good rows and uses the `continue` statement to reject the undesirable rows by skipping over them:

```
        if row.date == "date":
            continue
        yield row
```

This can be combined with the `row_merge()` function shown in the previous recipe to provide a list of the desirable rows of good data that's useful:

```
>>> row_gen = row_merge(log_rows)
>>> tail_gen = skip_header_date(row_gen)
>>> pprint(list(tail_gen))
[CombinedRow(date='10/25/13', engine_on_time='08:24:00 AM', engine_on_
fuel_height='29', filler_1='', engine_off_time='01:15:00 PM', engine_off_
fuel_height='27', filler_2='', other_notes="calm seas -- anchor solomon's
island", filler_3=''),
 CombinedRow(date='10/26/13', engine_on_time='09:12:00 AM', engine_on_
fuel_height='27', filler_1='', engine_off_time='06:25:00 PM', engine_off_
fuel_height='22', filler_2='', other_notes="choppy -- anchor in jackson's
creek", filler_3='')]
```

The `row_merge()` function on the first line is a generator that produces a sequence of `CombinedRow` objects; we've assigned the generator to the `row_gen` variable. The `skip_header_date()` function on the second line consumes data from the `row_gen` generator, and then produces a sequence of `CombinedRow` objects. We've assigned this to the `tail_gen` variable, because this data is the tail of the file.

We created a list of the objects to show the two good rows in the example data. Printing this list shows the collected data.

Creating more useful row objects

The dates and times in each row aren't very useful as separate strings. We'd really like rows with the dates and times combined into `datetime.datetime` objects. The function we'll write can have a slightly different form because it applies to all the rows in a simple way. For these kinds of transformations, we don't need to write the `for` statement inside the function; it can be applied externally to the function:

1. Define a new `NamedTuple` instance that specifies a more useful type for the time values:

```
class DatetimeRow(NamedTuple):
    date: datetime.date
    engine_on: datetime.datetime
    engine_on_fuel_height: str
    engine_off: datetime.datetime
    engine_off_fuel_height: str
    other_notes: str
```

2. Define a simple mapping function to convert one `CombinedRow` instance into a single `DatetimeRow` instance. We'll create an explicit generator expression to use this single-row function on an entire collection of data:

```
def convert_datetime(row: CombinedRow) -> DatetimeRow:
```

3. The body of this function will perform a number of date-time computations and create a new `DatetimeRow` instance. This function's focus is on date and time conversions. Other conversions can be deferred to other functions:

```
travel_date = datetime.datetime.strptime(
    row.date, "%m/%d/%y").date()
start_time = datetime.datetime.strptime(
    row.engine_on_time, "%I:%M:%S %p").time()
start_datetime = datetime.datetime.combine(
    travel_date, start_time)

end_time = datetime.datetime.strptime(
    row.engine_off_time, "%I:%M:%S %p").time()
end_datetime = datetime.datetime.combine(
    travel_date, end_time)

return DatetimeRow(
    date=travel_date,
    engine_on=start_datetime,
```

```
            engine_off=end_datetime,
            engine_on_fuel_height=row.engine_on_fuel_height,
            engine_off_fuel_height=row.engine_off_fuel_height,
            other_notes=row.other_notes
        )
```

We can stack the transformation functions to merge rows, exclude the header, and perform date time conversions. The processing may look like this:

```
>>> row_gen = row_merge(log_rows)
>>> tail_gen = skip_header_date(row_gen)
>>> datetime_gen = (convert_datetime(row) for row in tail_gen)
```

Here's the output from the preceding processing:

```
>>> pprint(list(datetime_gen))
[DatetimeRow(date=datetime.date(2013, 10, 25), engine_on=datetime.
datetime(2013, 10, 25, 8, 24), engine_on_fuel_height='29', engine_
off=datetime.datetime(2013, 10, 25, 13, 15), engine_off_fuel_height='27',
other_notes="calm seas -- anchor solomon's island"),
 DatetimeRow(date=datetime.date(2013, 10, 26), engine_on=datetime.
datetime(2013, 10, 26, 9, 12), engine_on_fuel_height='27', engine_
off=datetime.datetime(2013, 10, 26, 18, 25), engine_off_fuel_height='22',
other_notes="choppy -- anchor in jackson's creek")]
```

The expression `(convert_datetime(row) for row in tail_gen)` applies the `convert_datetime()` function to each of the rows produced by the `tail_gen` generator expression. This expression has the valid rows from the source data.

We've decomposed the reformatting, filtering, and transformation problems into three separate functions. Each of these three steps does a small part of the overall job. We can test each of the three functions separately. More important than being able to test is being able to fix or revise one step without completely breaking the entire stack of transformations.

How it works...

When we write a generator function, the argument value can be a collection of items, or it can be any other kind of iterable source of items. Since generator functions are iterators, it becomes possible to create a *pipeline* of generator functions.

A mapping generator function consumes an item from the input, applies a small transformation, and produces an item as output. In the case of a filter, more than one item could be consumed for each item that appears in the resulting iterator.

When we decompose the overall processing into separate transformations, we can make changes to one without breaking the entire processing pipeline.

Consider this stack of three generator functions:

```
>>> row_gen = row_merge(log_rows)
>>> tail_gen = skip_header_date(row_gen)
>>> datetime_gen = (convert_datetime(row) for row in tail_gen)
>>> for row in datetime_gen:
...     print(f"{row.date}: duration {row.engine_off-row.engine_on}")
```

In effect, the `datetime_gen` object is a composition of three separate generators: the `row_merge()` function, the `skip_header_date()` function, and an expression that involves the `convert_datetime()` function. The final `for` statement shown in the preceding example will be gathering values from the `datetime_gen` generator expression by evaluating the `next()` function repeatedly.

Here's the step-by-step view of what will happen to create the needed result:

1. The `for` statement will consume a value from the `datetime_gen` generator.
2. The `(convert_datetime(row) for row in tail_gen)` expression must produce a value for its consumer. To do this, a value must be consumed from the `tail_gen` generator. The value is assigned to the `row` variable, then transformed by the `convert_datetime()` function.
3. The `tail_gen` generator must produce a value from the `skip_header_date()` generator function. This function may read several rows from its source until it finds a row where the `date` attribute is not the column header string, `"date"`. The source for this is the output from the `row_merge()` function.
4. The `row_merge()` generator function will consume multiple rows from its source until it can assemble a `CombinedRow` instance from nine source cells spread across three input rows. It will yield the combined row. The source for this is a list-of-lists collection of the raw data.
5. The source collection of rows will be processed by a `for` statement inside the body of the `row_merge()` function. This statement will consume rows from the `log_rows` generator.

Each individual row of data will pass through this pipeline of steps. Small, incremental changes are made to the data to yield rows of distinct types. Some stages of the pipeline will consume multiple source rows for a single result row, restructuring the data as it is processed. Other stages consume and transform a single value.

The entire pipeline is driven by demand from the client. Each individual row is processed separately. Even if the source is a gigantic collection of data, processing can proceed very quickly. This technique allows a Python program to process vast volumes of data quickly and simply.

There's more...

There are a number of other conversions required to make this data useful. We'll want to transform the start and end time stamps into a duration. We also need to transform the fuel height values into floating-point numbers instead of strings.

We have three ways to handle these derived data computations:

1. We can add the computations as properties of the `NamedTuple` definition.
2. We can create additional transformation steps in our stack of generator functions.
3. We can also add `@property` methods to the class definition. In many cases, this is optimal.

The second approach is often helpful when the computations are very complex or involve collecting data from external sources. While we don't need to follow this approach with this specific recipe, the design is a handy way to see how transformations can be stacked to create a sophisticated pipeline.

Here's how we can compute a new `NamedTuple` that includes a duration attribute. First, we'll show the new `DurationRow` definition:

```
class DurationRow(NamedTuple):
    date: datetime.date
    engine_on: datetime.datetime
    engine_on_fuel_height: str
    engine_off: datetime.datetime
    engine_off_fuel_height: str
    duration: float
    other_notes: str
```

Objects of this class can be produced by a function that transforms a `DatetimeRow` into a new `DurationRow` instance. Here's a function that's used to build new objects from the existing data:

```
def duration(row: DatetimeRow) -> DurationRow:
    travel_hours = round(
        (row.engine_off-row.engine_on).total_seconds()/60/60, 1
    )
    return DurationRow(
        date=row.date,
        engine_on=row.engine_on,
        engine_off=row.engine_off,
        engine_on_fuel_height=row.engine_on_fuel_height,
        engine_off_fuel_height=row.engine_off_fuel_height,
        other_notes=row.other_notes,
```

```
            duration=travel_hours
        )
```

Many of the fields are simply preserved without doing any processing. Only one new field is added to the tuple definition.

A more complete definition of the leg of a journey would involve a more useful measure of fuel height. Here's the relevant class definition:

```
class Leg(NamedTuple):
    date: datetime.date
    engine_on: datetime.datetime
    engine_on_fuel_height: float
    engine_off: datetime.datetime
    engine_off_fuel_height: float
    duration: float
    other_notes: str
```

Here's a function that's used to build `Leg` objects from the `DurationRow` objects built previously:

```
def convert_height(row: DurationRow) -> Leg:
    return Leg(
        date=row.date,
        engine_on=row.engine_on,
        engine_off=row.engine_off,
        duration=row.duration,
        engine_on_fuel_height=
            float(row.engine_on_fuel_height),
        engine_off_fuel_height=
            float(row.engine_off_fuel_height),
        other_notes=row.other_notes
    )
```

This concept drives the definition of a composite `leg_duration_iter()` function. This function is composed of a number of functions, each of which can be applied to items of collections. We've stacked the functions into a series of transformations, as shown here:

```
def leg_duration_iter(source: Iterable[str]) -> Iterator[Leg]:
    merged_rows = row_merge(log_rows)
    tail_gen = skip_header_date(merged_rows)
    datetime_gen = (convert_datetime(row) for row in tail_gen)
    duration_gen = (duration(row) for row in datetime_gen)
    height_gen = (convert_height(row) for row in duration_gen)
    return height_gen
```

The transformations in this stack fall into two general types:

- Generator functions, `row_merge()` and `skip_header_date()`: These two functions have a `for` statement and some complex additional processing. The `row_merge()` function has an internal list, `cluster`, that accumulates three rows before yielding a result. The `skip_header_date()` function can consume more than one row before emitting a row; it's a filter, not a transformation.
- Generator expressions that map a function against a collection of data: The functions `convert_datetime()`, `duration()`, and `convert_height()` all perform small transformations. We use a generator expression to apply the function to each item in the source collection.

We now have a sophisticated computation that's defined in a number of small and (almost) completely independent chunks. We can modify one piece without having to think deeply about how the other pieces work.

The filter processing of `skip_header_date()` can be built using the `built-in filter()` higher-order function. We'll look at filtering in the *Picking a subset – three ways to filter recipe* in this chapter.

The generator expression `(duration(row) for row in datetime_gen)` can also be written as `map(duration, datetime_gen)`. Both apply a function against a source of data. When first looking at a stack of transformations, it seems easier to work with an explicit generator expression. Later, it can be replaced with the slightly simpler-looking built-in `map()` function.

See also

- See the *Writing generator functions with the yield statement* recipe for an introduction to generator functions.
- See the *Slicing and dicing a list* recipe in *Chapter 4, Built-In Data Structures Part 1: Lists and Sets*, for more information on the fuel consumption dataset.
- See the *Combining map and reduce transformations* recipe for another way to combine operations.
- The *Picking a subset – three ways to filter* recipe covers the filter function in more detail.

Picking a subset – three ways to filter

Choosing a subset of relevant rows can be termed filtering a collection of data. We can view a filter as rejecting bad rows or including the desirable rows. There are several ways to apply a filtering function to a collection of data items.

In the *Using stacked generator expressions* recipe, we wrote the `skip_header_date()` generator function to exclude some rows from a set of data. The `skip_header_date()` function combined two elements: a rule to pass or reject items and a source of data. This generator function had a general pattern that looks like this:

```
def data_filter_iter(source: Iterable[T]) -> Iterator[T]:
    for item in source:
        if item should be passed:
            yield item
```

The `data_filter_iter()` function's type hints emphasize that it consumes items from an iterable source collection. Because a generator function is a kind of iterator, it will produce items of the same type for another consumer. This function design pattern exposes a common underlying pattern.

Mathematically, we might summarize this as follows:

$$N = \{ x \mid x \in S \textbf{ if } f(x) \}$$

The new collection, *N*, is each item, x, of the source, S, where a filter function, $f(x)$, is true. This mathematical summary emphasizes the filter function, $f(x)$, separating it from the details of consuming the source and producing the result.

This mathematical summary suggests the `for` statement is little more than scaffolding code. Because it's less important than the filter rule, it can help to refactor a generator function and extract the filter from the other processing.

If the `for` statement is scaffolding, how else can we apply a filter to each item of a collection? There are three techniques we can use:

- We can write an explicit `for` statement. This was shown in the previous recipe, *Using stacked generator expressions*, in this chapter.
- We can write a generator expression.
- We can use the built-in `filter()` function.

Getting ready...

In this recipe, we'll look at the web log data from the *Writing generator functions with the yield statement* recipe. This had `date` as a string that we would like to transform into a proper timestamp.

The text lines from the log were converted into `RawLog` objects. While these were handy because the attributes were cleanly separated from each other, this representation had a problem. Because the attribute values are strings, the datetime value is difficult to work with. Here's the example data, shown as a sequence of `RawLog` objects.

In the *Applying transformations to a collection* recipe shown earlier in this chapter, we used a generator function, `parse_date_iter()`, to transform each `RawLog` object into a more useful `DatedLog` instance. This made more useful data, as shown in the following example:

```
>>> data = [
... DatedLog(date=datetime.datetime(2016, 4, 24, 11, 5, 1, 462000),
level='INFO', module='module1', message='Sample Message One'),
... DatedLog(date=datetime.datetime(2016, 4, 24, 11, 6, 2, 624000),
level='DEBUG', module='module2', message='Debugging'),
... DatedLog(date=datetime.datetime(2016, 4, 24, 11, 7, 3, 246000),
level='WARNING', module='module1', message='Something might have gone
wrong')
... ]
```

It's often necessary to focus on a subset of the `DatedLog` instances. We may need to focus on a particular module, or date range. This leads to a need to extract a useful subset from a larger set.

For this example, we'll focus initially on filtering the data using the module name attribute of each `DatedLog` instance. This decision can be made on each row in isolation.

There are three distinct ways to create the necessary filters. We can write a generator function, we can use a generator expression, or we can use the built-in `filter()` function. In all three cases, we have to separate some common for-and-if code from the unique filter condition. We'll start with the explicit `for` and `if` statements, then show two other ways to filter this data.

How to do it...

The first part of this recipe will use explicit `for` and `if` statements to filter a collection of data:

1. Start with a draft version of a generator function with the following outline:

    ```
    def draft_module_iter(
            source: Iterable[DatedLog]
            ) -> Iterator[DatedLog]:
        for row in source:
            if row.module == "module2":
                yield row
    ```

2. The `if` statement's decision can be refactored into a function that can be applied to a single row of the data. It must produce a `bool` value:

    ```
    def pass_module(row: DatedLog) -> bool:
        return row.module == "module2"
    ```

3. The original generator function can now be simplified:

```
def module_iter(
        source: Iterable[DatedLog]) -> Iterator[DatedLog]:
    for item in source:
        if pass_module(item):
            yield item
```

The `pass_module()` function can be used in three ways. As shown here, it can be part of a generator function. It can also be used in a generator expression, and with the `filter()` function. We'll look at these as separate parts of this recipe.

While this uses two separate function definitions, it has the advantage of separating the filter rule from the boilerplate `for` and `if` processing. The `pass_module()` function helps to highlight the possible reasons for change. It keeps this separate from the parts of the processing unlikely to change.

There are two other ways we can write this function: in a generator expression and with the built-in `filter()` function. We'll show these in the next two sections.

Using a filter in a generator expression

A generator expression includes three parts – the item, a `for` clause, and an `if` clause – all enclosed by `()`:

1. Write the output object, which is usually the variable from the `for` clause. The variable will be assigned to each individual item from the overall collection:

    ```
    item
    ```

2. Write a `for` clause that assigns objects to the variable used previously. This value comes from some iterable collection, which is `source` in this example:

    ```
    for item in source
    ```

3. Write an `if` clause using the filter rule function, `pass_module()`:

    ```
    if pass_module (item)
    ```

4. The expression can be the return value from a function that provides suitable type hints for the source and the resulting expression. Here's the entire function, since it's so small:

    ```
    def module_iter(
            source: Iterable[DatedLog]) -> Iterator[DatedLog]:
        return (item for item in source if pass_module(item))
    ```

This is a generator expression that applies the `pass_module()` function to each item in the `source` collection to determine whether it passes and is kept, or whether it is rejected.

Using the filter() function

Using the `filter()` function includes two parts – the decision function and the source of data – as arguments:

1. Use the `filter()` function to apply the function to the source data:

   ```
   filter(pass_module, data)
   ```

2. We can use this as follows:

   ```
   >>> for row in filter(pass_module, data):
   ...     pprint(row)
   ```

The `filter()` function is an iterator that applies the `pass_module()` function as a rule to pass or reject each item from the `data` iterable. It yields the rows for which the `pass_module()` function returns true.

It's important to note that the `pass_module` name, without `()`, is a reference to the function object. It's a common error to think the function must be evaluated and include extra `()`.

How it works...

A generator expression must include a `for` clause to provide a source of data items from a collection. The optional `if` clause can apply a condition that preserves the items. A final expression defines the resulting collection of objects. Placing a filter condition in an `if` clause can make the combination of a source filter and final expression very clear and expressive of the algorithm.

Generator expressions have an important limitation. As expressions, they cannot use statement-oriented features of Python. One important statement is a try-except block to handle exceptional data conditions. Because this can't be used in a simple generator expression, we may resort to a more elaborate for-and-if construct.

The `filter()` function replaces the common boilerplate code. We can imagine that the definition for the built-in function looks something like this:

```
def filter(
        f: Callable[[P], bool], source: Iterable[P]
        ) -> Iterator[P]:
    for item in source:
        if f(item):
            yield item
```

Or, we can imagine that the built-in `filter()` function looks like this:

```
def filter(
        f: Callable[[P], bool], source: Iterable[P]
```

```
        ) -> Iterator[P]:
    return (item for item in source if f(item))
```

Both of these definitions summarize the core feature of the `filter()` function: some data is passed and some data is rejected. This is handy shorthand that eliminates some boilerplate code for using a function to test each item in an iterable source of data.

There's more...

Sometimes, it's difficult to write a simple rule to pass data. It may be clearer if we write a rule to reject data. For example, a rule to reject all names that match a regular expression might be easier to imagine than the logically equivalent pass rule:

```
pattern = re.compile(r"module\d+")
def reject_modules(row: DatedLog) -> bool:
    return bool(pattern.match(row.module))
```

We can use a reject rule instead of a pass rule in a number of ways. Here's a `for...if...continue...yield` pattern of statements. This will use the `continue` statement to skip the rejected items and yield the remaining items:

```
>>> def reject_modules_iter(
...         source: Iterable[DatedLog]) -> Iterator[DatedLog]:
...     for item in source:
...         if reject_modules(item):
...             continue
...         yield item
```

This has the advantage of letting us write rejected rows to a log for debugging purposes. The simpler alternative is this:

```
for item in collection:
    if not reject_modules(item):
        yield item
```

We can also use a generator expression like this:

```
(item for item in data if not reject_modules(item))
```

We can't, however, easily use the `filter()` function with a rule that's designed to reject data. The `filter()` function is designed to work with pass rules only.

We can, however, create a `lambda` object to compute the inverse of the `reject` function, turning it into a `pass` function. The following example shows how this works:

```
filter(lambda item: not reject_modules(item), data)
```

The `lambda` object is a small, anonymous function. A lambda is effectively a function that's been reduced to just two elements: the parameter list and a single expression. We wrapped the `reject_modules()` function to create a kind of `not_reject_modules()` function via a `lambda` object.

In the `itertools` module, we use the `filterfalse()` function. We can also use `from itertools import filterfalse`. This function lets us work with reject rules instead of pass rules.

See also

- In the *Using stacked generator expressions* recipe, earlier in this chapter, we placed a function like this in a stack of generators. We built a composite function from a number of individual mapping and filtering operations written as generator functions.

Summarizing a collection – how to reduce

A reduction is the generalized concept behind computing a sum or a product of a collection of numbers. Computing statistical measures like mean or variance are also reductions. In this recipe, we'll look at several summary techniques.

In the introduction to this chapter, we noted that there are three processing patterns that Python supports elegantly: map, filter, and reduce. We saw examples of mapping in the *Applying transformations to a collection* recipe and examples of filtering in the *Picking a subset – three ways to filter* recipe. It's relatively easy to see how these higher-level functions define generic operations.

The third common pattern is reduction. In the *Designing classes with lots of processing* and *Extending a collection: a list that does statistics* recipes, we looked at class definitions that computed a number of statistical values. These definitions relied—almost exclusively—on the built-in `sum()` function. This is one of the more common reductions.

In this recipe, we'll look at a way to generalize summation, leading to ways to write a number of different kinds of reductions that are similar. Generalizing the concept of reduction will let us build on a reliable foundation to create more sophisticated algorithms.

Getting ready

One of the most common reductions is the sum. Other reductions include the product, minimum, maximum, average, variance, and even a simple count of values. The mathematics of summation help us to see how an operator is used to convert a collection of values into a single value.

This abstraction provides ways for us to understand Python's capabilities. With this foundation, it can be made clear how extensions to the built-in reductions can be designed.

Here's a way to think of the mathematical definition of the sum function using an operator, $+$, applied to values in a collection, *C*:

$$\sum_{c_i \in C} c_i = c_0 + c_1 + c_2 + \cdots + c_n$$

We've expanded the definition of sum by *folding* the $+$ operator into the sequence of values, $C = c_0, c_1, c_2, \ldots, c_n$. This idea of folding in the $+$ operator captures the meaning of the built-in `sum()` function.

Similarly, the definition of product looks like this:

$$\prod_{c_i \in C} c_i = c_0 \times c_1 \times c_2 \times \ldots \times c_n$$

Here, too, we've performed a different *fold* on a sequence of values. Folding involves two items: a binary operator and a base value. For sum, the operator was $+$ and the base value was zero. For product, the operator is $\times$ and the base value is one.

This idea of a fold is a generic concept that underlies Python's `reduce()`. We can apply this to many algorithms, potentially simplifying the definition.

How to do it...

Let's start by importing the function we need:

1. Import the `reduce()` function from the `functools` module:

   ```
   from functools import reduce
   ```

2. Pick the operator. For `sum`, it's $+$. For `product`, it's $*$. These can be defined in a variety of ways. Here's the long version. Other ways to define the necessary binary operators will be shown later:

   ```
   def mul(a, b):
       return a * b
   ```

3. Pick the base value required. For `sum`, it's zero. For `product`, it's one. This allows us to define a `prod()` function that computes a generic product:

   ```
   def prod(values):
       return reduce(mul, values, 1)
   ```

We can use this to define a function based on this product reduction. The function looks like this:

```
def factorial(n: int) -> int:
    return prod(range(1, n+1))
```

Here's the number of ways that a 52-card deck can be arranged. This is the value 52:

```
>>> factorial(52)
80658175170943878571660636856403766975289505440883277824000000000000
```

There are a lot of a ways a deck can be shuffled.

How many five-card hands are possible? The binomial calculation uses a factorial:

$$\binom{52}{5} = \frac{52!}{5!\,(52-5)!}$$

Here's the Python implementation:

```
>>> factorial(52)//(factorial(5)*factorial(52-5))
2598960
```

For any given shuffle, there are about 2.6 million different possible poker hands.

How it works...

The `reduce()` function behaves as though it has this definition:

```
T = TypeVar("T")
def reduce(
        fn: Callable[[T, T], T],
        source: Iterable[T],
        base: T) -> T:
    result = base
    for item in source:
        result = fn(result, item)
    return result
```

The type shows how there has to be a unifying type, `T`. The given function, `fn()`, must combine two values of type `T` and return another value of the same type `T`. The base value is an object of the type `T`, and the result of the `reduce()` function will be a value of this type also.

Furthermore, this `reduce` operation must iterate through the values from left to right. It will apply the given binary function, `fn()`, between the previous result and the next item from the source collection.

There's more...

When designing a new application for the `reduce()` function, we need to provide a binary operator. There are three ways to define the necessary binary operator. First, we can use a complete function definition like this:

```
def mul(a: int, b: int) -> int:
    return a * b
```

There are two other choices. We can use a `lambda` object instead of a complete function:

```
l_mul: Callable[[int, int], int] = lambda a, b: a * b
```

A `lambda` object is an anonymous function boiled down to just two essential elements: the parameters and the `return` expression. There are no statements inside a `lambda`, only a single expression. In this case, the expression uses the desired operator, `*`.

We can use a `lambda` object like this:

```
def prod2(values: Iterable[int]) -> int:
    return reduce(lambda a, b: a*b, values, 1)
```

This provides the multiplication function as a `lambda` object without the overhead of a separate function definition.

When the operation is one of Python's built-in operators, it can also import the definition from the `operator` module:

```
from operator import add, mul
```

This works nicely for all the built-in arithmetic operators.

Note that logical reductions using the Boolean operators `and` and `or` are different from other arithmetic reductions. Python's Boolean operators have a short-circuit feature: when we evaluate the expression `False and 3/0` and the result is `False`, the operation on the right-hand side of the `and` operator, `3/0`, is never evaluated; the exception won't be raised. The `or` operator is similar: when the left side is `True`, the right-hand side is never evaluated.

The built-in functions `any()` and `all()` are reductions using logic operators. The `any()` function is, effectively, a kind of `reduce()` using the `or` operator. Similarly, the `all()` function behaves as if it's a `reduce()` with the `and` operator.

Maxima and minima

We can use the `reduce()` function to compute a customized maximum or minimum as well. This is a little more complex because there's no trivial base value that can be used. We cannot start with zero or one because these values might be outside the range of values being minimized or maximized.

Also, the built-in `max()` and `min()` functions must raise exceptions for an empty sequence. These functions don't fit perfectly with the way the `sum()` and `reduce()` functions work. The `sum()` and `reduce()` functions have an identity element that is the result of why they're operating against an empty sequence. Some care must be exercised to define a proper identity element for a customized `min()` or `max()`.

We can imagine that the built-in `max()` function has a definition something like the following:

```
def mymax(source: Iterable[T]) -> T:
    try:
        base = source[0]
        max_rule = lambda a, b: a if a > b else b
        return reduce(max_rule, source, base)
    except IndexError:
        raise ValueError
```

This function will pick the first value from the sequence as a base value. It creates a `lambda` object, named `max_rule`, which selects the larger of the two argument values. We can then use this base value and the `lambda` object. The `reduce()` function will locate the largest value in a non-empty collection. We've captured the `IndexError` exception so that evaluating the `mymax()` function on an empty collection will raise a `ValueError` exception.

Potential for abuse

Note that a fold (or `reduce()`, as it's called in Python) can be abused, leading to poor performance. We have to be cautious about using a `reduce()` function without thinking carefully about what the resulting algorithm might look like. In particular, the operator being folded into the collection should be a simple operation such as adding or multiplying. Using `reduce()` changes the complexity of an $\mathbf{O}(1)$ operation into $\mathbf{O}(n)$.

Imagine what would happen if the operator being applied during the reduction involved a sort over a collection. A complex operator—with $\mathbf{O}(n\log n)$ complexity—being used in a `reduce()` function would change the complexity of the overall `reduce()` to $\mathbf{O}(n^2\log n)$. For a collection of 10,000 items, this goes from approximately 132,800 operations to over 1,328,000,000 operations. What may have taken 6 seconds could take almost 16 hours.

Combining the map and reduce transformations

In the other recipes in this chapter, we've been looking at `map`, `filter`, and `reduce` operations. We've looked at each of these in isolation:

- The *Applying transformations to a collection* recipe shows the `map()` function.
- The *Picking a subset – three ways to filter* recipe shows the `filter()` function.
- The *Summarizing a collection – how to reduce* recipe shows the `reduce()` function.

Many algorithms will involve combinations of functions. We'll often use mapping, filtering, and reduction to produce a summary of available data. Additionally, we'll need to look at a profound limitation of working with iterators and generator functions; namely, this limitation:

> An iterator can only produce values once.

If we create an iterator from a generator function and a collection of data, the iterator will only produce the data one time. After that, it will appear to be an empty sequence.

Here's an example:

```
>>> typical_iterator = iter([0, 1, 2, 3, 4])
>>> sum(typical_iterator)
10
>>> sum(typical_iterator)
0
```

We created an iterator over a sequence of values by manually applying the `iter()` function to a literal `list` object. The first time that the `sum()` function used the value of `typical_iterator`, it consumed all five values. The next time we try to apply any function to `typical_iterator`, there will be no more values to be consumed; the iterator will appear empty.

This one-time-only restriction may force us to cache intermediate results so that we can perform multiple reductions on the data. Creating intermediate collection objects will consume memory, leading to a need for the careful design of very complex processes for very large collections of data.

Getting ready

In the *Using stacked generator expressions* recipe, we looked at data that required a number of processing steps. We merged rows with a generator function. We filtered some rows to remove them from the resulting data. Additionally, we applied a number of mappings to the data to convert dates and times into more useful information.

We'd like to supplement this with two more reductions to get some average and variance information. These statistics will help us understand the data more fully.

In the *Using stacked generator expressions* recipe, earlier in this chapter, we looked at some sailboat data. The spreadsheet was badly organized, and a number of steps were required to impose a more useful structure on the data.

In that recipe, we looked at a spreadsheet that is used to record fuel consumption on a large sailboat. It has rows that look like this:

Date	**Engine on**	**Fuel height**
	Engine off	Fuel height
	Other notes	
10/25/2013	08:24	29
	13:15	27
	calm seas - anchor solomon's island	
10/26/2013	09:12	27
	18:25	22
	choppy - anchor in jackson's creek	

Example of saiboat fuel use

The initial processing was a sequence of operations to change the organization of the data, filter out the headings, and compute some useful values. We'll build on that earlier processing with some additional steps.

How to do it...

To do a complex transformation of a collection, it can help to restate each piece of the transformation. We want to look for examples of `map`, `filter`, and `reduce` operations. We can implement these individually and combine them into sophisticated composite operations built from easy-to-understand pieces. Let's get started:

1. It helps to start with the line of code as a goal. In this case, we'd like a function to sum the fuel use per hour. This can follow a common three-step design pattern. First, we normalize the data with `row_merge()`. Then, we use mapping and filtering to create more useful objects with `clean_data_iter()`.

Finally, we want to be summarize using the `total_fuel()` function. See the *Using stacked generator expressions* recipe for more information on this kind of design. Here's the goal expression:

```
>>> round(
...     total_fuel(clean_data_iter(row_merge(log_rows))),
...     3)
7.0
```

2. Define a generator for any structural normalization that's required. For this example, we have to combine three input rows to create each output row. We'll reuse the functions from earlier recipes:

```
from Chapter_09.ch08_r03 import row_merge, CombinedRow, log_rows
```

3. Define the target data structure created by the cleaning and enrichment step. We'll use a mutable dataclass in this example. The fields coming from the normalized `CombinedRow` object can be initialized directly. The other five fields will be computed by several separate functions. Because they'll be computed later, they're given an initial value of `field(init=False)`:

```
from dataclasses import dataclass, field

@dataclass
class Leg:
    date: str
    start_time: str
    start_fuel_height: str
    end_time: str
    end_fuel_height: str
    other_notes: str
    start_timestamp: datetime.datetime = field(init=False)
    end_timestamp: datetime.datetime = field(init=False)
    travel_hours: float = field(init=False)
    fuel_change: float = field(init=False)
    fuel_per_hour: float = field(init=False)
```

4. Define the overall data cleansing and enrichment data function. This will build the enriched `Leg` objects from the source `CombinedRow` objects. We'll build this from seven simpler functions. In addition to functions to compute the five derived fields, there's a function to do the initial conversion to a `Leg` instance, and a `filter` function to reject the header row that's present in the source data. The implementation is a stack of `map()` and `filter()` operations that will derive data from the source fields:

```
def clean_data(
        source: Iterable[CombinedRow]) -> Iterator[Leg]:
```

```
        leg_iter = map(make_Leg, source)
        fitered_source = filter(reject_date_header, leg_iter)
        start_iter = map(start_datetime, fitered_source)
        end_iter = map(end_datetime, start_iter)
        delta_iter = map(duration, end_iter)
        fuel_iter = map(fuel_use, delta_iter)
        per_hour_iter = map(fuel_per_hour, fuel_iter)
        return per_hour_iter
```

5. Write the `make_Leg()` function to create `Leg` instances from `CombinedRow` instances. This does the minimal amount of work required and doesn't compute any of the uninitialized fields:

```
    def make_Leg(row: CombinedRow) -> Leg:
        return Leg(
            date=row.date,
            start_time=row.engine_on_time,
            start_fuel_height=row.engine_on_fuel_height,
            end_time=row.engine_off_time,
            end_fuel_height=row.engine_off_fuel_height,
            other_notes=row.other_notes,
        )
```

6. Write the `reject_date_header()` function used by `filter()` to remove the heading rows. If needed, this can be expanded to remove blank lines or other bad data from the source. The idea is to pass good data as soon as possible in the processing stage. In this example, good data has only one rule – the `date` attribute is not equal to the string `"date"`:

```
    def reject_date_header(row: Leg) -> bool:
        return not (row.date == "date")
```

7. Write the data conversion functions. We'll start with the time strings, which need to become `datetime` objects. Both the start time and end time require similar algorithms. We can refactor the common code into a timestamp function that builds a single `datetime` object from a date string and time string:

```
    def timestamp(
            date_text: str, time_text: str
            ) -> datetime.datetime:
        date = datetime.datetime.strptime(
            date_text, "%m/%d/%y").date()
        time = datetime.datetime.strptime(
            time_text, "%I:%M:%S %p").time()
```

```
        timestamp = datetime.datetime.combine(
            date, time)
        return timestamp
```

8. Mutate the `Leg` instances with additional values. Both of these functions compute new values and also update the `Leg` object so it includes the computed values. This is an optimization that avoids the creation of intermediate objects:

```
    def start_datetime(row: Leg) -> Leg:
        row.start_timestamp = timestamp(
            row.date, row.start_time)
        return row

    def end_datetime(row: Leg) -> Leg:
        row.end_timestamp = timestamp(
            row.date, row.end_time)
        return row
```

9. Compute the derived duration from the time stamps. Here's a function that must be performed after the previous two:

```
    def duration(row: Leg) -> Leg:
        travel_time = row.end_timestamp - row.start_timestamp
        row.travel_hours = round(
            travel_time.total_seconds() / 60 / 60, 1)
        return row
```

10. Compute any other metrics that are needed for the analyses. This includes creating the height values that are converted into float numbers. The final calculation is based on two other calculated results:

```
    def fuel_use(row: Leg) -> Leg:
        end_height = float(row.end_fuel_height)
        start_height = float(row.start_fuel_height)
        row.fuel_change = start_height - end_height
        return row

    def fuel_per_hour(row: Leg) -> Leg:
        row.fuel_per_hour = row.fuel_change / row.travel_hours
        return row
```

The `fuel_per_hour()` function's calculation depends on the entire preceding stack of calculations. The travel hours duration is derived from the start and end time stamps. Each of these computations is done separately to clarify and emphasize the computation. This approach tends to divorce the computations from considerations about the overall data structure in use. It also permits changes to the computations separate from changes to the overall data structure.

How it works...

The idea is to create a composite operation that follows this template:

1. Normalize the structure. This often requires a generator function to read data in one structure and yield data in a different structure.
2. Filter and cleanse each item. This may involve a simple filter, as shown in this example. We'll look at more complex filters later.
3. Derive data via mappings or via lazy properties of class definitions. A class with lazy properties is a reactive object. Any change to the source property should cause changes to the computed properties.

In more complex applications, we might need to look up reference data or decode coded fields. All of the additional complexity can be refactored into separate functions.

Once we've completed the preliminary computations, we have data that can be used for a variety of analyses. Many times, this is a `reduce` operation. The initial example computes a sum of fuel use. Here are two other examples:

```
from statistics import *

def avg_fuel_per_hour(source: Iterable[Leg]) -> float:
    return mean(row.fuel_per_hour for row in source)

def stdev_fuel_per_hour(source: Iterable[Leg]) -> float:
    return stdev(row.fuel_per_hour for row in source)
```

These functions apply the `mean()` and `stdev()` functions to the `fuel_per_hour` attribute of each row of the enriched data.

We might use this as follows:

```
>>> round(
...     avg_fuel_per_hour(clean_data_iter(row_merge(log_rows))),
...     3)
0.48
```

Here, we've used the `clean_data_iter(row_merge(log_rows))` mapping pipeline to cleanse and enrich the raw data. Then, we applied a reduction to this data to get the value we're interested in.

We now know that a 30" tall tank is good for about 60 hours of motoring. At 6 knots, this sailboat can go about 360 nautical miles on a full tank of fuel. Additional data can refine this rough estimate into a range based on the variance or standard deviation of the samples.

There's more...

As we noted, we can only perform one iteration on an iterable source of data. If we want to compute several averages, or the average as well as the variance, we'll need to use a slightly different design pattern.

In order to compute multiple summaries of the data, we'll need to create a concrete object of some kind that can be summarized repeatedly:

```
def summary(raw_data: Iterable[List[str]]) -> None:
    data = tuple(clean_data_iter(row_merge(raw_data)))
    m = avg_fuel_per_hour(data)
    s = 2 * stdev_fuel_per_hour(data)
    print(f"Fuel use {m:.2f} ±{s:.2f}")
```

Here, we've created a `tuple` from the cleaned and enriched data. This `tuple` can produce any number of iterators. Having this capability means we can compute two summaries from this `tuple` object.

We can also use the `tee()` function in the `itertools` module for this kind of processing:

```
from itertools import tee
def summary_t(raw_data: Iterable[List[str]]):
    data1, data2 = tee(clean_data_iter(row_merge(raw_data)), 2)
    m = avg_fuel_per_hour(data1)
    s = 2 * stdev_fuel_per_hour(data2)
    print(f"Fuel use {m:.2f} ±{s:.2f}")
```

We've used `tee()` to create two clones of the iterable output from `clean_data_iter(row_merge(log_rows))`. We can use one of the clones to compute a mean and the other clone to compute a standard deviation.

This design involves a large number of transformations of source data. We've built it using a stack of `map`, `filter`, and `reduce` operations. This provides a great deal of flexibility.

Implementing "there exists" processing

The processing patterns we've been looking at can all be summarized with the universal quantifier, ∀, meaning *for all*. It's been an implicit part of all of the processing definitions:

- **Map**: For all items in the source, S, apply the `map` function, $m(x)$. We can change notation to have an explicit use of the universal quantifier: $\forall x \in X\big(m(x)\big)$.
- **Filter**: For all items in the source, pass those for which the `filter` function is `true`. Here, also, we've used the universal quantifier to make this explicit: $\forall x \in S\big(x \textbf{ if } f(x)\big)$.
- **Reduce**: For all items in the source, use the given operator and base value to compute a summary. The universal quantification is implicit in the definition of operators like $\sum_{x \in S} x$.

There are also cases where we are only interested in locating a single item. We often describe these cases as a **search** to show there exists at least one item where a condition is true. This can be called the existential quantifier, ∃, meaning *there exists*.

We'll need to use some additional features of Python to create generator functions that stop when the first value matches some predicate. This will let us build generators that locate a single item in ways that are similar to generators that work with all items.

Getting ready

Let's look at an example of an existence test.

We might want to know whether a number is prime or composite. A prime number has no factors other than 1 and itself. Other numbers, with multiple factors, are called composite. For example, the number 5 is prime because it has only the numbers 1 and 5 as factors. The number 42 is composite because it has the numbers 2, 3, and 7 as prime factors.

We can define a prime predicate, *P(n)*, like this:

$$P(n) = \neg\exists i(2 \le i < n \textbf{ if } n = 0 \mod i)$$

A number, *n*, is prime if there does not exist a value of *i* (between 2 and the number) that divides the number evenly. If *n* is zero and the modulus is *i*, then *i* is a factor of *n*.

We can move the negation around and rephrase this as follows:

$$\neg P(n) = \exists i(2 \le i < n \textbf{ if } n = 0 \mod i)$$

A number, *n*, is composite (non-prime) if there exists a value, *i*, between 2 and the number itself that divides the number evenly. For a test to see if a number is prime, we don't need to know **all** the factors. The existence of a single factor shows the number is composite.

The overall idea is to iterate through the range of candidate numbers. Once we've found a factor, we can break early from any further iteration. In Python, this early exit from a `for` statement is done with the `break` statement. Because we're not processing all values, we can't easily use any of the built-in higher-order functions such as `map()`, `filter()`, or `reduce()`. Because `break` is a statement, we can't easily use a generator expression, either; we're constrained to writing a generator function.

(The Fermat test is generally more efficient than this, but it doesn't involve a simple search for the existence of a factor.)

How to do it...

In order to build this kind of search function, we'll need to create a generator function that will complete processing at the first match. One way to do this is with the `break` statement, as follows:

1. Define a generator function to skip items until a test is passed. The generator can yield the first value that passes the predicate test. The generator will require a predicate function, `fn`. The definition can rely on `TypeVar` because the actual type doesn't matter. The type must match between the source of the data, `source`, and the predicate function, `fn`:

```
T_ = TypeVar("T_")
Predicate = Callable[[T_], bool]

def find_first(
        fn: Predicate, source: Iterable[T_]
        ) -> Iterator[T_]:
    for item in source:
        if fn(item):
            yield item
            break
```

2. Define the specific predicate function. For our purposes, a `lambda` object will do. Since we're testing for being prime, we're looking for any value that divides the target number, `n`, evenly. Here's the expression:

```
lambda i: n % i == 0
```

3. Apply the find_first() search function with the given range of values and predicate. If the factors iterable has an item, then n is composite. Otherwise, there are no values in the factors iterable, which means n is a prime number:

```
import math
def prime(n: int) -> bool:
    factors = find_first(
        lambda i: n % i == 0,
        range(2, int(math.sqrt(n)+1)) )
    return len(list(factors)) == 0
```

As a practical matter, we don't need to test every single number between two and n to see whether n is prime. It's only necessary to test values, i, such that $2 \leq i < \lfloor\sqrt{n}\rfloor$.

How it works...

In the find_first() function, we introduce a break statement to stop processing the source iterable. When the for statement stops, the generator will reach the end of the function and return normally.

The process that is consuming values from this generator will be given the StopIteration exception. This exception means the generator will produce no more values. The find_first() function raises an exception, but it's not an error. It's the normal way to signal that an iterable has finished processing the input values.

In this case, the StopIteration exception means one of two things:

- If a value has been yielded, the value is a factor of n.
- If no value was yielded, then n is prime.

This small change of breaking early from the for statement makes a dramatic difference in the meaning of the generator function. Instead of processing **all** values from the source, the find_first() generator will stop processing as soon as the predicate is true.

This is different from a filter, where all the source values will be consumed. When using the break statement to leave the for statement early, some of the source values may not be processed.

See also

- We looked at how to combine mapping and filtering in the *Using stacked generator expressions* recipe, earlier in this chapter.
- We look at lazy properties in the *Using properties for lazy attributes* recipe in *Chapter 7, Basics of Classes and Objects*. Also, this recipe looks at some important variations of map-reduce processing.

There's more...

In the `itertools` module, there is an alternative to the `find_first()` function. This will be shown in this example. The `takewhile()` function uses a predicate function to take values from the input while the predicate function is true. When the predicate becomes false, then the function stops processing values.

To use `takewhile()`, we need to invert our factor test. We need to consume values that are non-factors until we find the first factor. This leads to a change in the lambda from `lambda i: n % i == 0` to `lambda i: n % i != 0`.

Let's look at two examples. We'll test 47 and 49 for being prime. We need to check numbers in the range 2 to $\sqrt{49} = 7$:

```
>>> from itertools import takewhile
n = 47
list(takewhile(lambda i: n % i != 0, range(2, 8)))
[2, 3, 4, 5, 6, 7]
n = 49
list(takewhile(lambda i: n % i != 0, range(2, 8)))
[2, 3, 4, 5, 6]
```

For a prime number, like 47, none of the values are factors. All the non-factors pass the `takewhile()` predicate. The resulting list of non-factors is the same as the set of values being tested. The collection of non-factors from the `takewhile()` function and the `range(2, 8)` object are both `[2, 3, 4, 5, 6, 7]`.

For a composite number, like 49, many non-factors pass the `takewhile()` predicate until a factor is found. In this example, the values 2 through 6 are not factors of `49`. The collection of non-factors, `[2, 3, 4, 5, 6]`, is not the same as the set of values collection that was tested, `[2, 3, 4, 5, 6, 7]`.

Using the `itertooks.takewhile()` function leads us to a test that looks like this:

```
def prime_t(n: int) -> bool:
    tests = set(range(2, int(math.sqrt(n) + 1)))
    non_factors = set(takewhile(lambda i: n % i != 0, tests))
    return tests == non_factors
```

This creates two intermediate set objects, `tests` and `non_factors`. If all of the tested values are also not factors, the number is prime.

The built-in `any()` function is also an existential test. It can also be used to locate the first item that matches a given criteria. In the following example, we'll use `any()` to see if any of the test numbers in the `tests` range is a factor. If there are no factors, the number is prime:

```
def prime_any(n: int) -> bool:
    tests = range(2, int(math.sqrt(n) + 1))
    has_factors = any(n % t == 0 for t in tests)
    return not has_factors
```

The itertools module

There are a number of additional functions in the `itertools` module that we can use to simplify complex map-reduce applications:

- `filterfalse()`: It is the companion to the built-in `filter()` function. It inverts the predicate logic of the `filter()` function; it rejects items for which the predicate is `true`.
- `zip_longest()`: It is the companion to the built-in `zip()` function. The built-in `zip()` function stops merging items when the shortest iterable is exhausted. The `zip_longest()` function will supply a given fill value to pad short iterables so they match the longest ones.
- `starmap()`: It is a modification of the essential `map()` algorithm. When we perform `map(function, iter1, iter2)`, an item from each of the two iterables is provided as two positional arguments to the given function. `starmap()` expects a single iterable to provide a tuple that contains all the argument values for the function.

There are still other functions in this module that we might use, too:

- `accumulate()`: This function is a variation on the built-in `sum()` function. This will yield each partial total that's produced before reaching the final sum.
- `chain()`: This function will combine iterables in order.

- `compress()`: This function uses one iterable as a source of data and the other as a source of selectors. When the item from the selector is true, the corresponding data item is passed. Otherwise, the data item is rejected. This is an item-by-item filter based on true-false values.
- `dropwhile()`: While the predicate to this function is `true`, it will reject values. Once the predicate becomes `false`, it will pass all remaining values. See `takewhile()`.
- `groupby()`: This function uses a key function to control the definition of groups. Items with the same key value are grouped into separate iterators. For the results to be useful, the original data should be sorted into order by the keys.
- `islice()`: This function is like a `slice` expression, except it applies to an iterable, not a list. Where we use `list[1:]` to discard the first row of a list, we can use `islice(iterable, 1)` to discard the first item from an iterable.
- `takewhile()`: While the predicate is `true`, this function will pass values. Once the predicate becomes `false`, stop processing any remaining values. See `dropwhile()`.
- `tee()`: This splits a single iterable into a number of clones. Each clone can then be consumed separately. This is a way to perform multiple reductions on a single iterable source of data.

There are a variety of ways we can use generator functions. The `itertools` module provides a number of ready-built higher-order functions that we can extend with generator functions. Building on the `itertools` foundation can provide a great deal of confidence that the final algorithm will work reliably.

See also

- In the *Using stacked generator expressions* recipe, earlier in this chapter, we made extensive use of immutable class definitions.
- See `https://projecteuler.net/problem=10` for a challenging problem related to prime numbers less than 2 million. Parts of the problem seem obvious. It can be difficult, however, to test all those numbers for being prime.

Creating a partial function

When we look at functions such as `reduce()`, `sorted()`, `min()`, and `max()`, we see that we'll often have some argument values that change very rarely, if at all. In a particular context, they're essentially fixed. For example, we might find a need to write something like this in several places:

```
reduce(operator.mul, ..., 1)
```

Of the three parameters for `reduce()`, only one - the iterable to process - actually changes. The operator and the base value arguments are essentially fixed at `operator.mul` and `1`.

Clearly, we can define a whole new function for this:

```
def prod(iterable):
    return reduce(operator.mul, iterable, 1)
```

However, Python has a few ways to simplify this pattern so that we don't have to repeat the boilerplate `def` and `return` statements.

The goal of this recipe is different from providing general default values. A partial function doesn't provide a way for us to override the defaults. A partial function has specific values bound in a kind of permanent way. This leads to creating possibly many partial functions, each with specific argument values bound in advance.

Getting ready

Some statistical modeling is done with standard scores, sometimes called **z-scores**. The idea is to standardize a raw measurement onto a value that can be easily compared to a normal distribution, and easily compared to related numbers that are measured in different units.

The calculation is this:

$$z = \frac{x - \mu}{\sigma}$$

Here, x is a raw value, μ is the population mean, and σ is the population standard deviation. The value z will have a mean of 0 and a standard deviation of 1. We can use this value to spot **outliers** - values that are suspiciously far from the mean. We expect that (about) 99.7% of our z values will be between -3 and +3.

We could define a function to compute standard scores, like this:

```
def standardize(mean: float, stdev: float, x: float) -> float:
    return (x - mean) / stdev
```

This `standardize()` function will compute a z-score from a raw score, *x*. When we use this function in a practical context, we'll see that there are two kinds of argument values for the parameters:

- The argument values for `mean` and `stdev` are essentially fixed. Once we've computed the population values, we'll have to provide the same two values to the `standardize()` function over and over again.

- The value for the `x` parameter will vary each time we evaulate the `standardize()` function. The value of the `x` parameter will change frequently, but the values for the `mean` and `stdev` will remain essentially fixed each time the function is used.

Let's work with a collection of data samples with two variables, `x` and `y`. The data is defined by the `Row` class:

```
@dataclass
class Row:
    x: float
    y: float
```

A collection of these `Row` items looks like this:

```
data_1 = [Row(x=10.0, y=8.04),
 Row(x=8.0, y=6.95),
 Row(x=13.0, y=7.58),
 Row(x=9.0, y=8.81),
 Row(x=11.0, y=8.33),
 Row(x=14.0, y=9.96),
 Row(x=6.0, y=7.24),
 Row(x=4.0, y=4.26),
 Row(x=12.0, y=10.84),
 Row(x=7.0, y=4.82),
Row(x=5.0, y=5.68)]
```

As an example, we'll compute a standardized value for the `x` attribute. This means computing the mean and standard deviation for the `x` values. Then, we'll need to apply the mean and standard deviation values to standardize data in both of our collections. This looks like this:

```
import statistics
mean_x = statistics.mean(item.x for item in data_1)
stdev_x = statistics.stdev(item.x for item in data_1)

for row in data_1:
    z_x = standardize(mean_x, stdev_x, row.x)
    print(row, z_x)
```

Providing the `mean_x`, `stdev_x` values each time we evaluate the `standardize()` function can clutter an algorithm with details that aren't deeply important. In some more complex algorithms, the clutter can lead to more confusion than clarity. We can use a partial function to simplify this use of `standardize()` with some relatively fixed argument values.

How to do it...

To simplify using a function with a number of relatively fixed argument values, we can create a partial function. This recipe will show two ways to create a partial function:

- Using the `partial()` function from the `functools` module to build a new function from the full `standardize()` function.
- Creating a `lambda` object to supply argument values that don't change.

Using functools.partial()

1. Import the `partial` function from `functools`:

    ```
    from functools import partial
    ```

2. Create a new function using `partial()`. We provide the base function, plus the positional arguments that need to be included. Any parameters that are not supplied when the partial is defined must be supplied when the partial is evaluated:

    ```
    z = partial(standardize, mean_x, stdev_x)
    ```

We've provided fixed values for the first two parameters, `mean` and `stdev`, of the `standardize()` function. We can now use the `z()` function with a single value, `z(a)`, and it will apply `standardize(mean_x, stdev_x, a)`. Stated another way, the partial function, `z(a)`, is equivalent to a full function with values bound to `mean_x` and `stdev_x`.

Creating a lambda object

1. Define a `lambda` object that binds the fixed parameters:

    ```
    lambda x: standardize(mean_x, stdev_x, x)
    ```

2. Assign this `lambda` to a variable to create a callable object, `z()`:

    ```
    z = lambda x: standardize(mean_x, stdev_x, x)
    ```

This also provides fixed values for the first two parameters, `mean` and `stdev`, of the `standardize()` function. We can now use the `z()` lambda object with a single value, `z(a)`, and it will apply `standardize(mean_x, stdev_x, a)`.

How it works...

Both techniques create a callable object – a function – named `z()` that has the values for `mean_x` and `stdev_x` already bound to the first two positional parameters. With either approach, we can now have processing that can look like this:

```
for row in data_1:
    print(row, z(row.x))
```

We've applied the `z()` function to each set of data. Because the `z()` function has some parameters already applied, its use is simplified.

There's one significant difference between the two techniques for creating the `z()` function:

- The `partial()` function binds the actual values of the parameters. Any subsequent change to the variables that were used doesn't change the definition of the partial function that's created. After creating `z = partial(standardize(mean_x, stdev_x))`, changing the value of `mean_X` or `stdev_X` doesn't have an impact on the partial function, `z()`.
- The `lambda` object binds the variable name, not the value. Any subsequent change to the variable's value will change the way the lambda behaves. After creating `z = lambda x: standardize(mean_x, stdev_x, x)`, changing the value of `mean_x` or `stdev_x` changes the values used by the `lambda` object, `z()`.

We can modify the `lambda` slightly to bind specific values instead of names:

```
z = lambda x, m=mean_x, s=stdev_x: standardize(m, s, x)
```

This extracts the current values of `mean_x` and `stdev_x` to create default values for the `lambda` object. The values of `mean_x` and `stdev_x` are now irrelevant to the proper operation of the `lambda` object, `z()`.

There's more...

We can provide keyword argument values as well as positional argument values when creating a partial function. While this works nicely in general, there are a few cases where it doesn't work.

The `reduce()` function, interestingly, can't be trivially turned into a partial function. The parameters aren't in the ideal order for creating a partial. The `reduce()` function *appears* to be defined like this:

```
def reduce(function, iterable, initializer=None)
```

If this were the actual definition, we could do this:

```
prod = partial(reduce(mul, initializer=1))
```

Practically, the preceding example doesn't work because the definition of `reduce()` is a bit more complex than it might appear. The `reduce()` function doesn't permit named argument values.

This means that we're forced to use the `lambda` technique:

```
>>> from operator import mul
>>> from functools import reduce
>>> prod = lambda x: reduce(mul, x, 1)
```

We've used a `lambda` object to define a function, `prod()`, with only one parameter. This function uses `reduce()` with two fixed parameters and one variable parameter.

Given this definition for `prod()`, we can define other functions that rely on computing products. Here's a definition of the `factorial` function:

```
>>> factorial = lambda x: prod(range(2, x+1))
>>> factorial(5)
120
```

The definition of `factorial()` depends on `prod()`. The definition of `prod()` is a kind of partial function that uses `reduce()` with two fixed parameter values. We've managed to use a few definitions to create a fairly sophisticated function.

In Python, a function is an object. We've seen numerous ways that functions can be arguments to a function. A function that accepts or returns another function as an argument is sometimes called a **higher-order function**.

Similarly, functions can also return a function object as a result. This means that we can create a function like this:

```
def prepare_z(data):
    mean_x = statistics.mean(item.x for item in data_1)
    stdev_x = statistics.stdev(item.x for item in data_1)
    return partial(standardize, mean_x, stdev_x)
```

Here, we've defined a function over a set of (*x*, *y*) samples. We've computed the mean and standard deviation of the *x* attribute of each sample. We then created a partial function that can standardize scores based on the computed statistics. The result of this function is a function we can use for data analysis. The following example shows how this newly created function is used:

```
z = prepare_z(data_1)
for row in data_2:
    print(row, z(row.x))
```

When we evaluated the `prepare_z()` function, it returned a function. We assigned this function to a variable, `z`. This variable is a callable object; it's the function `z()`, which will standardize a score based on the sample mean and standard deviation.

Simplifying complex algorithms with immutable data structures

The concept of a `stateful` object is a common feature of object-oriented programming. We looked at a number of techniques related to objects and state in *Chapter 7, Basics of Classes and Objects*, and *Chapter 8, More Advanced Class Design*. A great deal of the emphasis of object-oriented design is creating methods that mutate an object's state.

When working with JSON or CSV files, we'll often be working with objects that have a Python `dict` object that defines the attributes. Using a `dict` object to store an object's attributes has several consequences:

- We can trivially add and remove new attributes to the dictionary. We're not limited to simply setting and getting defined attributes. This makes it difficult for `mypy` to check our design carefully. The `TypedDict` type hint suggests a narrow domain of possible key values, but it doesn't prevent runtime use of unexpected keys.
- A `dict` object uses a somewhat larger amount of memory than is minimally necessary. This is because dictionaries use a hashing algorithm to locate keys and values. The hash processing requires more memory than other structures such as `list` or `tuple`. For very large amounts of data, this can become a problem.

The most significant issue with stateful object-oriented programming is that it can be challenging to understand the state changes of an object. Rather than trying to understand the state changes, it may be easier to create entirely new objects with a state that can be simply mapped to the object's type. This, coupled with Python type hints, can sometimes create more reliable, and easier to test, software.

In some cases, we can also reduce the amount of memory by avoiding stateful objects in the first place. We have two techniques for doing this:

- Using class definitions with `__slots__`: See the *Optimizing small objects with __slots__* recipe for this. These objects are mutable, so we can update attributes with new values.
- Using immutable `tuples` or `NamedTuples`: See the *Designing classes with little unique processing* recipe for some background on this. These objects are immutable. We can create new objects, but we can't change the state of an object. The cost savings from less memory overall have to be balanced against the additional costs of creating new objects.

Immutable objects can be somewhat faster than mutable objects – but the more important benefit is for algorithm design. In some cases, writing functions that create new immutable objects from old immutable objects can be simpler and easier to test and debug than algorithms that work with stateful objects. Writing type hints can help with this process.

As we noted in the *Using stacked generator expressions* and *Implementing "there exists" processing* recipes, we can only process a generator once. If we need to process it more than once, the iterable sequence of objects must be transformed into a complete collection like a list or tuple.

This often leads to a multi-phase process:

- **Initial extraction of the data**: This might involve a database query or reading a `.csv` file. This phase can be implemented as a function that yields rows or even returns a generator function.
- **Cleansing and filtering the data**: This may involve a stack of generator expressions that can process the source just once. This phase is often implemented as a function that includes several map and filter operations.
- **Enriching the data**: This, too, may involve a stack of generator expressions that can process the data one row at a time. This is typically a series of map operations to create new, derived data from existing data. This often means separate class definitions for each enrichment step.
- **Reducing or summarizing the data**: This may involve multiple summaries. In order for this to work, the output from the enrichment phase needs to be a collection object that can be iterated over more than once.

In some cases, the enrichment and summary processes may be interleaved. As we saw in the *Creating a partial function* recipe, we might do some summarization followed by more enrichment.

Getting ready

Let's work with a collection of data samples with two variables, `x` and `y`. The data is defined by the `DataPair` class:

```
DataPair = NamedTuple("DataPair", [("x", float), ("y", float)])
```

A collection of these `DataPair` items looks like this:

```
data_1 = [DataPair(x=10.0, y=8.04),
 DataPair(x=8.0, y=6.95),
 DataPair(x=13.0, y=7.58),
 DataPair(x=9.0, y=8.81),
 DataPair(x=11.0, y=8.33),
 DataPair(x=14.0, y=9.96),
 DataPair(x=6.0, y=7.24),
 DataPair(x=4.0, y=4.26),
 DataPair(x=12.0, y=10.84),
```

```
DataPair(x=7.0, y=4.82),
DataPair(x=5.0, y=5.68)]
```

In this example, we'll apply a number of computations to rank order this data using the `y` value of each pair. This requires creating another data type for the `y`-value ranking. Computing this ranking value requires sorting the data first, and then yielding the sorted values with an additional attribute value, the `y` rank order.

There are two approaches to this. First, we can change the initial design in order to replace `NamedTuple` with a mutable class that allows an update for each `DataPair` with a y-rank value. The alternative is to use a second `NamedTuple` to carry the y-rank value.

Applying a rank-order value is a little bit like a state change, but it can be done by creating new immutable objects instead of modifying the state of existing objects.

How to do it...

We'll build immutable rank order objects that will contain our existing `DataPair` instances. This will involve defining a new class and a function to create instances of the new class:

1. Define the enriched `NamedTuple` subclass. We'll include the original data as an element of this class rather than copying the values from the original class:

```
class RankYDataPair(NamedTuple):
    y_rank: int
    pair: DataPair
```

2. The alternative definition can look like this. For simple cases, this can be helpful. The behavior is identical to the class shown previously:

```
RankYDataPair = NamedTuple("RankYDataPair", [
    ("y_rank", int),
    ("pair", DataPair)
])
```

3. Define the enrichment function. This will be a generator that starts with `DataPair` instances and yields `RankYDataPair` instances:

```
def rank_by_y(
          source: Iterable[DataPair]
        ) -> Iterator[RankYDataPair]:
```

4. Write the body of the enrichment. In this case, we're going to be rank ordering, so we'll need sorted data, using the original `y` attribute. We're creating new objects from the old objects, so the function yields instances of `RankYDataPair`:

```
    all_data = sorted(source, key=lambda pair: pair.y)
```

```
        for y_rank, pair in enumerate(all_data, start=1):
            yield RankYDataPair(y_rank, pair)
```

We can use this in a longer expression to parse the input text, cleanse each row, and then rank the rows. The use of type hints can make this clearer than an alternative involving stateful objects. In some cases, there can be a very helpful improvement in the clarity of the code.

How it works...

The result of the `rank_by_y()` function is a new object that contains the original object, plus the result of the enrichment. Here's how we'd use this stacked sequence of generators, that is, `rank_by_y()`, `cleanse()`, and `text_parse()`:

```
>>> data = rank_by_y(cleanse(text_parse(text_1)))
>>> pprint(list(data))
[RankYDataPair(y_rank=1, pair=DataPair(x=4.0, y=4.26)),
 RankYDataPair(y_rank=2, pair=DataPair(x=7.0, y=4.82)),
 RankYDataPair(y_rank=3, pair=DataPair(x=5.0, y=5.68)),
 RankYDataPair(y_rank=4, pair=DataPair(x=8.0, y=6.95)),
 RankYDataPair(y_rank=5, pair=DataPair(x=6.0, y=7.24)),
 RankYDataPair(y_rank=6, pair=DataPair(x=13.0, y=7.58)),
 RankYDataPair(y_rank=7, pair=DataPair(x=10.0, y=8.04)),
 RankYDataPair(y_rank=8, pair=DataPair(x=11.0, y=8.33)),
 RankYDataPair(y_rank=9, pair=DataPair(x=9.0, y=8.81)),
 RankYDataPair(y_rank=10, pair=DataPair(x=14.0, y=9.96)),
 RankYDataPair(y_rank=11, pair=DataPair(x=12.0, y=10.84))]
```

The data is in ascending order by the `y` value. We can now use these enriched data values for further analysis and calculation. The original immutable objects are part of the new ranked objects.

The Python type hints work well with the creation of new objects. Consequently, this technique can provide strong evidence that a complex algorithm is correct. Using **mypy** can make immutable objects more appealing.

Finally, we may sometimes see a small speed-up when we use immutable objects. This is not guaranteed and depends on a large number of factors. Using the `timeit` module to assess the performance of the alternative designs is essential.

We can use a test like the one shown in the following example to gather timing details:

```
import timeit
from textwrap import dedent

tuple_runtime = timeit.timeit(
    """list(rank_by_y(data))""",
    dedent("""
    from ch09_r09 import text_parse, cleanse, rank_by_y, text_1
    data = cleanse(text_parse(text_1))
    """),
)
print(f"tuple {tuple_runtime}")
```

This example imports the `timeit` module and a handy tool from the `textwrap` module to de-indent (`dedent`) text. This lets us have blocks of Python code as an indented string. The test code is `list(rank_by_y_dc(data))`. This will be processed repeatedly to gather basic timing information. The other block of code is the one-time setup. This is an import to bring in a number of functions and a statement to gather the raw data and save it in the variable data. This setup is done once; we don't want to measure the performance here.

There's more...

The alternative design uses a mutable dataclass. This relies on a type definition that looks like this:

```
@dataclass
class DataPairDC:
    x: float
    y: float
    y_rank: int = field(init=False)
```

This definition shows the two initial values of each data pair and the derived value that's computed during the rank ordering computation. We'll need a slightly different cleansing function. Here's a `cleanse_dc()` function to produce these `DataPairDC` objects:

```
def cleanse_dc(
        source: Iterable[List[str]]) -> Iterator[DataPairDC]:
    for text_item in source:
        try:
            x_amount = float(text_item[0])
            y_amount = float(text_item[1])
            yield DataPairDC(x=x_amount, y=y_amount)
        except Exception as ex:
            print(ex, repr(text_item))
```

This function is nearly identical to the `cleanse()` function for immutable objects. The principle difference is the class used in the `yield` statement and the related type hint.

Here's the ranking function:

```
def rank_by_y_dc(
        source: Iterable[DataPairDC]) -> Iterable[DataPairDC]:
    all_data = sorted(source, key=lambda pair: pair.y)
    for y_rank, pair in enumerate(all_data, start=1):
        pair.y_rank = y_rank
        yield pair
```

This does two things. First, it yields a sequence of `DataPairDC` instances. As a side effect, it also updates each object, setting the `y_rank` attribute. This additional state change can be obscure in a complex application.

See also

- In the *Using stacked generator expressions* recipe, earlier in this chapter, we also made extensive use of immutable class definitions.

Writing recursive generator functions with the yield from statement

Many algorithms can be expressed neatly as recursions. In the *Designing recursive functions around Python's stack limits* recipe, we looked at some recursive functions that could be optimized to reduce the number of function calls.

When we look at some data structures, we see that they involve recursion. In particular, JSON documents (as well as XML and HTML documents) can have a recursive structure. A JSON document might include a complex object that contains other complex objects within it.

In many cases, there are advantages to using generators for processing these kinds of structures. In this recipe, we'll look at ways to handle recursive data structures with generator functions.

Getting ready

In this recipe, we'll look at a way to search for all matching values in a complex data structure. When working with complex JSON documents, they often contain dict-of-dict, dict-of-list, list-of-dict, and list-of-list structures. Of course, a JSON document is not limited to two levels; dict-of-dict really means dict-of-dict-of.... Similarly, dict-of-list really means dict-of-list-of.... The search algorithm must descend through the entire structure looking for a particular key or value.

A document with a complex structure might look like this:

```
document = {
    "field": "value1",
    "field2": "value",
    "array": [
        {"array_item_key1": "value"},
        {"array_item_key2": "array_item_value2"}
    ],
    "object": {
        "attribute1": "value",
        "attribute2": "value2"
    },
}
```

This shows a document that has four keys, `field`, `field2`, `array`, and `object`. Each of these keys has a distinct data structure as its associated value. Some of the values are unique, while some are duplicated. This duplication is the reason why our search must find **all** instances inside the overall document.

The core algorithm is a depth-first search. The output from this function will be a list of paths that identify the target value. Each path will be a sequence of field names or field names mixed with index positions.

In the previous example, the value `"value"` can be found in three places:

- `["array", 0, "array_item_key1"]`: This path starts with the top-level field named `array`, then visits item zero of a list, then a field named `array_item_key1`.
- `["field2"]`: This path has just a single field name where the value is found.
- `["object", "attribute1"]`: This path starts with the top-level field named `object`, then the child, `attribute1`, of that field.

The `find_value()` function yields both of these paths when it searches the overall document for the target value. Before looking at the recipe itself, let's take a quick look at a conceptual overview of this search function. This is not intended to be useful code. Instead, it shows how the different types are handled. Consider the `if` statements in this snippet:

```
def find_path(value, node, path=None):
    path = path or []
    if isinstance(node, dict):
        for key in node.keys():
            # find_value(value, node[key], path+[key])
            # This may yield multiple values
    elif isinstance(node, list):
```

```
        for index in range(len(node)):
            # find_value(value, node[index], path+[index])
            # This may yield multiple values
    else:
        # a primitive type
        if node == value:
            yield path
```

There are three alternatives expressed in the `find_path()` `if` statement:

- When the `node` value is a dictionary, the value of each key must be examined. The values may be any kind of data, so we'll use the `find_path()` function recursively on each value. This will yield a sequence of matches.
- If the `node` value is a list, the items for each index position must be examined. The items may be any kind of data, so we'll use the `find_path()` function recursively on each value. This will yield a sequence of matches.
- The other choice is for the `node` value to be a primitive type, one of `int`, `float`, `str`, `bool`, or `None`. If the `node` value is the `target` value, we've found one instance, and can yield this path to this match.

There are two ways to handle the recursion. One is like this:

```
for match in find_value(value, node[key], path+[key]):
    yield match
```

The `for` statement seems to be scaffolding around a simple idea. The other way, using `yield from`, can be simpler and a bit clearer. This lets us remove a lot of `for` statement scaffolding.

How to do it...

We'll start by sketching out some replacement code for each branch in the conceptual code shown in the *Getting ready* section of this recipe. We will then create the complete function for traversing the complex data structure:

1. Start with a template function to examine the various alternatives:

```
def find_path(
    value: Any, node: JSON_DOC, path: Optional[List[Node_Id]]
= None
) -> Iterator[List[Node_Id]]:
    if path is None:
        path = []
    if isinstance(node, dict):
        # apply find_path to each key
```

```
    elif isinstance(node, list):
        # applu find_path to each item in the Last
    else:  # str, int, float, bool, None
        if node == value:
            yield path
```

2. For a recursive function reference, write out the complete `for` statement. Use this for initial debugging to ensure things work. Here's how to look at each key of a dictionary. This replaces the `# apply find_path to each key` line in the preceding code. Test this to be sure the recursion works properly:

```
for key in sorted(node.keys()):
    for match in find_path (value, node[key], path+[key]):
        yield match
```

3. Replace the inner `for` with a `yield from` statement once we're sure things work:

```
for key in sorted(node.keys()):
    yield from find_path(value, node[key], path+[key])
```

4. This has to be done for the list case as well. Start an examination of each item in the list:

```
for index in range(len(node)):
    for match in find_path(value, node[index], path + [index]):
        yield match
```

5. Replace the inner `for` with a `yield from` statement:

```
for index in range(len(node)):
    yield from find_path(value, node[index], path + [index])
```

The complete depth-first `find_path()` search function will look like this:

```
def find_path(
        value: Any,
        node: JSON_DOC,
        path: Optional[List[Node_Id]] = None
        ) -> Iterator[List[Node_Id]]:
    if path is None:
        path: List[Node_Id] = []
    if isinstance(node, dict):
        for key in sorted(node.keys()):
            yield from find_path(value, node[key], path + [key])
    elif isinstance(node, list):
        for index in range(len(node)):
            yield from find_path(
```

```
                value, node[index], path + [index])
    else: # str, int, float, bool, None
        if node == value:
            yield path
```

When we use the `find_path()` function, it looks like this:

```
>>> list(find_path('array_item_value2', document))
[['array', 1, 'array_item_key2']]
```

The `find_path()` function is an iterator, yielding a number of values. We consumed all the results to create a list. In this example, the list had one item, `['array', 1, 'array_item_key2']`. This item was the list of nodes on the `path` to the matching item.

We can then evaluate `document['array'][1]['array_item_key2']` to find the referenced value.

When we look for a non-unique value, we might see a list like this:

```
>>> list(find_value('value', document))
[['array', 0, 'array_item_key1'],
 ['field2'],
['object', 'attribute1']]
```

The resulting list has three items. Each of these is a list of keys on the path to an item with the target value of `value`.

How it works...

The `yield from X` statement is shorthand for:

```
for item in X:
    yield item
```

This lets us write a succinct recursive algorithm that will behave as an iterator and properly yield multiple values.

This can also be used in contexts that don't involve a recursive function. It's entirely sensible to use a `yield from` statement anywhere that an iterable result is involved. It's a big simplification for recursive functions, however, because it preserves a clearly recursive structure.

There's more...

Another common style of definition assembles a list using `append` operations. We can rewrite this into an iterator and avoid the overhead of building a `list` object.

When factoring a number, we can define the set of prime factors like this:

$$F(x) = \begin{cases} \{x\} & \textbf{if } x \text{ is prime} \\ \{n\} \cup F\left(\frac{x}{n}\right) & \textbf{if } x = 0 \mod n \end{cases}$$

If the value, x, is prime, it has only itself in the set of prime factors. Otherwise, there must be some prime number, *n*, which is the least factor of x. We can assemble a set of factors starting with *n* and then append all factors of $\frac{x}{n}$. To be sure that only prime factors are found, *n* must be prime. If we search ascending values of *n*, we'll find prime factors before finding composite factors.

The eager approach builds a complete list of factors. A lazy approach can generate factors for a consumer. Here's an eager list-building function:

```
import math
def factor_list(x: int) -> List[int]:
    limit = int(math.sqrt(x) + 1)
    for n in range(2, limit):
        q, r = divmod(x, n)
        if r == 0:
            return [n] + factor_list(q)
    return [x]
```

This `factor_list()` function will search all numbers, *n*, such that $2 \leq n < \sqrt{x}$. This function builds a `list` object. If a factor, *n*, is found, it will start a list with that factor. It will extend the list, `[n]`, with the factors built from `x // n`. If there are no factors of `x`, then the value is prime, and this returns a list with only the value of `x`.

Consider what happens when we evaluate `factor_list(42)`. When `n` is `2`, we'll compute `[2] + factor_list(21)`. Computing `factor_list(21)` leads to computing `[3] + factor_list(7)`. When `factor_list(7)` finds no factors, it returns `[7]`, and as the recursive invocations of this function finish their work, the final result is `[2, 3, 7]`.

This will search for composite numbers as well as prime numbers, wasting time. For example, after testing `2` and `3`, this will also test `4` and `6`, even though they're composite and all of their factors have already been tested.

We can rewrite this as an iterator by replacing the recursive calls with `yield from`. The function will look like this:

```
def factor_iter(x: int) -> Iterator[int]:
    limit = int(math.sqrt(x) + 1)
    for n in range(2, limit):
```

```
            q, r = divmod(x, n)
            if r == 0:
                yield n
                yield from factor_iter(q)
                return
        yield x
```

As with the list-building version, this will search numbers, *n*, such that $2 \leq n < \sqrt{x}$. When a factor is found, the function will yield the factor, followed by any other factors found by a recursive call to `factor_iter()`. If no factors are found, the function will yield the prime number and nothing more.

Using an iterator allows us to build any kind of collection from the factors. Instead of being limited to always creating a `list` object, we can create a multiset using the `collections.Counter` class. It would look like this:

```
>>> from collections import Counter
>>> Counter(factor_iter(384))
Counter({2: 7, 3: 1})
```

This shows us that:

$$384 = 2^7 \times 3$$

In some cases, this kind of multiset can be easier to work with than a simple list of factors.

What's important is that the multiset was created directly from the `factor_iter()` iterator without creating an intermediate `list` object. This kind of optimization lets us build complex algorithms that aren't forced to consume large volumes of memory.

See also

- In the *Designing recursive functions around Python's stack limits* recipe, earlier in this chapter, we covered the core design patterns for recursive functions. This recipe provides an alternative way to create the results.

10
Input/Output, Physical Format, and Logical Layout

Computing often works with persistent data. There may be source data to be analyzed, or output to be created using Python input and output operations. The map of the dungeon that's explored in a game is data that will be input to the game application. Images, sounds, and movies are data output by some applications and input by other applications. Even a request through a network will involve input and output operations. The common aspect to all of these is the concept of a file of data. The term **file** is overloaded with many meanings:

- The **operating system** (**OS**) uses a file as a way to organize bytes of data on a device. All of the wildly different kinds of content are reduced to a collection of bytes. It's the responsibility of application software to make sense of the bytes. Two common kinds of devices offer variations in terms of the features of OS files:
  - **Block devices** such as disks or **solid-state drives** (**SSD**): The bytes tend to be persistent. A file on this kind of device can seek any specific byte, making them particularly good for databases, where any row can be processed at any time.
  - **Character devices** such as a network connection, or a keyboard, or a GPS antenna. A file on this kind of device is viewed as a stream of individual bytes in transit to or from the device. There's no way to seek forward or backward; the bytes must be captured and processed as they arrive.

- The word *file* also defines a data structure used by the Python runtime. A uniform Python file abstraction wraps the various OS file implementations. When we open a Python file, there is a binding between the Python abstraction, an OS implementation, and the underlying collection of bytes on a block device or stream of bytes of a character device.

Python gives us two common modes for working with a file's content:

- In "b" (**binary**) mode, our application sees the bytes, without further interpretation. This can be helpful for processing media data like images, audio, and movies, which have complex encodings. These file formats can be rather complex, and difficult to work with. We'll often import libraries like `pillow` to handle the details of image file encoding into bytes.
- In "t" (**text**) mode, the bytes of the file are used to decode string values. Python strings are made of Unicode characters, and there are a variety of encoding schemes for translating between text and bytes. Generally, the OS has a preferred encoding and Python respects this. The UTF-8 encoding is popular. Files can have any of the available Unicode encodings, and it may not be obvious which encoding was used to create a file.

Additionally, Python modules like `shelve` and `pickle` have unique ways of representing more complex Python objects than simple strings. There are a number of `pickle` protocols available; all of them are based on binary mode file operations.

Throughout this chapter, we'll talk about how Python objects are **serialized**. When an object is written to a file, a representation of the Python object's state is transformed into a series of bytes. Often, the translation involves text objects as an intermediate notation. Deserialization is the reverse process: it recovers a Python object's state from the bytes of a file. Saving and transferring a representation of the object state is the foundational concept behind REST web services.

When we process data from files, we have two common concerns:

- **The physical format of the data**: This is the fundamental concern of how the bytes on the file can be interpreted to reconstruct a Python object. The bytes could represent a JPEG-encoded image or an MPEG-encoded movie. A common example is that the bytes of the file represent Unicode text, organized into lines. The bytes could encode text for **comma-separated values** (**CSV**) or the bytes could encode the text for a JSON document. All physical format concerns are commonly handled by Python libraries like `csv`, `json`, and `pickle`, among many others.
- **The logical layout of the data**: A given layout may have flexible positions or ordering for the data. The arrangement of CSV columns or JSON fields may be variable. In cases where the data includes labels, the logical layout can be handled with tremendous flexibility. Without labels, the layout is positional, and some additional schema information is required to identify what data items are in each position.

Both the physical format and logical layout are essential to interpreting the data on a file. We'll look at a number of recipes for working with different physical formats. We'll also look at ways to divorce our program from some aspects of the logical layout.

In this chapter, we'll look at the following recipes:

- Using `pathlib` to work with filenames
- Replacing a file while preserving the previous version
- Reading delimited files with the CSV module
- Using `dataclasses` to simplify working with CSV files
- Reading complex formats using regular expressions
- Reading JSON and YAML documents
- Reading XML documents
- Reading HTML documents
- Refactoring a `.csv DictReader` as a dataclass reader

In order to start doing input and output with files, we'll start by working with the OS filesystem. The common features of the directory structure of files and devices are described by Python's `pathlib` module. This module has consistent behavior across a number of operating systems, allowing a Python program to work similarly on Linux, macOS, and Windows.

Using pathlib to work with filenames

Most operating systems use a hierarchical path to identify a file. Here's an example filename, including the entire path:

```
/Users/slott/Documents/Writing/Python Cookbook/code
```

This full pathname has the following elements:

- The leading / means the name is absolute. It starts from the root of the directory of files. In Windows, there can be an extra letter in front of the name, such as `C:`, to distinguish between the directories on individual storage devices. Linux and macOS treat all the devices as a unified hierarchy.
- The names `Users`, `slott`, `Documents`, `Writing`, `Python Cookbook`, and `code` represent the directories (or "folders," as a visual metaphor) of the filesystem. The path names a top-level `Users` directory. This directory is expected to contain the `slot` subdirectory. This is true for each name in the path.
- / is a separator between directory names. The Windows OS uses \ to separate items on the path. Python running on Windows, however, can use / because it automatically converts the more common / into the Windows path separator character gracefully; in Python, we can generally ignore the Windows use of \.

There is no way to tell what kind of filesystem object the name at the end of the path, "code", represents. The name code might be a directory that contains the names of other files. It could be an ordinary data file, or a link to a stream-oriented device. The operating system retains additional directory information that shows what kind of filesystem object this is.

A path without the leading / is relative to the current working directory. In macOS and Linux, the cd command sets the current working directory. In Windows, the chdir command does this job. The current working directory is a feature of the login session with the OS. It's made visible by the shell.

This recipe will show you how we can work with pathlib.Path objects to get access to files in any OS directory structure.

Getting ready

It's important to separate two concepts:

- The path that identifies a file, including the name and metadata like creation timestamps and ownership
- The contents of the file

The path provides two things: an optional sequence of directory names and a mandatory filename. An OS directory includes each file's name, information about when each file was created, who owns the files, what the permissions are for each file, how many bytes the files use, and other details. The contents of the files are independent of the directory information: multiple directory entries can be linked to the same content.

Often, the filename has a suffix (or extension) as a hint as to what the physical format is. A file ending in .csv is likely a text file that can be interpreted as rows and columns of data. This binding between name and physical format is not absolute. File suffixes are only a hint and can be wrong.

In Python, the pathlib module handles all path-related processing. The module makes several distinctions among paths:

- Pure paths that may or may not refer to an actual file
- Concrete paths that are resolved; these refer to an actual file

This distinction allows us to create pure paths for files that our application will likely create or refer to. We can also create concrete paths for those files that actually exist on the OS. An application can resolve a pure path to a concrete path.

The `pathlib` module also makes a distinction between Linux path objects and Windows path objects. This distinction is rarely needed; most of the time, we don't want to care about the OS-level details of the path. An important reason for using `pathlib` is because we want processing that is isolated from details of the underlying OS. The cases where we might want to work with a `PureLinuxPath` object are rare.

All of the mini recipes in this section will leverage the following:

```
>>> from pathlib import Path
```

We rarely need any of the other definitions from `pathlib`.

We'll also presume the `argparse` module is used to gather the file or directory names. For more information on `argparse`, see the *Using argparse to get command-line input* recipe in *Chapter 6, User Inputs and Outputs*. We'll use the `options` variable as a namespace that contains the `input` filename or directory name that the recipe works with.

For demonstration purposes, a mock argument parsing is shown by providing the following `Namespace` object:

```
>>> from argparse import Namespace
>>> options = Namespace(
...     input='/path/to/some/file.csv',
...     file1='data/ch10_file1.yaml',
...     file2='data/ch10_file2.yaml',
... )
```

This `options` object has three mock argument values. The `input` value is an absolute path. The `file1` and `file2` values are relative paths.

How to do it...

We'll show a number of common pathname manipulations as separate mini recipes. These will include the following manipulations:

- Making the output filename by changing the input filename's suffix
- Making a number of sibling output files
- Creating a directory and a number of files in the directory
- Comparing file dates to see which is newer
- Removing a file
- Finding all files that match a given pattern

We'll start by creating an output filename based on an input filename. This reflects a common kind of application pattern where a source file in one physical format is transformed into a file in a distinct physical format.

Making the output filename by changing the input filename's suffix

Perform the following steps to make the output filename by changing the input suffix:

1. Create the `Path` object from the input filename string. In this example, the `PosixPath` class is displayed because the author is using macOS. On a Windows machine, the class would be `WindowsPath`. The `Path` class will properly parse the string to determine the elements of the path. Here's how we create a path from a string:

```
>>> input_path = Path(options.input)
>>> input_path
PosixPath('/path/to/some/file.csv')
```

2. Create the output `Path` object using the `with_suffix()` method:

```
>>> output_path = input_path.with_suffix('.out')
>>> output_path
PosixPath('/path/to/some/file.out')
```

All of the filename parsing is handled seamlessly by the `Path` class. The `with_suffix()` method saves us from manually parsing the text of the filename.

Making a number of sibling output files with distinct names

Perform the following steps to make a number of sibling output files with distinct names:

1. Create a `Path` object from the input filename string. In this example, the `PosixPath` class is displayed because the author uses Linux. On a Windows machine, the class would be `WindowsPath`. The `Path` class will properly parse the string to determine the elements of the path:

```
>>> input_path = Path(options.input)
>>> input_path
PosixPath('/path/to/some/file.csv')
```

2. Extract the parent directory and the stem from the filename. The stem is the name without the suffix:

```
>>> input_directory = input_path.parent
>>> input_stem = input_path.stem
```

3. Build the desired output name. For this example, we'll append _pass to the filename. An input file of file.csv will produce an output of file_pass.csv:

```
>>> output_stem_pass = f"{input_stem}_pass"
>>> output_stem_pass
'file_pass'
```

4. Build the complete Path object:

```
>>> output_path = (
...     input_directory / output_stem_pass
...     ).with_suffix('.csv')
>>> output_path
PosixPath('/path/to/some/file_pass.csv')
```

The / operator assembles a new path from path components. We need to put the / operation in parentheses to be sure that it's performed first to create a new Path object. The input_directory variable has the parent Path object, and output_stem_pass is a simple string. After assembling a new path with the / operator, the with_suffix() method ensures a specific suffix is used.

Creating a directory and a number of files in the directory

The following steps are for creating a directory and a number of files in the newly created directory:

1. Create the Path object from the input filename string. In this example, the PosixPath class is displayed because the author uses Linux. On a Windows machine, the class would be WindowsPath. The Path class will properly parse the string to determine the elements of the path:

```
>>> input_path = Path(options.input)
>>> input_path
PosixPath('/path/to/some/file.csv')
```

2. Create the Path object for the output directory. In this case, we'll create an output directory as a subdirectory with the same parent directory as the source file:

```
>>> output_parent = input_path.parent / "output"
>>> output_parent
PosixPath('/path/to/some/output')
```

3. Create the output filename using the output Path object. In this example, the output directory will contain a file that has the same name as the input with a different suffix:

```
>>> input_stem = input_path.stem
>>> output_path = (
...     output_parent / input_stem).with_suffix('.src')
```

We've used the / operator to assemble a new `Path` object from the parent `Path` and a string based on the stem of a filename. Once a `Path` object has been created, we can use the `with_suffix()` method to set the desired suffix for the path.

Comparing file dates to see which is newer

The following are the steps to see newer file dates by comparing them:

1. Create the `Path` objects from the input filename strings. The `Path` class will properly parse the string to determine the elements of the path:

   ```
   >>> file1_path = Path(options.file1)
   >>> file2_path = Path(options.file2)
   ```

2. Use the `stat()` method of each `Path` object to get timestamps for the file. This method returns a `stat` object; within that `stat` object, the `st_mtime` attribute of that object provides the most recent modification time for the file:

   ```
   >>> file1_path.stat().st_mtime
   1464460057.0
   >>> file2_path.stat().st_mtime
   1464527877.0
   ```

The values are timestamps measured in seconds. We can compare the two values to see which is newer.

If we want a timestamp that's sensible to people, we can use the `datetime` module to create a proper `datetime` object from this:

```
>>> import datetime
>>> mtime_1 = file1_path.stat().st_mtime
>>> datetime.datetime.fromtimestamp(mtime_1)
datetime.datetime(2016, 5, 28, 14, 27, 37)
```

We can use the `strftime()` method to format the `datetime` object or we can use the `isoformat()` method to provide a standardized display. Note that the time will have the local time zone offset implicitly applied to the OS timestamp; depending on the OS configuration(s), a laptop may not show the same time as the server that created it because they're in different time zones.

Removing a file

The Linux term for removing a file is **unlinking**. Since a file may have many links, the actual data isn't removed until all links are removed. Here's how we can unlink files:

1. Create the `Path` object from the input filename string. The `Path` class will properly parse the string to determine the elements of the path:

```
>>> input_path = Path(options.input)
>>> input_path
PosixPath('/path/to/some/file.csv')
```

2. Use the `unlink()` method of this `Path` object to remove the directory entry. If this was the last directory entry for the data, then the space can be reclaimed by the OS:

```
>>> try:
...     input_path.unlink()
... except FileNotFoundError as ex:
...     print("File already deleted")
File already deleted
```

If the file does not exist, a `FileNotFoundError` is raised. In some cases, this exception needs to be silenced with the `pass` statement. In other cases, a warning message might be important. It's also possible that a missing file represents a serious error.

Additionally, we can rename a file using the `rename()` method of a `Path` object. We can create new soft links using the `symlink_to()` method. To create OS-level hard links, we need to use the `os.link()` function.

Finding all files that match a given pattern

The following are the steps to find all the files that match a given pattern:

1. Create the `Path` object from the input directory name. The `Path` class will properly parse the string to determine the elements of the path:

```
>>> Path(options.file1)
PosixPath('data/ch09_file1.yaml')
>>> directory_path = Path(options.file1).parent
>>> directory_path
PosixPath('data')
```

2. Use the `glob()` method of the `Path` object to locate all files that match a given pattern. By default, this will not recursively walk the entire directory tree (add `keyword-argument recursive=True` to the `glob` call to walk the whole tree):

```
>>> list(directory_path.glob("*.csv"))
[PosixPath('data/wc1.csv'), PosixPath('data/ex2_r12.csv'),
 PosixPath('data/wc.csv'), PosixPath('data/ch07_r13.csv'),
 PosixPath('data/sample.csv'),
```

```
PosixPath('data/craps.csv'), PosixPath('data/output.csv'),
PosixPath('data/fuel.csv'), PosixPath('data/waypoints.csv'),
PosixPath('data/quotient.csv'),
PosixPath('data/summary_log.csv'), PosixPath('data/fuel2.csv')]
```

With this, we've seen a number of mini recipes for using `pathlib.Path` objects for managing the file resources. This abstraction is helpful for simplifying access to the filesystem, as well as providing a uniform abstraction that works for Linux, macOS, and Windows.

How it works...

Inside the OS, a path is a sequence of directories (a folder is a visual depiction of a directory). In a name such as `/Users/slott/Documents/writing`, the root directory, /, contains a directory named `Users`. This contains a subdirectory, `slott`, which contains `Documents`, which contains `writing`.

In some cases, a simple string representation can be used to summarize the navigation from root to directory, through to the final target directory. The string representation, however, makes many kinds of path operations into complex string parsing problems.

The `Path` class definition simplifies operations on paths. These operations on `Path` include the following examples:

- Extract the parent directory, as well as a sequence of all enclosing directory names.
- Extract the final name, the stem of the final name, and the suffix of the final name.
- Replace the suffix with a new suffix or replace the entire name with a new name.
- Convert a string into a `Path`. Also, convert a `Path` into a string. Many OS functions and parts of Python prefer to use filename strings.
- Build a new `Path` object from an existing `Path` joined with a string using the / `operator`.

A concrete `Path` represents an actual filesystem resource. For concrete `Paths`, we can do a number of additional manipulations of the directory information:

- Determine what kind of directory entry this is; that is, an ordinary file, a directory, a link, a socket, a named pipe (or FIFO), a block device, or a character device.
- Get the directory details, including information such as timestamps, permissions, ownership, size, and so on. We can also modify many of these things.
- Unlink (that is, remove) the directory entry.

Just about anything we might want to do with directory entries for files can be done with the `pathlib` module. The few exceptions are part of the `os` or `os.path` module.

There's more...

When we look at other file-related recipes in the rest of this chapter, we'll use `Path` objects to name the files. The objective is to avoid trying to use strings to represent paths.

The `pathlib` module makes a small distinction between Linux pure `Path` objects and Windows pure `Path` objects. Most of the time, we don't care about the OS-level details of the path.

There are two cases where it can help to produce pure paths for a specific operating system:

- If we do development on a Windows laptop, but deploy web services on a Linux server, it may be necessary to use `PureLinuxPath` in unit test cases. This allows us to write test cases on the Windows development machine that reflect actual intended use on a Linux server.
- If we do development on a macOS (or Linux) laptop, but deploy exclusively to Windows servers, it may be necessary to use `PureWindowsPath`.

The following snippet shows how to create Windows-specific `Path` objects:

```
>>> from pathlib import PureWindowsPath
>>> home_path = PureWindowsPath(r'C:\Users\slott')
>>> name_path = home_path / 'filename.ini'
>>> name_path
PureWindowsPath('C:/Users/slott/filename.ini')
>>> str(name_path)
'C:\\Users\\slott\\filename.ini'
```

Note that the / characters are normalized from Windows to Python notation when displaying the `WindowsPath` object. Using the `str()` function retrieves a path string appropriate for the Windows OS.

When we use the generic `Path` class, we always get a subclass appropriate to the user's environment, which may or may not be Windows. By using `PureWindowsPath`, we've bypassed the mapping to the user's actual OS.

See also

- In the *Replacing a file while preserving the previous version* recipe, later in this chapter, we'll look at how to leverage the features of a `Path` to create a temporary file and then rename the temporary file to replace the original file.
- In the *Using argparse to get command-line input* recipe in *Chapter 6, User Inputs and Outputs*, we looked at one very common way to get the initial string that will be used to create a `Path` object.

Replacing a file while preserving the previous version

We can leverage the power of `pathlib` to support a variety of filename manipulations. In the *Using pathlib to work with filenames* recipe, earlier in this chapter, we looked at a few of the most common techniques for managing directories, filenames, and file suffixes.

One common file processing requirement is to create output files in a fail-safe manner. That is, the application should preserve any previous output file, no matter how or where the application fails.

Consider the following scenario:

1. At time t_0, there's a valid `output.csv` file from the previous run of the `long_complex.py` application.
2. At time t_1, we start running the `long_complex.py` application. It begins overwriting the `output.csv` file. Until the program finishes, the bytes are unusable.
3. At time t_2, the application crashes. The partial `output.csv` file is useless. Worse, the valid file from time t_0 is not available either since it was overwritten.

We need a way to preserve the previous state of the file, and only replace the file when the new content is complete and correct. In this recipe, we'll look at an approach to creating output files that's safe in the event of a failure.

Getting ready

For files that don't span across physical devices, fail-safe file output generally means creating a new copy of the file using a temporary name. If the new file can be created successfully, then the old file should be replaced using a single, atomic rename operation.

The goal is to create files in such a way that at any time prior to the final rename, a crash will leave the original file in place. Subsequent to the final rename, the new file should be in place.

We can add capabilities to preserve the old file as well. This provides a recovery strategy. In case of a catastrophic problem, the old file can be renamed manually to make it available as the original file.

There are several ways to approach this. The `fileinput` module has an `inplace=True` option that permits reading a file while redirecting standard output to write a replacement of the input file. We'll show a more general approach that works for any file. This uses three separate files and does two renames:

- The important output file we want to preserve in a valid state at all times, for example, `output.csv`.

- A temporary version of the file: `output.csv.new`. There are a variety of conventions for naming this file. Sometimes, extra characters such as ~ or # are placed on the filename to indicate that it's a temporary, working file; for example, `output.csv~`. Sometimes, it will be in the `/tmp` filesystem.
- The previous version of the file: `name.out.old`. Any previous `.old` file will be removed as part of finalizing the output. Sometimes, the previous version is `.bak`, meaning "backup."

To create a concrete example, we'll work with a file that has a very small but precious piece of data: a `Quotient`. Here's the definition for this `Quotient` object:

```
from dataclasses import dataclass, asdict, fields

@dataclass
class Quotient:
    numerator: int
    denominator: int
```

The following function will write this object to a file in CSV notation:

```
def save_data(
        output_path: Path, data: Iterable[Quotient]) -> None:
    with output_path.open("w", newline="") as output_file:
        headers = [f.name for f in fields(Quotient)]
        writer = csv.DictWriter(output_file, headers)
        writer.writeheader()
        for q in data:
            writer.writerow(asdict(q))
```

We've opened a file with a context manager to be guaranteed the file will be closed. The `headers` variable is the list of attribute names in the `Quotient` dataclass. We can use these headers to create a CSV writer, and then emit all the given instances of the `Quotient` dataclass.

Some typical contents of the file are shown here:

```
numerator,denominator
87,32
```

Yes. This is a silly little file. We can imagine that it might be an important part of the security configuration for a web server, and changes must be managed carefully by the administrators.

In the unlikely event of a problem when writing the `data` object to the file, we could be left with a corrupted, unusable output file. We'll wrap this function with another to provide a reliable write.

How to do it...

We start creating our wrapper by importing the classes we need:

1. Import the `Path` class from the `pathlib` module:

```
from pathlib import Path
```

2. Define a "wrapper" function to encapsulate the `save_data()` function with some extra features. The function signature is the same as it is for the `save_data()` function:

```
def safe_write(
        output_path: Path, data: Iterable[Quotient]
        ) -> None:
```

3. Save the original suffix and create a new suffix with `.new` at the end. This is a temporary file. If it is written properly, with no exceptions, then we can rename it so that it's the target file:

```
    ext = output_path.suffix
    output_new_path = output_path.with_suffix(f'{ext}.new')
    save_data(output_new_path, data)
```

4. Before saving the current file, remove any previous backup copy. We'll remove an `.old` file, if one exists. If there's no `.old` file, we can use the `missing_ok` option to ignore the `FileNotFound` exception:

```
    output_old_path = output_path.with_suffix(f'{ext}.old')
    output_old_path.unlink(missing_ok=True)
```

5. Now, we can preserve the current file with the name of `.old` to save it in case of problems:

```
    try:
        output_path.rename(output_old_path)
    except FileNotFoundError as ex:
        # No previous file. That's okay.
        pass
```

6. The final step is to make the temporary `.new` file the official output:

```
    try:
        output_new_path.rename(output_path)
    except IOError as ex:
        # Possible recovery...
        output_old_path.rename(output_path)
```

This multi-step process uses two rename operations:

- Rename the current version to a version with `.old` appended to the suffix.
- Rename the new version, with `.new` appended to the suffix, to the current version of the file.

A `Path` object has a `replace()` method. This always overwrites the target file, with no warning if there's a problem. The choice depends on how our application needs to handle cases where old versions of files may be left in the filesystem. We've used `rename()` in this recipe to try and avoid overwriting files in the case of multiple problems. A variation could use `replace()` to always replace a file.

How it works...

This process involves the following three separate OS operations: an unlink and two renames. This leads to a situation in which the `.old` file is preserved and can be used to recover the previously good state.

Here's a timeline that shows the state of the various files. We've labeled the content as version 1 (the previous contents) and version 2 (the revised contents):

Time	Operation	.csv.old	.csv	.csv.new
t_0		version 0	version 1	
t_1	Mid-creation	version 0	version 1	Will appear corrupt if used
t_2	Post-creation, closed	version 0	version 1	version 2
t_3	After unlinking `.csv.old`		version 1	version 2
t_4	After renaming `.csv` to `.csv.old`	version 1		version 2
t_5	After renaming `.csv.tmp` to `.csv`	version 1	version 2	

Timeline of file operations

While there are several opportunities for failure, there's no ambiguity about which file is valid:

- If there's a `.csv` file, it's the current, valid file.
- If there's no `.csv` file, then the `.csv.old` file is a backup copy, which can be used for recovery.

Since none of these operations involve actually copying the files, the operations are all extremely fast and reliable.

There's more...

In some enterprise applications, output files are organized into directories with names based on timestamps. This can be handled gracefully by the `pathlib` module. We might, for example, have an archive directory for old files:

```
archive_path = Path("/path/to/archive")
```

We may want to create date-stamped subdirectories for keeping temporary or working files:

```
import datetime
today = datetime.datetime.now().strftime("%Y%m%d_%H%M%S")
```

We can then do the following to define a working directory:

```
working_path = archive_path / today
working_path.mkdir(parents=True, exists_ok=True)
```

The `mkdir()` method will create the expected directory, including the `parents=True` argument, which ensures that all parent directories will also be created. This can be handy the very first time an application is executed. `exists_ok=True` is handy so that if a directory already exists, it can be reused without raising an exception.

`parents=True` is not the default. With the default of `parents=False`, when a parent directory doesn't exist, the method will raise a `FileNotFoundError` exception because the required file doesn't exist.

Similarly, `exists_ok=True` is not the default. By default, if the directory exists, a `FileExistsError` exception is raised. Including options to make the operation silent when the directory already exists can be helpful.

Also, it's sometimes appropriate to use the `tempfile` module to create temporary files. This module can create filenames that are guaranteed to be unique. This allows a complex server process to create temporary files without regard to filename conflicts.

See also

- In the *Using pathlib to work with filenames* recipe, earlier in this chapter, we looked at the fundamentals of the `Path` class.
- In *Chapter 11*, *Testing*, we'll look at some techniques for writing unit tests that can ensure that parts of this will behave properly.
- In *Chapter 6*, *User Inputs and Outputs*, the *Using contexts and context managers* recipe shows additional details regarding working with the `with` statement to ensure file operations complete properly, and that all of the OS resources are released.

Reading delimited files with the CSV module

One commonly used data format is **comma-separated values** (**CSV**). We can generalize this to think of the comma character as simply one of many candidate separator characters. For example, a CSV file can use the | character as the separator between columns of data. This generalization for separators other than the comma makes CSV files particularly powerful.

How can we process data in one of the wide varieties of CSV formats?

Getting ready

A summary of a file's content is called a schema. It's essential to distinguish between two aspects of the schema.

The physical format of the file: For CSV, this means the file's bytes encode text. The text is organized into rows and columns using a row separator character (or characters) and a column separator character. Many spreadsheet products will use , (comma) as the column separator and the `\r\n` sequence of characters as the row separator. The specific combination of punctuation characters in use is called the *CSV dialect*.

The logical layout of the data in the file: This is the sequence of data columns that are present. There are several common cases for handling the logical layout in CSV files:

- The file has one line of headings. This is ideal and fits nicely with the way the CSV module works. It can be helpful when the headings are also proper Python variable names.
- The file has no headings, but the column positions are fixed. In this case, we can impose headings on the file when we open it.
- If the file has no headings and the column positions aren't fixed, additional schema information is required to interpret the columns of data.
- Some files can have multiple lines of headings. In this case, we have to write special processing to skip past these lines. We will also have to replace complex headings with something more useful in Python.
- An even more difficult case is where the file is not in proper **First Normal Form** (**1NF**). In 1NF, each row is independent of all other rows. When a file is not in this normal form, we'll need to add a generator function to rearrange the data into 1NF. See the *Slicing and dicing a list* recipe in *Chapter 4, Built-In Data Structures Part 1: Lists and Sets*, and the *Using stacked generator expressions* recipe in the online chapter, *Chapter 9, Functional Programming Features* (link provided in the *Preface*), for other recipes that work on normalizing data structures.

We'll look at a CSV file that has some real-time data recorded from the log of a sailboat. This is the `waypoints.csv` file. The data looks as follows:

```
lat,lon,date,time
32.8321666666667,-79.9338333333333,2012-11-27,09:15:00
31.6714833333333,-80.93325,2012-11-28,00:00:00
30.7171666666667,-81.5525,2012-11-28,11:35:00
```

This data contains four columns named in the first line of the file: `lat`, `lon`, `date`, and `time`. These describe a waypoint and need to be reformatted to create more useful information.

How to do it...

1. Import the `csv` module and the `Path` class:

```
import csv
from pathlib import Path
```

2. Examine the data file to confirm the following features:
   - The column separator character is ',', which is the default.
   - The row separator characters are '`\r\n`', also widely used in both Windows and Linux. Python's universal newlines feature means that the Linux standard '`\n`' will work just as well as a row separator.
   - There is a single-row heading. If it isn't present, the headings should be provided separately when the reader object is created.
3. Define the `raw()` function to read raw data from a `Path` that refers to the file:

```
def raw(data_path: Path) -> None:
```

4. Use the `Path` object to open the file in a `with` statement:

```
    with data_path.open() as data_file:
```

5. Create the CSV reader from the open file object. This is indented inside the `with` statement:

```
        data_reader = csv.DictReader(data_file)
```

6. Read (and process) the various rows of data. This is properly indented inside the `with` statement. For this example, we'll only print the rows:

```
        for row in data_reader:
            print(row)
```

Here's the function that we created:

```
def raw(data_path: Path) -> None:
    with data_path.open() as data_file:
```

```
        data_reader = csv.DictReader(data_file)
        for row in data_reader:
            print(row)
```

The output from the `raw()` function is a series of dictionaries that looks as follows:

```
{'date': '2012-11-27',
 'lat': '32.8321666666667',
 'lon': '-79.9338333333333',
 'time': '09:15:00'}
```

We can now process the data by referring to the columns as dictionary items, using syntax like, for example, `row['date']`. Using the column names is more descriptive than referring to the column by position; for example, `row[0]` is hard to understand.

To be sure that we're using the column names correctly, the `typing.TypedDict` type hint can be used to provide the expected column names.

How it works...

The `csv` module handles the physical format work of separating the rows from each other, and also separating the columns within each row. The default rules ensure that each input line is treated as a separate row and that the columns are separated by ",".

What happens when we need to use the column separator character as part of data? We might have data like this:

```
lan,lon,date,time,notes
32.832,-79.934,2012-11-27,09:15:00,"breezy, rainy"
31.671,-80.933,2012-11-28,00:00:00,"blowing ""like stink"""
```

The `notes` column has data in the first row, which includes the "," column separator character. The rules for CSV allow a column's value to be surrounded by quotes. By default, the quoting characters are ". Within these quoting characters, the column and row separator characters are ignored.

In order to embed the quote character within a quoted string, it is doubled. The second example row shows how the value `blowing "like stink"` is encoded by doubling the quote characters when they are part of the value of a column. These quoting rules mean that a CSV file can represent any combination of characters, including the row and column separator characters.

The values in a CSV file are always strings. A string value like `7331` may look like a number to us, but it's always text when processed by the `csv` module. This makes the processing simple and uniform, but it can be awkward for our Python application programs.

When data is saved from a manually prepared spreadsheet, the data may reveal the quirks of the desktop software's internal rules for data display. It's surprisingly common, for example, to have a column of data that is displayed as a date on the desktop software but shows up as a floating-point number in the CSV file.

There are two solutions to the date-as-number problem. One is to add a column in the source spreadsheet to properly format the date as a string. Ideally, this is done using ISO rules so that the date is represented in `YYYY-MM-DD` format. The other solution is to recognize the spreadsheet date as a number of seconds past some epochal date. The epochal dates vary slightly, but they're generally either Jan 1, 1900 or Jan 1, 1904.

There's more...

As we saw in the *Combining map and reduce transformations* recipe in *Chapter 9, Functional Programming Features*, there's often a pipeline of processing that includes cleaning and transforming the source data. In this specific example, there are no extra rows that need to be eliminated. However, each column needs to be converted into something more useful.

To transform the data into a more useful form, we'll use a two-part design. First, we'll define a row-level cleansing function. In this case, we'll create a dictionary object by adding additional values that are derived from the input data. A `clean_row()` function can look like this:

```
import datetime
Raw = Dict[str, Any]
Waypoint = Dict[str, Any]

def clean_row(source_row: Raw) -> Waypoint:
    ts_date = datetime.datetime.strptime(
        source_row["date"], "%Y-%m-%d"
    ).date()
    ts_time = datetime.datetime.strptime(
        source_row["time"], "%H:%M:%S"
    ).time()

    return dict(
        date=source_row["date"],
        time=source_row["time"],
        lat=source_row["lat"],
        lon=source_row["lon"],
        lat_lon=(
            float(source_row["lat"]),
            float(source_row["lon"])
        ),
```

```
            ts_date=ts_date,
            ts_time=ts_time,
            timestamp = datetime.datetime.combine(
                ts_date, ts_time
            )
        )
```

Here, we've created some new column values. The column named `lat_lon` has a two-tuple with proper floating-point values instead of strings. We've also parsed the date and time values to create `datetime.date` and `datetime.time` objects. We've combined the date and time into a single, useful value, which is the value of the `timestamp` column.

Once we have a row-level function for cleaning and enriching our data, we can map this function to each row in the source of data. We can use `map(clean_row, reader)` or we can write a function that embodies this processing loop:

```
def cleanse(reader: csv.DictReader) -> Iterator[Waypoint]:
    for row in reader:
        yield clean_row(cast(Raw, row))
```

This can be used to provide more useful data from each row:

```
def display_clean(data_path: Path) -> None:
    with data_path.open() as data_file:
        data_reader = csv.DictReader(data_file)
        clean_data_reader = cleanse(data_reader)
        for row in clean_data_reader:
            pprint(row)
```

We've used the `cleanse()` function to create a very small stack of transformation rules. The stack starts with `data_reader`, and only has one other item in it. This is a good beginning. As the application software is expanded to do more computations, the stack will expand.

These cleansed and enriched rows look as follows:

```
{'date': '2012-11-27',
 'lat': '32.8321666666667',
 'lat_lon': (32.8321666666667, -79.9338333333333),
 'lon': '-79.9338333333333',
 'time': '09:15:00',
 'timestamp': datetime.datetime(2012, 11, 27, 9, 15),
 'ts_date': datetime.date(2012, 11, 27),
 'ts_time': datetime.time(9, 15)}
```

We've added columns such as `lat_lon`, which have proper numeric values instead of strings. We've also added `timestamp`, which has a full date-time value that can be used for simple computations of elapsed time between waypoints.

We can leverage the `typing.TypedDict` type hint to make a stronger statement about the structure of the dictionary data that will be processed. The initial data has known column names, each of which has string data values. We can define the raw data as follows:

```
from typing import TypedDict
class Raw_TD(TypedDict):
    date: str
    time: str
    lat: str
    lon: str
```

The cleaned data has a more complex structure. We can define the output from a `clean_row_td()` function as follows:

```
class Waypoint_TD(Raw_TD):
    lat_lon: Tuple[float, float]
    ts_date: datetime.date
    ts_time: datetime.time
    timestamp: datetime.datetime
```

The `Waypoint_TD TypedDict` definition extends `Raw_TD TypedDict` to make the outputs from the `cleanse()` function explicit. This lets us use the `mypy` tool to confirm that the `cleanse()` function – and any other processing – adheres to the expected keys and value types in the dictionary.

See also

- See the *Combining map and reduce transformations* recipe in *Chapter 9, Functional Programming Features*, for more information on the idea of a processing pipeline or stack.
- See the *Slicing and dicing a list* recipe in *Chapter 4, Built-In Data Structures Part 1: Lists and Sets*, and the *Using stacked generator expressions* recipe in the online chapter, *Chapter 9, Functional Programming Features* (link provided in the *Preface*), for more information on processing a CSV file that isn't in a proper 1NF.
- For more information on the `with` statement, see the *Reading and writing files with context managers* recipe in *Chapter 7, Basics of Classes and Objects*.

Using dataclasses to simplify working with CSV files

One commonly used data format is known as CSV. Python's `csv` module has a very handy `DictReader` class definition. When a file contains a one-row header, the header row's values become keys that are used for all the subsequent rows. This allows a great deal of flexibility in the logical layout of the data. For example, the column ordering doesn't matter, since each column's data is identified by a name taken from the header row.

This leads to dictionary-based references to a column's data. We're forced to write, for example, `row['lat']` or `row['date']` to refer to data in specific columns. While this isn't horrible, it would be much nicer to use syntax like `row.lat` or `row.date` to refer to column values.

Additionally, we often have derived values that should - perhaps - be properties of a class definition instead of a separate function. This can properly encapsulate important attributes and operations into a single class definition.

The dictionary data structure has awkward-looking syntax for the column references. If we use dataclasses for each row, we can change references from `row['name']` to `row.name`.

Getting ready

We'll look at a CSV file that has some real-time data recorded from the log of a sailboat. This file is the `waypoints.csv` file. The data looks as follows:

```
lat,lon,date,time
32.8321666666667,-79.9338333333333,2012-11-27,09:15:00
31.6714833333333,-80.93325,2012-11-28,00:00:00
30.7171666666667,-81.5525,2012-11-28,11:35:00
```

The first line contains a header that names the four columns, `lat`, `lon`, `date`, and `time`. The data can be read by a `csv.DictReader` object. However, we'd like to do more sophisticated work, so we'll create a `@dataclass` class definition that can encapsulate the data and the processing we need to do.

How to do it...

We need to start with a dataclass that reflects the available data, and then we can use this dataclass with a dictionary reader:

1. Import the definitions from the various libraries that are needed:

```
from dataclasses import dataclass, field
import datetime
from typing import Tuple, Iterator
```

2. Define a `dataclass` narrowly focused on the input, precisely as it appears in the source file. We've called the class `RawRow`. In a complex application, a more descriptive name than `RawRow` would be appropriate. This definition of the attributes may change as the source file organization changes:

```
@dataclass
class RawRow:
    date: str
    time: str
    lat: str
    lon: str
```

3. Define a second dataclass where objects are built from the source dataclass attributes. This second class is focused on the real work of the application. The source data is in a single attribute, `raw`, in this example. Fields computed from this source data are all initialized with `field(init=False)` because they'll be computed after initialization:

```
@dataclass
class Waypoint:
    raw: RawRow
    lat_lon: Tuple[float, float] = field(init=False)
    ts_date: datetime.date = field(init=False)
    ts_time: datetime.time = field(init=False)
    timestamp: datetime.datetime = field(init=False)
```

4. Add the `__post_init__()` method to initialize all of the derived fields:

```
def __post_init__(self):
    self.ts_date = datetime.datetime.strptime(
        self.raw.date, "%Y-%m-%d"
    ).date()
    self.ts_time = datetime.datetime.strptime(
        self.raw.time, "%H:%M:%S"
```

```
        ).time()
        self.lat_lon = (
            float(self.raw.lat),
            float(self.raw.lon)
        )
        self.timestamp = datetime.datetime.combine(
            self.ts_date, self.ts_time
        )
```

5. Given these two dataclass definitions, we can create an iterator that will accept individual dictionaries from a `csv.DictReader` object and create the needed `Waypoint` objects. The intermediate representation, `RawRow`, is a convenience so that we can assign attribute names to the source data columns:

```
def waypoint_iter(reader: csv.DictReader) ->
Iterator[Waypoint]:
    for row in reader:
        raw = RawRow(**row)
        yield Waypoint(raw)
```

The `waypoint_iter()` function creates `RawRow` objects from the input dictionary, then creates the final `Waypoint` objects from the `RawRow` instances. This two-step processing is helpful for managing changes to the source or the processing.

We can use the following function to read and display the CSV data:

```
def display(data_path: Path) -> None:
    with data_path.open() as data_file:
        data_reader = csv.DictReader(data_file)
        for waypoint in waypoint_iter(data_reader):
            pprint(waypoint)
```

This function uses the `waypoint_iter()` function to create `Waypoint` objects from the dictionaries read by the `csv.DictReader` object. Each `Waypoint` object contains a reference to the original raw data:

```
Waypoint(
    raw=RawRow(
        date='2012-11-27',
        time='09:15:00',
        lat='32.8321666666667',
        lon='-79.9338333333333'),
    lat_lon=(32.8321666666667, -79.9338333333333),
    ts_date=datetime.date(2012, 11, 27),
```

```
        ts_time=datetime.time(9, 15),
        timestamp=datetime.datetime(2012, 11, 27, 9, 15)
    )
```

Having the original input object can sometimes be helpful when diagnosing problems with the source data or the processing.

How it works...

The source dataclass, the `RawRow` class in this example, is designed to match the input document. The dataclass definition has attribute names that are exact matches for the source column names, and the attribute types are all strings to match the CSV input types.

Because the names match, the `RawRow(**row)` expression will work to create an instance of the `RawRow` class from the `DictReader` dictionary.

From this initial, or raw, data, we can derive the more useful data, as shown in the `Waypoint` class definition. The `__post_init__()` method transforms the initial value in the `self.raw` attribute into a number of more useful attribute values.

We've separated the `Waypoint` object's creation from reading raw data. This lets us manage the following two kinds of common changes to application software:

1. The source data can change because the spreadsheet was adjusted manually. This is common: a person may change column names or change the order of the columns.
2. The required computations may change as the application's focus expands or shifts. More derived columns may be added, or the algorithms may change. We want to isolate this application-specific processing from reading the raw data.

It's helpful to disentangle the various aspects of a program so that we can let them evolve independently. Gathering, cleaning, and filtering source data is one aspect of this. The resulting computations are a separate aspect, unrelated to the format of the source data.

There's more...

In many cases, the source CSV file will have headers that do not map directly to valid Python attribute names. In these cases, the keys present in the source dictionary must be mapped to the column names. This can be managed by expanding the `RawRow` class definition to include a `__post_init__()` method. This will help build the `RawRow` dataclass object from a dictionary built from CSV row headers that aren't useful Python key names.

The following example defines a class called `RawRow_HeaderV2`. This reflects a variant spreadsheet with different row names. We've defined the attributes with `field(init=False)` and provided a `__post_init__()` method, as shown in this code block:

```
@dataclass
class RawRow_HeaderV2:
    source: Dict[str, str]
    date: str = field(init=False)
    time: str = field(init=False)
    lat: str = field(init=False)
    lon: str = field(init=False)

    def __post_init__(self):
        self.date = self.source['Date of Travel (YYYY-MM-DD)']
        self.time = self.source['Arrival Time (HH:MM:SS)']
        self.lat = self.source['Latitude (degrees N)']
        self.lon = self.source['Logitude (degrees W)']
```

This `RawRow_HeaderV2` class creates objects that are compatible with the `RawRow` class. Either of these classes of objects can also be transformed into `Waypoint` instances.

For an application that works with a variety of data sources, these kinds of "raw data transformation" dataclasses can be handy for mapping the minor variations in a logical layout to a consistent internal structure for further processing.

As the number of input transformation classes grows, additional type hints are required. For example, the following type hint provides a common name for the variations in input format:

```
Raw = Union[RawRow, RawRow_HeaderV2]
```

This type hint helps to unify the original `RawRow` and the alternative `RawRow_HeaderV2` as alternative type definitions with compatible features. This can also be done with a `Protocol` type hint that spells out the common attributes.

See also

- The *Reading delimited files with the CSV module* recipe, earlier in this chapter, also covers CSV file reading.
- In *Chapter 6, User Inputs and Outputs*, the *Using dataclasses for mutable objects* recipe also covers ways to use Python's dataclasses.

Reading complex formats using regular expressions

Many file formats lack the elegant regularity of a CSV file. One common file format that's rather difficult to parse is a web server log file. These files tend to have complex data without a single, uniform separator character or consistent quoting rules.

When we looked at a simplified log file in the *Writing generator functions with the yield statement* recipe in the online chapter, *Chapter 9, Functional Programming Features* (link provided in the *Preface*), we saw that the rows look as follows:

```
[2016-05-08 11:08:18,651] INFO in ch09_r09: Sample Message One
[2016-05-08 11:08:18,651] DEBUG in ch09_r09: Debugging
[2016-05-08 11:08:18,652] WARNING in ch09_r09: Something might have
gone wrong
```

There are a variety of punctuation marks being used in this file. The `csv` module can't handle this complexity.

We'd like to write programs with the elegant simplicity of CSV processing. This means we'll need to encapsulate the complexities of log file parsing and keep this aspect separate from analysis and summary processing.

Getting ready

Parsing a file with a complex structure generally involves writing a function that behaves somewhat like the `reader()` function in the `csv` module. In some cases, it can be easier to create a small class that behaves like the `DictReader` class.

The core feature of reading a complex file is a function that will transform one line of text into a dictionary or tuple of individual field values. This job can often be done by the `re` package.

Before we can start, we'll need to develop (and debug) the regular expression that properly parses each line of the input file. For more information on this, see the *String parsing with regular expressions* recipe in *Chapter 1, Numbers, Strings, and Tuples*.

For this example, we'll use the following code. We'll define a pattern string with a series of regular expressions for the various elements of the line:

```
import re
pattern_text = (
    r"\[   (?P<date>.*?)  \]\s+"
    r"     (?P<level>\w+)    \s+"
    r"in\s+(?P<module>\S?)"
    r":\s+ (?P<message>.+)"
)
pattern = re.compile(pattern_text, re.X)
```

We've used the `re.X` option so that we can include extra whitespace in the regular expression. This can help to make it more readable by separating prefix and suffix characters.

There are four fields that are captured and a number of characters that are part of the template, but they never vary. Here's how this regular expression works:

- The date-time stamp contains digits, hyphens, colons, and a comma; it's surrounded by [and]. We've had to use \[and \] to escape the normal meaning of [and] in a regular expression. This is saved as date in the resulting group dictionary.
- The severity level is a single run of "word" characters, \w. This is saved as level in the dictionary of groups created by parsing text with this regular expression.
- The module name has a preface of the characters in; these are not captured. After this preface, the name is a sequence of non-whitespace characters, matched by \S. The module is saved as a group named module.
- Finally, there's a message. This has a preface of an extra ':' character we can ignore, then more spaces we can also ignore. Finally, the message itself starts and extends to the end of the line.

When we write a regular expression, we can wrap the interesting sub-strings to capture in (). After performing a match() or search() operation, the resulting Match object will have values for the matched substrings. The groups() method of a Match object and the groupdict() method of a Match object will provide the captured strings.

Note that we've used the \s+ sequence to quietly skip one or more space-like characters. The sample data appears to always use a single space as the separator. However, when absorbing whitespace, using \s+ seems to be a slightly more general approach because it permits extra spaces.

Here's how this pattern works:

```
>>> sample_data = '[2016-05-08 11:08:18,651] INFO in ch10_r09: Sample
Message One'
>>> match = pattern.match(sample_data)
>>> match.groups()
('2016-05-08 11:08:18,651', 'INFO', 'ch10_r09', 'Sample Message One')
>>> match.groupdict()
{'date': '2016-05-08 11:08:18,651',
'level': 'INFO',
'module': 'ch10_r09',
'message': 'Sample Message One'}
```

We've provided a line of sample data in the sample_data variable. The match object, has a groups() method that returns each of the interesting fields. The value of the groupdict() method of a match object is a dictionary with the name provided in the ?P<name> preface to the regular expression in brackets, ().

How to do it...

This recipe is split into two parts. The first part defines a `log_parser()` function to parse a single line, while the second part uses the `log_parser()` function for each line of input.

Defining the parse function

Perform the following steps to define the `log_parser()` function:

1. Define the compiled regular expression object. It helps us use the `(?P<name>...)` regular expression construct to create a dictionary key for each piece of data that's captured. The resulting dictionary will then contain useful, meaningful keys:

```
import re
pattern_text = (
    r"\[   (?P<date>.*?)  \]\s+"
    r"     (?P<level>\w+)    \s+"
    r"in\s+(?P<module>.+?)"
    r":\s+ (?P<message>.+)"
)
pattern = re.compile(pattern_text, re.X)
```

2. Define a class to model the resulting complex data object. This can have additional derived properties or other complex computations. Minimally, a `NamedTuple` must define the fields that are extracted by the parser. The field names should match the regular expression capture names in the `?P<name>` prefix:

```
class LogLine(NamedTuple):
    date: str
    level: str
    module: str
    message: str
```

3. Define a function that accepts a line of text as an argument:

```
def log_parser(source_line: str) -> LogLine:
```

4. Apply the regular expression to create a `match` object. We've assigned it to the `match` variable and also checked to see if it is not `None`:

```
    if match := pattern.match(source_line):
```

5. When the match is not `None`, return a useful data structure with the various pieces of data from this input line. The `cast(Match, match)` expression is necessary to help `mypy`; it states that the `match` object will not be `None`, but will always be a valid instance of the `Match` class. It's likely that a future release of `mypy` will not need this:

```
        data = cast(Match, match).groupdict()
        return LogLine(**data)
```

6. When the match is `None`, either log the problem or raise an exception to stop processing because there's a problem:

```
raise ValueError(f"Unexpected input {source_line=}")
```

Here's the `log_parser()` function, all gathered together:

```
def log_parser(source_line: str) -> LogLine:
    if match := pattern.match(source_line):
        data = cast(Match, match).groupdict()
        return LogLine(**data)
    raise ValueError(f"Unexpected input {source_line=}")
```

The `log_parser()` function can be used to parse each line of input. The text is transformed into a `NamedTuple` instance with field names and values based on the fields found by the regular expression parser. These field names must match the field names in the `NamedTuple` class definition.

Using the log_parser() function

This portion of the recipe will apply the `log_parser()` function to each line of the input file:

1. From `pathlib`, import the `Path` class definition:

   ```
   from pathlib import Path
   ```

2. Create the `Path` object that identifies the file:

   ```
   data_path = Path("data") / "sample.log"
   ```

3. Use the `Path` object to open the file in a `with` statement:

   ```
   with data_path.open() as data_file:
   ```

4. Create the log file reader from the open file object, `data_file`. In this case, we'll use the built-in `map()` function to apply the `log_parser()` function to each line from the source file:

   ```
       data_reader = map(log_parser, data_file)
   ```

5. Read (and process) the various rows of data. For this example, we'll just print each row:

   ```
       for row in data_reader:
           pprint(row)
   ```

The output is a series of `LogLine` tuples that looks as follows:

```
LogLine(date='2016-06-15 17:57:54,715', level='INFO', module='ch10_r10',
message='Sample Message One')
LogLine(date='2016-06-15 17:57:54,715', level='DEBUG', module='ch10_r10',
message='Debugging')
```

```
LogLine(date='2016-06-15 17:57:54,715', level='WARNING', module='ch10_
r10', message='Something might have gone wrong')
```

We can do more meaningful processing on these tuple instances than we can on a line of raw text. These allow us to filter the data by severity level, or create a `Counter` based on the module providing the message.

How it works...

This log file is in **First Normal Form** (**1NF**): the data is organized into lines that represent independent entities or events. Each row has a consistent number of attributes or columns, and each column has data that is atomic or can't be meaningfully decomposed further. Unlike CSV files, however, this particular format requires a complex regular expression to parse.

In our log file example, the timestamp contains a number of individual elements - year, month, day, hour, minute, second, and millisecond - but there's little value in further decomposing the timestamp. It's more helpful to use it as a single `datetime` object and derive details (like hour of the day) from this object, rather than assembling individual fields into a new piece of composite data.

In a complex log processing application, there may be several varieties of message fields. It may be necessary to parse these message types using separate patterns. When we need to do this, it reveals that the various lines in the log aren't consistent in terms of the format and number of attributes, breaking one of the 1NF assumptions.

We've generally followed the design pattern from the *Reading delimited files with the CSV module* recipe, so that reading a complex log is nearly identical to reading a simple CSV file. Indeed, we can see that the primary difference lies in one line of code:

```
data_reader = csv.DictReader(data_file)
```

As compared to the following:

```
data_reader = map(log_parser, data_file)
```

This parallel construct allows us to reuse analysis functions across many input file formats. This allows us to create a library of tools that can be used on a number of data sources.

There's more...

One of the most common operations when reading very complex files is to rewrite them into an easier-to-process format. We'll often want to save the data in CSV format for later processing.

Some of this is similar to the *Using multiple contexts for reading and writing files* recipe in *Chapter 7, Basics of Classes and Objects*, which also shows multiple open contexts. We'll read from one file and write to another file.

The file writing process looks as follows:

```
import csv

def copy(data_path: Path) -> None:
    target_path = data_path.with_suffix(".csv")
    with target_path.open("w", newline="") as target_file:
        writer = csv.DictWriter(target_file, LogLine._fields)
        writer.writeheader()

        with data_path.open() as data_file:
            reader = map(log_parser, data_file)
            writer.writerows(row._asdict() for row in reader)
```

The first portion of this script defines a CSV writer for the target file. The path for the output file, `target_path`, is based on the input name, `data_path`. The suffix changed from the original filename's suffix to `.csv`.

The target file is opened with the newline character, which is turned off by the `newline=''` option. This allows the `csv.DictWriter` class to insert newline characters appropriate for the desired CSV dialect.

A `DictWriter` object is created to write to the given file. The sequence of column headings is provided by the `LogLines` class definition. This makes sure the output CSV file will contain column names matching the `LogLines` subclass of the `typing.NamedTuple` class.

The `writeheader()` method writes the column names as the first line of output. This makes reading the file slightly easier because the column names are provided. The first row of a CSV file can be a kind of explicit schema definition that shows what data is present.

The source file is opened, as shown in the preceding recipe. Because of the way the `csv` module writers work, we can provide the `reader` generator expression to the `writerows()` method of the writer. The `writerows()` method will consume all of the data produced by the `reader` generator. This will, in turn, consume all the rows produced by the open file.

We don't need to write any explicit `for` statements to ensure that all of the input rows are processed. The `writerows()` function makes this a guarantee.

The output file looks as follows:

```
date,level,module,message
"2016-05-08 11:08:18,651",INFO,ch10_r10,Sample Message One
"2016-05-08 11:08:18,651",DEBUG,ch10_r10,Debugging
"2016-05-08 11:08:18,652",WARNING,ch10_r10,Something might have gone
wrong
```

The file has been transformed from the rather complex input format into a simpler CSV format, suitable for further analysis and processing.

See also

- For more information on the `with` statement, see the *Reading and writing files with context managers* recipe in *Chapter 7, Basics of Classes and Objects*.
- The *Writing generator functions with the yield statement* recipe in the online chapter, *Chapter 9, Functional Programming Features* (link provided in the *Preface*), shows other processing of this log format.
- In the *Reading delimited files with the CSV module* recipe, earlier in this chapter, we looked at other applications of this general design pattern.
- In the *Using dataclasses to simplify working with CSV files* recipe, earlier in this chapter, we looked at other sophisticated CSV processing techniques.

Reading JSON and YAML documents

JavaScript Object Notation (**JSON**) is a popular syntax for serializing data. For details, see `http://json.org`. Python includes the `json` module in order to serialize and deserialize data in this notation.

JSON documents are used widely by web applications. It's common to exchange data between RESTful web clients and servers using documents in JSON notation. These two tiers of the application stack communicate via JSON documents sent via the HTTP protocol.

The YAML format is a more sophisticated and flexible extension to JSON notation. For details, see `https://yaml.org`. Any JSON document is also a valid YAML document. The reverse is not true: YAML syntax is more complex and includes constructs that are not valid JSON.

To use YAML, an additional module has to be installed. The PyYAML project offers a `yaml` module that is popular and works well. See `https://pypi.org/project/PyYAML/`.

In this recipe, we'll use the `json` or `yaml` module to parse JSON format data in Python.

Getting ready

We've gathered some sailboat racing results in `race_result.json`. This file contains information on teams, legs of the race, and the order in which the various teams finished each individual leg of the race. JSON handles this complex data elegantly.

An overall score can be computed by summing the finish position in each leg: the lowest score is the overall winner. In some cases, there are null values when a boat did not start, did not finish, or was disqualified from the race.

When computing the team's overall score, the null values are assigned a score of one more than the number of boats in the competition. If there are seven boats, then the team is given eight points for their failure to finish, a hefty penalty.

The data has the following schema. There are two fields within the overall document:

- `legs`: An array of strings that shows the starting port and ending port.
- `teams`: An array of objects with details about each team. Within each `teams` object, there are several fields of data:
    - `name`: String team name.
    - `position`: Array of integers and nulls with position. The order of the items in this array matches the order of the items in the `legs` array.

The data looks as follows:

```
{
  "teams": [
    {
      "name": "Abu Dhabi Ocean Racing",
      "position": [
        1,
        3,
        2,
        2,
        1,
        2,
        5,
        3,
        5
      ]
    },
    ...
  ],
  "legs": [
    "ALICANTE - CAPE TOWN",
    "CAPE TOWN - ABU DHABI",
    "ABU DHABI - SANYA",
    "SANYA - AUCKLAND",
    "AUCKLAND - ITAJA\u00cd",
    "ITAJA\u00cd - NEWPORT",
    "NEWPORT - LISBON",
```

```
        "LISBON - LORIENT",
        "LORIENT - GOTHENBURG"
      ]
    }
```

We've only shown the first team. There was a total of seven teams in this particular race. Each team is represented by a Python dictionary, with the team's name and their history of finish positions on each leg. For the team shown here, Abu Dhabi Ocean Racing, they finished in first place in the first leg, and then third place in the next leg. Their worst performance was fifth place in both the seventh and ninth legs of the race, which were the legs from Newport, Rhode Island, USA to Lisbon, Portugal, and from Lorient in France to Gothenburg in Sweden.

The JSON-formatted data can look like a Python dictionary that t lists within it. This overlap between Python syntax and JSON syntax can be thought of as a happy coincidence: it makes it easier to visualize the Python data structure that will be built from the JSON source document.

JSON has a small set of data structures: null, Boolean, number, string, list, and object. These map to objects of Python types in a very direct way. The `json` module makes the conversions from source text into Python objects for us.

One of the strings contains a Unicode escape sequence, `\u00cd`, instead of the actual Unicode character Í. This is a common technique used to encode characters beyond the 128 ASCII characters. The parser in the `json` module handles this for us.

In this example, we'll write a function to disentangle this document and show the team finishes for each leg.

How to do it...

This recipe will start with importing the necessary modules. We'll then use these modules to transform the contents of the file into a useful Python object:

1. We'll need the `json` module to parse the text. We'll also need a `Path` object to refer to the file:

   ```
   import json
   from pathlib import Path
   ```

2. Define a `race_summary()` function to read the JSON document from a given `Path` instance:

   ```
   def race_summary(source_path: Path) -> None:
   ```

3. Create a Python object by parsing the JSON document. It's often easiest to use `source_path.read_text()` to read the file named by `Path`. We provided this string to the `json.loads()` function for parsing. For very large files, an open file can be passed to the `json.load()` function; this can be more efficient than reading the entire document into a string object and loading the in-memory text:

```
        document = json.loads(source_path.read_text())
```

4. Display the data: This document creates a dictionary with two keys, `teams` and `legs`. Here's how we can iterate through each leg, showing the team's position in the leg:

```
    for n, leg in enumerate(document['legs']):
        print(leg)
        for team_finishes in document['teams']:
            print(
                team_finishes['name'],
                team_finishes['position'][n])
```

The data for each team will be a dictionary with two keys: `name` and `position`. We can navigate down into the team details to get the name of the first team:

```
>>> document['teams'][6]['name']
'Team Vestas Wind'
```

We can look inside the `legs` field to see the names of each leg of the race:

```
>>> document['legs'][5]
'ITAJAÍ - NEWPORT'
```

Note that the JSON source file included a '`\u00cd`' Unicode escape sequence. This was parsed properly, and the Unicode output shows the proper Í character.

How it works...

A JSON document is a data structure in JavaScript Object Notation. JavaScript programs can parse the document trivially. Other languages must do a little more work to translate the JSON to a native data structure.

A JSON document contains three kinds of structures:

- **Objects that map to Python dictionaries**: JSON has a syntax similar to Python: `{"key": "value"}`. Unlike Python, JSON only uses `"` for string quotation marks. JSON notation is intolerant of an extra `,` at the end of the dictionary value. Other than this, the two notations are similar.

- **Arrays that map to Python lists**: JSON syntax uses `[item, ...]`, which looks like Python. JSON is intolerant of an extra `,` at the end of the array value.
- **Primitive values**: There are five classes of values: string, number, `true`, `false`, and `null`. Strings are enclosed in `"` and use a variety of `\escape` sequences, which are similar to Python's. Numbers follow the rules for floating-point values. The other three values are simple literals; these parallel Python's `True`, `False`, and `None` literals. As a special case, numbers with no decimal point become Python `int` objects. This is an extension of the JSON standard.

There is no provision for any other kinds of data. This means that Python programs must convert complex Python objects into a simpler representation so that they can be serialized in JSON notation.

Conversely, we often apply additional conversions to reconstruct complex Python objects from the simplified JSON representation. The `json` module has places where we can apply additional processing to the simple structures to create more sophisticated Python objects.

There's more...

A file, generally, contains a single JSON document. The JSON standard doesn't provide an easy way to encode multiple documents in a single file. If we want to analyze a web log, for example, the original JSON standard may not be the best notation for preserving a huge volume of information.

There are common extensions, like Newline Delimited JSON, `http://ndjson.org`, and JSON Lines, `http://jsonlines.org`, to define a way to encode multiple JSON documents into a single file.

There are two additional problems that we often have to tackle:

- Serializing complex objects so that we can write them to files, for example, a datetime object
- Deserializing complex objects from the text that's read from a file

When we represent a Python object's state as a string of text characters, we've serialized the object. Many Python objects need to be saved in a file or transmitted to another process. These kinds of transfers require a representation of the object state. We'll look at serializing and deserializing separately.

Serializing a complex data structure

Many common Python data structures can be serialized into JSON. Because Python is extremely sophisticated and flexible, we can also create Python data structures that cannot be directly represented in JSON.

The serialization to JSON works out the best if we create Python objects that are limited to values of the built-in `dict`, `list`, `str`, `int`, `float`, `bool`, and `None` types. This subset of Python types can be used to build objects that the `json` module can serialize and can be used widely by a number of programs written in different languages.

One commonly used data structure that doesn't serialize easily is the `datetime.datetime` object. Here's what happens when we try:

```
>>> import datetime
>>> example_date = datetime.datetime(2014, 6, 7, 8, 9, 10)
>>> document = {'date': example_date}
```

Here, we've created a simple document with a dictionary mapping a string to a `datetime` instance. What happens when we try to serialize this in JSON?

```
>>> json.dumps(document)
Traceback (most recent call last):
  ...
TypeError: datetime.datetime(2014, 6, 7, 8, 9, 10) is not JSON
serializable
```

This shows that objects will raise a `TypeError` exception when they cannot be serialized. Avoiding this exception can done in one of two ways. We can either convert the data into a JSON-friendly structure before building the document, or we can add a default type handler to the JSON serialization process that gives us a way to provide a serializable version of the data.

To convert the `datetime` object into a string prior to serializing it as JSON, we need to make a change to the underlying data. In the following example, we replaced the `datetime.datetime` object with a string:

```
>>> document_converted = {'date': example_date.isoformat()}
>>> json.dumps(document_converted)
'{"date": "2014-06-07T08:09:10"}'
```

This uses the standardized ISO format for dates to create a string that can be serialized. An application that reads this data can then convert the string back into a `datetime` object. This kind of transformation can be difficult for a complex document.

The other technique for serializing complex data is to provide a function that's used by the `json` module during serialization. This function must convert a complex object into something that can be safely serialized. In the following example, we'll convert a `datetime` object into a simple string value:

```
def default_date(object: Any) -> Union[Any, Dict[str, Any]]:
    if isinstance(object, datetime.datetime):
        return {"$date": object.isoformat()}
    return object
```

We've defined a function, `default_date()`, which will apply a special conversion rule to `datetime` objects. Any datetime instance will be massaged into a dictionary with an obvious key – `"$date"` – and a string value. This dictionary of strings can be serialized by functions in the `json` module.

We provide this function to the `json.dumps()` function, assigning the `default_date()` function to the `default` parameter, as follows:

```
>>> example_date = datetime.datetime(2014, 6, 7, 8, 9, 10)
>>> document = {'date': example_date}
>>> print(
...     json.dumps(document, default=default_date, indent=2))
{
  "date": {
    "$date": "2014-06-07T08:09:10"
  }
}
```

When the `json` module can't serialize an object, it passes the object to the given `default` function. In any given application, we'll need to expand this function to handle a number of Python object types that we might want to serialize in JSON notation. If there is no default function provided, an exception is raised when an object can't be serialized.

Deserializing a complex data structure

When deserializing JSON to create Python objects, there's a *hook* that can be used to convert data from a JSON dictionary into a more complex Python object. This is called `object_hook` and it is used during processing by the `json.loads()` function. This hook is used to examine each JSON dictionary to see if something else should be created from the dictionary instance.

The function we provide will either create a more complex Python object, or it will simply return the original dictionary object unmodified:

```
def as_date(object: Dict[str, Any]) -> Union[Any, Dict[str, Any]]:
    if {'$date'} == set(object.keys()):
        return datetime.datetime.fromisoformat(object['$date'])
    return object
```

This function will check each object that's decoded to see if the object has a single field, and that single field is named `$date`. If that is the case, the value of the entire object is replaced with a `datetime` object. The return type is a union of `Any` and `Dict[str, Any]` to reflect the two possible results: either some object or the original dictionary.

We provide a function to the `json.loads()` function using the `object_hook` parameter, as follows:

```
>>> source = '''{"date": {"$date": "2014-06-07T08:09:10"}}'''
>>> json.loads(source, object_hook=as_date)
{'date': datetime.datetime(2014, 6, 7, 8, 9, 10)}
```

This parses a very small JSON document that meets the criteria for containing a date. The resulting Python object is built from the string value found in the JSON serialization.

We may also want to design our application classes to provide additional methods to help with serialization. A class might include a `to_json()` method, which will serialize the objects in a uniform way. This method might provide class information. It can avoid serializing any derived attributes or computed properties. Similarly, we might need to provide a static `from_json()` method that can be used to determine if a given dictionary object is actually an instance of the given class.

See also

- The *Reading HTML documents* recipe, later in this chapter, will show how we prepared this data from an HTML source.

Reading XML documents

The XML markup language is widely used to represent the state of objects in a serialized form. For details, see `http://www.w3.org/TR/REC-xml/`. Python includes a number of libraries for parsing XML documents.

XML is called a markup language because the content of interest is marked with tags, and also written with a start `<tag>` and an end `</tag>` to clarify the structure of the data. The overall file text includes both the content and the XML markup.

Because the markup is intermingled with the text, there are some additional syntax rules that must be used to distinguish markup from text. In order to include the < character in our data, we must use XML character entity references. We must use `<` to include < in our text. Similarly, `>` must be used instead of >, `&`, which is used instead of &. Additionally, `"` is also used to embed a " character in an attribute value delimited by " characters. For the most part, XML parsers will handle this transformation when consuming XML.

A document, then, will have items as follows:

```
<team><name>Team SCA</name><position>...</position></team>
```

The `<team>` tag contains the `<name>` tag, which contains the text of the team's name. The `<position>` tag contains more data about the team's finish position in each leg of a race.

Most XML processing allows additional `\n` and space characters in the XML to make the structure more obvious:

```
<team>
    <name>Team SCA</name>
    <position>...</position>
</team>
```

As shown in the preceding example, content (like team name) is surrounded by the tags. The overall document forms a large, nested collection of containers. We can think of a document as a tree with a root tag that contains all the other tags and their embedded content. Between tags, there is some additional content. In some applications, the additional content between the ends of tags is entirely whitespace.

Here's the beginning of the document we'll be looking at:

```
<?xml version="1.0"?>
  <results>
    <teams>
      <team>
        <name>
          Abu Dhabi Ocean Racing
        </name>
        <position>
          <leg n="1">
            1
          </leg>
          ...
        </position>
        ...
      </team>
      ...
    </teams>
  </results>
```

The top-level container is the `<results>` tag. Within this is a `<teams>` tag. Within the `<teams>` tag are many repetitions of data for each individual team, enclosed in the `<team>` tag. We've used ... to show where parts of the document were elided.

It's very, very difficult to parse XML with regular expressions. We need more sophisticated parsers to handle the syntax of nested tags.

There are two binary libraries that are available in Python for parsing: XML-SAX and Expat. Python includes the modules `xml.sax` and `xml.parsers.expat` to exploit these two libraries directly.

In addition to these, there's a very sophisticated set of tools in the `xml.etree` package. We'll focus on using the `ElementTree` module in this package to parse and analyze XML documents.

In this recipe, we'll use the `xml.etree` module to parse XML data.

Getting ready

We've gathered some sailboat racing results in `race_result.xml`. This file contains information on teams, legs, and the order in which the various teams finished each leg.

A team's overall score is the sum of the finish positions. Finishing first, or nearly first, in each leg will give a very low score. In many cases, there are empty values where a boat did not start, did not finish, or was disqualified from the race. In those cases, the team's score will be one more than the number of boats. If there are seven boats, then the team is given eight points for the leg. The inability to compete creates a hefty penalty.

The root tag for this data is a `<results>` document. This has the following schema:

- The `<legs>` tag contains individual `<leg>` tags that name each leg of the race. The leg names contain both a starting port and an ending port in the text.
- The `<teams>` tag contains a number of `<team>` tags with details of each team. Each team has data structured with internal tags:
    - The `<name>` tag contains the team name.
    - The `<position>` tag contains a number of `<leg>` tags with the finish position for the given leg. Each leg is numbered, and the numbering matches the leg definitions in the `<legs>` tag.

The data for all the finish positions for a single team looks as follows:

```
<?xml version="1.0"?>
  <results>
    <teams>
      <team>
        <name>
          Abu Dhabi Ocean Racing
        </name>
        <position>
          <leg n="1">
            1
          </leg>
          <leg n="2">
            3
```

```
        </leg>
        <leg n="3">
          2
        </leg>
        <leg n="4">
          2
        </leg>
        <leg n="5">
          1
        </leg>
        <leg n="6">
          2
        </leg>
        <leg n="7">
          5
        </leg>
        <leg n="8">
          3
        </leg>
        <leg n="9">
          5
        </leg>
      </position>
    </team>
      ...
  </teams>
  <legs>
  ...
  </legs>
</results>
```

We've only shown the first team. There was a total of seven teams in this particular race around the world.

In XML notation, the application data shows up in two kinds of places. The first is between the start and the end of a tag – for example, `<name>Abu Dhabi Ocean Racing</name>`. The tag is `<name>`, while the text between `<name>` and `</name>` is the value of this tag, `Abu Dhabi Ocean Racing`.

Also, data shows up as an attribute of a tag; for example, in `<leg n="1">`. The tag is `<leg>`; the tag has an attribute, `n`, with a value of `1`. A tag can have an indefinite number of attributes.

The `<leg>` tags point out an interesting problem with XML. These tags include the leg number given as an attribute, `n`, and the position in the leg given as the text inside the tag. The general approach is to put essential data inside the tags and supplemental, or clarifying, data in the attributes. The line between essential and supplemental is blurry.

XML permits a **mixed content model**. This reflects the case where XML is mixed in with text, where there is text inside and outside XML tags. Here's an example of mixed content:

```
<p>This has <strong>mixed</strong> content.</p>
```

The content of the `<p>` tag is a mixture of text and a tag. The data we're working with does not rely on this kind of mixed content model, meaning all the data is within a single tag or an attribute of a tag. The whitespace between tags can be ignored.

We'll use the `xml.etree` module to parse the data. This involves reading the data from a file and providing it to the parser. The resulting document will be rather complex.

We have not provided a formal schema definition for our sample data, nor have we provided a **Document Type Definition** (**DTD**). This means that the XML defaults to mixed content mode. Furthermore, the XML structure can't be validated against the schema or DTD.

How to do it...

Parsing XML data requires importing the `ElementTree` module. We'll use this to write a `race_summary()` function that parses the XML data and produces a useful Python object:

1. We'll need the `xml.etree.ElementTree` class to parse the XML text. We'll also need a `Path` object to refer to the file. We've used the `import... as...` syntax to assign a shorter name of `XML` to the `ElementTree` class:

   ```
   import xml.etree.ElementTree as XML
   from pathlib import Path
   ```

2. Define a function to read the XML document from a given `Path` instance:

   ```
   def race_summary(source_path: Path) -> None:
   ```

3. Create a Python `ElementTree` object by parsing the XML text. It's often easiest to use `source_path.read_text()` to read the file named by `Path`. We provided this string to the `XML.fromstring()` method for parsing. For very large files, an incremental parser is sometimes helpful:

   ```
       source_text = source_path.read_text(encoding='UTF-8')
       document = XML.fromstring(source_text)
   ```

4. Display the data. This document creates a dictionary with two keys, `"teams"` and `"legs"`. Here's how we can iterate through each leg, showing the team's position in the leg:

   ```
       legs = cast(XML.Element, document.find('legs'))
   ```

```
        teams = cast(XML.Element, document.find('teams'))

        for leg in legs.findall('leg'):
            print(cast(str, leg.text).strip())
            n = leg.attrib['n']

            for team in teams.findall('team'):
                position_leg = cast(XML.Element,
                    team.find(f"position/leg[@n='{n}']"))
                name = cast(XML.Element, team.find('name'))
                print(
                    cast(str, name.text).strip(),
                    cast(str, position_leg.text).strip()
                )
```

Once we have the document object, we can then search the object for the relevant pieces of data. In this example, we used the `find()` method to locate the two tags containing legs and teams.

Within the `legs` tag, there are a number of `leg` tags. Each of those tags has the following structure:

```
<leg n="1">
    ALICANTE - CAPE TOWN
</leg>
```

The expression `leg.attrib['n']` extracts the value of the attribute named `n`. The expression `leg.text.strip()` is all the text within the `<leg>` tag, stripped of extra whitespace.

It's central to note that the results of the `find()` function have a type hint of `Optional[XML.Element]`. We have two choices to handle this:

- Use an `if` statement to determine if the result is not `None`.
- Use `cast(XML.Element, tag.find(...))` to claim that the result is never going to be `None`. For some kinds of output from automated systems, the tags are always going to be present, and the overhead of numerous `if` statements is excessive.

For each leg of the race, we need to print the finish positions, which are represented in the data contained within the `<teams>` tag. Within this tag, we need to locate a tag containing the name of the team. We also need to find the proper `leg` tag with the finish position for this team on the given leg.

We need to use a complex XPath search, `f"position/leg[@n='{n}']"`, to locate a specific instance of the `position` tag. The value of `n` is the leg number. For the ninth leg, this search will be the string `"position/leg[@n='9']"`. This will locate the `position` tag containing a `leg` tag that has an attribute `n` equal to `9`.

Because XML is a mixed content model, all the `\n`, `\t`, and space characters in the content are perfectly preserved in the data. We rarely want any of this whitespace, and it makes sense to use the `strip()` method to remove all extraneous characters before and after the meaningful content.

How it works...

The XML parser modules transform XML documents into fairly complex objects based on a standardized document object model. In the case of the `etree` module, the document will be built from `Element` objects, which generally represent tags and text.

XML can also include processing instructions and comments. We'll ignore them and focus on the document structure and content here.

Each `Element` instance has the text of the tag, the text within the tag, attributes that are part of the tag, and a tail. The tag is the name inside `<tag>`. The attributes are the fields that follow the tag name. For example, the `<leg n="1">` tag has a tag name of `leg` and an attribute named `n`. Values are always strings in XML; any conversion to a different data type is the responsibility of the application using the data.

The text is contained between the start and end of a tag. Therefore, a tag such as `<name>Team SCA</name>` has `"Team SCA"` for the value of the `text` attribute of the `Element` that represents the `<name>` tag.

Note that a tag also has a tail attribute. Consider this sequence of two tags:

```
<name>Team SCA</name>
<position>...</position>
```

There's a `\n` whitespace character after the closing `</name>` tag and before the opening of the `<position>` tag. This extra text is collected by the parser and put into the tail of the `<name>` tag. The tail values can be important when working with a mixed content model. The tail values are generally whitespace when working in an element content model.

There's more...

Because we can't trivially translate an XML document into a Python dictionary, we need a handy way to search through the document's content. The `ElementTree` module provides a search technique that's a partial implementation of the **XML Path Language** (**XPath**) for specifying a location in an XML document. The XPath notation gives us considerable flexibility.

The XPath queries are used with the `find()` and `findall()` methods. Here's how we can find all of the team names:

```
>>> for tag in document.findall('teams/team/name'):
...     print(tag.text.strip())
Abu Dhabi Ocean Racing
Team Brunel
Dongfeng Race Team
MAPFRE
Team Alvimedica
Team SCA
Team Vestas Wind
```

Here, we've looked for the top-level `<teams>` tag. Within that tag, we want `<team>` tags. Within those tags, we want the `<name>` tags. This will search for all the instances of this nested tag structure.

Note that we've omitted the type hints from this example and assumed that all the tags will contain text values that are not `None`. If we use this in an application, we may have to add checks for `None`, or use the `cast()` function to convince `mypy` that the tags or the text attribute value is not `None`.

We can search for attribute values as well. This can make it handy to find how all the teams did on a particular leg of the race. The data for this can be found in the `<leg>` tag, within the `<position>` tag for each team.

Furthermore, each `<leg>` has an attribute named `n` that shows which of the race legs it represents. Here's how we can use this to extract specific data from the XML document:

```
>>> for tag in document.findall("teams/team/position/leg[@n='8']"):
...     print(tag.text.strip())
3
5
7
4
6
1
2
```

This shows us the finishing positions of each team on leg 8 of the race. We're looking for all tags with `<leg n="8">` and displaying the text within that tag. We have to match these values with the team names to see that team number 3, Team SCA, finished first, and that team number 2, Dongfeng Race Team, finished last on this leg.

See also

- The *Reading HTML documents* recipe, later in this chapter, shows how we prepared this data from an HTML source.

Reading HTML documents

A great deal of content on the web is presented using HTML markup. A browser renders the data very nicely. How can we parse this data to extract the meaningful content from the displayed web page?

We can use the standard library `html.parser` module, but it's not as helpful as we'd like. It only provides low-level lexical scanning information; it doesn't provide a high-level data structure that describes the original web page.

Instead, we'll use the Beautiful Soup module to parse HTML pages into more useful data structures. This is available from the **Python Package Index** (**PyPI**). See `https://pypi.python.org/pypi/beautifulsoup4`.

This must be downloaded and installed. Often, this is as simple as doing the following:

```
python -m pip install beautifulsoup4
```

Using the `python -m pip` command ensures that we will use the `pip` command that goes with the currently active virtual environment.

Getting ready

We've gathered some sailboat racing results in `Volvo Ocean Race.html`. This file contains information on teams, legs, and the order in which the various teams finished each leg. It's been scraped from the Volvo Ocean Race website, and it looks wonderful when opened in a browser.

Except for very old websites, most HTML notation is an extension of XML notation. The content is surrounded by `<tag>` marks, which show the structure and presentation of the data. HTML predates XML, and an XHTML standard reconciles the two. Note that browser applications must be tolerant of older HTML and improperly structured HTML. The presence of damaged HTML can make it difficult to analyze some data from the World Wide Web.

HTML pages can include a great deal of overhead. There are often vast code and style sheet sections, as well as invisible metadata. The content may be surrounded by advertising and other information.

Generally, an HTML page has the following overall structure:

```
<html>
```

```
    <head>...</head>
    <body>...</body>
</html>
```

Within the <head> tag, there will be links to JavaScript libraries and links to **Cascading Style Sheet** (**CSS**) documents. These are used to provide interactive features and to define the presentation of the content.

The bulk of the content is in the <body> tag. It can be difficult to track down the relevant data on a web page. This is because the focus of the design effort is on how people see it more than how automated tools can process it.

In this case, the race results are in an HTML <table> tag, making them easy to find. What we can see here is the overall structure for the relevant content in the page:

```
<table>
    <thead>
        <tr>
            <th>...</th>
            ...
        </tr>
    </thead>
    <tbody>
        <tr>
            <td>...</td>
            ...
        </tr>
        ...
    </tbody>
</table>
```

The <thead> tag includes the column titles for the table. There's a single table row tag, <tr>, with table heading, <th>, tags that include the content. Each of the <th> tags contains two parts. It looks like this:

```
<th tooltipster data-title="<strong>ALICANTE - CAPE TOWN</strong>"
data-theme="tooltipster-shadow" data-htmlcontent="true" data-
position="top">LEG 1</th>
```

The essential display is a number for each leg of the race, `LEG 1`, in this example. This is the content of the tag. In addition to the displayed content, there's also an attribute value, `data-title`, that's used by a JavaScript function. This attribute value is the name of the leg, and it is displayed when the cursor hovers over a column heading. The JavaScript function pops up the leg's name.

The <tbody> tag includes the team name and the results for each race. The table row, <tr>, tag, contains the details for each team. The team name (and graphic and overall finish rank) is shown in the first three columns of the table data, <td>. The remaining columns of table data contain the finishing position for a given leg of the race.

Because of the relative complexity of sailboat racing, there are additional notes in some of the table data cells. These are included as attributes to provide supplemental data regarding the reason why a cell has a particular value. In some cases, teams did not start a leg, did not finish a leg, or retired from a leg.

Here's a typical <tr> row from the HTML:

```
<tr class="ranking-item">
    <td class="ranking-position">3</td>
    <td class="ranking-avatar">
        <img src="..."> </td>
    <td class="ranking-team">Dongfeng Race Team</td>
    <td class="ranking-number">2</td>
    <td class="ranking-number">2</td>
    <td class="ranking-number">1</td>
    <td class="ranking-number">3</td>
    <td class="ranking-number" tooltipster data-
title="<center><strong>RETIRED</strong><br>Click for more info</
center>" data-theme="tooltipster-3" data-position="bottom" data-
htmlcontent="true"><a href="/en/news/8674_Dongfeng-Race-Team-breaks-
mast-crew-safe.html" target="_blank">8</a><div  class="status-dot
dot-3"></div></td>
    <td class="ranking-number">1</td>
    <td class="ranking-number">4</td>
    <td class="ranking-number">7</td>
    <td class="ranking-number">4</td>
    <td class="ranking-number total">33<span class="asterix">*</
span></td>
</tr>
```

The <tr> tag has a class attribute that defines the style for this row. The `class` attribute on this tag helps our data gathering application locate the relevant content. It also chooses the CSS style for this class of content.

The <td> tags also have class attributes that define the style for the individual cells of data. Because the CSS styles reflect the content, the class also clarifies what the content of the cell means. Not all CSS class names are as well defined as these.

One of the cells has no text content. Instead, the cell has an `<a>` tag and an empty `<div>` tag. That cell also contains several attributes, including `data-title`, `data-theme`, `data-position`, and others. These additional tags are used by a JavaScript function to display additional information in the cell. Instead of text stating the finish position, there is additional data on what happened to the racing team and their boat.

An essential complexity here is that the `data-title` attribute contains HTML content. This is unusual, and an HTML parser cannot detect that an attribute contains HTML markup. We'll set this aside for the *There's more...* section of this recipe.

How to do it...

We'll start by importing the necessary modules. The function for parsing down the data will have two important sections: the list of legs and the team results for each leg. These are represented as headings and rows of an HTML table:

1. We'll need the `BeautifulSoup` class from the `bs4` module to parse the text. We'll also need a `Path` object to refer to the file. We've used a `# type: ignore` comment because the bs4 module didn't have complete type hints at the time of publication:

   ```
   from bs4 import BeautifulSoup  # type: ignore
   from pathlib import Path
   ```

2. Define a function to read the HTML document from a given `Path` instance:

   ```
   def race_extract(source_path: Path) -> Dict[str, Any]:
   ```

3. Create the soup structure from the HTML content. We'll assign it to a variable, `soup`. We've used a context manager to access the file. As an alternative, we could also read the content using the `Path.read_text()` method:

   ```
       with source_path.open(encoding="utf8") as source_file:
           soup = BeautifulSoup(source_file, "html.parser")
   ```

4. From the `Soup` object, we can navigate to the first `<table>` tag. Within that, we need to find the first `<thead>` tag. Within that heading, we need to find the `<tr>` tag. This row contains the individual heading cells. Navigating to the first instance of a tag means using the tag name as an attribute; each tag's children are available as attributes of the tag:

   ```
       thead_row = soup.table.thead.tr
   ```

5. We can accumulate data from each `<th>` cell within the row. There are three variations of the heading cells. Some have no text, some have text, and some have text and a `data-title` attribute value. For this first version, we'll capture all three variations. The tag's `text` attribute contains this content. The tag's `attrs` attribute contains the various attribute values:

   ```
       legs: List[Tuple[str, Optional[str]]] = []
   ```

```
for tag in thead_row.find_all("th"):
    leg_description = (
        tag.string, tag.attrs.get("data-title")
    legs.append(leg_description)
```

6. From the `Soup` object, we can navigate to the first `<table>` tag. Within that, we need to find the first `<tbody>` tag. We can leverage the way Beautiful Soup makes the first instance of any tag into an attribute of the parent's tag:

```
tbody = soup.table.tbody
```

7. Within that body, we need to find all the `<tr>` tags in order to visit all of the rows of the table. Within the `<tr>` tags for a row, each cell is in a `<td>` tag. We want to convert the content of the `<td>` tags into team names and a collection of team positions, depending on the attributes available:

```
teams: List[Dict[str, Any]] = []
for row in tbody.find_all("tr"):
    team: Dict[str, Any] = {
        "name": None,
        "position": []}
    for col in row.find_all("td"):
        if "ranking-team" in col.attrs.get("class"):
            team["name"] = col.string
        elif (
            "ranking-number" in col.attrs.get("class")
        ):
            team["position"].append(col.string)
        elif "data-title" in col.attrs:
            # Complicated explanation with nested HTML
            # print(col.attrs, col.string)
            Pass
    teams.append(team)
```

8. Once the legs and teams have been extracted, we can create a useful dictionary that will contain the two collections:

```
document = {
    "legs": legs,
    "teams": teams,
}
return document
```

We've created a list of legs showing the order and names for each leg, and we parsed the body of the table to create a dict-of-list structure with each leg's results for a given team. The resulting object looks like this:

```
{'legs': [(None, None),
          ('LEG 1', '<strong>ALICANTE - CAPE TOWN</strong>'),
          ('LEG 2', '<strong>CAPE TOWN - ABU DHABI</strong>'),
          ('LEG 3', '<strong>ABU DHABI - SANYA</strong>'),
          ('LEG 4', '<strong>SANYA - AUCKLAND</strong>'),
          ('LEG 5', '<strong>AUCKLAND - ITAJAÍ</strong>'),
          ('LEG 6', '<strong>ITAJAÍ - NEWPORT</strong>'),
          ('LEG 7', '<strong>NEWPORT - LISBON</strong>'),
          ('LEG 8', '<strong>LISBON - LORIENT</strong>'),
          ('LEG 9', '<strong>LORIENT - GOTHENBURG</strong>'),
          ('TOTAL', None)],
 'teams': [{'name': 'Abu Dhabi Ocean Racing',
            'position': ['1', '3', '2', '2', '1', '2', '5', '3',
'5', '24']},
           {'name': 'Team Brunel',
            'position': ['3', '1', '5', '5', '4', '3', '1', '5',
'2', '29']},
           {'name': 'Dongfeng Race Team',
            'position': ['2', '2', '1', '3', None, '1', '4', '7',
'4', None]},
           {'name': 'MAPFRE',
            'position': ['7', '4', '4', '1', '2', '4', '2', '4',
'3', None]},
           {'name': 'Team Alvimedica',
            'position': ['5', None, '3', '4', '3', '5', '3', '6',
'1', '34']},
           {'name': 'Team SCA',
            'position': ['6', '6', '6', '6', '5', '6', '6', '1',
'7', None]},
           {'name': 'Team Vestas Wind',
            'position': ['4',
                         None,
                         None,
                         None,
                         None,
                         None,
                         None,
```

```
'2',
'6',
'60']}]}
```

This structure is the content of the source HTML table, unpacked into a Python dictionary we can work with. Note that the titles for the legs include embedded HTML within the attribute's value.

Within the body of the table, many cells have `None` for the final race position, and a complex value in `data-title` for the specific `<TD>` tag. We've avoided trying to capture the additional results data in this initial part of the recipe.

How it works...

The `BeautifulSoup` class transforms HTML documents into fairly complex objects based on a **document object model** (**DOM**). The resulting structure will be built from instances of the `Tag`, `NavigableString`, and `Comment` classes.

Generally, we're interested in the tags that contain the string content of the web page. These are instances of the `Tag` class, as well as the `NavigableString` class.

Each `Tag` instance has a name, string, and attributes. The name is the word inside < and >. The attributes are the fields that follow the tag name. For example, `<td class="ranking-number">1</td>` has a tag name of `td` and an attribute named `class`. Values are often strings, but in a few cases, the value can be a list of strings. The string attribute of the `Tag` object is the content enclosed by the tag; in this case, it's a very short string, `1`.

HTML is a mixed content model. This means that a tag can contain child tags, in addition to navigable text. When looking at the children of a given tag, there will be a sequence of `Tag` and `NavigableText` objects freely intermixed.

One of the most common features of HTML is small blocks of navigable text that contain only newline characters. When we have HTML like this:

```
<tr>
    <td>Data</td>
</tr>
```

There are three children within the `<tr>` tag. Here's a display of the children of this tag:

```
>>> example = BeautifulSoup('''
...     <tr>
...         <td>data</td>
...     </tr>
... ''', 'html.parser')
```

```
>>> list(example.tr.children)
['\n', <td>data</td>, '\n']
```

The two newline characters are peers of the `<td>` tag. These are preserved by the parser. This shows how `NavigableText` objects often surround a child `Tag` object.

The `BeautifulSoup` parser depends on another, lower-level library to do some of the parsing. It's easy to use the built-in `html.parser` module for this. There are alternatives that can be installed as well. These may offer some advantages, like better performance or better handling of damaged HTML.

There's more...

The `Tag` objects of Beautiful Soup represent the hierarchy of the document's structure. There are several kinds of navigation among tags:

- All tags except a special root `container` will have a parent. The top `<html>` tag will often be the only child of the root `container`.
- The `parents` attribute is a generator for all parents of a tag. It's a path "upward" through the hierarchy from a given tag.
- All `Tag` objects can have children. A few tags such as `<img/>` and `<hr/>` have no children. The `children` attribute is a generator that yields the children of a tag.
- A tag with children may have multiple levels of tags under it. The overall `<html>` tag, for example, contains the entire document as descendants. The `children` attribute contains the immediate children; the `descendants` attribute generates all children of children, recursively.
- A tag can also have siblings, which are other tags within the same container. Since the tags have a defined order, there's the `next_sibling` and `previous_sibling` attributes to help us step through the peers of a tag.

In some cases, a document will have a straightforward organization, and a simple search by the `id` attribute or `class` attribute will find the relevant data. Here's a typical search for a given structure:

```
>>> ranking_table = soup.find('table', class_="ranking-list")
```

Note that we have to use `class_` in our Python query to search for the attribute named `class`. The token `class` is a reserved word in Python and cannot be used as a parameter name. Given the overall document, we're searching for any `<table class="ranking-list">` tag. This will find the first such table in a web page. Since we know there will only be one of these, this attribute-based search helps distinguish between what we are trying to find and any other tabular data on a web page.

Here's the list of parents of this `<table>` tag:

```
>>> list(tag.name for tag in ranking_table.parents)
['section', 'div', 'div', 'div', 'div', 'body', 'html', '[document]']
```

We've displayed just the tag name for each parent above the given `<table>`. Note that there are four nested `<div>` tags that wrap the `<section>` that contains `<table>`. Each of these `<div>` tags likely has a different class attribute to properly define the content and the style for the content.

`[document]` is the overall `BeautifulSoup` container that holds the various tags that were parsed. This is displayed distinctively to emphasize that it's not a real tag, but a container for the top-level `<html>` tag.

See also

- The *Reading JSON documents* and *Reading XML documents* recipes, shown earlier in this chapter, both use similar data. The example data was created for them by scraping the original HTML page using these techniques.

Refactoring a .csv DictReader as a dataclass reader

When we read data from a CSV format file, the `csv` module offers two general choices for the kind of reader to create:

- When we use `csv.reader()`, each row becomes a list of column values.
- When we use `csv.DictReader`, each row becomes a dictionary. By default, the contents of the first row become the keys for the row dictionary. An alternative is to provide a list of values that will be used as the keys.

In both cases, referring to data within the row is awkward because it involves rather complex-looking syntax. When we use the `csv.reader()` function, we must use syntax like `row[2]` to refer to a cell; the semantics of index 2 are completely obscure.

When we use `csv.DictReader`, we can use `row['date']`, which is less obscure, but this is still a lot of extra syntax. While this has a number of advantages, it requires a CSV with a single-row header of unique column names, which is something not ubiquitous in practice.

In some real-world spreadsheets, the column names are impossibly long strings. It's hard to work with `row['Total of all locations\nexcluding franchisees']`.

We can use a dataclass to replace this complex list or dictionary syntax with something simpler. This lets us replace an opaque index position or column names with a useful name.

Getting ready

One way to improve the readability of programs that work with spreadsheets is to replace a list of columns with a `typing.NamedTuple` or `dataclass` object. These two definitions provide easy-to-use names defined by the class instead of the possibly haphazard column names in the `.csv` file.

More importantly, it permits much nicer syntax for referring to the various columns; for example, we can use `row.date` instead of `row['date']` or `row[2]`.

The column names (and the data types for each column) are part of the schema for a given file of data. In some CSV files, the first line of the column titles provides part of the schema for the file. The schema that gets built from the first line of the file is incomplete because it can only provide attribute names; the target data types aren't known and have to be managed by the application program.

This points to two reasons for imposing an external schema on the rows of a spreadsheet:

- We can supply meaningful names
- We can perform data conversions where necessary

We'll look at a CSV file that contains some real-time data that's been recorded from the log of a sailboat. This is the `waypoints.csv` file, and the data looks as follows:

```
lat,lon,date,time
32.8321666666667,-79.9338333333333,2012-11-27,09:15:00
31.6714833333333,-80.93325,2012-11-28,00:00:00
30.7171666666667,-81.5525,2012-11-28,11:35:00
```

The data contains four columns, `lot`, `lon`, `date`, and `time`. Two of the columns are the latitude and longitude of the waypoint. It contains a column with the date and the time as separate values. This isn't ideal, and we'll look at various data cleansing steps separately.

In this case, the column titles happen to be valid Python variable names. This is rare, but it can lead to a slight simplification. The more general solution involves mapping the given column names to valid Python attribute names.

A program can use a dictionary-based reader that looks like the following function:

```
def show_waypoints_raw(data_path: Path) -> None:
    with data_path.open() as data_file:
        data_reader = csv.DictReader(data_file)
        for row in data_reader:
            ts_date = datetime.datetime.strptime(
                row['date'], "%Y-%m-%d"
            ).date()
```

```
            ts_time = datetime.datetime.strptime(
                row['time'], "%H:%M:%S"
            ).time()
            timestamp = datetime.datetime.combine(
                ts_date, ts_time)
            lat_lon = (
                float(row['lat']),
                float(row['lon'])
            )
            print(
                f"{timestamp:%m-%d %H:%M}, "
                f"{lat_lon[0]:.3f} {lat_lon[1]:.3f}"
            )
```

This function embodies a number of assumptions about the available data. It combines the physical format, logical layout, and processing into a single operation. A small change to the layout - for example, a column name change - can be difficult to manage.

In this recipe, we'll isolate the various layers of processing to create some kind of immunity from change. This separation of concerns can create a much more flexible application.

How to do it...

We'll start by defining a useful dataclass. We'll create functions to read raw data, and create dataclass instances from this cleaned data. We'll include some of the data conversion functions in the dataclass definition to properly encapsulate it. We'll start with the target class definition, `Waypoint_1`:

1. Import the modules and definitions required. We'll be introducing a dataclass, and we'll also need to define optional attributes of this dataclass:

   ```
   from dataclasses import dataclass, field
   from typing import Optional
   ```

2. Define a base dataclass that matches the raw input from the CSV file. The names here should be defined clearly, irrespective of the actual headers in the CSV file. This is an initial set of attributes, to which we'll add any derived values later:

   ```
   @dataclass
   class Waypoint_1:
       arrival_date: str
       arrival_time: str
       lat: str
       lon: str
   ```

3. Add any derived attributes to this dataclass. This should focus on attributes with values that are expensive to compute. These attributes will be a cache for the derived value to avoid computing it more than once. These will have a type hint of `Optional`, and will use the `field()` function to define them as `init=False` and provide a default value, which is usually `None`:

```
_timestamp: Optional[datetime.datetime] = field(
    init=False, default=None
)
```

4. Write properties to compute the expensive derived values. The results are cached as an attribute value of the dataclass. In this example, the conversion of text date and time fields into a more useful `datetime` object is a relatively expensive operation. The result is cached in an attribute value, `_timestamp`, and returned after the initial computation:

```
@property
def arrival(self):
    if self._timestamp is None:
        ts_date = datetime.datetime.strptime(
            self.arrival_date, "%Y-%m-%d"
        ).date()
        ts_time = datetime.datetime.strptime(
            self.arrival_time, "%H:%M:%S"
        ).time()
        self._timestamp = datetime.datetime.combine(
            ts_date, ts_time)
    return self._timestamp
```

5. Refactor any relatively inexpensive computed values as properties of the dataclass. These values don't need to be cached because the performance gains from a cache are so small:

```
@property
def lat_lon(self):
    return float(self.lat), float(self.lon)
```

6. Define a static method to create instances of this class from source data. This method contains the mapping from the source column names in the CSV file to more meaningful attribute names in the application. Note the type hint for this method must use the class name with quotes – `'Waypoint_1'` – because the class is not fully defined when the method is created. When the body of the method is evaluated, the class will exist, and a quoted name is not used:

```
@staticmethod
def from_source(row: Dict[str, str]) -> 'Waypoint_1':
```

```
        name_map = {
            'date': 'arrival_date',
            'time': 'arrival_time',
            'lat': 'lat',
            'lon': 'lon',
        }
        return Waypoint_1(
            **{name_map[header]: value
                for header, value in row.items()}
        )
```

7. Write a generator expression to use the new dataclass when reading the source data:

```
def show_waypoints_1(data_path: Path) -> None:
    with data_path.open() as data_file:
        data_reader = csv.DictReader(data_file)
        waypoint_iter = (
            Waypoint_1.from_source(row)
                for row in data_reader
        )
        for row in waypoint_iter:
            print(
                f"{row.arrival:%m-%d %H:%M}, "
                f"{row.lat_lon[0]:.3f} "
                f"{row.lat_lon[1]:.3f}"
            )
```

Looking back at the *Reading delimited files with the CSV module* recipe, earlier in this chapter, the structure of this function is similar to the functions in that recipe. Similarly, this design also echoes the processing shown in the *Using dataclasses to simplify working with CSV files* recipe, earlier in this chapter.

The expression `(Waypoint_1.from_source(row) for row in data_reader)` provides each raw dictionary with the `Waypoint_1.from_source()` static function. This function will map the source column names to class attributes, and then create an instance of the `Waypoint_1` class.

The remaining processing has to be rewritten so that it uses the attributes of the new dataclass that was defined. This often leads to simplification because row-level computations of derived values have been refactored into the class definition, removing them from the overall processing. The remaining overall processing is a display of the detailed values from each row of the source CSV file.

How it works...

There are several parts to this recipe. Firstly, we've used the `csv` module for the essential parsing of rows and columns of data. We've also leveraged the *Reading delimited files with the CSV module* recipe to process the physical format of the data.

Secondly, we've defined a dataclass that provides a minimal schema for our data. The minimal schema is supplemented with the `from_source()` function to convert the raw data into instances of the dataclass. This provides a more complete schema definition because it has a mapping from the source columns to the dataclass attributes.

Finally, we've wrapped the `csv` reader in a generator expression to build dataclass objects for each row. This change permits the revision of the remaining code in order to focus on the object defined by the dataclass, separate from CSV file complications.

Instead of `row[2]` or `row['date']`, we can now use `row.arrival_date` to refer to a specific column. This is a profound change; it can simplify the presentation of complex algorithms.

There's more...

A common problem that CSV files have is blank rows that contain no useful data. Discarding empty rows requires some additional processing when attempting to create the row object. We need to make two changes:

1. Expand the `from_source()` method so that it has a slightly different return value. It often works out well to change the return type from `'Waypoint_1'` to `Optional['Waypoint_1']` and return a `None` object instead of an empty or invalid `Waypoint_1` instance.
2. Expand the `waypoint_iter` expression in order to include a filter to reject the `None` objects.

We'll look at each of these separately, starting with the revision to the `from_source()` method.

Each source of data has unique rules for what constitutes valid data. In this example, we'll use the rule that all four fields must be present and have data that fits the expected patterns: dates, times, or floating-point numbers.

This definition of valid data leads to a profound rethinking of the way the dataclass is defined. The application only uses two attributes: the arrival time is a `datetime.datetime` object, while the latitude and longitude is a `Tuple[float, float]` object.

A more useful class definition, then, is this:

```
@dataclass
```

```
class Waypoint_2:
    arrival: datetime.datetime
    lat_lon: Tuple[float, float]
```

Given these two attributes, we can redefine the `from_source()` method to build this from a row of raw data:

```
@staticmethod
def from_source(row: Dict[str, str]) -> Optional['Waypoint_2']:
    try:
        ts_date = datetime.datetime.strptime(
            row['date'], "%Y-%m-%d"
        ).date()
        ts_time = datetime.datetime.strptime(
            row['time'], "%H:%M:%S"
        ).time()
        arrival = datetime.datetime.combine(
            ts_date, ts_time)
        return Waypoint_2(
            arrival=arrival,
            lat_lon=(
                float(row['lat']),
                float(row['lon'])
            )
        )
    except (ValueError, KeyError):
        return None
```

This function will locate the source values, `row['date']`, `row['time']`, `row['lat']`, and `row['lon']`. It assumes the fields are all valid and attempts to do a number of complex conversions, including the date-time combination and float conversion of the latitude and longitude values. If any of these conversions fail, an exception will be raised and a `None` value will be returned. If all the conversions are successful, then an instance of the `Waypoint_2` class can be built and returned from this function.

Once this change is in place, we can make one more change to the main application:

```
def show_waypoints_2(data_path: Path) -> None:
    with data_path.open() as data_file:
        data_reader = csv.DictReader(data_file)
        waypoint_iter = (
            Waypoint_2.from_source(row)
                for row in data_reader
```

```
        )
        for row in filter(None, waypoint_iter):
            print(
                f"{row.arrival:%m-%d %H:%M}, "
                f"{row.lat_lon[0]:.3f} "
                f"{row.lat_lon[1]:.3f}"
            )
```

We've changed the `for` statement that consumes values from the `waypoint_iter` generator expression. This change introduces the `filter()` function in order to exclude `None` values from the source of data. Combined with the change to the `from_source()` method, we can now exclude bad data and tolerate source file changes without complex rewrites.

See also

- In the *Reading delimited files with the csv module* recipe, earlier in this chapter, we looked at the basics of using the `csv` module to parse files.
- The *Using dataclasses to simplify working with CSV files* recipe, earlier in this chapter, covered a different approach to working with complex data mappings.

11
Testing

Testing is central to creating working software. Here's the canonical statement describing the importance of testing:

> *Any program feature without an automated test simply doesn't exist.*

That's from Kent Beck's book, *Extreme Programming Explained: Embrace Change*.

We can distinguish several kinds of testing:

- **Unit testing**: This applies to independent *units* of software: functions, classes, or modules. The unit is tested in isolation to confirm that it works correctly.
- **Integration testing**: This combines units to be sure they integrate properly.
- **System testing**: This tests an entire application or a system of interrelated applications to be sure that the aggregated suite of software components works properly (also often known as **end-to-end testing**). This is often used for **acceptance testing**, to confirm software is fit for use.
- **Performance testing**: This assures that a unit, subsystem, or whole system meets performance objectives (also often known as **load testing**). In some cases, performance testing includes the study of resources such as memory, threads, or file descriptors. The goal is to be sure that software makes appropriate use of system resources.

These are some of the more common types. There are even more ways to use testing to identify software defects or potential defects. In this chapter, we'll focus on unit testing.

It's sometimes helpful to summarize a test following the Gherkin language. In this test specification language, each scenario is described by *GIVEN-WHEN-THEN* steps. Here's an example:

- **GIVEN** n = 52
- **AND** k = 5
- **WHEN** we compute binomial coefficient, c = binom(n, k)
- **THEN** the result, c, is 2,598,960

This approach to writing tests describes the given starting state, the action to perform, and the resulting state after the action. It can help us provide meaningful names for unit test cases even when we're not using Gherkin-based tools.

In this chapter, we'll look at the following recipes:

- Test tool setup
- Using docstrings for testing
- Testing functions that raise exceptions
- Handling common `doctest` issues
- Unit testing with the `unittest` module
- Combining `unittest` and `doctest` tests
- Unit testing with the `pytest` module
- Combining `pytest` and `doctest` tests
- Testing things that involve dates or times
- Testing things that involve randomness
- Mocking external resources

We'll start with setting up test tools. Python comes with everything we need. However, the `pytest` tool is so handy, it seems imperative to install it first. Once this tool is available, we can use it to run a variety of kinds of unit tests.

Test tool setup

Python has two built-in testing frameworks. The `doctest` tool examines docstrings for examples that include the `>>>` prompt. While this is widely used for unit testing, it can also be used for some kinds of integration testing.

The other built-in testing framework uses classes defined in the `unittest` module. The tests are extensions to the `TestCase` class. This, too, is designed primarily for unit testing, but can also be applied to integration and performance testing. These tests are run using the `unittest` tool.

It turns out there's a tool that lets us run both kinds of tests. It's very helpful to install the `pytest` tool. This mini-recipe will look at installing the `pytest` tool and using it for testing.

How to do it...

This needs to be installed separately with a command like the following:

```
python -m pip install pytest
```

Why it works...

The `pytest` tool has sophisticated test discovery. It can locate `doctest` test cases, as well as `unittest` test cases. It has its own, slightly simpler approach to writing tests.

We have to follow a couple of simple guidelines:

- Put all the tests into modules with names that begin with `test_`
- If an entire package of tests will be created, it helps to have the directory named `tests`

All the examples from this book use the `pytest` tool to be sure they're correct.

The `pytest` tool searches modules with the appropriate name, looking for the following:

- `unittest.TestCase` subclass definitions
- Functions with names that start with `test_`

When executed with the `--doctest-modules` option, the tool looks for blocks of text that appear to have `doctest` examples in them.

There's more...

The `pytest` tool has very handy integration with the `coverage` package, allowing you to run tests and see which lines of code were exercised during the testing and which need to be tested. The `pytest-cov` plugin can be useful for testing complex software.

When using the `pytest-cov` plugin, it's important to pass the `--cov` option to define which modules need to be tracked by the coverage tool. In many projects, all of the project's Python files are collected into a single directory, often named `src`. This makes it easy to use `--cov=src` to gather test coverage information on the application's modules.

Using docstrings for testing

Good Python includes docstrings inside every module, class, function, and method. Many tools can create useful, informative documentation from docstrings. Here's an example of a function-level docstring, from the *Writing clear documentation strings with RST markup* recipe in *Chapter 3, Function Definitions*:

```
def Twc(T: float, V: float) -> float:
    """Computes the wind chill temperature

    The wind-chill, :math:'T_{wc}', is based on
    air temperature, T, and wind speed, V.

    :param T: Temperature in °C
    :param V: Wind Speed in kph
    :returns: Wind-Chill temperature in °C
    :raises ValueError: for low wind speeds or high Temps
    """
    if V < 4.8 or T > 10.0:
        raise ValueError(
            "V must be over 4.8 kph, T must be below 10°C")
    return (
         13.12 + 0.6215 * T
         - 11.37 * V ** 0.16 + 0.3965 * T * V ** 0.16
    )
```

One important element of a docstring is an example. The examples provided in docstrings can become unit-test cases. An example often fits the *GIVEN-WHEN-THEN* model of testing because it shows a unit under test, a request to that unit, and a response.

In this recipe, we'll look at ways to turn examples into proper automated test cases.

Getting ready

We'll look at a small function definition as well as a class definition. Each of these will include docstrings that include examples that can be used as automated tests.

We'll use a function to compute the binomial coefficient of two numbers. It shows the number of combinations of *n* things taken in groups of size *k*. For example, how many ways a 52-card deck can be dealt into 5-card hands is computed like this:

$$\binom{n}{k} = \frac{n!}{k! \times (n-k)!}$$

This can be implemented by a Python function that looks like this:

```
from math import factorial

def binom(n: int, k: int) -> int:
    return factorial(n) // (factorial(k) * factorial(n-k))
```

This function does a computation and returns a value. Since it has no internal state, it's relatively easy to test. This will be one of the examples used for showing the unit testing tools available.

We'll also look at a class that uses lazy calculation of the mean and median. This is similar to the classes shown in *Chapter 7, Basics of Classes and Objects*. The *Designing classes with lots of processing* and *Using properties for lazy attributes* recipes both have classes similar to this.

This `Summary` class uses an internal `Counter` object that can be interrogated to determine the mode:

```
from statistics import median
from collections import Counter

class Summary:

def __init__(self) -> None:
    self.counts: Counter[int] = collections.Counter()

def __str__(self) -> str:
    return f"mean = {self.mean:.2f}\nmedian = {self.median:d}"

def add(self, value: int) -> None:
    self.counts[value] += 1

@property
def mean(self) -> float:
    s0 = sum(f for v, f in self.counts.items())
    s1 = sum(v * f for v, f in self.counts.items())
    return s1 / s0

@property
def median(self) -> float:
    return statistics.median(self.counts.elements())
```

The `add()` method changes the state of this object. Because of this state change, we'll need to provide more sophisticated examples to show how an instance of the `Summary` class behaves.

How to do it...

We'll show two variations in this recipe. The first variation can be applied to largely stateless operations, such as the computation of the `binom()` function. The second is more appropriate for stateful operations, such as the `Summary` class. We'll look at them together because they're very similar, even though they apply to different kinds of applications.

The general outline of both recipes will be the following:

1. Put examples of the function or class into the docstrings for the module, function, method, or class. The exact location is chosen to provide the most clarity to someone reading the code.
2. Run the `doctest` module as a program:

```
python -m doctest Chapter_11/ch11_r01.py
```

Writing examples for stateless functions

This recipe starts by creating the function's docstring, and then adds an example of how the function works:

1. Start the docstring with a summary:

```
def binom(n: int, k: int) -> int:
    """
    Computes the binomial coefficient.
    This shows how many combinations exist of
    *n* things taken in groups of size *k*.
```

2. Include the parameter definitions:

```
    :param n: size of the universe
    :param k: size of each subset
```

3. Include the return value definition:

```
    :returns: the number of combinations
```

4. Mock up an example of using the function at Python's `>>>` prompt:

```
    >>> binom(52, 5)
    2598960
```

5. Close the docstring with the appropriate quotation marks:

```
"""
```

Writing examples for stateful objects

This recipe also starts with writing a docstring. The docstring will show several steps using the stateful object to show the state changes:

1. Write a class-level docstring with a summary. It can help to leave some blank lines in front of the `doctest` example:

```
class Summary:
    """
    Computes summary statistics.
```

2. Extend the class-level docstring with concrete examples. In this case, we'll write two. The first example shows that the `add()` method has no return value but changes the state of the object. The `mean()` method reveals this state, as does the `__str__()` method:

```
    >>> s = Summary()
    >>> s.add(8)
    >>> s.add(9)
    >>> s.add(9)
    >>> round(s.mean, 2)
    8.67
    >>> s.median
    9
    >>> print(str(s))
    mean = 8.67
    median = 9
```

3. Finish with the triple quotes to end the docstring for this class:

```
    """
```

4. Write the method-level docstring with a summary. Here's the `add()` method:

```
    def add(self, value: int) -> None:
        """
        Adds a value to be summarized.

        :param value: Adds a new value to the collection.
        """
        self.counts[value] += 1
```

5. Here's the `mean()` property. A similar string is required for the `median()` property and all other methods of the class:

```
@property
def mean(self) -> float:
    """
    Returns the mean of the collection.
    """
    s0 = sum(f for v, f in self.counts.items())
    s1 = sum(v * f for v, f in self.counts.items())
    return s1 / s0
```

Because this uses floating-point values, we've rounded the result of the mean. Floating-point might not have the exact same text representation on all platforms and an exact test for equality may fail tests unexpectedly because of minor platform number formatting differences.

When we run the `doctest` program, we'll generally get a silent response because the test passed. We can add a `-v` command-line option to see an enumeration of the tests run.

What happens when something doesn't work? Imagine that we changed the expected output to have a wrong answer. When we run `doctest`, we'll see output like this:

```
*********************************************************************
File "Chapter_11/ch11_r01.py", line 80, in ch10_r01.Summary
Failed example:
    s.median
Expected:
    10
Got:
    9
```

This shows where the error is. It shows an expected value from the test example, and the actual answer that failed to match the expected answer. At the end of the entire test run, we might see a summary line like the following:

```
*********************************************************************
1 items had failures:
   1 of   7 in ch11_r01.Summary
13 tests in 13 items.
12 passed and 1 failed.
***Test Failed*** 1 failures.
```

This final summary of the testing shows how many tests were found in the docstring examples, and how many of those tests passed and failed.

How it works...

The `doctest` module includes a main program—as well as several functions—that scan a Python file for examples. The scanning operation looks for blocks of text that have a characteristic pattern of a `>>>` line followed by lines that show the response from the command.

The `doctest` parser creates a small test case object from the prompt line and the block of response text. There are three common cases:

- **No expected response text**: We saw this pattern when we defined the tests for the `add()` method of the `Summary` class.
- **A single line of response text**: This was exemplified by the `binom()` function and the `mean()` method.
- **Multiple lines of response**: Responses are bounded by either the next `>>>` prompt or a blank line. This was exemplified by the `str()` example of the `Summary` class.

The `doctest` module executes each line of code shown with a `>>>` prompt. It compares the actual results with the expected results. Unless special annotations are used, the output text must precisely match the expectation text. In general cases, every space counts.

The simplicity of this testing protocol imposes some software design requirements. Functions and classes must be designed to work from the `>>>` prompt. Because it can become awkward to create very complex objects as part of a docstring example, our class design must be kept simple enough that it can be demonstrated at the interactive prompt. These constraints can be beneficial to keep a design understandable.

The simplicity of the comparison of the results can create some complications. Note, for example, that we rounded the value of the mean to two decimal places. This is because the display of floating-point values may vary slightly from platform to platform.

As a specific example, Python 3.5.1 (on macOS) shows `8.666666666666666` where the old, unsupported, Python 2.6.9 (also on macOS) showed `8.6666666666666661`. The values are equal in many of the decimal digits. We'll address this float comparison issue in detail in the *Handling common doctest issues* recipe later in this chapter.

There's more...

One of the important considerations in test design is identifying edge cases. An **edge case** generally focuses on the limits for which a calculation is designed.

There are, for example, two edge cases for the binomial function:

$$\binom{n}{0} = \binom{n}{n} = 1$$

We can add these to the examples to be sure that our implementation is sound; this leads to a function that looks like the following:

```
def binom(n: int, k: int) -> int:
    """
    Computes the binomial coefficient.
    This shows how many combinations exist of
    *n* things taken in groups of size *k*.

    :param n: size of the universe
    :param k: size of each subset

    :returns: the number of combinations

    >>> binom(52, 5)
    2598960
    >>> binom(52, 0)
    1
    >>> binom(52, 52)
    1
    """
    return factorial(n) // (factorial(k) * factorial(n - k))
```

In some cases, we might need to test values that are outside the valid range of values. These cases aren't really ideal for putting into the docstring, because they can clutter an explanation of what is supposed to happen with details of things that should never normally happen.

In addition to reading docstrings, the tool also looks for test cases in a global variable named `__test__`. This variable must refer to a mapping. The keys to the mapping will be test case names, and the values of the mapping must be `doctest` examples. Generally, each value will need to be a triple-quoted string.

Because the examples in the `__test__` variable are not inside the docstrings, they don't show up when using the built-in `help()` function. Nor do they show up when using other tools to create documentation from source code. This might be a place to put examples of failures or complex exceptions.

We might add something like this:

```
__test__ = {
"GIVEN_binom_WHEN_0_0_THEN_1":
    """
    >>> binom(0, 0)
    1
    """,
"GIVEN_binom_WHEN_52_52_THEN_1":
    """
    >>> binom(52, 52)
    1
    """,
    }
```

In this `__test__` mapping, the keys are descriptions of the test. The values are the expected behavior we'd like to see at the Python `>>>` prompt. Indentation is used to help separate the keys from the values.

These test cases are found by the `doctest` program and included in the overall suite of tests. We can use this for tests that don't need to be as visible as the docstring examples.

See also

- In the *Testing functions that raise exceptions* and *Handling common doctest issues recipes* later in this chapter, we'll look at two additional `doctest` techniques. These are important because exceptions can often include a traceback, which may include object IDs that can vary each time the program is run.

Testing functions that raise exceptions

Good Python includes docstrings inside every module, class, function, and method. One important element of a docstring is an example. This can include examples of common exceptions. There's one complicating factor, however, to including exceptions.

When an exception is raised, the traceback messages created by Python are not completely predictable. The message may include object ID values that are impossible to predict or module line numbers that may vary slightly depending on the context in which the test is executed. The matching rules `doctest` uses to compare expected and actual results aren't appropriate when exceptions are involved.

Our testing frameworks provide ways to be sure the right exceptions are raised by a test case. This will involve using a special `doctest` provision for identifying the traceback messages exceptions produce.

Getting ready

We'll look at a small function definition as well as a class definition. Each of these will include docstrings that include examples that can be used as formal tests.

Here's a function from the *Using docstrings for testing* recipe, shown earlier in this chapter, that computes the binomial coefficient of two numbers. It shows the number of combinations of *n* things taken in groups of *k*. For example, it shows how many ways a 52-card deck can be dealt into 5-card hands. Here's the formal definition:

$$\binom{n}{k} = \frac{n!}{k! \times (n-k)!}$$

This defines a small Python function that we can write like this:

```
def binom(n: int, k: int) -> int:
    """
    Computes the binomial coefficient.
    This shows how many combinations of
    *n* things taken in groups of size *k*.

    :param n: size of the universe
    :param k: size of each subset

    :returns: the number of combinations

    >>> binom(52, 5)
    2598960
    >>> binom(52, 0)
    1
    >>> binom(52, 52)
    1
    """
    return factorial(n) // (factorial(k) * factorial(n - k))
```

This function does a simple calculation and returns a value. We'd like to include some additional test cases in the `__test__` variable to show what this does when given values outside the expected ranges.

How to do it...

We start by running the `binom` function we defined previously:

1. Run the function at the interactive Python prompt to collect the actual exception details.
2. Create a global `__test__` variable at the end of the module. One approach is to build the mapping from all global variables with names that start with `test_`:

```
__test__ = {
    n: v
    for n, v in locals().items()
    if n.startswith("test_")
}
```

3. Define each test case as a global variable with a block of text containing the `doctest` example. These must come before the final creation of the `__test__` mapping. We've included a note about the test as well as the data copied and pasted from interactive Python:

```
test_GIVEN_n_5_k_52_THEN_ValueError = """

GIVEN n=5, k=52 WHEN binom(n, k) THEN exception

>>> binom(52, -5)
Traceback (most recent call last):
  File "/Users/slott/miniconda3/envs/cookbook/lib/python3.8/
doctest.py", line 1328, in __run
    compileflags, 1), test.globs)
  File "<doctest __main__.__test__.GIVEN_binom_WHEN_wrong_
relationship_THEN_ValueError[0]>", line 1, in <module>
    binom(5, 52)
  File "/Users/slott/Documents/Python/Python Cookbook 2e/Code/
ch11_r01.py", line 24, in binom
    return factorial(n) // (factorial(k) * factorial(n-k))
ValueError: factorial() not defined for negative values
"""
```

4. Change the function call in the example to include a `doctest` directive comment, `IGNORE_EXCEPTION_DETAIL`. The three lines that start with `File...` will be ignored. The `ValueError:` line will be checked to be sure that the test produces the expected exception. The `>>> binom(5, 52)` line in the example must be changed to this:

```
>>> binom(5, 52)  # doctest: +IGNORE_EXCEPTION_DETAIL
```

We can now use a command like this to test the entire module's features:

```
python -m doctest -v Chapter_11/ch11_r01.py
```

Because each test is a separate global variable, we can easily add test scenarios. All of the names starting with `test_` will become part of the final `__test__` mapping that's used by `doctest`.

How it works...

The `doctest` parser has several directives that can be used to modify the testing behavior. The directives are included as special comments with the line of code that performs the test action.

We have two ways to handle tests that include an exception:

- We can use a `# doctest: +IGNORE_EXCEPTION_DETAIL` directive and provide a full traceback error message. This was shown in the recipe. The details of the traceback are ignored, and only the final exception line is matched against the expected value. This makes it very easy to copy an actual error and paste it into the documentation.
- We can use a `# doctest: +ELLIPSIS` directive and replace parts of the traceback message with `...`. This, too, allows an expected output to elide details and focus on the last line that has the actual error. This requires manual editing, a way to introduce problems into the test case.

For this second kind of exception example, we might include a test case like this:

```
test_GIVEN_negative_THEN_ValueError = """
GIVEN n=52, k=-5 WHEN binom(n, k) THEN exception
>>> binom(52, -5)  # doctest: +ELLIPSIS
Traceback (most recent call last):
...
ValueError: factorial() not defined for negative values
"""
```

The test case uses the `+ELLIPSIS` directive. The details of the error traceback have had irrelevant material replaced with `...`. The relevant material has been left intact and the actual exception message must match the expected exception message precisely.

This requires manual editing of the traceback message. A mistake in the editing can lead to a test failing not because the code is broken, but because the traceback message was edited incorrectly.

These explicit directives help make it perfectly clear what our intent is. Internally, `doctest` can ignore everything between the first `Traceback...` line and the final line with the name of the exception. It's often helpful to people reading examples to be explicit by using directives.

There's more...

There are several more comparison directives that can be provided to individual tests:

- `+ELLIPSIS`: This allows an expected result to be generalized by replacing details with `...`.
- `+IGNORE_EXCEPTION_DETAIL`: This allows an expected value to include a complete traceback message. The bulk of the traceback will be ignored, and only the final exception line is checked.
- `+NORMALIZE_WHITESPACE`: In some cases, the expected value might be wrapped onto multiple lines to make it easier to read. Or, it might have spacing that varies slightly from standard Python values. Using this directive allows some flexibility in the whitespace for the expected value.
- `+SKIP`: The test is skipped. This is sometimes done for tests that are designed for a future release. Tests may be included prior to the feature being completed. The test can be left in place for future development work, but skipped in order to release a version on time.
- `+DONT_ACCEPT_TRUE_FOR_1`: This covers a special case that was common in Python 2. Before `True` and `False` were added to the language, values `1` and `0` were used instead. The `doctest` algorithm for comparing expected results to actual results can honor this older scheme by matching `True` nd `1`.
- `+DONT_ACCEPT_BLANKLINE`: Normally, a blank line ends an example. In the case where the example output includes a blank line, the expected results must use the special syntax `<blankline>`. Using this shows where a blank line is expected, and the example doesn't end at this blank line. When writing a test for the `doctest` module itself, the expected output will actually include the characters `<blankline>`. Outside `doctest`'s own internal tests, this directive should not be used.

See also

- See the *Using docstrings for testing* recipe earlier in this chapter. This recipe shows the basics of `doctest`.
- See the *Handling common doctest issues* recipe later in this chapter. This shows other special cases that require `doctest` directives.

Handling common doctest issues

Good Python includes docstrings inside every module, class, function, and method. One important element of a docstring is an example. While `doctest` can make the example into a unit test case, the literal matching of the expected text output against the actual text can cause problems. There are some Python objects that do not have a consistent text representation.

For example, object hash values are randomized. This often results in the order of elements in a set collection being unpredictable. We have several choices for creating test case example output:

- Write tests that can tolerate randomization (often by converting to a sorted structure)
- Stipulate a value for the `PYTHONHASHSEED` environment variable
- Require that Python be run with the `-R` option to disable hash randomization entirely

There are several other considerations beyond simple variability in the location of keys or items in a set. Here are some other concerns:

- The `id()` and `repr()` functions may expose an internal object ID. No guarantees can be made about these values
- Floating-point values may vary across platforms
- The current date and time cannot meaningfully be used in a test case
- Random numbers using the default seed are difficult to predict
- OS resources may not exist, or may not be in the proper state

`doctest` examples require an exact match with the text. This means our test cases must avoid unpredictable results stemming from hash randomization or floating-point implementation details.

Getting ready

We'll look at three separate versions of this recipe. The first will include a function where the output includes the contents of a set. Because the order of items in a set can vary, this isn't as easy to test as we'd like. There are two solutions to this kind of problem: we can make our software more testable by sorting the set, or we can make the test more flexible by eliding some details of the results.

Here's a definition of a `Row` object that's read by the `raw_reader()` function. The function creates a set of expected column names from `Row._fields`. If the actual header field names don't match the expected field names, an exception is raised, and the exception contains the value of the set object in the `expected` variable:

```
import csv
from typing import Iterator, NamedTuple, TextIO

class Row(NamedTuple):
    date: str
    lat: str
    lon: str
    time: str

def raw_reader(data_file: TextIO) -> Iterator[Row]:
    """
    Read from a given file if the data has columns that match Row's
definition.
    """
    row_field_names = set(Row._fields)
    data_reader = csv.DictReader(data_file)
    reader_field_names = set(
        cast(Sequence[str], data_reader.fieldnames))
    if not (reader_field_names >= row_field_names):
        raise ValueError(f"Expected {row_field_names}")
    for row in data_reader:
        yield Row(**{k: row[k] for k in row_field_names})
```

Testing the preceding function is difficult because the exception exposes the value of a set, `row_field_names`, and the order of items within a set is unpredictable.

The second example will be a class that doesn't have a `__repr__()` definition. The default definition of the `__repr__()` method will expose an internal object ID. Since these vary, the test results will vary. There are two solutions here also: we can change the class definition to provide a more predictable string output from `__repr__()` or we can change the test to ignore the details:

```
class Point:
    def __init__(self, lat: float, lon: float) -> None:
        self.lat = lat
        self.lon = lon

    @property
    def text(self):
        ns_hemisphere = "S" if self.lat < 0 else "N"
        ew_hemisphere = "W" if self.lon < 0 else "E"
```

```
        lat_deg, lat_ms = divmod(abs(self.lat), 1.0)
        lon_deg, lon_ms = divmod(abs(self.lon), 1.0)
        return (
            f"{lat_deg:02.0f}°{lat_ms*60:4.3f}'{ns_hemisphere} "
            f"{lon_deg:03.0f}°{lon_ms*60:4.3f}'{ew_hemisphere}"
        )
```

We'll also look at a real-valued function so that we can work with floating-point values:

$$\phi(n) = \frac{1}{2}\left[1 + \text{erf}\left(\frac{n}{\sqrt{2}}\right)\right]$$

This function is the cumulative probability density function for standard z-scores. After normalizing a variable, the mean of the z-score values for that variable will be zero, and the standard deviation will be one. See the *Creating a partial function* recipe in *Chapter 9, Functional Programming Features* (link provided in *Preface*), for more information on the idea of normalized scores.

This function, $\phi(n)$, tells us what fraction of the population is below a given z-score. For example, $\phi(0) = 0.5$: half the population has a z-score below zero.

Here's the Python implementation:

```
from math import sqrt, pi, exp, erf

def phi(n: float) -> float:
    return (1 + erf(n / sqrt(2))) / 2


def frequency(n: float) -> float:
    return phi(n) - phi(-n)
```

These two functions involve some rather complicated numeric processing. The unit tests have to reflect the floating-point precision issues.

How to do it...

We'll look at set ordering and object representation in three mini-recipes. We'll start with set ordering, then look at object IDs, and finally, floating-point values.

Writing doctest examples with unpredictable set ordering

We'll start by importing the libraries we need.

1. Import the necessary libraries and define the `raw_reader()` function, as shown earlier.
2. Create a "happy path" `doctest` example that shows how the function is expected to work. Rather than creating a file for this kind of test, we can use an instance of the `StringIO` class from the `io` package. We can show the expected behavior with a file that has the expected column names:

```
>>> from io import StringIO
>>> mock_good_file = StringIO('''lat,lon,date,time
... 32.8321,-79.9338,2012-11-27,09:15:00
... ''')
>>> good_row_iter = iter(raw_reader(mock_good_file))
>>> next(good_row_iter)
Row(date='2012-11-27', lat='32.8321', lon='-79.9338',
time='09:15:00')
```

3. Create a `doctest` that shows the exception raised when the function is provided with improper data. Again, we'll create a file-like object using a `StringIO` object:

```
>>> from io import StringIO
>>> mock_bad_file = StringIO('''lat,lon,date-time,notes
... 32.8321,-79.9338,2012-11-27T09:15:00,Cooper River"
... ''')
>>> bad_row_iter = iter(raw_reader(mock_bad_file))
>>> next(bad_row_iter)
Traceback (most recent call last):
  File "/Applications/PyCharm CE.app/Contents/plugins/python-ce/
helpers/pycharm/docrunner.py", line 138, in __run
    exec(compile(example.source, filename, "single",
  File "<doctest ch11_r03.raw_reader[6]>", line 1, in <module>
    next(bad_row_iter)
  File "Chapter_11/ch11_r03.py", line 74, in raw_reader
    raise ValueError(f"Expected {expected}")
ValueError: Expected {'lat', 'lon', 'time', 'date'}
```

4. This test has a problem. The `ValueError` results will tend to be inconsistent. One alternative for fixing this is to change the function to raise `ValueError(f"Expected {sorted(expected)}")`. This imposes a known order on the items by creating a sorted list.

5. An alternative is to change the test to use a `# doctest: +ELLIPSIS` directive. This means changing the `>>> next(bad_row_iter)` line in the test, and using ellipsis on the exception displayed in the expected output to look like this:

```
>>> from io import StringIO
>>> mock_bad_file = StringIO('''lat,lon,date-time,notes
... 32.8321,-79.9338,2012-11-27T09:15:00,Cooper River"
... ''')
>>> bad_row_iter = iter(raw_reader(mock_bad_file))
>>> next(bad_row_iter)  # doctest: +ELLIPSIS
Traceback (most recent call last):
  File "/Applications/PyCharm CE.app/Contents/plugins/python-ce/
helpers/pycharm/docrunner.py", line 138, in __run
    exec(compile(example.source, filename, "single",
  File "<doctest ch11_r03.raw_reader[6]>", line 1, in <module>
    next(bad_row_iter)
  File "Chapter_11/ch11_r03.py", line 74, in raw_reader
    raise ValueError(f"Expected {expected}")
ValueError: Expected {...}
```

When writing a `doctest`, we must impose an order on the items in the set, or we must tolerate unpredictable item ordering in the displayed value of the set. In this case, we used `doctest: +ELLIPSIS`. The expected output of `ValueError: Expected {...}` omitted the unpredictable details of the error message.

Writing doctest examples with object IDs

Ideally, our applications won't display object IDs. These are highly variable and essentially impossible to predict. In some cases, we want to test a piece of code that may involve displaying an object ID:

1. Import the necessary libraries and define the `Point` class, as shown earlier.

2. Define a "happy path" `doctest` scenario to show that the class performs its essential methods correctly. In this case, we'll create a `Point` instance and use the `text` property to see a representation of the `Point`:

```
>>> Point(36.8439, -76.2936).text
'36°50.634′N 076°17.616′W'
```

3. When we define a test that displays the object's representation string, the test will include results that include the unpredictable object ID. The `doctest` might look like the following:

```
>>> Point(36.8439, -76.2936)
<ch11_r03.Point object at 0x107910610>
```

4. We need to change the test by using a `# doctest: +ELLIPSIS` directive. This means changing the `>>> Point(36.8439, -76.2936)` line in the test, and using an ellipsis on the exception displayed in the expected output to look like this:

```
>>> Point(36.8439, -76.2936)  # doctest: +ELLIPSIS
<ch11_r03.Point object at ...>
```

Either we must define `__repr__()` or avoid tests where `__repr__()` may be used. Or, we must tolerate unpredictable IDs in the displayed value. In this case, we used `# doctest: +ELLIPSIS` to change the expected output to `<ch11_r03.Point object at ...>`, which elided the object ID from the expected output.

The `PYTHONPATH` environment variable value can have an impact on the class names that are displayed. In order to be sure this test works in all contexts, it's helpful to include an ellipsis before the module name as well:

```
>>> Point(36.8439, -76.2936)  #doctest: +ELLIPSIS
<...ch11_r03.Point object at ...>
```

The ellipsis in front of the module name allows some changes in the test context. For example, it allows the same unit test to be run from an IDE or after the module has been installed in a virtual environment.

Writing doctest examples for floating-point values

We have two choices when working with float values. We can round the values to a certain number of decimal places. An alternative is to use the `math.isclose()` function. We'll show both:

1. Import the necessary libraries and define the `phi()` and `frequency()` functions as shown previously.
2. For each example, include an explicit use of `round()`:

```
>>> round(phi(0), 3)
0.5
>>> round(phi(-1), 3)
0.159
>>> round(phi(+1), 3)
0.841
```

3. An alternative is to use the `isclose()` function from the `math` module:

```
>>> from math import isclose
>>> isclose(phi(0), 0.5)
True
>>> isclose(phi(1), 0.8413, rel_tol=.0001)
True
>>> isclose(phi(2), 0.9772, rel_tol=1e-4)
```

Because float values can't be compared exactly, it's best to display values that have been rounded to an appropriate number of decimal places. It's sometimes nicer for readers of examples to use `round()` because it may be slightly easier to visualize how the function works, compared to the `isclose` alternative.

How it works...

Because of hash randomization, the hash keys used for sets are unpredictable. This is an important security feature, used to defeat a subtle denial-of-service attack. For details, see `http://www.ocert.org/advisories/ocert-2011-003.html`.

Since Python 3.7, dictionary keys are guaranteed to be kept in insertion order. This means that an algorithm that builds a dictionary will provide a consistent sequence of key values even if the internal hashing used for key lookup is randomized.

The same ordering guarantee is not made for sets. Interestingly, sets of integers tend to have a consistent ordering because of the way hash values are computed for numbers. Sets of other types of objects, however, will not show consistent ordering of items.

When confronted with unpredictable results like set ordering or internal object identification revealed by `__repr__()`, we have a testability issue. We can either change the software to be more testable, or we can change the test to tolerate some unpredictability.

Most floating-point implementations are reasonably consistent. However, there are few formal guarantees about the last few bits of any given floating-point number. Rather than trusting that all of the bits have exactly the right value, it's often a good practice to round the value to a precision consistent with other values in the problem domain.

Being tolerant of unpredictability can be taken too far, allowing the test to tolerate bugs. In general, we often need to move beyond the capabilities of `doctest`. We should use `doctest` to demonstrate the happy path features, but edge cases and exceptions may be better handled with `pytest` cases.

There's more...

We can run the tests using this command-line option too:

```
python3 -R -m doctest Chapter_11/ch11_r03.py
```

This will turn off hash randomization while running `doctest` on a specific file, `ch11_r03.py`.

The `tox` tool will report the value of the `PYTHONHASHSEED` environment variable used when the test was run. We often see something like this in the output:

```
python run-test-pre: PYTHONHASHSEED='803623355'
```

(Your output may be different because the seed value is random.) This line of output provides the specific hash seed value used for randomization. We can set this environment value when running a test. Forcing a specific hash seed value will lead to consistent ordering of items in sets.

See also

- The *Testing things that involve dates or times* recipe, in particular, the `now()` method of datetime requires some care.
- The *Testing things that involve randomness* recipe shows how to test processing that involves `random`.
- This recipe focused on set ordering, object ID, and floating-point issues with `doctest` expected results. We'll look at `datetime` and `random` in the *Testing things that involve dates or times* and *Testing things that involve randomness* recipes later in this chapter.
- We'll look at how to work with external resources in the *Mocking external resources* recipe later in this chapter.

Unit testing with the unittest module

The `unittest` module allows us to step beyond the examples used by `doctest`. Each test case can have one more scenario built as a subclass of the `unittest.TestCase` class. These use result checks that are more sophisticated than the literal text matching used by the `doctest` tool.

The `unittest` module also allows us to package tests outside docstrings. This can be helpful for tests for edge cases that might be too detailed to be helpful documentation. Often, `doctest` cases focus on the **happy path**—the most common use cases, where everything works as expected. We can use the `unittest` module to define test cases that are both on as well as off the happy path.

This recipe will show how we can use the `unittest` module to create more sophisticated tests. It will step beyond simple text comparison to use the more sophisticated assertion methods of the `unittest.TestCase` class.

Getting ready

It's sometimes helpful to summarize a test following ideas behind the Gherkin language. In this test specification language, each scenario is described by *GIVEN-WHEN-THEN* steps. For this case, we have a scenario like this:

```
Scenario: Summary object can add values and compute statistics.

  Given a Summary object
  And numbers in the range 0 to 1000 (inclusive) shuffled randomly
  When all numbers are added to the Summary object
  Then the mean is 500
  And the median is 500
```

The `unittest.TestCase` class doesn't precisely follow this three-part structure. A `TestCase` generally has these two parts:

- A `setUp()` method must implement the *Given* steps of the test case. It can also handle the *When* steps. This is rare but can be helpful in cases where the *When* steps are very closely bound to the *Given* steps.
- A `runTest()` method must handle the *Then* steps to confirm the results using a number of assertion methods to confirm the actual results match the expected results. Generally, it will also handle the *When* steps.

An optional `tearDown()` method is available for those tests that need to perform some cleanup of left-over resources. This is outside the test's essential scenario specification.

The choice of where to implement the *When* steps is tied to the question of reuse. For example, a class or function may have a number of methods to take different actions or make a number of state changes. In this case, it makes sense to pair each *When* step with a distinct *Then* step to confirm correct operation. A `runTest()` method can implement both *When* and *Then* steps. A number of subclasses can share the common `setUp()` method.

As another example, a class hierarchy may offer a number of alternative implementations for the same algorithm. In this case, the *Then* step confirmation of correct behavior is in the `runTest()` method. Each alternative implementation has a distinct subclass with a unique `setup()` method for the *Given* and *When* steps.

We'll create some tests for a class that is designed to compute some basic descriptive statistics. We'd like to provide sample data that's larger than anything we'd ever choose to enter as `doctest` examples. We'd like to use thousands of data points rather than two or three.

Here's an outline of the class definition that we'd like to test. We'll only provide the methods and some summaries, omitting implementation details. The bulk of the code was shown in the *Using docstrings for testing* recipe earlier in this chapter:

```
import collections
from statistics import median
from typing import Counter


class Summary:

    def __init__(self) -> None: ...

    def __str__(self) -> str: ...

    def add(self, value: int) -> None: ...

    @property
    def mean(self) -> float: ...

    @property
    def median(self) -> float: ...

    @property
    def count(self) -> int: ...

    @property
    def mode(self) -> List[Tuple[int, int]]: ...
```

Because we're not looking at the implementation details, we can think of this as opaque-box testing; the implementation details are not known to the tester. To emphasize that, we replaced code with ... placeholders as if this was a type stub definition.

We'd like to be sure that when we use thousands of samples, the class performs correctly. We'd also like to ensure that it works quickly; we'll use this as part of an overall performance test, as well as a unit test.

How to do it...

We'll need to create a test module and a subclass of `unittest.TestCase` in that module. It's common to keep the tests separate from the module's code:

1. Create a file with a name related to the module under test. If the module was named `summary.py`, then a good name for a test module would be `test_summary.py`. Using the "`test_`" prefix makes the test easier to find by tools like `pytest`.
2. We'll use the `unittest` module for creating test classes. We'll also be using the `random` module to scramble the input data:

    ```
    import unittest
    import random
    ```

3. Import the module under test:

    ```
    from Chapter_11.ch11_r01 import Summary
    ```

4. Create a subclass of `unittest.TestCase`. Provide this class with a name that shows the intent of the test. If we try to adopt a name based on the *Given*, *When*, and *Then* steps, the names could become very long. Since we rely on `unittest` to discover all subclasses of `TestCase`, we don't have to type this class name more than once, and the length isn't a real problem:

    ```
    class GIVEN_data_WHEN_1k_samples_THEN_mean_median(
        unittest.TestCase):
    ```

5. Define a `setUp()` method in this class that handles the *Given* step of the test. We've created a collection of `1,001` samples ranging in value from `0` to `1,000`. The mean is `500` exactly, and so is the median. We've shuffled the data into a random order. This creates a context for the test scenario:

    ```
        def setUp(self):
            self.summary = Summary()
            self.data = list(range(1001))
            random.shuffle(self.data)
    ```

6. Define a `runTest()` method that handles the *When* step of the test. This performs the state changes:

    ```
        def runTest(self):
            for sample in self.data:
                self.summary.add(sample)
    ```

7. Add assertions to implement the *Then* steps of the test. This confirms that the state changes worked properly:

    ```
            self.assertEqual(500, self.summary.mean)
            self.assertEqual(500, self.summary.median)
    ```

8. To make it very easy to run, we might want to add a main program section. With this, the test can be run at the OS command prompt by running the test module itself:

```
if __name__ == "__main__":
    unittest.main()
```

If our test module is called `test_summary.py`, we can also use this command to find `unittest.TestCase` classes in a module and run them:

```
python -m unittest tests/test_summary.py
```

We can also run tests with the `pytest` tool using the following command:

```
python -m pytest tests/test_summary.py
```

These commands will find all the test cases in the given file. The resulting collection of cases will be executed. If all of the assertions pass, then the test suite will pass and the test run will be successful overall.

How it works...

We're using several parts of the `unittest` module:

- The `TestCase` class is used to define one test case. The class can have a `setUp()` method to create the unit and possibly the request. The class must have at least a `runTest()` to make a request of the unit and check the response.
- The `unittest.main()` function does several things:
  - It creates an empty `TestSuite` that will contain all the `TestCase` objects.
  - It uses a default loader to examine a module and find all of the `TestCase` instances in the current module. These classes are loaded into the `TestSuite` object.
  - It then runs the `TestSuite` object and displays a summary of the results.

When we run this module, we'll see output that looks like this:

```
----------------------------------------------------------------------
Ran 1 test in 0.005s


OK
```

As each test is passed, a `.` is displayed. This shows that the test suite is making progress. The summary shows the number of tests run and the time. If there are failures or exceptions, the counts shown at the end will reflect these.

Finally, there's a summary line of `OK` to show – in this example – all the tests passed.

If we change the test slightly to be sure that it fails, we'll see the following output:

```
F
======================================================================
FAIL: test_mean (Chapter_11.test_ch11_r04.GIVEN_Summary_WHEN_1k_samples_
THEN_mean_median)
----------------------------------------------------------------------
Traceback (most recent call last):
  File "Chapter_11/ch11_r04.py", line 22, in runTest
    self.assertEqual(501, self.summary.mean)
AssertionError: 501 != 500.0
----------------------------------------------------------------------
Ran 1 test in 0.004s
FAILED (failures=1)
```

Instead of a `.` for a passing test, a failing test displays an `F`. This is followed by the traceback from the assertion that failed. To force the test to fail, we changed the expected mean to `501`, which is not the computed mean value of `500.0`.

There's a final summary of `FAILED`. This includes `(failures=1)` to show the reason why the suite as a whole is a failure.

There's more...

In this example, we have two *Then* steps inside the `runTest()` method. If one fails, the test stops as a failure, and the other step is not exercised.

This is a weakness in the design of this test. If the first assertion fails, we may not get all of the diagnostic information we might want. We should avoid having a sequence of otherwise independent assertions in the `runTest()` method. When multiple assertions can be true or false independently, we can break these into multiple, separate `TestCase` instances. Each independent failure may provide more complete diagnostic information.

In some cases, a test case may involve multiple assertions with a clear dependency. When one assertion fails, the remaining assertions are expected to fail. In this case, the first failure generally provides all the diagnostic information that's required.

These two scenarios suggest that clustering the test assertions is a design trade-off between simplicity and diagnostic detail. There's no single, best approach. We want the test case failures to provide help in locating the root cause bug.

When we want more diagnostic details, we have two general choices:

- Use multiple test methods instead of `runTest()`. Instead of a single method, we can create multiple methods with names that start with `test_`. The default implementation of the test loader will execute the `setUp()` method and each separate `test_` method when there is no overall `runTest()` method. This is often the simplest way to group a number of related tests together.
- Use multiple subclasses of the `testcase` subclass, each with a separate *Then* step. Since `setUp()` is common, this can be inherited.

Following the first alternative, the test class would look like this:

```
class GIVEN_Summary_WHEN_1k_samples_THEN_mean_median(
        unittest.TestCase):
    def setUp(self):
        self.summary = Summary()
        self.data = list(range(1001))
        random.shuffle(self.data)
        for sample in self.data:
            self.summary.add(sample)

    def test_mean(self):
        self.assertEqual(500, self.summary.mean)

    def test_median(self):
        self.assertEqual(500, self.summary.median)
```

We've refactored the `setUp()` method to include the *Given* and *When* steps of the test. The two independent *Then* steps are refactored into their own separate `test_mean()` and `test_median()` methods. Because there is no `runTest()` method, there are two separate test methods for separate *Then* steps.

Since each test is run separately, we'll see separate error reports for problems with computing mean or computing median.

Some other assertions

The `TestCase` class defines numerous assertions that can be used as part of the *Then* steps; here are a few of the most commonly used:

- `assertEqual()` and `assertNotEqual()` compare actual and expected values using the default `==` operator.
- `assertTrue()` and `assertFalse()` require a single Boolean expression.

- `assertIs()` and `assertIsNot()` use the `is` comparison to determine whether the two arguments are references to the same object.
- `assertIsNone()` and `assertIsNotNone()` use `is` to compare a given value with `None`.
- `assertIn()` and `assertNotIn()` use the `in` operator to see if an item exists in a given collection.
- `assertIsInstance()` and `assertNotIsInstance()` use the `isinstance()` function to determine whether a given value is a member of a given class (or tuple of classes).
- `assertAlmostEqual()` and `assertNotAlmostEqual()` round the given values to seven decimal places to see whether most of the digits are equal.
- `assertGreater()`, `assertGreateEqual()`, `assertLess()`, and `assertLessEqual()` all implement the comparison operations between the two argument values.
- `assertRegex()` and `assertNotRegex()` compare a given string using a regular expression. This uses the `search()` method of the regular expression to match the string.
- `assertCountEqual()` compares two sequences to see whether they have the same elements, irrespective of order. This can be handy for comparing dictionary keys and sets too.

There are still more assertion methods available in the `TestCase` class. A number of them provide ways to detect exceptions, warnings, and log messages. Another group provides more type-specific comparison capabilities. This large number of specialized methods is one reason why the `pytest` tool is used as an alternative to the `unittest` framework.

For example, the mode feature of the `Summary` class produces a list. We can use a specific `assertListEqual()` assertion to compare the results:

```
class GIVEN_Summary_WHEN_1k_samples_THEN_mode(unittest.TestCase):
    def setUp(self):
        self.summary = Summary()
        self.data = [500] * 97
        # Build 903 elements: each value of n occurs n times.
        for i in range(1, 43):
            self.data += [i] * i
        random.shuffle(self.data)
        for sample in self.data:
            self.summary.add(sample)

    def test_mode(self):
        top_3 = self.summary.mode[:3]
```

```
        self.assertListEqual(
            [(500, 97), (42, 42), (41, 41)], top_3)
```

First, we built a collection of `1,000` values. Of those, `97` are copies of the number `500`. The remaining `903` elements are copies of numbers between `1` and `42`. These numbers have a simple rule—the frequency is the value. This rule makes it easier to confirm the results.

The `setUp()` method shuffled the data into a random order. Then the `Summary` object was built using the `add()` method.

We used a `test_mode()` method. This allows expansion to include other *Then* steps in this test. In this case, we examined the first three values from the mode to be sure it had the expected distribution of values. `assertListEqual()` compares two `list` objects; if either argument is not a list, we'll get a more specific error message showing that the argument wasn't of the expected type.

A separate tests directory

In larger projects, it's common practice to sequester the test files into a separate directory, often called `tests`. When this is done, we can rely on the discovery application that's part of the `unittest` framework and the `pytest` tool. Both applications can search all of the files of a given directory for test files. Generally, these will be files with names that match the pattern `test*.py`. If we use a simple, consistent name for all test modules, then they can be located and run with a simple command.

The `unittest` loader will search each module in the directory for all classes that are derived from the `TestCase` class. This collection of classes within the larger collection of modules becomes the complete `TestSuite`. We can do this with the following command:

```
$ python -m unittest discover -s tests
```

This will locate all test cases in all test modules in the `tests` directory of a project.

See also

- We'll combine `unittest` and `doctest` in the *Combining unittest and doctest tests* recipe next in this chapter. We'll look at mocking external objects in the *Mocking external resources* recipe later in this chapter.
- The *Unit testing with the pytest module* recipe later in this chapter covers the same test case from the perspective of the `pytest` module.

Combining unittest and doctest tests

In some cases, we'll want to combine `unittest` and `doctest` test cases. For examples of using the `doctest` tool, see the *Using docstrings for testing* recipe earlier in this chapter. For examples of using the `unittest` tool, see the *Unit testing with the unittest module* recipe, earlier in this chapter.

The `doctest` examples are an essential element of the documentation strings on modules, classes, methods, and functions. The `unittest` cases will often be in a separate `tests` directory in files with names that match the pattern `test_*.py`.

In this recipe, we'll look at ways to combine a variety of tests into one tidy package.

Getting ready

We'll refer back to the example from the *Using docstrings for testing* recipe earlier in this chapter. This recipe created tests for a class, `Summary`, that does some statistical calculations. In that recipe, we included examples in the docstrings.

The class started with a docstring like this:

```
class Summary:
    """
    Computes summary statistics.

    >>> s = Summary()
    >>> s.add(8)
    >>> s.add(9)
    >>> s.add(9)
    >>> round(s.mean, 2)
    8.67
    >>> s.median
    9
    >>> print(str(s))
    mean = 8.67
    median = 9
    """
```

The methods have been omitted here so that we can focus on the example provided in the class docstring.

In the *Unit testing with the unittest module* recipe earlier in this chapter, we wrote some `unittest.TestCase` classes to provide additional tests for this class. We created test class definitions like this:

```
class GIVEN_Summary_WHEN_1k_samples_THEN_mean_median(
        unittest.TestCase):
    def setUp(self):
        self.summary = Summary()
        self.data = list(range(1001))
        random.shuffle(self.data)
        for sample in self.data:
            self.summary.add(sample)

    def test_mean(self):
        self.assertEqual(500, self.summary.mean)

    def test_median(self):
        self.assertEqual(500, self.summary.median)
```

This test creates a `Summary` object; this is the implementation of the *Given* step. It then adds a number of values to that `Summary` object. This is the *When* step of the test. The two `test_` methods implement two *Then* steps of this test.

It's common to see a project folder structure that looks like this:

```
project-name/
    statstools/
        summary.py
    tests/
        test_summary.py
    README.rst
    requirements.txt
    tox.ini
```

We have a top-level folder, `project-name`, that matches the project name in the source code repository.

Within the top-level directory, we would have some overheads that are common to large Python projects. This would include files such as `README.rst` with a description of the project, `requirements.txt`, which can be used with `pip` to install extra packages, and perhaps `tox.ini` to automate testing.

The directory `statstools` contains a module file, `summary.py`. This has a module that provides interesting and useful features. This module has docstring comments scattered around the code. (Sometimes this directory is called `src`.)

The directory `tests` should contain all the module files with tests. For example, the file `tests/test_summary.py` has the `unittest` test cases in it. We've chosen the directory name `tests` and a module named `test_*.py` so that they fit well with automated test discovery.

We need to combine all of the tests into a single, comprehensive test suite. The example we'll show uses `ch11_r01` instead of some cooler name such as `summary`. Ideally, a module should have a memorable, meaningful name. The book content is quite large, and the names are designed to match the overall chapter and recipe outline.

How to do it...

To combine unittests and doctests we'll start with an existing test module, and add a `load_tests()` function to include the relevant doctests with the existing unittest test cases. The name must be `load_tests()` to be sure the `unittest` loader will use it:

1. Locate the `unittest` file and the module being tested; they should have similar names. For this example, the code available for this book has a module of `ch11_r01.py` and tests in `test_ch11_r04.py`. These example names don't match very well. In most cases, they can have names that are more precise parallels. To use `doctest` tests, import the `doctest` module. We'll be combining `doctest` examples with `TestCase` classes to create a comprehensive test suite. We'll also need the `random` module so we can control the random seeds in use:

   ```
   import doctest
   import unittest
   import random
   ```

2. Import the module that contains the module with strings that have `doctest` examples in them:

   ```
   import Chapter_11.ch11_r01
   ```

3. To implement the `load_tests` protocol, include a `load_tests()` function in the test module. We'll combine the standard tests, automatically discovered by `unittest` with the additional tests found by the `doctest` module:

   ```
   def load_tests(loader, standard_tests, attern):
       dt = doctest.DocTestSuite(Chapter_11.ch11_r01)
       standard_tests.addTests(dt)
       return standard_tests
   ```

The `loader` argument to the `load_test()` function is the test case loader currently being used; this is generally ignored. The `standard_tests` value will be all of the tests loaded by default. Generally, this is the suite of all subclasses of `TestCase`. The function updates this object with the additional tests. The `pattern` value was the value provided to the `loader` to locate tests; this is also ignored.

When we run this from the OS command prompt, we see the following:

```
(cookbook) slott@MacBookPro-SLott Modern-Python-Cookbook-Second-Edition %
PYTHONPATH=. python -m unittest -v Chapter_11/test_ch11_r04.py
test_mean (Chapter_11.test_ch11_r04.GIVEN_Summary_WHEN_1k_samples_THEN_
mean_median) ... ok
test_median (Chapter_11.test_ch11_r04.GIVEN_Summary_WHEN_1k_samples_THEN_
mean_median) ... ok
test_mode (Chapter_11.test_ch11_r04.GIVEN_Summary_WHEN_1k_samples_THEN_
mode) ... ok
runTest (Chapter_11.test_ch11_r04.GIVEN_data_WHEN_1k_samples_THEN_mean_
median) ... ok
Summary (Chapter_11.ch11_r01)
Doctest: Chapter_11.ch11_r01.Summary ... ok
test_GIVEN_n_5_k_52_THEN_ValueError (Chapter_11.ch11_r01.__test__)
Doctest: Chapter_11.ch11_r01.__test__.test_GIVEN_n_5_k_52_THEN_ValueError
... ok
test_GIVEN_negative_THEN_ValueError (Chapter_11.ch11_r01.__test__)
Doctest: Chapter_11.ch11_r01.__test__.test_GIVEN_negative_THEN_ValueError
... ok
test_GIVEN_str_THEN_TypeError (Chapter_11.ch11_r01.__test__)
Doctest: Chapter_11.ch11_r01.__test__.test_GIVEN_str_THEN_TypeError ...
ok
binom (Chapter_11.ch11_r01)
Doctest: Chapter_11.ch11_r01.binom ... ok

----------------------------------------------------------------------
Ran 9 tests in 0.032s

OK
```

This shows us that the `unittest` test cases were included as well as `doctest` test cases.

How it works...

The `unittest.main()` application uses a test loader to find all of the relevant test cases. The loader is designed to find all classes that extend `TestCase`. We can supplement the standard tests with tests created by the `doctest` module. This is implemented by including a `load_tests()` function. This name is used to locate additional tests. The `load_tests()` name (with all three parameters) is required to implement this feature.

Generally, we can import a module under test and use the `DocTestSuite` to build a test suite from the imported module. We can, of course, import other modules or even scan the `README.rst` documentation for more examples to test.

There's more...

In some cases, a module may be quite complicated; this can lead to multiple test modules. The test modules may have names such as `tests/test_module_feature_X.py` to show that there are tests for separate features of a very complex module. The volume of code for test cases can be quite large, and keeping the features separate can be helpful.

In other cases, we might have a test module that has tests for several different but closely related small modules. A single test module may employ inheritance techniques to cover all the modules in a package.

When combining many smaller modules, there may be multiple suites built in the `load_tests()` function. The body might look like this:

```
import doctest

import Chapter_11.ch11_r01 as ch11_r01
import Chapter_11.ch11_r08 as ch11_r08
import Chapter_11.ch11_r09 as ch11_r09


def load_tests(loader, standard_tests, pattern):
    for module in (
        ch11_r01, ch11_r08, ch11_r09
    ):
        dt = doctest.DocTestSuite(module)
        standard_tests.addTests(dt)
    return standard_tests
```

This will incorporate doctests from multiple modules into a single, large test suite. Note that the examples from `ch11_r03.py` can't be included in this test. The tests include some object `repr()` strings in the `test_point` examples that don't precisely match when the test is combined into a suite in this way. Rather than fix the tests, we'll change tools and use `pytest`.

See also

- For examples of `doctest`, see the *Using docstrings for testing* recipe, earlier in the chapter. For examples of `unittest`, see the *Unit testing with the unittest module* recipe, earlier in this chapter.

Unit testing with the pytest module

The `pytest` tool allows us to step beyond the examples used by `doctest`. Instead of using a subclass of `unittest.TestCase`, the `pytest` tool lets us use function definitions. The `pytest` approach uses Python's built-in `assert` statement, leaving the test case looking somewhat simpler. The `pytest` test design avoids using the complex mix of assertion methods.

The `pytest` tool is not part of Python; it needs to be installed separately. Use a command like this:

```
python -m pip install pytest
```

In this recipe, we'll look at how we can use `pytest` to simplify our test cases.

Getting ready

The ideas behind the Gherkin language can help to structure a test. In this test specification language, each scenario is described by *GIVEN-WHEN-THEN* steps. For this recipe, we have a scenario like this:

```
Scenario: Summary object can add values and compute statistics.

  Given a Summary object
  And numbers in the range 0 to 1000 (inclusive) shuffled randomly
  When all numbers are added to the Summary object
  Then the mean is 500
  And the median is 500
```

A `pytest` test function doesn't precisely follow the Gherkin three-part structure. A test function generally has two parts:

- If necessary, fixtures, which can establish some of the *Given* steps. In some cases, fixtures are designed for reuse and don't do everything required by a specific test. A fixture can also tear down resources after a test has finished.
- The body of the function will usually handle the *When* steps to exercise the object being tested and the *Then* steps to confirm the results. In some cases, it will also handle the *Given* steps to prepare the object's initial state.

We'll create some tests for a class that is designed to compute some basic descriptive statistics. We'd like to provide sample data that's larger than anything we'd ever enter as `doctest` examples. We'd like to use thousands of data points rather than two or three.

Here's an outline of the class definition that we'd like to test. We'll only provide the methods and some summaries. The bulk of the code was shown in the *Using docstrings for testing* recipe. This is just an outline of the class, provided as a reminder of what the method names are:

```
import collections
from statistics import median
from typing import Counter


class Summary:

    def __init__(self) -> None: ...

    def __str__(self) -> str: ...

    def add(self, value: int) -> None: ...

    @property
    def mean(self) -> float: ...

    @property
    def median(self) -> float: ...

    @property
    def count(self) -> int: ...

    @property
    def mode(self) -> List[Tuple[int, int]]: ...
```

Because we're not looking at the implementation details, we can think of this as opaque box testing. The code is in an opaque box. To emphasize that, we omitted the implementation details from the preceding code, using ... placeholders as if this was a type stub definition.

We'd like to be sure that when we use thousands of samples, the class performs correctly. We'd also like to ensure that it works quickly; we'll use this as part of an overall performance test, as well as a unit test.

How to do it...

We'll begin by creating our test file:

1. Create a test file with a name similar to the module under test. If the module was named `summary.py`, then a good name for a test module would be `test_summary.py`. Using the `test_ prefix` makes the test easier to find.
2. We'll use the `pytest` module for creating test classes. We'll also be using the `random` module to scramble the input data. We've included a `# type: ignore` comment because the release of `pytest` used for this book (version 5.2.2) lacks type hints:

```
from pytest import *  # type: ignore
import random
```

3. Import the module under test:

```
from Chapter_11.ch11_r01 import Summary
```

4. Implement the *Given* step as a fixture. This is marked with the `@fixture` decorator. It creates a function that can return a useful object, data for creating an object, or a mocked object. The type needs to be ignored by the `mypy` tool:

```
@fixture  # type: ignore
def flat_data():
    data = list(range(1001))
    random.shuffle(data)
    return data
```

5. Implement the *When* and *Then* steps as a test function with a name visible to `pytest`. This means the name must begin with `test_`. When a parameter to a test function is the name of a fixture function, the results of the fixture function are provided at runtime. This means the shuffled set of 1001 values will be provided as an argument value for the `flat_data` parameter:

```
def test_flat(flat_data):
```

6. Implement a *When* step to perform an operation on an object:

```
summary = Summary()
for sample in flat_data:
    summary.add(sample)
```

7. Implement a *Then* step to validate the outcome:

```
assert summary.mean == 500
assert summary.median == 500
```

If our test module is called `test_summary.py`, we can often execute it with a command like the following:

```
python -m pytest tests/test_summary.py
```

This will invoke the `pytest` package as a main application. It will search the given file for functions with names starting with `test_` and execute those test functions.

How it works...

We're using several parts of the `pytest` package:

- The `@fixture` decorator can be used to create reusable test fixtures with objects in known states, ready for further processing.
- The `pytest` application does several things:
  - It searches the given path for all functions with names that start with `test_` in a given module. It can search for modules with names that begin with `test_`. Often, we'll collect these files in a directory named `tests`.
  - All functions marked with `@fixture` are eligible to be executed automatically as part of the test setup. This makes it easy to provide a list of fixture names as parameters. When the test is run, `pytest` will evaluate each of these functions.
  - It then runs all of the `test_*` functions and displays a summary of the results.

When we run the `pytest` command, we'll see output that looks like this:

```
====================== test session starts ======================
platform darwin -- Python 3.8.0, pytest-5.2.2, py-1.8.0, pluggy-0.13.0
rootdir: /Users/slott/Documents/Writing/Python/Python Cookbook 2e/Modern-Python-Cookbook-Second-Edition
collected 1 item

Chapter_11/test_ch11_r06.py .                                    [100%]
```

```
======================= 1 passed in 0.02s ========================
```

As each test is passed, a `.` is displayed. This shows that the test suite is making progress. The summary shows the number of tests run and the time. If there are failures or exceptions, the counts on the last line will reflect this.

If we change the test slightly to be sure that it fails, we'll see the following output:

```
===================== test session starts ======================
platform darwin -- Python 3.8.0, pytest-5.2.2, py-1.8.0, pluggy-0.13.0
rootdir: /Users/slott/Documents/Writing/Python/Python Cookbook 2e/Modern-
Python-Cookbook-Second-Edition
collected 2 items

Chapter_11/test_ch11_r06.py F.                                   [100%]

=========================== FAILURES ===========================
__________________________ test_flat ___________________________

flat_data = [540, 395, 212, 290, 121, 370, ...]

    def test_flat(flat_data):
        summary = Summary()
        for sample in flat_data:
            summary.add(sample)
        assert summary.mean == 500
>       assert summary.median == 501
E       assert 500 == 501
E        +  where 500 = <Chapter_11.ch11_r01.Summary object at
0x10ce56910>.median

Chapter_11/test_ch11_r06.py:26: AssertionError
================= 1 failed, 1 passed in 0.06s ==================
```

Instead of a `.` for a passing test, a failing test displays an `F`. This is followed by a comparison between actual and expected results showing the `assert` statement that failed.

There's more...

In this example, we have two *Then* steps inside the `test_flat()` function. These are implemented as two `assert` statements. If the first one fails, the test stops as a failure, and the other step is not exercised. This test failure mode means we won't get all of the diagnostic information we might want.

When we want more diagnostic details, we can use multiple test functions. All of the functions can share a common fixture. In this case, we might want to create a second fixture that depends on the `flat_data` fixture and builds the `Summary` object to be used by a number of tests:

```
@fixture  # type: ignore
def summary_object(flat_data):
    summary = Summary()
    for sample in flat_data:
        summary.add(sample)
    return summary

def test_mean(summary_object):
    assert summary_object.mean == 500

def test_median(summary_object):
    assert summary_object.median == 500
```

Since each test is run separately, we'll see separate error reports for problems with the computing mean or computing median.

See also

- The *Unit testing with the unittest module* recipe in this chapter covers the same test case from the perspective of the `unittest` module.

Combining pytest and doctest tests

In most cases, we'll have a combination of `pytest` and `doctest` test cases. For examples of using the `doctest` tool, see the *Using docstrings for testing* recipe. For examples of using the `pytest` tool, see the *Unit testing with the pytest module* recipe.

The `doctest` examples are an essential element of the documentation strings on modules, classes, methods, and functions. The `pytest` cases will often be in a separate `tests` directory in files with names that match the pattern `test_*.py`.

In this recipe, we'll combine the `doctest` examples and the `pytest` test cases into one tidy package.

Getting ready

We'll refer back to the example from the *Using docstrings for testing* recipe. This recipe created tests for a class, `Summary`, that does some statistical calculations. In that recipe, we included examples in the docstrings.

The class started like this:

```
class Summary:
    """
    Computes summary statistics.

    >>> s = Summary()
    >>> s.add(8)
    >>> s.add(9)
    >>> s.add(9)
    >>> round(s.mean, 2)
    8.67
    >>> s.median
    9
    >>> print(str(s))
    mean = 8.67
    median = 9
    """
```

The methods have been omitted here so that we can focus on the example provided in the docstring.

In the *Unit testing with the pytest module* recipe, we wrote some test functions to provide additional tests for this class. These tests were put into a separate module, with a name starting with `test_`, specifically `test_summary.py`. We created fixtures and function definitions like these:

```
@fixture  # type: ignore
def flat_data():
    data = list(range(1001))
    random.shuffle(data)
    return data
```

```
def test_flat(flat_data):
    summary = Summary()
    for sample in flat_data:
        summary.add(sample)
    assert summary.mean == 500
    assert summary.median == 500
```

This test creates a `Summary` object; this is the *Given* step. It then adds a number of values to that `Summary` object. This is the *When* step of the test. The two `assert` statements implement the two *Then* steps of this test.

It's common to see a project folder structure that looks like this:

```
project-name/
    statstools/
        summary.py
    tests/
        test_summary.py
    README.rst
    requirements.txt
    tox.ini
```

We have a top-level folder, `project-name`, that matches the project name in the source code repository.

The directory `tests` should contain all the module files with tests. For example, it should contain the `tests/test_summary.py` module with unit test cases in it. We've chosen the directory name `tests` and a module named `test_*.py` so that they fit well with the automated test discovery features of the `pytest` tool.

We need to combine all of the tests into a single, comprehensive test suite. The example we'll show uses `ch11_r01` instead of a cooler name such as `summary`. As a general practice, a module should have a memorable, meaningful name. The book's content is quite large, and the names are designed to match the overall chapter and recipe outline.

How to do it...

It turns out that we don't need to write any Python code to combine the tests. The `pytest` module will locate test functions. It can also be used to locate `doctest` cases:

1. Locate the unit test file and the module being tested. In general, the names should be similar. For this example, we have the `ch11_r01.py` module with the code being tested. The test cases, however, are in `test_ch11_r06.py` because they were demonstrated earlier in this chapter, *in Unit testing with the pytest module.*

2. Create a shell command to run the unit test suite, as well as to examine a module for `doctest` cases:

```
pytest Chapter_11/test_ch11_r06.py --doctest-modules
Chapter_11/ch11_r01.py
```

When we run this from the OS command prompt we see the following:

```
$ pytest Chapter_11/test_ch11_r06.py --doctest-modules Chapter_11/ch11_
r01.py
===================== test session starts ======================
platform darwin -- Python 3.8.0, pytest-5.2.2, py-1.8.0, pluggy-0.13.0
rootdir: /Users/slott/Documents/Writing/Python/Python Cookbook 2e/Modern-
Python-Cookbook-Second-Edition
collected 9 items

Chapter_11/test_ch11_r06.py ....                                 [ 44%]
Chapter_11/ch11_r01.py .....                                     [100%]

====================== 9 passed in 0.05s =======================
```

The `pytest` command worked with both files. The dots after `Chapter_11/test_ch11_r06.py` show that four test cases were found in this file. This was 44% of the test suite. The dots after `Chapter_11/ch11_r01.py` show that five test cases were found; this was the remaining 66% of the suite.

This shows us that the `pytest` test cases were included as well as `doctest` test cases. What's helpful is that we don't have to adjust anything in either of the test suites to execute all of the available test cases.

How it works...

The `pytest` application has a variety of ways to search for test cases. The default is to search the given paths for all functions with names that start with `test_` in a given module. It will also search for all subclasses of `unittest.TestCase`. If we provide a directory, it will search it for all modules with names that begin with `test_`. Often, we'll collect these files in a directory named `tests`.

The `--doctest-modules` command-line option is used to mark modules that contain `doctest` examples. These examples are also processed by `pytest` as test cases.

This level of sophistication in finding and executing a variety of types of tests makes `pytest` a very powerful tool. It makes it easy to create tests in a variety of forms to create confidence that our software will work as intended.

There's more...

Adding the `-v` option provides a more detailed view of the tests found by `pytest`. Here's how the additional details are displayed:

```
==================== test session starts =====================
platform darwin -- Python 3.8.0, pytest-5.2.2, py-1.8.0, pluggy-0.13.0 --
/Users/slott/miniconda3/envs/cookbook/bin/python
cachedir: .pytest_cache
rootdir: /Users/slott/Documents/Writing/Python/Python Cookbook 2e/Modern-
Python-Cookbook-Second-Edition
collected 9 items

Chapter_11/test_ch11_r06.py::test_flat PASSED                 [ 11%]
Chapter_11/test_ch11_r06.py::test_mean PASSED                 [ 22%]
Chapter_11/test_ch11_r06.py::test_median PASSED               [ 33%]
Chapter_11/test_ch11_r06.py::test_biased PASSED               [ 44%]
Chapter_11/ch11_r01.py::Chapter_11.ch11_r01.Summary PASSED [ 55%]
Chapter_11/ch11_r01.py::Chapter_11.ch11_r01.__test__.test_GIVEN_n_5_k_52_
THEN_ValueError PASSED [ 66%]
Chapter_11/ch11_r01.py::Chapter_11.ch11_r01.__test__.test_GIVEN_negative_
THEN_ValueError PASSED [ 77%]
Chapter_11/ch11_r01.py::Chapter_11.ch11_r01.__test__.test_GIVEN_str_THEN_
TypeError PASSED [ 88%]
Chapter_11/ch11_r01.py::Chapter_11.ch11_r01.binom PASSED [100%]

===================== 9 passed in 0.05s ======================
```

Each individual test is identified, providing us with a detailed explanation of the test processing. This can help confirm that all of the expected `doctest` examples were properly located in the module under test.

Another handy feature for managing a large suite of tests is the `-k` option to locate a subset of tests; for example, we can use `-k median` to locate the test with `median` in the name. The output looks like this:

```
$ pytest -v Chapter_11/test_ch11_r06.py --doctest-modules Chapter_11/
ch11_r01.py -k 'median'
==================== test session starts =====================
platform darwin -- Python 3.8.0, pytest-5.2.2, py-1.8.0, pluggy-0.13.0 --
/Users/slott/miniconda3/envs/cookbook/bin/python
cachedir: .pytest_cache
```

```
rootdir: /Users/slott/Documents/Writing/Python/Python Cookbook 2e/Modern-Python-Cookbook-Second-Edition
collected 9 items / 8 deselected / 1 selected


Chapter_11/test_ch11_r06.py::test_median PASSED            [100%]


=============== 1 passed, 8 deselected in 0.02s ================
```

This is one of many tools for focusing the test processing on tests that have failed recently to help the process of debugging and retesting.

See also

- For examples of `doctest`, see the *Using docstrings for testing* recipe earlier in this chapter.
- The *Unit testing with the pytest module* recipe, earlier in this chapter, has the `pytest` test cases used for this recipe.
- For examples of the `unittest` version of these tests, see the *Unit testing with the unittest module* recipe earlier in this chapter.

Testing things that involve dates or times

Many applications rely on functions like `datetime.datetime.now()` or `time.time()` to create a timestamp. When we use one of these functions with a unit test, the results are essentially impossible to predict. This is an interesting dependency injection problem here: our application depends on a class that we would like to replace only when we're testing. The `datetime` package must be tested separately and a replacement used when testing our application.

One option is to design our application to avoid `now()` and `utcnow()`. Instead of using these methods directly, we can create a factory function that emits timestamps. For test purposes, this function can be replaced with one that produces known results. It seems awkward to avoid using the `now()` method in a complex application.

Another option is to avoid direct use of the `datetime` class entirely. This requires designing classes and modules that wrap the `datetime` class. A wrapper class that produces known values for `now()` can then be used for testing. This, too, seems needlessly complex.

In this recipe, we'll write tests with `datetime` objects. We'll need to create mock objects for `datetime` instances to create repeatable test values.

Getting ready

We'll work with a small function that creates a CSV file. This file's name will include the date and time in the format of YYYYMMDDHHMMSS as a long string of digits. We'll create files with names that look like this:

```
extract_20160704010203.json
```

This kind of file-naming convention might be used by a long-running server application. The name helps match a file and related log events. It can help to trace the work being done by the server.

We'll use a function like this to create these files:

```
import datetime
import json
from pathlib import Path
from typing import Any

def save_data(base: Path, some_payload: Any) -> None:
    now_date = datetime.datetime.utcnow()
    now_text = now_date.strftime("extract_%Y%m%d%H%M%S")
    file_path = (base / now_text).with_suffix(".json")
    with file_path.open("w") as target_file:
        json.dump(some_payload, target_file, indent=2)
```

This function has the use of `utcnow()`, which produces a distinct value each time this is run. Since this value is difficult to predict, it makes test assertions difficult to write.

To create a reproducible test output, we can create a mock version of the `datetime` module. We can patch the test context to use this mock object instead of the actual `datetime` module. Within the mocked module, we can create a mock class with a mock `utcnow()` method that will provide a fixed, easy-to-test response.

For this case, we have a scenario like this:

```
Scenario: save_date function writes JSON data to a date-stamped file.

  Given a base directory Path
  And a payload object {"primes": [2, 3, 5, 7, 11, 13, 17, 19]}
  And a known date and time of 2017-9-10 11:12:13 UTC
  When save_data(base, payload) function is executed
  Then the output file of "extract_20170910111213.json"
    is found in the base directory
  And the output file has a properly serialized version
```

```
    of the payload
  And the datetime.datetime.utcnow() function was called once
    to get the date and time
```

This can be implemented as a `pytest` test case.

How to do it...

This recipe will focus on using the `pytest` tool for testing, as well as patching mock objects into the context required by the object under test:

1. We'll need to import a number of modules required by the module we're testing:

   ```
   import datetime
   import json
   from pathlib import Path
   ```

2. We'll also need the core tools for creating mock objects and test fixtures. The `pytest` module doesn't seem to have complete type hints, so we'll use a special comment to tell `mypy` to ignore this module:

   ```
   from unittest.mock import Mock, patch
   from pytest import *  # type: ignore
   ```

3. Also, we'll need the module we're going to test:

   ```
   import Chapter_11.ch11_r08
   ```

4. We must create an object that will behave like the `datetime` module for the purposes of the test scenario. This module must contain a class, also named `datetime`. The class must contain a method, `utcnow()`, which returns a known object rather than a date that changes each time the test is run. We'll create a fixture, and the fixture will return this mock object with a small set of attributes and behaviors defined:

   ```
   @fixture  # type: ignore
   def mock_datetime():
       return Mock(
           wraps="datetime",
           datetime=Mock(
               utcnow=Mock(
                   return_value=datetime.datetime(
                       2017, 9, 10, 11, 12, 13))
           ),
       )
   ```

5. We also need a way to isolate the behavior of the filesystem into test directories. The `tmpdir` fixture is built in to `pytest` and provides temporary directories into which test files can be written safely.
6. We can now define a test function that will use the `mock_datetime` fixture, which creates a mock object; the `tmpdir` fixture, which creates an isolated working directory for test data; and the `monkeypatch` fixture, which lets us adjust the context of the module under test (by omitting any type hints, we'll avoid scrutiny from `mypy`):

```
def test_save_data(mock_datetime, tmpdir, monkeypatch):
```

7. We can use the `monkeypatch` fixture to replace an attribute of the `Chapter_11.ch11_r08` module. The `datetime` attribute will be replaced with the object created by the `mock_datetime` fixture. Between the fixture definitions and this patch, we've created a *Given* step that defines the test context:

```
    monkeypatch.setattr(
        Chapter_11.ch11_r08, "datetime", mock_datetime)
```

8. We can now exercise the `save_data()` function in a controlled test environment. This is the *When* step that exercises the code under test:

```
    data = {"primes": [2, 3, 5, 7, 11, 13, 17, 19]}
    Chapter_11.ch11_r08.save_data(Path(tmpdir), data)
```

9. Since the date and time are fixed by the mock object, the output file has a known, predictable name. We can read and validate the expected data in the file. Further, we can interrogate the mock object to be sure it was called exactly once with no argument values. This is a *Then* step to confirm the expected results:

```
    expected_path = (
        Path(tmpdir) / "extract_20170910111213.json")
    with expected_path.open() as result_file:
        result_data = json.load(result_file)
        assert data == result_data

    mock_datetime.datetime.utcnow.assert_called_once_with()
```

We can execute this test with `pytest` to confirm that our `save_data()` function will create the expected file with the proper content.

How it works...

The `unittest.mock` module has a wonderfully sophisticated class definition, the `Mock` class. A `Mock` object can behave like other Python objects, but generally only offers a limited subset of behaviors. In this example, we've created three different kinds of `Mock` objects.

The `Mock(wraps="datetime", ...)` object mocks a complete module. It will behave, to the extent needed by this test scenario, like the standard library `datetime` module. Within this object, we created a mock class definition but didn't assign it to any variable.

The `Mock(utcnow=...)` object is the mock class definition inside the mock module. We've created an attribute with the `return_value` attribute. This acts like a method definition and returns a mock object.

The `Mock(return_value=...)` object behaves like a function or method. We provide the return value required for this test.

When we create an instance of `Mock` that provides the `return_value` (or `side_effect`) attribute, we're creating a callable object. Here's an example of a mock object that behaves like a very dumb function:

```
>>> from unittest.mock import *
>>> dumb_function = Mock(return_value=12)
>>> dumb_function(9)
12
>>> dumb_function(18)
12
```

We created a mock object, `dumb_function`, that will behave like a callable—a function—that only returns the value `12`. For unit testing, this can be very handy, since the results are simple and predictable.

What's more important is this feature of the `Mock` object:

```
>>> dumb_function.mock_calls
[call(9), call(18)]
```

The `dumb_function()` tracked each call. We can then make assertions about these calls. For example, the `assert_called_with()` method checks the last call in the history:

```
>>> dumb_function.assert_called_with(18)
```

If the last call really was `dumb_function(18)`, then this succeeds silently. If the last call doesn't match the assertion, then this raises an `AssertionError` exception that the `unittest` module will catch and register as a test failure.

We can see more details like this:

```
>>> dumb_function.assert_has_calls([call(9), call(18)])
```

This assertion checks the entire call history. It uses the `call()` function from the `Mock` module to describe the arguments provided in a function call.

The `patch()` function can reach into a module's context and change any reference in that context. In this example, we used `patch()` to tweak a definition in the `__main__` module—the one currently running. In many cases, we'll import another module, and will need to patch that imported module. Because the `import` statement is part of running the module under test, the details of patching depend on the execution of the `import` and `import as` statements. It can sometimes help to use the debugger to see the context that's created when a module under test is executed.

There's more...

In this example, we created a mock for the `datetime` module that had a very narrow feature set for this test. The module contained a class, named `datetime`.

The `Mock` object that stands in for the `datetime` class has a single attribute, `utcnow()`. We used the special `return_value` keyword when defining this attribute so that it would return a fixed `datetime` instance. We can extend this pattern and mock more than one attribute to behave like a function. Here's an example that mocks both `utcnow()` and `now()`:

```
@fixture  # type: ignore
def mock_datetime_now():
    return Mock(
        name='mock datetime',
        datetime=Mock(
            name='mock datetime.datetime',
            utcnow=Mock(
                return_value=datetime.datetime(
                    2017, 7, 4, 1, 2, 3)
            ),
            now=Mock(
                return_value=datetime.datetime(
                    2017, 7, 4, 4, 2, 3)
            )
        )
    )
```

The two mocked methods, `utcnow()` and `now()`, each create a different `datetime` object. This allows us to distinguish between the values. We can more easily confirm the correct operation of a unit test.

We can add the following assertion to confirm that the `utcnow()` function was used properly by the unit under test:

```
mock_datetime_now.datetime.utcnow.assert_called_once_with()
```

This will examine the `self.mock_datetime` mock object. It looks inside this object at the `datetime` attribute, which we've defined to have a `utcnow` attribute. We expect that this is called exactly once with no argument values.

If the `save_data()` function has a bug and doesn't make a proper call to `utcnow()`, this assertion will detect that problem. We see the following two parts in each test with a mock object:

- The result of the mocked `datetime` was used properly by the unit being tested
- The unit being tested made appropriate requests to the mocked `datetime` object

In some cases, we might need to confirm that an obsolete or deprecated method is never called. We might have something like this to confirm that another method is not used:

```
assert mock_datetime_now.datetime.now.mock_calls == []
```

This kind of testing is used when refactoring software. In this example, the previous version may have used the `now()` method. After the change, the function is required to use the `utcnow()` method. We've included a test to be sure that the `now()` method is no longer being used.

See also

- The *Unit testing with the unittest module* recipe earlier in this chapter has more information about the basic use of the `unittest` module.

Testing things that involve randomness

Many applications rely on the `random` module to create random values or put values into a random order. In many statistical tests, repeated random shuffling or random selection is done. When we want to test one of these algorithms, any intermediate results or details of the processing are essentially impossible to predict.

We have two choices for trying to make the `random` module predictable enough to write meaningful unit tests:

- Set a known seed value; this is common, and we've made heavy use of this in many other recipes
- Use `unittest.mock` to replace the `random` module with something predictable

In this recipe, we'll look at ways to unit test algorithms that involve randomness.

Getting ready

Given a sample dataset, we can compute a statistical measure such as a mean or median. A common next step is to determine the likely values of these statistical measures for some overall population. This can be done by a technique called **bootstrapping**.

The idea is to resample the initial set of data repeatedly. Each of the resamples provides a different estimate of the statistical measures for the population. This can help us understand the population from which the sample was taken.

In order to be sure that a resampling algorithm will work, it helps to eliminate randomness from the processing. We can resample a carefully planned set of data with a non-randomized version of the `random.choice()` function. If this works properly, then we have confidence the randomized version will also work.

Here's our candidate resampling function. This does sampling with replacement:

```
import random
from typing import List, Iterator

def resample(population: List[int], N: int) -> Iterator[int]:
    for i in range(N):
        sample = random.choice(population)
        yield sample
```

We would normally apply this random `resample()` function to populate a `Counter` object that tracks each distinct value for a particular statistical measure. For our example, we'll track alternative values of the mean based on resampling. The overall resampling procedure looks like this:

```
def mean_distribution(population: List[int], N: int):
    means: Counter[float] = collections.Counter()
    for _ in range(1000):
        subset = list(resample(population, N))
        measure = round(statistics.mean(subset), 1)
        means[measure] += 1
    return means
```

This evaluates the `resample()` function `1000` times. This will lead to a number of subsets, each of which may have a distinct value for the measure we're estimating, the mean. These values are used to populate the `means` collection.

The histogram for `mean_distribution` will provide a helpful estimate for population variance. This estimate of the variance will help bracket a range for the overall population's most likely mean values.

Here's what the output looks like:

```
>>> random.seed(42)
>>> population = [8.04, 6.95, 7.58, 8.81, 8.33, 9.96, 7.24, 4.26, 10.84,
4.82, 5.68]
>>> mean_distribution(population, 4).most_common(5)
[(7.8, 51), (7.2, 45), (7.5, 44), (7.1, 41), (7.7, 40)]
```

This shows us that the most likely value for the mean of the overall population could be between `7.1` and `7.8`. There's more to this kind of analysis than we're showing here. Our focus is on testing the `resample()` function.

The test for `resample` involves a scenario like the following:

```
Given a random number generator where choice() always return the sequence
[23, 29, 31, 37, 41, 43, 47, 53]
When we evaluate resample(any 8 values, 8)
Then the expected results are [23, 29, 31, 37, 41, 43, 47, 53]
And the random choice() was called 8 times
```

This scenario describes a configuration where the `random.choice()` function provides a fixed sequence of values. Given a fixed sequence, then the `resample()` function will also provide a fixed sequence of values.

How to do it...

We'll define a mock object that can be used instead of the `random.choice()` function. With this fixture in place, the results are fixed and predictable:

1. We'll also need the core tools for creating mock objects and test fixtures. `pytest` doesn't seem to have complete type hints, so we'll use a special comment to tell `mypy` to ignore this module:

   ```
   from types import SimpleNamespace
   from unittest.mock import Mock, patch, call
   from pytest import *  # type: ignore
   ```

2. Also, we'll need the module we're going to test:

   ```
   import Chapter_11.ch11_r09
   ```

3. We'll need an object that will behave like the `choice()` function inside the `random` module. We'll create a fixture, and the fixture will return both the mocked function and the expected data that the mock object will use. We'll package the two items into an object using `SimpleNamespace` as a container. The resulting object will have attributes based on the local variables created inside this function:

```
@fixture  # type: ignore
def mock_random_choice():
    expected_resample_data = [
        23, 29, 31, 37, 41, 43, 47, 53]
    mock_choice=Mock(
        name='mock random.choice()',
        side_effect=expected_resample_data)
    return SimpleNamespace(**locals())
```

4. We can now define a test function that will use the `mock_random_choice` fixture, which creates a mock object, and the `monkeypatch` fixture, which lets us adjust the context of the module under test (by omitting any type hints, we'll avoid scrutiny from `mypy`):

```
def test_resample(mock_random_choice, monkeypatch):
```

5. We can use the `monkeypatch` fixture to replace an attribute of the `random` module that was imported in the `Chapter_11.ch11_r08` module. The `choice` attribute will be replaced with the mock function created by the `mock_random_choice` fixture. Between the fixture definitions and this patch, we've created a *Given* step that defines the test context:

```
    monkeypatch.setattr(
        Chapter_11.ch11_r09.random,
        "choice",
        mock_random_choice.mock_choice)
```

6. We can now exercise the `resample()` function in a controlled test environment. This is the *When* step that exercises the code under test:

```
    data = [2, 3, 5, 7, 11, 13, 17, 19]
    resample_data = list(
        Chapter_11.ch11_r09.resample(data, 8))
```

7. Since the random choices are fixed by the mock object, the result is fixed. We can confirm that the data created by the `mock_random` module was used for resampling. We can also confirm that the mocked choice function was properly called with the input data:

```
    assert (
        resample_data ==
```

```
            mock_random_choice.expected_resample_data)
        mock_random_choice.mock_choice.assert_has_calls(
            8 * [call(data)])
```

We can execute this test with `pytest` to confirm that our `resample()` function will create the output based on the given input and the `random.choice()` function.

How it works...

When we create an instance of the `Mock` class, we must provide the methods and attributes of the resulting object. When the `Mock` object includes a named argument value, this will be saved as an attribute of the resulting object.

When we create an instance of `Mock` that provides the `side_effect` named argument value, we're creating a callable object. The callable object will return the next value from the `side_effect` sequence each time the `Mock` object is called. This gives us a handy way to mock iterators.

Here's an example of a mock object that uses the `side_effect` attribute to behave like an iterator:

```
>>> from unittest.mock import *
>>> mocked_iterator = Mock(side_effect=[11, 13])
>>> mocked_iterator()
11
>>> mocked_iterator()
13
>>> mocked_iterator()
Traceback (most recent call last):
  File "/Users/slott/miniconda3/envs/cookbook/lib/python3.8/doctest.py",
line 1328, in __run
    compileflags, 1), test.globs)
  File "<doctest examples.txt[53]>", line 1, in <module>
    mocked_iterator()
  File "/Users/slott/miniconda3/envs/cookbook/lib/python3.8/unittest/
mock.py", line 965, in __call__
    return _mock_self._mock_call(*args, **kwargs)
  File "/Users/slott/miniconda3/envs/cookbook/lib/python3.8/unittest/
mock.py", line 1027, in _mock_call
    result = next(effect)
StopIteration
```

First, we created a `Mock` object and assigned it to the name `mocked_iterator`. The `side_effect` attribute of this `Mock` object provides a shortlist of two distinct values that will be returned.

The example then evaluates `mocked_iterator()` two times. Each time, the next value is returned from the `side_effect` list. The third attempt raises a `StopIteration` exception that would end the processing of the `for` statement.

We can see the call history using the `mock_calls` attribute of a `Mock` object:

```
>>> mocked_iterator.mock_calls
[call(), call(), call()]
```

This behavior allows us to write a test that detects certain kinds of improper uses of a function or a method. In particular, checking the `mock_calls` attribute reveals how many times the function was used, and what argument values were used with each call.

There's more...

The `resample()` function has an interesting pattern to it. When we take a step back from the details, we see this:

```
def resample(X, Y):
    for _ in range(Y):
        yield another_function(X)
```

The `X` argument value (called `population` in the actual code) is simply passed through to another function. For testing purposes, it doesn't matter what the value of `X` is. What we're testing is that the parameter's value in the `resample()` function is provided as the argument to the `another_function()` function, untouched.

The `mock` library provides an object called `sentinel` that can be used to create an argument value in these circumstances. When we refer to an attribute name as `sentinel`, it creates a distinct object. We might use `sentinel.POPULATION` as a kind of mock for a collection of values. The exact collection doesn't matter since it's simply passed as an argument to another function (called `random.choice()` in the actual code).

In this kind of pattern, the object is opaque. It passes through the `resample()` function untouched and unexamined. In this case, an object created by `sentinel` is a useful alternative to creating a list of realistic-looking values.

Here's how this use of sentinels can change this test:

```
def test_resample_2(monkeypatch):
        mock_choice=Mock(
            name='mock random.choice()',
```

```
            side_effect=lambda x: x
    )
    monkeypatch.setattr(
        Chapter_11.ch11_r09.random,
        "choice",
        mock_choice)

    resample_data = list(Chapter_11.ch11_r09.resample(
        sentinel.POPULATION, 8))

    assert resample_data == [sentinel.POPULATION]*8
    mock_choice.assert_has_calls(
        8 * [call(sentinel.POPULATION)])
```

We still need to mock the `random.choice()` function. We've used a variation of the mock object's `side_effect` feature. Given a callable object (like a lambda) the `side_effect` object is called to produce the answer. In this case, it's a lambda object that returns the argument value.

We provide the `sentinel.POPULATION` object to the `resample()` function. The same sentinel should be provided to the mocked `random.choice()` function. Because the `random.choice()` function was monkey-patched to be a mock object, we can examine the mock. The `Mock` object yields the original argument value, `sentinel.POPULATION`. We expect this to be called a total of `N` times, where the `N` parameter is set to `8` in the test case.

The value of `8` appears twice in the expected results. This creates a "brittle" test. A small change to the code or to the *Given* step conditions may lead to several changes in the *Then* steps expected results. This assures us that the test did not work by accident, but can only be passed when the software truly does the right thing.

When an object passes through a mock untouched, we can write test assertions to confirm this expected behavior. If the code we're testing uses the population object improperly, the test can fail when the result is not the untouched sentinel object. Also, the test may raise an exception because sentinel objects have almost no usable methods or attributes.

This test gives us confidence the population of values is provided, untouched, to the `random.choice()` function and the `N` parameter value is the size of the returned set of items from the population. We've relied on a sentinel object because we know that this algorithm should work on a variety of Python types.

See also

- The *Using set methods and operators* and *Creating dictionaries – inserting and updating* recipes in *Chapter 4, Built-In Data Structures Part 1: Lists and Sets*, and the *Using cmd for creating command-line applications* recipe in *Chapter 6, User Inputs and Outputs*, show how to seed the random number generator to create a predictable sequence of values.
- In *Chapter 7, Basics of Classes and Objects*, there are several other recipes that show an alternative approach, for example, *Using a class to encapsulate data + processing, Designing classes with lots of processing, Optimizing small objects with __slots__*, and *Using properties for lazy attributes*.
- Also, in *Chapter 8, More Advanced Class Design*, see the *Choosing between inheritance and extension – the is-a question, Separating concerns via multiple inheritance, Leveraging Python's duck typing, Creating a class that has orderable objects*, and *Defining an ordered collection* recipes.

Mocking external resources

In earlier recipes in this chapter, *Testing things that involve dates or times* and *Testing things that involve randomness*, we wrote tests for involving resources with states that we could predict and mock. In one case, we created a mock `datetime` module that had a fixed response for the current time. In the other case, we created a mock `random` module that returned a fixed response from the `choice()` function.

In some cases, we need to mock objects that have more complex state changes. A database, for example, would require mock objects that respond to create, retrieve, update, and delete requests. Another example is the overall OS with a complex mixture of stateful devices, including the filesystem, and running processes.

In the *Testing things that involve dates or times* recipe, we looked briefly at how the pytest tool provides a `tmpdir` fixture. This fixture creates a temporary directory for each test, allowing us to run tests without conflicting with other activities going on in the filesystem. Few things are more horrifying than testing an application that deletes or renames files and watching the test delete important files unexpectedly and raise havoc.

A Python application can use the `os`, `subprocess`, and `pathlib` modules to make significant changes to a running computer. We'd like to be able to test these external requests in a safe environment, using mocked objects, and avoid the horror of corrupting a working system with a misconfigured test.

In this recipe, we'll look at ways to create more sophisticated mock objects. These will allow the safe testing of changes to precious OS resources like files, directories, processes, users, groups, and configuration files.

Getting ready

We'll revisit an application that makes a number of OS changes. In *Chapter 10, Input/Output, Physical Format, and Logical Layout*, the *Replacing a file while preserving the previous version* recipe showed how to write a new file and then rename it so that the previous copy was always preserved.

A thorough set of test cases would present a variety of failures. This would help provide confidence that the function behaves properly.

The essential design was a definition of a class of objects, and a function to write one of those objects to a file. Here's the code that was used:

```
from pathlib import Path
import csv
from dataclasses import dataclass, asdict, fields
from typing import Callable, Any


@dataclass
class Quotient:
    numerator: int
    denominator: int


def save_data(output_path: Path, data: Quotient) -> None:
    with output_path.open("w", newline="") as output_file:
        headers = [f.name for f in fields(Quotient)]
        writer = csv.DictWriter(output_file, headers)
        writer.writeheader()
        writer.writerow(asdict(data))
```

This solves the core problem of replacing a file's content. Beyond this core problem, we want to be sure that the output file is always available in a form that's usable.

Consider what happens when there's a failure in the middle of the `save_data()` function. For example, the supplied data is invalid. In this case, the file would be partially rewritten, and useless to other applications. Leaving a corrupted file presents a potentially serious problem in a complex application like a web server where many clients need access to this file. When it becomes corrupted, a number of users may see the website crash.

Here's a function that wraps the `save_data()` function with some more sophisticated file handling:

```
def safe_write(
        output_path: Path, data: Iterable[Quotient]) -> None:
    ext = output_path.suffix
    output_new_path = output_path.with_suffix(f"{ext}.new")

    save_data(output_new_path, data)

    # Clear any previous .{ext}.old
    output_old_path = output_path.with_suffix(f"{ext}.old")
    output_old_path.unlink(missing_ok=True)

    # Try to preserve current as old
    try:
        output_path.rename(output_old_path)
    except FileNotFoundError as ex:
        # No previous file. That's okay.
        Pass

    # Try to replace current .{ext} with new .{ext}.new
    try:
        output_new_path.rename(output_path)
    except IOError as ex:
        # Possible recovery...
        output_old_path.rename(output_path)
```

The `safe_write()` function uses the `save_data()` function to do the core work of preserving the objects. Additionally, it handles a number of failure scenarios.

It's important to test failures in each one of the steps of this function. This leads us to one of a number of scenarios:

1. Everything works – sometimes called the "happy path"
2. The `save_data()` function raises an exception, leaving a file corrupted
3. The `output_old_path.unlink()` function raises an exception other than a `FileNotFoundError` exception
4. The `output_path.rename()` function raises an exception other than a `FileNotFoundError` exception
5. The `output_new_path.rename()` function raises an exception other than an `IOError` exception

There's a sixth scenario that requires a complex double failure. The `output_new_path.rename()` function must raise an `IOError` exception followed by a problem performing an `output_old_path.rename()`. This scenario requires the `output_path` to be successfully renamed to the `output_old_path`, but after that, the `output_old_path` cannot be renamed back to its original name. This situation indicates a level of filesystem damage that will require manual intervention to repair. It also requires a more complex mock object, with a list of exceptions for the `side_effect` attribute.

Each of the scenarios listed previously can be translated into Gherkin to help clarify precisely what it means; for example:

```
Scenario: save_data() function is broken.
  Given A faulty set of data, faulty_data, that causes a failure in
the save_data() function
  And an existing file, "important_data.csv"
  When safe_write("important_data.csv", faulty_data)
  Then safe_write raises an exception
  And the existing file, "important_data.csv" is untouched
```

This can help use the `Mock` objects to provide the various kinds of external resource behaviors we need. Each scenario implies a distinct fixture to reflect a distinct failure mode.

Among the five scenarios, three describe failures of an OS request made via one of the various `Path` objects that get created. This suggests a fixture to create a mocked `Path` object. Each scenario is a different parameter value for this fixture; the parameters have different points of failure.

How to do it...

We'll use separate testing techniques. The `pytest` package offers the `tmpdir` and `tmp_path` fixtures, which can be used to create isolated files and directories. In addition to an isolated directory, we'll also want to use a mock to stand in for parts of the application we're not testing:

1. Identify all of the fixtures required for the various scenarios. For the happy path, where the mocking is minimal, the `pytest.tmpdir` fixture is all we need. For scenario two, where the `save_data()` function is broken, the mocking involves part of the application, not OS resources. For the other three, methods of `Path` objects will raise exceptions.
2. This test will use a number of features from the `pytest` and `unittest.mock` modules. It will be creating `Path` objects, and test functions defined in the `Chapter_10.ch10_r02` module:

```
from unittest.mock import Mock, sentinel
from pytest import *  # type: ignore
```

```
from pathlib import Path
import Chapter_10.ch10_r02
```

3. Write a test fixture to create the original file, which should not be disturbed unless everything works correctly. We'll use a `sentinel` object to provide some text that is unique and recognizable as part of this test scenario:

```
@fixture  # type: ignore
def original_file(tmpdir):
    precious_file = tmpdir/"important_data.csv"
    precious_file.write_text(
        hex(id(sentinel.ORIGINAL_DATA)), encoding="utf-8")
    return precious_file
```

4. Write a function that will replace the `save_data()` function. This will create mock data used to validate that the `safe_write()` function works. In this, too, we'll use a `sentinel` object to create a unique string that is recognizable later in the test:

```
def save_data_good(path, content):
    path.write_text(
        hex(id(sentinel.GOOD_DATA)), encoding="utf-8")
```

5. Write the "happy path" scenario. The `save_data_good()` function can be given as the `side_effect` of a `Mock` object and used in place of the original `save_data()` function. This confirms that the `safe_write()` function implementation really does use the `save_data()` function to create the expected resulting file:

```
def test_safe_write_happy(original_file, monkeypatch):
    mock_save_data = Mock(side_effect=save_data_good)
    monkeypatch.setattr(
        Chapter_10.ch10_r02, 'save_data', mock_save_data)

    data = [
        Chapter_10.ch10_r02.Quotient(355, 113)
    ]
    Chapter_10.ch10_r02.safe_write(
        Path(original_file), data)

    actual = original_file.read_text(encoding="utf-8")
    assert actual == hex(id(sentinel.GOOD_DATA))
```

6. Write a mock for scenario two, in which the `save_data()` function fails to work correctly. This requires the test to include a `save_data_failure()` function to write recognizably corrupt data, and then raise an unexpected exception. This simulates any of a large number of OS exceptions related to file access permissions, resource exhaustion, as well as other problems like running out of memory:

```
def save_data_failure(path, content):
    path.write_text(
        hex(id(sentinel.CORRUPT_DATA)), encoding="utf-8")
    raise RuntimeError("mock exception")
```

7. Finish scenario two, using this alternate function as the `side_effect` of a `Mock` object. In this test, we need to confirm that a `RuntimeError` exception was raised, and we also need to confirm that the corrupt data did not overwrite the original data:

```
def test_safe_write_scenario_2(original_file, monkeypatch):
    mock_save_data = Mock(side_effect=save_data_failure)
    monkeypatch.setattr(
        Chapter_10.ch10_r02, 'save_data', mock_save_data)

    data = [
        Chapter_10.ch10_r02.Quotient(355, 113)
    ]
    with raises(RuntimeError) as ex:
        Chapter_10.ch10_r02.safe_write(
            Path(original_file), data)

    actual = original_file.read_text(encoding="utf-8")
    assert actual == hex(id(sentinel.ORIGINAL_DATA))
```

This produces two test scenarios that confirm the `safe_write()` function will work in a number of common scenarios. We'll turn to the remaining three scenarios in the *There's more...* section later in this recipe.

How it works...

When testing software that makes OS, network, or database requests, it's imperative to include cases where the external resource fails. The principal tool for doing this is the `pytest.monkeypatch` fixture; we can replace Python library functions with mock objects that raise exceptions instead of working correctly.

In this recipe, we used the `monkeypatch.setattr()` method to replace an internal function, `save_data()`, used by the function we're testing, `safe_write()`. For the happy path scenario, we replaced the `save_data()` function with a `Mock` object that wrote some recognizable data. Because we're using the `pytest.tmpdir` fixture, the file was written into a safe, temporary directory, where it could be examined to confirm that new, good data replaced the original data.

For the first of the failure scenarios, we used the `monkeypatch` fixture to replace the `save_data()` function with a function that both wrote corrupt data and also raised an exception. This is a way to simulate a broad spectrum of application failures. We can imagine that `save_data()` represents a variety of external requests including database operations, RESTful web service requests, or even computations that could strain the resources of the target system.

We have two ways to provide sensible failures. In this scenario, the `save_data_failure()` function was used by a `Mock` object. This function replaced the `save_data()` function and raised an exception directly. The other way to provide a failure is to provide an exception or exception class as the value of the `side_effect` parameter when creating a `Mock` object; for example:

```
>>> a_mock = Mock(side_effect=RuntimeError)
>>> a_mock(1)
Traceback (most recent call last):
...
RuntimeError
```

This example creates a mock object, `a_mock`, that always raises a `RuntimeError` when it's called.

Because the `side_effect` attribute can also work with a list of values, we can use the following to create an unreliable resource:

```
>>> b_mock = Mock(side_effect=[42, RuntimeError])
>>> b_mock(1)
42
>>> b_mock(2)
Traceback (most recent call last):
...
RuntimeError
```

This example creates a mock object, `b_mock`, which will return an answer for the first request, but will raise a specified exception for the second request.

These test scenarios also made use of the `sentinel` object. When we reference any `sentinel` attribute, a unique object is created. This means that `sentinel.GOOD_DATA` is never equal to `sentinel.CORRUPT_DATA`. `sentinel` objects aren't strings, but we can use `hex(id(sentinel.GOOD_DATA))` to create a unique string that can be used within the test to confirm that an object provided as an argument value was used without further processing or tampering.

There's more...

The remaining three scenarios are very similar; they all have the following test function:

```
def test_safe_write_scenarios(
        original_file, mock_pathlib_path, monkeypatch):
    mock_save_data = Mock(side_effect=save_data_good)
    monkeypatch.setattr(
        Chapter_10.ch10_r02, 'save_data', mock_save_data)

    data = [
        Chapter_10.ch10_r02.Quotient(355, 113)
    ]
    with raises(RuntimeError) as exc_info:
        Chapter_10.ch10_r02.safe_write(mock_pathlib_path, data)
    assert exc_info.type == RuntimeError
    assert exc_info.value.args in {("3",), ("4",), ("5",)}

    actual = original_file.read_text(encoding="utf-8")
    assert actual == hex(id(sentinel.ORIGINAL_DATA))
    assert mock_save_data.called_once()
    assert mock_pathlib_path.rename.called_once()
```

This function provides the `save_data_good()` mock for the `save_data()` function. Each scenario will raise a `RuntimeError` exception, but the exception will be from different `Path` operations. In all three cases, the new data is inaccessible, but the original data remains usable in the original file. This is confirmed by checking the original file's content to be sure it has the original data.

We want to use three different versions of the `mock_pathlib_path` mock object to implement the three different scenarios. When we look inside the `safe_write()` function, we see that the original `Path` object is used to create two additional paths, one for the new file and one as the path for a backup of the previous edition of the original file.

These two additional path instances are created by using the `with_suffix()` method of a `Path`. This leads us to the following sketch of what the mock object needs to contain:

```
new_path = Mock(rename=Mock(side_effect= ? ))
old_path = Mock(unlink=Mock(side_effect= ? ))
original_path = Mock(
    with_suffix=Mock(side_effect=[new_path, old_path]),
    rename=Mock(side_effect= ? )
)
```

The `original_path` mock will be returned by the fixture. This `Mock` object behaves like a `Path` object and provides the `with_suffix()` method to create the mock representation for the new path and the old path. Each of these paths is used in slightly different ways.

The `old_path` has the `unlink()` method used. In scenario three, this fails to work.

In addition to providing the other path objects, the `original_path` must be renamed to become a backup. In scenario four, this fails to work.

The `new_path` will have a rename performed to make it the replacement copy of the file. In scenario five, this fails to work, forcing the function to put the old file back into place.

These small changes replace the `?`'s in the preceding outline. We can use a parameterized fixture to spell out these three alternatives. First, we'll package the choices as three separate dictionaries that provide the `side_effect` values:

```
scenario_3 = {
    "original": None, "old": RuntimeError("3"), "new": None}
scenario_4 = {
    "original": RuntimeError("4"), "old": None, "new": None}
scenario_5 = {
    "original": None, "old": None, "new": RuntimeError("5")}
```

Given these three definitions, we can plug the values into a fixture via the `request.params` object provided by `pytest`. We've marked the fixture to be ignored by `mypy`:

```
@fixture(params=[scenario_3, scenario_4, scenario_5])  # type: ignore
def mock_pathlib_path(request):
    new_path = Mock(rename=Mock(side_effect=request.param["new"]))
    old_path = Mock(unlink=Mock(side_effect=request.param["old"]))
    original_path = Mock(
        with_suffix=Mock(side_effect=[new_path, old_path]),
        rename=Mock(side_effect=request.param["original"])
    )
    return original_path
```

Because this fixture has three parameters, any test using this fixture is run three times, once with each of the parameter values. This lets us reuse the `test_safe_write_scenarios` test case to be sure it works with a variety of system failures.

Here's what the output from `pytest` looks like. It shows the two unique scenarios followed by `test_safe_write_scenarios` using three different parameter values:

```
Chapter_11/test_ch11_r10.py::test_safe_write_happy PASSED
[ 20%]
Chapter_11/test_ch11_r10.py::test_safe_write_scenario_2 PASSED
[ 40%]
Chapter_11/test_ch11_r10.py::test_safe_write_scenarios[mock_pathlib_
path0] PASSED [ 60%]
Chapter_11/test_ch11_r10.py::test_safe_write_scenarios[mock_pathlib_
path1] PASSED [ 80%]
Chapter_11/test_ch11_r10.py::test_safe_write_scenarios[mock_pathlib_
path2] PASSED [100%]
```

We've created a variety of mock objects to inject failures throughout a complex function. This sequence of tests helps provide confidence that the implementation supports the five defined scenarios.

See also

- The *Testing things that involve dates or times* and *Testing things that involve randomness* recipes earlier in this chapter show techniques for dealing with unpredictable data.
- The *Reading complex formats using regular expressions* recipe in *Chapter 10, Input/Output, Physical Format, and Logical Layout*, shows how to parse a complex log file. In the *Using multiple contexts for reading and writing files* recipe in *Chapter 10, Input/Output, Physical Format, and Logical Layout*, the complex log records were written to a `CSV` file.
- For information on chopping up strings to replace parts, see the *Rewriting an immutable string* recipe in *Chapter 1, Numbers, Strings, and Tuples*.
- Elements of this can be tested with the `doctest` module. See the *Using docstrings for testing* recipe earlier in this chapter for examples. It's also important to combine these tests with any doctests. See the *Combining unittest and doctest tests* recipe earlier in this chapter for more information on how to do this.

12
Web Services

Many problems can be solved by offering a centralized software service to a number of remote clients. Since the 90s, this kind of networking has been called the World Wide Web, and the centralized applications are called web services. Web clients have evolved to include browsers, mobile applications, and other web services, creating a sophisticated, interlinked network of computing. Providing a web service involves solving several interrelated problems. The applicable protocols must be followed, each with its own unique design considerations. One of the foundations for providing web services is the various standards that define the **Hypertext Transfer Protocol** (**HTTP**).

One of the use cases for HTTP is to provide web services. In this case, the standard HTTP requests and responses will exchange data in formats other than HTML and images preferred by browsers. One of the most popular formats for encoding information is JSON. We looked at processing JSON documents in the *Reading JSON documents* recipe in *Chapter 10, Input/ Output, Physical Format, and Logical Layout*.

A web service client can prepare documents in JSON. The server includes a Python application that creates response documents, also in JSON notation. The HTTP status codes are used to indicate the success or failure of each individual request. A status of `200 OK` often indicates success, and `400 Bad Request` indicates an error in the request.

The documents exchanged by a web service and a client encode a representation of an object's state. A client application in JavaScript may have an object state that is sent to a server. A server in Python may transfer a representation of an object state to a client. This concept is called **Representational State Transfer** (**REST**). A service using REST processing is often called RESTful.

Most Python web service applications follow the **Web Services Gateway Interface** (**WSGI**). The WSGI standard defines a web service as a function that returns a response document. The web service function is given a standardized request implemented as a dictionary, plus a secondary function used to set a status and headers.

There are several places to look for detailed information on the overall WSGI standard:

- **PEP 3333**: See `https://www.python.org/dev/peps/pep-3333/`.
- **The Python standard library**: It includes the `wsgiref` module. This is the reference implementation in the standard library.
- **The Werkzeug project**: See `http://werkzeug.pocoo.org`. This is an external library with numerous WSGI utilities. This is used widely to implement WSGI applications.

A good RESTful implementation should also provide a great deal of information about the service being used. One way to provide this information is through the OpenAPI specification. For information on the OpenAPI (formerly known as Swagger) specification, see `http://swagger.io/specification/`.

The core of the OpenAPI specification is a JSON schema specification. For more information on this, see `http://json-schema.org`.

The two foundational ideas are as follows:

1. We write a specification for the requests that are accepted by the service and the responses returned by the service. This specification is written in JSON, making it accessible to client applications written in a variety of languages.
2. We provide the specification at a fixed URL, often `/openapi.yaml`. This can be queried by a client to determine the details of how the service works.

Creating OpenAPI documents can be challenging. The `swagger-spec-validator` project can help. See `https://github.com/p1c2u/openapi-spec-validator`. This is a Python package that we can use to confirm that a document meets the OpenAPI requirements.

In this chapter, we'll look at a number of recipes for creating RESTful web services and also serving static or dynamic content. We'll look at the following recipes:

- Defining the card model
- Using the Flask framework for RESTful APIs
- Parsing the query string in a request
- Making REST requests with urllib
- Parsing the URL path
- Parsing a JSON request
- Implementing authentication for web services

Central to web services is a WSGI-based application server. The Flask framework provides this. Flask allows us to write view functions that handle the detailed processing of a request to create a response. We'll start with a data model for playing cards and then move to a simple Flask-based server to present instances of `Card` objects. From there, we'll add features to make a more useful web service.

Defining the card model

In several of these recipes, we'll look at a web service that emits playing cards from either a deck or a shoe. This means we'll be transferring the representation of `Card` objects.

This is often described as Representational State Transfer - REST. We need to define our class of objects so we can create a useful representation of the state of each `Card` instance. A common representation is JSON notation.

It might be helpful to think of this as recipe zero. This data model is based on a recipe from *Chapter 7, Basics of Classes and Objects*. We'll expand it here in this chapter and use it as a foundation for the remaining recipes in this chapter. In the GitHub repo for this chapter, this recipe is available as `card_model.py`

Getting ready

We'll rely on the `Card` class definition from the *Using dataclasses for mutable objects* recipe in *Chapter 7, Basics of Classes and Objects*. We'll also rely on JSON notation. We looked at parsing and creating JSON notation in *Chapter 10, Input/Output, Physical Format, and Logical Layout*, in the *Reading JSON and YAML documents* recipe.

How to do it...

We'll decompose this recipe into an initial step, followed by steps for each individual method of the class:

1. Define the overall class, including the attributes of each `Card` instance. We've used the `frozen=True` option to make the object immutable:

```
from dataclasses import dataclass, asdict

@dataclass(frozen=True)
class Card:
    rank: int
    suit: str
```

2. Add a method to create a version of the card's attributes in a form that's readily handled by the JSON serialization. We'll call this the `serialize()` method. Because the attributes are an integer and a string, we can use the `dataclasses.asdict()` function to create a useful, serializable representation. We've created a dictionary with a key that names the class, `__class__`, and a key that contains a dictionary used to create instances of the dataclass `__init__`:

```
def serialize(self) -> Dict[str, Any]:
    return {
        "__class__": self.__class__.__name__,
        "__init__": asdict(self)
    }
```

3. Add a method to deserialize the preceding object into a new instance of the `Card` class. We've made this a class method, so the class will be provided as an initial parameter value. This isn't necessary but seems to be helpful if we want to make this a superclass of a class hierarchy:

```
@classmethod
def deserialize(cls: Type, document: Dict[str, Any]) ->
'Card':
    if document["__class__"] != cls.__name__:
        raise TypeError(
            f"Cannot make {cls.__name__} "
            f"from {document['__class__']}"
        )
    return Card(**document["__init__"])
```

4. This needs to be a separate module, `card_model.py`, so it can be imported into other recipes. Unit tests are appropriate to be sure that the various methods work as promised.

Given this class, we can create an instance of the class like this:

```
>>> c = Card(1, "\\u2660")
>>> repr(c)
"Card(rank=1, suit='♠')"
>>> document = c.serialize()
>>> document
{'__class__': 'Card', '__init__': {'rank': 1, 'suit': '♠'}}
```

The `serialize()` method of the object, `c`, provides a dictionary of integer and text values. We can then dump this in JSON notation as follows:

```
>>> json.dumps(document)
'{"__class__": "Card", "__init__": {"rank": 1, "suit": "\\\\u2660"}}'
```

This shows the JSON-syntax string created from the serialized `Card` instance.

We can use `Card.deserialize()` on the document to recreate a copy of the `Card` instance. This pair of operations lets us prepare a `Card` for the transfer of the representation of the internal state, and build on the object that reflects the representation of the state.

How it works...

We've broken the web resource into three distinct pieces. At the core is the `Card` class that models a single playing card, with rank and suit attributes. We've included methods to create Python dictionaries from the `Card` object. Separately, we can dump and load these dictionaries as JSON-formatted strings. We've kept the various representations separated.

In our applications, we'll work with the essential `Card` objects. We'll only use the serialization and JSON formatting for transfer between client and server applications.

See `http://docs.oasis-open.org/odata/odata-json-format/v4.0/odata-json-format-v4.0.html` for more information on the JSON-formatting of data for web services.

There's more...

We'll also need a `Deck` class as a container of `Card` instances. An instance of this `Deck` class can create `Card` objects. It can also act as a stateful object that can deal cards. Here's the class definition:

```
import random
from typing import List, Iterator, Union, overload

class Deck:
    SUITS = (
        "\N{black spade suit}",
        "\N{white heart suit}",
        "\N{white diamond suit}",
        "\N{black club suit}",
    )
```

```
    def __init__(self, n: int = 1) -> None:
        self.n = n
        self.create_deck(self.n)

    def create_deck(self, n: int = 1) -> None:
        self.cards = [
            Card(r, s)
            for r in range(1, 14)
            for s in self.SUITS for _ in range(n)
        ]
        random.shuffle(self.cards)
        self.offset = 0

    def deal(self, hand_size: int = 5) -> List[Card]:
        if self.offset + hand_size > len(self.cards):
            self.create_deck(self.n)
        hand = self.cards[self.offset : self.offset + hand_size]
        self.offset += hand_size
        return hand

    def __len__(self) -> int:
        return len(self.cards)

    @overload
    def __getitem__(self, position: int) -> Card:
        ...

    @overload
    def __getitem__(self, position: slice) -> List[Card]:
        ...

    def __getitem__(self, position: Union[int, slice]) -> Union[Card,
List[Card]]:
        return self.cards[position]

    def __iter__(self) -> Iterator[Card]:
        return iter(self.cards)
```

The `create_deck()` method uses a generator to create all 52 combinations of the thirteen ranks and four suits. Each suit is defined by a single character: ♣, ◊, ♡, or ♠. The example spells out the Unicode character names using `\N{}` sequences in the class variable, `SUITS`.

If a value of `n` is provided when creating the `Deck` instance, the container will create multiple copies of the 52-card deck. This multideck shoe is sometimes used to speed up play by reducing the time spent shuffling. It can also make card counting somewhat more difficult. Furthermore, a shoe can be used to take some cards out of play. Once the sequence of `Card` instances has been created, it is shuffled using the random module. For repeatable test cases, a fixed seed can be provided.

The `deal()` method will use the value of `self.offset` to determine where to start dealing. This value starts at `0` and is incremented after each hand of cards is dealt. The `hand_size` argument determines how many cards will be in the next hand. This method updates the state of the object by incrementing the value of `self.offset` so that the cards are dealt just once.

The various `@overload` definitions of `__getitem__()` are required to match the way Python deals with `list[position]` and `list[index:index]`. The first form has the type hint `__getitem__(self, position: int) -> Any`. The second form has the type hint `__getitem__(self, position: slice) -> Any`. We need to provide both overloaded type hints. The implementation passes the argument value - either an integer or a `slice` object - through to the underlying `self.cards` instance variable, which is a list collection.

Here's one way to use this class to create `Card` objects:

```
>>> from Chapter_12.card_model import Deck
>>> import random
>>> random.seed(42)
>>> deck = Deck()
>>> cards = deck.deal(5)
>>> cards
[Card(rank=3, suit='♡'), Card(rank=6, suit='♣'),
 Card(rank=7, suit='♡'), Card(rank=1, suit='♣'),
 Card(rank=6, suit='♡')]
```

To create a sensible test, we provided a fixed seed value. The script created a single deck using `Deck()`. We can then deal a hand of five `Card` instances from the deck.

In order to use this as part of a web service, we'll also need to produce useful output in JSON notation. Here's an example of how that would look:

```
>>> import json
>>> json_cards = list(card.to_json() for card in deck.deal(5))
>>> print(json.dumps(json_cards, indent=2, sort_keys=True))
[
  {
    "__class__": "Card",
```

```
    "rank": 10,
    "suit": "\u2662"
  },
  {
    "__class__": "Card",
    "rank": 5,
    "suit": "\u2660"
  },
  {
    "__class__": "Card",
    "rank": 10,
    "suit": "\u2663"
  },
  {
    "__class__": "Card",
    "rank": 5,
    "suit": "\u2663"
  },
  {
    "__class__": "Card",
    "rank": 3,
    "suit": "\u2663"
  }
]
```

We've used `deck.deal(5)` to deal a hand with five more cards from the deck. The expression `list(card.to_json() for card in deck.deal(5))` will use the `to _json()` method of each `Card` object to emit the small dictionary representation of that object. The list of dictionary structure was then serialized into JSON notation. The `sort_keys=True` option is handy for creating a repeatable test case. It's not generally necessary for RESTful web services.

Now that we have a definition of `Card` and `Deck`, we can write RESTful web services to provide `Card` instances from the `Deck` collection. We'll use these definitions throughout the remaining recipes in this chapter.

Using the Flask framework for RESTful APIs

Many web applications have several layers. The layers often follow this pattern:

- A **presentation** layer. This might run on a mobile device or a computer's browser. This is the visible, external view of the application. Because of the variety of mobile devices and browsers, there may be many clients for an application.
- An **application** layer. This is often implemented as a RESTful API to provide web services. This layer does the processing to support the web or mobile presentation. This can be built using Python and the Flask framework.
- A **persistence** layer. This handles the retention of data and transaction state over a single session as well as across multiple sessions from a single user. This is often a database, but in some cases the OS filesystem is adequate.

The Flask framework is very helpful for creating the application layer of a web service. It can serve HTML and JavaScript to provide a presentation layer. It can work with the filesystem or any database to provide persistence.

Getting ready

First, we'll need to add the Flask framework to our environment. This generally relies on using `pip` or `conda` to install the latest release of Flask and the other related projects, `itsdangerous`, `Jinja2`, `click`, `MarkupSafe`, and `Werkzeug`.

This book was written using the `conda` environment manager. This creates virtual environments that permit easy upgrades and the installation of additional packages. Other virtual environment managers can be used as well. In the following example, a conda environment named `temp` was the current active environment.

The installation looks like the following:

```
(temp) % pip install flask
Collecting flask
  Using cached Flask-1.1.1-py2.py3-none-any.whl (94 kB)
Collecting Werkzeug>=0.15
  Downloading Werkzeug-1.0.0-py2.py3-none-any.whl (298 kB)
     |████████████████████████████████| 298 kB 1.7 MB/s
Collecting Jinja2>=2.10.1
  Downloading Jinja2-2.11.1-py2.py3-none-any.whl (126 kB)
     |████████████████████████████████| 126 kB 16.2 MB/s
Collecting click>=5.1
```

```
  Downloading click-7.1.1-py2.py3-none-any.whl (82 kB)
     |████████████████████████████████| 82 kB 2.5 MB/s
Collecting itsdangerous>=0.24
  Using cached itsdangerous-1.1.0-py2.py3-none-any.whl (16 kB)
Collecting MarkupSafe>=0.23
  Downloading MarkupSafe-1.1.1-cp38-cp38-macosx_10_9_x86_64.whl (16 kB)
Installing collected packages: Werkzeug, MarkupSafe, Jinja2, click,
itsdangerous, flask
Successfully installed Jinja2-2.11.1 MarkupSafe-1.1.1 Werkzeug-1.0.0
click-7.1.1 flask-1.1.1 itsdangerous-1.1.0
```

We can see that `Werkzeug`, `Jinja2`, and `MarkupSafe` were installed in this environment. The `Flask` project identified these dependencies and the `conda` tool downloaded and installed them for us.

The Flask framework allows us to create our application as a Python module. Functions in the module can be used to handle a specific pattern of URL paths.

We'll look at some core card-dealing functions using the class definitions shown in the *card model* recipe earlier in this chapter. The `Card` class defines a simple playing card. The `Deck` class defines a deck or shoe of cards.

For our RESTful web service, we'll define a route to a resource that looks like this:

```
/dealer/hand/?cards=5
```

This route can be part of a complete URL: `http://127.0.0.1:5000/dealer/hand/?cards=5`.

The route has three important pieces of information:

- The first part of the path, `/dealer/`, is an overall web service. In a more complex environment, this can be to send requests to the appropriate processor.
- The next part of the path, `hand/`, is a specific resource, a hand of cards.
- The query string, `?cards=5`, defines the `cards` parameter for the query. The numeric value is the size of the hand being requested. It should be limited to a range of 1 to 52 cards. A value that's out of range will get a `400` status code because the query is invalid.

We'll leverage Flask's route parsing to separate the path elements and map them to view function definitions. The return value from a Flask view function has an implicit status of `200 OK`. We can use the `abort()` function to stop processing with a different status code.

How to do it...

We'll build a Flask application to create Card instances from a Deck object. This will require the card_model module. It will also require various elements of the Flask framework. We'll define a function to manage the Deck object. Finally, we'll map a specific path to a view function to deal Card instances:

1. Import some core definitions from the flask package. The Flask class defines the overall application. The request object holds the current web request. The jsonify() function returns a JSON-format object from a Flask view function. The abort() function returns an HTTP error status and ends the processing of the request. The Response object is used as a type hint:

   ```
   from flask import Flask, jsonify, request, abort, Response
   from http import HTTPStatus
   from typing import Optional
   ```

2. Import the underlying classes, Card and Deck. Ideally, these are imported from a separate module. It should be possible to test all of their features outside the web services environment:

   ```
   from Chapter_12.card_model import Card, Deck
   ```

3. In order to control the shuffle, we'll also need the random module. This can be used to force a specific seed for testing or pick a suitably random seed for normal use:

   ```
   import os
   import random
   ```

4. Create the Flask object. This is the overall web services application. We'll call the Flask application dealer, and we'll also assign the object to a global variable, dealer:

   ```
   dealer = Flask("dealer")
   ```

5. Create any objects used throughout the application. Be sure to create a unique name that doesn't conflict with any of Flask's internal attributes. Stateful global objects must be able to work in a multi-threaded environment, or threading must be explicitly disabled:

   ```
   deck: Optional[Deck] = None
   ```

   For this recipe, the implementation of the Deck class is not thread-safe, so we'll rely on having a single-threaded server. For a multi-threaded server, the deal() method would use the Lock class from the threading module to define an exclusive lock to ensure proper operation with concurrent threads.

6. Define a function to access or initialize the global object. When request processing first starts, this will initialize the object. Subsequently, the cached object can be returned. This can be extended to apply thread locks and handle persistence if needed:

```
def get_deck() -> Deck:
    global deck
    if deck is None:
        random.seed(os.environ.get("DEAL_APP_SEED"))
        deck = Deck()
    return deck
```

7. Define a route—a URL pattern—to a view function that performs a specific request. This is a decorator, placed immediately in front of the function. It will bind the function to the Flask application:

```
@dealer.route("/dealer/hand")
```

8. Define the view function for this route. A view function retrieves data or updates the application state. In this example, the function does both:

```
def deal() -> Response:
    try:
        hand_size = int(request.args.get("cards", 5))
        assert 1 <= hand_size < 53
    except Exception as ex:
        abort(HTTPStatus.BAD_REQUEST)
    deck = get_deck()
    cards = deck.deal(hand_size)
    response = jsonify([card.to_json() for card in cards])
    return response
```

Flask parses the string after the `?` in the URL—the query string—to create the `request.args` value. A client application or browser can set this value with a query string such as `?cards=13`. This will deal 13-card hands for bridge.

If the hand size value from the query string is validated, then using the `int()` function will check the syntax, and the assert statement will check the range of values. If the value is inappropriate, the `abort()` function will end processing and return an HTTP status code of `400`. This indicates that the request was unacceptable. This is a minimal response, with no more detailed content. Adding a text message is often a good idea to clarify why the request was deemed invalid.

The real work of this route is the statement `cards = deck.deal(hand_size)`. The idea here is to wrap existing functionality in a web framework. Ideally, the features can be fully tested without the web application; the web application embeds the application's processing in the RESTful protocol.

The response is created by the `jsonify()` function: this creates a `Response` object. The body of the response will be a Python list of `Card` objects represented in JSON notation. If we need to add headers to the response, we can update the `response.headers` attribute to include additional information.

Here's the main program that runs the server:

```
if __name__ == "__main__":
    dealer.run(use_reloader=True, threaded=False)
```

We've included the `debug=True` option to provide rich debugging information in the browser as well as the Flask log file. Once the server is running, we can open a browser to see `http://localhost:5000/`. This will return a batch of five cards. Each time we refresh, we get a different batch of cards.

Entering a URL in the browser executes a `GET` request with a minimal set of headers. Since our WSGI application doesn't require any specific headers and responds to all HTTP methods, it will return a result.

The result is a JSON document with five cards. Each card is represented by `class name`, `rank`, and `suit` information:


```
[
 {
   "__class__": "Card",
   "suit": "\u2663",
   "rank": 6
 },
 {
   "__class__": "Card",
   "suit": "\u2662",
   "rank": 8
 },
 {
   "__class__": "Card",
   "suit": "\u2660",
   "rank": 8
 },
 {
   "__class__": "Card",
   "suit": "\u2660",
   "rank": 10
 },
 {
   "__class__": "Card",
```

```
    "suit": "\u2663",
    "rank": 11
  }
]
```

To see more than five cards, the URL can be modified. For example, this will return a bridge hand: `http://127.0.0.1:5000/dealer/hand/?cards=13`.

How it works...

A Flask application consists of an application object with a number of individual view functions. In this recipe, we created a single view function, `deal()`. Applications often have numerous functions. A complex website may have many applications, each of which has many functions.

A route is a mapping between a URL pattern and a view function. This makes it possible to have routes that contain parameters that can be used by the view function.

The `@dealer.route` decorator is the technique used to add each route and view function into the overall Flask instance. The view function is bound into the overall application based on the route pattern.

The `run()` method of a `Flask` object does the following kinds of processing. This isn't precisely how Flask works, but it provides a broad outline of some important steps:

- It waits for an HTTP request. Flask follows the WSGI standard: the request arrives in the form of a dictionary, known as "the WSGI environment."
- It creates a Flask `Request` object from the WSGI environment. The `request` object has all of the information from the request, including all of the URL elements, query string elements, and any attached documents.
- Flask then examines the various routes, looking for a route that matches the request's path:
    - If a route is found, then the view function is executed. The function's return value must be a `Response` object.
    - If a route is not found, a `404 NOT FOUND` response is sent automatically.
- The WSGI interface includes a function that's used to send a status and headers. This function also starts sending the response. The `Response` object that was returned from the view function is provided as a stream of bytes to the client.

A Flask application can contain a number of methods that make it very easy to provide a web service with multiple routes and access to a number of related resources.

There's more...

If we're writing a complex RESTful application server, we often want some additional qualification tests applied to each request. Some web services can provide responses in a variety of formats, including JSON and HTML. A client needs to specify which format of response it wants. There are two common ways to handle this:

- An `Accept` header can describe the syntax the client software expects.
- A query string with `$format=json` in it is another way to specify what format the response should be.

This rule will reject requests that lack an `Accept` header. The rule will also reject requests with an `Accept` header that fails to specifically mention JSON. This is quite restrictive and means the web server won't respond unless JSON is specifically requested.

We've seen the Flask `@dealer.route` decorator. Flask has a number of other decorators that can be used to define various stages in request and response processing. In order to apply a test to the incoming request, we can use the `@dealer.before_request` decorator. All of the functions with this decoration will be invoked prior to the request being processed.

We can add a function here to examine the request to see if it's possible for the Flask server to return the expected response format. The function looks like this:

```
@dealer.before_request
def check_json() -> Optional[Response]:
    if "json" in request.headers.get("Accept", "*/*"):
        return None
    if "json" == request.args.get("$format", "html"):
        return None
    abort(HTTPStatus.BAD_REQUEST)
```

When a `@flask.before_request` decorator fails to return a value (or returns `None`), then processing will continue. The routes will be checked, and a view function will be evaluated to compute the response. If a value is returned by this function, that is the result of the web service's request. In this case, the `abort()` function was used to stop processing and create a response. A little more friendly `check_json()` function might include an error message in the `abort()` function.

In this example, if the `Accept` header includes `json` or the `$format` query parameter is `json`, then the function returns `None`. This means that the normal view function will then be found to process the request.

We can now use a browser's address window to enter a URL like the following:

```
http://127.0.0.1:5000/dealer/hand/?cards=13&$format=json
```

This will return a 13-card hand, and the request now explicitly requests the result in JSON format. It is instructive to try other values for `$format` as well as omitting the `$format` key entirely.

> This example has a subtle semantic issue. The `GET` method changes the state of the server. It is generally a bad idea to have `GET` requests with inconsistent results. Having consistent results from a `GET` request is termed "idempotent."

HTTP supports a number of methods that parallel database `CRUD` operations. `Create` is done with `POST`, `Retrieve` is done with `GET`, `Update` is done with `PUT`, and `Delete` maps to `DELETE`.

This idea leads to the idea that a web service's `GET` operation should be idempotent. A series of `GET` operations - without any other `POST`, `PUT`, or `DELETE` - should return the same result each time. In this example, each `GET` returns a different result. Since the deal service is not idempotent, the `GET` method may not be the best choice.

To make it easy to explore using a browser, we've avoided checking the method in the Flask route. If this was changed to responding to `POST` requests, the route decorator should look like the following:

```
@dealer.route('/dealer/hand/', methods=['POST'])
```

Doing this makes it difficult to use a browser to see that the service is working. In the *Making REST requests with urllib* recipe, we'll look at creating a client, and switching to using `POST` for this method.

See also

- See `https://flask.palletsprojects.com/en/1.1.x/` to learn more about the Flask framework. There are a number of closely related projects, all used widely to build web services.
- Also, `https://www.packtpub.com/web-development/mastering-flask` has more information on mastering Flask.

Parsing the query string in a request

A URL is a complex object. It contains at least six separate pieces of information. More information can be included via optional elements.

A URL such as `http://127.0.0.1:5000/dealer/hand/?cards=13&$format=json` has several fields:

- `http` is the scheme. `https` is for secure connections using encrypted sockets.
- `127.0.0.1` can be called the authority, although "network location" is a more common term. Sometimes it's called the host. This particular IP address means the localhost and is a kind of loopback to your computer. The name localhost maps to this IP address.
- `5000` is the port number and is part of the authority.
- `/dealer/hand/` is the path to a resource.
- `cards=13&$format=json` is a query string, and it's separated from the path by the `?` character.

The query string can be quite complex. While not an official standard, it's possible (and common) for a query string to have a repeated key. The following query string is valid, though perhaps confusing:

```
?cards=6&cards=4&cards=4
```

We've repeated the `cards` key. The web service should provide a six-card hand and two separate four-card hands.

The ability to repeat a key in the query string complicates the possibility of using a Python dictionary to keep the keys and values from a URL query string. There are several possible solutions to this problem:

- Each key in the dictionary can be associated with a `list` that contains all of the values. This is awkward for the most common case where a key is not repeated. In the common case, each key's list of values would have only a single item. This solution is implemented via the `parse_qs()` function in the `urllib.parse` module.
- Each key is only saved once and the first (or last) value is kept; the other values are dropped. This is awful and isn't the way the query string was designed to be used.
- Instead of a dictionary, the query string can be represented as a list of (`key, value`) pairs. This also allows keys to be duplicated. For the common case with unique keys, the list can be converted to a dictionary. For the uncommon case, the duplicated keys can be handled some other way. This is implemented by the `parse_qsl()` function in the `urllib.parse` module.

There are better ways to handle a query string. We'll look at a more sophisticated structure that behaves like a dictionary with single values for the common case and a more complex object for the rare cases where a field key is duplicated and has multiple values. This will let us model the common case as well as the edge cases comfortably.

Getting ready

Flask depends on another project, `Werkzeug`. When we install Flask using `pip`, the requirements will lead `pip` to also install the `Werkzeug` toolkit. `Werkzeug` has a data structure that provides an excellent way to handle query strings.

We'll be extending the *Using the Flask framework for RESTful APIs* recipe from earlier in this chapter.

How to do it...

We'll start with the code from the *Using the Flask framework for RESTful APIs* recipe to use a somewhat more complex query string. We'll add a second route that deals multiple hands. The size of each hand will be specified in a query string that allows repeated keys:

1. Start with the *Using the Flask framework for RESTful APIs* recipe. We'll be adding a new view function to an existing web application.
2. Define a `route`—a URL pattern—to a view function that performs a specific request. This is a decorator, placed immediately in front of the function. It will bind the function to the Flask application. We've used hands in the route to suggest multiple hands will be dealt:

```
@dealer.route("/dealer/hands")
```

3. Define a view function that responds to requests sent to the particular route:

```
def multi_hand() -> Response:
```

4. Within the `multi_hand()` view function, there are two methods to extract the values from a query string. We can use the `request.args.get()` method for a key that will occur once. For repeated keys, use the `request.args.getlist()` method. This returns a list of values. Here's a view function that looks for a query string such as `?card=5&card=5` to deal two five-card hands:

```
    dealer.logger.debug(f"Request: {request.args}")
    try:
        hand_sizes = request.args.getlist(
            "cards", type=int)
    except ValueError as ex:
        abort(HTTPStatus.BAD_REQUEST)
    dealer.logger.info(f"{hand_sizes=}")
    if len(hand_sizes) == 0:
        hand_sizes = [13, 13, 13, 13]
    if not(1 <= sum(hand_sizes) < 53):
```

```
            abort(HTTPStatus.BAD_REQUEST)
        deck = get_deck()
        hands = [
            deck.deal(hand_size) for hand_size in hand_sizes]
    response = jsonify(
        [
            {
                "hand": i,
                "cards": [
                    card.to_json()
                    for card in hand
                ]
            }
            for i, hand in enumerate(hands)
        ]
    )
    return response
```

This function will get all of the `cards` keys from the query string. If the values are all integers, and each value is in the range 1 to 52 (inclusive), then the values are valid, and the view function will return a result. If there are no `cards` key values in the query, then four hands of 13 cards will be dealt.

The response will be a JSON representation of a list of hands. Each hand is represented as a dictionary with two keys. The "`hand`" key has a hand ID. The "`cards`" key has the sequence of individual `Card` instances. Each `Card` instance is expanded into a dictionary using the `to_json()` method of the `Card` class.

Here's the small main program that will run this module as a Flask server:

```
if __name__ == "__main__":
    dealer.run(use_reloader=True, threaded=False)
```

Once the server is running, we can open a browser to see this URL:

`http://localhost:5000/?cards=5&cards=5&$format=json`

The result is a JSON document with two hands of five cards. We've used ... to elide some details to emphasize the structure of the response:

```
[
 {
   "cards": [
     {
```

```
            "__class__": "Card",
            "rank": 11,
        "suit": "\u2660"
          },
          {
            "__class__": "Card",
            "rank": 8,
            "suit": "\u2662"
          },
          ...
        ],
        "hand": 0
      },
      {
        "cards": [
          {
            "__class__": "Card",
            "rank": 3,
            "suit": "\u2663"
          },
          {
            "__class__": "Card",
            "rank": 9,
            "suit": "\u2660"
          },
          ...
        ],
        "hand": 1
      }
    ]
```

Because the web service parses the query string, it's trivial to add more complex hand sizes to the query string. The example includes the `$format=json` based on the *Using the Flask framework for RESTful APIs* recipe.

How it works...

The `werkzeug` module defines a `Multidict` class. This is a handy data structure for working with headers and query strings. This is an extension to the built-in dictionary. It allows multiple, distinct values for a given key.

We can build something like this using the `defaultdict` class from the `collections` module. The definition would be `defaultdict(list)`. The problem with this definition is that the value of every key is a list, even when the list only has a single item as a value.

The advantage provided by the `Multidict` class is the variations on the `get()` method. The `get()` method returns the first value when there are many copies of a key or the only value when the key occurs only once. This has a `default` parameter, as well. This method parallels the method of the built-in `dict` class.

The `getlist()` method, however, returns a list of all values for a given key. This method is unique to the `Multidict` class. We can use this method to parse more complex query strings.

One common technique that's used to validate query strings is to pop items as they are validated. This is done with the `pop()` and `poplist()` methods. These will remove the key from the `Multidict` class. If any keys remain after checking all the valid keys, these extras can be considered syntax errors, and the web request can be rejected with `abort(HTTPStatus.BAD_REQUEST)`. Adding an error message with details would be a helpful addition to the arguments to this function.

There's more...

The query string uses relatively simple syntax rules. There are one or more key-value pairs using `=` as the punctuation between the key and value. The separator between each pair is the `&` character. Because of the meaning of other characters in parsing a URL, there is one other rule that's important – the keys and values must be encoded.

The URL encoding rules require that certain characters be replaced with HTML entities. The technique is called percent encoding. The "&" character, for example, needs to be encoded as `%26`. Here's an example showing this encoding:

```
>>> from urllib.parse import urlencode
>>> urlencode({'n':355,'d':113})
'n=355&d=113'
>>> urlencode({'n':355,'d':113,'note':'this&that'})
'n=355&d=113&note=this%26that'
```

The value `this&that` was encoded to `this%26that`, replacing the `&` with `%26`. This transformation is undone by request parsing in Flask.

There's a short list of characters that must have the `%`-encoding rules applied. This comes from *RFC 3986* – refer to *section 2.2, Reserved Characters*. The list includes these characters:

```
! * ' ( ) ; : @ & = + $ , / ? # [ ] %
```

Generally, the JavaScript code associated with a web page will handle encoding query strings. If we're writing an API client in Python, we need to use the `urlencode()` function to properly encode query strings. Flask handles the decoding automatically for us.

There's a practical size limit on the query string. Apache HTTPD, for example, has a `LimitRequestLine` configuration parameter with a default value of `8190`. This limits the overall URL to this size.

In the OData specifications (`http://docs.oasis-open.org/odata/odata/v4.0/`), there are several kinds of values that are suggested for the query options. This specification suggests that our web services should support the following kinds of query option:

- For a URL that identifies an entity or a collection of entities, the `$expand` and `$select` options can be used. Expanding a result means that the query will provide additional details such as related items. The `select` query will impose additional criteria to filter the collection.
- A URL that identifies a collection should support `$filter`, `$search`, `$orderby`, `$skip`, and `$top` options. These options don't make sense for a URL that returns a single item. The `$filter` and `$search` options accept complex conditions for finding data. The `$orderby` option defines a particular order to impose on the results. The `$top` and `$skip` options are used to page through data. If the count is large, it's common to use the `$top` option to limit the results to a specific number that will be shown on a web page. The value of the `$skip` option determines which page of data will be shown. For example, `$top=20&$skip=40` would be page 3 of the results—the top `20` after skipping `40`.
- A collection URL can also support a `$count` option. This changes the query fundamentally to return the count of items instead of the items themselves.

Generally, it can be helpful for all URLs to support the `$format` option to specify the format of the result. We've been focusing on JSON, but a more sophisticated service might offer CSV or YAML output or even XML. With the format in the URL as part of the query string, special headers aren't required and some preliminary exploration can be done with browser queries.

See also

- See the *Using the Flask framework for RESTful APIs* recipe earlier in this chapter for the basics of using Flask for web services.
- In the *Making REST requests with urllib* recipe, later in this chapter, we'll look at how to write a client application that can prepare complex query strings.

Making REST requests with urllib

A web application has two essential parts:

- **A client**: This can be a user's browser, but may also be a mobile device app. In some cases, a web server may be a client of other web servers.
- **A server**: This provides the web services and resources we've been looking at, in the *Using the Flask framework for RESTful APIs*, and *Parsing the query string in a request* recipes, as well as other recipes, such as *Parsing a JSON request and Implementing authentication for web services*.

A browser-based client will generally be written in JavaScript. Mobile apps are written in a variety of languages, with a focus on Java or Kotlin for Android devices and Objective-C with Swift for iOS devices.

There are several user stories that involve RESTful API clients written in Python. How can we create a Python program that is a client of RESTful web services?

Getting ready

We'll assume that we have a web server based on the *Using the Flask framework for RESTful APIs*, and the *Parsing the query string in a request* recipes earlier in this chapter. Currently, these server examples do not provide an OpenAPI specification. In the *Parsing the URL path* recipe, later in this chapter, we'll add an OpenAPI specification.

A server should provide a formal OpenAPI specification of its behavior. For the purposes of this recipe, we'll assume that an OpenAPI specification exists. We'll break the specification down into the major sections of the document.

First, the `openapi` block states which version of the OpenAPI specification will be followed:

```
openapi: 3.0.3
```

The `info` block provides some identifying information about the service:

```
info:
  title: Python Cookbook Chapter 12, recipe 4.
  description: Parsing the query string in a request
  version: "1.0"
```

A client will often check the version to be sure of the server's version. An unexpected version number may mean the client is out of date and should suggest an upgrade to the user.

The `servers` block is one way to identify the base URL for all of the individual paths that the server handles. This is often redundant since the client gets the specification by making an initial request to the server:

```
servers:
- url: "http://127.0.0.1:5000/dealer"
```

The `paths` block lists each of the paths and describes the kinds of requests that each path can handle. In this case, there are two paths. The first path is `/hands` and expects a query string with the hand sizes; this uses HTML form-encoding of the data values. Here's what this fragment looks like in YAML notation:

```
paths:
  /hands:
    get:
      parameters:
      - name: cards
        in: query
        style: form
        explode: true
        schema:
          type: integer
      responses:
        "200":
          description: cards for each hand size in the query
          content:
            application/json:
              schema:
                type: array
                items:
                  type: object
                  properties:
                    hand:
                      type: integer
                    cards:
                      type: array
                      items:
                        $ref: "#/components/schemas/Card"
```

A `components` block in the OpenAPI specification provides common definitions shared by the paths. A value with a `$ref` key can have a value of a path to an item in the `components` block. This often provides schema details used to validate requests and replies.

The OpenAPI document provides us with some guidance on how to consume these services using Python's `urllib` module. It also describes what the expected responses should be, giving us guidance on how to handle the responses.

The detailed resource definitions are provided in the `paths` section of the specification. The `/hands` path, for example, shows the details of how to make a request for multiple hands.

When we provide a URL built from the `server url` value and the path in the OpenAPI specification, we also need to provide a method. When the HTTP method is `get`, then the specification declares the parameters must be provided in the query. The `cards` parameter in the query provides an integer number of cards, and it can be repeated multiple times.

The response will include at least the response described. In this case, the HTTP status will be `200`, and the body of the response has a minimal description. It's possible to provide a more formal schema definition for the response, but we'll omit that from this example.

We can combine the built-in `urllib` library with OpenAPI specification details to make RESTful API requests.

How to do it...

1. Import the `urllib` components that are required. We'll be making URL requests, and building more complex objects, such as query strings. We'll need the `urllib.request` and `urllib.parse` modules for these two features. Since the expected response is in JSON, then the `json` module will be useful as well:

   ```
   import urllib.request
   import urllib.parse
   import json
   from typing import Dict, Any
   ```

2. Define a function to make the request to be sent to the server:

   ```
   def query_build_1() -> None:
   ```

3. Define the query string that will be used. In this case, all of the values happen to be fixed. In a more complex application, some might be fixed and some might be based on user inputs:

   ```
       query = {"hand": 5}
   ```

4. Use the query to build the pieces of the full URL. We can use a `ParseResult` object to hold the relevant parts of the URL. This class isn't graceful about missing items, so we must provide explicit `""` values for parts of the URL that aren't being used:

   ```
       full_url = urllib.parse.ParseResult(
           scheme="http",
           netloc="127.0.0.1:5000",
   ```

```
        path="/dealer" + "/hand",
        params="",
        query=urllib.parse.urlencode(query),
        fragment="",
    )
```

5. Build a final `Request` instance. We'll use the URL built from a variety of pieces. We'll explicitly provide an HTTP method (browsers tend to use `GET` as a default). Also, we can provide explicit headers, including the `Accept` header to state the results accepted by the client. We've provided the `HTTP Content-Type` header to state the request consumed by the server, and provided by our client script:

```
    request2 = urllib.request.Request(
        url=urllib.parse.urlunparse(full_url),
        method="GET",
        headers={"Accept": "application/json",},
    )
```

6. Open a context to process the response. The `urlopen()` function makes the request, handling all of the complexities of the HTTP protocol. The final `result` object is available for processing as a response:

```
        with urllib.request.urlopen(request2) as response:
```

7. Generally, there are three attributes of the response that are of particular interest:

```
            print(response.getcode())
            print(response.headers)
            print(json.loads(response.read().decode("utf-8")))
```

The `status` is the final status code from the server. We expect a status `200` for a normal, successful request. The code values are defined in the `http` module. The `headers` attribute includes all of the headers that are part of the `response`. We might, for example, want to check that the `response.headers['Content-Type']` is the expected `application/json`.

The value of `response.read()` is the bytes downloaded from the server. We'll often need to decode these to get proper Unicode characters. The `utf-8` encoding scheme is very common. The `Content-Type` header can provide an override in the rare case this encoding is not used. We can use `json.loads()` to create a Python object from the JSON document.

When we run this, we'll see the following output:

```
200
Content-Type: application/json
Content-Length: 367
```

```
Server: Werkzeug/0.11.10 Python/3.5.1
Date: Sat, 23 Jul 2016 19:46:35 GMT


[{'suit': '♣', 'rank': 4, '__class__': 'Card'},
 {'suit': '♡', 'rank': 4, '__class__': 'Card'},
 {'suit': '♠', 'rank': 9, '__class__': 'Card'},
 {'suit': '♣', 'rank': 1, '__class__': 'Card'},
 {'suit': '♣', 'rank': 2, '__class__': 'Card'}]
```

The initial `200` is the status, showing that everything worked properly. There were four headers provided by the server. Finally, the internal Python object was an array of small dictionaries that provided information about the cards that were dealt.

To reconstruct `Card` objects, we'd need to use a slightly more clever JSON parser. See the *Reading JSON documents* recipe in *Chapter 10, Input/Output, Physical Format, and Logical Layout*.

How it works...

We've built up the request through several explicit steps:

1. The query data started as a dictionary with keys and values, `{"hand": 5}`.
2. The `urlencode()` function turned the query data into a query string, properly encoded.
3. The URL as a whole started as individual components in a `ParseResult` object. This makes each piece visible, and changeable. For this particular API, the pieces are largely fixed. In other APIs, the path and the query portion of the URL might both have dynamic values.
4. A `Request` object was built from the URL, method, and a dictionary of headers. This example did not provide a separate document as the body of a request. If a complex document is sent, or a file is uploaded, this is also done by providing details to the `Request` object.
5. The `urllib.request.urlopen()` function sends the request and will read the response.

The step-by-step assembly isn't required for a simple application. In simple cases, a literal string value for the URL might be acceptable. At the other extreme, a more complex application may print out intermediate results as a debugging aid to be sure that the request is being constructed correctly.

The other benefit of spelling out the details like this is to provide a handy avenue for unit testing. See *Chapter 11, Testing*, for more information. We can often decompose a web client into request building and request processing. The request building can be tested carefully to be sure that all of the elements are set properly. The request processing can be tested with dummy results that don't involve a live connection to a remote server.

There's more...

User authentication is often an important part of a web service. For HTML-based websites – where user interaction is emphasized – people expect the server to understand a long-running sequence of transactions via a session. The person will authenticate themselves once (often with a username and password) and the server will use this information until the person logs out or the session expires.

For RESTful web services, there is rarely the concept of a session. Each request is processed separately, and the server is not expected to maintain a complex long-running transaction state. This responsibility shifts to the client application. The client is required to make appropriate requests to build up a complex document that can be presented as a single transaction.

For RESTful APIs, each request may include authentication information. We'll look at this in detail in the *Implementing authentication for web services* recipe later in this chapter. For now, we'll look at providing additional details via headers. This will fit comfortably with our RESTful client script.

There are a number of ways that authentication information is provided to a web server:

- Some services use the `HTTP Authorization` header. When used with the Basic mechanism, a client can provide a username and password with each request.
- Some services will use a header with a name such as `Api-Key`. The value for this header might be a complex string that has encoded information about the requestor.
- Some services will invent a header with a name such as `X-Auth-Token`. This may be used in a multi-step operation where a username and password credentials are sent as part of an initial request. The result will include a string value (a token) that can be used for subsequent API requests. Often, the token has a short expiration period and must be renewed.

Generally, all of these methods require the **Secure Socket Layer** (**SSL**) protocol to transmit the credentials securely. This is available as the `https` scheme. In order to handle the SSL protocol, the servers (and sometimes the clients) must have proper certificates. These are used as part of the negotiation between client and server to set up the encrypted socket pair.

All of these authentication techniques have a feature in common – they rely on sending additional information in headers. They differ slightly in which header is used, and what information is sent. In the simplest case, we might have something like the following:

```
request = urllib.request.Request(
    url = urllib.parse.urlunparse(full_url),
    method = "GET",
    headers = {
        'Accept': 'application/json',
        'X-Authentication': 'seekrit password',
    }
)
```

This hypothetical request would be for a web service that requires a password provided in an `X-Authentication` header. In the *Implementing authentication for web services* recipe later in this chapter, we'll add an authentication feature to the web server.

The OpenAPI specification

Many servers will explicitly provide a specification as a file at a fixed, standard URL path of `/openapi.yaml` or `/openapi.json`. The OpenAPI specification was formerly known as **Swagger**.

If it's available, we may be able get a website's OpenAPI specification in the following way:

```
def get_openapi_spec() -> Dict[str, Any]:
    with urllib.request.urlopen(
        "http://127.0.0.1:5000/dealer/openapi.json"
    ) as spec_request:
        openapi_spec = json.load(spec_request)
    return openapi_spec
```

Not all servers offer OpenAPI specifications. It's widely used, but not required.

The OpenAPI specification can be in JSON or YAML notation. While JSON is very common, some people find YAML easier to work with. Most of the examples for this book were prepared in YAML notation for that reason.

Once we have the specification, we can use it to get the details for the service or resource. We can use the technical information in the specification to build URLs, query strings, and headers.

Adding the OpenAPI resource to the server

For our little demonstration server, an additional view function is required to provide the OpenAPI specification. We can update the `ch12_r02.py` module to respond to a request for `openapi.yaml`.

There are several ways to handle this important information:

- A separate, static file: Flask can serve static content, but it's often more efficient to have a server like Gunicorn handle static files.
- Embed the specification as a large blob of text in the module: We could, for example, provide the specification as the docstring for the module or another global variable.
- Create a Python specification object in proper Python syntax: This can then be encoded into JSON and transmitted.

Here's a view function to send a separate file:

```
from flask import send_file
@dealer.route('/dealer/openapi.yaml')
def openapi_1() -> Response:
    # Note. No IANA registered standard as of this writing.
    response = send_file(
        "openapi.yaml",
          mimetype="application/yaml")
    return response
```

This doesn't involve too much application programming. The drawback of this approach is that the specification is separate from the implementation module. While it's not difficult to coordinate the implementing module and the specification, any time two things must be synchronized it invites problems.

A second approach is to embed the OpenAPI specification into the module docstring. Often, we'll need to parse the docstring to use it in the server to validate input from clients. We can use `yaml.load()` to build the specification as a Python object from the string. Here's a view function to send the module docstring:

```
from flask import make_response
specification = yaml.load(__doc__, Loader=yaml.SafeLoader)

@dealer.route("/dealer/openapi.yaml")
def openapi_2() -> Response:
    response = make_response(
        yaml.dump(specification).encode("utf-8"))
    response.headers["Content-Type"] = "application/yaml"
    return response
```

This has the advantage of being part of the module that implements the web service. It has the disadvantage of requiring that we check the syntax of the docstring to be sure that it's valid YAML. This is in addition to validating that the module implementation actually conforms to the specification.

A third option is to write the OpenAPI specification as a Python document and serialize this into JSON notation:

```
from flask import make_response
specification = {
    "openapi": "3.0.3",
    "info": {
        "description": "Parsing the query string in a request",
        "title": "Python Cookbook Chapter 12, recipe 2.",
        "version": "1.0",
    },
    "servers": [{"url": "http://127.0.0.1:5000/dealer"}],
    "paths": {
        ...
    },
    "components": {
        ...
    }
}
@dealer.route("/dealer/openapi.json")
def openapi_3() -> Response:
    return jsonify(specification)
```

This makes use of Flask's `jsonify()` function to translate a specification written as a Python data structure into JSON notation.

In all cases, there are several benefits to having a formal specification available:

1. Client applications can download the specification to confirm the server's features.
2. When examples are included, the specification becomes a series of test cases for both client and server. This can form a contract used to validate clients as well as servers.
3. The various details of the specification can also be used by the server application to provide validation rules, defaults, and other details. If the OpenAPI specification is a Python data structure, pieces of it can be used to create JSON schema validators.

As seen previously, there are only a few lines of code required to provide the OpenAPI specification. It provides helpful information to clients. The largest cost is the intellectual effort to carefully define the API and write down the contract in the formal language of the OpenAPI specification.

See also

- The *Parsing the query string in a request* recipe earlier in this chapter introduces the core web service.
- The *Implementing Authentication for web services* recipe later in this chapter will add authentication to make the service more secure.

Parsing the URL path

A URL is a complex object. It contains at least six separate pieces of information. More data can be included via optional elements.

A URL such as `http://127.0.0.1:5000/dealer/hand/player_1?$format=json` has several fields:

- `http` is the **scheme**. `https` is for secure connections using encrypted sockets.
- `127.0.0.1` can be called the *authority*, although **network location** is more commonly used.
- `5000` is the **port number** and is often considered to be part of the authority.
- `/dealer/hand/player_1` is the **path** to a resource.
- `$format=json` is a **query string**.

The path to a resource can be quite complex. It's common in RESTful web services to use the path information to identify groups of resources, individual resources, and even relationships among resources.

In this recipe, we'll see how Flask lets us parse complex URL patterns.

Getting ready

Most web services provide access to some kind of resource. In the *Using the Flask framework for RESTful APIs*, and *Parsing the query string in a request* recipes earlier in this chapter, the resource was identified on the URL path as a hand or hands. This is - in a way - misleading.

There are actually two resources that are involved in the example web service:

- A `deck`, which can be shuffled to produce one or more random hands
- A `hand`, which was treated as a transient response to a request

To make matters potentially confusing, the `hand` resource was created via a `GET` request instead of the more common `POST` request. This is confusing because a `GET` request is never expected to change the state of the server. Ideally, each time a `GET` request is made, the response is the same; however, in this case, we've broken that expectation.

For simple explorations and technical spikes, GET requests are helpful. Because a browser can make GET requests, these are a handy way to explore some aspects of web services design.

We'll redesign this service to provide explicit access to a randomized instance of the Deck class. One feature of each deck will be hands of cards. This parallels the idea of Deck as a collection and Hands as a resource within the collection:

- /dealer/decks: A POST request will create a new deck object. The response to this request is a token in the form of a string that is used to identify the unique deck.
- /dealer/deck/{id}/hands: A GET request to this will get a hand object from the given deck identifier. The query string will specify how many cards. The query string can use the $top option to limit how many hands are returned. It can also use the $skip option to skip over some hands and get cards for later hands.

These queries will be difficult to perform from a browser; they will require an API client. One possibility is to use the Postman tool. We'll leverage the *Making REST requests with urllib* recipe earlier in this chapter as the starting point for a client to process these more complex APIs.

How to do it...

We'll decompose this into two parts: server and client.

Server

We'll build the server based on previous examples. Start with the *Parsing the query string in a request* recipe earlier in this chapter as a template for a Flask application. We'll be changing the view functions in that example:

1. We'll import the various modules needed to make use of the Flask framework. We'll define a Flask application and set a few handy global configuration parameters to make debugging slightly easier:

```
from http import HTTPStatus
from flask import (
    Flask, jsonify, request, abort, url_for, Response
    )
from Chapter_12.card_model import Card, Deck

dealer = Flask("ch12_r04")
dealer.DEBUG = True
dealer.TESTING = True
```

2. Import any additional modules. In this case, we'll use the `uuid` module to create a unique token string to identify a shuffled deck:

   ```
   import uuid
   ```

3. Define the global state. This includes the collection of decks. It also includes the random number generator. For testing purposes, it can help to have a way to force a particular seed value:

   ```
   import os
   import random
   decks: Optional[Dict[str, Deck]] = None
   ```

4. Define a function to create or access the global state information. When request processing first starts, this will initialize the object. Subsequently, the cached object can be returned:

   ```
   def get_decks() -> Dict[str, Deck]:
       global decks
       if decks is None:
           random.seed(os.environ.get("DEAL_APP_SEED"))
           # Database connection might go here.
           decks = {}
       return decks
   ```

5. Define a route – a URL pattern – to a view function that performs a specific request. Because creating a deck is a state change, the route should only handle `HTTP POST` requests. In this example, the route creates a new instance in the collection of decks. Write the decorator, placed immediately in front of the function. It will bind the function to the Flask application:

   ```
   @dealer.route("/dealer/decks", methods=["POST"])
   ```

6. Define the view function that supports this resource. We'll use the parsed query string for the number of decks to create. Any exception from an invalid number of decks will lead to a bad request response. The response will include the `UUID` for a newly created deck. This will also be in the `Location` header of the response:

   ```
   def make_deck() -> Response:
       try:
           dealer.logger.info(f"make_deck {request.args}")
           n_decks = int(request.args.get("decks", 1))
           assert 1 <= n_decks
       except Exception as ex:
           abort(HTTPStatus.BAD_REQUEST)

       decks = get_decks()
   ```

```
    id = str(uuid.uuid1())
    decks[id] = Deck(n=n_decks)

    response_json = jsonify(status="ok", id=id)
    response = make_response(
        response_json, HTTPStatus.CREATED)
    response.headers["Location"] = url_for(
        "get_one_deck_count", id=id)
    response.headers["Content-Type"] = "application/json"
    return response
```

The response has a status of `201 Created` instead of the default `200 OK`. The body will be a small JSON document with a `status` field and the `id` field to identify the deck created.

7. Define a route to get a hand from a given deck. In this case, the route must include the specific deck ID to deal from. The `<id>` makes this a path template instead of a simple, literal path. Flask will extract the `<id>` field from the path in the request URL:

```
@dealer.route("/dealer/decks/<id>", methods=["GET"])
```

8. Define a view function that has parameters that match the template. Since the template included `<id>`, the view function has a parameter named `id` as well. Flask handles the URL parsing, making the value available as a parameter. There are three parts: validating the request, doing the work, and creating the final `response` object:

```
def get_hands(id: str) -> Response:
    decks = get_decks()
    if id not in decks:
        dealer.logger.error(id)
        abort(HTTPStatus.NOT_FOUND)
    try:
        cards = int(request.args.get("cards", 13))
        top = int(request.args.get("$top", 1))
        skip = int(request.args.get("$skip", 0))
        assert (
            skip * cards + top * cards
            <= len(decks[id].cards)
        ), "$skip, $top, and cards larger than the deck"
    except (ValueError, AssertionError) as ex:
        dealer.logger.error(ex)
        abort(HTTPStatus.BAD_REQUEST)
```

```
        subset = decks[id].cards[
            skip * cards : skip * cards + top * cards]
        hands = [
            subset[h * cards : (h + 1) * cards]
            for h in range(top)
        ]

        response = jsonify(
            [
                {
                    "hand": i,
                    "cards": [card.to_json() for card in hand]
                } for i, hand in enumerate(hands)
            ]
        )
        return response
```

The validation checks several parts of the request:

- The value of the `id` parameter must be one of the keys to the `decks` collection. Otherwise, the function makes a `404 NOT FOUND` response. In this example, we don't provide much of an error message. A more complete error might use the optional description, like this: `abort(HTTPStatus.NOT_FOUND, description=f"{id} not found")`
- The values of `$top`, `$skip`, and `cards` are extracted from the query string. For this example, all of the values should be integers, so the `int()` function is used for each value. A rudimentary sanity check is performed on the query parameters. An additional check on the combination of values is also a good idea; you are encouraged to add checks.

The real work of the view function creates a hand of cards. The `subset` variable is the portion of the deck being dealt. We've sliced the deck to start after `skip` sets of cards; we've included just `top` sets of `cards` in this slice. From that slice, the `hands` sequence decomposes the subset into the `top` number of hands, each of which has `cards` in it.

The response preparation converts the sequence of `Card` objects to JSON via the `jsonify()` function. The default status set by the `jsonify()` function is `200 OK`, which is appropriate here because this query is an idempotent `GET` request. Each time a query is sent, the same set of cards will be returned.

Client

This will be similar to the client module from the *Making REST requests with urllib* recipe:

1. Import the essential modules for working with RESTful APIs:

    ```
    import urllib.request
    import urllib.parse
    import urllib.error
    import json
    ```

2. Define a function to make the `POST` request that will create a new, shuffled deck. We've called this `no_spec_create_new_deck()` to emphasize that it doesn't rely on the OpenAPI specification. The return value will be a document containing the deck's unique identifier assigned by the server:

    ```
    def no_spec_create_new_deck(
            size: int = 6) -> Dict[str, Any]:
    ```

3. This starts by defining the query and using the query to create the URL. The URL is built in pieces, by creating a `ParseResult` object manually. This will be collapsed into a single string:

    ```
        query = {"size": size}
        full_url = urllib.parse.urlunparse(
            urllib.parse.ParseResult(
                scheme="http",
                netloc="127.0.0.1:5000",
                path="/dealer" + "/decks",
                params="",
                query=urllib.parse.urlencode({"size": size}),
                fragment=""
            )
        )
    ```

4. Build a `Request` object from the URL, method, and headers:

    ```
        request = urllib.request.Request(
            url=full_url,
            method="POST",
            headers={"Accept": "application/json",}
        )
    ```

5. Send the request and process the response object. For debugging purposes, it can be helpful to print status and header information. We need to make sure that the status was the expected `201`. The response document should be a JSON serialization of a Python dictionary. This client confirms the `status` field in the response document is `ok` before using the value in the `id` field:

```
    try:
        with urllib.request.urlopen(request) as response:
            assert (
                response.getcode() == 201
            ), f"Error Creating Deck: {response.status}"

            print(response.headers)
            document = json.loads(
                response.read().decode("utf-8"))

        print(document)
        assert document["status"] == "ok"
        return document
    except Exception as ex:
        print("ERROR: ex")
        print(ex.read())
        raise
```

6. Define the function to make the `GET` request to fetch one or more hands from the new deck. We've called this `no_spec_get_hands()` to emphasize that it doesn't rely on the OpenAPI specification. The `id` parameter is the unique deck ID from the document returned by the `no_spec_create_new_deck()` function. The return value will be a document containing the requested hands:

```
def no_spec_get_hands(
        id: str,
        cards: int = 13,
        limit: int = 4
) -> Dict[str, Any]:
```

7. This starts by defining the query and using the query to create the URL. The URL is built in pieces, by creating a `ParseResult` object manually. This will be collapsed into a single string:

```
    query = {"$top": limit, "cards": cards}
    full_url = urllib.parse.urlunparse(
        urllib.parse.ParseResult(
```

```
                scheme="http",
                netloc="127.0.0.1:5000",
                path="/dealer" + f"/decks/{id}/hands",
                params="",
                query=urllib.parse.urlencode(query),
                fragment=""
            )
        )
```

8. Make the `Request` object using the full URL, the method, and the standard headers:

```
        request = urllib.request.Request(
            url=full_url,
            method="GET",
            headers={"Accept": "application/json",}
        )
```

9. Send the request and process the response. We'll confirm that the response is `200 OK`. The response can then be parsed to get the details of the cards that are part of the requested hand:

```
        with urllib.request.urlopen(request) as response:
            assert (
                response.getcode() == 200
            ), f"Error Fetching Hand: {response.status}"
            hands = json.loads(
                response.read().decode("utf-8"))
        return hands
```

We have two functions that produce the expected results. We can combine them like this:

```
create_doc = no_spec_create_new_deck(6)
print(create_doc)
id = create_doc["id"]
hands = no_spec_get_hands(id, cards=6, limit=2)

for hand in hands:
    print(f"Hand {hand['hand']}")
    pprint(hand['cards'])
    print()
```

This will produce output that looks like this:

```
{'id': '53f7c70e-adcc-11ea-8e2d-6003089a7902', 'status': 'ok'}
Hand 0
[{'__class__': 'Card', '__init__': {'rank': 3, 'suit': '♣'}},
 {'__class__': 'Card', '__init__': {'rank': 5, 'suit': '♡'}},
 {'__class__': 'Card', '__init__': {'rank': 8, 'suit': '♢'}},
 {'__class__': 'Card', '__init__': {'rank': 12, 'suit': '♠'}},
 {'__class__': 'Card', '__init__': {'rank': 12, 'suit': '♣'}},
 {'__class__': 'Card', '__init__': {'rank': 6, 'suit': '♣'}}]

Hand 1
[{'__class__': 'Card', '__init__': {'rank': 13, 'suit': '♣'}},
 {'__class__': 'Card', '__init__': {'rank': 10, 'suit': '♢'}},
 {'__class__': 'Card', '__init__': {'rank': 4, 'suit': '♢'}},
 {'__class__': 'Card', '__init__': {'rank': 2, 'suit': '♠'}},
 {'__class__': 'Card', '__init__': {'rank': 13, 'suit': '♢'}},
 {'__class__': 'Card', '__init__': {'rank': 5, 'suit': '♣'}}]
```

Your results will vary because of the use of a random shuffle in the server. For integration testing purposes, the random seed should be set in the server to produce fixed sequences of cards. The first line of output shows the ID and status from creating the deck. The next block of output is the two hands of six cards each.

How it works...

The server defines two routes that follow a common pattern for a collection and an instance of the collection. It's typical to define collection paths with a plural noun, `decks`. Using a plural noun means that the CRUD operations (Create, Retrieve, Update, and Delete) are focused on creating instances within the collection.

In this case, the Create operation is implemented with a `POST` method of the `/dealer/decks` path. Retrieve could be supported by writing an additional view function to handle the `GET` method of the `/dealer/decks` path. This would expose all of the deck instances in the decks collection.

If Delete is supported, this could use the `DELETE` method of `/dealer/decks`. Update (using the `PUT` method) doesn't seem to fit with the idea of a server that creates random decks.

Within the `/dealer/decks` collection, a specific deck is identified by the `/dealer/decks/<id> path`. The design calls for using the `GET` method to fetch several hands of cards from the given deck.

The remaining CRUD operations—Create, Update, and Delete—don't make much sense for this kind of `Deck` object. Once the `Deck` object is created, then a client application can interrogate the deck for various hands.

Deck slicing

The dealing algorithm makes several slices of a deck of cards. The slices are based on the fact that the size of a deck, *D*, must contain enough cards for the number of hands, *h*, and the number of cards in each hand, *c*. The number of hands and cards per hand must be no larger than the size of the deck:

$$h \times c \leq D$$

The social ritual of dealing often involves cutting the deck, which is a very simple shuffle done by the non-dealing player. We'll ignore this nuance since we're asking an impartial server to shuffle for us.

Traditionally, each hth card is assigned to each hand, H_n:

$$H_n = \{D_{n+h\times i} \mid 0 \leq i < c\}$$

The idea in the preceding formula is that hand H_0 has cards $H_0 = \{D_0, D_h, D_{2h}, \ldots, D_{c\times h}\}$, hand H_1 has cards $H_1 = \{ D_1, D_{1+h}, D_{1+2h}, \ldots, D_{1+c\times h}\}$, and so on. This distribution of cards looks fairer than simply handing each player the next batch of c cards.

This social ritual isn't really necessary for our software, and our Python program deals cards using slices that are slightly easier to compute with Python:

$$H_n = \{D_{i+n\times c} \mid 0 \leq i < c\}$$

The Python code creates hand H_0 with cards $H_0 = \{ D_0, D_1, D_2, \ldots, D_{c-1}\}$, hand H_1 has cards $H_1 = \{ D_c, D_{c+1}, D_{c+2}, \ldots, D_{2c-1}\}$, and so on. Given a random deck, this is just as fair as any other allocation of cards. It's slightly simpler to enumerate in Python because it involves a simpler kind of list slicing. For more information on slicing, see the *Slicing and dicing a list* recipe in *Chapter 4, Built-In Data Structures Part 1: Lists and Sets*.

The client side

The client side of this transaction is a sequence of RESTful requests. The first request, to create a new deck, uses `POST`. The response includes the identity of the created object. The server put the information in two places in the response:

1. It was in the body of the document, a JSON-encoded dictionary, in the `id` key.
2. It was in a `Location` header in the response.

This kind of redundancy is common, and it allows the client more flexibility. The value in the body of the response document is only the UUID for the deck. The value in the header, however, is the full URL required to get the details of the deck.

Looking at the client code, there's a fair number of lines tied up with building URL strings. It would be simpler for the URLs to be provided by the server. This is a design pattern called **Hypertext as the Engine of State** (**HATEOS**.) It's advantageous to have the server provide relevant URLs, and save the client from the complication of computing a value that's already part of the server's internal processing. Not all RESTful servers do this well, but examples like the GitHub API are worth careful study because of their sophisticated use of URL links in the responses.

There's more...

We'll look at some features that we should consider adding to the server:

- Checking for JSON in the `Accept` header
- Providing the OpenAPI specification

It's common to use a header to distinguish between RESTful API requests and other requests to a server. The `Accept` header can provide a MIME type that distinguishes requests for JSON content from requests for user-oriented content.

The `@dealer.before_request` decorator can be used to inject a function that filters each request. This filter can distinguish proper RESTful API requests based on the following requirements:

- The `Accept` header must include a MIME type that includes `json`. Typically, the full MIME string is `application/json`.
- Additionally, we can make an exception for the `openapi.json` and `openapi.yaml` files. These specific cases can be treated as a RESTful API request irrespective of any other indicators, like a proper Accept header, slightly simplifying debugging for client applications.

Here's the additional code to implement this:

```
@dealer.before_request
def check_json() -> Optional[Response]:
    exceptions = {"/dealer/openapi.yaml", "/dealer/openapi.json"}
    if request.path in exceptions:
        return None
    if "json" in request.headers.get("Accept", "*/*"):
        return None
    if "json" == request.args.get("$format", "html"):
```

```
            return None
        abort(HTTPStatus.BAD_REQUEST)
```

If the Accept header or the $format query string parameter doesn't specify a JSON response document, this filter will abort the request with a 400 BAD REQUEST response. A more explicit error message must not divulge too much information about the server's implementation. With care, we can expand abort() with the optional description parameter to return a more detailed message, focused carefully on a failure to meet the specification, avoiding any information about the implementation.

Providing an OpenAPI specification

A well-behaved RESTful API provides the OpenAPI specification for the various services available. This is generally packaged in the /openapi.json or /openapi.yaml route. This doesn't necessarily mean that a literal file is available. Instead, this path is used as a focus to provide the detailed interface specification in JSON notation following the OpenAPI 3.0 specification.

We've defined the route, /openapi.json, and bound a function, openapi3_json(), to this route. This function will create a JSON representation of a global object, specification:

```
@dealer.route("/dealer/openapi.json")
def openapi3_json() -> Response:
    response = make_response(
        json.dumps(specification, indent=2).encode("utf-8"))
    response.headers["Content-Type"] = "application/json"
    return response
```

The specification object has the following outline. Some of the details have been replaced with ... to emphasize the overall structure. The overview is as follows:

```
spec_yaml = """
openapi: 3.0.3
info:
  title: Python Cookbook Chapter 12, recipe 4.
  description: Parsing the URL path
  version: "1.0"
servers:
- url: http://127.0.0.1:5000/dealer
paths:
  /decks:
    ...
  /decks/{id}:
    ...
```

```
  /decks/{id}/hands:
    ...
components:
  schemas:
    ...
  parameters:
    ...
"""
specification = yaml.load(spec_yaml, Loader=yaml.SafeLoader)
```

It seems slightly easier to write the OpenAPI specification in YAML notation. We can parse the block of text, and emit either YAML or JSON notation as required.

Two of the paths correspond to the two `@dealer.route` decorators in the server. We've included a third, potentially helpful path in the specification. It's often helpful to start the design of a server with an OpenAPI specification, discuss the design when it's still only a document, and then build the code to meet the specification.

Note the small syntax difference. Flask uses `/decks/<id>/hands` where the OpenAPI specification uses `/decks/{id}/hands`. This small thing means we can't trivially copy and paste between Python and OpenAPI documents.

Here are the details of the `/decks` path. This shows the input parameters that come from the query string. It also shows the details of the `201` response that contains the deck ID information:

```
/decks:
  post:
    operationId: make_deck
    parameters:
    - name: size
      in: query
      description: number of decks to build and shuffle
      schema:
        type: integer
        default: 1
    responses:
      "201":
        description: Create a deck, returns a unique deck id.
        headers:
          Location:
            schema:
              type: string
```

```
          format: uri
        description: URL for new deck
    content:
      application/json:
        schema:
          type: object
          properties:
            id:
              description: deck_id used for later queries
              type: string
            status:
              description: response status
              type: string
              enum: ["ok", "problem"]
  "400":
    description: Request doesn't accept JSON or size invalid
    content: {}
```

The response includes the `Location` header in addition to the content of the form `application/json`. The `Location` header can be used by a client to confirm the object created by the server.

The `/decks/{id}/hands` path has a similar structure. It defines all of the parameters that are available in the query string. It also defines the various responses: a `200` response that contains the cards and defines the `404` response when the ID value was not found.

We've omitted some of the details of the parameters for each path. We've also omitted details on the structure of the deck. The outline, however, summarizes the RESTful API:

- The `openapi` key must be at least 3.0.3. The standard follows semantic versioning standards. See `https://swagger.io/specification/#versions`.
- The `info` section can provide a great deal of information. This example only has the minimal requirements of title, description, and version.
- The `servers` section defines a base URL used for this service.
- The `paths` section identifies all of the paths that provide a response on this server. This shows the `/decks` and the `/decks/{id}/hands` paths.

The `openapi3_json()` function transforms this Python object into JSON notation and returns it. This implements what the client will see as a page named `openapi.json`. The internal specification object, however, is a Python data structure that can be used as a contract to permit the consistent validation of request documents and parameter values.

Using the OpenAPI specification

In the client programming, we used literal values for building the URL. The examples looked like the following:

```
full_url = urllib.parse.urlunparse(
    urllib.parse.ParseResult(
        scheme="http",
        netloc="127.0.0.1:5000",
        path="/dealer" + "/decks",
        params="",
        query=urllib.parse.urlencode({"size": size}),
        fragment=""
    )
)
```

Rather than building a URL, we can gather the information from the OpenAPI specification. When we look at the `/decks` path, shown above, we see the `operationId` key associated with the path and method. The value of this key can be used to provide unique, visible names to each path and method combination. This can serve as a useful index for a client.

Here's an overview of the steps to make use of `operationId` values:

```
path, operation = find_path_op(openapi_spec, "make_deck")
base_url = openapi_spec["servers"][0]["url"]

query = {"size": size}
query_text = urllib.parse.urlencode(query)
full_url = f"{base_url}{path}?{query_text}"
```

First, we searched all of the paths for the path with an `operationId` value of `"make_deck"`. The `base_url` value is found in the servers block at the top of the OpenAPI specification. The `query_text` value is a URL encoded form of a dictionary with the required parameter. The value of the `full_url` variable combines the `base_url`, `path`, and the `query_text`.

The OpenAPI specification is a formal contract for working with a RESTful API. Rather than building a URL, the details for the URL were extracted from known locations in the OpenAPI specification. This can simplify client applications. It also supports automated testing for clients and servers. Finally, using the OpenAPI specification avoids the client making assumptions about how the server works.

See also

- See the *Making REST requests with urllib* and *Parsing the query string in a request* recipes earlier in this chapter for more examples of RESTful web services.

Parsing a JSON request

Many web services involve a request to create a new persistent object or make an update to an existing persistent object. In order to implement these kinds of operations, the application will need input from the client.

A RESTful web service will generally accept input (and produce output) in the form of JSON documents. For more information on JSON, see the *Reading JSON documents* recipe in *Chapter 10, Input/Output, Physical Format, and Logical Layout*.

Flask provides the capability to parse JSON input from web clients. This makes it possible to have a client provide sophisticated documents to a web server.

Getting ready

We'll extend the Flask application from the *Parsing the query string in a request* recipe earlier in this chapter to add a user registration feature; this will add a player who can then request cards. The player is a resource that will involve the essential CRUD operations:

- A client can do a POST to the /players path to create a new player. This will include a payload of a document that describes the player. The service will validate the document, and if it's valid, create a new, persistent Player instance. The response will include the ID assigned to the player. If the document is invalid, a response will be sent back detailing the problems.
- A client can do a GET to the /players path to get the list of players.
- A client can do a GET to the /players/<id> path to get the details of a specific player.
- A client can do a PUT to the /players/<id> path to update the details of a specific player. As with the initial POST, this requires a payload document that must be validated.
- A client can do a DELETE to the /players/<id> path to remove a player.

As with the *Parsing the query string in a request* recipe, earlier in this chapter, we'll implement both the client and the server portion of these services. The server will handle the essential POST and one of the GET operations. We'll leave the PUT and DELETE operations as exercises for the reader.

We'll need a JSON validator. See https://pypi.python.org/pypi/jsonschema/2.5.1. This is particularly good. It's helpful to have an OpenAPI specification validator as well. See https://pypi.python.org/pypi/swagger-spec-validator.

If we install the `swagger-spec-validator` package, this also installs the latest copy of the `jsonschema` project. Here's how the whole sequence might look:

```
(cookbook) % python -m pip install swagger-spec-validator
Collecting swagger-spec-validator
  Downloading https://files.pythonhosted.org/packages/bf/09/03a8d574d4a7
6a0ffee0a0b0430fb6ba9295dd48bb09ea73d1f3c67bb4b4/swagger_spec_validator-
2.5.0-py2.py3-none-any.whl
Requirement already satisfied: six in /Users/slott/miniconda3/envs/
cookbook/lib/python3.8/site-packages (from swagger-spec-validator)
(1.12.0)
Collecting jsonschema
  Using cached https://files.pythonhosted.org/packages/c5/8f/51e89ce52a0
85483359217bc72cdbf6e75ee595d5b1d4b5ade40c7e018b8/jsonschema-3.2.0-py2.
py3-none-any.whl
Requirement already satisfied: pyyaml in /Users/slott/miniconda3/envs/
cookbook/lib/python3.8/site-packages (from swagger-spec-validator)
(5.1.2)
Requirement already satisfied: attrs>=17.4.0 in /Users/slott/miniconda3/
envs/cookbook/lib/python3.8/site-packages (from jsonschema->swagger-spec-
validator) (19.3.0)
Requirement already satisfied: setuptools in /Users/slott/miniconda3/
envs/cookbook/lib/python3.8/site-packages (from jsonschema->swagger-spec-
validator) (42.0.2.post20191203)
Requirement already satisfied: pyrsistent>=0.14.0 in /Users/slott/
miniconda3/envs/cookbook/lib/python3.8/site-packages (from jsonschema-
>swagger-spec-validator) (0.15.5)
Installing collected packages: jsonschema, swagger-spec-validator
Successfully installed jsonschema-3.2.0 swagger-spec-validator-2.5.0
```

We used the `python -m pip` command to install the `swagger-spec-validator` package. This installation also checked that `six`, `jsonschema`, `pyyaml`, `attrs`, `setuptools`, and `pyrsistent` were already installed. Once all of these packages are installed, we can use the `openapi_spec_validator` module that is installed by the `swagger-spec-validator` project.

How to do it...

We'll decompose this recipe into three parts: the OpenAPI specification that's provided by the server, the server, and an example client.

The OpenAPI specification

Let's start by defining the outline.

1. Here's the outline of the OpenAPI specification, defined as text in YAML notation:

   ```
   spec_yaml = """
   openapi: 3.0.3
   info:
     title: Python Cookbook Chapter 12, recipe 5.
     description: Parsing a JSON request
     version: "1.0"
   servers:
   - url: http://127.0.0.1:5000/dealer
   paths:
     /players:
       ...
     /players/{id}:
       ...
   components:
     schemas:
       ...
     parameters:
       ...
   ```

   The first fields, `openapi`, `info`, and `servers`, are essential boilerplate for RESTful web services. The `paths` and `components` will be filled in with the URLs and the schema definitions that are part of the service.

2. Here's the schema definition used to validate a new player. This goes inside the `schemas` section under `components` in the overall specification. The overall input document is formally described as having a type of object. There are four properties of that object:

   - An email address, which is a string with a specific format
   - A name, which is a string
   - A Twitter URL, which is a string with a given format
   - A `lucky_number`, which is an integer:

   ```
   Player:
     type: object
     properties:
       email:
   ```

```
      type: string
      format: email
    name:
      type: string
    twitter:
      type: string
      format: uri
    lucky_number:
      type: integer
```

3. Here's the overall `players` path that's used to create a new player. This path defines the `POST` method to create a new player. This parameter for this method will be provided the body of the request, and it follows the player schema shown previously, included in the `components` section of the document:

```
/players:
  post:
    operationId: make_player
    requestBody:
      content:
        application/json:
          schema:
            $ref: '#/components/schemas/Player'
    responses:
      "201":
        description: Player created
        content:
          application/json:
            schema:
              type: object
              properties:
                player:
                  $ref: "#/components/schemas/Player"
                id:
                  type:
                      string
```

```
        "403":
          description: Player is invalid or a duplicate
          content: {}
```

4. Here's the definition of a path to get details about a specific player. That path is similar to the one shown in the *Parsing the URL path* recipe. The `player` key is provided in the URL. The response when a player ID is valid is shown in detail. The response has a defined schema that also uses the player schema definition in the `definitions` section:

```
  /players/{id}:
    get:
      operationId: get_one_player
      parameters:
      - $ref: "#/components/parameters/player_id"
      responses:
        "200":
          description: The details of a specific player
          content:
            application/json:
              schema:
                type: object
                properties:
                  player:
                    $ref: '#/components/schemas/Player'
                example:
                  player:
                    email: example@example.com
                    name: example
                    twitter: https://twitter.com/PacktPub
                    lucky_number: 13
        "404":
          description: Player ID not found
          content: {}
```

This specification will be part of the server. It can be provided by a view function defined in the `@dealer.route('/openapi.json')` route.

Server

We'll begin by leaning on one of the recipes from earlier in this chapter:

1. Start with the *Parsing the query string in a request* recipe as a template for a Flask application. We'll be changing the view functions:

```
from http import HTTPStatus
from flask import (
    Flask, jsonify, request, abort, url_for, Response)
```

2. Import the additional libraries required. We'll use the JSON schema for validation. We'll also compute hashes of strings to serve as useful external identifiers in URLs. Because there aren't type hints in this library, we'll have to use the `#type: ignore` comment so the `mypy` tool doesn't examine this code closely:

```
from jsonschema import validate  # type: ignore
from jsonschema.exceptions import ValidationError  # type:
ignore
import hashlib
```

3. Create the application. The specification is a global variable with a large block of text in YAML notation. We'll parse this block of text to create a useful Python data structure:

```
from Chapter_12.card_model import Card, Deck
specification = yaml.load(
    spec_yaml, Loader=yaml.SafeLoader)

dealer = Flask("ch12_r05")
```

4. Define the global state. This includes the collection of players. In this example, we don't have a more sophisticated type definition than `Dict[str, Any]`. We'll rely on the JSONSchema validation using the schema defined in the OpenAPI specification:

```
JSON_Doc = Dict[str, Any]
players: Optional[Dict[str, JSON_Doc]] = None
```

5. Define a function to create or access the global state information. When request processing first starts, this will initialize the object. Subsequently, the cached object can be returned:

```
def get_players() -> Dict[str, JSON_Doc]:
    global players
    if players is None:
        # Database connection and fetch might go here
        players = {}
    return players
```

6. Define the route for posting to the overall collection of `players`:

```
@dealer.route("/dealer/players", methods=["POST"])
```

7. Define the function that will parse the input document, validate the content, and then create the persistent `player` object. This function can follow a common four-step design for making persistent changes:

    - Validate the input JSON document. The schema is exposed as part of the overall OpenAPI specification. We'll extract a particular piece of this document and use it for validation.
    - Create a key and confirm that it's unique. Often we'll use a hash that's derived from the data as a key. In this case, we'll hash their Twitter ID to create an easy-to-process unique key. We might also create unique keys using the `uuid` module.
    - Persist the new document in the database. In this example, it's only a single statement, `players[id] = document`. This follows the ideal that a RESTful API is built around classes and functions that already provide a complete implementation of the features.
    - Build a response document.

    Here's how this function can be implemented:

```
def make_player() -> Response:
    try:
        document = request.get_json()
    except Exception as ex:
        # Document wasn't proper JSON.
        abort(HTTPStatus.BAD_REQUEST)
    player_schema = (
        specification["components"]["schemas"]["Player"]
    )
    try:
        validate(document, player_schema)
    except ValidationError as ex:
        # Document did't pass schema rules
        abort(
            HTTPStatus.BAD_REQUEST,
            description=ex
        )

    players = get_players()
```

```
    id = hashlib.md5(
        document["twitter"].encode("utf-8")).hexdigest()

    if id in players:
        abort(
            HTTPStatus.BAD_REQUEST,
            description="Duplicate player")

    players[id] = document
    response = make_response(
        jsonify(player=document, id=id),
        HTTPStatus.CREATED)
    response.headers["Location"] = url_for(
        "get_one_player", id=str(id))
    response.headers["Content-Type"] = "application/json"
    return response
```

We can add other methods to see multiple players or individual players. These will follow the essential designs of the *Parsing the URL path* recipe. We'll look at these in the next section.

Client

This will be similar to the client module from the *Parsing the URL path* recipe, earlier in this chapter:

1. Import several essential modules for working with RESTful APIs. Because the `openapi_spec_validator` module, version 0.2.8 doesn't have type hints, we need to make sure `mypy` ignores it, and use a `# type: ignore` comment:

```
import urllib.request
import urllib.parse
import json
from openapi_spec_validator import validate_spec  # type: ignore
from typing import Dict, List, Any, Union, Tuple
```

2. Write a function to get and validate the server's OpenAPI specification. We'll make two additional checks, first to make sure the title is for the expected service, and second, that it's the expected version of the service:

```
def get_openapi_spec() -> ResponseDoc:
    """Get the OpenAPI specification."""
```

```
    openapi_request = urllib.request.Request(
        url="http://127.0.0.1:5000/dealer/openapi.json",
        method="GET",
        headers={"Accept": "application/json",},
    )

    with urllib.request.urlopen(openapi_request) as response:
        assert response.getcode() == 200
        openapi_spec = json.loads(
            response.read().decode("utf-8"))
    validate_spec(openapi_spec)
    assert (
        openapi_spec["info"]["title"]
        == "Python Cookbook Chapter 12, recipe 5."
    )
    assert (
        openapi_spec["info"]["version"] == "1.0"
    )

    return openapi_spec
```

3. We'll use a small helper function to transform the specification into a mapping. The mapping will use `OperationId` to refer to a given path and operation. This makes it easier to locate the path and method required to perform the desired operation:

```
Path_Map = Dict[str, Tuple[str, str]]


def make_path_map(openapi_spec: ResponseDoc) -> Path_Map:
    operation_ids = {
        openapi_spec["paths"][path][operation]
        ["operationId"]: (path, operation)
    for path in openapi_spec["paths"]
        for operation in openapi_spec["paths"][path]
            if (
                "operationId" in
                openapi_spec["paths"][path][operation]
            )
    }
    return operation_ids
```

4. Define a structure for the user-supplied input to this client. Since many web service clients are browser-based applications, there may be a form presented to the user. This dataclass contains the inputs supplied from the user's interaction with the client application:

```
@dataclass
class Player:
    player_name: str
    email_address: str
    other_field: int
    handle: str
```

5. Define a function to create a player. This function uses the OpenAPI specification to locate the path for a specific operation. This function creates a document with the required attributes. From the URL and the document, it builds a complete `Request` object. In the second part, it makes the HTTP request. Here's the first part:

```
def create_new_player(
        openapi_spec: ResponseDoc,
        path_map: Path_Map,
        input_form: Player) -> ResponseDoc:
    path, operation = path_map["make_player"]
    base_url = openapi_spec["servers"][0]["url"]
    full_url = f"{base_url}{path}"

    document = {
        "name": input_form.player_name,
        "email": input_form.email_address,
        "lucky_number": input_form.other_field,
        "twitter": input_form.handle,
    }

    request = urllib.request.Request(
        url=full_url,
        method="POST",
        headers={
            "Accept": "application/json",
            "Content-Type": "application/json",
        },
        data=json.dumps(document).encode("utf-8"),
    )
```

6. Once the request object has been created, we can use `urllib` to send it to the server to create a new player. According to the OpenAPI specification, the response document should include a field named status. In addition to the status code of `201`, we'll also check this field's value:

```
try:
    with urllib.request.urlopen(request) as response:
        assert (
            response.getcode() == 201
        )
        document = json.loads(
            response.read().decode("utf-8"))
    print(document)
    return document
except urllib.error.HTTPError as ex:
    print(ex.getcode())
    print(ex.headers)
    print(ex.read())
    raise
```

We can also include other queries in this client. We might want to retrieve all players or retrieve a specific player. These will follow the design shown in the *Parsing the URL path* recipe.

How it works...

Flask automatically examines inbound documents to parse them. We can simply use `request.json` to leverage the automated JSON parsing that's built into Flask.

If the input is not actually JSON, then the Flask framework will return a `400 BAD REQUEST` response. This can happen when our server application references the `json` property of the request and the document isn't valid JSON. We can use a `try` statement to capture the `400 BAD REQUEST` response object and make changes to it, or possibly return a different response.

We've used the `jsonschema` package to validate the input document against the schema defined in the OpenAPI specification. This validation process will check a number of features of the JSON document:

- It checks if the overall type of the JSON document matches the overall type of the schema. In this example, the schema required an object, which is a dictionary-like JSON structure.

- For each property defined in the schema and present in the document, it confirms that the value in the document matches the schema definition. This starts by confirming the value fits one of the defined JSON types. If there are other validation rules, like a format or a range specification, or a number of elements for an array, these constraints are checked also. This check proceeds recursively through all levels of the schema.
- If there's a list of required fields, it checks that all of these are actually present in the document.

For this recipe, we've kept the details of the schema to a minimum. A common feature that we've omitted in this example is the list of required properties. We should provide considerably more detailed attribute descriptions.

We've kept the database update processing to a minimum in this example. In some cases, the database insert might involve a much more complex process where a database client connection is used to execute a command that changes the state of a database server. The `get_decks()` and `get_players()` functions, for example, can involve more processing to get a database connection and configure a client object.

There's more...

The OpenAPI specification allows examples of response documents. This is often helpful in several ways:

- It's common to start a design by creating the sample documents to be sure they cover all the necessary use cases. If the examples demonstrate that the application will be useful, a schema specification can be written to describe the examples.
- Once the OpenAPI specification is complete, a common next step is to write the server-side programming. Example documents in the schema serve as seeds for growing unit test cases and acceptance test cases.
- For users of the OpenAPI specification, a concrete example of the response can be used to design the client and write unit tests for the client-side programming.

We can use the following code to confirm that a server has a valid OpenAPI specification. If this raises an exception, either there's no OpenAPI document or the document doesn't properly fit the OpenAPI schema:

```
>>> from openapi_spec_validator import validate_spec_url
>>> validate_spec_url('http://127.0.0.1:5000/dealer/openapi.json')
```

If the URL provides a valid OpenAPI specification, there's no further output. If the URL doesn't work or doesn't provide a valid specification, an `OpenAPIValidationError` exception is raised.

Location header

The `201 CREATED` response included a small document with some status information. The status information included the key that was assigned to the newly created record.

It's also possible for a `201 CREATED` response to have an additional `Location` header in the response. This header will provide a URL that can be used to recover the document that was created. For this application, the location would be a URL, like the following example: `http://127.0.0.1:5000/dealer/players/75f1bfbda3a8492b74a33ee2832664 9c`. The `Location` header can be saved by a client. A complete URL is slightly simpler than creating a URL from a URL template and a value.

A good practice is to provide both the key and the full URL in the body of the response. This allows a server to also provide multiple URLs for related resources, allowing the client to choose among the alternatives, avoiding the client having to build URLs to the extent possible.

The server can build the URLs using the Flask `url_for()` function. This function takes the name of a view function and any parameters that come from the URL path. It then uses the route for the view function to construct a complete URL. This will include all the information for the currently running server. After the header is inserted, the `Response` object can be returned.

Additional resources

The server should be able to respond with a list of players. Here's a minimal implementation that simply transforms the data into a large JSON document:

```
@dealer.route("/dealer/players", methods=["GET"])
def get_all_players() -> Response:
    players = get_players()
    response = make_response(jsonify(players=players))
    response.headers["Content-Type"] = "application/json"
    return response
```

A more sophisticated implementation would support the `$top` and `$skip` query parameters to page through the list of players. Additionally, a `$filter` option might be useful to implement a search for a subset of players.

In addition to the generic query for all players, we need to implement a method that will return an individual player. This kind of view function looks like the following code:

```
@dealer.route("/dealer/players/<id>", methods=["GET"])
def get_one_player(id: str) -> Response:
    players = get_players()
    if id not in players:
        abort(HTTPStatus.NOT_FOUND,
```

```
            description=f"Player {id} not found")

    response = make_response(jsonify(player=players[id]))
    response.headers["Content-Type"] = "application/json"
    return response
```

This function confirms that the given ID is a proper key value in the database. If the key is not in the database, the database document is transformed into JSON notation and returned.

See also

- See the *Parsing the URL path* recipe earlier in this chapter for other examples of URL processing.
- The *Making REST requests with urllib* recipe earlier in this chapter shows other examples of query string processing.

Implementing authentication for web services

Security is a pervasive issue throughout application design, implementation, and ongoing operational support. Every part of an application will have security considerations. Parts of the implementation of security will involve two closely related issues:

- **Authentication**: A client must provide some evidence of who they are. This might involve signed certificates or it might involve credentials like a username and password. It might involve multiple factors, such as an SMS message to a phone that the user should have access to. The web server must validate this authentication.
- **Authorization**: A server must define areas of authority and allocate these to groups of users. Furthermore, individual users must be defined as members of the authorization groups.

Application software must implement authorization decisions. For Flask, the authorization can be part of each view function. The connection of individual to group and group to view function defines the resources available to any specific user.

There are a variety of ways that authentication details can be provided from a web client to a web server. Here are a few of the alternatives:

- **Certificates**: Certificates that are encrypted and include a digital signature as well as a reference to a **Certificate Authority** (**CA**): These are exchanged by the **Secure Socket Layer** (**SSL**) as part of setting up an encrypted channel. In some environments, both client and server must have certificates and perform mutual authentication. In other environments, the server provides a certificate of authenticity, but the client does not.

- **HTTP headers**:
  - Usernames and passwords can be provided in the `Authorization` header. There are a number of schemas; the Basic schema is simple but requires SSL.
  - The `Api-Key` header can be used to provide a key used to authorize access to APIs or services.
  - Bearer tokens from third parties can be provided in the `Authorization` header using a bearer token. For details, see `http://openid.net`.

Additionally, there's a question of how the user authentication information gets loaded into a web server. There are a lot of business models for granting access to web services. For this example, we'll look at a model where users access the "sign in" form and fill in their essential information.

This kind of design leads to a mixture of routes. Some routes must be authorized for an anonymous user - someone who has not yet signed up. Some routes must be authorized to allow a user to log in. Once a user logs in with valid credentials, they are no longer anonymous, and other routes are authorized to known users.

In this recipe, we'll configure HTTPS in a Flask container to support secure connections. With a secure connection, we can leverage the `Authorization` header to provide credentials with each request. This means we'll need to use the secure password hashing capabilities of the Werkzeug project.

Getting ready

We'll implement a version of HTTP-based authentication using the `Authorization` header. There are two variations on this theme in use with secure sockets:

- **HTTP basic authentication**: This uses a simple username and password string. It relies on the SSL layer to encrypt the traffic between the client and server.
- **HTTP bearer token authentication**: This uses a token generated by a separate authorization server. The authorization server does two important things for user access control. First, it validates user credentials and issues an access token. Second, it validates access tokens to confirm they are valid. This implies the access token is an opaque jumble of characters.

Both of these variations require SSL. Because SSL is so pervasive, it means HTTP basic authentication can be used without fear of exposing user credentials. This can be a simplification in RESTful API processing since each request can include the `Authorization` header when secure sockets are used between the client and server.

Configuring SSL

Much of the process of getting and configuring certificates is outside of the realm of Python programming. What is relevant for secure data transfers is having clients and servers that both use SSL to communicate. The protocol either requires both sides to have certificates signed by a CA, or both sides to share a common self-signed certificate.

For this recipe, we'll share a self-signed certificate between web clients and the web server. The `OpenSSL` package provides tools for creating self-signed certificates.

There are two parts to creating a certificate with `OpenSSL`:

1. Create a configuration file with a name like `cert.conf` that looks like the following:

```
[req]
distinguished_name = req_distinguished_name
x509_extensions = v3_req
prompt = no

[req_distinguished_name]
countryName = "US"
stateOrProvinceName = "Nevada"
localityName = "Las Vegas"
organizationName = "ItMayBeAHack"
organizationalUnitName = "Chapter 12"
commonName = www.yourdomain.com
# req_extensions
[ v3_req ]
# http://www.openssl.org/docs/apps/x509v3_config.html
subjectAltName  = IP:127.0.0.1
```

   You'll need to change the values associated with `countryName`, `stateOrProvinceName`, `localityName`, `organizationName`, and `commonName` to be more appropriate to where you live. The `subjectAltName` must be the name the server will be using. In our case, when running from the desktop, the server is almost always known by the localhost IP address of `127.0.0.1`.

2. Run the Open SSL application to create a secret key as well as the certificate with a public key. The command is rather long. Here's how it looks:

```
% openssl req -x509 -nodes -days 365 -newkey rsa:2048 \
-keyout demo.key -out demo.cert -config cert.conf
```

This makes a request (`req`) to create a self-signed certificate (`-x509`) with no encryption of the private key (`-nodes`). The certificate will be good for the next 365 days (`-days 365`). A new RSA key pair will be created using 2,048 bits (`-newkey rsa:2048`) and it will be written to a local file named demo.key (`-keyout demo.key`). The certificate is written to demo.cert (`-out demo.cert`).

These two steps create two files: `demo.key` and `demo.cert`. We'll use these files to secure the server. The certificate file, `demo.cert`, can be shared with all clients to create a secure channel with the server. The clients don't get the private key in the `demo.key` file; that's private to the server configuration, and should be treated carefully. The private key is required to decode any SSL requests encrypted with the public key.

To work with secure servers, we'll use the `requests` library. The `urllib` package in the standard library can work with HTTPS, but the setup is complex and confusing; it's easier to work with `requests`.

The installation looks like the following:

```
% python -m pip install requests
Collecting requests
  Downloading https://files.pythonhosted.org/packages/1a/70/1935c770cb3be
6e3a8b78ced23d7e0f3b187f5cbfab4749523ed65d7c9b1/requests-2.23.0-py2.py3-
none-any.whl (58kB)
     |████████████████████████████████| 61kB 1.3MB/s
Requirement already satisfied: idna<3,>=2.5 in /Users/slott/miniconda3/
envs/cookbook/lib/python3.8/site-packages (from requests) (2.8)
Requirement already satisfied: certifi>=2017.4.17 in /Users/slott/
miniconda3/envs/cookbook/lib/python3.8/site-packages (from requests)
(2020.4.5.1)
Requirement already satisfied: chardet<4,>=3.0.2 in /Users/slott/
miniconda3/envs/cookbook/lib/python3.8/site-packages (from requests)
(3.0.4)
Requirement already satisfied: urllib3!=1.25.0,!=1.25.1,<1.26,>=1.21.1 in
/Users/slott/miniconda3/envs/cookbook/lib/python3.8/site-packages (from
requests) (1.25.6)
Installing collected packages: requests
Successfully installed requests-2.23.0
```

This shows how `requests` has been added to our current virtual environment via a `pip` install.

Users and credentials

In order for users to be able to supply a username and a password, we'll need to store some user information on the server. There's a very important rule about user credentials:

> Never store credentials. Never.

It should be clear that storing plain text passwords is an invitation to a security disaster. What's less obvious is that we can't even store encrypted passwords. When the key used to encrypt the passwords is compromised, that will also lead to a loss of all of the user identities.

How can a user's password be checked if we do not store the password?

The solution is to store a hash of the original password. Each time a user wants to log in, the user's password input is hashed and compared with the original hash. If the two hash values match, then the new password entered must have matched the original password when the hash was saved. What's central is the extreme difficulty of recovering a password from a hash value.

There is a three-step process to create the initial hash value for a password:

1. Create a random **salt** value. Generally, at least 16 bytes from `os.urandom()` can be used. The Python secrets module has some handy functions for creating a string of bytes usable for salt.
2. Use the **salt** plus the password to create a **hash** value. Generally, one of the `hashlib` functions is used. The most secure hashes come from `hashlib.pbkdf2_hmac()`.
3. Save the digest algorithm name, the **salt** value, and the final **hash** value. Often this is combined into a single string that looks like `method$salt$hash`. The method is the hash method, for example, `md5`. The `$` separates the algorithm name, the `salt`, and the **hash** values. The password is not saved.

The output might look like this:

```
md5$vvASgIJS$df7b094ce72240a0cf05c603c2396e64
```

This example password hash records an algorithm of `md5`, a salt of `vvASgIJS`, and a hex-encoded hash of the salt plus the password.

The presence of a unique, random salt assures that two people with the same password will not have the same hash value. This means exposure of the hashed credentials is relatively unhelpful because each hash is unique even if all of the users chose the password "Hunter2."

When a password needs to be checked, a similar process is followed to create a hash of the candidate password:

1. Given the username, locate the saved hash value. This will have a three-part structure of `method$salt$hash`. The method is the algorithm name, for example, `md5`.
2. Use the named method, the saved salt (`vvASgIJS` in the example above), plus the candidate password to create a computed `hash` value.
3. If the computed hash bytes match the original `hash` portion of the saved password, the password must match. We've made sure the digest algorithm and salt values both match; therefore, the password is the only degree of freedom. The password is never saved nor checked directly. The password cannot (easily) be recovered from the hash, only guessed. Using a slow algorithm like PBKDF2 makes guessing difficult.

We don't need to write these algorithms ourselves. We can rely on the `werkzeug.security` module to provide a `generate_password_hash()` function to hash a password and a `check_password_hash()` function to check a password. These use a hash method named `pbkdf2:sha256` to create very secure hashes of passwords.

We'll define a simple class to retain user information as well as the hashed password. We can use Flask's `g` object to save the user information during request processing.

The Flask view function decorator

There are several alternatives for handling authentication checks:

- If almost every route has the same security requirements, then the `@dealer.before_request` function can be used to validate all `Authorization` headers. This would require some exception processing for the `/openapi.json` route and the self-service route that allows an unauthorized user to create their new username and password credentials.
- When some routes require authentication and some don't, it works out well to introduce a decorator for the routes that need authentication.

A Python decorator is a function that wraps another function to extend its functionality. The core technique looks like this:

```
from functools import wraps
def decorate(function):
    @wraps(function)
    def decorated_function(*args, **kw):
        # processing before
        result = function(*args, **kw)
        # processing after
```

```
        return result
    return decorated_function
```

The idea is to replace a given function with a new function, `decorated_function`, built by the operation of the decorator. Within the body of this new, decorated function, it executes the original function. Some processing can be done before and some processing can be done after the function is decorated.

In a Flask context, we must put our application-specific decorators **after** the `@route` decorator:

```
@dealer.route('/path/to/resource')
@decorate
def view_function():
    return make_result('hello world', 200)
```

We've wrapped a function, `view_function()`, with the `@decorate decorator`. We can write a decorator to check authentication to be sure that the user is known.

How to do it...

We'll decompose this recipe into four parts:

- Defining the `User` class
- Defining a view decorator
- Creating the server
- Creating an example client

The `User` class definition will include password hashing and comparison algorithms. This will isolate the details from the rest of the application. The view decorator will be applied to most of the functions in the server. Once we've built a server, it helps to have a client we can use for integration and acceptance testing.

Defining the User class

This class definition provides an example of a definition of an individual `User` class:

1. Import modules that are required to create a `User` class definition and check the password:

    ```
    from dataclasses import dataclass, field, asdict
    from typing import Optional
    from werkzeug.security import (
        generate_password_hash, check_password_hash)
    ```

2. Start the definition of the `User` class. We'll base this on the dataclass because it provides a number of useful methods for initialization and object serialization:

   ```
   @dataclass
   class User:
   ```

3. Most of the time, we'll create users from a JSON document. We'll expect the field names to match these attribute names. This allows us to use `User(**doc)` to build a `User` object from a JSON document that has been deserialized into a dictionary:

   ```
       name: str
       email: str
       twitter: str
       lucky_number: int
       password: Optional[str] = field(
           default="md5$x$", repr=False)
   ```

4. Define a method for setting the password hash. This uses the `generate_password_hash()` function from the `werkzeug.security` module:

   ```
       def set_password(self, password: str) -> None:
           self.password = generate_password_hash(
               password
           )
   ```

5. Define an algorithm for checking a password hash value. This also relies on the `werkzeug.security` module for the `check_password_hash()` function:

   ```
       def check_password(self, password: str) -> bool:
           return check_password_hash(
               self.password, password)
   ```

Here's a demonstration of how this class is used:

```
>>> details = {'name': 'Noriko',
...     'email': 'x@example.com',
...     'lucky_number': 8,
...     'twitter': 'https://twitter.com/PacktPub'}

>>> u = User(**details)
>>> u.set_password('OpenSesame')
>>> u.check_password('opensesame')
False
>>> u.check_password('OpenSesame')
True
```

We created a user with details that might have been provided by filling out an HTML form, designed to allow first-time users to sign in. The password is provided separately because it is not stored with the rest of the data.

This test case can be included in the class docstring. See the *Using docstrings for testing* recipe in *Chapter 11, Testing*, for more information on this kind of test case.

We can use `json_dumps(asdict(u))` to create a JSON serialization of each `User` object. This can be saved in a database to register website users.

Defining a view decorator

The decorator will be applied to view functions that require authorization. We'll decorate most view functions, but not all of them. The decorator will inject an authorization test in front of the view function processing:

1. We'll need a number of type definitions:

   ```
   from typing import Dict, Optional, Any, Callable, Union

   from http import HTTPStatus
   from flask import (
       Flask, jsonify, request, abort, url_for, Response)
   ```

2. Import the `@wraps` decorator from `functools`. This helps define decorators by assuring that the new function has the original name and docstring copied from the function that is being decorated:

   ```
   from functools import wraps
   ```

3. In order to check passwords, we'll need the `base64` module to help decompose the value of the `Authorization` header. We'll also need to report errors and update the Flask processing context using the global `g` object:

   ```
   from functools import wraps
   import base64
   from flask import g
   ```

4. We'll provide a type hint for the decorator. This defines the two classes of view functions that can be decorated. Some view functions have parameter values parsed from the URL path. Other view functions don't receive parameter values. All view functions return `flask.Response` objects:

   ```
   ViewFunction = Union[
       Callable[[Any], Response],
       Callable[[], Response]]
   ```

5. As a global, we'll also create a default `User` instance. This is the user identity when no valid user credentials are available. This ensures there is always a `User` object available. A default can be simpler than a lot of `if` statements looking for a `None` object instead of a valid `User` instance:

```
DEFAULT_USER = User(name="", email="", twitter="", lucky_
number=-1)
```

6. Define the decorator function. All decorators have this essential outline. We'll replace the `processing here` line in the next step:

```
def authorization_required(view_function: ViewFunction) ->
ViewFunction:
    @wraps(view_function)
    def decorated_function(*args, **kwargs):
        processing here
    return decorated_function
```

7. Here are the processing steps to examine the header. In case of a request without any authorization information, default values are provided that are expected to (eventually) fail. The idea is to make all processing take a consistent amount of time and avoid any timing differences. When a problem is encountered during an authorization check, the decorator will abort processing with `401 UNAUTHORIZED` as the status code with no additional information. To prevent hackers from exploring the algorithm, there are no helpful error messages; all of the results are identical even though the root causes are different:

```
header_value = request.headers.get(
    "Authorization", "BASIC :")
kind, data = header_value.split()
if kind == "BASIC":
    credentials = base64.b64decode(data)
else:
    credentials = base64.b64decode("Og==")
usr_bytes, _, pwd_bytes = credentials.partition(b":")
username = usr_bytes.decode("ascii")
password = pwd_bytes.decode("ascii")
user_database = get_users()
user = user_database.get(username, DEFAULT_USER)
if not user.check_password(password):
    abort(HTTPStatus.UNAUTHORIZED)
g.user = user_database[username]
return view_function(*args, **kwargs)
```

There are a number of conditions that must be successfully passed before the view function is executed:

- An `Authorization` header must be present. If not, a default is provided that will fail.
- The header must specify BASIC authentication. If not, a default is provided that will fail.
- The value must include a username:password string encoded using `base64`. If not, a default is provided that will fail.
- The username must be a known username. If not, the value of `DEFAULT_USER` is used; this user has a hashed password that's invalid, leading to an inevitable failure in the final step.
- The computed hash from the given password must match the expected password hash.

Failure to follow these rules will lead to a `401 UNAUTHORIZED` response. To prevent leaking information about the service, no additional information on the details of the failure are provided.

For more information on status codes in general, see `https://tools.ietf.org/html/rfc7231`. For details on the `401` status, see `https://tools.ietf.org/html/rfc7235#section-3.1`.

Creating the server

This parallels the server shown in the *Parsing a JSON request* recipe. We'll define two kinds of routes. The first route has no authentication requirements because it's used to sign up new users. The second route will require user credentials:

1. Create a local self-signed certificate. For this recipe, we'll assume the two filenames are `demo.cert` and `demo.key`.
2. Import the modules required to build a server. Also import the `User` class definition:

```
from flask import Flask, jsonify, request, abort, url_for
from http import HTTPStatus
from Chapter_12.ch12_r06_user import User, asdict
```

3. Include the `@authorization_required` decorator definition.
4. Define a route with no authentication. This will be used to create new users. A similar view function was defined in the `Parsing a JSON request` recipe:

```
@dealer.route("/dealer/players", methods=["POST"])
```

5. Define the function to handle the route. This function will validate the JSON document to be sure it matches the required schema, then build and save the new `User` instance. The schema is defined by the OpenAPI specification. This first half of the view function will validate the JSON document:

```
def make_player() -> Response:
    try:
        document = request.json
    except Exception as ex:
        # Document wasn't even JSON.
        # We can fine-tune the error message here.
        abort(HTTPStatus.BAD_REQUEST)
    player_schema = (
        specification["components"]["schemas"]["Player"]
    )
    try:
        validate(document, player_schema)
    except ValidationError as ex:
        abort(
            HTTPStatus.BAD_REQUEST, description=ex.message)
```

6. Continue the view function by first ensuring the user is not already present in the collection. After checking to prevent duplication, create and save the new `User` instance. The response will include information about the `User` object, including a `Location` header with the link to the new resource:

```
    user_database = get_users()
    id = hashlib.md5(
        document["twitter"].encode("utf-8")).hexdigest()
    if id in user_database:
        abort(
            HTTPStatus.BAD_REQUEST,
            description="Duplicate player")

    password = document.pop('password')
    new_user = User(**document)
    new_user.set_password(password)
    user_database[id] = new_user

    response = make_response(
        jsonify(
```

```
                player=redacted_asdict(new_user),
                id=id),
            HTTPStatus.CREATED
        )
        response.headers["Location"] = url_for(
            "get_player", id=str(id))
        return response
```

Each user gets assigned a cryptic internal ID. The assigned ID is computed from a hex digest of their Twitter handle. The idea is to use a value that's likely to be unique based on some external resource identification.

7. Define a route to show user details. This requires authentication. A similar view function was defined in the *Parsing a JSON request* recipe. This version uses the `@authorization_required` decorator. This also uses a function to redact passwords from the user database record:

```
@dealer.route("/dealer/players/<id>", methods=["GET"])
@authorization_required
def get_player(id) -> Response:
    user_database = get_users()
    if id not in user_database:
        abort(HTTPStatus.NOT_FOUND,
            description=f"{id} not found")

    response = make_response(
        jsonify(
            player=redacted_asdict(user_database[id])
        )
    )
    response.headers["Content-Type"] = "application/json"
    return response
```

8. Here's the `redacted_asdict()` function. This applies `asdict()` and then removes the `password` attribute to be sure even the hash value derived from the password isn't disclosed:

```
def redacted_asdict(user: User) -> Dict[str, Any]:
    """Build the dict of a User, but redact 'password'."""
    document = asdict(user)
    document.pop("password", None)
    return document
```

Most of the other routes will have similar `@authorization_required` decorators. Some routes, such as the `/openapi.json` route, will not require authorization.

Starting the server

To be secure, the Flask server requires **Secure Socket Layer** (**SSL**) protocols. These require a certificate and a key for the certificate. These were created in the *Configuring SSL* section, earlier in this recipe, leaving two files, `demo.key` and `demo.cert`. We can use those when we start a Flask server from the command line:

```
% export PYTHONPATH=Chapter_12
% FLASK_APP=Chapter_12.ch12_r06_server flask run --cert demo.cert --key
demo.key
* Serving Flask app "Chapter_12.ch12_r06_server"
 * Environment: production
   WARNING: This is a development server. Do not use it in a production
deployment.
   Use a production WSGI server instead.
 * Debug mode: off
 * Running on https://127.0.0.1:5000/ (Press CTRL+C to quit)
```

The export `PYTHONPATH` sets an environment variable to be sure `Chapter_12` is seen by Python as a place to search for importable modules.

The `FLASK_APP=Chapter_12.ch12_r06_server flask run --cert demo.cert --key demo.key` command does these two things:

- First, it sets the `FLASK_APP` variable naming the specific module to look for a Flask instance to execute.
- Second, it executes the `flask run` command using the self-signed certificate and key we created earlier. This will start a server that uses the HTTPS protocol.

This works well for testing and demonstration purposes. For production use, access is more commonly handled by embedding the Flask application in a server like the Gunicorn server. See `https://flask.palletsprojects.com/en/1.1.x/deploying/wsgi-standalone/?highlight=gunicorn#gunicorn` for the basics of running a Flask app from within a Gunicorn server. The Gunicorn command has options to employ the SSL certificate and key files.

When you try to use this with a browser, you will be warned by the browser that the certificate is self-signed and may not be trustworthy.

Creating an example client

It's always helpful to create a client for a web service. It's useful for integration and performance testing because it can rigorously test the conformance of the service against the OpenAPI specification. It also serves as a sample for client implementations in other languages to show how the API should be used:

1. Import the libraries required. The OpenAPI Spec Validator project we're using doesn't have complete type hints, so we'll use `# type: ignore` to prevent `mypy` from scrutinizing it:

   ```
   from pprint import pprint
   from typing import Dict, List, Any, Union, Tuple

   import requests
   from openapi_spec_validator import validate_spec  # type:
   ignore
   ```

2. We'll define two generic type hints to describe two slightly different classes of objects that happen to use a common underlying representation. The `OpenAPI` spec type hint and the generic `ResponseDoc` type hint both describe one aspect of generic JSON data structures: they are often a dictionary with string keys and a variety of values. We provide two names because these are used in different contexts. As this application evolves, these types may also evolve. The reasons for changes could potentially be distinct, so we'll give them different type hints:

   ```
   OpenAPISpec = Dict[str, Any]
   ResponseDoc = Dict[str, Any]
   ```

3. We'll define a handy function to fetch the server's OpenAPI specification. We'll make a few checks to confirm that it's the expected specification and the version is usable by this client:

   ```
   def get_openapi_spec() -> OpenAPISpec:
       response = requests.get(
           url="https://127.0.0.1:5000/dealer/openapi.json",
           headers={"Accept": "application/json",},
           verify="demo.cert",
       )
       assert response.status_code == 200
       openapi_spec = response.json()

       validate_spec(openapi_spec)
       assert (
           openapi_spec["info"]["title"] ==
           "Python Cookbook Chapter 12, recipe 6."
       )
       assert (
   ```

```
            openapi_spec["info"]["version"] == "1.0"
        )
        pprint(openapi_spec)

        return openapi_spec
```

4. Once we have the OpenAPI specification, we'll need to create a useful mapping from the `operationId` attribute values to the operation and path information required to make a request:

```
Path_Map = Dict[str, Tuple[str, str]]


def make_path_map(openapi_spec: OpenAPISpec) -> Path_Map:
    """Mapping from operationId values to path and
operation."""
    operation_ids = {
        openapi_spec["paths"][path][operation]["operationId"]:
(path, operation)
        for path in openapi_spec["paths"]
        for operation in openapi_spec["paths"][path]
        if "operationId" in openapi_spec["paths"][path]
[operation]
    }
    return operation_ids
```

5. When we create a player, it adds a username and password to the server's database. This requires a document that fits the defined schema in the Open API specification. We'll define a function that has an open-ended type hint of `Dict[str, Any]`. The document's validity will be checked by the server. We must also provide a verify option to the `requests.post()` function. Because our server is working with a self-signed certificate, we must provide either `verify=False` (to bypass the validation of the certificate) or a path to locate known certificates that are trustworthy even if they're not signed by a CA. Since we created our own certificate, both the client and server can share it:

```
def create_new_player(
        openapi_spec: OpenAPISpec,
        path_map: Path_Map,
        document: Dict[str, Any]
    ) -> ResponseDoc:
    path, operation = path_map["make_player"]
    base_url = openapi_spec["servers"][0]["url"]
    full_url = f"{base_url}{path}"
```

```
    response = requests.post(
        url=full_url,
        headers={"Accept": "application/json"},
        json=document,
        verify="demo.cert"
    )

    assert response.status_code == 201
    document = response.json()
    assert "id" in document
    return document
```

6. Instead of error checking and logging, we've used `assert` statements. These can be helpful for debugging and creating the first version. A more complete implementation would have more detailed error checking.
7. Create a function to query the new `Player` information. This request requires basic-style authentication, which the `requests` module handles for us. We can provide a two-tuple with the assigned ID and the password. This will be used to build a proper `Authorization` header:

```
def get_one_player(
        openapi_spec: ResponseDoc,
        path_map: Path_Map,
        credentials: Tuple[str, str],
        player_id: str,
    ) -> ResponseDoc:
    path_template, operation = path_map["get_one_player"]
    base_url = openapi_spec["servers"][0]["url"]
    path_instance = path_template.replace(
        "{id}", player_id)
    full_url = f"{base_url}{path_instance}"

    response = requests.get(
        url=full_url,
        headers={"Accept": "application/json"},
        auth=credentials,
        verify="demo.cert"
    )
```

```
        assert response.status_code == 200
        player_response = response.json()
        return player_response["player"]
```

8. The `verify="demo.cert"` assures that the SSL protocol is used with the expected host. The `auth=credentials` option assures that the given username and password are used to get access to the requested resources.
9. The main script to create and query a player might look like the following step. We can start by getting the OpenAPI specification and extracting the relevant path information. A new player document is defined and used with the `create_new_payer()` function. The return value is the assigned player ID. The assigned ID, paired with the original password, can be used to query password-protected resources on the server:

```
    def main():
        spec = get_openapi_spec()
        paths = make_path_map(spec)

        player = {
            "name": "Noriko",
            "email": "nori@example.com",
            "lucky_number": 7,
            "twitter": "https://twitter.com/PacktPub",
            "password": "OpenSesame",
        }

        create_doc = create_new_player(spec, paths, player)
        id = create_doc["id"]

        credentials = (id, "OpenSesame")
        get_one_player(spec, paths, credentials, id)
```

Because the client and server both share a copy of the self-signed certificate, the client will find the server to be trustworthy. The use of certificates to secure the channel is an important part of overall network security in these kinds of RESTful APIs.

How it works...

There are three parts to this recipe:

- **Using SSL to provide a secure channel**: A secure channel makes it possible to exchange usernames and passwords directly. The use of a common certificate assures both parties can trust each other.
- **Using best practices for password hashing**: Saving passwords in any form is a security risk. Rather than saving plain passwords or even encrypted passwords, we save a computed hash value. This hash includes the password and a random salt string. This assures us that it's expensive and difficult to reverse engineer passwords from hashed values.
- **Using a decorator for secure view functions**: This decorator distinguishes between routes that require authentication and routes that do not require authentication. This permits a server to provide an OpenAPI specification to clients, but no other resources until proper credentials are provided.

The combination of techniques is important for creating trustworthy RESTful web services. What's helpful here is that the security check on the server is a short `@authorization_required` decorator, making it easy to add to be sure that it is in place on the appropriate view functions.

There's more...

When we start testing the various paths that lead to the use of `abort()`, we'll find that our RESTful interface doesn't completely provide JSON responses. The default behavior of Flask is to provide an HTML error response when the `abort()` function is used. This isn't ideal, and it's easy to correct.

We need to do the following two things to create JSON-based error messages:

- We need to provide some error handling functions to our Flask application that will provide the expected errors using the `jsonify()` function.
- We'll also find it helpful to supplement each `abort()` function with a description parameter that provides additional details of the error.

Here's a snippet from the `make_player()` function. This is where the input JSON document is validated to be sure it fits with the OpenAPI specification. This shows how the error message from validation is used by the description parameter of the `abort()` function:

```
try:
    validate(document, player_schema)
except ValidationError as ex:
    abort(HTTPStatus.BAD_REQUEST, description=ex.message)
```

Once we provide descriptions to the `abort()` function, we can then add error handler functions for each of the `HTTPStatus` codes returned by the application's view functions. Here's an example that creates a JSON response for `HTTPStatus.BAD_REQUEST` errors:

```
@dealer.errorhandler(HTTPStatus.BAD_REQUEST)
def badrequest_error(ex):
    return jsonify(
        error=str(ex)
    ), HTTPStatus.BAD_REQUEST
```

This will create a JSON response whenever the statement `abort(HTTPStatus.BAD_REQUEST)` is used to end processing. This ensures that your error messages have the expected content type. It also provides a consistent way to end processing when it can't be successful.

See also

- The proper SSL configuration of a server generally involves using certificates signed by a CA. This involves a certificate chain that starts with the server and includes certificates for the various authorities that issued the certificates. See `https://www.ssl.com/faqs/what-is-a-certificate-authority/` for more information.
- Many web service implementations use servers such as Gunicorn or NGINX. These servers generally handle HTTP and HTTPS issues outside our application. They can also handle complex chains and bundles of certificates. For details, see `http://docs.gunicorn.org/en/stable/settings.html#ssl` and also `http://nginx.org/en/docs/http/configuring_https_servers.html`.
- More sophisticated authentication schemes include OAuth. See `https://oauth.net/2/` for information on other ways to handle user authentication.

13
Application Integration: Configuration

Python's concept of an extensible library gives us rich access to numerous computing resources. The language provides avenues to make even more resources available. This makes Python programs particularly strong at integrating components to create sophisticated composite processing. In this chapter, we'll address the fundamentals of creating complex applications: managing configuration files, logging, and a design pattern for scripts that permits automated testing.

These new recipes are based on recipes shown earlier. Specifically, in the *Using argparse to get command-line input*, *Using cmd for creating command-line applications*, and *Using the OS environment settings* recipes in *Chapter 6, User Inputs and Outputs*, some specific techniques for creating top-level (main) application scripts were shown. In *Chapter 10, Input/Output, Physical Format, and Logical Layout*, we looked at filesystem input and output. In *Chapter 12, Web Services*, we looked at creating servers, which are the main applications that receive requests from clients.

All of these examples show some aspects of application programming in Python. There are some additional techniques that are helpful, such as processing configuration from files. In the *Using argparse to get command-line input* recipe in *Chapter 6, User Inputs and Outputs*, we showed techniques for parsing command-line arguments. In the *Using the OS environment settings* recipe, we touched on other kinds of configuration details. In this chapter, we'll look at a number of ways to handle configuration files. There are many file formats that can be used to store long-term configuration information:

- The INI file format as processed by the `configparser` module.
- The YAML file format is very easy to work with but requires an add-on module that's not currently part of the Python distribution. We'll look at this in the *Using YAML for configuration files* recipe.

- The Properties file format is typical of Java programming and can be handled in Python without writing too much code. The syntax overlaps with Python scripts.
- For Python scripts, a file with assignment statements looks a lot like a Properties file, and is very easy to process using the `compile()` and `exec()` functions. We'll look at this in the *Using Python for configuration files* recipe.
- Python modules with class definitions is a variation that uses Python syntax but isolates the settings into separate classes. This can be processed with the `import` statement. We'll look at this in the *Using class-as-namespace for configuration* recipe.

This chapter will extend some of the concepts from *Chapter 7, Basics of Classes and Objects*, and *Chapter 8, More Advanced Class Design*, and apply the idea of the command design pattern to Python programs.

In this chapter, we'll look at the following recipes:

- Finding configuration files
- Using YAML for configuration files
- Using Python for configuration files
- Using `class-as-namespace` for configuration values
- Designing scripts for composition
- Using logging for control and audit output

We'll start with a recipe for handling multiple configuration files that must be combined. This gives users some helpful flexibility. From there, we can dive into the specifics of various common configuration file formats.

Finding configuration files

Many applications will have a hierarchy of configuration options. The foundation of the hierarchy is often the default values built into a particular release. These might be supplemented by server-wide (or cluster-wide) values from centralized configuration files. There might be user-specific files, or perhaps even configuration files provided when starting a program.

In many cases, configuration parameters are written in text files, so they are persistent and easy to change. The common tradition in Linux is to put system-wide configuration in the `/etc` directory. A user's personal changes would be in their home directory, often named `~username` or `$HOME`.

In this recipe, we'll see how an application can support a rich hierarchy of locations for configuration files.

Getting ready

The example we'll use is a web service that provides hands of cards to users. The service is shown in several recipes throughout *Chapter 12, Web Services*. We'll gloss over some of the details of the service so we can focus on fetching configuration parameters from a variety of filesystem locations.

We'll follow the design pattern of the Bash shell, which looks for configuration files in the following places:

1. It starts with the `/etc/profile` file.
2. After reading that file, it looks for one of these files, in this order:
    1. `~/.bash_profile`
    2. `~/.bash_login`
    3. `~/.profile`

In a POSIX-compliant operating system, the shell expands the ~ to be the home directory for the logged-in user. This is defined as the value of the `HOME` environment variable. In general, the Python `pathlib` module can handle this automatically via the `Path.home()` method. This technique applies to Windows and Linux derivatives, as well as macOS.

The design pattern from the Bash shell can use a number of separate files. When we include defaults that are part of the release, application-wide settings as part of an installation, and personal settings, we can consider three levels of configuration. This can be handled elegantly with a mapping and the `ChainMap` class from the `collections` module.

In later recipes, we'll look at ways to parse and process specific formats of configuration files. For the purposes of this recipe, we won't pick a specific format. Instead, we'll assume that a function, `load_config_file()`, has been defined that will load a specific configuration mapping from the contents of the file. The function looks like this:

```
def load_config_file(config_path: Path) -> Dict[str, Any]:
    """Loads a configuration mapping object with the contents
    of a given file.

    :param config_path: Path to be read.
    :returns: mapping with configuration parameter value
    """
    # Details omitted.
```

We'll look at a number of different ways to implement this function.

Why so many choices?

There's a side topic that sometimes arises when discussing this kind of design—Why have so many choices? Why not specify exactly two places?

The answer depends on the context for the application. When creating entirely new software, it may be possible to limit the choices to exactly two locations. However, when replacing legacy applications, it's common to have a new location that's better in some ways than the legacy location. This often means the legacy location still needs to be supported. After several such evolutionary changes, it's common to see a number of alternative locations for files.

Also, because of variations among Linux distributions, it's common to see variations that are typical for one distribution, but atypical for another. And, of course, when dealing with Windows, there will be variant file paths that are unique to that platform.

How to do it...

We'll make use of the `pathlib` module to provide a handy way to work with files in various locations. We'll also use the `collections` module to provide the very useful `ChainMap` class:

1. Import the `Path` class and the `collections` module. There are several type hints that are also required:

```
from pathlib import Path
import collections
from typing import TextIO, Dict, Any, ChainMap
```

2. Define an overall function to get the configuration files:

```
def get_config() -> ChainMap[str, Any]:
```

3. Create paths for the various locations of the configuration files. These are called pure paths because there's no relationship with the filesystem. They start as names of *potential* files:

```
    system_path = Path("/etc") / "profile"
    local_paths = [
        Path.home() / ".bash_profile",
        Path.home() / ".bash_login",
        Path.home() / ".profile",
    ]
```

4. Define the application's built-in defaults:

```
    configuration_items = [
        dict(
            some_setting="Default Value",
            another_setting="Another Default",
```

```
                some_option="Built-In Choice",
            )
        ]
```

5. Each individual configuration file is a mapping from keys to values. Each of these mapping objects is combined to form a `list`; this becomes the final `ChainMap` configuration mapping. We'll assemble the `list` of maps by appending items, and then reverse the order after the files are loaded so that the last loaded file becomes the first in the `map`.
6. If a system-wide configuration file exists, load this file:

```
    if system_path.exists():
        configuration_items.append(
            load_config_file(system_path))
```

7. Iterate through other locations looking for a file to load. This loads the first file that it finds and uses a `break` statement to stop after the first file is found:

```
    for config_path in local_paths:
        if config_path.exists():
            configuration_items.append(
                load_config_file(config_path))
            break
```

8. Reverse the `list` and create the final `ChainMap`. The `list` needs to be reversed so that the local file is searched first, then the system settings, and finally the application default settings:

```
    configuration = collections.ChainMap(
        *reversed(configuration_items))
    return configuration
```

Once we've built the `configuration` object, we can use the final configuration like a simple mapping. This object supports all of the expected dictionary operations.

How it works...

One of the most elegant features of any object-oriented language is being able to create collections of objects. In this case, one of these collections of objects includes filesystem `Path` objects.

As noted in the *Using pathlib to work with file names* recipe in *Chapter 10, Input/Output, Physical Format, and Logical Layout*, the `Path` object has a `resolve()` method that can return a concrete `Path` built from a pure `Path`. In this recipe, we used the `exists()` method to determine if a concrete path could be built. The `open()` method, when used to read a file, will resolve the pure `Path` and open the associated file.

In the *Creating dictionaries – inserting and updating* recipe in *Chapter 4, Built-In Data Structures Part 1: Lists and Sets*, we looked at the basics of using a dictionary. Here, we've combined several dictionaries into a chain. When a `key` is not located in the first dictionary of the chain, then later dictionaries in the chain are checked. This is a handy way to provide default values for each `key` in the mapping.

Here's an example of creating a `ChainMap` manually:

```
>>> import collections
>>> config = collections.ChainMap(
...     {'another_setting': 2},
...     {'some_setting': 1},
...     {'some_setting': 'Default Value',
...      'another_setting': 'Another Default',
...      'some_option': 'Built-In Choice'})
```

The `config` object is built from three separate mappings. The first might be details from a local file such as `~/.bash_login`. The second might be system-wide settings from the `/etc/profile` file. The third contains application-wide defaults.

Here's what we see when we query this object's values:

```
>>> config['another_setting']
2
>>> config['some_setting']
1
>>> config['some_option']
'Built-In Choice'
```

The value for any given `key` is taken from the first instance of that `key` in the chain of maps. This is a very simple way to have local values that override system-wide values that override the built-in defaults.

There's more...

In the *Mocking external resources* recipe in *Chapter 11, Testing*, we looked at ways to mock external resources so that we could write a unit test that wouldn't accidentally delete files. A test for the code in this recipe needs to mock the filesystem resources by mocking the `Path` class.

To work with `pytest` test cases, it helps to consolidate the `Path` operations into a fixture that can be used to test the `get_config()` function:

```
from pathlib import Path
```

```
from pytest import *  # type: ignore
from unittest.mock import Mock, patch, mock_open, MagicMock, call
import Chapter_13.ch13_r01

@fixture  # type: ignore
def mock_path(monkeypatch, tmpdir):
    mocked_class = Mock(
        wraps=Path,
        return_value=Path(tmpdir / "etc"),
        home=Mock(return_value=Path(tmpdir / "home")),
    )
    monkeypatch.setattr(
        Chapter_13.ch13_r01, "Path", mocked_class)

    (tmpdir / "etc").mkdir()
    (tmpdir / "etc" / "profile").write_text(
        "exists", encoding="utf-8")
    (tmpdir / "home").mkdir()
    (tmpdir / "home" / ".profile").write_text(
        "exists", encoding="utf-8")
    return mocked_class
```

This `mock_path` fixture creates a module-like `Mock` object that can be used instead of the `Path` class. When the code under test uses `Path()` it will always get the `etc/profile` file created in the `tmpdir` location. The `home` attribute of this `Mock` object makes sure that `Path.home()` will provide a name that's part of the temporary directory created by `tmpdir`. By pointing the `Path` references to the temporary directory that's unique to the test, we can then load up this directory with any combination of files.

This fixture creates two directories, and a file in each directory. One file is `tmpdir/etc/profile`. The other is `tmpdir/home/.profile`. This allows us to check the algorithm for finding the system-wide profile as well as a user's local profile.

In addition to a fixture that sets up the files, we'll need one more fixture to mock the details of the `load_config_file()` function, which loads one of the configuration files. This allows us to define multiple implementations, confident that the overall `get_config()` function will work with any implementation that fills the contract of `load_config_file()`.

The fixture looks like this:

```
@fixture  # type: ignore
def mock_load_config(monkeypatch):
    mocked_load_config_file = Mock(return_value={})
    monkeypatch.setatt(
        Chapter_13.ch13_r01,
```

```
        "load_config_file",
        mocked_load_config_file
    )
    return mocked_load_config_file
```

Here are some of the tests that will confirm that the path search works as advertised. Each test starts by applying two patches to create a modified context for testing the `get_config()` function:

```
def test_get_config(mock_load_config, mock_path):
    config = Chapter_13.ch13_r01.get_config()

    assert mock_path.mock_calls == [
        call("/etc"),
        call.home(),
        call.home(),
        call.home(),
    ]
    assert mock_load_config.mock_calls == [
        call(mock_path.return_value / "profile"),
        call(mock_path.home.return_value / ".profile"),
    ]
```

The two fixtures mock the `Path` class and also mock the `load_config_file()` function that the `get_config()` function relies on. The assertion shows that several path requests were made, and two individual files were eventually loaded. This is the purpose behind this particular `get_config()` function; it loads two of the files it finds. To be complete, of course, the test suite needs to have two more fixtures and two more tests to examine the other two locations for user-specific configuration files.

See also

- In the *Using YAML for configuration files* and *Using Python for configuration files* recipes in this chapter, we'll look at ways to implement the `load_config_file()` function.
- In the *Mocking external resources* recipe in *Chapter 11, Testing*, we looked at ways to test functions such as this, which interact with external resources.
- Variations on the implementation are covered in the *Using YAML for configuration files* and *Using Python for configuration files* recipes of this chapter.
- The `pathlib` module can help with this processing. This module provides the `Path` class definition, which provides a great deal of sophisticated information about the OS's files. For more information, see the *Using pathlib to work with filenames* recipe in *Chapter 10, Input/Output, Physical Format, and Logical Layout*.

Using YAML for configuration files

Python offers a variety of ways to package application inputs and configuration files. We'll look at writing files in YAML notation because this format is elegant and simple.

It can be helpful to represent configuration details in YAML notation.

Getting ready

Python doesn't have a YAML parser built in. We'll need to add the `pyyaml` project to our library using the `pip` package management system. Here's what the installation looks like:

```
(cookbook) slott@MacBookPro-SLott Modern-Python-Cookbook-Second-Edition % python -m pip install pyyaml
Collecting pyyaml
  Downloading https://files.pythonhosted.org/packages/64/c2/b80047c7ac2478f9501676c988a5411ed5572f35d1beff9cae07d321512c/PyYAML-5.3.1.tar.gz (269kB)
     |████████████████████████████████| 276kB 784kB/s
Building wheels for collected packages: pyyaml
  Building wheel for pyyaml (setup.py) ... done
  Created wheel for pyyaml: filename=PyYAML-5.3.1-cp38-cp38-macosx_10_9_x86_64.whl size=44624 sha256=7450b3cc947c2afd5d8191ebe35cb1c8cdd5e212e0478121cd49ce52c835ddaa
  Stored in directory: /Users/slott/Library/Caches/pip/wheels/a7/c1/ea/cf5bd31012e735dc1dfea3131a2d5eae7978b251083d6247bd
Successfully built pyyaml
Installing collected packages: pyyaml
Successfully installed pyyaml-5.3.1
```

The elegance of the YAML syntax is that simple indentation is used to show the structure of the document. Here's an example of some settings that we might encode in YAML:

```
query:
  mz:
    - ANZ532
    - AMZ117
    - AMZ080
url:
  scheme: http
  netloc: forecast.weather.gov
  path: /shmrn.php
```

```
description: >
  Weather forecast for Offshore including the Bahamas
```

This document can be seen as a specification for a number of related URLs that are all similar to `http://forecast.weather.gov/shmrn.php?mz=ANZ532`. The document contains information about building the URL from a scheme, net location, base path, and several query strings. The `yaml.load()` function can load this YAML document; it will create the following Python structure:

```
{'description': 'Weather forecast for Offshore including the
Bahamas\n',
 'query': {'mz': ['ANZ532', 'AMZ117', 'AMZ080']},
 'url': {'netloc': 'forecast.weather.gov',
         'path': 'shmrn.php',
         'scheme': 'http'}}
```

This `dict-of-dict` structure can be used by an application to tailor its operations. In this case, it specifies a sequence of URLs to be queried to assemble a larger weather briefing.

We'll often use the *Finding configuration files* recipe, shown earlier in this chapter, to check a variety of locations for a given configuration file. This flexibility is often essential for creating an application that's easy to use on a variety of platforms.

In this recipe, we'll build the missing part of the previous example, the `load_config_file()` function. Here's the template that needs to be filled in:

```
def load_config_file(config_path: Path) -> Dict[str, Any]:
    """Loads a configuration mapping object with contents
    of a given file.

    :param config_path: Path to be read.
    :returns: mapping with configuration parameter values
    """
    # Details omitted.
```

In this recipe, we'll fill in the space held by the `Details omitted` line to load configuration files in YAML format.

How to do it...

This recipe will make use of the `yaml` module to parse a YAML-format file. This will create a dictionary from the YAML-format source. This can be part of building a `ChainMap` of configurations:

1. Import the `yaml` module along with the `Path` definition and the type hints required by the `load_config_file()` function definition:

```
from pathlib import Path
from typing import Dict, Any
import yaml
```

2. Use the `yaml.load()` function to load the YAML-syntax document:

```
def load_config_file(config_path: Path) -> Dict[str, Any]:
    """Loads a configuration mapping object with contents
    of a given file.

    :param config_path: Path to be read.
    :returns: mapping with configuration parameter values
    """
    with config_path.open() as config_file:
        document = yaml.load(
            config_file, Loader=yaml.SafeLoader)
    return document
```

This function can be fit into the design from the *Finding configuration files* recipe to load a configuration file using YAML notation.

How it works...

The YAML syntax rules are defined at `http://yaml.org`. The idea of YAML is to write JSON-like data structures in a more flexible, human-friendly syntax. JSON is a special case of the more general YAML syntax.

The trade-off here is that some spaces and line breaks in JSON don't matter—there is visible punctuation to show the structure of the document. In some of the YAML variants, line breaks and indentation determine the structure of the document; the use of white-space means that line breaks will matter with YAML documents.

The essential data structures available in JSON syntax are as follows:

- **Sequence**: [item, item, ...]
- **Mapping**: {`key: value`, `key: value`, ...}
- **Scalar**:
  - **String**: "`value`"
  - **Number**: `3.1415926`
  - **Literal**: `true`, `false`, and `null`

JSON syntax is one style of YAML; it's called a `flow` style. In this style, the document structure is marked by explicit indicators. The syntax requires {...} and [...] to show the structure.

The alternative that YAML offers is `block` style. The document structure is defined by line breaks and indentation. Furthermore, string scalar values can use plain, quoted, and folded styles of syntax. Here is how the alternative YAML syntax works:

- **Block sequence**: We preface each line of a sequence with a `-`. This looks like a bullet list and is easy to read. When loaded, it will create a dictionary with a `list` of strings in Python: `{zoneid: ['ANZ532', 'AMZ117', 'AMZ080']}`. Here's an example:

```
zoneid:
  - ANZ532
  - AMZ117
  - AMZ080
```

- **Block mapping**: We can use simple `key: value` syntax to associate a `key` with a simple scalar. We can use `key:` on a line by itself; the value is indented on the following lines. This creates a nested dictionary that looks like this in Python: `{'url': {'scheme': 'http', 'netloc': 'marine.weather.gov'}}`. Here's an example:

```
url:
  scheme: http
  netloc: marine.weather.gov
```

Some more advanced features of YAML will make use of this explicit separation between key and value:

- For short string scalar values, we can leave them plain, and the YAML rules will simply use all the characters with leading and trailing white-space stripped away. The examples all use this kind of assumption for string values.
- Quotes can be used for strings, exactly as they are in JSON, when necessary.
- For longer strings, YAML introduces the | prefix; the lines after this are preserved with all of the spacing and newlines intact. It also introduces the > prefix, which preserves the words as a long string of text—any newlines are treated as single white-space characters. This is common for running text.
- In some cases, the value may be ambiguous. For example, a US ZIP code is all digits—22102. This should be understood as a `string`, even though the YAML rules will interpret it as a number. Quotes, of course, can be helpful. To be even more explicit, a local tag of `!!str` in front of the value will force a specific data type. `!!str 22102`, for example, assures that the digits will be treated as a string object.

There's more...

There are a number of additional features in YAML that are not present in JSON:

- The comments, which begin with # and continue to the end of the line. They can go almost anywhere. JSON doesn't tolerate comments.
- The document start, which is indicated by the `---` line at the start of a new document. This allows a YAML file to contain a stream of separate documents.
- Document end. An optional `...` line is the end of a document in a stream of documents.
- Complex keys for mappings. JSON mapping keys are limited to the available scalar types—`string`, `number`, `true`, `false`, and `null`. YAML allows mapping keys to be considerably more complex. We have to honor Python's restriction that keys must be immutable.

Here are some examples of these features. In this first example, we'll look at a stream that contains two documents.

Here is a YAML file with two separate documents, something that JSON does not handle well:

```
>>> import yaml
>>> yaml_text = '''
... ---
... id: 1
... text: "Some Words."
... ---
... id: 2
... text: "Different Words."
... '''
>>> document_iterator = yaml.load_all(yaml_text)
>>> document_1 = next(document_iterator)
>>> document_1['id']
1
>>> document_2 = next(document_iterator)
>>> document_2['text']
'Different Words.'
```

The `yaml_text` string is a stream with two YAML documents, each of which starts with `---`. The `load_all()` function is an iterator that loads the documents one at a time. An application must iterate over the results of this to process each of the documents in the stream.

YAML provides a way to create complex objects for mapping keys. What's important is that Python requires a hashable, immutable object for a mapping key. This means that a complex key must be transformed into an immutable `Python` object, often a tuple. In order to create a Python-specific object, we need to use a more complex local tag. Here's an example:

```
>>> mapping_text = '''
... ? !!python/tuple ["a", "b"]
... : "value"
... '''
>>> yaml.load(mapping_text, Loader=yaml.UnsafeLoader)
{('a', 'b'): 'value'}
```

This example uses `?` and `:` to mark the `key` and `value` of a mapping. We've done this because the `key` is a complex object. The `key` value uses a local tag, `!!python/tuple`, to create a tuple instead of the default, which would have been a `list`. The text of the `key` uses a flow-type YAML value, `["a", "b"]`.

Because this steps outside the default type mappings, we also have to use the special `UnsafeLoader`. This is a way of acknowledging that a wide variety of Python objects can be created this way.

JSON has no provision for a `set` collection. YAML allows us to use the `!!set` tag to create a `set` instead of a simple sequence. The items in the `set` must be identified by a `?` prefix because they are considered keys of a mapping for which there are no values.

Note that the `!!set` tag is at the same level of indentation as the values within the `set` collection. It's indented inside the `dictionary` key of `data_values`:

```
>>> import yaml
>>> set_text = '''
... document:
...     id: 3
...     data_values:
...       !!set
...       ? some
...       ? more
...       ? words
... '''

>>> some_document = yaml.load(set_text, Loader=yaml.SafeLoader)
>>> some_document['document']['id']
3
>>> some_document['document']['data_values'] == {
```

```
...         'some', 'more', 'words'}
True
```

The `!!set` local tag modifies the following sequence to become a `set` object instead of the default `list` object. The resulting set is equal to the expected Python set object, `{'some', 'more', 'words'}`.

Items in a `set` must be immutable objects. While the YAML syntax allows creating a set of mutable list objects, it's impossible to build the document in Python. A run-time error will reveal the problem when we try to collect mutable objects into a `set`.

Python objects of almost any class can be described using YAML local tags. Any class with a simple `__init__()` method can be built from a YAML serialization.

Here's a small class definition:

```
class Card:
    def __init__(self, rank: int, suit: str) -> None:
        self.rank = rank
        self.suit = suit

    def __repr__(self) -> str:
        return f"{self.rank} {self.suit}"
```

We've defined a class with two positional attributes. Here's the YAML serialization of an instance of this class:

```
!!python/object/apply:Chapter_13.ch13_r02.Card
kwds:
    rank: 7
    suit: ♣
```

We've used the `kwds` key to provide two keyword-based argument values to the `Card` constructor function. The Unicode ♣ character works well because YAML files are text written using UTF-8 encoding.

See also

- See the *Finding configuration files* recipe earlier in this chapter to see how to search multiple filesystem locations for a configuration file. We can easily have application defaults, system-wide settings, and personal settings built into separate files and combined by an application.

Using Python for configuration files

Python offers a variety of ways to package application inputs and configuration files. We'll look at writing files in Python notation because it's elegant and simple.

A number of packages use assignment statements in a separate module to provide configuration parameters. The Flask project, in particular, supports this. We looked at Flask in the *Using the Flask framework for RESTful APIs* recipe and a number of related recipes in *Chapter 12, Web Services*.

In this recipe, we'll look at how we can represent configuration details in Python notation.

Getting ready

Python assignment statements are particularly elegant. The syntax can be simple, easy to read, and extremely flexible. If we use assignment statements, we can import an application's configuration details from a separate module. This could have a name like `settings.py` to show that it's focused on configuration parameters.

Because Python treats each imported module as a `global Singleton` object, we can have several parts of an application all use the `import settings` statement to get a consistent view of the current, global application configuration parameters.

For some applications, we might want to choose one of several alternative settings files. In this case, we want to load a file using a technique that's more flexible than the fixed `import` statement.

We'd like to be able to provide definitions in a text file that look like this:

```
"""Weather forecast for Offshore including the Bahamas
"""
query = {'mz': ['ANZ532', 'AMZ117', 'AMZ080']}
url = {
  'scheme': 'http',
  'netloc': 'forecast.weather.gov',
  'path': '/shmrn.php'
}
```

This is Python syntax. The parameters include two variables, `query` and `url`. The value of the `query` variable is a dictionary with a single key, `mz`, and a sequence of values.

This can be seen as a specification for a number of related URLs that are all similar to `http://forecast.weather.gov/shmrn.php?mz=ANZ532`.

We'll often use the *Finding configuration files* recipe to check a variety of locations for a given configuration file. This flexibility is often essential for creating an application that's easily used on a variety of platforms.

In this recipe, we'll build the missing part of the first recipe, the `load_config_file()` function. Here's the template that needs to be filled in:

```
def load_config_file(config_path: Path) -> Dict[str, Any]:
    """Loads a configuration mapping object with contents
    of a given file.

    :param config_path: Path to be read.
    :returns: mapping with configuration parameter values
    """
    # Details omitted.
```

In this recipe, we'll fill in the space held by the `Details omitted` line to load configuration files in Python format.

How to do it...

We can make use of the `pathlib` module to locate the files. We'll leverage the built-in `compile()` and `exec()` functions to process the code in the configuration file:

1. Import the `Path` definition and the type hints required by the `load_config_file()` function definition:

```
from pathlib import Path
from typing import Dict, Any
```

2. Use the built-in `compile()` function to compile the `Python` module into an executable form. This function requires the source text as well as the filename from which the text was read. The filename is essential for creating trace-back messages that are useful and correct:

```
def load_config_file(config_path: Path) -> Dict[str, Any]:
    code = compile(
        config_path.read_text(),
        config_path.name,
        "exec")
```

   In rare cases where the code doesn't come from a file, the general practice is to provide a name such as `<string>` for the filename.

3. Execute the code object created by the `compile()` function. This requires two contexts. The global context provides any previously imported modules, plus the `__builtins__` module. The local context is the `locals` dictionary; this is where new variables will be created:

```
    locals: Dict[str, Any] = {}
```

```
        exec(code, {"__builtins__": __builtins__}, locals)
        return locals
```

How it works...

The details of the Python language–the syntax and semantics–are embodied in the built-in `compile()` and `exec()` functions. When we launch a Python application or script, the process is essentially this:

1. Read the text. Compile it with the `compile()` function to create a code object.
2. Use the `exec()` function to execute the code object.

The `__pycache__` directory holds code objects, and saves the work of recompiling text files that haven't changed.

The `exec()` function reflects the way Python handles `global` and `local` variables. There are two namespaces (`mappings`) provided to this function. These are visible to a script that's running via the `globals()` and `locals()` functions.

When code is executed at the very top level of a script file—often inside the `if __name__ == "__main__"` condition—it executes in the global context; the `globals` and `locals` variable collections are the same. When code is executed inside a `function`, `method`, or `class` definition, the local variables for that context are separate from the global variables.

Here, we've created a separate `locals` object. This makes sure the imported statements don't make unexpected changes to any other global variables.

We provided two distinct dictionaries:

- A dictionary of global objects. The most common use is to provide access to the imported modules, which are always global. The `__builtins__` module is often provided in this dictionary. In some cases, other modules like `pathlib` should be added.
- The dictionary provided for the locals is updated by each assignment statement. This local dictionary allows us to capture the variables created within the `settings` module.

The `locals` dictionary will be updated by the `exec()` function. We don't expect the `globals` to be updated and will ignore any changes that happen to this collection.

There's more...

This recipe suggests a configuration file is entirely a sequence of `name = value` assignments. The assignment statement is in Python syntax, as are the variable names and the literal syntax. This permits Python's large collection of built-in types.

Additionally, the full spectrum of Python statements is available. This leads to some engineering trade-offs.

Because any statement can be used in the configuration file, it can lead to complexity. If the processing in the configuration file becomes too complex, the file ceases to be configuration and becomes a first-class part of the application. Very complex features should be implemented by modifying the application programming, not hacking around with the configuration settings. Since Python applications include the full source, as it is generally easier to fix the source than create hyper-complex configuration files. The goal is for a configuration file to provide values to tailor operations, not provide plug-in functionality.

We might want to include the OS environment variables as part of the global variables used for configuration. This ensures that the configuration values match the current environment settings. This can be done with the `os.environ` mapping.

It can also be sensible to do some processing simply to make a number of related settings easier to organize. For example, it can be helpful to write a configuration file with a number of related paths like this:

```
"""Config with related paths"""
if environ.get("APP_ENV", "production"):
    base = Path('/var/app/')
else:
    base = Path.cwd("var")
log = base/'log'
out = base/'out'
```

The values of `log` and `out` are used by the application. The value of `base` is only used to ensure that the other two paths share a common parent directory.

This leads to the following variation on the `load_config_file()` function shown earlier. This version includes some additional modules and global classes:

```
from pathlib import Path
import platform
import os

def load_config_file_xtra(config_path: Path) -> Dict[str, Any]:
    def not_allowed(*arg, **kw) -> None:
        raise RuntimeError("Operation not allowed")

    code = compile(
        config_path.read_text(),
        config_path.name,
        "exec")
```

```
    safe_builtins = cast(Dict[str, Any], __builtins__).copy()
    for name in ("eval", "exec", "compile", "__import__"):
        safe_builtins[name] = not_allowed

    globals = {
        "__builtins__": __builtins__,
        "Path": Path,
        "platform": platform,
        "environ": os.environ.copy()
    }
    locals: Dict[str, Any] = {}
    exec(code, globals, locals)
    return locals
```

Including `Path`, `platform`, and a copy of `os.environ` in the globals means that a configuration file can be written without the overhead of `import` statements. This can make the settings simpler to prepare and maintain.

We've also removed four built-in functions: `eval()`, `exec()`, `compile()`, and `__import__()`. This will reduce the number of things a Python-language configuration file is capable of doing. This involves some fooling around inside the `__builtins__` collection. This module behaves like a dictionary, but the type is not simply `Dict[str, Any]`. We've used the `cast()` function to tell `mypy` that the `__builtins__.copy()` method will work even though it's not obviously part of the module's type.

See also

- See the *Finding configuration files* recipe earlier in this chapter to learn how to search multiple filesystem locations for a configuration file.

Using class-as-namespace for configuration

Python offers a variety of ways to package application inputs and configuration files. We'll continue to look at writing files in Python notation because it's elegant and the familiar syntax can lead to easy-to-read configuration files.

A number of projects allow us to use a class definition to provide configuration parameters. The use of a class hierarchy means that inheritance techniques can be used to simplify the organization of parameters. The `Flask` package, in particular, can do this. We looked at Flask in the *Using the Flask framework for RESTful APIs* recipe, and a number of related recipes.

In this recipe, we'll look at how we can represent configuration details in Python class notation.

Getting ready

Python notation for defining the attributes of a class can be simple, easy to read, and reasonably flexible. We can, with a little work, define a sophisticated configuration language that allows someone to change configuration parameters for a Python application quickly and reliably.

We can base this language on class definitions. This allows us to package a number of configuration alternatives in a single module. An application can load the module and pick the relevant class definition from the module.

We'd like to be able to provide definitions that look like this:

```
class Configuration:
    """
    Generic Configuration
    """
    url = {
        "scheme": "http",
        "netloc": "forecast.weather.gov",
        "path": "/shmrn.php"}
    query = {"mz": ["ANZ532"]}
```

We can create this class definition in a `settings.py` file to create a `settings` module. To use the `configuration`, the main application could do this:

```
from settings import Configuration
```

The application will gather the settings using the fixed module name of `settings` with a fixed class name of Configuration. We have two ways to add flexibility to using a module as a configuration file:

- We can use the `PYTHONPATH` environment variable to list a number of locations for configuration modules
- We can use multiple inheritance and mix in class definitions to combine defaults, system-wide settings, and localized settings into a configuration class definition

These techniques can be helpful because the configuration file locations follow Python's rules for finding modules. Rather than implementing our own search for the configuration, we can leverage Python's search of `sys.path`.

In this recipe, we'll build the missing part of the previous example, the `load_config_file()` function. Here's the template that needs to be filled in:

```
def load_config_file(
        config_path: Path, classname: str = "Configuration"
```

```
) -> Dict[str, Any]:
"""Loads a configuration mapping object with contents
of a given file.

:param config_path: Path to be read.
:returns: mapping with configuration parameter values
"""
# Details omitted.
```

We've used a similar template in a number of recipes in this chapter. For this recipe, we've added a parameter to this definition. The `classname` parameter is not present in previous recipes, but it is used here to select one of the many classes from a module at the location in the filesystem named by the `config_path` parameter.

How to do it...

We can make use of the `pathlib` module to locate the files. We'll leverage the built-in `compile()` and `exec()` functions to process the code in the configuration file. The result is not a dictionary, and isn't compatible with previous `ChainMap`-based configurations:

1. Import the `Path` definition and the type hints required by the `load_config_file()` function definition:

   ```
   from pathlib import Path
   import platform
   from typing import Dict, Any, Type
   ```

2. Since the point of this configuration is to return a class, we'll provide a type hint for any class definition:

   ```
   ConfigClass = Type[object]
   ```

3. Use the built-in `compile()` function to compile the `Python` module into an executable form. This function requires the source text as well as a filename from which the text was read. The filename is essential for creating trace-back messages that are useful and correct:

   ```
   def load_config_file(
           config_path: Path, classname: str = "Configuration"
       ) -> ConfigClass:
       code = compile(
           config_path.read_text(),
           config_path.name,
           "exec")
   ```

4. Execute the code object created by the `compile()` method. We need to provide two contexts. The global context can provide the `__builtins__` module, plus the `Path` class and the `platform` module. The local context is where new variables will be created:

```
globals = {
    "__builtins__": __builtins__,
    "Path": Path,
    "platform": platform}
locals: Dict[str, ConfigClass] = {}
exec(code, globals, locals)
return locals[classname]
```

This locates the named class in the `locals` mapping. This mapping will have all the local variables set when the module was executed; these local variables will include all class and function definitions in addition to assigned variables. The value of `locals[classname]` will be the named class in the definitions created by the module that was executed.

How it works...

The details of the Python language—syntax and semantics—are embodied in the `compile()` and `exec()` functions. The `exec()` function reflects the way Python handles global and local variables. There are two namespaces provided to this function. The global `namespace` instance includes `__builtins__` plus a class and module that might be used in the file.

The local variable namespace will have the new class created in it. The local namespace has a `__dict__` attribute that makes it accessible via dictionary methods. Because of this, we can then extract the class by name using `locals[classname]`. The function returns the `class` object for use throughout the application.

We can put any kind of object into the attributes of a class. Our example showed mapping objects. There's no limitation on what can be done when creating attributes at the class level.

We can have complex calculations within the `class` statement. We can use this to create attributes that are derived from other attributes. We can execute any kind of statement, including `if` statements and `for` statements, to create attribute values.

We will not, however, ever create an instance of the class. Ordinary methods of the class will not be used. If a function-like definition is helpful, it would have to be decorated with `@classmethod` to be useful.

There's more...

Using a class definition means that we can leverage inheritance to organize the configuration values. We can easily create multiple subclasses of `Configuration`, one of which will be selected for use in the application. The configuration might look like this:

```
class Configuration:
    """
    Generic Configuration
    """
    url = {
        "scheme": "http",
        "netloc": "forecast.weather.gov",
        "path": "/shmrn.php"}

class Bahamas(Configuration):
    """
    Weather forecast for Offshore including the Bahamas
    """
    query = {"mz": ["AMZ117", "AMZ080"]}

class Chesapeake(Configuration):
    """
    Weather for Chesapeake Bay
    """
    query = {"mz": ["ANZ532"]}
```

This means that our application must choose an appropriate class from the available classes in the `settings` module. We might use an OS environment variable or a command-line option to specify the class name to use. The idea is that our program can be executed like this:

```
python3 some_app.py -c settings.Chesapeake
```

This would locate the `Chesapeake` class in the settings module. Processing would then be based on the details in that particular configuration class. This idea leads to an extension to the `load_config_module()` function.

In order to pick one of the available classes, we'll provide an additional parameter with the class name:

```
import importlib
def load_config_module(name: str) -> ConfigClass:
    module_name, _, class_name = name.rpartition(".")
    settings_module = importlib.import_module(module_name)
```

```
        result: ConfigClass = vars(settings_module)[class_name]
        return result
```

Rather than manually compiling and executing the module, we've used the higher-level `importlib` module. This module implements the `import` statement semantics. The requested module is imported; compiled and executed; and the resulting module object is assigned to the variable named `settings_module`.

We can then look inside the module's variables and pick out the class that was requested. The `vars()` built-in function will extract the internal dictionary from a module, a class, or even the local variables.

Now we can use this function as follows:

```
>>> configuration = Chapter_13.ch13_r04.load_config_module(
...     'Chapter_13.settings.Chesapeake')
>>> configuration.__doc__.strip()
'Weather for Chesapeake Bay'
>>> configuration.query
{'mz': ['ANZ532']}
>>> configuration.url['netloc']
'forecast.weather.gov'
```

We've located the `Chesapeake` configuration class in the `settings` module and extracted the various settings the application needs from this class.

Configuration representation

One consequence of using a class like this is the default display isn't very informative. When we try to print the configuration, it looks like this:

```
>>> print(configuration)
<class 'settings.Chesapeake'>
```

This isn't very helpful. It provides one nugget of information, but that's not nearly enough for debugging.

We can use the `vars()` function to see more details. However, this shows local variables, not inherited variables:

```
>>> pprint(vars(configuration))
mappingproxy({'__doc__': '\n    Weather for Chesapeake Bay\n    ',
              '__module__': 'Chapter_13.settings',
              'query': {'mz': ['ANZ532']}})
```

This is a little better, but it remains incomplete.

In order to see all of the settings, we need something a little more sophisticated. Interestingly, we can't simply define `__repr__()` for a class. A method defined in a class is used by the instances of this class, not the class itself.

Each class object we create is an instance of the built-in `type` class. We can, using a meta-class, tweak the way the `type` class behaves, and implement a slightly nicer `__repr__()` method, which looks through all parent classes for attributes.

We'll extend the built-in type with a `__repr__` that does a somewhat better job at displaying the working configuration:

```
class ConfigMetaclass(type):
    """Displays a subclass with superclass values injected"""
    def __repr__(self) -> str:
        name = (
            super().__name__
            + "("
            + ", ".join(b.__name__ for b in super().__bases__)
            + ")"
        )
        base_values = {
            n: v
            for base in reversed(super().__mro__)
            for n, v in vars(base).items()
            if not n.startswith("_")
        }
        values_text = [f"class {name}:"] + [
            f"    {name} = {value!r}"
            for name, value in base_values.items()
        ]
        return "\n".join(values_text)
```

The class name is available from the superclass, `type`, as the `__name__` attribute. The names of the base classes are included as well, to show the inheritance hierarchy for this configuration class.

The `base_values` are built from the attributes of all of the base classes. Each class is examined in reverse **Method Resolution Order** (**MRO**). Loading all of the attribute values in reverse MRO means that all of the defaults are loaded first. These values are then overridden with subclass values.

Names with the _ prefix are quietly ignored. This emphasizes the conventional practice of treating these as implementation details that aren't part of a public interface. This kind of name shouldn't really be used for a configuration file.

The resulting values are used to create a text representation that resembles a class definition. This does not recreate the original class source code; it's the net effect of the original class definition and all the superclass definitions.

Here's a `Configuration` class hierarchy that uses this metaclass. The base class, `Configuration`, incorporates the metaclass, and provides default definitions. The subclass extends those definitions with values that are unique to a particular environment or context:

```
class Configuration(metaclass=ConfigMetaclass):
    unchanged = "default"
    override = "default"
    feature_x_override = "default"
    feature_x = "disabled"

class Customized(Configuration):
    override = "customized"
    feature_x_override = "x-customized"
```

This is the kind of output our meta-class provides:

```
>>> print(Customized)
class Customized(Configuration):
    unchanged = 'default'
    override = 'customized'
    feature_x_override = 'x-customized'
    feature_x = 'disabled'
```

The output here can make it a little easier to see how the subclass attributes override the superclass defaults. This can help to clarify the resulting configuration used by an application.

We can leverage all of the power of Python's multiple inheritance to build `Configuration` class definitions. This can provide the ability to combine details on separate features into a single configuration object.

See also

- We'll look at class definitions in *Chapter 7, Basics of Classes and Objects*, and *Chapter 8, More Advanced Class Design*.

Designing scripts for composition

Many large applications are amalgamations of multiple smaller applications. In enterprise terminology, they are often called application systems comprising individual command-line application programs.

Some large, complex applications include a number of commands. For example, the `Git` application has numerous individual commands, such as `git pull`, `git commit`, and `git push`. These can also be seen as separate applications that are part of the overall `Git` system of applications.

An application might start as a collection of separate Python script files. At some point during its evolution, it can become necessary to refactor the scripts to combine features and create new, composite scripts from older disjoint scripts. The other path is also possible: a large application might be decomposed and refactored into a new organization of smaller components.

In this recipe, we'll look at ways to design a script so that future combinations and refactoring are made as simple as possible.

Getting ready

We need to distinguish between several aspects of a Python script.

We've seen several aspects of gathering input:

- Getting highly dynamic input from a command-line interface and environment variables. See the *Using argparse to get command-line input* recipe in *Chapter 6, User Inputs and Outputs*.
- Getting slower-changing configuration options from files. See the *Finding configuration files*, *Using YAML for configuration files*, and *Using Python for configuration files* recipes.
- For reading any input file, see the *Reading delimited files with the CSV module*, *Reading complex formats using regular expressions*, *Reading JSON documents*, *Reading XML documents*, and *Reading HTML documents* recipes in *Chapter 10, Input/Output, Physical Format, and Logical Layout*.

There are several aspects to producing output:

- Creating logs and offering other features that support audit, control, and monitoring. We'll look at some of this in the *Using logging for control and audit output* recipe.
- Creating the main output of the application. This might be printed or written to an output file using some of the same library modules used to parse inputs.

And finally, there's the real work of the application. This is made up of the essential features disentangled from the various input parsing and output formatting considerations. The real work is an algorithm working exclusively with Python data structures.

This *separation of concerns* suggests that an application, no matter how simple, should be designed as several separate functions. These should then be combined into the complete script. This lets us separate the input and output from the core processing. The processing is the part we'll often want to reuse. The input and output formats should be easy to change.

As a concrete example, we'll look at an application that creates sequences of dice rolls. Each sequence will follow the rules of the game of *Craps*. Here are the rules:

1. The first roll of two dice is the come out roll:
   - A roll of `2`, `3`, or `12` is an immediate loss. The sequence has a single value, for example, `[(1, 1)]`.
   - A roll of `7` or `11` is an immediate win. This sequence also has a single value, for example, `[(3, 4)]`.
2. Any other number establishes a point. The sequence starts with the point value and continues until either a `7` or the point value is rolled:
   - A final `7` is a loss, for example, `[(3, 1), (3, 2), (1, 1), (5, 6), (4, 3)]`.
   - A final match of the original point value is a win. There will be a minimum of two rolls. There's no upper bound on the length of a game, for example, `[(3, 1), (3, 2), (1, 1), (5, 6), (1, 3)]`.

The output is a sequence of items. Each item has a different structure. Some will be short lists. Some will be long lists. This is an ideal place for using YAML format files.

This output can be controlled by two inputs—how many sample sequences to create, and whether or not to seed the random number generator. For testing purposes, it can help to have a fixed seed.

How to do it...

This recipe will involve a fair number of design decisions. We'll start by considering the different kinds of output. Then we'll refactor the application around the kinds of output and the different purposes for the output:

1. Separate the output display into two broad areas:
   - Functions (or classes) that do no processing but display result objects. In this example, this is the sequence of throws for each individual game.
   - Logging used for monitoring and control, as well as audit or debugging. This is a cross-cutting concern that will be embedded throughout an application.

The sequence of rolls needs to be written to a file. This suggests that the `write_rolls()` function is given an iterator as a parameter. Here's a function that iterates and dumps values to a file in YAML notation:

```
def write_rolls(
        output_path: Path,
        game_iterator: Iterable[Game_Summary]
    ) -> Counter[int]:
    face_count: Counter[int] = collections.Counter()
    with output_path.open("w") as output_file:
        for game_outcome in game_iterator:
            output_file.write(
                yaml.dump(
                    game_outcome,
                    default_flow_style=True,
                    explicit_start=True
                )
            )
            for roll in game_outcome:
                face_count[sum(roll)] += 1
    return face_count
```

2. The monitoring and control output should display the input parameters used to control the processing. It should also provide the counts that show that the dice were fair. As a general practice, this kind of extra control information, separate from the primary output, is often written to standard error:

```
def summarize(
        configuration: argparse.Namespace,
        counts: Counter[int]
    ) -> None:
    print(configuration, file=sys.stderr)
    print(counts, file=sys.stderr)
```

3. Design (or refactor) the essential processing of the application to look like a single function:
    - All inputs are parameters.
    - All outputs are produced by `return` or `yield`. Use `return` to create a single result. Use `yield` to generate each item of an iterator that will produce multiple results.

In this example, we can easily make the core feature a function that iterates over the interesting values. This generator function relies on a `craps_game()` function to generate the requested number of samples. Each sample is a full game, showing all of the dice rolls. The `roll_iter()` function provides the `face_count` counter to this lower-level function to accumulate some totals to confirm that everything worked properly.

```
def roll_iter(
        total_games: int,
        seed: Optional[int] = None
    ) -> Iterator[Game_Summary]:
    random.seed(seed)
    for i in range(total_games):
        sequence = craps_game()
        yield sequence
```

4. The `craps_game()` function implements the *Craps* game rules to emit a single sequence of one or more rolls. This comprises all the rolls in a single game. We'll look at this `craps_game()` function later.
5. Refactor all of the input gathering into a function (or class) that gathers the various input sources. This can include environment variables, command-line arguments, and configuration files. It may also include the names of multiple input files. This function gathers command-line arguments. It also checks the `os.environ` collection of environment variables:

```
def get_options(
        argv: List[str] = sys.argv[1:]
    ) -> argparse.Namespace:
```

6. The argument parser will handle the details of parsing the `-samples` and `-output` options. We can leverage additional features of `argparse` to better validate the argument values:

```
    parser = argparse.ArgumentParser()
    parser.add_argument("-s", "--samples", type=int)
    parser.add_argument("-o", "--output")
    options = parser.parse_args(argv)

    if options.output is None:
        parser.error("No output file specified")
```

7. The value of `output_path` is created from the value of the `-output` option. Similarly, the value of the `RANDOMSEED` environment variable is validated and placed into the `options` namespace. This use of the `options` object keeps all of the various arguments in one place:

```
    options.output_path = Path(options.output)

    if "RANDOMSEED" in os.environ:
        seed_text = os.environ["RANDOMSEED"]
        try:
            options.seed = int(seed_text)
        except ValueError:
            parser.error(
                f"RANDOMSEED={seed_text!r} invalid seed")
    else:
        options.seed = None
    return options
```

8. Write the overall `main()` function, which incorporates the three previous elements, to create the final, overall script:

```
def main() -> None:
    options = get_options(sys.argv[1:])
    face_count = write_rolls(
        options.output_path,
        roll_iter(
            options.samples, options.seed
        )
    )
    summarize(options, face_count)
```

This brings the various aspects of the application together. It parses the command-line and environment options.

The `roll_iter()` function is the core processing. It takes the various options, and it emits a sequence of rolls.

The primary output from the `roll_iter()` method is collected by `write_rolls()` and written to the given output path. Additional control output is written by a separate function, `summarize()`, so that we can change the summary without an impact on the primary output.

How it works...

The central premise here is the separation of concerns. There are three distinct aspects to the processing:

- **Inputs**: The parameters from the command-line and environment variables are gathered by a single function, `get_options()`. This function can grab inputs from a variety of sources, including configuration files.
- **Outputs**: The primary output was handled by the `write_rolls()` function. The other control output was handled by accumulating totals in a `Counter` object and then dumping this output at the end.
- **Process**: The application's essential processing is factored into the `roll_iter()` function. This function can be reused in a variety of contexts.

The goal of this design is to separate the `roll_iter()` function from the surrounding application details.

The output from this application looks like the following example:

```
slott$ python Chapter_13/ch13_r05.py --samples 10 --output=x.yaml
Namespace(output='x.yaml', output_path=PosixPath('x.yaml'), samples=10,
seed=None)
Counter({5: 7, 6: 7, 7: 7, 8: 5, 4: 4, 9: 4, 11: 3, 10: 1, 12: 1})
```

The command line requested ten samples and specifies an output file of `x.yaml`. The control output is a simple dump of the options. It shows the values for the parameters plus the additional values set in the `options` object.

The control output includes the counts from ten samples. This provides some confidence that values such as `6`, `7`, and `8` occur more often. It shows that values such as `3` and `12` occur less frequently.

The output file, `x.yaml`, might look like this:

```
slott$ more x.yaml
--- [[5, 4], [3, 4]]
--- [[3, 5], [1, 3], [1, 4], [5, 3]]
--- [[3, 2], [2, 4], [6, 5], [1, 6]]
--- [[2, 4], [3, 6], [5, 2]]
--- [[1, 6]]
--- [[1, 3], [4, 1], [1, 4], [5, 6], [6, 5], [1, 5], [2, 6], [3, 4]]
--- [[3, 3], [3, 4]]
--- [[3, 5], [4, 1], [4, 2], [3, 1], [1, 4], [2, 3], [2, 6]]
--- [[2, 2], [1, 5], [5, 5], [1, 5], [6, 6], [4, 3]]
--- [[4, 5], [6, 3]]
```

Consider the larger context for this kind of simulation. There might be one or more analytical applications to make use of the simulation output. These applications could perform some statistical analyses on the sequences of rolls.

After using these two applications to create rolls and summarize them, the users may determine that it would be advantageous to combine the roll creation and the statistical overview into a single application. Because the various aspects of each application have been separated, we can rearrange the features and create a new application.

We can now build a new application that will start with the following two imports to bring in the useful functions from the existing applications:

```
from generator import roll_iter, craps_rules
from stats_overview import summarize
```

Ideally, a new application can be built without any changes to the other two applications. This leaves the original suite of applications untouched by the introduction of new features.

More importantly, the new application did not involve any copying or pasting of code. The new application imports working software. Any changes made to fix one application will also fix latent bugs in other applications.

Reuse via copy and paste creates technical debt. Avoid copying and pasting the code.

When we try to copy code from one application and paste it into a new application, we create a confusing situation. Any changes made to one copy won't magically fix latent bugs in the other copy. When changes are made to one copy, and the other copy is not kept up to date, this is an example of code rot.

There's more...

In the previous section, we skipped over the details of the `craps_rules()` function. This function creates a sequence of dice rolls that comprise a single game of *Craps*. It can vary from a single roll to a sequence of indefinite length. About 98% of the games will consist of thirteen or fewer throws of the dice.

The rules depend on the total of two dice. The data captured include the two separate faces of the dice. In order to support these details, it's helpful to have a `NamedTuple` instance that has these two, related properties:

```
class Roll(NamedTuple):
    faces: List[int]
    total: int


def roll(n: int = 2) -> Roll:
```

```
    faces = list(random.randint(1, 6) for _ in range(n))
    total = sum(faces)
    return Roll(faces, total)
```

This `roll()` function creates a `Roll` instance with a sequence that shows the `faces` of the dice, as well as the `total` of the dice. The `craps_game()` function will generate enough `Roll` objects to be one complete game:

```
Game_Summary = List[List[int]]


def craps_game() -> Game_Summary:
    """Summarize the game as a list of dice pairs."""
    come_out = roll()
    if come_out.total in [2, 3, 12]:
        return [come_out.faces]
    elif come_out.total in [7, 11]:
        return [come_out.faces]
    elif come_out.total in [4, 5, 6, 8, 9, 10]:
        sequence = [come_out.faces]
        next = roll()
        while next.total not in [7, come_out.total]:
            sequence.append(next.faces)
            next = roll()
        sequence.append(next.faces)
        return sequence
    else:
        raise Exception(f"Horrifying Logic Bug in {come_out}")
```

The `craps_game()` function implements the rules for *Craps*. If the first roll is `2`, `3`, or `12`, the sequence only has a single value, and the game is a loss. If the first roll is `7` or `11`, the sequence also has only a single value, and the game is a win. The remaining values establish a point. The sequence of rolls starts with the point value. The sequence continues until it's ended by seven or the point value.

The horrifying logic bug exception represents a way to detect a design problem. The `if` statement conditions are quite complex. As we noted in the *Designing complex if...elif chains* recipe in *Chapter 2, Statements and Syntax*, we need to be absolutely sure the `if` and `elif` conditions are complete. If we've designed them incorrectly, the `else` statement should alert us to the failure to correctly design the conditions.

Refactoring a script to a class

The close relationship between the `roll_iter()`, `roll()`, and `craps_game()` methods suggests that it might be better to encapsulate these functions into a single class definition. Here's a class that has all of these features bundled together:

```
class CrapsSimulator:
    def __init__(self, /, seed: int = None) -> None:
        self.rng = random.Random(seed)
        self.faces: List[int]
        self.total: int

    def roll(self, n: int = 2) -> int:
        self.faces = list(
            self.rng.randint(1, 6) for _ in range(n))
        self.total = sum(self.faces)
        return self.total

    def craps_game(self) -> List[List[int]]:
        self.roll()
        if self.total in [2, 3, 12]:
            return [self.faces]
        elif self.total in [7, 11]:
            return [self.faces]
        elif self.total in [4, 5, 6, 8, 9, 10]:
            point, sequence = self.total, [self.faces]
            self.roll()
            while self.total not in [7, point]:
                sequence.append(self.faces)
                self.roll()
            sequence.append(self.faces)
            return sequence
        else:
            raise Exception("Horrifying Logic Bug")

    def roll_iter(
            self, total_games: int) -> Iterator[List[List[int]]]:
        for i in range(total_games):
            sequence = self.craps_game()
            yield sequence
```

This class includes an initialization of the simulator to include its own random number generator. It will either use the given seed value, or the internal algorithm will pick the seed value.

The `roll()` method will set the `self.total` and `self.faces` instance variables. There's no clear benefit to having the `roll()` method return a value and also cache the current value of the dice in the `self.total` attribute. Eliminating `self.total` is left as an exercise for the reader.

The `craps_game()` method generates one sequence of rolls for one game of *Craps*. It uses the `roll()` method and the two instance variables, `self.total` and `self.faces`, to track the state of the dice.

The `roll_iter()` method generates the sequence of games. Note that the signature of this method is not exactly like the preceding `roll_iter()` function. This class separates random number seeding from the game creation algorithm.

Rewriting the `main()` function to use the `CrapsSimulator` class is left as an exercise for the reader. Since the method names are similar to the original function names, the refactoring should not be terribly complex.

See also

- See the *Using argparse to get command-line input* recipe in *Chapter 6, User Inputs and Outputs*, for background on using `argparse` to get inputs from a user.
- See the *Finding configuration files* recipe earlier in this chapter for a way to track down configuration files.
- The *Using logging for control and audit output* recipe later in this chapter looks at logging.
- In the *Combining two applications into one* recipe, in *Chapter 14, Application Integration: Combination*, we'll look at ways to combine applications that follow this design pattern.

Using logging for control and audit output

In the *Designing scripts for composition* recipe earlier in this chapter, we examined three aspects of an application:

- Gathering input
- Producing output
- The essential processing that connects input and output

There are several different kinds of output that applications produce:

- The main output that helps a user make a decision or take action
- Control information that confirms that the program worked completely and correctly
- Audit summaries that are used to track the history of state changes in persistent databases
- Any error messages that indicate why the application didn't work

It's less than optimal to lump all of these various aspects into `print()` requests that write to standard output. Indeed, it can lead to confusion because too many different outputs are interleaved in a single stream.

The OS provides each running process with two output files, standard output and standard error. These are visible in Python through the `sys` module with the names `sys.stdout` and `sys.stderr`. By default, the `print()` method writes to the `sys.stdout` file. We can change this and write the control, audit, and error messages to `sys.stderr`. This is an important step in the right direction.

Python also offers the `logging` package, which can be used to direct the ancillary output to a separate file (and/or other output channels, such as a database). It can also be used to format and filter that additional output.

In this chapter we'll look at good ways to use the `logging` module.

Getting ready

In the *Designing scripts for composition* recipe, earlier in this chapter, we looked at an application that produced a YAML file with the raw output of a simulation in it. In this recipe, we'll look at an application that consumes that raw data and produces some statistical summaries. We'll call this application `overview_stats.py`.

Following the design pattern of separating the input, output, and processing, we'll have an application, `main()`, that looks something like this:

```
def main(argv: List[str] = sys.argv[1:]) -> None:
    options = get_options(argv)
    if options.output is not None:
        report_path = Path(options.output)
        with report_path.open("w") as result_file:
            process_all_files(result_file, options.file)
    else:
        process_all_files(sys.stdout, options.file)
```

This function will get the options from various sources. If an output file is named, it will create the output file using a `with` statement context manager. This function will then process all of the command-line argument files as input from which statistics are gathered.

If no output file name is provided, this function will write to the `sys.stdout` file. This will display output that can be redirected using the OS shell's > operator to create a file.

The `main()` function relies on a `process_all_files()` function. The `process_all_files()` function will iterate through each of the argument files and gather statistics from that file. Here's what that function looks like:

```
def process_all_files(
        result_file: TextIO,
        file_paths: Iterable[Path]
    ) -> None:
    for source_path in file_paths:
        with source_path.open() as source_file:
            game_iter = yaml.load_all(
                source_file,
                Loader=yaml.SafeLoader)
            statistics = gather_stats(game_iter)
            result_file.write(
                yaml.dump(
                    dict(statistics),
                    explicit_start=True))
```

The `process_all_files()` function applies `gather_stats()` to each file in the `file_names` iterable. The resulting collection is written to the given `result_file` file.

The function shown here conflates processing and output in a design that is not ideal. We'll address this design flaw in the *Combining two applications into one* recipe.

The essential processing is in the `gather_stats()` function. Given a path to a file, this will read and summarize the games in that file. The resulting `summary` object can then be written as part of the overall display or, in this case, appended to a sequence of YAML-format summaries:

```
def gather_stats(
        game_iter: Iterable[List[List[int]]]
    ) -> Counter[Outcome]:
    counts: Counter[Outcome] = collections.Counter()
    for game in game_iter:
        if len(game) == 1 and sum(game[0]) in (2, 3, 12):
            outcome = "loss"
```

```
        elif len(game) == 1 and sum(game[0]) in (7, 11):
            outcome = "win"
        elif len(game) > 1 and sum(game[-1]) == 7:
            outcome = "loss"
        elif len(game) > 1 and sum(game[0]) == sum(game[-1]):
            outcome = "win"
        else:
            detail_log.error("problem with %r", game)
            raise Exception(
                f"Wait, What? "
                f"Inconsistent len {len(game)} and
                f"final {sum(game[-1])} roll"
            )
        event = (outcome, len(game))
        counts[event] += 1
    return counts
```

This function determines which of the four game termination rules were applied to the sequence of dice rolls. It starts by opening the given source file and using the `load_all()` function to iterate through all of the YAML documents. Each document is a single game, represented as a sequence of dice pairs.

This function uses the first (and sometimes last) rolls to determine the overall outcome of the game. There are four rules, which should enumerate all possible logical combinations of events. In the event that there is an error in our reasoning, an exception will get raised to alert us to a special case that didn't fit the design in some way.

The game is reduced to a single event with an outcome and a length. These are accumulated into a `Counter` object. The outcome and length of a game are the two values we're computing. These are a stand-in for more complex or sophisticated statistical analyses that are possible.

We've carefully segregated almost all file-related considerations from this function. The `gather_stats()` function will work with any iterable source of game data.

Here's the output from this application. It's not very pretty; it's a YAML document that can be used for further processing:

```
slott$ python Chapter_13/ch13_r06.py x.yaml
---
? !!python/tuple [loss, 2]
: 2
? !!python/tuple [loss, 3]
: 1
```

```
? !!python/tuple [loss, 4]
: 1
? !!python/tuple [loss, 6]
: 1
? !!python/tuple [loss, 8]
: 1
? !!python/tuple [win, 1]
: 1
? !!python/tuple [win, 2]
: 1
? !!python/tuple [win, 4]
: 1
? !!python/tuple [win, 7]
: 1
```

We'll need to insert logging features into all of these functions to show which file is being read, and any errors or problems with processing the file.

Furthermore, we're going to create two logs. One will have details, and the other will have a minimal summary of files that are created. The first log can go to `sys.stderr`, which will be displayed at the console when the program runs. The other log will be appended to a long-term `log` file to cover all uses of the application.

One approach to having separate needs is to create two loggers, each with a different intent. The two loggers can have dramatically different configurations. Another approach is to create a single logger and use a `Filter` object to distinguish content intended for each logger. We'll focus on creating separate loggers because it's easier to develop and easier to unit test.

Each logger has a variety of methods reflecting the severity of the message. The severity levels defined in the `logging` package include the following:

- **DEBUG**: These messages are not generally shown since their intent is to support debugging.
- **INFO**: These messages provide information on the normal, happy-path processing.
- **WARNING**: These messages indicate that processing may be compromised in some way. The most sensible use case for a warning is when functions or classes have been deprecated: they still work, but they should be replaced.
- **ERROR**: Processing is invalid and the output is incorrect or incomplete. In the case of a long-running server, an individual request may have problems, but the server as a whole can continue to operate.
- **CRITICAL**: A more severe level of error. Generally, this is used by long-running servers where the server itself can no longer operate and is about to crash.

The method names are similar to the severity levels. We use `logging.info()` to write an **INFO** message.

How to do it...

We'll be building a more complete application, leveraging components from previous examples. This will add use of the `logging` module:

1. We'll start by implementing basic `logging` features into the existing functions. This means that we'll need the `logging` module, plus the other packages required by this app:

   ```
   import argparse
   import collections
   import logging
   from pathlib import Path
   import sys
   from typing import List, Iterable, Tuple, Counter, TextIO
   import yaml
   ```

2. We'll create two `logger` objects as module globals. Loggers have hierarchical names. We'll name the loggers using the application name and a suffix with the content. The `overview_stats.detail` logger will have processing details. The `overview_stats.write` logger will identify the files read and the files written; this parallels the idea of an audit log because the file writes track state changes in the collection of output files:

   ```
   detail_log = logging.getLogger("overview_stats.detail")
   write_log = logging.getLogger("overview_stats.write")
   ```

   We don't need to configure these loggers at this time. If we do nothing more, the two `logger` objects will silently accept individual log entries, but won't do anything further with the data.

3. We'll rewrite the `main()` function to summarize the two aspects of the processing. This will use the `write_log logger` object to show when a new file is created. We've added the `write_log.info()` line to put an information message into the log for files that have been written:

   ```
   def main(argv: List[str] = sys.argv[1:]) -> None:
       options = get_options(argv)
       if options.output is not None:
           report_path = Path(options.output)
           with report_path.open("w") as result_file:
               process_all_files(result_file, options.file)
   ```

```
            write_log.info("wrote %r", report_path)
        else:
            process_all_files(sys.stdout, options.file)
```

4. We'll rewrite the `process_all_files()` function to provide a note when a file is read. We've added the `detail_log.info()` line to put information messages in the detail log for every file that's read:

```
def process_all_files(
        result_file: TextIO,
        file_paths: Iterable[Path]
    ) -> None:
    for source_path in file_paths:
        detail_log.info("read %r", source_path)
        with source_path.open() as source_file:
            game_iter = yaml.load_all(
                source_file,
                Loader=yaml.SafeLoader)
            statistics = gather_stats(game_iter)
            result_file.write(
                yaml.dump(
                    dict(statistics),
                    explicit_start=True))
```

The `gather_stats()` function can have a log line added to it to track normal operations. Additionally, we've added a log entry for the logic error. The `detail_log` logger is used to collect debugging information. If we set the overall logging level to include debug messages, we'll see this additional output:

```
def gather_stats(
        game_iter: Iterable[List[List[int]]]
    ) -> Counter[Outcome]:
    counts: Counter[Outcome] = collections.Counter()
    for game in game_iter:
        if len(game) == 1 and sum(game[0]) in (2, 3, 12):
            outcome = "loss"
        elif len(game) == 1 and sum(game[0]) in (7, 11):
            outcome = "win"
        elif len(game) > 1 and sum(game[-1]) == 7:
            outcome = "loss"
        elif (len(game) > 1
```

```
            and sum(game[0]) == sum(game[-1])):
            outcome = "win"
        else:
            detail_log.error("problem with %r", game)
            raise Exception("Wait, What?")
        event = (outcome, len(game))
        detail_log.debug(
            "game %r -> event %r", game, event)
        counts[event] += 1
    return counts
```

5. The `get_options()` function will also have a debugging line written. This can help diagnose problems by displaying the options in the log:

```
def get_options(
        argv: List[str] = sys.argv[1:]
    ) -> argparse.Namespace:
    parser = argparse.ArgumentParser()
    parser.add_argument("file", nargs="*", type=Path)
    parser.add_argument("-o", "--output")
    options = parser.parse_args(argv)
    detail_log.debug("options: %r", options)
    return options
```

6. We can add a basic configuration to see the log entries. This works as a first step to confirm that there are two loggers and they're being used properly:

```
if __name__ == "__main__":
    logging.basicConfig(stream=sys.stderr, level=logging.INFO)
    main()
    logging.shutdown()
```

This logging configuration builds the default handler object. This object simply prints all of the log messages on the given stream. This handler is assigned to the root logger; it will apply to all children of this logger. Therefore, both of the loggers created in the preceding code will go to the same stream.

Here's an example of running this script:

```
(cookbook) % python Chapter_13/ch13_r06.py -o data/sum.yaml data/x.yaml
INFO:overview_stats.detail:read PosixPath('data/x.yaml')
INFO:overview_stats.write:wrote PosixPath('data/sum.yaml')
```

There are two lines in the log. Both have a severity of INFO. The first line is from the `overview_stats.detail` logger. The second line is from the `overview_stats.write logger`. The default configuration sends all loggers to `sys.stderr` so the logging output is kept separate from the main output of the application.

How it works...

There are three parts to introducing logging into an application:

- Creating `Logger` objects
- Placing log requests near important state changes
- Configuring the logging system as a whole

Creating loggers can be done in a variety of ways. A common approach is to create one logger with the same name as the module:

```
logger = logging.getLogger(__name__)
```

For the top-level, main script, this will have the name `"__main__"`. For imported modules, the name will match the module name.

In more complex applications, there will be a variety of loggers serving a variety of purposes. In these cases, simply naming a logger after a module may not provide the required level of flexibility.

It's also possible to use the `logging` module itself as the root logger. This means a module can use the `logging.info()` method, for example. This isn't recommended because the root logger is anonymous, and we sacrifice the possibility of using the logger name as an important source of information.

There are two concepts that can be used to assign names to the loggers. It's often best to choose one of them and stick with it throughout a large application:

- Follow the package and module hierarchy. This means that a logger specific to a class might have a name like `package.module.class`. Other classes in the same module would share a common parent logger name. It's then possible to set the logging level for the whole package, one of the specific modules, or just one of the classes.
- Follow a hierarchy based on the audience or use case. The top-level name will distinguish the audience or purpose for the log. We might have top-level loggers with names such as `event`, `audit`, and perhaps `debug`. This way, all of the `audit` loggers will have names that start with "`audit.`". This can make it easy to route all loggers under a given parent to a specific handler.

In the recipe, we used the first style of naming. The logger names parallel the software architecture.

Placing logging requests near all the important state changes means we can decide which of the interesting state changes in an application belong in a log:

- Any change to a persistent resource might be a good place to include a message of level `INFO`. This means any change to the OS state, for example removing a file or creating a directory, is a candidate for logging. Similarly, database updates and requests that should change the state of a web service should be logged.
- Whenever there's a problem making a persistent state change, there should be a message with a level of `ERROR`. Any OS-level exceptions can be logged when they are caught and handled.
- In long, complex calculations, it may be helpful to include `DEBUG` messages after particularly important assignment statements.
- Any change to an internal application resource deserves a `DEBUG` message so that object state changes can be tracked through the log.
- When the application enters an erroneous state. This should generally be in an exception handler. When exceptions are being silenced or transformed, then a `DEBUG` message might be more appropriate than a log entry at the `CRITICAL` level.

The third aspect of logging is configuring the loggers so that they route the requests to the appropriate destination. By default, with no configuration at all, the loggers will all quietly create log events but won't display them.

With minimal configuration, we can see all of the log events on the console. This can be done with the `basicConfig()` method and covers a large number of simple use cases without any real fuss. Instead of a stream, we can use a filename to provide a named file. Perhaps the most important feature is providing a simple way to enable debugging by setting the logging level on the root logger from the `basicConfig()` method.

The example configuration in the recipe used two common handlers—the `StreamHandler` and `FileHandler` classes. There are over a dozen more handlers, each with unique features for gathering and publishing log messages.

There's more...

In order to route the different loggers to different destinations, we'll need a more sophisticated configuration. This goes beyond what we can build with the `basicConfig()` function. We'll need to use the `logging.config` module, and the `dictConfig()` function. This can provide a complete set of configuration options. The easiest way to use this function is to write the configuration in YAML and then convert this to an internal `dict` object using the `yaml.load()` function:

```
from textwrap import dedent
config_yaml = dedent("""\
version: 1
```

```
formatters:
    default:
        style: "{"
        format: "{levelname}:{name}:{message}"
        #   Example: INFO:overview_stats.detail:read x.yaml
    timestamp:
        style: "{"
        format: "{asctime}//{levelname}//{name}//{message}"

handlers:
    console:
        class: logging.StreamHandler
        stream: ext://sys.stderr
        formatter: default
    file:
        class: logging.FileHandler
        filename: data/write.log
        formatter: timestamp

loggers:
    overview_stats.detail:
        handlers:
        -   console
    overview_stats.write:
        handlers:
        -   file
        -   console

root:
    level: INFO
""")
```

The YAML document is enclosed in a triple-quoted string. This allows us to write as much text as necessary. We've defined five things in the big block of text using YAML notation:

- The value of the `version` key must be `1`.
- The value of the `formatters` key defines the log format. If this is not specified, the default format shows only the message body, without any level or logger information:
    - The `default` formatter defined here mirrors the format created by the `basicConfig()` function.

- The `timestamp` formatter defined here is a more complex format that includes the datetime stamp for the record. To make the file easier to parse, a column separator of // was used.

- The `handlers` key defines the two handlers for the two loggers. The `console` handler writes to the `sys.stderr` stream. We specified the formatter this handler will use. This definition parallels the configuration created by the `basicConfig()` function. Unsurprisingly, the `FileHandler` class writes to a file. The default mode for opening the file is `a`, which will append to the file with no upper limit on the file size. There are other handlers that can rotate through multiple files, each of a limited size. We've provided an explicit filename, and the formatter that will put more detail into the file than is shown on the console.
- The `loggers` key provides a configuration for the two loggers that the application will create. Any logger name that begins with `overview_stats.detail` will be handled only by the console handler. Any logger name that begins with `overview_stats.write` will go to both the file handler and the console handler.
- The `root` key defines the top-level logger. It has a name of `''` (the empty string) in case we need to refer to it in code. Setting the level on the root logger will set the level for all of the children of this logger.

Use the configuration to wrap the `main()` function like this:

```
logging.config.dictConfig(
    yaml.load(config_yaml, Loader=yaml.SafeLoader))
main()
logging.shutdown()
```

This will start the logging in a known state. It will do the processing of the application. It will finalize all of the logging buffers and properly close any files.

See also

- See the *Designing scripts for composition* recipe earlier in this chapter for the complementary part of this application.

14
Application Integration: Combination

The Python language is designed to permit extensibility. We can create sophisticated programs by combining a number of smaller components. In this chapter, we'll look at ways to take a number of smaller components and create sophisticated combinations.

We'll look at the complications that can arise from composite applications and the need to centralize some features, like command-line parsing. This will enable us to create uniform interfaces for a variety of closely related programs.

We'll extend some of the concepts from *Chapter 7, Basics of Classes and Objects*, and *Chapter 8, More Advanced Class Design*, and apply the idea of the Command Design Pattern to Python programs. By encapsulating features in class definitions, we'll find it easier to combine features.

In this chapter, we'll look at the following recipes:

- Combining two applications into one
- Combining many applications using the Command Design Pattern
- Managing arguments and configuration in composite applications
- Wrapping and combining CLI applications
- Wrapping a program and checking the output
- Controlling complex sequences of steps

We'll start with a direct approach to combining multiple Python applications into a single, more sophisticated and useful application. We'll expand this to apply object-oriented design techniques and create an even more flexible composite. The next layer is to create uniform command-line argument parsing for composite applications.

Combining two applications into one

In the *Designing scripts for composition* recipe in *Chapter 13, Application Integration: Configuration*, we looked at a simple application that creates a collection of statistics by simulating a process. In the *Using logging for control and audit output* recipe in *Chapter 13, Application Integration: Configuration*, we looked at an application that summarizes a collection of statistics. In this recipe, we'll combine the separate simulation and summarizing applications to create a single, composite application that performs both a simulation and summarizes the resulting data.

There are several common approaches to combining multiple applications:

- A shell script can run the simulator and then run the summary.
- A Python program can stand in for the shell script and use the `runpy` module to run each program.
- We can build a composite application from the essential components of each application.

In the *Designing scripts for composition* recipe, we examined three aspects of an application. Here are the three aspects that many applications implement:

- Gathering input
- Producing output
- The essential processing that connects input and output

This separation of concerns can be helpful for suggesting how components can be selected from multiple applications and recombined into a new, larger application.

In this recipe, we'll look at a direct way to combine applications by writing a Python application that treats other applications as separate modules.

Getting ready

In the *Designing scripts for composition* and *Using logging for control and audit output* recipes in *Chapter 13, Application Integration: Configuration*, we followed a design pattern that separated the input gathering, the essential processing, and the production of output. The objective behind that design pattern was gathering the interesting pieces together to combine and recombine them into higher-level constructs.

Note that we have a tiny mismatch between the two applications, we can borrow a phrase from database engineering (and also electrical engineering) and call this an impedance mismatch. In electrical engineering, it's a problem with circuit design, and it's often solved by using a device called a transformer to match the impedance between circuit components.

In database engineering, this kind of problem surfaces when the database has normalized, flat data, but the programming language uses richly structured complex objects. For SQL databases, this is a common problem, and packages such as `SQLAlchemy` are used as an **Object-Relational Management** (**ORM**) layer. This layer is a transformer between flat database rows (often from multiple tables) and complex Python structures.

When building a composite application, the impedance mismatch that surfaces in this example is a cardinality problem. The simulator is designed to run more frequently than the statistical summarizer. We have several choices for addressing issues such as this one:

- **Total Redesign**: This may not be a sensible alternative because the two component applications have an established base of users. In other cases, the new use cases are an opportunity to make sweeping fixes and retire some technical debt.
- **Include the Iterator**: This means that when we build the composite application, we'll add a `for` statement to perform many simulation runs and then process this into a single summary. This parallels the original design intent.
- **List of One**: This means that the composite application will run one simulation and provide this single simulation output to the summarizer. This doesn't follow the original intent well, but it has the advantage of simplicity.

The choice between these design alternatives depends on the user story that leads to creating the composite application in the first place. It may also depend on the established base of users. For our purposes, we'll assume that the users have come to realize that 1,000 simulation runs of 1,000 samples is now their standard approach, and they would like to follow the *Include the Iterator* design to create a composite process.

How to do it...

We'll follow a design pattern that decomposes a complex process into functions that are independent of input or output details. See the *Designing scripts for composition* recipe in *Chapter 13, Application Integration: Configuration*, for details on this.

1. Import the essential functions from the working modules. In this case, the two modules have the relatively uninteresting names `ch13_r05` and `ch13_r06`:

```
from Chapter_13.ch13_r05 import roll_iter
from Chapter_13.ch13_r06 import gather_stats, Outcome
```

2. Import any other modules required. We'll use a `Counter` collection to prepare the summaries in this example:

```
import argparse
import collections
import logging
import time
import sys
from typing import List, Counter, Tuple, Iterable, Dict
```

3. Create a new function that combines the existing functions from the other applications. The output from one function is input to another:

```
def summarize_games(
        total_games: int, *, seed: int = None
    ) -> Counter[Outcome]:
    game_statistics = gather_stats(
        roll_iter(total_games, seed=seed))
    return game_statistics
```

4. Write the output-formatting functions that use this composite process. Here, for example, is a composite process that exercises the `summarize_games()` function. This also writes the output report:

```
def simple_composite(
        games: int = 100, rolls: int = 1_000) -> None:
    start = time.perf_counter()
    stats = summarize_games(games*rolls)
    end = time.perf_counter()

    games = sum(stats.values())
    print("games", games, "rolls", rolls)
    print(win_loss(stats))
    print(f"serial: {end-start:.2f} seconds")
```

5. Gathering command-line options can be done using the `argparse` module. There are examples of this in recipes such as the *Designing scripts for composition* recipe.

The combined functionality is now a function, `simple_composite()`, that we can invoke from a block of code like the following:

```
if __name__ == "__main__":
    logging.basicConfig(stream=sys.stderr, level=logging.INFO)
    simple_composite(games=1000, rolls=1000)
```

This gives us a combined application, written entirely in Python. We can write unit tests for this composite, as well as each of the individual steps that make up the overall application.

How it works...

The central feature of this design is the separation of the various concerns of the application into isolated functions or classes. The two component applications started with a design divided up among input, process, and output concerns. Starting from this base made it easier to import and reuse the processing. This also left the two original applications in place, unchanged.

The objective is to import functions from working modules and avoid copy-and-paste programming. Copying a function from one file and pasting it into another means that any change made to one is unlikely to be made to the other. The two copies will slowly diverge, leading to a phenomenon sometimes called code rot.

When a class or function does several things, the reuse potential is reduced. This leads to the Inverse power law of reuse—the re usability of a class or function, *R(c)*, is related to the inverse of the number of features in that class or function, *F(c)*:

$$\mathrm{R(c)} \propto \frac{1}{F(c)}$$

A single feature aids reuse. Multiple features reduce the opportunities for reuse of a component.

When we look at the two original applications from the *Designing scripts for composition* and *Using logging for control and audit output* recipes in *Chapter 13, Application Integration: Configuration*, we can see that the essential functions had few features. The `roll_iter()` function simulated a game and yielded results. The `gather_stats()` function gathered statistics from any source of data.

The idea of counting features depends, of course, on the level of abstraction. From a small-scale view, the functions do many small things. From a very large-scale view, the functions require several helpers to form a complete application; from this viewpoint, an individual function is only a part of a feature.

In this case, one application created files. The second application summarized files. Feedback from users may have revealed that the distinction was not important or perhaps confusing. This led to a redesign to combine the two original steps into a one-step operation.

There's more...

We'll look at three additional areas of rework of the application:

- **Structure**: The *Combining two applications into one* recipe did not do a good job of distinguishing between processing aspects and output aspects. When trying to create a composite application, we may need to refactor the component modules to look for better organization of the features.
- **Performance**: Running several `roll_iter()` instances in parallel to use multiple cores.
- **Logging**: When multiple applications are combined, the combined logging can become complex. When we need to observe the operations of the program for auditing and debugging purposes, we may need to refactor the logging.

We'll go through each area in turn.

Structure

In some cases, it becomes necessary to rearrange software to expose useful features. In one of the components, the `ch13_r06` module, the `process_all_files()` function seemed to do too much.

This function combined source file iteration, detailed processing, and output creation in one place. The `result_file.write()` output processing was a single, complex statement that seemed unrelated to gathering and summarizing data.

In order to reuse this file-writing feature between two distinct applications, we'll need to refactor the `ch13_r06` application so that the file output is not buried inside the `process_all_files()` function.

One line of code, `result_file.write(...)`, needs to be replaced with a separate function. This is a small change. The details are left as an exercise for the reader. When the output operation is defined as a separate function, it is easier to change to new physical formats or logical layouts of data.

This refactoring also makes the new function available for other composite applications. When multiple applications share a common function, then it's much more likely that outputs between the applications are actually compatible.

Performance

Running many simulations followed by a single summary is a kind of map-reduce design. The detailed simulations are a kind of mapping that creates raw data. These can be run concurrently, using multiple cores and multiple processors. The final summary is created from all of the simulations via a statistical reduction.

We often use OS features to run multiple concurrent processes. The POSIX shells include the `&` operator, which can be used to fork concurrent subprocesses. Windows has a `start` command, which is similar to the POSIX `&` operator. We can leverage Python directly to spawn a number of concurrent simulation processes.

One module for doing this is the `futures` module from the `concurrent` package. We can build a parallel simulation processor by creating an instance of `ProcessPoolExecutor`. We can submit requests to this executor and then collect the results from those concurrent requests:

```
from concurrent import futures

def parallel_composite(
        games: int = 100,
        rolls: int = 1_000,
        workers: Optional[int] = None) -> None:
    start = time.perf_counter()
    total_stats: Counter[Outcome] = collections.Counter()
```

```
    worker_list = []
    with futures.ProcessPoolExecutor(max_workers=workers) as
executor:
        for i in range(games):
            worker_list.append(
                executor.submit(summarize_games, rolls))
        for worker in worker_list:
            stats = worker.result()
            total_stats.update(stats)
    end = time.perf_counter()

    games = sum(total_stats.values())
    print("games", games, "rolls", rolls)
    print(win_loss(total_stats))
    if workers is None:
        workers = multiprocessing.cpu_count()
    print(f"parallel ({workers}): {end-start:.2f} seconds")
```

We've initialized three objects: `start`, `total_stats`, and `worker_list`. The `start` object has the time at which processing started; `time.perf_counter()` is often the most accurate timer available. `total_stats` is a `Counter` object that will collect the final statistical summary. `worker_list` will be a list of individual `Future` objects, one for each request that's made.

The `futures.ProcessPoolExecutor` method creates a processing context in which a pool of workers is available to handle requests. By default, the pool has as many workers as the number of processors. Each worker process will import the module that creates the pool. All functions and classes defined in that module are available to the workers.

The `submit()` method of an executor is given a function to execute along with arguments to that function. In this example, there will be 100 requests made, each of which will simulate 1,000 games and return the sequence of dice rolls for those games. `submit()` returns a `Future` object, which is a model for the working request.

After submitting all 100 requests, the results are collected. The `result()` method of a `Future` object waits for the processing to finish and gathers the resulting object. In this example, the result is a statistical summary of 1,000 games. These are then combined to create the overall `total_stats` summary.

Here's a comparison of serial and parallel execution on a four-core processor:

```
(cookbook) % export PYTHONPATH=.
(cookbook) slott@MacBookPro-SLott Modern-Python-Cookbook-Second-Edition %
python Chapter_14/ch14_r01.py --rolls 10_000 --serial
games 1000000 rolls 10000
```

```
Counter({'loss': 507921, 'win': 492079})
serial: 13.53 seconds
(cookbook) slott@MacBookPro-SLott Modern-Python-Cookbook-Second-Edition %
python Chapter_14/ch14_r01.py --rolls 10_000 --parallel
games 1000000 rolls 10000
Counter({'loss': 506671, 'win': 493329})
parallel: 8.15 seconds
```

Concurrent simulation cuts the elapsed processing time from 13.53 seconds to 8.15 seconds. The runtime improved by 40%. Since there are four cores in the processing pool for concurrent requests, why isn't the time cut to 1/4th of the original time, or 3.38 seconds?

There is considerable overhead in spawning the subprocesses, communicating the request data, and collecting the result data from those subprocesses. It's interesting to create more workers than CPUs to see if this improves performance. It's also interesting to switch from `ProcessPoolExecutor` to `ThreadPoolExector` to see which offers the best performance for this specific workload.

Logging

In the *Using logging for control and audit output* recipe in *Chapter 13, Application Integration: Configuration*, we looked at how to use the `logging` module for control, audit, and error outputs. When we build a composite application, we'll have to combine the logging features from each of the original applications.

Logging involves a three-part recipe:

1. Creating `logger` objects. This is generally a line such as `logger = logging.get_logger('some_name')`. It's generally done once at the class or module level.
2. Using the `logger` objects to collect events. This involves lines such as `logger.info('some message')`. These lines are scattered throughout an application.
3. Configuring the logging system as a whole. While this is not required, it is simplest when logging configuration is done only at the outermost, global scope of the application. This makes it easy to ignore when building composite applications. Ideally, it looks like this:

```
if __name__ == "__main__":
    # logging configuration should only go here.
    main()
    logging.shutdown()
```

When creating composite applications, we may wind up with multiple logging configurations. There are two approaches that a composite application can follow:

- The composite application is built with a final configuration, which intentionally overwrites all previously-defined loggers. This is the default behavior and can be stated explicitly via `incremental: false` in a YAML configuration document.

- The composite application preserves other application loggers and merely modifies the `logger` configurations, perhaps by setting the overall level. This is not the default behavior and requires including `incremental: true` in the YAML configuration document.

The use of incremental configuration can be helpful when combining Python applications that don't isolate the logging configuration. It can take some time to read and understand the code from each application in order to properly configure logging for composite applications to avoid duplicating data among the various logs from the various components of the application.

See also

- In the *Designing scripts for composition* recipe in *Chapter 13, Application Integration: Configuration*, we looked at the core design pattern for a composable application.

Combining many applications using the Command Design Pattern

Many complex suites of applications follow a design pattern similar to the one used by the `Git` program. There's a base command, `git`, with a number of subcommands. For example, `git pull`, `git commit`, and `git push`.

What's central to this design is the idea of a collection of individual commands under a common parent command. Each of the various features of `Git` can be thought of as a separate class definition that performs a given function.

In this recipe, we'll see how we can create families of closely related commands.

Getting ready

We'll imagine an application built from three commands. This is based on the applications shown in the *Designing scripts for composition* and *Using logging for control and audit output* recipes in *Chapter 13, Application Integration: Configuration*, as well as the *Combining two applications into one* recipe from earlier in this chapter. We'll have three applications–`simulate`, `summarize`, and a combined application called `simsum`.

These features are based on modules with names such as `ch13_r05`, `ch13_r06`, and `ch14_r01`. The idea is that we can restructure these separate modules into a single class hierarchy following the Command Design Pattern.

There are two key ingredients to this design:

1. The client depends only on the abstract superclass, `Command`.

2. Each individual subclass of the `Command` superclass has an identical interface. We can substitute any one of them for any other.

When we've done this, then an overall application script can create and execute any one of the `Command` subclasses.

How to do it...

We'll start by creating a superclass for all of the related commands. We'll then extend that superclass for each specific command that is part of the overall application.

1. The overall application will have a structure that attempts to separate the features into two categories—argument parsing and command execution. Each subcommand will include both processing and the output bundled together. We're going to rely on `argparse.Namespace` to provide a very flexible collection of options to each subclass. This is not required but will be helpful in the *Managing arguments and configuration in composite applications* recipe later in this chapter. Here's the `Command` superclass:

```
import argparse
class Command:
    def __init__(self) -> None:
        pass

    def execute(self, options: argparse.Namespace) -> None:
        pass
```

2. Create a subclass of the `Command` superclass for the `Simulate (command)` class. This will wrap the processing and output from the `ch13_r05` module in the `execute()` method of this class:

```
import Chapter_13.ch13_r05 as ch13_r05

class Simulate(Command):
    def __init__(self) -> None:
        super().__init__()
        self.seed: Optional[Any] = None
        self.game_path: Path

    def execute(self, options: argparse.Namespace) -> None:
        self.game_path = Path(options.game_file)
        if 'seed' in options:
            self.seed = options.seed
```

```
        data = ch13_r05.roll_iter(options.games, self.seed)
        ch13_r05.write_rolls(self.game_path, data)
        print(f"Created {str(self.game_path)}")
```

3. Create a subclass of the `Command` superclass for the `Summarize (command)` class. For this class, we've wrapped the file creation and the file processing into the `execute()` method of the class:

```
import Chapter_13.ch13_r06 as ch13_r06

class Summarize(Command):
    def execute(self, options: argparse.Namespace) -> None:
        self.summary_path = Path(options.summary_file)
        with self.summary_path.open("w") as result_file:
            game_paths = [Path(f) for f in options.game_files]
            ch13_r06.process_all_files(result_file, game_paths)
```

4. The overall composite processing can be performed by the following `main()` function:

```
def main() -> None:
    options_1 = Namespace(
        games=100, game_file="x.yaml")
    command1 = Simulate()
    command1.execute(options_1)

    options_2 = Namespace(
        summary_file="y.yaml", game_files=["x.yaml"])
    command2 = Summarize()
    command2.execute(options_2)
```

We've created two commands, an instance of the `Simulate` class, and an instance of the `Summarize` class. These can be executed to provide a combined feature that both simulates and summarizes data.

How it works...

Creating interchangeable, polymorphic classes for the various subcommands is a handy way to provide an extensible design. The Command Design Pattern strongly encourages each individual subclass to have an identical signature. Doing this makes it easier for the command subclasses to be created and executed. Also, new commands can be added that fit the framework.

One of the SOLID design principles is the **Liskov Substitution Principle** (**LSP**). Any of the subclasses of the `Command` abstract class can be used in place of the parent class.

Each `Command` instance has a simple interface. There are two features:

- The `__init__()` method expects a `Namespace` object that's created by the argument parser. Each class will pick only the needed values from this namespace, ignoring any others. This allows some global arguments to be ignored by a subcommand that doesn't require them.
- The `execute()` method does the processing and writes any output. This is based entirely on the values provided during initialization.

The use of the Command Design Pattern makes it easy to be sure that `Command` subclasses can be interchanged with each other. The overall `main()` script can create instances of the `Simulate` or `Summarize` classes. The substitution principle means that either instance can be executed because the interfaces are the same. This flexibility makes it easy to parse the command-line options and create an instance of either of the available classes. We can extend this idea and create sequences of individual command instances.

There's more...

One of the more common extensions to this design pattern is to provide for composite commands. In the *Combining two applications into one* recipe, we showed one way to create composites. This is another way, based on defining a new command that implements a combination of existing commands:

```
class Sequence(Command):
    def __init__(self, *commands: Type[Command]) -> None:
        super().__init__()
        self.commands = [command() for command in commands]

    def execute(self, options: argparse.Namespace) -> None:
        for command in self.commands:
            command.execute(options)
```

This class will accept other `Command` classes via the `*commands` parameter. This sequence will combine all of the positional argument values. From the classes, it will build the individual class instances.

We might use this `Sequence` class like this:

```
options = Namespace(
    games=100,
    game_file="x.yaml",
    summary_file="y.yaml",
    game_files=["x.yaml"]
)
both_command = Sequence(Simulate, Summarize)
both_command.execute(options)
```

We created an instance of `Sequence` built from two other classes—`Simulate` and `Summarize`. The `__init__()` method will build an internal sequence of the two objects. The `execute()` method of the `sim_sum_command` object will then perform the two processing steps in sequence.

This design, while simple, exposes some implementation details. In particular, the two class names and the intermediate `x.yaml` file are details that can be encapsulated into a better class design.

We can create a slightly nicer subclass of the `Sequence` argument if we focus specifically on the two commands being combined. This will have an `__init__()` method that follows the pattern of other `Command` subclasses:

```
class SimSum(Sequence):
    def __init__(self) -> None:
        super().__init__(Simulate, Summarize)

    def execute(self, options: argparse.Namespace) -> None:
        self.intermediate = (
            Path("data") / "ch14_r02_temporary.yaml"
        )
        new_namespace = Namespace(
            game_file=str(self.intermediate),
            game_files=[str(self.intermediate)],
            **vars(options)
        )
        super().execute(new_namespace)
```

This class definition incorporates two other classes into the already defined `Sequence` class structure. `super().__init__()` invokes the parent class initialization with the `Simulate` and `Summarize` classes.

This provides a composite application definition that conceals the details of how a file is used to pass data from the first step to a subsequent step. This is purely a feature of the composite integration and doesn't lead to any changes in either of the original applications that form the composite.

See also

- In the *Designing scripts for composition* and *Using logging for control and audit output* recipes in *Chapter 13, Application Integration: Configuration*, we looked at the constituent parts of this composite application.
- In the *Combining two applications into one* recipe earlier in this chapter, we looked at the constituent parts of this composite application. In most cases, we'll need to combine elements of all of these recipes to create a useful application.
- We'll often need to follow the *Managing arguments and configuration in composite applications* recipe, which comes next in this chapter.

Managing arguments and configuration in composite applications

When we have a complex suite (or system) of individual applications, it's common for several applications to share common features. When we have completely separate applications, **external Command-Line Interfaces** (**CLIs**) are is tied directly to the software architecture. It becomes awkward to refactor the software components because changes will also alter the visible CLI.

The coordination of common features among many applications can become awkward. As a concrete example, imagine defining the various, one-letter abbreviated options for command-line arguments. We might want all of our applications to use `-v` for verbose output: this is an example of an option that would require careful coordination. Ensuring that there are no conflicts might require keeping some kind of master list of options, outside all of the individual applications.

This kind of common configuration should be kept in only one place in the code somewhere. Ideally, it would be in a common module, used throughout a family of applications.

Additionally, we often want to divorce the modules that perform useful work from the CLI. This lets us refactor the design without changing the user's understanding of how to use the application.

In this recipe, we'll look at ways to ensure that a suite of applications can be refactored without creating unexpected changes to the CLI. This means that complex additional design notes and instructions to users aren't required.

Getting ready

Many complex suites of applications follow a design pattern similar to the one used by `Git`. There's a base command, `git`, with a number of subcommands. For example, `git pull`, `git commit`, and `git push`. The core of the CLI can be centralized by the `git` command. The subcommands can then be organized and reorganized as needed with fewer changes to the visible CLI.

We'll imagine an application built from three commands. This is based on the applications shown in the *Designing scripts for composition* and *Using logging for control and audit output* recipes in *Chapter 13, Application Integration: Configuration*, and the *Combining two applications into one* recipe earlier in this chapter. We'll have three applications with three commands: `craps simulate`, `craps summarize`, and the combined application, `craps simsum`.

We'll rely on the subcommand design from the *Combining many applications using the Command Design Pattern* recipe earlier in this chapter. This will provide a handy hierarchy of `Command` subclasses:

- The `Command` class is an `abstract` superclass.
- The `Simulate` subclass performs the simulation functions from the *Designing scripts for composition* recipe.
- The `Summarize` subclass performs summarization functions from the *Using logging for control and audit output* recipe.
- A `SimSum` subclass can perform combined simulation and summarization, following the ideas of the *Combining two applications into one* recipe.

In order to create a simple command-line application, we'll need appropriate argument parsing.

This argument parsing will rely on the subcommand parsing capability of the `argparse` module. We can create a common set of command options that apply to all subcommands. We can also create unique options for each subcommand.

How to do it...

This recipe will start with a consideration of what the CLI commands need to look like. This first step might involve some prototypes or examples to be sure that the commands are truly useful to the user. After that, we'll implement the argument definitions in each of the `Command` subclasses.

1. Define the CLI. This is an exercise in **User Experience** (**UX**) design. While most UX is focused on web and mobile device applications, the core principles are appropriate for CLI applications and servers, as well. Earlier, we noted that the root application will be *Craps*. It will have the following three subcommands:

```
craps simulate -o game_file -g games
craps summarize -o summary_file game_file ...
craps simsum -g games
```

2. Define the root Python application. Consistent with other files in this book, we'll call it `ch14_r02.py`. At the OS level, we can provide an alias or a link to make the visible interface match the user expectation of a command like `craps`.
3. We'll import the class definitions from the *Combining many applications using the Command Design Pattern* recipe. This will include the `Command` superclass and the `Simulate`, `Summarize`, and `SimSum` subclasses. We'll extend the `Command` class with an additional method, `arguments()`, to set the unique options in the argument parser for this command. This is a class method and is called on the class as a whole, not an instance of the class:

```
class Command:
    @classmethod
    def arguments(
            cls,
            sub_parser: argparse.ArgumentParser
    ) -> None:
        Pass

    def __init__(self) -> None:
        pass

    def execute(self, options: argparse.Namespace) -> None:
        pass
```

4. Here are the unique options for the `Simulate` command. We won't repeat the entire class definition, only the new `arguments()` method. This creates the arguments unique to the `craps simulate` command:

```
class Simulate(Command):
    @classmethod
    def arguments(
            cls,
            simulate_parser: argparse.ArgumentParser
        ) -> None:
        simulate_parser.add_argument(
            "-g", "--games", type=int, default=100000)
        simulate_parser.add_argument(
            "-o", "--output", dest="game_file")
```

```
        simulate_parser.add_argument(
            "--seed",
            default=os.environ.get("CH14_R03_SEED", None)
        )
        simulate_parser.set_defaults(command=cls)
```

5. Here is the new `arguments()` method of the `Summarize` command. This method creates arguments unique to the `craps summarize` command:

```
class Summarize(Command):
    @classmethod
    def arguments(
            cls,
            summarize_parser: argparse.ArgumentParser
    ) -> None:
        summarize_parser.add_argument(
            "-o", "--output", dest="summary_file")
        summarize_parser.add_argument(
            "game_files", nargs="*", type=Path)
        summarize_parser.set_defaults(command=cls)
```

6. Here is the new `arguments()` method for the composite command, `SimSum`. This method creates arguments appropriate for the combined command:

```
class SimSum(Command):

    @classmethod
    def arguments(
            cls,
            simsum_parser: argparse.ArgumentParser
    ) -> None:
        simsum_parser.add_argument(
            "-g", "--games", type=int, default=100000)
        simsum_parser.add_argument(
            "-o", "--output", dest="summary_file")
        simsum_parser.add_argument(
            "--seed",
            default=os.environ.get("CH14_R03_SEED", None)
        )
        simsum_parser.set_defaults(command=cls)
```

7. Create the overall argument parser. Use this to create a subparser builder. For each command, create a parser and add arguments that are unique to that command. The `subparsers` object will be used to create each subcommand's argument definition:

```
import argparse
def get_options(
        argv: List[str] = sys.argv[1:]
    ) -> argparse.Namespace:
    parser = argparse.ArgumentParser(prog="craps")
    subparsers = parser.add_subparsers()
    simulate_parser = subparsers.add_parser("simulate")
    Simulate.arguments(simulate_parser)

    summarize_parser = subparsers.add_parser("summarize")
    Summarize.arguments(summarize_parser)

    simsum_parser = subparsers.add_parser("simsum")
    SimSum.arguments(simsum_parser)
```

8. Parse the command-line values. In this case, the overall argument to the `get_options()` function is expected to be the value of `sys.argv[1:]`, which includes the arguments to the Python command. We can override the argument value for testing purposes:

```
options = parser.parse_args(argv)
if "command" not in options:
    parser.error("No command selected")
return options
```

The overall parser includes three subcommand parsers. One will handle the `craps simulate` command, another handles `craps summarize`, and the third handles `craps simsum`. Each subcommand has slightly different combinations of options.

The `command` option is set via the `set_defaults()` method. This includes useful additional information about the command to be executed. In this case, we've provided the class that must be instantiated. The class will be a subclass of `Command`, with a known interface.

The overall application is defined by the following `main()` function:

```
def main() -> None:
    options = get_options(sys.argv[1:])
    command = cast(Type[Command], options.command)()
    command.execute(options)
```

The options will be parsed. Each distinct subcommand sets a unique class value for the `options.command` argument. This class is used to build an instance of a `Command` subclass. This object will have an `execute()` method that does the real work of this command.

Implement the OS wrapper for the root command. For Linux or macOS, we might have a file named `craps`. The file would have `rx` permissions so that it was readable by other users. The content of the file could be this line:

```
python Chapter_14/ch14_r03.py $*
```

This small shell script provides a handy way to enter a command of `craps` and have it properly execute a Python script with a somewhat more complex name.

When the `PYTHONPATH` environment variable includes the applications we're building, we can also use this command to run them:

```
python -m Chapter_14.ch14_r03
```

This uses Python's `sys.path` to look for the package named `Chapter_14` and the `ch14_r03` module within that package.

How it works...

There are two parts to this recipe:

- Using the Command Design Pattern to define a related set of classes that are polymorphic. For more information on this, see the *Combining many applications using the Command Design Pattern* recipe. In this case, we pushed parameter definition, initialization, and execution down to each subcommand as methods of their respective subclasses.
- Using features of the `argparse` module to handle subcommands.

The `argparse` module feature that's important here is the `add_subparsers()` method of a parser. This method returns an object that is used to build each distinct subcommand parser. We assigned this object to the `subparsers` variable.

We also used the `set_defaults()` method of a parser to add a command argument to each of the `subparsers`. This argument will be populated by the defaults defined for one of the `subparsers`. The value assigned by the `set_defaults()` method actually used will show which of the subcommands was invoked.

Each sub parser is built using the `add_parser()` method of the `subparsers` object. The `parser` object that is returned can then have arguments and defaults defined.

When the overall parser is executed, it will parse any arguments defined outside the subcommands. If there's a subcommand, this is used to determine how to parse the remaining arguments.

Look at the following command:

```
craps simulate -g 100 -o x.yaml
```

This command will be parsed to create a `Namespace` object that looks like this:

```
Namespace(command=<class '__main__.Simulate'>, game_file='x.yaml',
games=100)
```

The `command` attribute in the `Namespace` object is the default value provided as part of the subcommand definition. The values for `game_file` and `games` come from the `-o` and `-g` options.

There's more...

The `get_optionsO` function has an explicit list of classes that it is incorporating into the overall command. As shown, a number of lines of code are repeated, and this could be optimized. We can provide a data structure that replaces a number of lines of code:

```
def get_options_2(argv: List[str] = sys.argv[1:]) -> argparse.
Namespace:
    parser = argparse.ArgumentParser(prog="craps")
    subparsers = parser.add_subparsers()

    sub_commands = [
        ("simulate", Simulate),
        ("summarize", Summarize),
        ("simsum", SimSum),
    ]
    for name, subc in sub_commands:
        cmd_parser = subparsers.add_parser(name)
        subc.arguments(cmd_parser)

    options = parser.parse_args(argv)
    if "command" not in options:
        parser.error("No command selected")
    return options
```

This variation on the `get_options()` function uses a sequence of two-tuples to provide the command name and the relevant class to implement the command. Iterating through this list assures that all of the various subclasses of `Command` are processed in a perfectly uniform manner.

We have one more optimization, but this relies on an internal feature of Python class definitions. Each class has references to subclasses built from the class, available via the `__subclasses__()` method. We can leverage this to create options that do not have an explicit list of classes. This doesn't always work out well, because any abstract subclasses aren't excluded from the list. For a very complex hierarchy, additional processing is required to confirm the classes are concrete:

```
def get_options_3(argv: List[str] = sys.argv[1:]) -> argparse.
Namespace:
    parser = argparse.ArgumentParser(prog="craps")
    subparsers = parser.add_subparsers()

    for subc in Command.__subclasses__():
        cmd_parser = subparsers.add_parser(subc.__name__.lower())
        subc.arguments(cmd_parser)

    options = parser.parse_args(argv)
    if "command" not in options:
        parser.error("No command selected")
    return options
```

In this example, all the subclasses of `Command` are concrete classes. Using the `Command.__subclasses__()` list does not present any unusual or confusing options. It has the advantage of letting us create new subclasses and have them appear on the command line without any other code changes to expose them to users.

See also

- See the *Designing scripts for composition* and *Using logging for control and audit output* recipes in *Chapter 13, Application Integration: Configuration*, for the basics of building applications focused on being composable.
- See the *Combining two applications into one* recipe from earlier in this chapter for the background on the components used in this recipe.
- See the *Using argparse to get command-line input* recipe in *Chapter 6, User Inputs and Outputs*, for more on the background of argument parsing.

Wrapping and combining CLI applications

One common kind of automation involves running several programs, none of which are Python applications. Since the programs aren't written in Python, it's impossible to refactor each program to create a composite Python application. When using a non-Python application, we can't follow the *Combining two applications into one* recipe shown earlier in this chapter.

Instead of aggregating the Python components, an alternative is to wrap the other programs in Python, creating a composite application. The use case is very similar to the use case for writing a shell script. The difference is that Python is used instead of a shell language. Using Python has some advantages:

- Python has a rich collection of data structures. Most shell languages are limited to strings and arrays of strings.
- Python has several outstanding unit test frameworks. Rigorous unit testing gives us confidence that the combined application will work as expected.

In this recipe, we'll look at how we can run other applications from within Python.

Getting ready

In the *Designing scripts for composition* recipe in *Chapter 13, Application Integration: Configuration*, we identified an application that did some processing that led to the creation of a rather complex result. For the purposes of this recipe, we'll assume that the application is not written in Python.

We'd like to run this program several hundred times, but we don't want to copy and paste the necessary commands into a script. Also, because the shell is difficult to test and has so few data structures, we'd like to avoid using the shell.

For this recipe, we'll pretend that the `ch13_r05` application is a native binary application. We'll act as if it was written in `C++`, `Go`, or `Fortran`. This means that we can't simply import a `Python` module that comprises the application. Instead, we'll have to process this application by running a separate OS process.

For the purposes of pretending this application is a binary executable, we can add a "shebang" line as the first line in the file. In many cases, the following can be used:

```
#!python3
```

When this is the first line of the file, most OSes will execute Python with the script file as the command-line argument. For macOS and Linux, use the following to change the mode of the file to executable:

```
chmod +x Chapter_14/ch14_r05.py
```

Marking a file as executable means using the `Chapter_14/ch14_r05.py` command directly at the command prompt will run our application. See `https://docs.python.org/3/using/windows.html#shebang-lines` and the *Writing Python script and module files* recipe in *Chapter 2, Statements and Syntax*.

We can use the `subprocess` module to run any application program at the OS level. There are two common use cases for running another program from within Python:

- The other program doesn't produce any output, or we don't want to gather the output in our Python program. The first situation is typical of OS utilities that return a status code when they succeed or fail. The second situation is typical of programs that update files and produce logs.
- The other program produces the output; the Python wrapper needs to capture and process it.

In this recipe, we'll look at the first case—the output isn't something we need to capture. In the *Wrapping a program and checking the output* recipe, we'll look at the second case, where the output is scrutinized by the Python wrapper program.

In many cases, one benefit of wrapping an existing application with Python is the ability to dramatically rethink the UX. This lets us redesign how the CLI works.

Let's look at wrapping a program that's normally started with the following command:

```
python Chapter_14/ch14_r05.py --samples 10 --output game_${n}.yaml
```

The output filename needs to be flexible so that we can run the program hundreds of times. This means creating files with numbers injected into the filenames. We've shown the placeholder for this number with `${n}` in the command-line example.

We'd want the CLI to have only two positional parameters, a directory and a number. The program startup would look like this, instead:

```
python -m Chapter_14.ch14_r04 $TMPDIR 100
```

This simpler command frees us from having to provide filenames. Instead, we provide the directory and the number of games to simulate, and our Python wrapper will execute the given app, `Chapter_14/ch14_r05.py`, appropriately.

How to do it...

In this recipe, we'll start by creating a call to `subprocess.run()` that starts the target application. This is a spike solution (`https://wiki.c2.com/?SpikeSolution`) that we will use to be sure that we understand how the other application works. Once we have the command, we can wrap this in a function call to make it easier to use.

1. Import the `argparse` and `subprocess` modules and the `Path` class. We'll also need the `sys` module and a type hint:

    ```
    import argparse
    import subprocess
    from pathlib import Path
    import sys
    from typing import List, Optional
    ```

2. Write the core processing, using `subprocess` to invoke the target application. This can be tested separately to ensure that this really is the shell command that's required. In this case, `subprocess.run()` will execute the given command, and the `check=True` option will raise an exception if the status is non-zero. Here's the spike solution that demonstrates the essential processing:

```
directory, n = Path("/tmp"), 42
filename = directory / f"game_{n}.yaml"

command = [
    "python",
    "Chapter_13/ch13_r05.py",
    "--samples",
    "10",
    "--output",
    str(filename),
]
subprocess.run(command, check=True)
```

3. Wrap the spike solution in a function that reflects the desired behavior. The new design requires only a directory name and a number of files. This requires a `for` statement to create the required collection of files. Each unique filename is created with an f-string that includes a number in a template name. The processing looks like this:

```
def make_files(directory: Path, files: int = 100) -> None:
    """Create sample data files."""
    for n in range(files):
        filename = directory / f"game_{n}.yaml"
        command = [
            "python",
            "Chapter_13/ch13_r05.py",
            "--samples",
            "10",
            "--output",
            str(filename),
        ]
        subprocess.run(command, check=True)
```

4. Write a function to parse the command-line options. In this case, there are two positional parameters: a directory and a number of games to simulate. The function looks like this:

```
def get_options(
        argv: Optional[List[str]] = None
) -> argparse.Namespace:
    if argv is None:
        argv = sys.argv[1:]

    parser = argparse.ArgumentParser()
    parser.add_argument("directory", type=Path)
    parser.add_argument("games", type=int)
    options = parser.parse_args(argv)
    return options
```

5. Combine the parsing and execution into a `main` function:

```
def main():
    options = get_options()
    make_files(options.directory, options.games)
```

We now have a function that's testable using any of the Python unit testing frameworks. This can give us real confidence that we have a reliable application built around an existing non-Python application.

How it works...

The `subprocess` module is how Python programs run other programs available on a given computer. The `run()` function in this module does a number of things for us.

In a POSIX (such as Linux or macOS) context, the steps are similar to the following sequence:

1. Prepare the `stdin`, `stdout`, and `stderr` file descriptors for the child process. In this case, we've accepted the defaults, which means that the child inherits the files being used by the parent. If the child process prints to `stdout`, it will appear on the console being used by the parent.
2. Invoke a function like the `os.execve()` function to start the child process with the given `stdin`, `stdout`, and `stderr` files.
3. While the child is running, the parent is waiting for the child process to finish and return the final status.
4. Since we used the `check=True` option, a non-zero status is transformed into an exception by the `run()` function.

An OS shell, such as `bash`, conceals these details from application developers. The `subprocess.run()` function, similarly, hides the details of creating and waiting for a child process.

Python, via the `subprocess` module, offers many features similar to the shell. Most importantly, Python offers several additional sets of features:

- A much richer collection of data structures than the shell.
- Exceptions to identify problems that arise. This can be much simpler and more reliable than inserting `if` statements throughout a shell script to check status codes.
- A way to unit test the script without using OS resources.

Using the subprocess module to run a separate executable allows Python to integrate a wide variety of software components into a unified whole. Using Python instead of the shell for application integration provides clear advantages over writing difficult-to-test shell scripts.

There's more...

We'll add a simple clean-up feature to this script. The idea is that all of the output files should be created as an atomic operation. We want all of the files or none of the files. We don't want an incomplete collection of data files.

This fits with the ACID properties:

- **Atomicity**: The entire set of data is available or it is not available. The collection is a single, indivisible unit of work.
- **Consistency**: The filesystem should move from one internally consistent state to another consistent state. Any summaries or indices will properly reflect the actual files.
- **Isolation**: If we want to process data concurrently, then having multiple, parallel processes should work. Concurrent operations should not interfere with each other.
- **Durability**: Once the files are written, they should remain on the filesystem. This property almost goes without saying for files. For more complex databases, it becomes necessary to consider transaction data that might be acknowledged by a database client but is not actually written yet to a server.

Isolation and durability are already part the OS filesystem's semantics. Generally, OS processes with separate working directories work out well. The atomicity and consistency properties, however, can lead to a need for a clean-up operation in the event of an application failure leaving corrupt files.

In order to clean up, we'll need to wrap the core processing in a `try:` block. We'll write a second function, `make_files_clean()`, that uses the original `make_files()` function to include a clean-up feature. A new overall function, `make_files_clean()`, would look like this:

```
def make_files_clean(directory: Path, files: int = 100) -> None:
    """Create sample data files, with cleanup after a failure."""
```

```
    try:
        make_files(directory, files)
    except subprocess.CalledProcessError as ex:
        # Remove any files.
        for partial in directory.glob("game_*.yaml"):
            partial.unlink()
        raise
```

The exception-handling block does two things. First, it removes any incomplete files from the current working directory. Second, it re-raises the original exception so that the failure will propagate to the client application.

Unit test

We have two scenarios to confirm. These scenarios can be described in `Gherkin` as follows:

```
Scenario: Everything Worked
Given An external application, Chapter_14/ch14_r05.py, that works
correctly
When The application is invoked 3 times
Then The subprocess.run() function will be called 3 times
And The output file pattern has 3 matches.

Scenario: Something failed
Given An external application, Chapter_14/ch14_r05.py, that works once,
then fails after the first run
When The application is invoked 3 times
Then The subprocess.run() function will be called 2 times
And The output file pattern has 0 matches.
```

The *Given* steps suggest we'll need to isolate the external application. We'll need two different mock objects to replace the `run()` function in the subprocess module. We can use mocks because we don't want to actually run the other process; we want to be sure that the `run()` function is called appropriately by the `make_files()` function.

One of the mocked `run()` functions needs to act as if the subprocess finished normally. The other mock needs to behave as if the called process fails.

Testing with mock objects means we never run the risk of accidentally overwriting or deleting useful files when testing. This is a significant benefit of using Python for this kind of automation.

Here are two fixtures to create a `Mock` object to succeed as well as a `Mock` object to fail:

```
from pathlib import Path
from subprocess import CalledProcessError
from unittest.mock import Mock, patch, call
from pytest import *  # type: ignore
import Chapter_14.ch14_r04


@fixture  # type: ignore
def mock_subprocess_run_good():
    def make_file(command, check):
        Path(command[5]).write_text("mock output")
    run_function = Mock(
        side_effect=make_file
    )
    return run_function


@fixture  # type: ignore
def mock_subprocess_run_fail():
    def make_file(command, check):
        Path(command[5]).write_text("mock output")
    run_function = Mock(
        side_effect=[
            make_file,
            CalledProcessError(13, ['mock', 'command'])
        ]
    )
    return run_function
```

The `mock_subprocess_run_good` fixture creates a `Mock` object. `monkeypatch` can use this in place of the standard library's `subprocess.run()` function. This will create some files that are stand-ins for the real work of the underlying `Chapter_14/ch14_r05.py` application that's being wrapped.

`mock_subprocess_run_fail` creates a `Mock` object that will work once, but on the second invocation, it will raise a `CalledProcessError` exception and fail. This fixture will also create a mock of the output file. In this case, because of the exception, we'd like the file to be cleaned up.

We also need to use the `pytest.tmpdir` fixture. This provides a temporary directory in which we can create and destroy files safely.

Here's a test case for the "everything worked" scenario:

```
def test_make_files_clean_good(
        mock_subprocess_run_good,
        monkeypatch,
        tmpdir):
    monkeypatch.setattr(
        Chapter_14.ch14_r04.subprocess,
        'run',
        mock_subprocess_run_good)

    directory = Path(tmpdir)
    Chapter_14.ch14_r04.make_files_clean(directory, files=3)

    expected = [
        call(
            [
                "python",
                "Chapter_13/ch13_r05.py",
                "--samples",
                "10",
                "--output",
                str(tmpdir/"game_0.yaml"),
            ],
            check=True,
        ),
        call(
            [
                "python",
                "Chapter_13/ch13_r05.py",
                "--samples",
                "10",
                "--output",
                str(tmpdir/"game_1.yaml"),
            ],
            check=True,
        ),
        call(
            [
                "python",
```

```
                "Chapter_13/ch13_r05.py",
                "--samples",
                "10",
                "--output",
                str(tmpdir/"game_2.yaml"),
            ],
            check=True,
        ),
    ]
    assert expected == mock_subprocess_run_good.mock_calls
    assert len(list(directory.glob("game_*.yaml"))) == 3
```

The `monkeypatch` fixture is used to replace the `subprocess.run()` function with the `Mock` object created by our `mock_subprocess_run_good` fixture. This will write mock results into the given files. This implements the scenario's *Given* step.

The *When* step is implemented by invoking the `make_files_clean()` function. The *Then* step needs to confirm a couple of things:

- That each of the calls to `subprocess.run()` has the expected parameters.
- That the expected number of output files has been created.

A second test case is required for the second scenario. This will use the `mock_subprocess_run_fail` fixture. The *Then* step will confirm that there were two expected calls. The most important part of this second scenario is confirming that zero files were left behind after the clean-up operation.

These unit tests provide confidence that the processing will work as advertised. The testing is done without accidentally deleting the wrong files.

See also

- This kind of automation is often combined with other Python processing. See the *Designing scripts for composition* recipe in *Chapter 12, Web Services*.
- The goal is often to create a composite application; see the *Managing arguments and configuration in composite applications* recipe earlier in this chapter.
- For a variation on this recipe, see the *Wrapping a program and checking the output* recipe, which is next in this chapter.

Wrapping a program and checking the output

One common kind of automation involves running several programs, none of which are actually Python applications. In this case, it's impossible to refactor the programs to create a composite Python application. In order to properly aggregate the functionality, the other programs must be wrapped as a Python class or module to provide a higher-level construct.

The use case for this is very similar to the use case for writing a shell script. The difference is that Python can be a better programming language than the OS's built-in shell languages.

In some cases, the advantage Python offers is the ability to perform detailed aggregation and analysis of the output files. A Python program might transform, filter, or summarize the output from a subprocess.

In this recipe, we'll see how to run other applications from within Python, collecting and processing the other applications' output.

Getting ready

In the *Designing scripts for composition* recipe in *Chapter 13, Application Integration: Configuration*, we identified an application that did some processing, leading to the creation of a rather complex result. We'd like to run this program several hundred times, but we don't want to copy and paste the necessary commands into a script. Also, because the shell is difficult to test and has so few data structures, we'd like to avoid using the shell.

For this recipe, we'll assume that the `ch13_r05` application is a native binary application written in `Go`, `Fortran`, or `C++`. This means that we can't simply import the `Python` module that comprises the application. Instead, we'll have to process this application by running a separate OS process.

We will use the `subprocess` module to run an application program at the OS level. There are two common use cases for running another binary program from within Python:

- Either there isn't any output, or we don't want to process the output file in our Python program.
- We need to capture and possibly analyze the output to retrieve information or ascertain the level of success. We might need to transform, filter, or summarize the log output.

In this recipe, we'll look at the second case—the output must be captured and summarized. In the *Wrapping and combining CLI applications* recipe earlier in this chapter, we looked at the first case, where the output is simply ignored.

Here's an example of running the `ch13_r05` application:

```
(cookbook) % python Chapter_14/ch14_r05.py --samples 10 --output=data/x.
yaml
Namespace(output='data/x.yaml', output_path=PosixPath('data/x.yaml'),
samples=10, seed=None)
Counter({7: 8, 9: 6, 5: 6, 6: 6, 8: 4, 3: 3, 10: 3, 4: 3, 11: 2, 2: 1,
12: 1})
```

There are two lines of output that are written to the OS standard output file. The first has a summary of the options, starting with the string `Namespace`. The second line of output is a summary of the file's data, starting with the string `Counter`. We want to capture the details of these `Counter` lines from this application and summarize them.

How to do it...

We'll start by creating a spike solution (`https://wiki.c2.com/?SpikeSolution`) that shows the command and arguments required to run another application from inside a Python application. We'll transform the spike solution into a function that captures output for further analysis.

1. Import the `argparse` and `subprocess` modules and the `Path` class. We'll also need the `sys` module and several type hints:

```
import argparse
from pathlib import Path
import subprocess
import sys
from typing import Counter, List, Any, Iterable, Iterator
```

2. Write the core processing, using subprocess to invoke the target application. This can be tested separately to be sure that this really is the shell command that's required. In this case, `subprocess.run()` will execute the given command, and the `check=True` option will raise an exception if the status is non-zero. In order to collect the output, we've provided an open file in the `stdout` parameter to `subprocess.run()`. In order to be sure that the file is properly closed, we've used that file as the context manager for a `with` statement. Here's a spike solution that demonstrates the essential processing:

```
directory, n = Path("/tmp"), 42
filename = directory / f"game_{n}.yaml"
temp_path = directory / "stdout.txt"

command = [
    "python",
```

```
            "Chapter_13/ch13_r05.py",
            "--samples",
            "10",
            "--output",
            str(filename),
        ]
        with temp_path.open('w') as temp_file:
            process = subprocess.run(
                command,
                stdout=temp_file,
                check=True,
               text=True)
        output_text = temp_path.read_text()
```

3. Wrap the initial spike solution in a function that reflects the desired behavior. We'll decompose this into two parts, delegating command creation to a separate function. This function will consume the commands to execute from an iterable source of commands. This generator function will yield the lines of output gathered as each command is executed. Separating command building from command execution is often helpful when the commands can change. The core use of `subprocess.run()` is less likely to change. The processing looks like this:

```
    def command_output_iter(
            temporary: Path,
            commands: Iterable[List[str]]
        ) -> Iterator[str]:
        for command in commands:
            temp_path = temporary/"stdout"
            with temp_path.open('w') as temp_file:
                process = subprocess.run(
                    command,
                    stdout=temp_file,
                    check=True,
                    text=True)
            output_text = temp_path.read_text()
            output_lines = (
                l.strip() for l in output_text.splitlines())
            yield from output_lines
```

4. Here's the generator function to create the commands for the `command_output_iter()` generator function. Because this has been separated, it's slightly easier to respond to design changes in the underlying `Chapter_13/ch13_r05.py` application. Here's a generator that produces the commands:

```
def command_iter(
        directory: Path,
        files: int
    ) -> Iterable[List[str]]:
    for n in range(files):
        filename = directory / f"game_{n}.yaml"
        command = [
            "python",
            "Chapter_13/ch13_r05.py",
            "--samples",
            "10",
            "--output",
            str(filename),
        ]
        yield command
```

5. The overall purpose behind this application is to collect and process the output from executing each command. Here's a function to extract the useful information from the command output. This function uses the built-in `eval()` to parse the output and reconstruct the original `Counter` object. In this case, the output happens to fit within the kind of things that `eval()` can parse. The generator function looks like this:

```
import collections

def collect_batches(output_lines_iter: Iterable[str]) ->
Iterable[Counter[Any]]:
    for line in output_lines_iter:
        if line.startswith("Counter"):
            batch_counter = eval(line)
            yield batch_counter
```

6. Write the function to summarize the output collected by the `collect_batches()` function. We now have a stack of generator functions. The `command_sequence` object yields commands. The `output_lines_iter` object yields the lines of output from each command. The `batch_summaries` object yields the individual `Counter` objects:

```
def summarize(
        directory: Path,
```

```
        games: int,
        temporary: Path
    ) -> None:
    total_counter: Counter[Any] = collections.Counter()

    command_sequence = command_iter(directory, games)
    output_lines_iter = command_output_iter(
        temporary, command_sequence)
    batch_summaries = collect_batches(output_lines_iter)
    for batch_counter in batch_summaries:
        print(batch_counter)
        total_counter.update(batch_counter)
    print("Total")
    print(total_counter)
```

7. Write a function to parse the command-line options. In this case, there are two positional parameters: a directory and a number of games to simulate. The function looks like this:

```
def get_options(
        argv: List[str] = sys.argv[1:]
    ) -> argparse.Namespace:
    parser = argparse.ArgumentParser()
    parser.add_argument("directory", type=Path)
    parser.add_argument("games", type=int)
    options = parser.parse_args(argv)
    return options
```

8. Combine the parsing and execution into a `main` function:

```
def main() -> None:
    options = get_options()
    summarize(
        directory=options.directory,
        games=options.games,
        temporary=Path("/tmp")
    )
```

Now we can run this new application and have it execute the underlying application and gather the output, producing a helpful summary. We've built this using Python instead of a bash (or other shell) script. Python offers more useful data structures and unit testing.

How it works...

The `subprocess` module is how Python programs run other programs available on a given computer. The `run()` function does a number of things for us.

In a POSIX (such as Linux or macOS) context, the steps are similar to the following:

- Prepare the `stdin`, `stdout`, and `stderr` file descriptors for the child process. In this case, we've arranged for the parent to collect output from the child. The child will produce an `stdout` file to a shared buffer (a pipe in Unix parlance) that is consumed by the parent. The `stderr` output, on the other hand, is left alone—the child inherits the same connection the parent has, and error messages will be displayed on the same console being used by the parent.
- Use a function like `os.execve()` to split the current process into parent and child, and then start the child process.
- The child process then starts, using the given `stdin`, `stdout`, and `stderr`.
- While the child is running, the parent is waiting for the child process to finish.
- Since we used the `check=True` option, a non-zero status is transformed into an exception.
- Once the child completes processing, the file opened by the parent for collecting standard output can be read by the parent.

The subprocess module gives us access to one of the most important parts of the operating system: launching a subprocess. Because we can tailor the environment, we have tremendous control over the application that is started by our Python application.

There's more...

Once we've wrapped `Chapter_13/ch13_r05.py` (assumed for the sake of exposition to be an executable file originally coded in whatever language its authors preferred!) within a Python application, we have a number of alternatives available to us for improving the output. In particular, the `summarize()` function in our wrapper application suffers from the same design problem the underlying `Chapter_13/ch13_r05.py` application suffers from; that is, the output is in Python's `repr()` format.

When we run it, we see the following:

```
(cookbook) % python Chapter_14/ch14_r05.py data 5
Counter({7: 6, 8: 5, 10: 5, 3: 4, 5: 3, 4: 3, 9: 2, 6: 2, 2: 1, 11: 1})
Counter({6: 7, 5: 5, 7: 5, 8: 3, 12: 3, 4: 2, 3: 2, 10: 1, 9: 1})
Counter({8: 7, 6: 5, 7: 4, 5: 4, 11: 4, 4: 4, 10: 3, 12: 2, 9: 2, 3: 1})
Counter({5: 7, 9: 6, 3: 5, 11: 4, 8: 4, 10: 3, 4: 3, 6: 3, 12: 2, 7: 2})
Counter({6: 6, 5: 6, 3: 5, 8: 5, 7: 4, 9: 3, 4: 3, 10: 2, 11: 2, 12: 1})
Total

Counter({5: 25, 8: 24, 6: 23, 7: 21, 3: 17, 4: 15, 10: 14, 9: 14, 11: 11,
12: 8, 2: 1})
```

An output file in standard JSON or CSV would be more useful.

Because we've wrapped the underlying application, we don't need to change the underlying `ch13_r05` application to change the results it produces. We can modify our wrapper program, leaving the original data generator intact.

We need to refactor the `summarize()` function to replace the `print()` function calls with a function that has a more useful format. A possible rewrite would change this function into two parts: one part would create the `Counter` objects, the other part would consume those `Counter` objects and write them to a file:

```
def summarize_2(
        directory: Path,
        games: int,
        temporary: Path
) -> None:

    def counter_iter(
            directory: Path,
            games: int,
            temporary: Path
    ) -> Iterator[Counter]:
        total_counter: Counter[Any] = collections.Counter()
        command_sequence = command_iter(directory, games)
        output_lines_iter = command_output_iter(
            temporary, command_sequence)
        batch_summaries = collect_batches(output_lines_iter)
        for batch_counter in batch_summaries:
            yield batch_counter
            total_counter.update(batch_counter)
        yield total_counter

    wtr = csv.writer(sys.stdout)
    for counter in counter_iter(directory, games, temporary):
        array = [counter[i] for i in range(20)]
        wtr.writerow(array)
```

This variation on the `summarize()` function emits output in CSV format. The internal `counter_iter()` generator does the essential processing to create a number of `Counter` summaries from each run of the simulation. This output is consumed by a `for` counter in the statement calling `counter_iter()`. Each `Counter` object is expanded into an array of values with game lengths from zero to twenty, and the frequency of games of the given length.

This rewrite didn't involve changing the underlying application. We were able to build useful features separately by creating layers of features. Leaving the underlying application untouched can help perform regression tests to be sure the core statistical validity has not been harmed by adding new features.

See also

- See the *Wrapping and combining CLI applications* recipe from earlier in this chapter for another approach to this recipe.
- This kind of automation is often combined with other Python processing. See the *Designing scripts for composition* recipe in *Chapter 13, Application Integration: Configuration*.
- The goal is often to create a composite application; see the *Managing arguments and configuration in composite applications* recipe from earlier in this chapter.
- Many practical applications will work with more complex output formats. For information on processing complex line formats, see the *String parsing with regular expressions* recipe in *Chapter 1, Numbers, Strings, and Tuples*, and the *Reading complex formats using regular expressions* recipe in *Chapter 8, More Advanced Class Design*. Much of *Chapter 10, Input/Output, Physical Format, and Logical Layout*, relates to the details of parsing input files.

Controlling complex sequences of steps

In the *Combining two applications into one* recipe earlier in this chapter, we looked at ways to combine multiple Python scripts into a single, longer, more complex operation. In the *Wrapping and combining CLI applications* and *Wrapping a program and checking the output* recipes earlier in this chapter, we looked at ways to use Python to wrap not-necessarily-Python executable programs.

We can combine these techniques to create even more flexible processing. We can create longer, more complex sequences of operations.

Getting ready

In the *Designing scripts for composition* recipe in *Chapter 13, Application Integration: Configuration*, we created an application that did some processing that led to the creation of a rather complex result. In the *Using logging for control and audit output* recipe in *Chapter 13, Application Integration: Configuration*, we looked at a second application that built on those results to create a sophisticated statistical summary.

The overall process looks like this:

1. Run the `ch13_r05` program 100 times to create 100 intermediate files.
2. Run the `ch13_r06` program to summarize those intermediate files.

For the purposes of this recipe, we'll assume that neither of these applications is written in Python. We'll pretend that they're written in Fortran or Ada or some other language that's not directly compatible with Python.

In the *Combining two applications into one* recipe, we looked at how we can combine Python applications. When applications are not written in Python, a little additional work is required.

This recipe uses the Command Design Pattern. This supports the expansion and modification of the sequences of commands by creating new subclasses of an abstract base class.

How to do it...

We'll use the Command Design Pattern to define classes to wrap the external commands. Using classes will let us assemble more complex sequences and alternative processing scenarios where `Python` objects act as proxies for external applications run as subprocesses.

1. We'll define an abstract `Command` class. The other commands will be defined as subclasses. The `execute()` method works by first creating the OS-level command to execute. Each subclass will provide distinct rules for the commands that are wrapped. Once the OS-level command has been built, the `run()` function of the `subprocess` module will process the OS command. In this recipe, we're using `subprocess.PIPE` to collect the output. This is only suitable for relatively small output files that won't overflow internal OS buffers.

   The `os_command()` method builds the sequence of text strings comprising a command to be executed by the OS. The value of the `options` parameter will be used to customize the argument values used to assemble the command. This superclass implementation provides some debugging information. Each subclass must override this method to create the unique OS command required to perform some useful work:

```
class Command:
    def execute(
            self,
            options: argparse.Namespace
    ) -> str:
        self.command = self.create_command(options)
        results = subprocess.run(
            self.command,
            check=True,
            stdout=subprocess.PIPE,
            text=True
        )
        self.output = results.stdout
        return self.output
```

```
    def os_command(
            self,
            options: argparse.Namespace
    ) -> List[str]:
        return [
            "echo", self.__class__.__name__, repr(options)]
```

2. We can create a `Command` subclass to define a command to simulate the game and create samples. In this case, we provided an override for the `execute()` method so this class can change the OS environment variables before executing the underlying OS command. This allows an integration test to set a specific random seed and confirm that the results match a fixed set of expected values:

```
import Chapter_13.ch13_r05 as ch13_r05

class Simulate(Command):
    def execute(
            self,
            options: argparse.Namespace
    ) -> str:
        if 'seed' in options:
            os.environ["RANDOMSEED"] = str(options.seed)
        return super().execute(options)
```

3. The `os_command()` method of the `Simulate` class emits the sequence of words for a command to execute the `ch13_r05` application. This converts the numeric value of `options.samples` to a string as required by the interface to the OS:

```
    def os_command(
            self,
            options: argparse.Namespace
    ) -> List[str]:
        return [
            "python",
            "Chapter_13/ch13_r05.py",
            "--samples",
            str(options.samples),
            "-o",
            options.game_file,
        ]
```

4. We can also extend the `Command` superclass to define a subclass, `Summarize`, to summarize the various simulation processes. In this case, we only implemented `os_command()`. This implementation provides the arguments for the `ch13_r06` command:

```
import Chapter_13.ch13_r06 as ch13_r06


class Summarize(Command):
    def os_command(
            self,
            options: argparse.Namespace
    ) -> List[str]:
        return [
            "python",
            "Chapter_13/ch13_r06.py",
            "-o",
            options.summary_file,
        ] + options.game_files
```

5. Given these two commands, the overall main program can follow the design pattern from the *Designing scripts for composition* recipe. We need to gather the options, and then use these options to execute the two commands:

```
def demo():
    options = Namespace(
        samples=100,
        game_file="data/x12.yaml",
        game_files=["data/x12.yaml"],
        summary_file="data/y12.yaml",
        seed=42
    )
    step1 = Simulate()
    step2 = Summarize()
    output1 = step1.execute(options)
    print(step1.os_cmd, output1)
    output2 = step2.execute(options)
    print(step2.os_cmd, output2)
```

This demonstration function, `demo()`, creates a `Namespace` instance with the parameters that could have come from the command line. It builds the two processing steps. Finally, it executes each step, displaying the collected output.

This kind of function provides a high-level script for executing a sequence of applications. It's considerably more flexible than the shell, because we can make use of Python's rich collection of data structures. Because we're using Python, we can more easily include unit tests as well.

How it works...

There are two interlocking design patterns in this recipe:

- The `Command` class hierarchy
- Wrapping external commands by using the `subprocess.run()` function

The idea behind a `Command` class hierarchy is to make each separate step or operation into a subclass of a common superclass. In this case, we've called that superclass `Command`. The two operations are subclasses of the `Command` class. This assures that we can provide common features to all of the classes.

Wrapping external commands has several considerations. One primary question is how to build the command-line options that are required. In this case, the `run()` function will use a list of individual words, making it very easy to combine literal strings, filenames, and numeric values into a valid set of options for a program.

The other primary question is how to handle the OS-defined standard input, standard output, and standard error files. In some cases, these files can be displayed on the console. In other cases, the application might capture those files for further analysis and processing.

The essential idea here is to separate two considerations:

1. The overview of the commands to be executed. This includes questions about sequences, iteration, conditional processing, and potential changes to the sequence. These are higher-level considerations related to the user stories.
2. The details of how to execute each command. This includes command-line options, output files used, and other OS-level considerations. These are more technical considerations of the implementation details.

Separating the two makes it easier to implement or modify the user stories. Changes to the OS-level considerations should not alter the user stories; the process might be faster or use less memory, but is otherwise identical. Similarly, changes to the user stories do not need to break the OS-level considerations. The user's interaction with the low-level applications is mediated by a flexible layer of Python.

What's central here is that a user story captures what the user needs to do. We often write them as "As a [persona...], I [want to...], [so that...]." This captures the user's goal in a form that we can use to build application software.

There's more...

A complex sequence of steps can involve iteration of one or more steps. Since the high-level script is written in Python, adding iteration is done with the `for` statement:

```
class IterativeSimulate(Command):
    """Iterative Simulation"""
    def execute(
            self,
            options: argparse.Namespace
    ) -> None:
        step1 = Simulate()
        options.game_files = []
        for i in range(options.simulations):
            options.game_file = f"data/game_{i}.yaml"
            options.game_files.append(options.game_file)
            step1.execute(options)
        step2 = Summarize()
        step2.execute(options)
```

This `IterativeSimulate` subclass of `Command` will process the `Simulate` step many times. It uses the `simulations` option to specify how many simulations to run. Each simulation will produce the expected number of samples.

This function will set a distinct value for the `game_file` option for each iteration of the processing. Each of the resulting filenames will be unique, leading to a number of sample files. The list of files is also collected into the `game_files` option.

When the next step, the `Summarize` class, is executed, it will have the proper list of files to process. The `Namespace` object, assigned to the `options` variable, can be used to track global state changes and provide this information to subsequent processing steps.

Because this is a subclass of `Command`, we can be sure that it is interchangeable with other commands. We may to also use the `Sequence` subclass of `Command` from the *Combining many applications using the Command Design Pattern* recipe to create more complex sequences of commands.

Building conditional processing

Since the high-level programming is written in Python, we can add additional processing that isn't based on the two applications that are wrapped. One feature might be an optional summarization step.

For example, if the options do not have a `summary_file` option, then any summarization processing can be skipped. This might lead to a subclass of the `Command` class that looks like this:

```
class ConditionalSummarize(Command):
    """Conditional Summarization"""
    def execute(
            self,
            options: argparse.Namespace
    ) -> str:
        step1 = Simulate()
        output = step1.execute(options)
        if "summary_file" in options:
            step2 = Summarize()
            output += step2.execute(options)
        return output
```

This `ConditionalSummarize` class will process the `Summarize` step conditionally. It will only create an instance of the `Summarize` class if there is a `summary_file` option.

We've used a subclass of `Command` to promote the idea of composability. We should be able to compose a more complex solution from individual components. In this case, the Python components are classes that wrap external commands and applications.

In this case, and the previous example, we've used Python programming to augment the two application programs with iteration and conditional features. This concept extends to error handling and recovery, also. We could use Python to clean up incomplete files. We can also use Python to handle a file rename to make sure that the latest and greatest results are always available after processing.

See also

- Generally, these kinds of processing steps are done for larger or more complex applications. See the *Combining two applications into one* and *Managing arguments and configuration in composite applications* recipes from earlier in this chapter for ways to work with larger and more complex composite applications.
- See *Replacing a file while preserving the previous version* in *Chapter 9, Functional Programming Features*, for a way to create output files so that a useful version is always available in spite of problems with unreliable networks or binary applications.
- See *Separating concerns via multiple inheritance* in *Chapter 7, Basics of Classes and Objects*, for some additional ideas for designing a `Command` class hierarchy to handle complex relationships among applications.
- When building more complex applications, consider the *Using logging for control and audit output* recipe in *Chapter 13, Application Integration: Configuration*, for ways to integrate logging as a consistent aspect of the various applications.
- For more information on user stories, see `https://www.atlassian.com/agile/project-management/user-stories`

15
Statistical Programming and Linear Regression

Data analysis and statistical processing are very import applications for modern programming languages. The subject area is vast. The Python ecosystem includes a number of add-on packages that provide sophisticated data exploration, analysis, and decision-making features.

We'll look at several topics, starting with some basic statistical calculations that we can do with Python's built-in libraries and data structures. This will lead to the question of correlation and how to create a regression model.

Statistical work also raises questions of randomness and the null hypothesis. It's essential to be sure that there really is a measurable statistical effect in a set of data. We can waste a lot of compute cycles analyzing insignificant noise if we're not careful.

Finally, we'll apply a common optimization technique. This can help to produce results quickly. A poorly designed algorithm applied to a very large set of data can be an unproductive waste of time.

In this chapter, we'll look at the following recipes:

- Using the built-in `statistics` library
- Average of values in a counter
- Computing the coefficient of a correlation
- Computing regression parameters

- Computing an autocorrelation
- Confirming that the data is random – the `null` hypothesis
- Locating outliers
- Analyzing many variables in one pass

We'll start by using the built-in `statistics` library. This provides useful results without requiring very sophisticated application software. It exemplifies the idea of the Python language having the batteries included – for some tasks, nothing more is needed.

Using the built-in statistics library

A great deal of **exploratory data analysis** (**EDA**) involves getting a summary of the data. There are several kinds of summary that might be interesting:

- **Central Tendency**: Values such as the mean, mode, and median can characterize the center of a set of data.
- **Extrema**: The minimum and maximum are as important as the central measures of a set of data.
- **Variance**: The variance and standard deviation are used to describe the dispersal of the data. A large variance means the data is widely distributed; a small variance means the data clusters tightly around the central value.

This recipe will show how to create basic descriptive statistics in Python.

Getting ready

We'll look at some simple data that can be used for statistical analysis. We've been given a file of raw data, called `anscombe.json`. It's a JSON document that has four series of (x,y) pairs.

We can read this data with the following command:

```
>>> from pathlib import Path
>>> import json
>>> from collections import OrderedDict
>>> source_path = Path('code/anscombe.json')
>>> data = json.loads(source_path.read_text())
```

We've defined the `Path` to the data file. We can then use the `Path` object to read the text from this file. This text is used by `json.loads()` to build a Python object from the JSON data.

We can examine the data like this:

```
>>> [item['series'] for item in data]
['I', 'II', 'III', 'IV']
>>> [len(item['data']) for item in data]
[11, 11, 11, 11]
```

The overall JSON document is a sequence of subdocuments with keys such as `I` and `II`. Each subdocument has two fields—`series` and `data`. The `series` key provides the name for the series. Within the `data` key, there is a list of observations that we want to characterize. Each observation has a pair of values.

The data looks like this:

```
[
  {
    "series": "I",
    "data": [
      {
        "x": 10.0,
        "y": 8.04
      },
      {
        "x": 8.0,
        "y": 6.95
      },
      ...
    ]
  },
  ...
]
```

We can call this a `List[Dict[str, Any]]`. This summary, however, doesn't fully capture the structure of the dictionary. Each of the `Series` dictionaries has a number of very narrow constraints.

This is very close to the kinds of structures defined by the `typing.TypedDict` definition. We can *almost* use definitions like the following:

```
class Point(TypedDict):
    x: float
    y: float
```

```
class Series(TypedDict, total=False):
    series: str
    data: List[Point]
```

These definitions don't work as well as we'd like, however. When we define a dictionary this way, we're compelled to use literal keys when referencing the items in the dictionary. This isn't ideal for what we're doing, so we'll use a slightly weaker set of type definitions.

These type definitions capture the essence of the document with our raw data:

```
Point = Dict[str, float]
Series = Dict[str, Union[str, float, List[Point]]]
```

We've described each point as a mapping from a string, either `x` or `y` to a `float` value. We've defined the series as a mapping from a `string`, either series or data, to one of the following types; either `str`, `float`, or a `List[Point]` collection.

This doesn't capture the following additional details:

- The `series` key maps to a `string`
- The `data` key maps to a `List[Point]` collection

The annotation suggests that additional keys with `float` values may be added to this dictionary. The file as a whole can be described as a `List[Series]`.

We'll look at the essential application of a few statistical functions to a number of closely related series of data. This core recipe serves as a basis for doing additional processing steps.

How to do it...

We'll start with a few steps to acquire the raw data. Once we've parsed the JSON document, we can define a collection of functions with a similar design pattern for gathering statistics.

1. Reading the raw data is a matter of using the `json.loads()` function to create a `List[Series]` structure that we can use for further processing. This was shown previously in the *Getting ready* section of this recipe.
2. We'll need a function to extract one of the variables from a `series` structure. This will return a generator that produces a sequence of values for a specific variable:

```
def data_iter(
        series: Series, variable_name: str) -> Iterable[Any]:
    return (
        item[variable_name]
        for item in cast(List[Point], series["data"])
    )
```

3. To compute summary statistics, we'll use a common template for a function. This has two comments to show where computations are done (`# Compute details here`) and where results are displayed (`# Display output here`):

```
def display_template(data: List[Series]) -> None:
    for series in data:
        for variable_name in 'x', 'y':
            samples = list(
                data_iter(series, variable_name))
            # Compute details here.
            series_name = series['series']
            print(
                f"{series_name:>3s} {variable_name}: "
                # Display output here.
            )
```

4. To compute measures of central tendency, such as `mean` and `median`, use the `statistics` module. For `mode`, we can use the `statistics` module or the `collections.Counter` class. This injects `mean()`, `median()`, and construction of a `Counter()` into the template shown in the previous step:

```
import statistics
import collections
def display_center(data: List[Series]) -> None:
    for series in data:
        for variable_name in 'x', 'y':
            samples = list(
                data_iter(series, variable_name))
            mean = statistics.mean(samples)
            median = statistics.median(samples)
            mode = collections.Counter(
                samples
            ).most_common(1)
            series_name = series['series']
            print(
                f"{series_name:>3s} {variable_name}: "
                f"mean={round(mean, 2)}, median={median}, "
                f"mode={mode}")
```

5. To compute the variance, we'll need a similar design. There's a notable change in this design. The previous example computed mean, median, and mode independently. The computations of variance and standard deviation depend on computation of the mean. This dependency, while minor in this case, can have performance consequences for a large collection of data:

```
def display_variance(data: List[Series]) -> None:
    for series in data:
        for variable_name in 'x', 'y':
            samples = list(
                data_iter(series, variable_name))
            mean = statistics.mean(samples)
            variance = statistics.variance(samples, mean)
            stdev = statistics.stdev(samples, mean)
            series_name = series['series']
            print(
                f"{series_name:>3s} {variable_name}: "
                f"mean={mean:.2f}, var={variance:.2f}, "
                f"stdev={stdev:.2f}")
```

The display_center() function produces a display that looks like the following:

```
I x: mean=9.0, median=9.0, mode=[(10.0, 1)]
I y: mean=7.5, median=7.58, mode=[(8.04, 1)]
II x: mean=9.0, median=9.0, mode=[(10.0, 1)]
II y: mean=7.5, median=8.14, mode=[(9.14, 1)]
III x: mean=9.0, median=9.0, mode=[(10.0, 1)]
III y: mean=7.5, median=7.11, mode=[(7.46, 1)]
IV x: mean=9.0, median=8.0, mode=[(8.0, 10)]
IV y: mean=7.5, median=7.04, mode=[(6.58, 1)]
```

The essential design pattern means that we can use a number of different functions to compute different descriptions of the raw data. We'll look at ways to generalize this in the *There's more...* section of this recipe.

How it works...

A number of useful statistical functions are generally first-class parts of the Python standard library. We've looked in three places for useful functions:

- The min() and max() functions are built-in.
- The collections module has the Counter class, which can create a frequency histogram. We can get the mode from this.

- The `statistics` module has `mean()`, `median()`, `mode()`, `variance()`, and `stdev()`, providing a variety of statistical measures.

Note that `data_iter()` is a generator function. We can only use the results of this generator once. If we only want to compute a single statistical summary value, that will work nicely.

When we want to compute more than one value, we need to capture the result of the generator in a `collection` object. In these examples, we've used `data_iter()` to build a `list` object so that we can process it more than once.

There's more...

Our original data structure, `data`, is a sequence of mutable dictionaries. Each dictionary has two keys—`series` and `data`. We can update this dictionary with the statistical summaries. The resulting object can be saved for subsequent analysis or display.

Here's a starting point for this kind of processing:

```
import statistics
def set_mean(data: List[Series]) -> None:
    for series in data:
        for variable_name in "x", "y":
            result = f"mean_{variable_name}"
            samples = data_iter(series, variable_name)
            series[result] = statistics.mean(samples)
```

For each one of the `data` series, we've used the `data_iter()` function to extract the individual samples. We've applied the `mean()` function to those samples. The result is used to update the `series` object, using a `string` key made from the function name, `mean`, the `_` character, and `variable_name`, showing which variable's `mean` was computed.

The output starts like this:

```
[{'data': [{'x': 10.0, 'y': 8.04},
           {'x': 8.0, 'y': 6.95},
           {'x': 13.0, 'y': 7.58},
           {'x': 9.0, 'y': 8.81},
           {'x': 11.0, 'y': 8.33},
           {'x': 14.0, 'y': 9.96},
           {'x': 6.0, 'y': 7.24},
           {'x': 4.0, 'y': 4.26},
           {'x': 12.0, 'y': 10.84},
           {'x': 7.0, 'y': 4.82},
```

```
            {'x': 5.0, 'y': 5.68}],
  'mean_x': 9.0,
  'mean_y': 7.500909090909091,
  'series': 'I'},
etc.
]
```

The other series are similar. Interestingly, mean values of all four series are nearly identical, even though the data is different.

If we want to extend this to include standard deviations or variance, we'd see that the outline of the processing doesn't change. The overall structure would have to be repeated using statistics.median(), min(), max(), and so on. Looking at changing the function from mean() to something else shows that there are two things that change in this boilerplate code:

- The result key that is used to update the series data
- The function that's evaluated for the selected sequence of samples

The similarities among all the statistical functions suggest that we can refactor this set_mean() function into a higher-order function that applies any function that summarizes data.

A summary function has a type hint like the following:

```
Summary_Func = Callable[[Iterable[float]], float]
```

Any Callable object that summarizes an Iterable collection of float values to create a resulting float should be usable. This describes a number of statistical summaries. Here's a more general set_summary() function to apply any function that meets the Summary_Func-type specification to a collection of Series instances:

```
def set_summary(
        data: List[Series], summary: Summary_Func) -> None:
    for series in data:
        for variable_name in "x", "y":
            summary_name = f"{summary.__name__}_{variable_name}"
            samples = data_iter(series, variable_name)
            series[summary_name] = summary(samples)
```

We've replaced the specific function, mean(), with a parameter name, summary, that can be bound to any Python function that meets the Summary_Func type hint. The processing will apply the given function to the results of data_iter(). This summary is then used to update the series dictionary using the function's name, the _ character, and variable_name.

We can use the `set_summary()` function like this:

```
for function in statistics.mean, statistics.median, min, max:
    set_summary(data, function)
```

This will update our document with four summaries based on `mean()`, `median()`, `max()`, and `min()`.

Because `statistics.mode()` will raise an exception for cases where there's no single modal value, this function may need a `try:` block to catch the exception and put some useful result into the `series` object. It may also be appropriate to allow the exception to propagate to notify the collaborating function that the data is suspicious.

Our revised document will look like this:

```
[
  {
    "series": "I",
    "data": [
      {
        "x": 10.0,
        "y": 8.04
      },
      {
        "x": 8.0,
        "y": 6.95
      },
      ...
    ],
    "mean_x": 9.0,
    "mean_y": 7.500909090909091,
    "median_x": 9.0,
    "median_y": 7.58,
    "min_x": 4.0,
    "min_y": 4.26,
    "max_x": 14.0,
    "max_y": 10.84
  },
  ...
]
```

We can save this expanded document to a file and use it for further analysis. Using `pathlib` to work with filenames, we might do something like this:

```
target_path = (
source_path.parent / (source_path.stem+'_stats.json')
)
target_path.write_text(json.dumps(data, indent=2))
```

This will create a second file adjacent to the source file. The name will have the same stem as the source file, but the stem will be extended with the string `_stats` and a suffix of `.json`.

Average of values in a counter

The `statistics` module has a number of useful functions. These are based on having each individual data `sample` available for processing. In some cases, however, the data has been grouped into bins. We might have a `collections.Counter` object instead of a simple list. Rather than a collection of raw values, we now have a collection of (value, frequency) pairs.

Given frequency information, we can do essential `statistical` processing. A summary in the form of (value, frequency) pairs requires less memory than raw data, allowing us to work with larger sets of data.

Getting ready

The general definition of the `mean` is the sum of all of the values divided by the number of values. It's often written like this:

$$\mu_C = \frac{\sum_{c_i \in C} c_i}{n}$$

We've defined some set of data, C, as a sequence of `n` individual values, $C = \{c_0, c_1, c_2, \ldots, c_{n-1}\}$. The `mean` of this collection, μ_C, is the sum of the values divided by the number of values, `n`.

There's a tiny change in this definition that helps to generalize the approach so we can work with `Counter` objects:

$$S(C) = \sum_{c_i \in C} c_i$$

$$n(C) = \sum_{c_i \in C} 1$$

The value of *S(C)* is the sum of the values. The value of *n(C)* is the sum using one instead of each value. In effect, *S(C)* is the sum of c_i^1 and *n(C)* is the sum of c_i^0. We can implement these two computations using the built-in `sum()` function.

We can reuse these definitions in a number of places. Specifically, we can now define the mean, μ_c, like this:

$$\mu_C = \frac{S(C)}{n(C)}$$

We will use this general idea to provide statistical calculations on data that's part of a `Counter` object. Instead of a collection of raw values, a `Counter` object has the raw values and frequencies. The data structure can be described like this:

$$F = \{v_0 : f_0, v_1 : f_1, v_2 : f_2, \dots, v_{n-1} : f_{n-1}\}$$

Each unique value, $v_i \in C$, is paired with a frequency, f_i. This makes two small changes to perform similar calculations for *S(F)* and *n(F)*:

$$S(F) = \sum_{v_i : f_i \in F} f_i \times v_i$$

$$n(F) = \sum_{v_i : f_i \in F} f_i \times 1$$

We've defined *S(F)* to use the product of frequency and value. Similarly, we've defined *n(F)* to use the frequencies.

In the *Using the statistics library* recipe, earlier in this chapter, we used a source of data that had a number of `Series`. Each `Series` had a name and a number of individual data `Point` instances.

Here's an overview of each `Series` and a list of `Point` data types:

```
Point = Dict[str, float]
class Series(TypedDict):
    series: str
    data: List[Point]
```

We've used `typing.TypedDict` to describe the `Series` dictionary object. It will have exactly two keys, `series` and `data`. The `series` key will have a `string` value and the `data` key will have a `list` of `Point` objects as the value.

These types are different from the types shown in the *Using the statistics library* recipe shown earlier in this chapter. These types reflect a more limited use for the `Series` object.

For this recipe, a `Series` object can be summarized by the following function:

```
def data_counter(
        series: Series, variable_name: str) -> Counter[float]:
    return collections.Counter(
        item[variable_name]
        for item in cast(List[Point], series["data"])
    )
```

This creates a `Counter` instance from one of the variables in the `Series`. In this recipe, we'll look at creating useful statistical summaries from a `Counter` object instead of a list of raw values.

How to do it...

We'll define a number of small functions that compute sums from `Counter` objects. We'll then combine these into useful statistics:

1. Define the sum of a `Counter` object:

```
def counter_sum(counter: Counter[float]) -> float:
    return sum(f*v for v, f in counter.items())
```

2. Define the total number of values in a `Counter` object:

```
def counter_len(counter: Counter[float]) -> int:
    return sum(f for v, f in counter.items())
```

3. We can now combine these to compute a `mean` of data that has been put into bins:

```
def counter_mean(counter: Counter[float]) -> float:
    return counter_sum(counter)/counter_len(counter)
```

We can use this function with `Counter`, like this:

```
>>> s_4_x
Counter({8.0: 10, 19.0: 1})
>>> print(
...     f"Series IV, variable x: "
...     f"mean={counter_mean(s_4_x)}"
... )
Series IV, variable x: mean=9.0
```

This shows how a `Counter` object can have essential statistics computed.

How it works...

A `Counter` is a dictionary. The keys of this dictionary are the actual values being counted. The values in the dictionary are the frequencies for each item. This means that the `items()` method will produce value and frequency information that can be used by our calculations.

We've transformed each of the definitions for *S(F)* and *S(F)* into sums of values created by generator expressions. Because Python is designed to follow the mathematical formalisms closely, the code follows the math in a relatively direct way.

There's more...

To compute the `variance` (and standard deviation), we'll need two more variations on this theme. We can define an overall `mean` of a frequency distribution, μ_F:

$$\mu_F = \frac{S(F)}{n(F)} = \frac{\sum_{v_i:f_i \in F} f_i \times v_i}{\sum_{v_i:f_i \in F} f_i}$$

Here, v_i is the key from the `Counter` object, *F*, and f_i is the frequency value for the given key from the `Counter` object.

The variance, VAR_F, can be defined in a way that depends on the mean, μ_F. The formula is this:

$$VAR_F = \frac{\sum_{v_i:f_i \in F} f_i \times (v_i - \mu_F)^2}{\{\sum_{v_i:f_i \in F} f_i\} - 1}$$

This computes the difference between each distinct value, v_i, and the mean, μ_F. This is weighted by the number of times this value occurs, f_i. The sum of these weighted differences is divided by the count, minus one.

The standard deviation, σ_F, is the square root of the variance:

$$\sigma_F = \sqrt{VAR_F}$$

This version of the standard deviation is quite stable mathematically, and therefore is preferred. It requires two passes through the data, which can be better than an erroneous result.

Another `variation` on the calculation does not depend on the `mean`, μ_F. This isn't as mathematically stable as the previous version. This variation separately computes the sum of squares of values, the sum of the values, and the count of the values:

$$\text{VAR}_F = \frac{1}{n(F) - 1} \times \left(\sum_{v_i : f_i \in F} f_i \times v_i^2 - \frac{\left(\sum_{v_i : f_i \in F} f_i \times v_i\right)^2}{n(F)} \right)$$

This requires one extra sum computation. We'll need to compute the sum of the values squared, $S^2(F) = \sum_{v_i : f_i \in F} f_i \times v_i^2$:

```
def counter_sum_2(counter: Counter[float]) -> float:
    return sum(f*v**2 for v, f in counter.items())
```

Given these three sum functions, $n(F)$, $S(F)$, and $S^2(F)$, we can define the `variance` for a `Counter` with values and frequencies, *F*:

```
def counter_variance(counter: Counter[float]) -> float:
    n = counter_len(counter)
    return (
        1/(n-1) *
        (counter_sum_2(counter) - (counter_sum(counter)**2)/n)
    )
```

The `counter_variance()` function fits the mathematical definition very closely, giving us reason to believe it's correct.

Using the `counter_variance()` function, we can compute the standard deviation:

```
import math
def counter_stdev(counter: Counter[float]) -> float:
    return math.sqrt(counter_variance(counter))
```

This allows us to see the following:

```
>>> counter_variance(series_4_x)
11.0
>>> round(counter_stdev(series_4_x), 2)
3.32
```

These small summary functions for counting, summing, and summing squares provide us with ways to perform simple data analysis without building large collections of raw data. We can work with smaller collections of summary data using `Counter` objects.

See also

- In the *Designing classes with lots of processing* recipe in *Chapter 7, Basics of Classes and Objects*, we looked at this from a slightly different perspective. In that recipe, our objective was simply to conceal a complex data structure.
- The *Analyzing many variables in one pass* recipe, later in this chapter, will address some efficiency considerations. In that recipe, we'll look at ways to compute multiple sums in a single pass through the data elements.

Computing the coefficient of a correlation

In the *Using the built-in statistics library* and *Average of values in a counter* recipes in this chapter, we looked at ways to summarize data. These recipes showed how to compute a central value, as well as variance and extrema.

Another common statistical summary involves the degree of correlation between two sets of data. One commonly used metric for correlation is called Pearson's r. The r-value is the number between `-1` and `+1` that expresses the degree to which the data values correlate with one another.

A value of zero says the data is random. A value of *0.95* suggests that 95% of the values correlate, and 5% don't correlate well. A value of *-0.95* says that 95% of the values have an inverse correlation: when one variable increases, the other decreases.

This is not directly supported by Python's standard library. We can follow a design pattern similar to those shown in the *Average of values in a counter* recipe, and decompose the larger computation into isolated pieces.

Getting ready

One expression for Pearson's *r* is this:

$$r_{xy} = \frac{n\sum x_i y_i - \sum x_i \sum y_i}{\sqrt{n\sum x_i^2 - (\sum x_i)^2}\sqrt{n\sum y_i^2 - (\sum y_i)^2}}$$

We've slightly simplified the summation notation. Instead of $\sum_{x_i \in X} x_i$, we've written only $\sum x_i$, assuming the range if the index is clear from the context.

This definition of correlation relies on a large number of individual summations of various parts of a dataset. Each of the $\sum z$ operators can be implemented via the Python `sum()` function with one of three transformations applied to the value:

- `sum(1 for x in X)` computes a count, shown as n in the definition of Pearson's r.
- `sum(x for x in X)` computes the expected sum, and can be simplified to `sum(X)`, shown as $\sum x_i$ and $\sum y_i$ in the preceding equation.
- `sum(x**2 for x in X)` computes the sum of squares, shown as $\sum x_i^2$ and $\sum y_i^2$ in the preceding equation.
- `sum(x*y for x, y in zip(X, Y))` computes the sum of products, shown as $\sum x_i y_i$.

We'll use data from the *Using the built-in statistics library* recipe earlier in this chapter. This data is composed of several individual `Series`; each `Series` object is a dictionary with two keys. The `series` key is associated with a `name`. The `data` key is associated with the `list` of individual `Point` objects. The following type definitions apply:

```
from typing import Iterable, TypedDict, List

class Point(TypedDict):
    x: float
    y: float

class Series(TypedDict):
    series: str
    data: List[Point]
```

These definitions can rely on `typing.TypedDict` because each reference to a `Series` object as well as each reference to a `Point` object uses string literal values that can be matched against the attributes by the `mypy` tool.

We can read this data with the following command:

```
>>> from pathlib import Path
>>> import json
>>> source_path = Path('code/anscombe.json')
>>> data: List[Series] = json.loads(source_path.read_text())
```

We've defined the `Path` to the data file. We can then use the `Path` object to read the text from this file. This text is used by `json.loads()` to build a `Python` object from the JSON data.

The overall JSON document is a `list` of `Series` dictionaries. The `data` key is associated with a `List[Point]` object. Each `Point` object is a dictionary with two keys, `x` and `y`. The `data` looks like this:

```
[
  {
    "series": "I",
    "data": [
      {
        "x": 10.0,
        "y": 8.04
      },
      {
        "x": 8.0,
        "y": 6.95
      },
      ...
    ]
  },
  ...
]
```

This set of `data` has a sequence of `Series` instances. We'd like to see whether the `x` and `y` values correlate with one another by computing the Pearson's coefficient of correlation.

How to do it...

We'll build a number of small sum-related functions first. Given this pool of functions, we can then combine them to create the necessary correlation coefficient:

1. Identify the various kinds of summaries required. For the definition, shown above in the *Getting ready* section of this recipe, we see the following:
   - $n = \sum_{x_i \in X} 1 = \sum_{y_i \in Y} 1$. This is the count of values. This can also be thought of as $\sum_{x_i \in X} x_i^0$ to be consistent with other definitions.

- $\sum x_i$
- $\sum y_i$
- $\sum x_i^2$
- $\sum y_i^2$
- $\sum x_i \times y_i$

2. Import the `sqrt()` function from the `math` module:

```
from math import sqrt
```

3. Define a function that wraps the calculation:

```
def correlation(series: List[Point]) -> float:
```

4. Write the various sums using the built-in `sum()` function. This is indented within the function definition. We'll use the value of the `series` parameter: a sequence of values from a given `series`. When we use `mypy` to check the code, it will try to confirm that the source data fits the `TypedDict` definition, having keys `x` and `y`:

```
    sumxy = sum(p["x"] * p["y"] for p in series)
    sumx = sum(p["x"] for p in series)
    sumy = sum(p["y"] for p in series)
    sumx2 = sum(p["x"] ** 2 for p in series)
    sumy2 = sum(p["y"] ** 2 for p in series)
    n = sum(1 for p in series)
```

5. Write the final calculation of *r* based on the various sums:

```
    r = (n * sumxy - sumx * sumy) / (
        sqrt(n*sumx2 - sumx**2) * sqrt(n*sumy2 - sumy**2)
    )
    return r
```

We can now use this to determine the degree of correlation between the various `series`:

```
>>> data = json.loads(source_path.read_text())
>>> for series in data:
...     r = correlation(series['data'])
...     print(f"{series['series']:>3s}, r={r:.2f}")
```

The output looks like this:

```
  I, r=0.82
 II, r=0.82
III, r=0.82
 IV, r=0.82
```

All four `series` have approximately the same coefficient of correlation. This doesn't mean the `series` are related to one another. It means that within each `series`, 82% of the `x` values predict a `y` value. This is almost exactly `9` of the `11` values in each `series`. The four `series` present interesting case studies in statistical analysis because the details are clearly distinct, but the summary statistics are similar.

How it works...

The overall formula looks rather complex. However, it decomposes into a number of separate sums and a final calculation that combines the sums. Each of the sum operations can be expressed very succinctly in Python.

Conventional mathematical notation might look like the following:

$$\sum_{p \in D} p_x$$

This translates to Python in a very direct way:

```
sum(p['x'] for p in data)
```

We can replace each complex-looking $\sum x_i$ with the slightly more Pythonic variable, S_x. This pattern can be followed to create S_y, S_{xy}, S_x^2, and S_y^2. These can make it easier to see the overall form of the equation:

$$r_{xy} = \frac{nS_{xy} - S_x S_y}{\sqrt{nS_x^2 - (S_x)^2}\sqrt{nS_y^2 - (S_y)^2}}$$

While the `correlation()` function defined above follows the formula directly, the implementation shown isn't optimal. It makes six separate passes over the data to compute each of the various reductions. As a proof of concept, this implementation works well. This implementation has the advantage of demonstrating that the programming works. It also serves as a starting point for creating unit tests and refactoring the algorithm to optimize the processing.

There's more...

The algorithm, while clear, is inefficient. A more efficient version would process the data once instead of repeatedly computing different kinds of sums. To do this, we'll have to write an explicit `for` statement that makes a single pass through the data. Within the body of the `for` statement, the various sums are computed.

An optimized algorithm looks like this:

```
def corr2(series: List[Point]) -> float:
    sumx = sumy = sumxy = sumx2 = sumy2 = n = 0.0
    for point in series:
        x, y = point["x"], point["y"]
        n += 1
        sumx += x
        sumy += y
        sumxy += x * y
        sumx2 += x ** 2
        sumy2 += y ** 2

    r = (n * sumxy - sumx * sumy) / (
        sqrt(n*sumx2 - sumx**2) * sqrt(n*sumy2 - sumy**2)
    )
    return r
```

We've initialized a number of results to zero, and then accumulated values into these results from a source of data items, `data`. Since this uses the data value once only, this will work with any `Iterable` data source.

The calculation of *r* from the sums doesn't change. The computation of the sums, however, can be streamlined.

What's important is the parallel structure between the initial version of the algorithm and the revised version that has been optimized to compute all of the summaries in one pass. The clear symmetry of the two versions helps validate two things:

- The initial implementation matches the rather complex formula.
- The optimized implementation matches the initial implementation and the complex formula.

This symmetry, coupled with proper test cases, provides confidence that the implementation is correct.

See also...

- The *Computing regression parameters* recipe, later in this chapter, will exploit the coefficient of correlation to create a linear model that can be used to predict values of the dependent variable.
- The *Analyzing many variables in one pass* recipe, later in this chapter, will address some efficiency considerations. In that recipe, we'll look at ways to compute multiple sums in a single pass through the data elements.

Computing regression parameters

Once we've determined that two variables have some kind of relationship, the next step is to determine a way to estimate the dependent variable from the value of the independent variable. With most real-world data, there are a number of small factors that will lead to random variation around a central trend. We'll be estimating a relationship that minimizes these errors, striving for a close fit.

In the simplest cases, the relationship between variables is linear. When we plot the data points, they will tend to cluster around a line. In other cases, we can adjust one of the variables by computing a logarithm or raising it to a power to create a linear model. In more extreme cases, a polynomial is required. The process of linear regression estimates a line that will fit the data with the fewest errors.

In this recipe, we'll show how to compute the linear regression parameters between two variables. This will be based on the correlation computed in *Computing the coefficient of correlation* recipe earlier in this chapter.

Getting ready

The equation for an estimated line is this:

$$\hat{y} = \alpha x + \beta$$

Given the independent variable, *x*, the estimated or predicted value of the dependent variable, *y*, is computed from the α and β parameters.

The goal is to find values of α and β that produce the minimal overall error between the estimated values, *y*, and the actual values for *y*. Here's the computation of β:

$$\beta = r_{xy} \times \frac{\sigma_y}{\sigma_x}$$

Where r_{xy} is the correlation coefficient. See the *Computing the coefficient of correlation* recipe earlier in this chapter. The definition of σ_x is the standard deviation of `x`. This value is given directly by the `statistics.stdev()` function.

Here's the computation of α:

$$\alpha = \mu_y - \beta \times \mu_x$$

Here, μ_y is the `mean` of y, and μ_x is the `mean` of x. This, also, is given directly by the `statistics.mean()` function.

We'll use data from the *Using the built-in statistics library* recipe earlier in this chapter. This data is composed of several individual `Series`; each `Series` object is a dictionary with two keys. The `series` key is associated with a `name`. The `data` key is associated with a `list` of individual `Point` objects. The following type definitions apply:

```
from typing import TypedDict, List

class Point(TypedDict):
    x: float
    y: float

class Series(TypedDict):
    series: str
    data: List[Point]
```

These definitions can rely on `typing.TypedDict` because each reference to a `Series` object, as well as each reference to a `Point` object, uses `string` literal values that can be matched against the attributes by the `mypy` tool.

We can read this data with the following command:

```
>>> from pathlib import Path
>>> import json
>>> source_path = Path('code/anscombe.json')
>>> data: List[Series] = json.loads(source_path.read_text)
```

We've defined the `Path` to the data file. We can then use the `Path` object to read the text from this file. This text is used by `json.loads()` to build a `Python` object from the JSON data.

This `set` of `data` has a sequence of `Series` instances. We'd like to compute the parameters for a linear model that predicts the `y` value given an `x` value.

How to do it...

We'll start by leveraging the `correlation()` function defined in the *Computing the coefficient of correlation* recipe earlier in this chapter. We'll use this to compute the regression parameters for a linear model:

1. Import the `correlation()` function and the `Point` type hint from the earlier recipe. We'll also need functions from the `statistics` module, as well as some common type hints:

   ```
   import statistics
   from typing import Iterable, TypedDict, List, NamedTuple
   from Chapter_15.ch15_r03 import correlation, Point
   ```

2. Define a type hint for the regression parameters. This is a tuple to keep the `alpha` and `beta` values together:

   ```
   class Regression(NamedTuple):
       alpha: float
       beta: float
   ```

3. Define a function that will produce the regression model parameters, `regression()`. This will return a two-tuple with the `alpha` and `beta` values:

   ```
   def regression(series: List[Point]) -> Regression:
   ```

4. Compute the various measures required:

   ```
       m_x = statistics.mean(p["x"] for p in series)
       m_y = statistics.mean(p["y"] for p in series)
       s_x = statistics.stdev(p["x"] for p in series)
       s_y = statistics.stdev(p["y"] for p in series)
       r_xy = correlation(series)
   ```

5. Compute the β and α values, and create the regression two-tuple.

   ```
       b = r_xy * s_y / s_x
       a = m_y - b * m_x
       return Regression(a, b)
   ```

We can use this `regression()` function to compute the regression parameters as follows:

```
>>> data = json.loads(source_path.read_text())
>>> for series in data:
...     a, b = regression(series['data'])
...     print(
...         f"{series['series']:>3s} "
```

```
...         f"y={round(a, 2)}+{round(b,3)}*x"
...     )
```

The output shows the formula that predicts an expected *y* value from a given *x* value. The output looks like this:

```
  I y=3.0+0.5*x
 II y=3.0+0.5*x
III y=3.0+0.5*x
 IV y=3.0+0.5*x
```

In all cases, the equations are $\hat{y} = 3 + {}^{1}/_{2}\,x$. This estimation appears to be a pretty good predictor of the actual values of *y*. The four data series were designed to have similar linear regression parameters in spite of having wildly different individual values.

How it works...

The two target formulas for α and β are not complex. The formula for β decomposes into the correlation value used with two standard deviations. The formula for α uses the β value and two means. Each of these is part of a previous recipe. The correlation calculation contains the actual complexity.

The core design technique is to build new features using as many existing features as possible. This spreads the test cases around so that the foundational algorithms are used (and tested) widely.

The analysis of the performance of *Computing the coefficient of a correlation* recipe is important, and applies here, as well. The `regression()` function makes five separate passes over the data to get the correlation as well as the various means and standard deviations. For large collections of data, this is a punishing computational burden. For small collections of data, it's barely measurable.

As a kind of proof of concept, this implementation demonstrates that the algorithm will work. It also serves as a starting point for creating unit tests. Given a working algorithm, then, it makes sense to refactor the code to optimize the processing.

There's more...

The regression algorithm shown earlier, while clear, is inefficient. In order to process the data once, we'll have to write an explicit `for` statement that makes a single pass through the data. Within the body of the `for` statement, we can compute the various sums required. Once the sums are available, we can compute values derived from the sums, including the `mean` and standard deviation:

```
def regr2(series: Iterable[Point]) -> Regression:

        sumx = sumy = sumxy = sumx2 = sumy2 = n = 0.0
        for point in series:
            x, y = point["x"], point["y"]
            n += 1
            sumx += x
            sumy += y
            sumxy += x * y
            sumx2 += x ** 2
            sumy2 += y ** 2
        m_x = sumx / n
        m_y = sumy / n
        s_x = sqrt((n * sumx2 - sumx ** 2) / (n * (n - 1)))
        s_y = sqrt((n * sumy2 - sumy ** 2) / (n * (n - 1)))
        r_xy = (n * sumxy - sumx * sumy) / (
            sqrt(n * sumx2 - sumx ** 2) * sqrt(n * sumy2 - sumy ** 2)
        )
        b = r_xy * s_y / s_x
        a = m_y - b * m_x
        return Regression(a, b)
```

We've initialized a number of sums to zero, and then accumulated values into these sums from a source of data items, `data`. Since this uses the data value once only, this will work with any `Iterable` data source.

The calculation of `r_xy` from these sums doesn't change from the previous examples, nor does the calculation of the α or β values, α and β. Since these final results are the same as the previous version, we have confidence that this optimization will compute the same answer, but do it with only one pass over the data.

See also

- The *Computing the coefficient of correlation* recipe earlier in this chapter, provides the `correlation()` function that is the basis for computing the model parameters.
- The *Analyzing many variables in one pass* recipe, later in this chapter, will address some efficiency considerations. In that recipe, we'll look at ways to compute multiple sums in a single pass through the data elements.

Computing an autocorrelation

In many cases, events occur in a repeating cycle. If the data correlates with itself, this is called an autocorrelation. With some data, the interval may be obvious because there's some visible external influence, such as seasons or tides. With some data, the interval may be difficult to discern.

If we suspect we have cyclic data, we can leverage the `correlation()` function from the *Computing the coefficient of correlation* recipe, earlier in this chapter, to compute an autocorrelation.

Getting ready

The core concept behind autocorrelation is the idea of a correlation through a shift in time, *T*. The measurement for this is sometimes expressed as $r_{xx}(T)$: the correlation between *x* and *x* with a time shift of *T*.

Assume we have a handy correlation function, $R(x, y)$. It compares two sequences of length *n*, $[x_0, x_1, x_2, ..., x_{n-1}]$ and $[y_0, y_1, y_2, ..., y_{n-1}]$, and returns the coefficient of correlation between the two sequences:

$$r_{xy} = R([x_0, x_1, x_2, ..., x_{n-1}], [y_0, y_1, y_2, ..., y_{n-1}])$$

We can apply this to autocorrelation by using it as a time shift in the index values:

$$r_{xx}(T) = R([x_0, x_1, x_2, ..., x_{n-1}], [x_{0+T}, x_{1+T}, x_{2+T}, ..., x_{n-1+T}])$$

We've computed the correlation between values of *x* where the indices are offset by *T*. If *T* = *0*, we're comparing each item with itself; the correlation is $r_{xx}(0) = 1$.

We'll use some data that we suspect has a seasonal signal in it. This is data from `http://www.esrl.noaa.gov/gmd/ccgg/trends/`. We can visit `ftp://ftp.cmdl.noaa.gov/ccg/co2/trends/co2_mm_mlo.txt` to download the file of the raw data.

The file has a preamble with lines that start with #. These lines must be filtered out of the data. We'll use the *Picking a subset – three ways to filter* recipe in online *Chapter 9, Functional Programming Features* (link provided in the *Preface*), that will remove the lines that aren't useful.

The remaining lines are in seven columns with spaces as the separators between values. We'll use the *Reading delimited files with the CSV module* recipe in *Chapter 10, Input/Output, Physical Format, and Logical Layout*, to read CSV data. In this case, the comma in CSV will be a space character. The result will be a little awkward to use, so we'll use the *Refactoring a CSV DictReader to a dataclass reader* recipe in *Chapter 10, Input/Output, Physical Format, and Logical Layout*, to create a more useful namespace with properly converted values.

To read the CSV-formatted files, we'll need the `csv` module as well as a number of type hints:

```
import csv
from typing import Iterable, Iterator, Dict
```

Here are two functions to handle the essential aspects of the physical format of the file. The first is a filter to reject comment lines; or, viewed the other way, pass non-comment lines:

```
def non_comment_iter(source: Iterable[str]) -> Iterator[str]:
    for line in source:
        if line[0] == "#":
            continue
        yield line
```

The `non_comment_iter()` function will iterate through the given source of lines and reject lines that start with `#`. All other lines will be passed untouched.

The `non_comment_iter()` function can be used to build a CSV reader that handles the lines of valid data. The reader needs some additional configuration to define the data columns and the details of the CSV dialect involved:

```
def raw_data_iter(
        source: Iterable[str]) -> Iterator[Dict[str, str]]:
    header = [
        "year",
        "month",
        "decimal_date",
        "average",
       "interpolated",
        "trend",
        "days",
    ]
    rdr = csv.DictReader(
        source, header, delimiter=" ", skipinitialspace=True)
    return rdr
```

The `raw_data_iter()` function defines the seven column headers. It also specifies that the column delimiter is a space, and the additional spaces at the front of each column of data can be skipped. The input to this function must be stripped of comment lines, generally by using a filter function such as `non_comment_iter()`.

The results of using these two functions are rows of data in the form of dictionaries with seven keys. These rows look like this:

```
    [{'average': '315.71', 'days': '-1', 'year': '1958', 'trend':
'314.62',
```

```
        'decimal_date': '1958.208', 'interpolated': '315.71', 'month':
'3'},
      {'average': '317.45', 'days': '-1', 'year': '1958', 'trend':
'315.29',
        'decimal_date': '1958.292', 'interpolated': '317.45', 'month':
'4'},
    etc.
```

Since the values are all strings, a pass of cleansing and conversion is required. Here's a row cleansing function that can be used in a generator to build a useful `NamedTuple`:

```
from typing import NamedTuple


class Sample(NamedTuple):
    year: int
    month: int
    decimal_date: float
    average: float
    interpolated: float
    trend: float
    days: int


def cleanse(row: Dict[str, str]) -> Sample:
    return Sample(
        year=int(row["year"]),
        month=int(row["month"]),
        decimal_date=float(row["decimal_date"]),
        average=float(row["average"]),
        interpolated=float(row["interpolated"]),
        trend=float(row["trend"]),
        days=int(row["days"]),
    )
```

This `cleanse()` function will convert each dictionary row to a `Sample` by applying a conversion function to the values in the raw input dictionary. Most of the items are floating-point numbers, so the `float()` function is used. A few of the items are integers, and the `int()` function is used for those.

We can write the following kind of generator expression to apply this cleansing function to each row of raw data:

```
cleansed_data = (cleanse(row) for row in raw_data)
```

This will apply the `cleanse()` function to each row of data. Generally, the expectation is that the rows ready for cleansing will come from the `raw_data_iter()` generator. Each of these raw rows comes from the `non_coment_iter()` generator.

These functions can be combined into a stack as follows:

```
def get_data(source_file: TextIO) -> Iterator[Sample]:
    non_comment_data = non_comment_iter(source_file)
    raw_data = raw_data_iter(non_comment_data)
    cleansed_data = (cleanse(row) for row in raw_data)
    return cleansed_data
```

This generator function binds all of the individual steps into a transformation pipeline. The `non_comment_iter()` function cleans out non-CSV lines. The `raw_data_iter()` function extracts dictionaries from the CSV source. The final generator expression applies the `cleanse()` function to each row to build `Sample` objects. We can add filters, or replace the parsing or cleansing functions in this `get_data()` function.

The context for using the `get_data()` function will look like this:

```
>>> source_path = Path('data/co2_mm_mlo.txt')
>>> with source_path.open() as source_file:
...     all_data = list(get_data(source_file))
```

This will create a `List[Sample]` object that starts like this:

```
[Sample(year=1958, month=3, decimal_date=1958.208, average=315.71,
interpolated=315.71, trend=314.62, days=-1),
Sample(year=1958, month=4, decimal_date=1958.292, average=317.45,
interpolated=317.45, trend=315.29, days=-1),
Sample(year=1958, month=5, decimal_date=1958.375, average=317.5,
interpolated=317.5, trend=314.71, days=-1),


...
]
```

Once we have the raw data, we can use this for statistical processing. We can combine this input pipeline with recipes shown earlier in this chapter to determine the autocorrelation among samples.

How to do it...

To compute the autocorrelation, we'll need to gather the data, select the relevant variables, and then apply the `correlation()` function:

1. Import the `correlation()` function from the `ch15_r03` module:

   ```
   from Chapter_15.ch15_r03 import correlation, Point
   ```

2. Get the relevant time series data item from the source data. In this case, we'll use the interpolated data. If we try to use the average data, there are reporting gaps that would force us to locate periods without the gaps. The interpolated data has values to fill in the gaps:

   ```
   source_path = Path("data") / "co2_mm_mlo.txt"
   with source_path.open() as source_file:
       co2_ppm = list(
           row.interpolated
           for row in get_data(source_file))
       print(f"Read {len(co2_ppm)} Samples")
   ```

3. For a number of time offsets, τ, compute the correlation. We'll use time offsets from `1` to `20` periods. Since the data is collected monthly, we suspect that $\tau = 12$ will have the highest correlation.

4. The `correlation()` function from the *Computing the coefficient of correlation* recipe expects a small dictionary with two keys: *x* and *y*. The first step is to build an array of these dictionaries. We've used the `zip()` function to combine two sequences of data:
   - `co2_ppm[:-tau]`
   - `co2_ppm[tau:]`

5. For different `tau` offsets from `1` to `20` months, we can create parallel sequences of data and correlate them:

   ```
   for tau in range(1, 20):
       data = [
           Point({"x": x, "y": y})
           for x, y in zip(co2_ppm[:-tau], co2_ppm[tau:])
       ]
       r_tau_0 = correlation(data[:60])
       r_tau_60 = correlation(data[60:120])
       print(f"r_{{xx}}(τ={tau:2d}) = {r_tau_0:6.3f}")
   ```

We've taken just the first 60 values to compute the autocorrelation with various time offset values. The data is provided monthly. The strongest correlation is among values that are 12 months apart. We've highlighted this row of output:

```
r_{xx}(τ= 1) =  0.862
r_{xx}(τ= 2) =  0.558
r_{xx}(τ= 3) =  0.215
r_{xx}(τ= 4) = -0.057
r_{xx}(τ= 5) = -0.235
r_{xx}(τ= 6) = -0.319
r_{xx}(τ= 7) = -0.305
r_{xx}(τ= 8) = -0.157
r_{xx}(τ= 9) =  0.141
r_{xx}(τ=10) =  0.529
r_{xx}(τ=11) =  0.857
r_{xx}(τ=12) =  0.981
r_{xx}(τ=13) =  0.847
r_{xx}(τ=14) =  0.531
r_{xx}(τ=15) =  0.179
r_{xx}(τ=16) = -0.100
r_{xx}(τ=17) = -0.279
r_{xx}(τ=18) = -0.363
r_{xx}(τ=19) = -0.349
```

When the time shift is `12`, $r_{xx}(12) = 0.981$. A similarly striking autocorrelation is available for almost any subset of the data. This high correlation confirms an annual cycle to the data.

The overall dataset contains almost 700 samples spanning over 58 years. It turns out that the seasonal variation signal is not as clear over the entire span of time as it is in the first 5 years' worth of data. This means that there is another, longer period signal that is drowning out the annual variation signal.

The presence of this other signal suggests that something more complex is going on with a timescale longer than 5 years. Further analysis is required.

How it works...

One of the elegant features of Python is the slicing concept. In the *Slicing and dicing a list* recipe in *Chapter 4, Built-In Data Structures Part 1: Lists and Sets*, we looked at the basics of slicing a list. When doing autocorrelation calculations, array slicing gives us a wonderful tool for comparing two subsets of the data with very little complexity.

The essential elements of the algorithm amounted to this:

```
data = [
    Point({"x": x, "y": y})
    for x, y in zip(co2_ppm[:-tau], co2_ppm[tau:])
]
```

The pairs are built from the `zip()` function, combing pairs of items from two slices of the `co2_ppm` sequence. One slice, `co2_ppm[:-tau]`, starts at the beginning, and the other slice, `co2_ppm[tau:]`, starts at an offset. These two slices build the expected `(x,y)` pairs that are used to create a temporary object, `data`. Given this `data` object, an existing `correlation()` function computed the correlation metric.

There's more...

We can observe the 12-month seasonal cycle repeatedly throughout the dataset using a similar array slicing technique. In the example, we used this:

```
r_tau_0 = correlation(data[:60])
```

The preceding code uses the first `60` samples of the available `699`. We could begin the slice at various places and use various sizes of the slice to confirm that the cycle is present throughout the data.

We can create a model that shows how the `12` months of `data` behave. Because there's a repeating cycle, the sine function is the most likely candidate for a model. We'd be having a fit using this:

$$\hat{y} = A\ \sin\big(f(x + \psi)\big) + K$$

The mean of the sine function itself is zero, so the *K* factor is the mean of a given `12`-month period. The function, $f(x + \psi)$, will convert monthly figures to proper values in the range $-2\pi \leq \mathrm{f}(\mathrm{x} + \psi) \leq 2\pi$. A function such as $\mathrm{f(x)} = 2\pi(\frac{x-6}{6})$ might be ideal for this conversion from period to radians. Finally, the scaling factor, *A*, scales the data to match the minimum and maximum for a given month.

Long-term model

This analysis exposes the presence of a long-term trend that obscures the annual oscillation. To locate that trend, it is necessary to reduce each `12`-month sequence of samples to a single, annual, central value. The `median`, or the `mean`, will work well for this.

We can create a sequence of monthly average values using the following generator expression:

```
from statistics import mean, median
monthly_mean = [
    Point(
        {"x": x, "y": mean(co2_ppm[x : x + 12])}
    )
    for x in range(0, len(co2_ppm), 12)
]
```

This generator builds a sequence of dictionaries. Each dictionary has the required `x` and `y` items that are used by the regression function. The `x` value is a simple surrogate for the year and month: it's a number that grows from `0` to `696`. The `y` value is the average of `12` monthly values for a given year.

The regression calculation is done as follows:

```
from Chapter_15.ch15_r04 import regression
alpha, beta = regression(monthly_mean)
print(f"y = {alpha}+x*{beta}")
```

This shows a pronounced line, with the following equation:

$$\hat{y} = 307.8 + 0.1276 \times x$$

The `x` value is a month number offset from the first month in the dataset, which is March 1958. For example, March of 1968 would have an `x` value of `120`. The yearly average CO_2 parts per million would be `y = 323.1`. The actual average for this year was `323.27`. As you can see, these are very similar values.

The r2 value for this model, which shows how the equation fits the data, is `0.98`. This rising slope is the strongest part of the signal, which, in the long run, dominates any seasonal fluctuations.

See also

- The *Computing the coefficient of a correlation* recipe earlier in this chapter shows the core function for the computing correlation between a series of values.
- The *Computing regression parameters* recipe earlier in this chapter gives additional background for determining the detailed regression parameters.

Confirming that the data is random – the null hypothesis

One of the important statistical questions is framed as the `null` hypothesis and an alternate hypothesis about sets of data. Let's assume we have two sets of data, S1 and S2. We can form two kinds of hypothesis in relation to the data:

- **Null**: Any differences are random effects and there are no significant differences.
- **Alternate**: The differences are statistically significant. Generally, we consider that the likelihood of this happening stochastically to samples that only differ due to random effects must be less than 5% for us to deem the difference "statistically significant."

This recipe will show one of many ways in which to evaluate data to see whether it's truly random or whether there's some meaningful variation.

Getting ready

The rare individual with a strong background in statistics can leverage statistical theory to evaluate the standard deviations of samples and determine whether there is a significant difference between two distributions. The rest of us, who are potentially weak in statistical theory, but have a strong background in programming, can do a little coding and achieve similar results.

The idea is to generate (or select) either a random subset of the data, or create a simulation of the process. If the randomized data matches the carefully gathered data, we should consider the `null` hypothesis, and try to find something else to measure. If the measurements don't match a randomized simulation, this can be a useful insight.

There are a variety of ways in which we can compare sets of data to see whether they're significantly different. The *Computing the coefficient of correlation* recipe from earlier in this chapter shows how we can compare two sets of data for correlation.

A simulation works best when a simulation is reasonably complete. Discrete events in casino gambling, for example, are easy to simulate. Some kinds of discrete events in web transactions, such as the items in a shopping cart, are also easy to simulate. Some phenomena are hard to simulate precisely.

In those cases where we can't do a simulation, we have a number of resampling techniques that are available. We can shuffle the data, use bootstrapping, or use cross-validation. In these cases, we'll use the data that's available to look for random effects.

We'll compare three subsets of the data in the *Computing an autocorrelation* recipe. We'll reuse the `get_data()` function to acquire the raw collection of `Sample` objects.

The context for using the `get_data()` function will look like this:

```
>>> source_path = Path('data/co2_mm_mlo.txt')
>>> with source_path.open() as source_file:
...     all_data = list(get_data(source_file))
```

This will create a `List[Sample]` objects that starts like this:

```
[Sample(year=1958, month=3, decimal_date=1958.208, average=315.71,
interpolated=315.71, trend=314.62, days=-1),
 Sample(year=1958, month=4, decimal_date=1958.292, average=317.45,
interpolated=317.45, trend=315.29, days=-1),
 Sample(year=1958, month=5, decimal_date=1958.375, average=317.5,
interpolated=317.5, trend=314.71, days=-1),
...
]
```

We want subsets of the data. We'll look at data values from two adjacent years and a third year that is widely separated from the other two. Each year has `12` samples, and we can compute the means of these groups:

```
>>> y1959 = [r.interpolated for r in all_data if r.year == 1959]
>>> y1960 = [r.interpolated for r in all_data if r.year == 1960]
>>> y2014 = [r.interpolated for r in all_data if r.year == 2014]
```

We've created three subsets for three of the available years of data. Each subset is created with a filter that creates a list of values for which the year matches a target value. We can compute statistics on these subsets as follows:

```
>>> from statistics import mean
>>> round(mean(y1959), 2)
315.97
>>> round(mean(y1960), 2)
316.91
>>> round(mean(y2014), 2)
398.61
```

The three `mean` values are different. Our hypothesis is that the differences between the `1959` and `1960` `mean` values are insignificant random variation, while the differences between the `1959` and `2014` `mean` values are statistically significant.

The permutation or shuffling technique for resampling works as follows:

1. Start with two collections of points to compare. For example, we can compare the data samples from 1959 and 1960, P_{1959} and P_{1960}. The observed difference between the means of the 1959 data, μ_{1959}, and the 1960 data, μ_{1960} is $316.91 - 315.97 = 0.94$. We can call this T_{obs}, the observed test measurement. We can then compute random subsets to compare arbitrary data to this specific grouping.
2. Combine the data from the two collections into a single population of data points, $P = P_{1959} \cup P_{1960}$.
3. For each permutation of the population of values, *P*:
   - Create two subsets from the permutation, *A*, and *B*, such that $\mathrm{P} = \mathrm{A} \cup \mathrm{B}$. This is the resampling step that gives the process its name.
   - Compute the difference between the means of each resampled subset, $\mathrm{T} = \mu_\mathrm{A} - \mu_\mathrm{B}$.
   - Count the number of differences, *L*, larger than T_{obs} and, *S*, smaller than T_{obs}.

If the differences between P_{1959} and P_{1960} are not statistically significant, all the random subsets of data will be scattered evenly around the observed measurement, T_{obs}. If there is a statistically significant difference, however, the distribution of random subsets will be highly skewed. A common heuristic threshold is to look for a 20:1 ratio between larger and smaller counts, *L*, and *S*.

The two counts show us how our observed difference compares with all possible differences. There can be many permutations. In our case, we know that the number of combinations of 24 samples taken 12 at a time is given by this formula:

$$\binom{n}{k} = \frac{n!}{k!\,(n-k)!}$$

We can compute the value for $n = 24$ and $k = 12$:

```
>>> from Chapter_03.ch03_r10 import fact_s
>>> def binom(n, k):
...     return fact_s(n)//(fact_s(k)*fact_s(n-k))
>>> binom(24, 12)
2704156
```

There are a fraction more than 2.7 million permutations of 24 values taken 12 at a time. We can use functions in the `itertools` module to generate these. The `combinations()` function will emit the various subsets. Processing all these combinations takes over 5 minutes (320 seconds).

An alternative plan is to use randomized subsets. Using `270,415` randomized samples can be done in under 30 seconds on a four-core laptop. Using 10% of the combinations provides an answer that's accurate enough to determine whether the two samples are statistically similar and the `null` hypothesis is true, or if the two samples are different.

How to do it...

To apply the shuffling technique, we'll leverage the `statistics` and `random` modules. We'll compute descriptive statistics for a number of random subsets.

1. We'll be using the `random` and `statistics` modules. The `shuffle()` function is central to randomizing the samples. We'll also be using the `mean()` function. While the process suggests two counts, values above and below the observed difference, T_{obs}, we'll instead create a `Counter` and quantize the counts in 2,000 fine-grained steps from `-0.001` to `+0.001`. This will provide some confidence that the differences are normally distributed:

```
import collections
import random
from statistics import mean
```

2. Define a function that accepts two separate sets of samples. These will be compared using the randomized shuffling procedure:

```
def randomized(
        s1: List[float],
        s2: List[float],
        limit: int = 270_415) -> None:
```

3. Compute the observed difference between the means, T_{obs}:

```
    T_obs = mean(s2) - mean(s1)
    print(
        f"T_obs = {mean(s2):.2f}-{mean(s1):.2f} "
        f"= {T_obs:.2f}"
    )
```

4. Initialize a `Counter` object to collect details:

```
    counts: Counter[int] = collections.Counter()
```

5. Create the combined universe of samples. We can concatenate the two lists:

```
    universe = s1 + s2
```

6. Use a `for` statement to perform a large number of resamples; `270,415` samples can take `35` seconds. It's easy to expand or contract the subset to balance a need for accuracy and the speed of calculation. The bulk of the processing will be nested inside this loop:

```
for resample in range(limit):
```

7. Shuffle the data:

```
random.shuffle(universe)
```

8. Pick two subsets that match the original sets of data in size. It seems easiest to slice the shuffled data cleanly into two subsets:

```
a = universe[:len(s2)]
b = universe[len(s2):]
```

9. Compute the difference between the means. In this case, we'll scale this by `1000` and convert to an integer so that we can accumulate a frequency distribution:

```
delta = int(1000*(mean(a) - mean(b)))
counts[delta] += 1
```

10. After the `for` loop, summarize the `counts` showing how many are above the observed difference, and how many are below it. If either value is less than 5%, this is a statistically significant difference:

```
T = int(1000*T_obs)
below = sum(v for k,v in counts.items() if k < T)
above = sum(v for k,v in counts.items() if k >= T)

print(
    f"below {below:,} {below/(below+above):.1%}, "
    f"above {above:,} {above/(below+above):.1%}"
)
```

When we run the `randomized()` function for the data from `1959` and `1960`, we see the following:

```
print("1959 v. 1960")
randomized(y1959, y1960)
```

The output looks like the following:

```
1959 v. 1960
T_obs = 316.91-315.97 = 0.93
below 239,491 88.6%, above 30,924 11.4%
```

This shows that 11% of the data was above the observed difference, while 88% was below it. This is well within the realm of normal statistical noise.

When we run this for data from `1959` and `2014`, we see the following output:

```
1959 v. 2014
T_obs = 398.61-315.97 = 82.64
below 270,415 100.0%, above 0 0.0%
```

The data here shows that none of the resampled subsets was above the observed difference in means, T_{obs}. We can conclude from this resampling exercise that the change from `1959` to `2014` is statistically significant.

How it works...

Computing all 2.7 million permutations gives the exact answer to a comparison of the given subsets with all possible subsets. It's faster to use many randomized subsets instead of computing all possible permutations. The Python random number generator is excellent, and it assures us that the randomized subsets will be fairly distributed.

We've used two techniques to compute randomized subsets of the data:

- Shuffle the entire universe with `random.shuffle(u)`.
- Partition the universe with code similar to `a,b = u[x:],u[:x]`.

Computing the means of the two partitions is done with the `statistics` module. We could define somewhat more efficient algorithms that did the shuffling, partitioning, and `mean` computation all in a single pass through the data.

The preceding algorithm turned each difference into a value between `-1000` and `+1000` using this:

```
delta = int(1000*(mean(a) - mean(b)))
```

This allows us to compute a frequency distribution with a `Counter`. This will indicate that most of the differences really are zero, something to be expected for normally distributed data. Seeing the distribution assures us that there isn't some hidden bias in the random number generation and shuffling algorithm.

Instead of populating a `Counter`, we could simply count the above and below values. The simplest form of this comparison between a permutation's difference and the observed difference, T_{obs}, is as follows:

```
if mean(a) - mean(b) > T_obs:
    above += 1
```

This counts the number of resampling differences that are larger than the observed difference. From this, we can compute the number below the observation via below = limit-above. This will give us a simple percentage value.

There's more...

We can speed processing up a tiny bit more by changing the way we compute the `mean` of each random subset.

Given a pool of numbers, *P*, we're creating two disjoint subsets, *A*, and *B*, such that:

$$A \cup B = P$$

$$A \cap B = \emptyset$$

The union of the *A* and *B* subsets covers the entire universe, *P*. There are no missing values because the intersection between *A* and *B* is an empty set.

The overall sum, S_p, can be computed just once:

$$S_P = \sum P_i$$

We only need to compute a sum for one subset, S_A:

$$S_A = \sum A_i$$

$$S_B = S_P - S_A$$

This means that the other subset sum is a subtraction. We don't need a costly process to compute a second sum.

The sizes of the sets, N_A, and N_B, similarly, are constant. The means, μ_A and μ_B, can be calculated a little more quickly than by using the `statistics.mean()` function:

$$\mu_A = \frac{S_A}{N_A}$$

$$\mu_B = \frac{(S_P - S_A)}{N_B}$$

This leads to a slight change in the resample function. We'll look at this in three parts. First, the initialization:

```
def faster_randomized(
        s1: List[float],
        s2: List[float],
        limit: int = 270_415) -> None:
    T_obs = mean(s2) - mean(s1)
    print(
        f"T_obs = {mean(s2):.2f}-{mean(s1):.2f} "
        f"= {T_obs:.2f}")

    counts: Counter[int] = collections.Counter()
    universe = s1 + s2
    a_size = len(s1)
    b_size = len(s2)
    s_u = sum(universe)
```

Three additional variables have been introduced: `a_size` and `b_size` are the sizes of the two original sets; `s_u` is the sum of all of the values in the universe. The sums of each subset must sum to this value, also.

Here's the second part of the function, which performs resamples of the full universe:

```
    for resample in range(limit):
        random.shuffle(universe)
        a = universe[: len(s1)]
        s_a = sum(a)
        m_a = s_a/a_size
        m_b = (s_u-s_a)/b_size
        delta = int(1000*(m_a-m_b))
        counts[delta] += 1
```

This resampling loop will compute one subset, and the `sum` of those values. The `sum` of the remaining values is computed by subtraction. The means, similarly, are division operations on these sums. The computation of the delta bin into which the difference falls is very similar to the original version.

Here's the final portion to display the results. This has not changed:

```
    T = int(1000 * T_obs)
    below = sum(v for k, v in counts.items() if k < T)
    above = sum(v for k, v in counts.items() if k >= T)
```

```
    print(
        f"below {below:,} {below/(below+above):.1%}, "
        f"above {above:,} {above/(below+above):.1%}"
    )
```

By computing just one sum, `s_a`, we shave considerable processing time off of the random resampling procedure. On a small four-core laptop, processing time dropped from 26 seconds to 3.6 seconds. This represents a considerable saving by avoiding computations on both subsets. We also avoided using the `mean()` function, and computed the means directly from the sums and the fixed counts.

This kind of optimization makes it quite easy to reach a statistical decision quickly. Using resampling means that we don't need to rely on a complex theoretical knowledge of statistics; we can resample the existing data to show that a given sample meets the `null` hypothesis or is outside of expectations, meaning that an alternative hypothesis is called for.

See also

- This process can be applied to other statistical decision procedures. This includes the *Computing regression parameters* and *Computing an autocorrelation* recipes earlier in this chapter.

Locating outliers

A set of measurements may include sample values that can be described as outliers. An outlier deviates from other samples, and may indicate bad data or a new discovery. Outliers are, by definition, rare events.

Outliers may be simple mistakes in data gathering. They might represent a software bug, or perhaps a measuring device that isn't calibrated properly. Perhaps a log entry is unreadable because a server crashed, or a timestamp is wrong because a user entered data improperly. We can blame high-energy cosmic ray discharges near extremely small electronic components, too.

Outliers may also be of interest because there is some other signal that is difficult to detect. It might be novel, or rare, or outside the accurate calibration of our devices. In a web log, this might suggest a new use case for an application or signal the start of a new kind of hacking attempt.

In this recipe, we'll look at one algorithm for identifying potential outliers. Our goal is to create functions that can be used with Python's `filter()` function to pass or reject outlier values.

Getting ready

An easy way to locate outliers is to normalize the values to make them Z-scores. A Z-score converts the measured value to a ratio between the measured value and the mean measured in units of standard deviation:

$$z_i = \frac{(x_i - \mu_x)}{\sigma_x}$$

Here, μ_x is the mean of a given variable, x, and σ_x is the standard deviation of that variable. We can compute the `mean` and standard deviation values using the `statistics` module.

This, however, can be somewhat misleading because the Z-scores are limited by the number of samples involved. If we don't have enough data, we may be too aggressive (or too conservative) on rejecting outliers. Consequently, the *NIST Engineering and Statistics Handbook, Section 1.3.5.17*, suggests using the modified Z-score, M_i, for detecting outliers:

$$M_i = 0.6745\frac{(x_i - \tilde{x})}{MAD}$$

Median Absolute Deviation (**MAD**) is used instead of the standard deviation for this outlier detection. The MAD is the `median` of the absolute values of the deviations between each sample, x_i, and the population median, $\tilde{x}$:

$$MAD = \text{median}\,|x_i - \tilde{x}|$$

The scaling factor of `0.6745` is used so that an M_i value greater than 3.5 can be identified as an outlier. This modified Z-score uses the population median, parallel to the way Z-scores use the sample variance.

We'll use data from the *Using the built-in statistics library* recipe shown earlier in this chapter. This data includes several individual `Series`, where each `Series` object is a dictionary with two keys. The `series` key is associated with a `name`. The `data` key is associated with a `list` of individual `Point` objects. The following type definitions apply:

```
from typing import Iterable, TypedDict, List, Dict

Point = Dict[str, float]

class Series(TypedDict):
    series: str
    data: List[Point]
```

The `Series` definition can rely on `typing.TypedDict` because each reference to a `Series` object uses string literal values that can be matched against the attributes by the `mypy` tool. The references to items within the `Point` dictionary will use variables instead of literal key values, making it impossible for the `mypy` tool to check the type hints fully.

We can read this data with the following command:

```
>>> from pathlib import Path
>>> import json
>>> source_path = Path('code/anscombe.json')
>>> data: List[Series] = json.loads(source_path.read_text)
```

We've defined the `Path` to the data file. We can then use the `Path` object to read the text from this file. This text is used by `json.loads()` to build a `Python` object from the JSON data.

This set of `data` has a sequence of `Series` instances. Each observation is a pair of measurements in a `Point` dictionary. In this recipe, we'll create a series of operations to locate outliers in the `x` or `y` attribute of each `Point` instance.

How to do it...

We'll need to start with the `median()` function of the `statistics` module. With this to create the threshold, we can build functions to work with the `filter()` function to pass or reject an outlier:

1. Import the `statistics` module. We'll be doing a number of `median` calculations. In addition, we can use some of the features of `itertools`, such as `compress()` and `filterfalse()`:

   ```
   import statistics
   import itertools
   ```

2. Define the `absdev()` function to map from absolute values to Z-scores. This will either use a given `median` or compute the actual `median` of the samples. It will then return a generator that provides all of the absolute deviations from the `median`:

   ```
   def absdev(
           data: Sequence[float],
           median: Optional[float] = None) -> Iterator[float]:
       if median is None:
           median = statistics.median(data)
       return (abs(x - median) for x in data)
   ```

3. Define a function to compute the `median` of deviations from the `median`, the `median_absdev()` function. This will locate the `median` of a sequence of absolute deviation values. This computes the `MAD` value used to detect outliers. This can compute a `median` or it can be given a `median` already computed:

```
def median_absdev(
        data: Sequence[float],
        median: Optional[float] = None) -> float:
    if median is None:
        median = statistics.median(data)
    return statistics.median(absdev(data, median=median))
```

4. Define the modified Z-score mapping, `z_mod()`. This will compute the `median` for the dataset, and use this to compute the MAD. The MAD value is then used to compute modified Z-scores based on this deviation value. The returned value is an iterator over the modified Z-scores. Because multiple passes are made over the data, the input can't be an `iterable` collection, so it must be a `list` object:

```
def z_mod(data: Sequence[float]) -> Iterator[float]:
    median = statistics.median(data)
    mad = median_absdev(data, median)
    return (0.6745 * (x - median) / mad for x in data)
```

   Interestingly, there's a possibility that the MAD value is zero. This can happen when the majority of the values don't deviate from the `median`. When more than half of the points have the same value, the `median` absolute deviation will be zero, and it's difficult to detect outliers with this method.

5. Define two outlier filters based on the modified Z mapping, `pass_outliers()`, and `reject_outliers()`. Any value over 3.5 can be labeled as an outlier. The statistical summaries can then be computed with and without the outlier values. The `itertools` module has a `compress()` function that can use a sequence of `Boolean` selector values to choose items from the original data sequence based on the results of the `z_mod()` computation:

```
def pass_outliers(data: Sequence[float]
                  ) -> Iterator[float]:
    return itertools.compress(
        data, (z >= 3.5 for z in z_mod(data)))


def reject_outliers(data: Sequence[float]
                    ) -> Iterator[float]:
    return itertools.compress(
        data, (z < 3.5 for z in z_mod(data)))
```

Most of these functions make multiple references to the input data parameter—an `iterable` cannot be used. These functions must be given a `Sequence` object so the data can be examined multiple times.

We can use `pass_outliers()` to locate the outlier values. This can be handy to identify the suspicious data values. We can use `reject_outliers()` to provide data with the outliers removed from consideration; this data would be used for other analysis steps.

How it works...

The stack of transformations can be summarized like this:

- Compute the overall population median.
- Map each value to an absolute deviation from the population median.
- Reduce the absolute deviations to create a median absolute deviation, MAD.
- Map each value to the modified Z-score using the population median and the MAD.
- Filter the results based on the modified Z-scores.

We've defined each transformation function in this stack separately. We can use recipes from the online *Chapter 9, Functional Programming Features* (link provided in the *Preface*), to create smaller functions and use the built-in `map()` and `filter()` functions to implement this process.

We can't easily use the built-in `reduce()` function to define a `median` computation. Efficient computation of the `median` involves a recursive algorithm to partition the data into smaller and smaller subsets, one of which has the `median` value. A less efficient alternative is to sort the data and choose the value in the middle.

Here's how we can apply the outlier detection to the given sample data:

```
def examine_all_series(source_path: Path) -> None:
    raw_data: List[Series] = json.loads(source_path.read_text())

    series_map = {
        series["series"]: series["data"]
        for series in raw_data}
    for series_name in series_map:
        print(series_name)
        series_data = series_map[series_name]
        for variable_name in 'x', 'y':
            values = [item[variable_name] for item in series_data]
            print(variable_name, values, end=" ")
            try:
```

```
            print("outliers", list(pass_outliers(values)))
        except ZeroDivisionError:
            print("Data Appears Linear")
    print()
```

We've iterated through each of the series in the source data. The computation of `series_data` extracts one of the `series` from the source data. Each of the `series` is a `list` of dictionaries with two keys, `x` and `y`. Within the `set` of samples, we can use the `pass_outliers()` function to locate outliers in the data.

The except clause handles a `ZeroDivisionError` exception. This exception is raised by the `z_mod()` function for a particularly pathological `set` of data. Here's the line of output that shows this odd-looking data:

```
x [8.0, 8.0, 8.0, 8.0, 8.0, 8.0, 8.0, 19.0, 8.0, 8.0, 8.0] Data Appears
Linear
```

In this case, more than half the values are the same, which leads the `mode` to also be the `median`. More than half the absolute deviations from the `median` will be zero, leaving the MAD to be zero. In this case, the idea of outliers is suspicious because the data doesn't seem to reflect ordinary statistical noise either.

When we find data like this, that does not fit the general model, and a different kind of analysis must be applied. It's possible, for example, that the cluster of identical values represents some kind of measurement error. Those values are invalid, and need to be rejected. This would leave a very small dataset with only a single valid point.

There's more...

The design shown in the recipe used two similar looking function definitions to the `pass_outliers()` and `reject_outliers()` functions. This design suffers from an unpleasant duplication of critical program logic; it breaks the DRY principle because a critical computation is repeated. Here are the two functions:

```
def pass_outliers(data: List[float]) -> Iterator[float]:
    return itertools.compress(
        data, (z >= 3.5 for z in z_mod(data)))


def reject_outliers(data: List[float]) -> Iterator[float]:
    return itertools.compress(
        data, (z < 3.5 for z in z_mod(data)))
```

The difference between `pass_outliers()` and `reject_outliers()` is tiny, and amounts to a logical negation of an expression. We have >= in one version and < in another. If the logic was more complex than a simple comparison, it may be difficult to be certain that the two logical expressions were opposites.

We can extract one version of the filter rule to create something like the following:

```
outlier = lambda z: z >= 3.5
```

We can then modify the two uses of the `compress()` function to make the logical negation explicit:

```
def pass_outliers_2(data: List[float]) -> Iterator[float]:
    return itertools.compress(
        data, (outlier(z) for z in z_mod(data)))


def reject_outliers_2(data: List[float]) -> Iterator[float]:
    return itertools.compress(
        data, (not outlier(z) for z in z_mod(data)))
```

The essential rule, `outlier()`, is like a separate `lambda` object. This helps reduce the code duplication and makes the logical negation more obvious. Now, the two versions can be compared easily to be sure that they have appropriate behavior.

We've used `itertools.compress()` to pass or reject outliers. This allows us to have a sequence of `Boolean` values and a sequence of `data` values. The function chooses `data` values where the matching `Boolean` value is `True`.

Another possible design alternative is to use the built-in `filter()` function. This leads to a radical transformation of the processing pipeline. The `filter()` higher-order function requires a decision function that creates a `Boolean` result for each raw value. Instead of comparing `z_mod()` results to a threshold, this version must compute the `z_mod()` value and also apply the decision threshold in a single function. The decision function for the `filter()` function is this:

$$\frac{0.6745(x_i - \tilde{x})}{\text{MAD}} \geq 3.5$$

This decision function requires two additional inputs—the population `median`, `x`, and the `MAD` value. This makes the filter decision function rather complex. It would look like this:

```
def filter_outlier(mad: float, median_x: float, x: float) -> bool:
    return 0.6745*(x - median_x)/mad >= 3.5
```

This `filter_outlier()` function can be used with `filter()` to pass outliers. It can be used with `itertools.filterfalse()` to reject outliers and create a subset that is free from erroneous values.

In order to use this `filter_outlier()` function, we'll need to create a pair of functions like these:

```
from functools import partial

def make_filter_outlier_partial(
        data: List[float]) -> Callable[[float], bool]:
    population_median = statistics.median(data)
    mad = median_absdev(data, population_median)
    outlier_partial = partial(
        filter_outlier, mad, population_median)
    return outlier_partial

def pass_outliers_3(data: List[float]) -> Iterator[float]:
    outlier_partial = make_filter_outlier_partial(data)
    return filter(outlier_partial, data)
```

The `make_filter_outlier_partial()` function creates a partial function built around the `filter_outlier()` function. This partial function provides fixed values for the `mad` and `median_x` parameters; the `x` parameter is the only remaining parameter.

To create the partial function, the `make_filter_outlier_partial()` function computes the two overall reductions: `population_median`, and `mad`. Given these two values, the partial function, `outlier_partial()` is created with two parameter values bound.

The `pass_outliers_3()` function is identical to previous `pass_outliers()` functions. It expects a sequence of data values. First, it creates the necessary partial function, and then it applies the partial function to pass `outlier` values. A similar function can be defined to reject outliers; the principal difference involves using the `itertools.filterfalse()` function instead of the built-in `filter()` function.

See also

- See `http://www.itl.nist.gov/div898/handbook/eda/section3/eda35h.htm` for details on algorithms that help with the detection of outlier values from a set of measurements.

Analyzing many variables in one pass

In many cases, we'll have data with multiple variables that we'd like to analyze. The data can be visualized as filling in a grid, with each row containing a specific outcome. Each outcome row has multiple variables in columns. Many recipes in this chapter have a very narrow grid with only two variables, `x` and `y`. Two recipes earlier in this chapter, *Computing an autocorrelation*, and *Confirming that the data is random – the null hypothesis*, have relied on data with more than two variables.

For many of these recipes, we have followed a pattern of treating the data as if it is provided in column-major order: the recipe processed each variable (from a column of data) independently. This leads to visiting each row of data multiple times. For a large number of rows, this can become inefficient.

The alternative is to follow a pattern of row-major order. This means processing all the variables at once for each row of data. This refactoring tends to make the functions a bit more complex-looking, but considerably more efficient.

We'll look at ways to optimize an algorithm to make a single pass through a set of data and collect several descriptive statistics all at once.

Getting ready

The variables that we might want to analyze will fall into a number of categories. For example, statisticians often segregate variables into categories such as the following:

- **Continuous real-valued data**: These variables are often measured by floating-point values, they have a well-defined unit of measure, and they can take on values with a precision limited by the accuracy of the measurement.
- **Discrete or categorical data**: These variables take on a value selected from a finite domain. In some cases, we can enumerate the domain in advance. Postal ZIP codes, for example, are often known in advance. In other cases, the domain's values must be discovered.
- **Ordinal data**: This provides a ranking or ordering. Generally, the ordinal value is a number; no other statistical summaries apply to this number. Since it's not really a measurement, it has no units, for example.
- **Count data**: This variable is a summary of individual discrete outcomes. It can be treated as if it were continuous by computing a real-valued mean of an otherwise discrete count.

Variables may be independent of each other, or a variable may depend on other variables. In the initial phases of a study, the dependence may not be known. In later phases, one objective of the software is to discover the dependencies. Later, software may be used to model the dependencies.

Because of the varieties of data, we need to treat each variable as a distinct item. We can't treat them all as simple floating-point values. Properly acknowledging the differences will lead to a hierarchy of class definitions. Each subclass will contain the unique features for a variable.

We have two overall design patterns:

- **Eager**: We can compute the various summaries as early as possible. In some cases, we don't have to accumulate very much data for this.
- **Lazy**: We compute the summaries as late as possible. This means that we'll be accumulating data, and using properties to compute the summaries.

For very large sets of data, we want to have a hybrid solution. We'll compute some summaries eagerly, and also use properties to compute the final results from those summaries.

We'll use some data from the *Using the built-in statistics library* recipe earlier in this chapter, and we'll also use some data from the *Computing an autocorrelation* recipe ealier in this chapter. In both cases, the data is a sequence of dictionaries. Each key is a column name. The values are mostly numbers, but it's a mixture of `integer` (discrete) values and floating-point (continuous) values.

The following type definitions apply

```
from typing import TypedDict, List, Dict

Sample = Dict[str, str]

class Series(TypedDict):
    series: str
    data: List[Sample]
```

The `Series` definition can rely on `typing.TypedDict` because each reference to a `Series` object uses `string` literal values that can be matched against the attributes by the `mypy` tool. The references to items within the `Point` dictionary will use variables instead of literal key values, making it impossible for the `mypy` tool to check the type hints fully.

This recipe will be designed to work with potentially invalid data. The `Sample` dictionary definition reflects this by expecting data with `string` values that will be cleansed and converted to more useful `Python` objects. We'll include this cleansing step in this recipe.

We can read this data with the following command:

```
>>> from pathlib import Path
>>> import json
>>> source_path = Path('code/anscombe.json')
>>> data: List[Series] = json.loads(source_path.read_text)
```

We've defined the `Path` to the data file. We can then use the `Path` object to read the text from this file. This text is used by `json.loads()` to build a `Python` object from the JSON data.

How can we examine all of the variables in a given `series` at once? We'll focus on an eager design that can work with very large volumes of data by minimizing the amount of raw data that's used.

How to do it...

We'll define a class that can include a number of summary values. The computations will rely on the data being kept in a separate object that is a collection of raw data. We'll define a hierarchy of classes for the various kinds of summaries:

1. Define a superclass for various kinds of analysis. This will act as a superclass for all more specialized analytics classes that may be required. We'll call this class `StatsGather` because that seems to summarize the general purpose:

   ```
   from abc import abstractmethod
   class StatsGather:
       def __init__(self, name: str) -> None:
           self.name = name

       @abstractmethod
       def add(self, value: Any) -> None:
           raise NotImplementedError

       @abstractmethod
       def summary(self) -> str:
           raise NotImplementedError
   ```

2. Define a class to handle the analysis of the variable. This should handle all conversions and cleansing. We'll eagerly compute the `count`, `sum`, and `sum` of squares values that can be used to compute the `mean` and standard deviation. We won't compute the final `mean` or standard deviation until these property values are requested:

   ```
   import math
   class SimpleStats(StatsGather):
       def __init__(self, name: str) -> None:
           super().__init__(name)
           self.count = 0
           self.sum = 0
   ```

```
        self.sum_2 = 0

    def cleanse(self, value: Any) -> float:
        return float(value)

    def add(self, value: Any) -> None:
        value = self.cleanse(value)
        self.count += 1
        self.sum += value
        self.sum_2 += value * value

    @property
    def mean(self) -> float:
        return self.sum / self.count

    @property
    def stdev(self) -> float:
        return math.sqrt(
            (self.count * self.sum_2 - self.sum ** 2)
            /
            (self.count * (self.count - 1))
        )

    def summary(self) -> str:
        return (
            f"{self.name} "
            f"mean={self.mean:.1f} stdev={self.stdev:.3f}"
        )
```

3. Define an `analyze()` function that creates multiple instances of the `SimpleStats` class and applies these to columns of data:

```
def analyze(
        series_data: Iterable[Sample],
        names: List[str]
) -> Dict[str, SimpleStats]:
```

4. Create a mapping from column names to instances of the `SimpleStats` class. Each of these objects will accumulate the summaries of the matching column of data:

```
column_stats = {
    key: SimpleStats(key) for key in names
}
```

5. Define a function to process all rows, using the `statistics`-computing objects for each column within each `row`. The outer `for` statement processes each `row` of data. The inner `for` statement processes each column of each `row`. The processing is clearly in `row`-major order:

```
for row in series_data:
    for column_name in column_stats:
        column_stats[column_name].add(row[column_name])

return column_stats
```

6. Display results or summaries from the various objects. The following snippet requires a `series_name`, and a `data_stream` which is an `iterable` over the `Point` types:

```
print(f"{series_name:>3s} var mean stddev")
column_stats = analyze(data_stream, ["x", "y"])
for column_key in column_stats:
    print(" ", column_stats[column_key].summary())
```

This gives an overview of each of the variables. We might see output like this for a series named `I`:

```
I
  x mean=9.0 stdev=3.317
  y mean=7.5 stdev=2.032
```

The `analyze()` function provides a summary, making a single pass through the data. This can be helpful for immense datasets that don't fit into the computer's memory.

How it works...

We've created the `SimpleStats` class to handle cleansing, filtering, and statistical processing for a continuous variable with a floating-point value. When confronted with other kinds of variables, for example, a discrete variable, we'll need additional class definitions. The idea is to be able to create a hierarchy of related classes, all of which have the essential `StatsGather` interface.

The `analyze()` function created an instance of the `SimpleStats` class for each specific column that we're going to analyze. For discrete or ordinal data, the computation of `mean` and standard deviation doesn't make sense, so a different summary object is required.

The `StatsGather` class is an `abstract` superclass requiring each subclass to provide an `add()` method and a `summary()` method. Each individual data value is provided to the `add()` method.

A subclass can provide any additional statistics that might be interesting. In this case, the `SimpleStats` class provided `mean` and `stdev` properties to compute summary statistics.

The `SimpleStats` class also defines an explicit `cleanse()` method. This can handle the data conversion needs. This can be extended to handle the possibility of invalid data. It might filter the values instead of raising an exception.

The overall `analyze()` function uses a collection of these `SimpleStats` statistics-processing objects. As a practical matter, there will be multiple classes involved in handling discrete variables and other kinds of data conversion processing. As each row of data is consumed by the `for` statement inside the `analyze()` function, all of the various `StatsGather` objects in the `column_stats` dictionary are updated using the `add()` method.

When all the rows have been consumed, the summaries in the `column_stats` dictionary can be displayed. This will provide summaries of the available data without loading huge datasets into memory.

There's more...

In this design, we've only considered the case where a variable is continuous and maps to a floating-point value. While this is common, there are a number of other categories of variables. One of the common alternatives is a discrete integer-valued variable.

We'll define an additional class, similar to `SimpleStats`, to handle this case. For discrete values, there's no good reason to use a measure of central tendency, like a `mean` or a `median`. A frequency distribution table, however, can be useful.

Here's a class that uses a `collection.Counter` object to compute the frequency of each discrete integer value:

```
class IntegerDiscreteStats:
    def __init__(self, name: str) -> None:
        self.name = name
        self.counts: Counter[int] = collections.Counter()

    def cleanse(self, value: Any) -> float:
        return int(value)
```

```
    def add(self, value: Any) -> None:
        value = self.cleanse(value)
        self.counts[value] += 1

    @property
    def mode(self) -> Tuple[int, int]:
        return self.counts.most_common(1)[0]

    @property
    def fq_dist(self) -> Counter[int]:
        return self.counts
```

This `IntegerDiscreteStats` class defines a `cleanse()` method to convert the source string to an integer. These integer values are then used to populate the `self.counts` object. The modal value is the most common value in the collection.

A more sophisticated class might check for several values with similar frequencies to expose the fact that the modal value is not unique. We've omitted any checking and simply reported the most common value and the count.

The `fq_dist` property is a reference to the underlying `Counter` object. This method isn't required, but this method can help to encapsulate internal processing, separating it from the return type provided by the property.

Our initial `analyze()` function built a dictionary mapping the column names provided in the names parameter to `SimpleStats` instances. This is limiting because it makes an assumption that all of the variables in the source data will fit the `SimpleStats` model. A better design would be to provide the collection of keys and statistical analyzers. A function like this works out better because it makes fewer assumptions about the data being analyzed:

```
def analyze2(
        series_data: Iterable[Sample],
        column_stats: Dict[str, StatsGather]
) -> Dict[str, StatsGather]:
    for row in series_data:
        for column_name in column_stats:
            column_stats[column_name].add(row[column_name])
    return column_stats
```

This function expects to be given a mapping from column names to `StatsGather` subclass instances. For example:

```
column_stats: Dict[str, StatsGather] = {
    "year": IntegerDiscreteStats("year"),
    "month":  IntegerDiscreteStats("month"),
    "decimal_date": SimpleStats("decimal_date"),
    "average": SimpleStats("average"),
    "interpolated": SimpleStats("interpolated"),
    "trend": SimpleStats("trend"),
    "days": IntegerDiscreteStats("days"),
}
```

could be used to analyze the more complex raw data used in the *Computing an autocorrelation* and *Confirming that the data is random – the null hypothesis* recipes earlier in this chapter.

See also

- See the *Designing classes with lots of processing* and *Using properties for lazy attributes* recipes in *Chapter 7, Basics of Classes and Objects*, for some additional design alternatives that fit into this overall approach.
- We can make use of the Command Design Patterns as well. See the *Combining many applications using the Command Design Pattern* section in *Chapter 14, Application Integration: Combination*, for ways to combine multiple individual `Command` classes into a composite `Command` class definition.

Other Books You May Enjoy

If you enjoyed this book, you may be interested in these other books by Packt:

Python Machine Learning – Third Edition

Sebastian Raschka, Vahid Mirjalili

ISBN: 978-1-78995-575-0

- Master the frameworks, models, and techniques that enable machines to 'learn' from data
- Use scikit-learn for machine learning and TensorFlow for deep learning
- Apply machine learning to image classification, sentiment analysis, intelligent web applications, and more

- Build and train neural networks, GANs, and other models
- Discover best practices for evaluating and tuning models
- Predict continuous target outcomes using regression analysis
- Dig deeper into textual and social media data using sentiment analysis

Python Automation Cookbook – Second Edition

Jaime Buelta

ISBN: 978-1-80020-708-0

- Learn data wrangling with Python and Pandas for your data science and AI projects
- Automate tasks such as text classification, email filtering, and web scraping with Python
- Use Matplotlib to generate a variety of stunning graphs, charts, and maps
- Automate a range of report generation tasks, from sending SMS and email campaigns to creating templates, adding images in Word, and even encrypting PDFs
- Master web scraping and web crawling of popular file formats and directories with tools like Beautiful Soup
- Build cool projects such as a Telegram bot for your marketing campaign, a reader from a news RSS feed, and a machine learning model to classify emails to the correct department based on their content
- Create fire-and-forget automation tasks by writing cron jobs, log files, and regexes with Python scripting

Leave a review - let other readers know what you think

Please share your thoughts on this book with others by leaving a review on the site that you bought it from. If you purchased the book from Amazon, please leave us an honest review on this book's Amazon page. This is vital so that other potential readers can see and use your unbiased opinion to make purchasing decisions, we can understand what our customers think about our products, and our authors can see your feedback on the title that they have worked with Packt to create. It will only take a few minutes of your time, but is valuable to other potential customers, our authors, and Packt. Thank you!

Index

Symbols

A

B

C

D

E

F

G

H

I

N

O

P

Q

R

S

T

U

V

W

X

Y

Z

CPSIA information can be obtained
at www.ICGtesting.com
Printed in the USA
BVHW020549180523
664380BV00007B/171

9 781800 207455